Northeast
Guide to

2nd Edition
Saltwater
Fishing and Boating

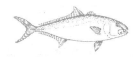

Edited by Vin T. Sparano

International Marine
Camden, Maine

About Our Experts

Pete Barrett is managing editor of *The Fisherman*, a magazine for East Coast recreational anglers, and his writing includes stories on fishing anywhere from Massachussetts to Florida. An active fisherman, he is a licensed charter captain operating out of Point Pleasant, New Jersey.

Eric B. Burnley has been fishing coastal waters from Cape Cod to Cape Hatteras for more than 40 years and has been a full-time outdoor writer for the past 20 years. A Delaware native, he currently lives in and guides out of Virginia Beach. Burnley has been involved in fisheries management issues on the local, state, and federal levels and has served on advisory boards for striped bass, summer flounder, black sea bass, and weakfish. He has contributed articles to all national outdoor publications and is author of *Surf Fishing the Atlantic Coast*. In 1990, Burnley was awarded Conservationist of the Year by the Virginia Beach Anglers Club.

Dean Travis Clarke is executive editor of *Sport Fishing* magazine, a regular contributor to most saltwater publications, and a specialist in marine electronics.

Gary Diamond, an outdoor writer for more than 20 years, photographer, and television producer and host, has fished inshore and offshore waters of the Atlantic from Maine to Key West, the Gulf of Mexico, and the Caribbean. His columns have appeared in such publications as *The Washington Post*, *Baltimore Sun*, *York Dispatch*, and the Journal Newspapers. His magazine credits include *The Fisherman*, *Saltwater Sportsman*, and *Chesapeake Bay Magazine*.

David R. Getchell, Sr., author of *Outboard Boater's Handbook*, was managing editor of *National Fisherman* for 22 years and founding editor of *The Mariner's Catalog* and *Small Boat Journal*. He was organizer and first Trail Director of the Maine Island Trail Association.

Jerry Gibbs is fishing editor of *Outdoor Life* and a member of the Fishing Hall of Fame.

Barry Gibson has been a charter captain in Boothbay Harbor, Maine, for 24 years, specializing in species ranging from bass and blues to sharks and giant tuna. A strong proponent of responsible fisheries management, he has been an advisor to the International Commission for the Conservation of Atlantic Tunas (ICCAT) and is currently completing a third term on the New England Fishery Management Council, of which he served as chairman in 1992. He is also active in numerous conservation and professional organizations. A world-record holder for bigeye tuna on fly, Gibson has fished extensively in North and South America.

Ed Jaworowski is a saltwater expert who writes regularly for *American Angler*, and *Fly Fishing Salt Water*, among other magazines.

 George Poveromo, field and boating editor for *Salt Water Sportsman*, is a nationally recognized sport fishing expert, writer, and photographer. The author of hundreds of articles, he has fished extensively along the U.S. coast, as well as in Europe, Australia, Bermuda, Mexico, the Bahamas, Africa, and numerous Caribbean, Central American, and South American destinations. In 1983, *Motor Boating & Sailing* magazine voted him one of the top eight U.S. anglers. Poveromo lives in South Florida.

John N. Raguso, an expert at taking a small boat offshore, is a regular contributor to *Sport Fishing*, *Boating*, *Trailer Boating*, *NY Outdoors*, *Fishing World*, and *Power and Motoryacht*.

Dusty Rhodes writes for *The Fisherman*, a magazine for East Coast recreational anglers. He also serves as a member of the Mid-Atlantic Fishery Management Council.

 Tom Richardson contributes many articles and photographs to *Salt Water Sportsman*, as well as writing its "New Gear" and "Traveling Fisherman" columns. He has fished the Caribbean and Central America, as well as many spots around the U.S., but his home waters are in Buzzards Bay, Massachusetts. Recently, Richardson was awarded first place in the Salt Water Magazine Category of the Outdoor Writers Association of America writing contest.

 Al Ristori has written thousands of newspaper and magazine articles and is the author of three books, including *North American Salt Water Fishing* and *Fishing for Bluefish*. Over his 29-year career as an outdoor writer, Ristori has fished all over the world and has held world records for bluefin tuna and mako shark. He is the past president of Save Our Stripers, has served on the Mid-Atlantic Fishery Management Council, and is currently on the Northeast Director's Recreational Advisory Committee of the National Marine Fisheries Service. He was honored as Mako Marine Outdoor Writer of the Year in 1984 and won the Saltwater Writing Award in the 1989 Outdoor Writers Association of America contest.

Nelson Sigelman, an avid fly-fisherman and part-time guide, is a reporter and fishing columnist for *The Martha's Vineyard Times.* He lives on the island with his wife, Norma, his five-year-old daughter, Marlan, and Tashmoo, their wayward black lab.

Mark Sosin is an award-winning writer, photographer, and television producer. During his 30-year writing career, he has authored 24 books on the outdoors and contributed more than 3,000 articles to major magazines. He is producer and host of "Mark Sosin's Saltwater Journal," a director of The Billfish Foundation, and a trustee of the University of Florida's  Whitney Laboratory. He is also a past president of the Outdoor Writers Association of America and the recipient of its Excellence in Craft Award, as well as its prestigious Ham Brown Award. Sosin is a member of many journalists' organizations and has been voted into both the International Fishing Hall of Fame and the Freshwater Fishing Hall of Fame.

To Betty,

Who shares my love of the sea, but
who has also learned to tolerate a husband
who chases fish and dreams.

————————————————

International Marine/
Ragged Mountain Press
A Division of The McGraw-Hill Companies

Published by International Marine®, with Vin T. Sparano
Communications, Inc.

10 9 8 7 6 5 4 3 2 1

Copyright © 1996 Vin T. Sparano

All rights reserved. The publisher takes no responsibility for
the use of any of the materials or methods described in this
book, nor for the products thereof. The name "International Marine" and the International Marine logo are trade-
marks of The McGraw-Hill Companies. Printed in the
United States of America.

Library of Congress Cataloging-in-Publication Data
Northeast guide to saltwater fishing and boating / edited
    by Vin T. Sparano.
    —2nd edition
        p.   cm.
        Includes index.
        ISBN 0-07-059893-2
        1. Saltwater fishing—Northeastern States—Guide-
books. 2. Boats and boating—Northeastern States—
Guidebooks. 3. Northeastern States—Guidebooks. 4.
Saltwater fishing—Northeastern States. 5. Boats and
boating—Northeastern States.   I. Sparano, Vin T.
SH464.N58N67   1996
799.1'6614—dc20   96-17826
                                CIP

Questions regarding the content of this book should be
addressed to:
    International Marine
    P.O. Box 220
    Camden, ME 04843

Questions regarding the ordering of this book should be
addressed to:
    The McGraw-Hill Companies
    Customer Service Department
    P.O. Box 547
    Blacklick, OH 43004
    Retail customers: 1-800-822-8158
    Bookstores: 1-800-722-4726

The Northeast Guide to Saltwater Fishing and Boating, Second Edition, is printed on acid-free paper.

Printed by Malloy Lithographing
Production and page layout by Janet Robbins
Edited by Jonathan Eaton, Tom McCarthy

Contents

Foreword

There's a sense of urgency about the time we spend in the outdoors today. Forecasters who sang of the great increase in leisure hours we were to have are silent now. New demands that zoom in from unexpected places make priceless each hour we can spend near the sea. To avoid wasting one moment of a fishing or boating trip, to live it safely, to be there when things are right normally demands extensive research of many sources on your part—another big time investment. No more. In your hands is the key to making that next adventure anywhere along our coast from Maine to Virginia, including Delaware and Chesapeake Bays, a brilliant success. It would take more free time than you have all year just trying to collect the amount of material Vin Sparano has distilled and organized in this guide.

That the premiere edition of the *Guide* was a resounding success is obvious, or there would not be this second, even better work. Just glance at the table of contents, then thumb quickly through the index. The fare of fascinating information is like an endless banquet for which you need exercise no restraint. Pick a place you want to fish or cruise or simply poke about. You'll learn how to access the spot by boat or afoot, what the services are, how the fishing's likely to be and for what. Want to spend just some of the time afloat? You'll learn how and where to find a charter or party boat or a small rental skiff to meet your needs.

If you want to do some further research on your own, you'll find the names and whereabouts of important state agencies to whom you can turn for more information. The latest in both boat and fishing tackle and their maintenance are here, too. Having trouble with your line kinking? Want to match tackle to the fish you're after, learn to catch bait better, or care for those fish you decide to keep? It's all here. So are helpful sections on boating electronics, mooring and anchoring safely, and making knots for every occasion.

And then there is this. Some of the coast's most knowledgeable saltwater anglers and boaters have supplied a selection of stories about their home waters— waters so familiar these experts could find their way as easily around them as around their homes when the lights go out. Read carefully, for their information can supply the core around which to build your own adventure trips for a particular species or for exploring areas off the usual beat of most visitors to an area.

For Vin Sparano, the sea has been that complex, lifelong mix of passion, learning ground, and source of renewal that she has for so many who love her. This is evident in the completeness of the *Guide,* which is certain to increase both the joy and the confidence of sportsmen and women exploring our ever-changing and always irresistible coast.

JERRY GIBBS,
Fishing Editor, *Outdoor Life*

No One Tackles Northeast Saltwater Fishing Like Penn.

Fishing along the Northeast Atlantic Coast is in a class all of its own. And so Penn brings you tackle all your own. Performance-matched rods and reels engineered exclusively for your rugged style of saltwater fishing.

Striper

Bluefish

The Northeast Is Penn Tackle Territory.

From Montauk to Nantucket… Cape May to the Kennebec… Northeast anglers who want to fish with the best fish with Penn. Rods and reels built to tackle the toughest fish and stand up to the nastiest saltwater conditions. Season after grueling season.

An American angling tradition for 60 years, Penn tackle has landed

more IGFA world records than any other brand. Including more than a few taken from the lumps, rips and wrecks of the Northeast.

Whether you're out to do battle with slammer blues, stripers,

weaks, 'togs or flounder, Penn quality, performance and reliability are your three best friends.

Specialized Penn Tackle Systems.

There's a Penn performance-matched rod and reel system for virtually every Northeast fishing technique. Casting, jigging, trolling or bottom fishing, live lining or surf fishing…name your style, we've got a system that's just right for you.

Each Penn system is optimized for the method you use and the fish you're after. And each one looks as great as it performs.

Summer Flounder

Visit Your Penn Fishing Center Today.

To learn more about the specialized Penn rod and reel systems for Northeast saltwater fishing, see your authorized "Penn Northeast Saltwater Retailer" today. Or send $2 ($5 outside North America) for your full-color Penn catalog.

Penn Fishing Tackle Mfg. Co., 3028 W. Hunting Park Ave., Dept.   , Philadelphia, PA 19132.

The Penn Wreck Fishing System™.
Penn Long Beach® 65 reel and
Penn Slammer® SLC-2701AX rod —
excellent for tautog and black sea bass.

The Penn Fluke System™. Penn 320GTi
Super Level Wind reel and Penn Power Stick®
PC-3811M rod — ideal for drifting for flounder.

PENN REELS

The Penn Wire Line System™. Penn Special Senator® 113H reel and Penn Sabre®
CS-2661RTC rod — custom made for trolling bunker spoons and bucktailing with wire line.

The Northeast Fishes With Penn.

TODAY'S RELEASE IS TOMORROW'S CATCH – SET A SENSIBLE LIMIT. OUR NATURAL RESOURCES ARE TOO PRECIOUS TO WASTE.

Y ou are holding the second edition of the *Northeast Guide to Saltwater Fishing & Boating.* I firmly believed that the first edition of this coastal guide was the most comprehensive book of its kind along the East Coast. Many fishermen must have agreed with me, because that first edition was a best-seller. It wasn't unbeatable, however, which I've proved with this second edition that is even better.

My mission with these guides, however, has not changed. The purpose of the *Northeast Guide* is to provide any inshore, offshore, or beach fisherman with the most comprehensive data available today, including advice from nationally known and local fishing experts. The new, updated edition of the *Northeast Guide to Saltwater Fishing & Boating* is once again a total package that will tell you when, where, and how to fish inshore and offshore for every saltwater gamefish.

How can I determine if I have done a thorough job? That's easy. With the completed manuscript in hand, I start fishing in Maine and follow the coast south. If I arrive at a state or region for which I can't find enough detailed information to plan a successful fishing trip, I know I have failed. But that hasn't happened yet! I have gathered huge amounts of fishing data and hot-spot locations for every coastal state. Much of the information included here is from local experts and fishing guides. I have also relied on state fish and game departments and private sources to compile complete listings of launch ramps, marinas, charter and party boats, beach access points, bait and tackle shops and other resources that traveling fishermen will find useful.

This book's usefulness is not limited to traveling fishermen. Regardless of how many years you've fished the salt water in your state, I am certain you can still find much to learn about your local waters. For example, while researching my home state of New Jersey, I discovered hot spots and techniques I'd never tried.

Books of this scope are never the work of one person. I want to thank Jon Eaton and Tom McCarthy at International Marine for their support, patience, and skill in handling a huge amount of data that would have driven many editors to a career change. Finally, I want to offer my sincere gratitude to all the federal and state marine fisheries divisions and local experts for their generous assistance.

This guide is for you . . . the coastal fisherman. If you like it, I want to know. More importantly, if you don't like it, or want more specific data, write to me and I'll try to fix it in the next edition. I can always be reached through International Marine, P.O. Box 220, Camden, Maine, 04843.

Good luck and good fishing.

VIN T. SPARANO, Fairfield and Barnegat Light, New Jersey, April 1996

Preface

Vin Sparano, right, and a sailfish he caught on the fly.

Part One

Fishing the Northeast, A Regional Guide

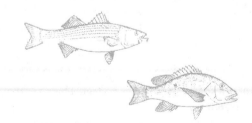

The Gulf of Maine

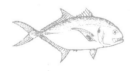

The great basin of water that lies to the east of Maine, New Hampshire, and Massachusetts is called the Gulf of Maine. About half its rim is formed by the bend in the Atlantic coast between Cape Sable, Nova Scotia, and Cape Cod, Massachusetts. The remainder is formed by a 300-mile-long chain of submerged mountainous plateaus rising 1,000 feet or more from the deep floor of the Gulf. These plateaus are the famous New England fishing banks, the largest of which, Georges Bank, Browns Bank, and Seal Island Ground, are separated from the mainland or each other by the deep passages of the Great South, Eastern (Northeast), and Northern Channels.

The composition and configuration of the shore along the Gulf of Maine are extremely varied. From West Quoddy Head, Maine, to Cape Elizabeth, Maine, the shore is almost continuously rocky; there are some 3,000 islands off the Maine coast, some as far as 20 miles from the mainland. The deep indentation of bays and passages gives this part of the Gulf, as viewed from a high-flying airplane, a serrated appearance.

About halfway between these capes, on Mount Desert Island, is the 1,500-foot granite summit of Cadillac Mountain, the highest point along the entire Atlantic coast. From Cape Elizabeth, Maine, to Scituate Harbor, Massachusetts, just south of Boston, the shore is characterized by a succession of gravelly or sandy beaches alternating with rocky headlands. The shoreline is more or less even except for the protuberance of Cape Ann and the indentation of Massachusetts Bay and Boston Harbor. Along this part of the Gulf there are few islands, except in Broad Sound and Boston Harbor, and no fjordlike indentations. South of Scituate Harbor the rocky shore gives way to the continuous sand beaches and even shoreline of Cape Cod. Cape Cod, which projects about 40 miles into the Atlantic and resembles the high upturned prow of a Norse ship, forms the southern mainland boundary of the Gulf of Maine.

A spectacular feature of the Gulf of Maine is the great rise and fall of the tides. At Monomoy Point, the southern end of Cape Cod, the tidal range is seldom over 4½ feet; but beginning on the Cape at Chatham, where tides average about 7 feet between high and low water, the range increases progressively to the north. In Gloucester, Massachusetts, the range is 10 feet; in Bar Harbor, Maine, 12 feet; and in the upper part of Passamaquoddy Bay it reaches 23 feet. Farther north in the upper reaches of the Bay of Fundy, within the Minas Basin, tides range from 45 to 55 feet. These are the greatest in the world.

The climate of the Gulf region is moist and cold. Winters are long, usually with heavy snowfalls and strong gales, mostly out of the north and west, though coastal winters are relatively mild compared with inland temperatures and snowfalls. Summers are generally mild, and although in certain sections there are periods when the air temperature exceeds 90°F, the heat is often tempered by onshore winds. At sea, fogs are heaviest during summer months when warm moist air is cooled in passing over the cold water of the Gulf. During the "dog days," from mid-June to September, wherever light winds from the southwest prevail, fogs become especially thick and may persist for days or even weeks. These disappear and the weather clears when the winds shift to the north or west. Normally the water temperature at the surface reaches its maximum of about 55° to 68°F during August and its minimum of 33° to 35°F during February. Water temperature at a depth of 300 feet reaches its maximum of 45° to 48°F during October or November and its minimum of 34° to 36°F during March or April.

Fishing has always been important to the people living along the Gulf of Maine. Long before the Vikings visited here late in the 10th century, Indians were catching fish, which they used not only for food but for fertilizer. The Basques "discovered" the land from Labrador to Cape Cod early in the 1500's while searching for whales. Other Europeans, more interested in fish than in whales, found an extraordinary abundance of cod. Indeed, it was dried cod, called bacalao, a universal article of trade, which brought large profits and motivated more people to venture to the New World. By the mid-1500's over 500 boats sailed annually from Portugal, France, England, and Spain to fish for cod along the Canadian and New England coasts. The need for food and supplies and the necessity of drying the fish ashore, a process requiring 3 or 4 months, led these fishermen to establish land bases. It was largely their daring and enterprise that made settlement in the New World a reality. By 1620, when the Pilgrims landed at Plymouth, Massachusetts, the entire length of the northeastern coast had been explored and its adjacent grounds fished. Competition for fishing grounds on the banks of Newfoundland, Nova Scotia, and New England was an important cause of the wars between France and England. Later, attempts by England to stop American exportation of cod to the Caribbean Islands was one of the major grievances leading to the Revolutionary War.

Because of its lush fertility, the Gulf of Maine supports a great abundance of fishes. Most of these live on or near the bottom or ground; hence, fishermen call them groundfish. Such are halibut, winter and smooth flounders, haddock, cod, cusk, wolffish, and most of the hakes. Even though fishermen have exploited this area for nearly 500 years, the decline in abundance due to overfishing of many species has taken place only since about the middle of the 20th century, a time marked by a great increase in fishing intensity.

Estuaries are important as breeding areas for some fishes and nursery areas for many others. Anadromous fishes, notably the Atlantic salmon, alewife, and blue-back herring, spawn in rivers within this area. The sexually mature fish must pass through the estuarine zone on their way upstream to spawn, and later the spawned-out fish and the juveniles must return by the same route on their way to the sea. Juveniles of our only catadromous fish, the eel, either pass through the estuarine zone on their way to fresh water or remain there to develop into adults. At maturity, adult eels move downstream, desert this zone, and swim offshore and south to spawn. Although not spawned in this area, many striped bass migrate here from southerly areas to spend the warm months feeding in the rivers and estuaries. The young of pollock and mackerel often find an abundance of food in estuaries and remain there during their juvenile life. Not only finfishes but shellfish live in estuaries—soft clams, hard clams, oysters, bay scallops, lobsters, and crabs.

Unfortunately, these extraordinarily fertile areas where saltwater and freshwater mix are being continually destroyed through unwise use. Encroachment on estuaries for housing and industrial development conflicts with increasing needs for food and open space.

Pollution, another serious problem for our natural resources, has also destroyed aquatic life in large portions of our waterways and has rendered other portions unusable, especially for harvesting shellfish. The total production from clam flats, scallop beds, and oyster bars has become greatly reduced. Many of the best soft-shell clamming areas in Maine, New Hampshire, and Massachusetts are closed, especially during the summer tourist season, when domestic pollution is at its peak.

An angler in Maine, New Hampshire, or Massachusetts who is not selling his catch does not need a license to fish in salt water. These states, however, have some saltwater regulations. Massachusetts, Maine and New Hampshire sets minimum size limits for a few marine fishes. Either the states or the coastal communities in each state have regulations governing the capture of anadromous fishes. Some communities also have regulations for shellfishing and worm digging, and some require permits.

It's important to note that fishing regulations are perishable, often changing from year to year. A prudent angler will check for the latest rules before dropping a hook.

To obtain copies of fishing and shellfishing regulations, contact the following:

- Maine—Department of Marine Resources, State House Station #21, Augusta, ME 04333; (207) 289-6500.
- New Hampshire—New Hampshire Fish & Game Department, Marine Fisheries Division, 37 Concord Ave., Durham, NH 03824; (603) 868-1095.
- Massachusetts—Massachusetts Division of Marine Fisheries, 100 Cambridge St., Boston, MA 02202; (617) 727-3193.

PASSAMAQUODDY BAY TO CASCO BAY

LAND CONFIGURATION AND WATER DEPTH

Nowhere along the east coast of the United States is the shore as serrated and rugged as it is from Passama-quoddy Bay to Cape Elizabeth. Worn by glacial action and battered by heavy seas churned up by storms, this area forms the famous Down East coastline, so called because sailing ships from Boston often ran downwind on an easterly course to come here. Extending out from the mainland into the sea like many fingers are the rocky headlands. Strewn all along the shore and extending in places 20 miles beyond the headlands are hundreds of islands, a feature which has struck every explorer of this region with wonder. The land near the sea seldom rises more than 100 or 200 feet, but the Camden Hills, which rise 1,400 feet, and the mountains of Mount Desert, which rise 1,500 feet, are exceptions. Between the headlands are river mouths, deeply indented bays, and inlets running far into the land. Here the depth of water is usually over 60 feet, in some places much deeper—it's more than 500 feet off Monroe Island. Seaward, the depth increases to 400 or 500 feet about 25 miles away from the mainland, the limit of these two maps.

FISH AND FISHING

Interestingly, recreational saltwater fishing from the Maine-Canadian border down through Penobscot Bay is light at best, despite the tremendous area of prime habitat for a number of species. The short summer season, averaging just eight weeks, serves to discourage the start-up of party- and charter-boat operations, and the dearth of summer tourists here, compared with regions in the southern part of the state, doesn't help matters. However, there are some fine fishing opportunities.

Mackerel are available, normally from mid-June on, in bays and harbors along the entire upper coastline. Although the smaller "tinkers" averaging 6 to 10 inches can be taken on pieces of fresh bait or tiny chrome-plated jigs from shoreside piers and floats, big "club" mackerel of a pound or more are best pursued from a trailerable outboard. Trolling a multiple-hook rig of colorful feathers or bright pieces of rubber surgical tubing (locally called mackerel rigs or "Christmas trees") available at any hardware or tackle store are preferred and are very effective. Add a 2- to 4-ounce diamond jig to the bitter end of the rig to get it down at least 10 feet, where mackerel do their feeding. Best spots to catch mackerel? The only answer is: Ask! Every coastal town and harbor in Maine has its pet mackerel grounds, and local fishermen are usually quite free with advice. But when in doubt, troll or jig outside the lobster-trap buoy line just offshore and around nearby islands.

Groundfish—cod, pollock, cusk, wolffish and hake—can be found all along the upper or "Down East" coast in waters from about 90 feet on out to 300 feet or more. Experienced private-boat anglers look for humps and ledges that rise up off the ocean floor, employing 8- to 16-ounce chrome-plated diamond or Norwegian-style jigs on 30- to 50-pound-class jigging outfits. Bait, such as sea clams or herring chunks, also works well, but often attracts dogfish, small sharks regarded as pests. Party boats for bottom-fishing along Maine's upper coastal region can be found in Eastport, Jones-port, Bar Harbor, Northeast Harbor, and Rockland. Some are half-day and others are full-day, and tackle is provided.

Striped bass are available in summer in a number of rivers in this region, particularly the Penobscot, but only a handful of anglers pursue them. Many regard this area as the "last frontier" for the species on the East Coast, but there's a lot of water to cover.

The stretch of shoreline from Penobscot Bay south to Casco Bay, sometimes called the "Mid-Coast Region," provides some excellent fishing. The Camden and Rockland area, on the lower west side of Penobscot Bay, is a jumping-off spot for private boaters going after mackerel, groundfish, and even bluefish on occasion. Thomaston, at the navigable head of the St. George River a few miles to the west, offers boaters access to both Penobscot and Muscongus bays. Island-dotted Muscongus Bay, as well as the Medomak River that empties into it, sees comparatively little recreational fishing pressure, although the potential is there, especially for striped bass.

The area from Pemaquid Neck, the peninsula that borders the western side of Muscongus Bay, to Cape Small, which marks the eastern side of Casco Bay, encompasses three major river systems and hosts some of the finest and most varied saltwater fishing in the state. Johns Bay, on the eastern side of Pemaquid, can be a good area for mackerel and bluefish in the summer. The Damariscotta River, adjacent just to the west and separated by Rutherford Island and the village of South Bristol, is a fertile ribbon of estuaries, channels, and flats that's navigable up to the town of Damariscotta on Route 1. Although not heavily fished, the Damariscotta can produce some excellent action with striped bass, and 50-plus-pounders have been taken.

Monhegan Island, some nine miles offshore southeast of Pemaquid Point, is a popular summer resort and a favorite cruising destination in summer. Although there are no charter boats or sportfishing facilities available, there's some productive bottom for cod and pollock over a series of deep-water humps that extend some three to six miles due southwest of the island.

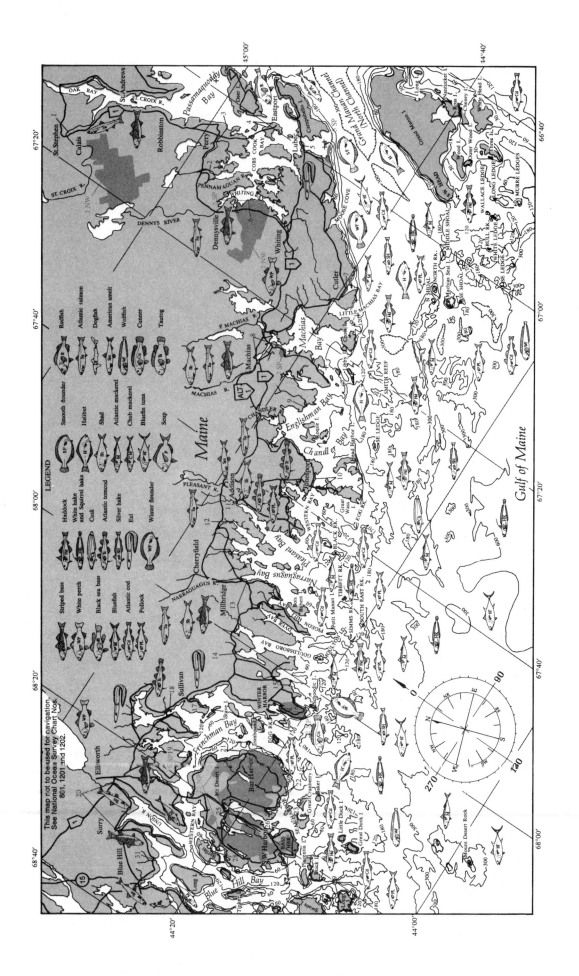

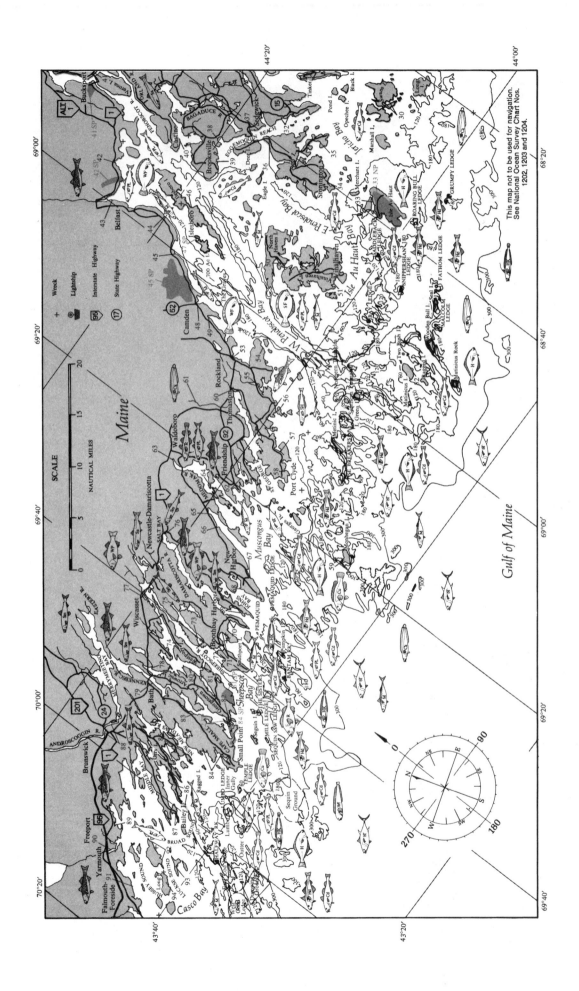

Additionally, if you can find any of a handful of sand or gravel patches a mile or two east of Monhegan in 100 to 150 feet of water, and lower down a fresh herring on a 7/0 or larger hook, you may just catch a halibut, Maine's ultimate bottom-fishing prize. These huge members of the flounder tribe can top 100 pounds, but a 30-pounder is more likely.

Just around the corner from Pemaquid Point, again to the west and working downcoast, is the Boothbay region, home to a fleet of three party boats and a half-dozen charter craft. Considered the East Coast's northernmost serious sportfishing destination, Boothbay Harbor is a bustling summer resort as well as an important commercial lobstering port.

The party boats target bottom fish—especially cod, pollock, hake and cusk—and often work an area known as the Kettle, a popular plateau-like expanse of bottom situated 10 miles south of Seguin Island that rises up as high as 200 feet from the ocean floor, although average depths are closer to 300 feet. The charter boats fish the same area for blue, mako and porbeagle sharks, and the Kettle has been very productive for bluefin tuna ranging in size from 150 to 800-plus pounds from mid-July through September since 1993. Boothay's charter boats also chase bluefish, striped bass and mackerel closer to shore, and private-boaters can launch at Boothbay Harbor, East Boothbay and West Boothbay Harbor to get in on the fun. Productive near-shore areas include the east side of Southport Island, the shoals just below Damariscove Island, and the mouth of the Sheepscot River. Trolled seven-inch swimming plugs in blue/white, silver/white or mackerel patterns are particularly effective for both bass and blues in this area.

The Sheepscot itself is an interesting river. It's one of Maine's coldest, year-round, yet never freezes. Bluefish cruise the wide mouth, known as Sheepscot Bay, during warm weather, and striped bass roam as far up as Wiscasset (on Route 1) and beyond, chasing schools of mackerel and menhaden, locally known as pogies, through September. The beach at Reid State Park on the western bank at the Sheepscot's mouth can provide some good surf-fishing for stripers.

The next river in the threesome is the famous Kennebec, which empties out to sea just three miles south of the Sheepscot. Once seriously polluted by industrial runoff many miles upriver, the Kennebec has benefited from new, stringent environmental laws and once again hosts populations of salmon, sturgeon, shad and striped bass, among others.

Arguably the best striper river in Maine, the Kennebec and its waterways that connect it to the Sheepscot system, including the Sasanoa River, Hockomock Bay and the famous Upper and Lower Hell Gates (well marked on chart #13293), annually produce thousands of bass from schoolie-size to 40-plus-pounders for hundreds of resident and visiting anglers. This is trailerboat country at its finest, with good access at Bath and Phippsburg (on the Kennebec) and Wiscasset (on the Sheepscot). There are several good river guide services in Bath, Edgecomb, Wiscasset and Boothbay Harbor. Popham Beach, at the mouth of the Kennebec, is a popular surf-fishing spot for both bass and blues. The coastline around the corner to the south is mostly sand beach dotted with rocky islands and ledges, with plenty of shoal water that provides ideal summer habitat for stripers and blues. Towering Sequin Island, less than two miles offshore, is surrounded by deeper water to 100 feet and more, a good area to troll or live-bait for both species. Good fishing, if you hit it right, extends westward three miles to Cape Small, the eastern gateway to Casco Bay.

CASCO BAY TO ISLES OF SHOALS

LAND CONFIGURATION AND WATER DEPTH

South of Casco Bay the shoreline is characterized by a succession of sandy or gravelly beaches alternating with rocky headlands. Compared with the coast of Maine to the east, there are only a few islands. The most notable ones are Boon Island and the Isles of Shoals, which consist of eight islands plus a number of islets, rocks, and ledges. The land along the seacoast from Casco Bay to the Isles of Shoals seldom rises more than 100 feet from the sea; usually it is less than 50 feet. From the sandy or gravelly beaches out a distance of about a quarter mile, the depth increases to 40 feet. Within a few hundred yards of the headlands the depth is 60 or 70 feet. For a distance of 15 or 20 miles offshore the bottom continues downward to about 600 feet and forms a deep pocket or depression called Jeffreys Basin. Continuing seaward from this basin the bottom rises rapidly to form Jeffreys Ledge, a bank about 3 miles wide by 45 miles long. Over this ledge the depth is usually less than 180 feet.

FISH AND FISHING

Casco Bay is the watery backyard of metropolitan Portland, Maine's largest city. Bounded by Cape Small to the east and Cape Elizabeth to the west, the bay is 18 miles wide at its mouth and extends inland nearly the same distance. Casco's myriad of southwesterly pointing granite, evergreen-carpeted island fingers, rocky shoals, coves and rivers—including the New Meadows, Harraseeket, Royal and Presumpscot—provide some good fishing for striped bass, bluefish, mackerel and even "market-size" cod, pollock and other groundfish from June through September.

7

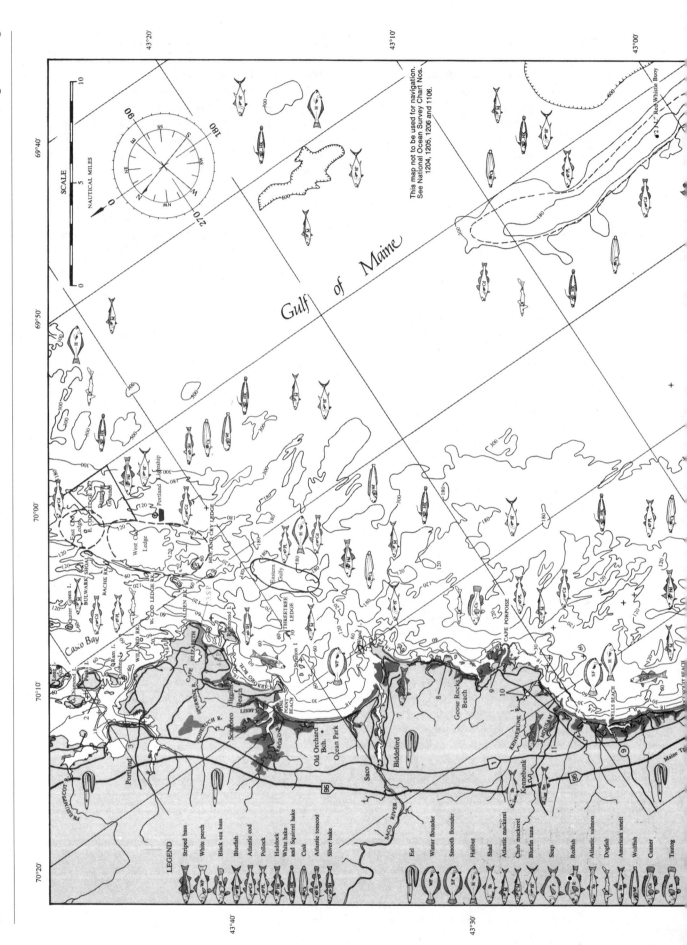

Gulf of Maine

This map not to be used for navigation.
See National Ocean Survey Chart Nos.
1204, 1205, 1206 and 1106.

SCALE
NAUTICAL MILES

LEGEND

Striped bass
White perch
Black sea bass
Bluefish
Atlantic cod
Pollock
Haddock
White hake
and Squirrel hake
Cusk
Atlantic tomcod
Silver hake

Eel
Water flounder
Smooth flounder
Halibut
Shad
Atlantic mackerel
Chub mackerel
Bluefin tuna
Scup
Redfish
Atlantic salmon
Dogfish
American smelt
Wolffish
Cunner
Tautog

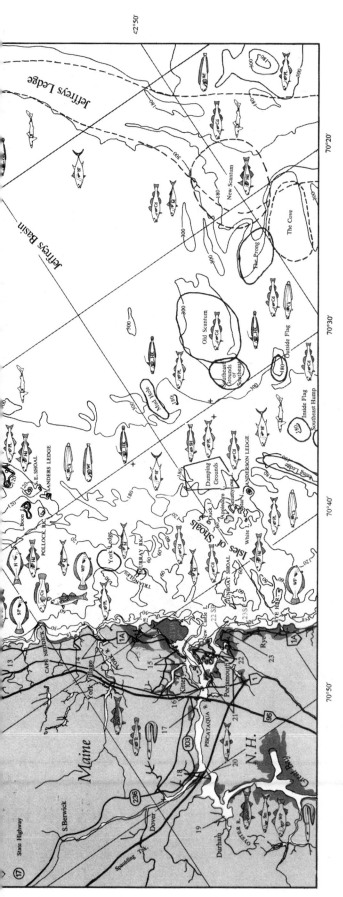

Blues can be taken almost anywhere on occasion, although few areas offer consistent day-to-day action. The ledges in the outer bay—including Temple, Lumbo, Halfway Rock, Bulwark Shoal and Alden Rock—are good spots to troll, yet bluefish will often chase bait right up into a foot of water in the expansive mud flats along the northwest side of the bay that stretch from Portland to Brunswick. This is prime striper habitat as well. Bottom fish can be taken around the numerous rocks, ledges, and underwater humps and outcroppings in the outer bay. Try depths of 90 to 150 feet over hard bottom, with six- or eight-ounce diamond jigs or pieces of fresh-cut bait. There are a number of good launch ramps and pleasure-boat marinas in the Portland area, and party and charter boats for groundfish, stripers, and blues, sharks and tuna are available in Portland, South Freeport and South Harpswell.

The Spurwink River marks the southerly natural border of Cape Elizabeth, and school-size stripers are plentiful from its banks in the summer—a great fly-fishing area. Adjacent is Higgins Beach, one of the state's top surf-fishing beaches for bass. Continuing south, crescent-shaped Saco Bay, home of famous Old Orchard Beach, terminates at Biddeford Pool and the mouth of the Saco River, another top Maine river for stripers and, on occasion, bluefish.

The five-mile stretch of coast from Biddeford Pool down to Cape Porpoise offers some inshore potential for bass, blues and mackerel. Just around the corner of Cape Arundel is the town of Kennebunkport, situated a mile or so up the Kennebunk River, home to several deep-sea party boats and a modest commercial bluefin tuna fleet in summer. Kennebunkport is also the closest jumping-off spot to the northern part of Jeffreys Ledge known as "The Fingers," 20 miles offshore, well known for its good catches of bottom fish and bluefin tuna.

The next harbor to the south is Wells Harbor, followed by Perkins Cove at Ogunquit, five miles farther down. Perkins Cove hosts a small fleet of party, commercial and pleasure boats, as does York Harbor, seven more miles downcoast, which provides good access to Boon Island and its adjacent ledges six miles offshore, where there can be some good bottom-fishing and occasional action with giant bluefin tuna. All of the ports along the state's south coast below Portland are jumping-off spots for productive Jeffreys Ledge, which ranges from 20 to 30 miles offshore, as well as the famous tuna and bottom-fish grounds farther to the east into the Gulf of Maine including Platts Bank and Cashes Ledge.

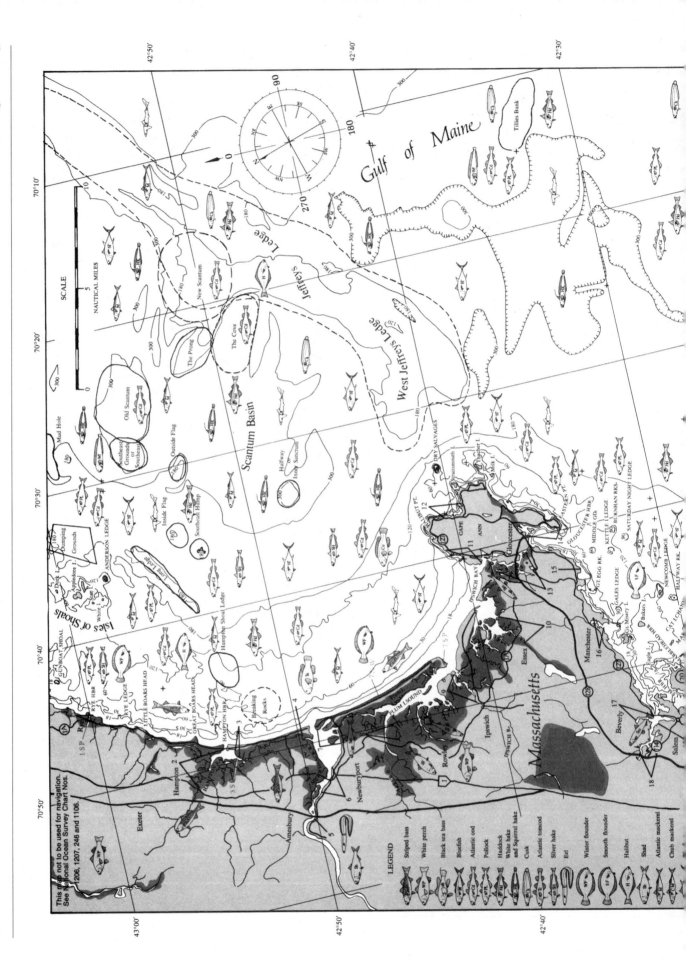

This map is not to be used for navigation.
See National Ocean Survey Chart Nos.
206, 1207, 246 and 1106.

SCALE

NAUTICAL MILES

LEGEND

Striped bass
White perch
Black sea bass
Bluefish
Atlantic cod
Pollock
Haddock
White hake
and Squirrel hake
Cusk
Atlantic tomcod
Silver hake
Eel
Winter flounder
Smooth flounder
Halibut
Shad
Atlantic mackerel
Chub mackerel

Gulf of Maine

Tillies Bank

Jeffreys Ledge

West Jeffreys Ledge

New Scantum

Scantum Basin

The Cove

The Prong

Old Scantum

Mud Hole

Southeast Grounds
or Southeast

Outside Flag

Inside Flag

Southeast Hump

Halfway
Inner Sanctum

Anderson Ledge

Hampton Shoal Ledge

Boon Ledge

Isles of Shoals

Gunboat Shoal

Rye Harbor

Rye Ledge

Little Boars Head

Great Boars Head

Breaking Rocks

Hampton Harbor

Dumping Grounds

White I.
Star I.
Duck I.
Appledore I.

Exeter

Hampton

Amesbury

Newburyport

Ipswich

Rowley

Massachusetts

Plum Island

Plum Sound

Ipswich Bay

Ipswich R.

Essex

Manchester

Beverly

Salem

Gloucester

Cape Ann

Halibut Pt.

Portsmouth

Straitsmouth I.
Thacher I.
Milk I.

Dry Salvages

Eastern Pt.

Gloucester Hbr.

Kettle I.

Middle Gd.

Gt. Egg Rk.
Burnham Rks.
Saturday Night Ledge

Gales Ledge

Baker's I.

Gt. Misery I.

Newcomb Ledge

Halfway Rk.

Eagle I.

Cat Chan.

Marblehead Hbr.

Marblehead

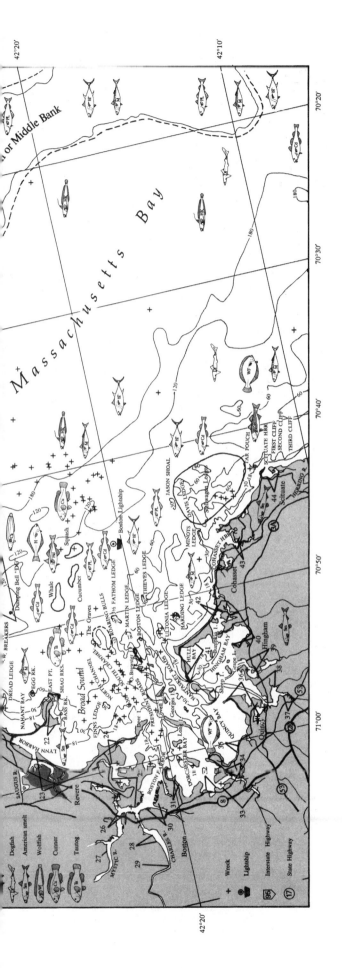

ISLES OF SHOALS TO SCITUATE HARBOR

LAND CONFIGURATION

The coastline from Rye Harbor to the Hampton River in New Hampshire is a succession of rocky headlands separated by sand or sand-gravel beaches. From Hampton River to Ipswich Bay in Massachusetts the beaches are mostly sandy. Plum Island, off the northern Massachusetts coast, is the first large barrier beach south of the United States-Canadian border. Coastal land formations from Rye Harbor to Ipswich Bay are relatively low, seldom rising more than 50 feet above sea level.

The rocky headlands of Cape Ann protrude seaward more than 7 miles from the general coastline of Massachusetts to form one of the most noticeable features along this section of coast. Small rocky islands, such as Dry Salvages, Thacher, and Milk Islands, lie about a mile beyond Cape Ann. The rocky shore of Cape Ann and south to about Marblehead rises 50 to 100 feet from the sea. Pool Hill, on Cape Ann, rises 235 feet and is the highest elevation along the coast from Rye Harbor to Scituate Harbor. The coastline from Cape Ann to Scituate is mostly rocky, although there are isolated stretches of sand such as the beaches of Marblehead, Lynn, Revere, Winthrop, and Nantasket. The many rocky islands in Greater Boston Bay more closely resemble the coast north of Casco Bay, Maine. With the exceptions of Deer Island, just north of Boston Harbor, and the islands and hills on the shore of Hingham and Hull Bays, some of which rise 150 feet or more, the land along the coast from Marblehead to Scituate rises no more than 50 feet.

BOTTOM CONFIGURATION AND WATER DEPTH

North of Cape Ann, proceeding away from shore about 20 miles, the depth of the water increases to 400 feet, the bottom of Scantum Basin. Another few miles offshore of this deep basin the bottom rises rapidly to about 150 feet on Jeffreys Ledge. Seaward of this ledge the depth increases to about 900 feet at the bottom of Wilkinson Basin, which is beyond the limit of the accompanying chart. South of Cape Ann, proceeding away from shore, the depth increases to 200 or 300 feet in Massachusetts Bay before the bottom rises rapidly to about 80 feet on Stellwagen Bank. Beyond Stellwagen Bank the bottom slopes downward to about 900 feet, the deepest part of Murray Basin. Near shore the bottom is composed mostly of sand or a sand-gravel mixture. Offshore the bottom is sand and mud, and in the basins entirely mud. Scattered from shore to the basins are boulders, rocky patches, and rock outcrops.

FISH AND FISHING

Kittery, Maine, and Portsmouth, New Hampshire, at the mouth of the Piscataqua River that marks the boundary between the two states, combine to host a large fleet of commercial groundfish and lobster boats, tuna vessels, party and charters boats, and recreational craft. Much of the fishing takes place out on Jeffreys Ledge, but there can be some good bottom-fishing around the Isles of Shoals.

The Portsmouth area also offers some fine inshore sport for the small-boater. The Piscataqua River and its islands and ledges at the mouth provide some excellent fishing for stripers, and many local experts favor live bait when targeting larger bass, which can top 40 pounds. Bluefish action can be fast and furious at times, especially in mid- to late summer, and schools of big mackerel can show up between late May and October.

A brace of 40-pound-plus striped bass taken from New England waters on trolled plugs. (VIN T. SPARANO)

Coho salmon, introduced into the Piscataqua a decade ago, are an occasional catch, but the number taken each season continues to dwindle.

New Hampshire's 15 or so miles of coastline consists mostly of beaches punctuated by rocky heads and ledges. The two main harbors below Portsmouth, Rye, and Hampton are home to several party and charter boats, as well as facilities for private boats. The beaches offer some good surf-casting for stripers and blues, although an influx of sun-worshipping tourists in summer may discourage daytime anglers. The beach extends southward across the border to Salisbury in Massachusetts, terminating at the mouth of the Merrimack River.

The Merrimack is perhaps Massachusetts' most important river in terms of fish and fishing. Primary access is via the city of Newburyport some three miles upriver, where a number of marinas, launch ramps, motels, restaurants, and party- and charter-boat services can be found. The river itself offers some outstanding small-boat fishing for striped bass. The expansive Joppa Flats along the southern shore can provide outstanding shallow-water fly-fishing for bass to 40 pounds, and the entire mouth of the river is consistently productive. Bluefish often invade the area in summer, and mackerel school up just outside the jetties in spring. Decent bottom-fishing for cod, pollock and flounder can be found over a number of local grounds just offshore.

Plum Island, a narrow strip of sand beach extending southward seven miles from the Merrimack, is bordered by the open Atlantic on the east and by sheltered Plum Sound on the inside. An historically productive surf-fishing beach for striped bass from spring through fall—and where die-hards used to catch cod at night in frigid mid-winter—Plum Island still offers some good fishing for stripers, although shore access and parking have become increasingly problematic due to the island's popularity as a nature preserve and the accompanying regulations.

Just south of Plum Island is Castle Neck, inside of which lies shallow Essex Bay, which hosts a myriad of islands, flats and creeks, a productive ground for striped bass in summer. Offshore is Ipswich Bay, the half-round expanse of water between Castle Neck and the northeast tip of Cape Ann. An important near-shore commercial fishing ground, Ipswich Bay produces whiting (silver hake), cod, pollock and flounder.

Cape Ann is the home of Gloucester, one of the Northeast's most famous commercial fishing ports, yet it provides some excellent sport for anglers as well. The Annisquam River, which separates Cape Ann from the mainland, hosted tremendous numbers of big winter flounder in years past, but fishing for this species has fallen off. Striped bass can be taken almost anywhere along the river and at its mouth at Ipswich Bay, and an occasional tautog may be boated as well. Cunners, small pollock, flounders and occasional striped bass can be taken almost anywhere from Cape Ann's rocky shoreline, and small-boaters can pick up these species plus mackerel, bluefish and small cod. Offshore, boaters with seaworthy craft can work Jeffreys Ledge, which starts 10 miles northeast of Cape Ann and stretches 30 miles to the north. With average depths of 150 to 200 feet, Jeffreys can offer some good bottom-fishing for cod, pollock, cusk, hake and the occasional haddock, although commercial overfishing has significantly reduced stocks of bottom fish in recent years. Bluefin tuna fishermen often work the grounds known as The Cove and New Scantum at the southern end of the ledge, as well as The Fingers at the northwest tip, which is actually closer to York and Kennebunkport in Maine. Another productive, and much closer, tuna area can be found just a few miles off Cape Ann's Halibut Point, a favorite spot for chummers using live or fresh whiting, mackerel or herring for bait. Launch ramps, bait-and-tackle stores, and marinas are abundant on Cape Ann, and Gloucester hosts an excellent fleet of party boats that target bottom fish, as well as charter boats that go after bass, blues and giant tuna.

The shoreline to the south of Cape Ann swings westward in a semicircle to form the upper rim of Massachusetts Bay known as the "North Shore." It encompasses Manchester, Beverly, Salem and Marblehead, harbors which ring island-studded Salem Sound, a tremendously diverse and productive area for stripers, blues, flounders and mackerel. The shallow Danvers River system is an especially good area for school-size stripers from late May into October, with easy access in the town of Danversport. Decent inshore bottom-fishing, as well as action with stripers and blues, can often be found around the ledges and over the rocky bottom from Marblehead Neck down to Nahant. Devereux Beach just below "The Neck" has been especially good for surf-casters chasing stripers during the past couple of seasons. This brings us out into Broad Sound, the outer reaches of famous Boston Harbor.

The waters of Boston Harbor, which surround its historic islands and make up its inner bays, has suffered from the excesses of the city of Boston and nearby communities for centuries. Long regarded as one of the most polluted ports in the nation, aggressive action is underway to reverse the trend, and some progress has been measured in the last several years. "Boston Bay," as this whole area used to be known, was probably the richest area in the world for winter flounder due to a lush, expansive habitat of flats, channels, shell beds and forage organisms. Commercial net-fishing was banned in the 1960's as stocks dwindled, and "blackbacks" rebounded in force in the 1970's, fueling the growth of party-boat and skiff-rental operations. Unfortunately, flounder populations here have diminished in the past

decade due to overfishing in other parts of the species' range, but good catches can still be made.

The most productive areas for flounder continue to be around the islands in Dorchester and Quincy bays down through Hingham and Hull bays. Late May, June, September, and early October are prime times, and seaworms top the list as bait. Sharp anglers will chum with crushed clam shells or canned kernel corn in ten to 30 feet of water, and calm, sunny days are often the most productive. Cunners and small cod are incidental catches, especially in deeper water.

Boston Harbor has also offered some excellent striped bass fishing during the past few seasons. Hot spots include Broad Head Bar off the beach at Winthrop, Great Faun Bar off Deer Island, the waters around Long Island, the crescent of Brewster Islands (Little, Great, Middle and Outer) and the Shag Rocks at the outer harbor. Live eels, chunks of pogy (menhaden) and trolled swimming plugs and spoons prove deadly. The area around Hull Gut, between Peddocks Island and Hull, is excellent also, and trolled umbrella rigs are good producers. Bluefish action has been decent in the Boston Harbor region, especially in the deeper water, but numbers are down due to the species' decline all along the coast.

The stretch of shoreline from Point Allerton at the northern tip of Nantasket Beach down to Cohasset hosts some outstanding bass fishing, and there have been rumors of a couple of 70-pound bass taken at night and hustled quietly away by paranoid anglers afraid that their secret hot spots would be discovered. Good striper fishing can be found in the waters around Cohasset Harbor, particularly around Shag Rock and Minots Ledge just offshore a mile or so to the northeast. Dependable bass fishing can also be found from Minots Beach and "The Cliffs" area below Scituate. This entire stretch of coastline below Boston hosts some good inshore boat-fishing opportunities for flounder in spring and fall, as well as cod and other bottom dwellers. Launch ramps and boating facilities are numerous.

Much of the offshore fishing done out of ports from Gloucester south through Cape Cod Bay centers on Stellwagen Bank, a half-moon of prolific bottom stretching from a point 30 miles due east of Boston southward to Provincetown on Cape Cod's tip. Designated a National Marine Sanctuary in 1993, Stellwagen's rich bottom composition of sand, gravel, clay, shell beds and rocky mounds in depths ranging from 90 to 150 feet provides ideal habitat for whiting and other species of hake, herring, mackerel, and sand eels, which in turn attract cod, haddock, pollock, striped bass and bluefin tuna. Heavily fished during the warmer months by a substantial fleet of commercial, party, charter and private vessels, Stellwagen Bank continues to provide decent catches despite immense fishing pressure.

SCITUATE HARBOR TO ROUND HILL POINT

CAPE COD

Cape Cod, the most prominent cape of the United States' Atlantic coast, extends from the mainland of Massachusetts about 40 miles east to Monomoy Point, thence 35 miles northwest to Race Point. Early explorers were impressed by the Cape's various features and used different names in their writings and on their maps to describe it. The Icelanders called it Kialarnes or Ship's Nose for its resemblance to the high upturned prow of the Norse ships; Estéban Gomez, a native of Portugal, called it Cabo de Arenas or Sandy Cape for its high sandy cliffs, some of which rise more than 150 feet from the sea; the Frenchmen Pierre de Monts and Samuel de Champlain called it Cap Blanc or White Cape for the color of its sandy cliffs; and the first Dutch explorers, apparently respecting the French name, called it Witte Hoeck, White Hook; Englishman Bartholomew Gosnold, in 1602, the first to make a direct passage to this region from Europe, called it Shoal Hope. His use of the word "shoal" may refer to his loss of hope when he found this area not to be Virginia, his intended destination, or to his discouragement during the long two months' voyage across the Atlantic. Regardless of the reason, Gosnold soon changed the name to Cape Cod in recognition of his excellent success at cod fishing.

LAND CONFIGURATION AND WATER DEPTH

Except for the rocky headlands at Manomet Point and the preponderance of rocks along the shore of Buzzards Bay, the shoreline south of Scituate Harbor is mostly sandy. Along many of the beaches and extending away from shore are scattered rocks and boulders. The shoreline is unbroken from Scituate, around Race Point, to Monomoy Island, except at New Inlet and where it is indented by a few bays and harbors such as Duxbury, Plymouth, Barnstable, Wellfleet, and Nauset. Though Captains Hill on Duxbury Bay and the sand hills and cliffs of Cape Cod between North Truro and Wellfleet, commonly called the Highlands, rise over 150 feet, most of the land bordering the sea seldom rises more than 125 feet. From Monomoy Island west to Woods Hole and around Buzzards Bay are many smaller bays and harbors, and the shoreline is more irregular than it is to the north. Although in this "south shore" area the maximum elevation is about 125 feet, the land seldom rises more than 50 feet above the sea.

The sea floor within Cape Cod Bay slopes downward to its maximum depth of 195 feet off Race Point.

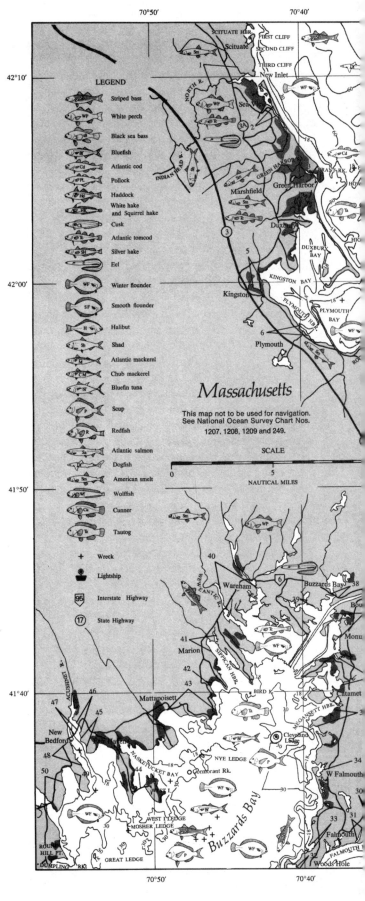

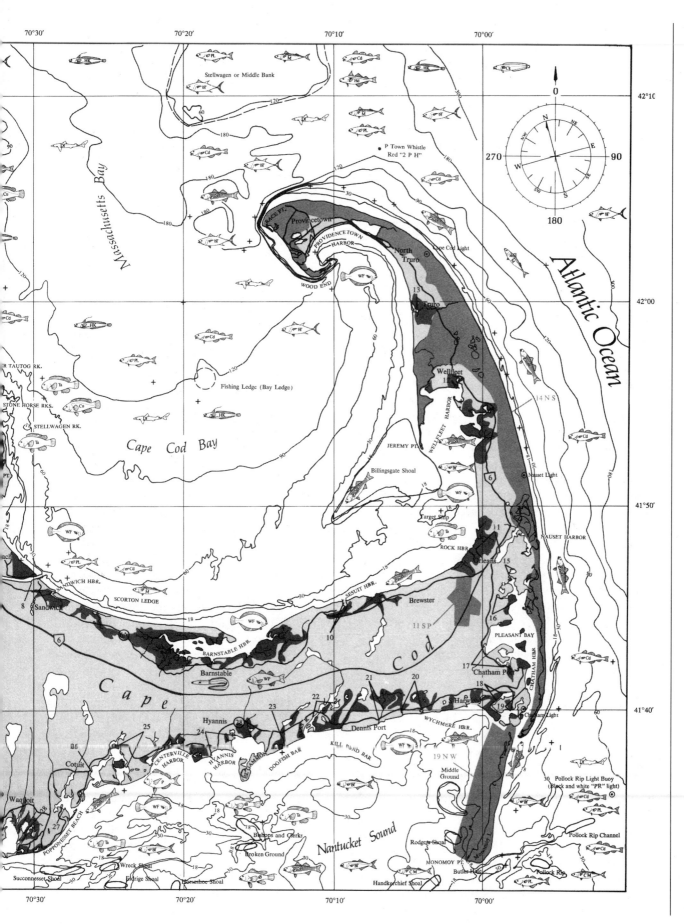

Starting from shore the composition of bottom sediments changes from sand to a sand-mud mixture and finally to mud in the deepest depths. Scattered throughout this bay are stones, boulders, and rock outcrops. Some of the better known ones are Farnham Rock, High Pine Ledge, Stone Horse Rocks, Stellwagen Rock, and Fishing Ledge.

Along the east side of Cape Cod the sea floor slopes downward rapidly to 600 feet. The bottom in this area is mostly sand, shell, and gravel. Along the southern shore of Cape Cod and in Buzzards Bay, the depths are usually less than 60 feet. Here the bottom is composed of sand, sand-mud, or gravel and is often interrupted by shoals, bars, and rocks, some protruding out of the water, but most hidden a few feet below the surface.

FISH AND FISHING: SCITUATE HARBOR TO ROUND HILL POINT

The coast from Scituate to upper Cape Cod, also called the South Shore, is typical of the Northeast—a patchwork of rugged surf-pounded headlands, cliffs, and craggy islands broken by beaches, estuaries, and sheltered tidal marshes. Offshore, the bottom of Cape Cod Bay is strewn with ledges, rocky reefs, sandy shoals, and huge underwater boulders, all courtesy of the last glacier.

During the winter months, things are quiet along the South Shore, although a few hardy New Englanders venture out in search of codfish. Cod are found closer to shore from November to April, and can sometimes be caught on clams or seaworms fished off harbor jetties and beaches. During stretches of calm weather, boat fishermen catch them over inshore ledges, sunken wrecks, and reefs. Tautog (blackfish) are also caught ocassionally in these same spots in the spring and fall, although this is about the northernmost range of the species. The numerous wrecks scattered along the bottom of Cape Cod Bay, in 60 to 100 feet of water, all hold cod, small pollock, and assorted bottom fish. Pollock Shoals off Scituate is a popular cod spot through the early spring. Travel further south off Green Harbor in Marshfield and you'll find them on ledges and rocky bottom, most often in 30 to 50 feet of water, while winter surf-casters sometimes catch them off the Duxbury beaches on clams and seaworms.

Mackerel are early-spring arrivals, entering Bay waters sometime in April. They can weigh up to two pounds and you'll find them around harbor jetties, points, and nearshore buoys, as well as migrating through the open water of the Bay in large schools. Locate a school and you can load up on them with small silver jigs or Christmas tree rigs—and they're loads of fun on the fly rod! Also in early spring, blackback flounder get active in mud-bottomed estuaries, bays, and marshes. After May, these fish move to deeper offshore waters. April sees shad entering the North

River system in Scituate, where anglers can catch them on flies, shiny spoons, and small jigs. White perch are another spring option, and can be caught in brackish marshes and estuaries on small flies, spinners, live killifish, and seaworms.

Come spring, South Shore anglers eagerly anticipate the arrival of the first striped bass of the season. Schoolies enter the area in mid- to late April, prowling the bottom around inshore rocks and ledges. Here, they forage for crabs, worms, and eels until the water warms and they begin to chase baitfish more aggressively. Bass can be found around virtually any jetty, beach, inlet, marsh, and rock pile during the spring migration. Beginning in late May and June, larger bass arrive, taking up residence around nearshore rocky areas. Here you'll often find them feeding right in the wash around the base of boulders and cliffs, waiting for baitfish to be tumbled by the swells.

One of the most productive places for striper-fishing throughout the season is the North River in Scituate and the ocean waters around its mouth. Third Cliff, Long Ledge, and Scituate Light also produce throughout the season. Green Harbor and the waters around Duxbury offer great schoolie action, and the deeper ocean ledges produce big fish through the hot months of summer.

As waters warm up in July, the bass head to deeper, darker haunts during the day. This is when drifting live eels or chunk baits at night around structure can be most productive, although this method also works during the day. Soaking chunk baits on the bottom of inlets and channels proves effective, too, with live eels becoming the primary bait by mid-summer. Deeper ledges, shoals, and reefs produce keeper bass through the hot summer months, when the fish tend to hold deep on bright days. Many troll wire line and umbrella rigs, tube lures, and parachute jigs around these spots. At night, any estuary, creek, or inlet can be counted on to produce action, too, especially on the outgoing tide.

Bluefish join the summer hit parade, and schools of five- to ten-pounders can be found feeding in inlets, on tidal flats, and around jetties when they make their appearance in June. By late July, blues have moved offshore to spawn, but return fatter and hungrier in late summer. Here they join schools of striped bass in feeding blitzes, both species tearing through schools of menhaden (pogies), herring, and mackerel that become trapped in protected bays, harbors, and inlets.

Bluefin tuna of all sizes, from 60-pound schoolies to 700-pound-plus giants, migrate into the Bay in late June or July and linger through the early fall. Trolling often produces the best results when the fish first arrive, while chunking is preferred after the fish settle down around structure and begin fattening up on bait. From the top of White Cliffs in Plymouth on a clear day, you can look far out over the Bay and see acre-wide schools of bass, blues, or tuna churning the surface as they tear into pods of baitfish.

Summer flounder, or fluke, take the place of winter flounder in late spring, the latter having moved offshore to deeper water. One of the most popular recreational species in the Northeast, fluke provide action around inlets, jetties, sandy shoals, and beaches. This is a quiet sport that's available all along the coast, and many a summer afternoon finds anglers anchored up or peacefully drifting sandworms on the bottom for fluke.

When the dog days of summer set in, causing a lull in inshore daylight action, many head offshore to Stellwagen Bank, which is accessible from any port along the South Shore. The Bank holds large amounts of mackerel, whiting, sand eels, and other baitfish, which in turn attract everything from giant bluefin tuna to sharks to pollock. Cod, stripers, and bluefish can all figure into a day's catch off Stellwagen, and there's sure to be a few whales around to keep things interesting.

After the exciting September and October action with blues and bass, the South Shore grows quiet again, although a few big bass may linger until December if a strong Nor'easter doesn't drive them out. Things eventually come full circle, with cod and pollock moving inshore again in October and November. Of course, many diehards extend the season by catching smelt, which enter harbors and rivers in late fall and can be caught through the winter.

Moving south to Cape Cod, the coast becomes progressively sandier. Scusset and Sagamore beaches near the east end of the Cape Cod Canal host outstanding striped bass fishing from June through early fall. Also popular is the mackerel fishing near the Canal entrance in spring, and small cod can be caught nearby from fall through March or April. Another spring option that few people know about is fishing for sea-run trout that swim near the mouth of Scorton Creek in Sandwich. (The tidal flats here also offer great action with blues and bass in May, June, and July.)

Then there's the Canal itself, a giant fish highway linking Buzzards Bay and Cape Cod Bay. Everything from sand eels to whales, bonito, seals, bluefish, tuna, and ocean sunfish use this manmade shortcut, where currents can reach eight knots; however, the "Big Ditch" is most famous for its bass fishing. The big stripers enter the Canal in May, initially taking up station near the mouth of the famous herring run, which leads up to Herring Pond in the town of Bourne. Many keepers are taken here each spring on—you guessed it—live herring. Throughout the summer and fall, monster blues and hefty stripers provide outstanding action for the fishermen who line the Canal's rocky banks. Baits, plugs, and flies all produce during slack water, when bass leave their bottom hideouts to chase bait, often on or near the surface. Best action comes at night and early morning, when sunlight and boat traffic are minimal.

There's nothing like fishing the Canal on a silent, gray morning, casting toward the sounds of busting stripers hidden in the fog.

Sand eels are the predominant summer visitors along the inner arm of Cape Cod, not surprising for a giant sandbar. This is where you'll find striped bass and bluefish feeding in the sandy shallows from Sandwich to Wellfleet on a rising tide. You can enjoy exciting surface action with topwater plugs and flies, or simply soak a chunk of mackerel on the bottom and hope a bass happens upon it. Speaking of mackerel, these light-tackle favorites enter the Bay in April, and can be found near buoys, jetties, and other structure. Or you can intercept them as they migrate northward through open water in large schools. Winter flounder are available in Barnstable Harbor early on, and striped bass and bluefish are caught here beginning in June. Barnstable also offers great shallow-water fishing for bass and blues, whether you wade or fish from a small boat.

As spring turns to summer, the inshore waters of the Cape fill with bait. Herring, squid, silversides, and shoals of sand eels all provide forage for the local game species. The sandy flats off Brewster, midway along the Cape, is the site of an exciting new fishery involving sight-fishing for stripers that cruise the shallows; it's just like fishing for bonefish, complete with skiffs and push-poles!

Billingsgate Shoal off Wellfleet is a well-known hot spot among Cape anglers, and striped bass line up here throughout the summer to nab bait being swept over the shallows by strong tides. Big bluefish are found feeding here, too, and giant bluefin tuna have even shown up on the Shoal in past summers. Wellfleet Harbor is another excellent spot to find blues and bass, especially in the main channel.

Another popular species is fluke, or summer flounder. These bottom fish can be caught throughout the Bay on tide-washed flats and shoals, as well as near channels and harbor mouths where they wait to intercept bait being swept by on the outgoing tide. Methods include drifting with clams and seaworms on spreader bars or slow-trolling live mummichogs and small "snapper" blues on spinner-blade rigs.

Moving to the tip of Cape Cod, you'll find outstanding action with stripers and bluefish from Truro around to the famous Race Point off Provincetown. Action here begins in April with school bass and runs through late fall. Jetties in Provincetown Harbor yield action with blues, bass, and flounder in summer, and even cod and pollock in the early spring and late fall. The tip of the Cape also marks the northernmost limit for summer visitors such as bonito and little tunny (false albacore), which can be found in rips formed over areas of uneven bottom. Here baitfish are tumbled in the strong currents, providing easy prey for these swift, powerful predators.

Any port from Provincetown to Barstable serves as a prime jumping-off spot for pursuing bluefin tuna in the Bay. These fish can be found cruising open water in large schools beginning in midsummer, then take up station around bottom structure. Stellwagen Bank is a good place to find them during August, when chunking can be productive.

The coastline from Provincetown along the surf-pounded outer beaches of the Cape Cod National Seashore are legendary among surf-fishermen, but those fishing from boats do just as well. This sandy stretch yields many huge stripers every year, and the fishing is getting better and better. Nauset Beach, Coast Guard Beach, and Head of the Meadow are some of the most famous striper haunts in all of surf-fishing, and during March and April, a fair share of small cod and pollock on bottom baits are fished close to shore. The secret to striper fishing here is to look for pockets, sand bars, and deep cuts at low tide, where bass will feed on the rising tide. Whether you soak a chunk of mackerel or an eel on the bottom or cast lures and flies into the surf, you can be sure that there are big stripers cruising nearby. and remember: the best action will come at night.

Along the deeper contours off the Cape, such as the 20-fathom line, you can find cod along the bottom in spring and late fall. Head out even farther to 50 fathoms and you may find bluefin tuna moving through in July and August.

Moving to the elbow of the Cape, great fishing continues. The classic shoal-water rips off Monomoy Island and Chatham are home to big bass, bluefish, bonito, and little tunny throughout summer and early fall. These spots can be productive right through the summer, even in bright daylight, although the most consistent action occurs on overcast days, at night, and in the early morning and evening hours. Fishermen do well by simply drifting through the roiling waters with live eels, live pogies, and cut bait, or by slow-trolling umbrella rigs, tube lures, and jigs on wire line. Recently, fly rodders have been scoring as well, especially with small sand eel imitations. Inside the protective line of beaches, there's outstanding flats action with bass in the marshes near Chatham. Here, fly fishermen play the sight-casting game as off Brewster. Record-size bass are also caught in deep pockets behind the Chatham bar and in the sheltered waters of Pleasant Bay, many at night on drifted chunks and eels. Flounder fishing can also be productive around any shoal or inlet with good tidal flow.

Moving west along the south side of the Cape, you'll find action with winter flounder and white perch in the marshes, tidal ponds, and estuaries in early spring and late fall. These places also offer excellent bass fishing beginning in May, particularly after dark on an outgoing tide. The Bass River near the towns of Yarmouth and Harwich is an excellent place to hunt for bass.

There's great action near its mouth and well upstream, especially at night.

The bottom of Nantucket Sound is laced with sandy shoals, all offering great fishing from May through November for blues and stripers, which are joined from July to October by bonito and little tunny. Flounder can be taken by drifting bottom baits (clams and seaworms are best) in these same spots, as well as along contour lines in 20 feet of water.

March and April and late fall are the best times to target tautog, which concentrate around inshore rockpiles, wrecks, and ledges. In fact, it's on the south side of the Cape that tautog fishing really begins to get productive. Anglers catch them by anchoring over bottom structure in 20 to 50 feet of water and sending down fiddler crabs or seaworms. Chumming helps to spark action.

The sandy flats skirting the shore off Osterville provide great action with small- to medium-sized bluefish in June and early July, while the bays, coves, and estuaries are home to school bass. Off Falmouth and Osterville, Horseshoe Shoal is a great spot to find bass, blues, and other summer visitors, while the swift waters of Woods Hole yield dependable yet frenetic action with bonito in late July, August, and September.

And who could overlook the famous "holes" of the Elizabeth Islands, arguably one of the best spots on earth to catch a trophy bass? Here strong currents flow between Buzzards Bay and Vineyard Sound, tumbling baitfish of all sorts and providing easy pickings for large stripers. Woods Hole, Robinsons Hole, Quicks Hole, and the rocky reefs such as Sows and Pigs all yield catches of enormous bass and bluefish throughout the summer, and few bass fanatics fail to recognize the name Cuttyhunk, once the site of the country's first bass-fishing clubs. On the Buzzards Bay side, the rocks of Weepecket and Penikese islands all hold plenty of bass.

While casting along the rocky shores of the Elizabeths can produce exciting action, experts find more consistent action by trolling parachute jigs, eels, and umbrella rigs on wire line in order to get down to where the biggest bass like to hide on bright days. Look for them near reefs, ledges and rocky bottom where they can get out of the current while waiting for a meal to pass by.

In the open water of Vineyard Sound, along the ocean side of the islands, you can encounter roving schools of bass, blues, bonito, albies, and even Spanish mackerel from mid-summer into October. Sound hot spots include Middle Ground and Lucas Shoal, which is also an outstanding spot for summer fluking. Ledges and rocky bottom throughout the Sound and along the Elizabeths are great spots to fish for tautog and scup in spring and late fall.

Moving into Buzzards Bay, the coast becomes more rocky. In March and April, white perch enter the brackish marshes and estuaries feeding into the Bay, providing light-tackle sport for those who can't wait for warmer weather. These cousins of the striped bass will take small flies, freshwater spinners, and live killifish (mummichogs). Mud-bottomed bays, marshes, and estuaries are also home to winter flounder from March through May. Look for them to get active once water temperatures rise into the 40's.

The many ledges and rockpiles scattered throughout Buzzards Bay offer some of New England's best tautog and scup fishing, especially in early spring when tautog move inshore to spawn. 'Tog retreat offshore during the warm months but return to the ledges in late fall. Upper Bay 'tog spots include Bird Island Reef, Dry Ledge, Sippican Neck, and Wings Neck at the west entrance of the Cape Cod Canal.

Beginning in April, the rocky coves, bays, rivers, and islands are the domain of striped bass. Schoolies provide great sport in the shallower reaches of the Upper Bay, where they gather around rocky points and any type of structure. April, May, and June find them feeding on herring in the local rivers and on squid on the flats. By July they have usually settled down around structure for the summer. The rule for summer bass fishing in the Upper Bay is simple: find some rocks and you'll find some bass. Best times are early morning and evening and during the two hours on either side of high tide. A few safe bets for plugging are Wings Neck, Bird Island, and Butler Point.

Another seasonal favorite is bluefish. Small blues from three to five pounds arrive around Memorial Day and roam the sandy flats through early July, feasting on squid and herring. In July they move offshore but return in the late summer and fall to prey on schools of menhaden, herring, mackerel and other baitfish, which they often drive into sheltered coves and rivers. In good years, Buzzards Bay bluefish action lasts well into October, and some of these fall fish can reach 20 pounds.

The west end of the Cape Cod Canal is a great fishing spot throughout the season. Bass, blues, and even bonito can be seen busting bait as the current rips through on its way to and from Cape Cod Bay. On an outgoing tide, the cooler water pouring in from Cape Cod Bay energizes the fish, bringing them to the surface to chase sand eels and silversides across the flats. Located next to the Canal, Onset Bay and the quiet, secluded Buttermilk Bay see lots of bass and blues throughout the season. Fluke fishing is also outstanding in the Canal, especially on the Mashnee Flats off Mashnee Island.

Upper Bay rivers like the Wareham and the Weweantic host annual migrations of shad and herring, and vast pods of menhaden are sometimes trapped in these confined waterways by schools of blues and bass. Every river, marsh, and creek in this region is loaded with eels, mummichugs, silversides, crabs, and seaworms—small wonder the place is alive with bass. Night is a special time in the quiet marshes and secret back rivers of Buzzards Bay. As bait is flushed out to sea on an outgoing

tide, stripers often feed with abandon. This can be lots of fun for light-tackle buffs and fly fishermen.

Deeper spots in the Bay such as Nyes Ledge, Wilkes Ledge, Cleveland Ledge, and Great Ledge hold big bass through the summer and fall, although you'll often have to get down deep with wire line to score during the day and when hot weather keeps them near the bottom. Drifting live eels and cut bait over these spots at night can also be very productive.

Along the west side of the Bay, you'll find bass around the rocks of Aucoot Cove and Converse Point off Marion. Mattapoisett Harbor, Mattapoisett Neck and Mattapoisett Ledge are all prime spots for bass and blues. This ledge also yields tautog in spring and fall. Try Ram Island for bass and blues, as well as Sconticut Neck and West Island off Fairhaven. The boulder-strewn shallows of this area are loaded with bass throughout the season—a good place for tossing plugs and flies.

Apponagansett Bay in South Dartmouth is the site of some famous late-season bluefish blitzes, with 20-pounders tearing into big schools of menhaden in the harbor. The protected marshes of the Westport River are home to stripers throughout the season, and nighttime action with schoolies can be sensational. Westport is also a great jumping-off spot for those who want to fish the Elizabeth Islands or Martha's Vineyard. There's also lots of deep ledges (Mishaum, Coxens) and wrecks that hold plenty of keeper bass, and the rocks around Barneys Joy Point, Gooseberry Neck, and Round Hill Point always yield big fish every year. Around the mouth of the Bay, ledges, wrecks, and rocks offer some outstanding tautog fishing in late fall and early spring. Cod are caught off Southwest Ledge in the early spring and fall, and Browns Ledge yields everything from cod and pollock to tautog to stripers in the course of the season.

Beginning in late August and early September, the Bay comes alive with huge schools of migratory gamefish preparing for their long trip south. Without a doubt, this is the best fishing of the year, especially on those calm, crisp autumn days. Bonito, striped bass, and bluefish are all possibilities on a fall day, and you can find them almost anywhere, feeding on schools of herring, squid, silversides, menhaden, and mackerel that pack into the Bay. If water temperatures stay at comfortable levels, and the bait isn't driven out by a big storm, then good fishing can last until November.

FISHING REGULATIONS

What follows are abstracts of fishing regulations for Maine, New Hampshire, and Massachusetts. This information should be used for general purposes only.

Because regulations change frequently, and because the regulations themselves are far more detailed than presented here, all anglers should contact the state agencies listed at the beginning and end of this chapter.

MAINE

No license is required for recreational fishing in the coastal waters except for Atlantic salmon. An Atlantic salmon license is required in all inland waters and certain coastal waters.

Atlantic Bluefin Tuna Permit

A federal permit is required to take Atlantic Bluefin Tuna. Permits are issued through the National Marine Fisheries Service.

A nonresident individual may fish for, take, possess, ship, transport, or sell tuna which he has taken, without a Commercial Fishing License, if he has a current special tuna permit.

Smelts

Taking of Smelts from the Coastal Waters of Maine: From March 15 to June 15, both days inclusive, it is unlawful to fish for or take smelts from coastal waters except by either hand dip net operated by one person or by angling with a hook and line. It is also illegal to take or possess more than two quarts of smelts in one day.

Striped Bass

It is unlawful to fish for or take striped bass in Maine water except by hook and line.

It is also unlawful to take or possess striped bass smaller than 36 inches in total length. It is unlawful to possess striped bass unless the fish is whole, with head on, and 36 inches or more in total length.

It is unlawful for any person to fish for or take striped bass in Maine waters except for personal use or to take or possess more than one striped bass each day.

Striped bass fishing is prohibited from December 1 through April 30 annually in all tidal waters of the Kennebec, Androscoggin, and Sheepscot Rivers and their adjacent coastal waters upstream and inside a line drawn from the outer point of Cape Small to the outer point of Salter Island, and from there to the outer point of Cape Newagen.

Due to conservation measures, possession limit and/or length may vary from year to year. Please contact your local Marine Patrol Officer for more information.

Other Species

Minimum size restrictions are in effect for the following marine species; all size limits are based on total length measurements—from the tip of the snout to the tip of the tail.

Cod: 19" total length
Haddock: 19" total length
Pollock: None
Witch flounder (gray sole): 14" total length
American plaice (dab): 14" total length
Yellowtail flounder: 13" total length
Winter flounder (blackback): 12" total length
Bluefish: No size limit, 10-fish-per-day possession limit
Summer flounder: 13" total length

Freshwater Fish in Coastal Waters

Method of Taking

It is illegal to fish for or take freshwater fish as defined in Section 1, 12 M.R.S.A. 6001 (17-A) by any means other than hook and line. The following freshwater fish species are so regulated: brown trout, large mouth bass, smallmouth bass, black crappie, rainbow trout, brook trout, chain pickerel, and landlocked salmon.

Minimum Length Limit for Landlocked Salmon, Brown Trout, and Rainbow Trout.

It is illegal to take or possess landlocked salmon, brown trout, or rainbow trout shorter than 14 inches in total length from Maine coastal waters.

Bag and Possession Limits for Landlocked Salmon, Brown Trout, Rainbow Trout, and Brook Trout.

It is illegal to take or possess more than five of the species listed above. Of those five, not more than two may be landlocked salmon, three brown trout, or three rainbow trout. All five may be brook trout.

Any fish caught in inland waters shall be counted against the bag and possession limits in coastal waters.

Minimum Length Limit for Brook Trout

It is illegal to take or possess brook trout shorter than 6 inches in total length from Maine coastal waters.

NEW HAMPSHIRE

Recreational fishermen are not required to be licensed to fish in salt water, except for smelt in Great Bay and for trout, shad and salmon in all state waters. A license is required to take all species of fish through the ice of Great Bay.

American Eel

Minimum length: 4"; no closed season. In the downstream portion of a river with a fishway, eels may be taken only from June 15 through October 1.

American Shad

Daily limit 2 fish; no length or weight limits. May be taken by angling only from salt and brackish water north of the Memorial Bridge in Ports-mouth. Fish taken by any other method must be immediately released. All-species fishing license required.

How to Survive In Cold Water

Even in mid-summer, water in the Gulf of Maine is frigid. Learning the dangers of cold water could save your life.

Statistics show that there are more fatal boating accidents when the water is cold than during the warm-weather months. Water at less than 70°F is considered "cold." How temperatures as low as 35° or 40° will affect a person in the water depends on the physical condition of that person.

Panic and shock are the first and most dangerous hazards of a capsizing. The shock of cold water places a severe strain on the body and can sometimes induce immediate cardiac arrest. Your breath will be literally driven from your body. If your face hits the water first, that first involuntary gasp for air will fill your lungs with water. You may also become disoriented and thrash wildly for nearly a minute before realizing what has happened.

It is critical that you wear your PFD (life jacket) at all times when out on the water in cold weather. It's a fact that cold water will numb your body and hands instantly, making it impossible to put on a PFD and tighten the straps, to grab and hold a rescue line or to hang onto a capsized boat. If you are not rescued in time, hypothermia will set in, followed by unconsciousness and death.

Cold water drains the body of heat 32 times faster than cold air. If you fall in or your boat capsizes, try to get out of the water as quickly as possible. The Pennsylvania Fish Commission claims that 90 percent of all fatal boating accidents in that state involve small boats with outboards less than 10 horsepower. With practice, most small boats can be righted and re-entered. Most small boats will also have flotation and will support the weight of the occupants. If you can, right your boat, climb into it and bail out the water. If the boat cannot be righted, climb on the hull and out of the water.

If you find yourself in cold water, avoid moving. Swimming, for example, will drain heat from your body much faster than remaining still in the water.

Besides, few people can swim very effectively or very far in cold water. Your best course of action may be to assume a protective posture in the water to protect your body's major heat-loss areas, such as your head, neck, armpits, chest and groin. If there is more than one person in the water, try huddling together to preserve body heat. You should only attempt to swim to safety if there is no chance of rescue.

Treatment of cold-water victims varies. If the person is rational and only shivering, dry clothes and blankets may be all that is necessary. Move a semi-conscious person to a warm place, and get him into dry clothes, but do not massage his arms and legs. The victim should be face-up on his back, head slightly lower than his feet, unless vomiting occurs. This position permits more blood flow to the brain.

Warming the victim is critical. If possible, place the person in a hot tub with a water temperature of 105 to 110 degrees. Keep the arms and legs out of the water to prevent drop-off, which happens when the cold blood from the limbs is forced back into the body, further lowering the core temperature. You can also apply hot towels to the victim's head, neck, chest, groin or abdomen—never the arms and legs. In a pinch, you can use your own body to warm a hypothermia victim.

Above all, never assume that a person recovered from cold water is dead. The body has a way of increasing its chances of survival through the "mammalian diving reflex," a reaction evident in whales, seals, and porpoises. The diving reflex, diverts blood from the extremities to the heart, brain, and lungs. The heartbeat may drop to only six beats a minute. These mammals can stay under water for as long as 30 minutes without brain or body damage.

We now know that humans can also experience this diving reflex, which means a rescuer might mistakenly assume a victim is dead. Don't give up resuscitation efforts until trained medical personnel arrive.

Alewives
Open to residents only. River herring (alewives and bluebacks) may not be taken by any method on Wednesdays. Inland netter's permit is required to take by any form of netting, including chicken wire.

Groundfish
Minimum mesh size for gillnets and mobile gear is 5½" to take, transport or possess cod, haddock, or yellowtail flounder. No mobile gear may be used to take finfish or crustaceans in Piscataqua River or its tributaries north of the Memorial Bridge in Portsmouth. Mobile gear may be used in state ocean waters from December 15 through April 15. For positive identification, all fillets must have skin intact while on or leaving state waters.

Groundfish Species
Minimum length: recreational and commercial
American Plaice—minimum length: 14"
Cod*—minimum length: 19"
Haddock*—minimum length: 19"
Yellow Flounder—minimum length: 13"
Pollock—minimum length: 19", no size limit if taken by
     angling.
Redfish—minimum length: 9"
Summer Flounder—minimum length: 13"
Winter Flounder—minimum length: 11"
*Must have head and tail intact or at least 12" fillets
with skin intact while on or leaving state waters.

Salmon
Sea-run salmon (coho, Atlantic, and chinook) may be
taken by angling only. All-species fishing license
required. Daily limit: 2 fish; minimum length: 15".

    Snagging (foul-hooking) not allowed. Any salmon
snagged must be immediately released unharmed.

    Pacific salmon (coho and chinook) may be taken
through the ice December 1 through March 31, min.
length 15".

Saltwater Smelt
May be taken by angling with either an All Species or
Warm-water fishing license. Daily limit, 10 quarts liquid measure of smelt with head and tail intact. Use of
nets or weirs prohibited from March 1 through December 15 north of Memorial Bridge in Newington-
Portsmouth. No license required to take by hook and
line from the Piscataqua River and its tributaries seaward of the Memorial Bridge, from the Hampton River
and its tributaries, and from Rye Harbor and its tributaries. Hand-held bow nets and dip nets may be used in
these rivers: Oyster, Squamscott, Bellamy, and Lamprey
between December 16 through February 28. Inland netter's permit required for bow netting and dip netting.
Daily limit of 10 quarts applies. Saltwater smelt may be
sold. Commercial fishing license required to sell smelt
taken by net.

Striped Bass
Minimum length: 36"; daily limit 1 fish; no closed season. Sale of striped bass is prohibited, regardless of origin. Netting is prohibited. Head and tail must remain
intact.

Sturgeon
Possession prohibited.

MASSACHUSETTS

Licenses
Saltwater licenses are not required for sportfishermen
in Massachusetts. The sale of fish, however, may require
a license from the Division of Marine Fisheries. To
obtain an abstract of marine fishing laws or other information concerning the Massachusetts coastal fishery,
contact the Division of Marine Fisheries.

Special Regulations: Minimum Size
American Eel: 4" total length.
Atlantic salmon: 15" total length. Fishery closed until
     further notice.
Bluefish: No size limit. 10 fish possession limit.
Cod: 19" total length.
Coho salmon: 15" total length: Mar. 1 to Aug. 31. Limit
     of two fish per day. No snagging allowed.
     No size restriction. Sept. 1 to Feb. 28.
Flounders: American dab, 14" total length; Grey sole,
     14" total length; Summer flounder, 14" total
     length; Windowpane, 12" total length; Win-
     ter flounder, 12" total length; Yellowtail, 13"
     total length.
Haddock: 19" total length.
Marlin: Blue, 86" total length. 1 fish limit; White, 62"
     total length. 1 fish limit.
Pollock: no size restriction.
Redfish: 9" total length.
Red drum: 4" total length.
Sailfish: 57" total length. 1 fish limit.
Shad: No size restriction. May be taken by hook and
     line only. No snagging allowed.
Smelt: No size restriction. May be taken by angling
     only. Closed season March 15 to June 15, inclu-
     sive.
Striped Bass: 34" total length. May be taken by hook
     and line only. Daily limit 1. Possession
     limit 1.
Scup: 9" total length.
Sea Bass: 12" total length.
Sturgeon (Atlantic): 72" total length.
Tautog: 12" total length.

Maine's Marvelous Makos

by Barry Gibson

The little yellow balloon dipped briefly under the glassy surface, then bobbed back to the top. Nothing. Then it dipped again, and sort of jiggled. I watched it intently as I picked the rod out of its holder.

It bobbed a third time, but didn't go completely under. "Get outta here!" I hollered at what was most certainly a pesky dogfish annoying the fresh-dead mackerel we had been drifting some 30 yards behind the boat. I quickly reeled in the slack, pointed the rod tip at the balloon, and struck hard, half-expecting a five-pound "barker" to come skidding across the top of the water at me.

The rod bent into a predictable arc, but the tip suddenly shot downward and 50-pound line crackled off the reel. This was no dogfish.

I handed the outfit to 19-year-old Nathan Eldridge of Belfast, and the mate and I quickly cranked in the other two rigs. Nathan held on as the fish slowed, then appeared to stop. "I think he's gone," Nathan informed us as he wound in 20 feet of seemingly slack line.

Just at that moment my eye caught an indigo shadow ghosting under the water off the port side. Suddenly it came into focus, just six feet below the surface right beneath me. Then the hair on the back of my neck stood straight up. The tail. The base of its tail was almost a foot wide. It could only be a . . .

"Mako!" I yelled. "It's a mako!" As if on cue the shark muscled its way underneath the stern, ripping line from the reel, and launched itself 20 feet in the air while executing a pair of somersaults. When it hit the water it looked—and sounded—like a picnic table being dropped upside-down from a helicopter. The shark dove, then went airborne again within seconds, this time managing a perfect triple-axel before crashing back into the water on its side. Dean and I were stunned. Nathan had the good sense to keep his rod tip high as the mako streaked off.

Nathan Eldridge of Belfast, Maine, displays a 270-pound mako he caught on Captain Barry Gibson's Shark IV off Boothbay Harbor. Makos like this—and larger—are becoming more common off the Maine coast each summer.
(BARRY GIBSON)

Interestingly, this shark never went deep. It worked its way back and forth on the surface, its triangular dorsal fin high in the air, as Nathan carefully gained line back. Then it hung tough off the port quarter, resisting the sideways pressure that was inching it toward the boat. I finally finished hyperventilating.

"We oughta' get the harpoon," I suggested to Dean, at the same time noticing that my mouth was unusually dry and that my knees seemed a bit rubbery. I fumbled under the gunwale for the five-inch straight gaff.

Nathan expertly worked the big mako closer and closer, finally within reach. There was a burst of spray and lots of hollering. Rope burned through my hands. It seemed that everyone was leaning over the side. But in less than a minute we had the shark trussed-up and quieted down, all 270 pounds of him. Nathan was jubilant.

Makos in Maine? What's this all about?

Nobody's really sure. The fact is, though, that the last two summer seasons have produced over a dozen big "genuine" makos—and a couple of really small ones, or "micros" as the longliners call them—off the lower third of the state's coastline. and, interestingly, almost all these sabre-toothed sharks have been taken relatively close to shore, within 20 miles. So the big question is: What's changed? Why have makos suddenly shown up?

The answer is that they may well have been here all along but that nobody's really employed the right tactics to catch them. I have photos I took of a 500-pounder Capt. Arno Rogers harpooned out near Cashes Ledge in the mid-80's and have heard of a number of others, although I suspect some may have actually been porbeagles, a similar species I'll get to in a minute.

But do makos really belong in the Gulf of Maine? It seems that they might, although documentation is sketchy. The shortfin mako (the one we caught), which ranges in size up to 1,000 or more pounds, is found in almost all tropical and warm-temperate ocean waters of the world. Many have been recorded taken off Cape Cod in the summertime over the years, and makos have been reported as far north as Seguin Island in Maine, according to one source.

The fact is, though, they're here. "I think they've followed the bluefish up," says Cal Robinson of Saco Bay Tackle, an expert sharker who closely monitors mako catches. "Bluefish make up about 80 percent of a mako's diet in this area," he says, "and we have plenty of those. Plus, our summer water temperature averages 62 to 67 degrees, which is just right."

Now that we know they're here, the question facing Maine sharkers is: How do you target makos? How do techniques differ from fishing for blue sharks?

The quick answer is that there's not a big difference. Many Maine makos (like the one we caught) are incidental catches, almost accidental. The best advice is to concentrate your efforts where makos are likely to be found. Robinson has some definite ideas on this. "Boon Island Ledge is a known mako haunt," he told me, "as is the area southeast of the Portland LNB since it's got tide rips, bluefish, and access to deep water from which the sharks can come in. Makos will move inshore to feed on the bluefish, so many anglers drive right over them as they blast out towards deep water. Blue sharks like the thermal structure offshore, but makos are more apt to be in close. Just look for the bluefish."

As for tackle, you'll have to make a decision. If you're just generally shark fishing and there are lots of blue sharks in the area, then 20- or 30-pound tackle is fine, and quite sporting. However, if you really want a mako, go with a good 50- or 80-pound stand-up outfit, complete with gimbal belt and shoulder harness. It would be better to over-gun a few blue sharks than to lose a 300-pound mako on tackle that was just too light.

Cal recommends a "double-wire" leader (two lengths of single-strand twisted together) and a tuna-quality hook such as the offset Mustad 7698R, in a 9/0 size. An alternate choice is "combo" leader made up of 12 feet or more of 300-pound mono, a swivel, and 18 inches to 4 feet of single or double wire or braided cable. This rig (the one I've been using for years) is easier to handle when a shark is at boatside, and you just change the short wire section when necessary—the mono will last quite a while. Sure, you'll ruin a few of these rigs on blue sharks, but again, the light single-strand stainless leaders and thin-wire hooks appropriate for blues just may not hold up against an airborne mako.

What's the best bait for a mako?

These sharks feed on herring, mackerel and other open-ocean baitfish, squid, bluefish, and swordfish—yes, swordfish! As a matter of fact there have been a number of makos caught with whole, or parts of, swordfish in their stomachs, and biologists generally agree that swords and makos are mortal enemies.

Outside of $6-per-pound swordfish steaks, the best bait for Maine makos is probably a live bluefish or a fillet, although New Jersey sharkers favor a "sandwich" of squid and mackerel strips. Many top mako anglers, too, like to use a brightly colored rubber skirt over the bait, in the belief that it adds a bit of visual appeal to the offering. Take your pick. Cal's and my best advice, though, is to stick with these pelagic baits rather than cod, whiting, hake or other bottom dwellers. Sure, makos must eat these fish as well, but we think they're more geared towards "open-ocean" forage species.

As for fishing techniques, simply use the same ones you'd employ for blue sharks. Either drift or anchor depending on sea conditions, and get a good chum slick going with a pail of frozen ground-up pogy or herring, or by cutting whole baitfish or bluefish into small chunks. Dribble a little fish oil over the side every now and then for some extra scent, and Cal says some bluefish scales added to your chum slick is a real turn-on for makos.

Stagger your baits in the water column from just a few feet below the surface to 90 feet or more. You might need a bit of weight to keep your bait down, and a small balloon or styrofoam net float makes a good sea-going "bobber."

OK. You've hooked up! But what kind of shark is on the business end of your line? If it rockets well up into the air and either spins or somersaults, it's a mako, period. No other shark found in our waters will do this.

If it doesn't jump, but just dogs deep or tries to follow the boat while staying down out of sight, it could be a mako, a porbeagle, or a big blue shark. Or it could be a tuna, but that's a subject for another article.

Assuming it's a shark, here's how to identify the species at boatside (see Chapter 6 for further details on identifying sharks): If it's long and relatively slender, with small, triangular teeth, a

bright blue back and white underbelly, and floppy, fleshy pectoral fins, it's probably a blue shark. If it's cobalt blue on top with a wide caudal keel, sharp snout, short, wide pectorals and teeth that look like backward-curving claws extending outside its lower jaw, it's probably a mako. If it's similar to a mako but is a brownish-gray or bluish-gray on top, is full-bodied, has less-fierce-looking teeth, and a distinctive white patch at the back end of the dorsal fin, it's undoubtedly a porbeagle.

This brings us to the porbeagle, or mackerel shark, a cool-water cousin of the mako that's far more common in Maine waters. Their numbers, however, have been reduced by commercial longlining in the past decade. Size in our waters ranges from about 25 pounds to upwards of 400 pounds, and although Capt. Terry Lewis and I caught a 298-pounder in 1979 from my old *Shark II* on a chin-rigged mackerel trolled on a tuna handline, most rod-and-reel taken specimens are considerably smaller. The current Maine state record is an 83.7-pounder, taken by Daniel F. X. Angerman aboard Tim Tower's well-known party boat *Bunny Clark* out of Ogunquit.

Porbeagles are creatures of the open ocean, feeding on herring, mackerel and bottom fish. They can occasionally be seen basking on the surface during the summer months, yet have been snared in gillnets as deep as 500 feet. Although porbeagles are actually very fast swimmers, they're not known for a sizzling fight at the end of a line.

Targeting porbeagles specifically on rod and reel can probably best be described as an exercise in frustration, as they're rarely plentiful in any particular area. Your best bet is to use the same tactics you would on blues and makos—with a mackerel or herring as bait—and cross your fingers. But one bit of personal advice: if you think a porbeagle has taken your bait, give him plenty of time to swallow it (assuming you intend to keep the shark). We pulled the hook on an estimated 200-pounder in 1990 after spotting it on the surface and feeding it a dead mackerel for only 30 seconds. The fight lasted 20 exciting minutes with lots of boat maneuvering, but the shark just wasn't hooked well. I wish we'd given it more time to eat the bait, and so did our disappointed charter party!

If you are lucky enough to hook and land a mako or porbeagle, be advised that both are terrific food fish. The firm, white flesh is very similar in appearance and taste to swordfish, and steaks are especially tasty when marinated and grilled. However, it makes the best conservation sense to release the really big ones (most of which are female), and to take only an occasional smaller one instead, which is probably better eating anyway. Besides, what are you going to do with 300 pounds of shark meat?

Finally, keep in mind that most game and food shark species such as the mako are overfished in U.S. waters, and some stocks are seriously depleted. A federal shark plan, implemented last year, places restrictions and daily bag limits on most sharks for recreational fishermen, and prohibits the sale of sharks to anyone (including a fish market or restaurant) unless the fisherman has a valid Commercial Shark Permit. For information on shark regulations and commercial permits contact the National Marine Fisheries Service, 1335 East-West Highway, Silver Spring, MD 20910, (301) 713-2347. ∎

Spotlight: Boothbay Harbor, Maine

by Barry Gibson

Aaaah, Maine. To most people, the mere mention of this state conjures up visions of pine trees, rocky coastline, blueberries and succulent oiled-lobster dinners. To freshwater fishermen Maine means landlocked salmon and bright brook trout, but to saltwater anglers Maine means— what?—catching cod on a handline?

Not any more. The Maine coast offers an exciting variety of saltwater sportfishing opportunities, and its image has dramatically changed over the past decade. Certainly cod and other bottom species comprise a large portion of the annual sport catch, but mackerel, bluefish, striped bass, sharks and bluefin tuna have collectively earned top billing in recent years and a successful sport fishery thrives in the summer months.

The little seaside town of Boothbay Harbor, about a third of the way up Maine's coast and 35 miles north of the major city of Portland, may have the dubious distinction of being about the northernmost sport fishing port on the East Coast. Once a bustling hub of commercial fishing activity, Boothbay's two biggest industries are now tourism and lobstering, but recreational fishing isn't far behind. Boasting four party boats and as many as six charter boats, plus marina services, accommodations, and launch ramps, Boothbay has something for just about every fisherman.

Bottom fish are the primary targets of the *Yellowbird* and *Bingo*, the two deep-sea party boats. They spend a lot

Vin Sparano with a chunky 35 pound-plus striped bass. Forty-pound bass are not uncommon in Boothbay Harbor. Live or cut bait, as well as cast or trolled plugs, will catch these stripers. (VIN T. SPARANO)

of time fishing an area known locally as the Kettle Bottom, which lies ten miles due south of Seguin Island, a 20-mile run or so run from the harbor. Ranging in depths from 250 to 400 feet, the plateau-like Kettle can yield good catches of cod in the 3- to 20-pound range as well as the occasional 40-pounder. Pollock, hake, cusk and wolffish are also taken with regularity here. Other productive bottomfish areas include the "Humps" five miles southwest of Monhegan Island, Great Ledge south of Damariscove Island, and for those with smaller boats, the shoal waters to 200 feet deep off Pumpkin Rock and below Bantam Rock Buoy.

The best bet for bottom fish is a stout jigging outfit loaded with 30- to 50-pound mono or Dacron, and an 8- to 16-ounce diamond or Norwegian-style chrome-plated jig. Brightly colored (pink is consistently hot) surgical tube or soft plastic teasers tied in just above the jig work very well and can result in doubleheaders of cod and pollock. Bait such as clams and squid can also be used but may attract unwanted pests such as dogfish.

Bluefish in the 8- to 17-pound range generally show up off Boothbay in July, and can provide fast fishing right through the month of September. Most Mainers troll lipped swimming plugs such as the Rapala CD18, Bomber Long A and the Storm Big Mac, and throw topwater poppers on spinning gear when schools are encountered on top, particularly around mid-day before afternoon breezes come up. Productive areas include the mouth of Booth Bay

Boothbay Harbor at a Glance

Marinas

(All area codes 207)
Brown's Wharf 633-5440
    (VHF ch. 9)
Carousel Marina 633-2922
    (VHF ch. 9)
Rocktide Motor Inn 633-4455
Fisherman's Wharf Inn 633-5090
Tugboat Inn 633-4434

Charter and Party Boats

Yellowbird and *Buccaneer* (party) 633-3244
Bingo (party) 633-3775
Breakaway (party/charter) 633-4414

Lucky Star (charter) 633-4446
Hopscotch (charter) 633-7221
Shark Five (charter) 633-3416

NOAA Charts

#13260 for offshore
#13288 for inshore
#13293 for river systems

Accommodations

Contact the Boothbay Harbor
    Region Chamber of Commerce
    at 633-2353 and ask for their
    "Annual Boothbay Harbor
    Guide."

Loran Tds for Fishing Areas (approximate)

Kettle Bottom 13120 × 25860
Great Ledge 13070 × 25868
Pumpkin Rock Shoals 13020 × 25890
Bantam Rock Shoals 13050 × 25890

---

around Cuckolds Lighthouse, the west side of Damariscove Island, nearby John's Bay, the mouth of the Sheepscot River, and the waters surrounding Seguin Island. These last two areas, as well as the Kennebec River all the way up to the city of Bath, also produce some excellent striped bass action. Twenty- to 40-pounders aren't uncommon, even during daylight hours, on live or cut bait or trolled and cast plugs.

Boothbay Harbor has hosted a small but active sport bluefin tuna fleet for many years, and although recent catches of these 200- to 800-pound-plus gamesters can't compare with those of the 1960's and 1970's, some nice fish are brought in every summer. Most of the charter boats are geared up to catch them, but anglers in their own boats have an equal chance. The above-mentioned Kettle Bottom attracts schools of bluefins from July through September, and on weekends there can be as many as 100 sport and commercial craft out there, most of which chum with fresh herring, mackerel or whiting. Slowly trolled spreader rigs of

fresh mackerel or plastic squid also take tuna here, and some of the best action is just after sunup.

Shark fishing is almost a sure bet off Boothbay and is increasingly popular each season. Blue sharks from 100 to 200 pounds are common, and 400-plus-pounders have been hooked. Porbeagles, threshers and makos turn up now and then too. Again the Kettle Bottom is a productive shark area, as is almost any offshore hump from 5 to 15 miles offshore, although the deeper mud gullies often provide the best blue shark fishing. Good baits include mackerel, pogy and herring, and 30-pound-class stand-up tackle provides top sport.

Boothbay Harbor is easy to fish from in the summer. Situated four miles from the open sea at the juncture of two large peninsulas, Linekin Neck and Southport Island, it is well protected, yet surrounding waters are deep. Carousel Marina, the first on the right as you enter the harbor from seaward, offers transient slips, moorings, fuel, a deli and a full ship's store. Next door is Brown's Wharf, which offers tie-up space, 80

sunset-facing motel rooms and a first-class restaurant. Farther up into the harbor, Rocktide Motor Inn, Fisherman's Wharf Inn and Tugboat Inn offer limited tie-up space, moorings and adjacent accommodations. For those who plan on trailering a boat, there's a launch ramp at Carousel Marina and in East Boothbay, although parking is limited. Your best bet is to park your rig, after launching, at one of the low-cost lots just outside town.

Best of all, though, Boothbay Harbor is fun. The charter- and party-boat skippers have a sense of camaraderie as well as Down East humor, and in most cases are willing to share fishing information over the VHF (they normally monitor channels 16 and 11), providing you're reasonably polite and your out-of-state accent isn't too thick. Apres-fishing socializing at any of the half-dozen or so on-the-water cafes, bars and restaurants is considered de rigeur in Boothbay, and you'll no doubt make some new friends in the process.

Those of us who fish there wouldn't trade it for anything! ∎

Small-Boat Handling Along the Western Maine Coast

by David R. Getchell, Sr.

Estuaries and Rivers

Only a few of Maine's rivers and streams have estuaries extensive enough to interest the small-boat skipper—with one notable exception: The coast from Harpswell Neck in Casco Bay all the way east to Muscongus Bay is dominated by large islands separated from the mainland by narrow saltwater streams and sounds. It is laced with a spider's web of coves, small bays, creeks, marshes, and swift-flowing rivers.

Much of this area offers superb travel for the small-boater, with only three major danger spots: the Upper and Lower Hellgates on the Sasanoa and the mouth of the Kennebec and Small Point. The two Hellgates, roughly two miles apart, can be safely navigated by most boats during the upper third of the tide cycle, when their swiftest dangers are flooded out. Otherwise, great caution is needed. An alternative route around the back side of Beal Island will bring you to Little Hellgate, which may offer a safer route.

The mouth of the Kennebec can be one of the most dangerous places on the entire coast for small boats. Very narrow at its mouth at Fort Popham, the big river spouts an awesome amount of water into the ocean on a dropping tide, and if this swift-flowing stream comes up against incoming waves generated by sea swell or southerly winds, a nasty mix of short, steep waves and breaking water can result. The best time to enter the river is on the top half of the tide.

The estuary of the Sheepscot, extending all the way to Head Tide some eight miles above Wiscasset, seems made for small boats. Its lower reaches are split by islands, deep coves, small bays, and a fascinating tidal stream crossing against the grain named, most appropriately, Cross River.

Like the Sheepscot, the Damariscotta River estuary extends inland for miles. At the twin towns of Newcastle and Damariscotta the river narrows into a swift and at times hazardous flow between the Route 1A bridge in town and the Route 1 bridge a mile upriver.

From the foot of Bremen Long Island north to the town of Waldoboro, the Medomak estuary is a maze of wooded islands, coves snaking into the mainland, and swirling tidal currents. Much of this turns to mud flats at low water, so as with most estuaries, one is best off exploring on the top half of the tide.

The St. George can be navigated on all tides nearly to Warren, several miles upstream of Thomaston. The Narrows, about a mile above Thomaston, is a fast ride or a slow haul, depending on which way the tide is running, but it is always a good idea to go with the flow when you are exploring saltwater rivers. Those fish you see sputtering at the surface from time to time are probably alewives, present in the river for the early months of summer; larger splashes, and large fish rolling and occasionally jumping are striped bass or bluefish feasting on alewives.

The Bays

Maine's big bays are a poor place for inexperienced boaters in small boats. Casco Bay has more ships and boats plying its waters at any given moment than any other on the coast. The heaviest concentrations of vessels of all sizes are in the main ship channel from Portland Head to Spring Point, the inner harbor between Portland and South Portland, and Hussey Sound between Peaks and Long islands. Regular traffic in the main channel includes tankers, freighters, ferries, tugboats, barges, and other large craft, most of which cannot maneuver around you. The channel and Hussey Sound, as well as most of the passages between islands, also see a steady parade of pleasure craft.

The best areas for small boats are the inner sounds and the wide reaches of Middle and Maquoit bays and the saltwater rivers, small bays, coves, and generally protected waters of the eastern bay between Harpswell Neck and Small Point.

Casco Bay abounds with reefs, rocks, mud flats, and sand bars lurking just under the surface at various stages of the tide. These are shown on the chart, and are reason enough why one should navigate by chart. Fog is common, especially in late afternoon and early morning in summer; when it is forecast, small boats should plan to be in protected low-traffic waters.

The mouth of Sheepscot Bay is narrow and exposed, and since the river drains a wide area, an outgoing tide meeting a southerly breeze can kick up a remarkably rough sea.

Bounded on the west by Pemaquid Point and on the east by Marshall Point and Port Clyde, Muscongus Bay is a demanding and thrilling place for competent small-boat sailors. The five-mile shore between Pemaquid Point and the entrance to Muscongus Sound is steep-sided rock and unforgiving, except for the narrow entrance to New Harbor. Most of the outer islands are swept by ocean swells and offer little protection.

The bay is a major lobstering area, and during much of the summer its waters are dotted with a colorful—and propeller-tangling—array of buoys. One will see fishermen working from their boats much of the time, and since they work their boats in all directions when hauling, it will be to your benefit and theirs to stay well clear.

Penobscot Bay. Penobscot Bay is more than 40 miles wide at its mouth from Marshall Point on the west to Brooklin's Naskeag Point on the east. However, Maine's shattered coastline means that such a great distance will be broken by multiple land forms. Thus, we will deal with the bay in sections.

All of this vast area can be navigated by well-found small boats in the hands of skilled skippers at one time or another, but don't forget that untold numbers of competent and not-so-competent mariners have lost their lives while fishing, cruising, and working these waters. Penobscot Bay is a poor place to discover how much you don't know. A welcome summer breeze on the streets of Castine can be a life-threatening gale to a man and his family caught just a few miles away off Cape Rosier in a 16-foot motorboat.

Muscle Ridge. You mean *M-u-s-s-e-l* Ridge, don't you? No, it's Muscle (the old English spelling of Mussel) Ridge, an archipelago of islands, small bays, several interesting gunkholes, and a busy ship channel. Heading into Penobscot Bay from the west, you can pass inside Mosquito Island on any tide in your small boat, although you will want to keep a sharp eye out for "bricks," as underwater ledges and rocks are called along the coast. Once past the cliffs of Mosquito Head, you soon enter island country, and with artful chart reading and rock dodging, you can pretty much stay "inside" all the way to Rockland Harbor. The "outside" islands, those on the eastern side of Muscle Ridge Channel, have a foundation of beautiful granite, and it is worth a cruise just for the sheer beauty of it. Remember, though, that all the islands are private, and should not be visited without the owners' permission.

The West Bay. By itself, the west bay would be one of Maine's largest. Its wide entrance is open ocean. We've crossed the 10 miles from Two Bush Island to Vinalhaven a number of times in our open 18-foot aluminum skiff, but always when the weather was rock-solid steady with light winds and no fog. The view up the bay on a September day is a sight one won't forget. We've crossed these same waters in larger boats when the wind was up, and only one thing was certain—the boat we were in was not big enough!

The east "side" of the west bay is made up of the western shores of Vinalhaven and North Haven and the mid-bay Islesboro chain of islands.

The west bay is big and open, with steep, rocky shores and few places where you can dodge in out of the weather. This side of the bay can be deceiving when the wind is out of the west and south. It may be calm at the launching ramp, while a mile or so offshore it is gusty and rough. It will probably get rougher the farther east you go. Frequently the afternoon sea breeze blows hard out of Rockland Harbor.

The outgoing tide pushing into a sea swell and perhaps an onshore wind builds an unusually heavy sea for a mile or so out of Rockland Harbor—treacherous going for small boats, especially if the waves are breaking.

Belfast and the Upper Bay. This area includes bay waters north of Turtle Head on Islesboro. Frequently calm on a summer's morning, it begins to ruffle up by mid-day, and a couple hours later may be covered with whitecaps. Everywhere, that is, except Belfast Harbor, which lies in the northwest corner of the bay out of the blow of the sea breeze.

A few miles out, off Fort Point, the main channel of the Penobscot pours out between the point and Fort Point Ledge, and when the current is running strong and the sea breeze is whistling up the bay, a steep breaking chop can be dangerous for small boats. If you must run up the river from the bay under these conditions, head east of the ledge. However, the outflow from any big river running against the wind can be hazardous, and the river between Fort Point and Odum Ledge above Sandy Point is rough going on many summer afternoons. The East Channel around Verona Island is a pleasant alternative if the main river is frothy.

East Penobscot Bay. Saddleback Ledge sits at the mouth of the east bay, more than 30 miles south of Fort Point, giving an idea of the size of this exciting stretch. For the most part the east bay is bounded by islands, a world that few mainlanders would recognize. The east bay is vast, confusing, gentle, deadly, and wonderful. An inexperienced small-boat skipper trying to find his way across this wilderness may add a few adjectives of his own. Carry a chart.

Some tips:

• It is quite possible that the upper part of the bay will be rougher than the lower part on a summer day because of the increasing speed of the cool sea breeze as it approaches the sun-warmed land. Strong tidal currents just west of Western Island to the south of Cape Rosier make for nasty going when the wind is up. Similar conditions may be found between some of the islands where the flow is pinched and piled up.

• If you must buck the chop, hop from the lee of one island to the lee of the next, softening the upwind beat.

• The long line of islands dominated by Islesboro can be pierced by traveling the length of Gilkey Harbor and rounding Pendleton Point on the south end of the big island. South of Little Thrumcap Island in Gilkey Harbor, hold to the east side just outside the moored boats. A ledge extends down much of the middle of this section, and many a boat and yacht have come to grief on these rocks lying just under the surface. This route is a real relief if you are pounding west for the Lincolnville Beach launching ramp.

• If you're heading east toward Blue Hill Bay, Eggemoggin Reach is a fine alternative for rounding Deer Isle.

• The east bay has a number of shoals and reefs. A long prop-twister lies on an east-west axis in the middle of the broad expanse between Bradbury and Pickering islands. Several others lurk just out of sight between Butter Island and North Haven. The Brandies off Isle au Haut and the entire east side of Vinalhaven also call for caution.

Deer Isle-Isle au Haut. On a sunny day this area is close to heaven; when the fog rolls in it can be world-class confusion.

Three major routes cut through this maze of islands: Eggemoggin Reach on the north, Deer Isle Thorofare off Stonington, and Merchant Row just north of Isle au Haut. The next route down is south of Isle au Haut, 10 miles away and out to sea. The Deer Isle region is prime lobster-fishing country.

Blue Hill Bay. Big and beautiful, Blue Hill Bay is unlike any other on the coast, with its shallow, rock-lined water in the southwest, long, deep reaches north and east, big islands, few villages, and fewer boats. The mid-bay islands—Black, Eagle, Pond, Tinker, and smaller satellites—are private and surrounded by shallows, and the big upper-bay islands like Hardwood, Bartlett, and Long are off-limits. The small-boater will find the most interesting waters in the north end, in the smaller bays and coves such as Blue Hill Harbor, Morgan Bay, Union River Bay, and Western Bay.

Caution Areas

• The Falls at South Blue Hill are not easily seen on a rising tide, and it would be easy to be caught in the powerful flow under the Route 175 bridge.

• A good portion of the water in Blue Hill Bay flows out through Eastern Passage between Placentia Island and Swan's Island on a dropping tide, and

the resulting seas can be awesome.

• Casco Passage on the west side of Swan's is narrow and often rough, while its western leg south of Johns Island cuts through a maze of reefs. You'll need local knowledge.

• Mt. Desert Narrows dries out at low tide. From mid-tide down, the half mile east of the bridge is dicey going; plan passage through this section on the top of a tide.

Frenchman Bay. Other than its upper end, Frenchman Bay is one big pool north of the Porcupine Islands and one big ocean to the south of them, and it is probably the least kind to small boaters.

Caution Areas

• Bars on the east side of Stave and Jordon islands extend to the mainland.

Currents are strong, and if the wind is blowing, they can be nasty. The Stave Island Bar dries out on a drain tide and is rarely passable at any low tide.

• The Mt. Desert coast south of Bar Harbor has long stretches where there is no place to hide or to land. Occasional swells breaking on hidden offshore reefs and the sometimes frightening reflective waves bouncing away from the cliffs and sweeping out from shore meet incoming swells explosively. Any power loss on your boat within a half mile of shore is serious business.

• The same conditions exist on the eastern side of the bay where Schoodic Peninsula juts far out to sea. ∎

FISHING ACCESS

MAINE

Town	Public Shore Access
Addison	Pleasant River
Bath	Kennebec River
Bar Harbor	Frenchman Bay
Belfast	Belfast Bay
Boothbay	Linekin River
Biddeford	Saco River, Hills Beach
Biddeford Pool	Fortune's Rocks Beach
Blue Hill	Blue Hill Harbor
Bristol	Colonial Pemaquid (Ft. Wm. Henry) Historic Site. *Open May 30 through Labor Day, weekends September-October.*
Brunswick	Buttermilk Cove
Calais	St. Croix River
Cape Elizabeth	Crescent Beach State Park. *Open approximately May 30 to September 30.*
Chelsea	Kennebec River
Damariscotta	Damariscotta Harbor
Dennysville	Cobscook Bay State Park. *Open approximately May 15 to October 30.*
Edmonds Twp.	Cobscook Bay
Eliot	Piscataqua River
Ellsworth	Union River
Frankfort	Penobscot River
Gardiner	Kennebec River
Georgetown	Reid State Park. *Open all year.*
Kennebunk	Libby's Point; Parson's Beach
N. Edgecomb	Fort Edgecomb Historic Site. *Open May 30 through Labor Day, weekends September-October.*
Ocean Park	Ocean Park Beach
Old Orchard	Old Orchard Beach
Orrington	Penobscot River
Penobscot	Penobscot River
Phippsburg	Head Beach / Popham Beach State Park. *Open all year.*
Portland	Casco Bay
Popham Beach	Fort Popham Historic Site. *Open May 30 through September 30, weekends September-October.*
Roque Bluffs	Roque Bluffs State Park. *Open approximately May 15 to September 30.*
Saco	Camp Ellis
Scarborough	Pine Point / Scarborough Beach State Park. *Open approximately May 30 to Labor Day.*

Searsport — Searsport Harbor

Stockton Springs — Fort Point (Fort Pownal) State Park. *Open approximately May 30 through Labor Day.*

NEW HAMPSHIRE

Town	Public Shore Access
Badger's Island	Memorial Bridge to Kittery. Fished infrequently.
Dover	Eliot Bridge, Salmon Falls River. Fished moderately by local sportsmen for striped bass and eels with fair success.
Dover Point	Bellamy Bridge (Scammel Bridge), Route 4. Fishing on southbound side of bridge only. Good location for striped bass. Also fished for flounder. Very popular.
Hampton	East side of Hampton-Seabrook Bridge and North Jetty, Hampton Beach State Park. (Jetty designed with 1,000-foot walkway for sportfishing.) Heavily used. Flounder, pollock, some mackerel, and striped bass. Hampton-Seabrook Bridge, Route 1-A. Reportedly fished heavily by Hampton Beach summer residents. Flounder, pollock, some mackerel and striped bass are caught. Hampton State Pier. Off Route 1-A, adjacent to the Seabrook Bridge. Open year-round. Fee, parking. Handicapped accessible: ramp down to floats.
Newington to Dover Point	General Sullivan Bridge. Route 4. Fishing on southbound side of bridge only. Excellent fishing for striped bass. Heavily fished (20-per-day average).
Portsmouth	Bridge to Pierce's Island. Infrequently used. Portsmouth Fish Pier, on Pierce Island opposite Prescott Park. Open year-round. No fee. Handicapped accessible; public restroom is accessible. Prescott Park. Small flounder, small school pollock, cunner, and smelt. Heavily utilized. Popular due to immediate availability of parking and proximity to downtown Portsmouth.
Portsmouth to Goat Island	Bridge on Route 1-B. Flounder, occasional striped bass on early morning incoming tides.
Rye	Jetty at Rye Harbor State Park. Pollock, flounder. Frequently fished (more than twelve persons per day). Admission fee. Rye Harbor Marina, on Route 1-A. Open year-round. Fee, parking. Handicapped accessible: ramp down to floats.
Seabrook	Seabrook Harbor, west of Route 1-A. Sandy beach area provides fishing for winter flounder, striped bass, mackerel, and pollock, as well as various other species. Bait, tackle facilities nearby.
Stratham-Newfields line	Stratham Bridge, Route 108. Infrequently used in the summer.

MASSACHUSETTS

The following information includes launch ramps, jetties, and piers, by town, statewide. (P) designates paved ramps; (S), sand ramps; (G), gravel; unless otherwise specified, ramps are good at all tides.

Town	Public Shore Access
Amesbury	Town landing, Merrimac Street (P)
Barnstable	Harbor (P); Bay Street (P); East Bay Road (P); Lewis Bay Road (P); Ocean View Avenue, Cotuit (S); Old Shore Road, Pope's Beach (S); Price Avenue, Marstons Mills (P); Scudder Lane (P); Shore Road, Hyannis (P)
Blish Point	Haywood Rd. (P); Bridge St. (S)
Beverly	River St. (P); Water St. (P)
Boston	Castle Island, S. Boston, jetty and pier; Charleston Navy Yard, Pier 4, pier; Puopolo Park, Chas. River Res., Commercial St., pier; Rainbow Park, Commercial St., Dorchester, pier
Bourne	Barlows Landing (P); Electric Ave. (P); Hen Cove (P); Monument Beach (P); Red Brook Harbor (P)
Chatham	Bridge St., pier, (P); Oyster River (S); Ryder's Cove (S); Crows Pond (P)
Chilmark	Nashaquitsa Pond, South Rd., (P)
Cohasset	Parker Ave. (P), half tide

Danvers	Danversport Marine Ctr., Harbor Street (P)	Kingston	Town landing, River Street (P)
Dartmouth	Demerest Lloyd State Park (P), half tide; Padanaram Bridge, pier, (P)	Lynn	General Edwards Bridge, pier; Lynn Harbor Marine, Blossom Street (P); MDC playground (P); Mercury Outboard Center (P)
Dennis	Cold Storage Rd., pier, (P); Follins Pond (P); Sesuit Neck Road (P); Uncle Freeman's Way (P) Cove Rd.(P); Horsefoot Cove (P)		
		Manchester	Town hall (P)
		Marblehead	Causeway (P)
		Marshfield	Brick Kiln Road (canoe only) (G); Green Harbor Marine (P); Humarock (residents only) (G); Humarock Marine (P); Mary's Livery (P); Town Pier, Green Harbor (P); Union Street, (canoe only) (G)
Duxbury	Bay Marine Corp. (P); Hicks Point Bay Rd. (P); Mattakeesett Ct., 2 piers, (P)		
Eastham	Rock Harbor, jetty, (P) Rt.6 Town Cove (P); Hemenway Rd. (P)		
Edgartown	Edgartown Great Pond, Wilson Landing (S); Katama Bay, Edgartown Bay Road (P)	Mashpee	Daniels Island Road (P); Great Neck Road (Ockway Bay) (P); Mashpee Neck Road (P)
Essex	Essex Marina, Dodge Street (P); Pike's Marina, Main Street (P);	Mattapoisett	Town dock, Water Street (P); Town landing, Matt Neck Road (G) half tide
Fairhaven	Earl's Marina, West Island (P); Pease Park, Middle Street (P); Seaview Ave., Sconticut Neck (P)		
		Nahant	Town Wharf (P)
		Nantucket	Madaket Harbor, H Street (P); Nantucket Harbor (P)
Fall River	Brownell Street (P)	New Bedford	East Rodney French Blvd. (P); West Rodney French Blvd. (P)
Falmouth	Child's River, off Rte. 28 (P); Falmouth Inner Harbor, Robbins Road, jetty, (P); Great Pond Marine, Harrington St. jetty, (P); Megannsett Harbor, County Rd. (P); Seapit Road, Waquoit, jetty, (P); West Falmouth Harbor, Old Dock Road, (P); Wild Harbor, Old Silver Beach (P); Woods Hole, Great Harbor, pier, (P)		
		Newburyport	Cashman Park (P); Marri-Mar Yacht Basin (P); Three-R Marine (P); Water Street (P), half tide
		Norwell	Bridge Steet (P), non-residents after Labor Day
		Oak Bluffs	Oak Bluffs Harbor, East Chop Dr. (P)
		Orleans	Cove Road (P); Goose Hummock Shop (P); House Pond, River Road (P); Mill Pond (P); Paw Wah Pond (P); Quanset Road (P); Rock Harbor (P)
Freetown	Water Street, Assonet (P), half tide		
Gay Head	Menemsha Creek, Lobsterville, jetty, (P)		
Gloucester	Blyman Canal at high school (P); Lanes Cove half tide(P); Corliss Landing half tide (P); Long Wharf (Jones River), Atlantic Street (P)	Pembroke	Adams Bait & Tackle, ramp (no info. on surface) canoe only, Bricklin Rd.
		Plymouth	Taylor Avenue (S) 4WD only; Town wharf, pier, (P)
Harwich	Allens Harbor, jetty, (P); Herring River (P); Round Cove (P); Saquatucket Harbor (P)	Provincetown	West End parking lot, Commercial Street (P), half tide
		Quincy	Anchor Marine 666, Southern Artery (P); Bay's Water Marine (P), half tide; Hurley's Boat Rental, 136 Bayview Avenue, pier (P)
Hingham	Iron Horse statue, Route 3A (P)		
Hull	"A" Street Marine, pier (P); Goulds Boat Shop (P); Pemberton Point, pier, (P); Priscilla Sails (P) half tide		
		Rockport	Granite Pier (P)
		Rowley	Perley's Marina (P)
Ipswich	Town landing, East Street (P); Water Street, pier, (P)	Salem	Kernwood Bridge (P); Winter Island (P)

Salisbury	State beach, 3 jetties (P)
Sandwich	Canal Basin, Canal Sides 2 jetties (P)
Saugus	Fishermen's Oulet (P)
Scituate	Cole Parkway (P); Driftway Recreation Area (G); North River Marine (P); Scituate Harbor, 1 jetty, 3 piers (P)
Somerset	Somerset Village, Marine Park, Main Street (P)
Swansea	Ocean Grove (P)
Tisbury	Lagoon Pond, Beach Road, jetty (P); Tashmoo Pond, Lake Avenue, jetty (P)
Truro	Pamet Harbor, jetty (P)
Wareham	East Blvd., Onset (P); Maco's (P); Oak Street, Tempest Knob (P); Rose Point (G); Rte. 195 Eastbound, Rest Area (P)
Wellfleet	Town Pier (P)
Westport	Gooseberry Island (P), half tide; Rte. 88 Bridge (P); Westport Pt. (P)
Weymouth	Wessagusset, George E. Lane Beach, Neck Street (P)
Winthrop	Shirley Street (P)
Yarmouth	Bayview Street (P) half tide; Center Street, Bass Hole (P) half tide; Follins Point Rd. (S); High Bank Rd. (P); New Hampshire Ave., Englewood Beach (P); Pleasant St. Beach (P), half tide; Sea Gull Beach (P); Ship Shops, Pleasant Street (P), half tide; Bass River Beach, South Street (P)

LAUNCH RAMPS

MAINE

Town	Comments
Addison	Pleasant River. Hard-surfaced, usable at all tides.
Augusta	Kennebec River. Hard-surfaced, usable at all tides.
	Kennebec River. Landing facility.
Bangor	Penobscot River. Landing facility.
Bar Harbor	Frenchman Bay. Hard-surfaced, usable at all tides.
Bath	Kennebec River. Hard-surfaced, usable at all tides.
	Kennebec River. Landing facility.
Belfast	Belfast Bay. Hard-surfaced, usable at all tides.
Biddeford	Saco River. Hard-surfaced, usable at all tides.
Blue Hill	Blue Hill Harbor. Hard-surfaced, not usable at all tides.
Boothbay	Linekin Bay. Hard-surfaced, not usable at all tides.
Bowdoinham	Cathance River. Hard-surfaced, usable at all tides.
Bristol	Pemaquid River. Hard-surfaced, usable at all tides. Pemaquid Historic Site.
Brunswick	Androscoggin River. Hard-surfaced, usable at all tides.
	Buttermilk Cove. Hard-surfaced, not usable at all tides, town.
	Middle Bay. Hard-surfaced, not usable at all tides.
	New Meadows River. Hard-surfaced, usable at all tides.
Calais	St. Croix River. Hard-surfaced, usable at all tides.
Chelsea	Kennebec River. Gravel, usable at all tides.
Cherryfield	Narraguagus River. Hard-surfaced, not usable at all tides.
Damariscotta	Damariscotta River. Hard-surfaced, usable at all tides.
Edmunds Township	Cobscook Bay. Hard-surfaced, usable at all tides, fee, Cobscook Bay State Park.
Eliot	Piscataqua River. Hard-surfaced, usable at all tides.
Ellsworth	Union River. Hard-surfaced, usable at all tides.
Frankfort	Penobscot River. Hard-surfaced, usable at all tides.
Gardiner	Kennebec River. Hard-surfaced, usable at all tides.
Hallowell	Kennebec River. Hard-surfaced, usable at all tides.
Hampden	Penobscot River. Hard-surfaced, usable at all tides.
Jonesport	Chandler Bay. Hard-surfaced, usable at all tides.
Lamoine	Frenchman Bay. Hard-surfaced, usable at all tides, fee, Lamoine State Park.
Lubec	Johnson Bay. Hard-surfaced, usable at all tides.
Machias	Machias River. Hard-surfaced, usable at all tides.
Milbridge	Narraguagus River. Hard-surfaced, usable at all tides.

Orrington	Penobscot River. Hard-surfaced, not usable at all tides.
Penobscot	No. Bay & Bagaduce River. Hard-surfaced, not usable at all tides.
Perry	Gleason Cove. Hard-surfaced, not usable at all tides.
Phippsburg	Kennebec River (at center). Gravel, usable at all tides.
Portland	Casco Bay. Hard-surfaced, not usable at all tides, fee.
Richmond	Kennebec River. Hard-surfaced, usable at all tides.
Robbinston	St. Croix River. Hard-surfaced, usable at all tides.
Rockland	Rockland Harbor. Hard-surfaced, usable at all tides.
Rockport	Rockport Harbor. Hard-surfaced, usable at all tides, fee.
St. George	Port Clyde. Hard-surfaced, usable at all tides.
	Tenants Harbor. Hard-surfaced, Nonesuch River. Hard-surfaced, not usable at all tides.
Searsport	Searsport Harbor. Hard-surfaced, usable at all tides.
South Portland	Fore River. Hard-surfaced, usable at all tides, fee.
Southwest Harbor	Hard-surfaced, usable at all tides.
Stockton Springs	Hard-surfaced, usable at all tides.
Swans Island	Mackerel Cove. Hard-surfaced, usable at all tides.
Tremont	Seal Cove. Hard-surfaced, usable at all tides.
Verona	Penobscot River. Hard-surfaced, usable at all tides.
Vinalhaven	Carvers Harbor. Hard-surfaced, usable at all tides.
Waldoboro	Medomak River. Hard-surfaced, not usable at all tides.
Westport	Back River. Hard-surfaced, usable at all tides.

MASSACHUSETTS

See page 30.

NEW HAMPSHIRE

Town	Comments
Dover	Hilton Park
Durham	Adams Point
	Cedar Point
	Jackson's Landing
	Shipyard Landing
Greenland	Stratham Depot Landing, limited Greenland Town Landing
Hampton Falls	Hampton Falls Boat Ramp
New Castle	New Castle Town Landing
Newfields	Newfields Town Landing
Newmarket	Newmarket Town Landing Lamprey River Access
Portsmouth	Pierce's Island Boat Ramp
Seabrook	Seabrook Town Dock

FISH RECORDS

MAINE

Bluefish: 20.32 lbs.; Bailey's Island; 1990
Bluefin Tuna: 819 lbs.; Portland Light Buoy; 1979
Blue Shark: 391 lbs.; 20 miles southeast of Portland; 1989
Cod: 77 lbs.; no location given; 1989
Striped Bass: 67 lbs.; Sheepscot River; 1987
Goosefish: 37 lbs. 11 oz.; no location given; 1988
Haddock: 11 lbs. 11 oz.; no location given; 1991
Halibut: 210 lbs. 8 oz.; no location given; 1985
Mako Shark: 680 lbs.; 20 miles east of Saco Bay; 1990
Pollock: 46 lbs. 10.9 oz.; no location given; 1990
Thresher Shark: 385 lbs.; no location given; 1989
Wolffish: 32.5 lbs.; no location given; 1989
Winter Flounder: 4 lbs. 3 oz.; no location given; 1989
White Hake: 46 lbs. 4 oz.; no location given; 1986

NEW HAMPSHIRE

Chinook Salmon: 19 lbs. 4 oz.; Exeter River; 1985
Coho Salmon: 16 lbs. 3 oz.; Piscataqua River; 1984
Cod: 98 lbs. 12 oz.; Isles of Shoals, Hampton; 1969
Bluefish: 21 lbs.; Great Bay, Durham; 1975
Striped Bass: 60 lbs.; Great Bay, Dover; 1980
Pollock: 47 lbs.; Atlantic, Portsmouth; 1981
Winter Flounder: 2 lbs. 4 oz.; Hampton Harbor, Hampton; 1986
Mackerel: 3 lbs.; Gulf of Maine, Hampton; 1988
Haddock: 10 lbs. 10.75 oz.; Gulf of Maine, Rye; 1988

MASSACHUSETTS

Bluefish: 27 lbs. 4 oz.; Graves Light; 1982
Bluefin Tuna: 1228 lbs.; Cape Cod Bay;, 1984
Blue Marlin: 637 lbs.; Atlantis Canyon; 1990
Blue Shark: (tie) 410 lbs.; Rockport; 1960; and Rockport, 1967
Bonito: 11 lbs. 2 oz.; Edgartown; 1990
Cod: 92 lbs.; Jeffreys Ledge; 1987
Coho Salmon: 18 lbs. 8 oz.; North River; 1986

Cusk: 34 lbs. 4 oz.; Stellwagen Bank; 1990

False Albacore: 19 lbs. 5 oz.; Edgartown; 1990

Fluke: 21 lbs. 8 oz.; Nomans Island; 1980

Haddock: (tie) 20 lbs.; Stellwagen Bank; 1972; and
Boston Lightship; 1974

Halibut: 255 lbs. 4 oz.; Cape Ann; 1989

Mackerel: (tie) 3 lbs.; Gulf of Maine; 1989; and Cape
Cod Bay, 1989

Mako Shark: 700 lbs.; Cape Cod Bay; 1989

Pollock: 44 lbs. 7 oz.; Cashes Ledge; 1981

Scup: 5 lbs. 14 oz.; Nomans Island; 1983

Sea Bass: 8 lbs.; Cotuit; 1985

Striped Bass: (three-way tie) 73 lbs.; Quick's Hole; 1933;
Sow and Pigs; 1967; Nauset Beach; 1981

Swordfish: 646 lbs.; Nomans Island; 1972

Tautog: 22 lbs. 9 oz.; Gay Head; 1978

Weakfish: 18 lbs. 12 oz.; Buzzards Bay, 1984

White Marlin: 131 lbs.; Nantucket; 1982

Winter Flounder: (tie) 6 lbs.; and Massachusetts Bay;
1982; Magnolia; 1987

Wolffish: 52 lbs.; Georges Bank; 1986

Yellowfin Tuna: 187 lbs.; Nantucket; 1990

Massachusetts Saltwater Fishing Derby Rules and Regulations

Sponsored by the Massachusetts Division of Marine Fisheries. The Commonwealth of Massachusetts, Division of Marine Fisheries, will acknowledge catches of outstanding saltwater gamefish that meet certain requirements. Eligible species and minimum qualifying weights are listed below.

At the end of each derby year, trophies will be awarded to anglers who landed the heaviest fish in each species category. Winners will be chosen in three divisions—men, women and junior (age fifteen and younger).

The derby runs from April 1 through October 31 each year and is open to all age groups. Fish entered must be caught in a fair and sporting manner on hook and line and must be measured and weighed at an official weigh-station on a certified scale. Weighmasters can be found at most local marinas and tackle shops.

Special awards are offered for new state records. If your catch exceeds the weight listed on the current list of Massachusetts Saltwater Gamefish Records, you may qualify for a special award. All weigh-stations have been provided with a copy of the current list. When applying for a new state record you must supply an affidavit accompanied by a clear photograph of your catch, with your name, address and telephone number printed on the back.

Eligible Species	Minimum Weight (pounds)
Bluefin Tuna	300
Bluefish	10
Blue Shark	150
Cod	25
Coho Salmon	10
Haddock	8
Halibut	50
Mackerel	2
Mako Shark	100
Pollock	20
Scup	2
Sea Bass	3
Striped Bass	30
Summer Flounder (Fluke)	5
Swordfish	150
Tautog	8
Weakfish	10
White Marlin	60
Winter Flounder	2

LOCATING PARTY, CHARTER OR RENTAL BOATS

For the most up-to-date information on party, charter, or rental boats, call the chamber of commerce or the state agency with jurisdiction in the area you're interested in visiting.

At the various coastal ports, you will find party boats and crews inspected and licensed by the U.S. Coast Guard to take people on coastal fishing cruises. The vessels are equipped with safety and communications devices, and many have electronic systems for depth recording and fish finding. The crews are experienced and knowledgeable about locating fish, and their guidance will help you have a good catch. A charter boat carries up to six people and is hired at a fixed price per boat per day. A headboat carries more (average capacity is 30, but at present some carry as many as 100) and operates on a fixed price per person per day or may be chartered for private groups. Advance reservations for trips on either type of vessel are a good idea.

Charter boats operate out of many Gulf of Maine harbors from Eastport and Lubec to York. Ports with higher concentrations of charter boats include Mount Desert Island at Bar Harbor and Southwest Harbor, Rockland, Boothbay Harbor, Ogunquit, Biddeford, Portland, Kennebunkport, and York.

The coastal waters of New Hampshire contain a great variety of food and gamefishes. At almost anytime of day during the March to October season, anglers can be seen trying their luck from banks and bridges. For those who want to increase their chances without the bother and expense of owning a boat, passenger-boat fishing is the logical choice. Whether for a half day, a full day, or longer, a fishing trip on a passenger boat is an inexpensive treat for an individual, a family, or a business or social group. And while every fisherman knows that the sport offers no guarantees, the waters of the New Hampshire coast have been known for their abundance for centuries. Bottom dwellers such as cod, cusk, haddock, hake, and wolffish abound in the cold, deep Gulf of Maine and annual migrations of ocean fishes such as mackerel and bluefish provide a great deal of excitement as well as a wonderful meal at the end of the day.

You can find charter operators in Seabrook, Hampton, Hampton Beach, and Rye Harbor.

MAINE

(All area codes 207)

Bath
Kayla D. and *Obsession* charters
4 Patricia Drive
Topsham 04086
442-8581
Bromos
Bald Head Rd.
Arrowsic 04530
443-3954

Bar Harbor
Dolphin
Bar Harbor 04609
288-3322

Biddeford
Steve Brettell
336 Guinea Rd.
Biddeford 04005
283-4129
Trina Lynn
14 Rathier Street
Biddeford 04005
284-2352

Boothbay Harbor
Breakaway
Box 860, Royal Road East
Boothbay Harbor 04544
633-4414
Bingo & Bingo Charter
P.O. Box 463
Boothbay Harbor 04538
633-3775
Lucky Star II
P.O. Box 161
Boothbay Harbor 04538
633-4446
Buccaneer & Yellow Bird
65 Atlantic Ave.
Boothbay Harbor 04538
633-3244
Hopscotch
Green Landing Rd.
E. Boothbay 04544
633-7221

Shark V
4 Puritan Rd.
Brown's Wharf
Boothbay Harbor 04535
633-3416
Redhook
Pension Ridge Rd.
Boothbay 04537
633-3807

Cape Small
Red Dog
Hermit Island Campground
443-2101
Yankee Cruises Charter
Small Point
443-2101

Eastport
Quoddy Dam
RR #1 Box 58
Eastport 04631
853-4303

Edgecomb
Charger
Rte. 27
Edgecomb 04556
882-9309

Falmouth
Maven's Heaven
187 Middle Rd.
Falmouth 04105
781-3904

Freeport
Big Fish
157 Durham Rd.
Freeport 04032
865-6561

Jonesport
Chief
RR Box 990
Jonesport 04649
497-5933

Kennebunk
Nerus
4 Western Ave. Rear
Kennebunk 04043
967-5507

Kennebunkport
Deep Water
P.O. Box 2775
Kennebunkport 04046
967-4938
Your Pleasure
c/o Chick's Marina
Ocean Ave.
Kennebunkport 04046
967-2782
Cape Arundel Cruises/
Whale Watch
Rte. #9, P.O. Box 840
Kennebunkport 04046
967-5595
Captain Al
RR # 4 Box 363D
Biddeford 04005
985-3436

Kittery
Eliot Charters
8 Forest Ave.
Kittery 03904
439-5233
Safari Charters
7 Island Ave.
Kittery 03904
439-5068

Lubec
Seafarer
9 High St.
Lubec 04652
733-5584

Millbridge
Foxy Lady II
Wyman Rd.
Millbridge 04658
546-7218

North Edgecomb
Catch 22
RR# 1 Box 3265
Union 04862
785-2408

Northeast Harbor
Poor Richard
P.O. Box 321

Northeast Harbor 04662
276-3785
Ogunquit
Ruth Bee II
P.O. Box 205
Ogunquit 03907
646-4074
Bunny Clark
P.O. Box 837
Ogunquit 03907
646-2214
Finestkind Scenic Cruises
P.O. Box 1828
Ogunquit 03907
646-5227
Ugly Anne
P.O. Box 863
Ogunquit 03907
646-7202
Old Orchard Beach
Salt Shaker
9 Banks Brook Rd.
Old Orchard Beach 04064
934-0886
Main Inspiration
190 Portland Ave.
Old Orchard Beach 04064
934-7073
Portland
Devil's Den
P.O. Box 272
Scarborough 04074
761-4466
First Choice Charters
17 Farwell Ave.
Portland 04102
829-4184
Seaquest
P.O. Box 894
N. Windham 04062
893-1261
Indian II Odyssey
634 Cape Rd.
Standish 04084
642-3270
Warlock
445 Brighton Ave.
Portland 04102
775-3486
Rockland
Henrietta
P.O. Box 128
Spruce Head Island 04859
594-5411
Scarborough
Mary Jean

8 Church St.
Scarborough 04074
883-2698
Shy Ann
28 Snow Rd.
Scarborough 04074
883-4691
San R Marie
74 E. Grand Ave.
Scarborough 04074
883-5002
Rock n Reel
21 Snow Rd.
Scarborough 04074
883-1015
South Freeport
Anjin-San
210 Prospect St.
Portland 04103
772-7168
Atlantic Sea Cruises
25 Main St.
865-6112
South Harpswell
Happy Hooker II
P.O. Box 842
South Harpswell 04079
Southwest Harbor
Acadia Naturalist Cruise (follow
Swans Island ferry signs)
244-5365
Thomaston
Sandpiper
Saltwater Farm Campground
Thomaston 04861
354-8713
Wells Harbor
Sea Time
P.O. Box 307
Moody 04054
646-8001
York/York Harbor
Enterprise
42 Sheru La.
York 03909
363-5634
E-Z
Town Dock
York 03909
363-5634
F.V. Blackback
P.O. Box 218
York 03909
363-5675
Shearwater
P.O. Box 472

York Harbor 03911
363-5324
Tom Cat
P.O. Box 368
York Beach 03910
363-7535

**Striped Bass Fishing Guides,
Kennebec River Area**
Mike Augut, 443-5941
Steve Brettel, 283-4129
Forrest Faulkingham, 882-7973
Barry Gibson, 633-3416
Doug Jowett, 725-4573
Pat Keliher, 865-6561
Dean Krah, 586-6422
Dave Pecci, 729-3997
Russell Troy, 785-2408
Harvey Wheeler, 781-3908

NEW HAMPSHIRE

(All area codes 603)
Atlantic Fishing Fleet
P.O. Box 678
Rye Harbor 03870
964-5220
Eastman Fishing & Marine
River St.
Seabrook 03874
474-3461
Al Gauron Deep Sea Fishing
State Pier
Hampton Beach 03842
926-2469
Smith & Gilmore
A Ocean Blvd.
Hampton Beach 03842
926-3503

MASSACHUSETTS

Barnstable
Apache
125 Chadwell Ave.
Sandwich
(508) 888-2907
Aquarius
171 Ryder St.
Buzzards Bay
(508) 759-3866
Heather Jean
100 Sullivan Rd.
West Yarmouth
(508) 775-3795
Kembe
19 O'Neil

Stoughton
(617) 334-4667
Lady J
67 Bayview
Wareham
(508) 295-8552
Malsie B
2 Pine Needle La.
East Sandwich
(508) 888-6454
Peregrine
12 Kristi Way
West Barnstable
(508) 428-2557
Striper
R.D. #1, 34 Pine Street
South Dennis
(508) 398-2179
Turnstone
Box 181
West Barnstable
(508) 771-1930
Beverly
Sweet Dream
110 Judith E. Drive
Tewksbury
(508) 851-4152
Boston
Miss Atlantic
7 Elwood Street
Charlestown
(617) 242-2470
Charters Unlimited
57 Cliffmont Street
Boston
(617) 328-9224
Midnight III
(617) 335-3298
Sea King
68 Edward St.
Boston
(617) 396-4096
Bourne
White Wave
34 Crestview Dr.
E. Sandwich
(508) 833-0614
Chilmark
Bass n Blue
RFD 314B
Chilmark
(508) 645-2993
Bass Ackwards
Box 166
Chilmark
(508) 645-2915

Hattie Attie
(508) 693-3779
Kathie C
Box 213
Chilmark
(508) 645-2614
Cohasset
Wardi
345 Howard Street
Rockland
(617)871-2754
Cuttyhunk
Aggravator
8 Grinnell Street
S. Dartmouth
(508) 993-5754
Jig M Up
(508) 996-3902
Lindesider
Cuttyhunk Island
(508) 991-7352
Rudy J.
Cuttyhunk
(508) 993-7427
Danvers
Reel Thing
70 Martin Ave.
N. Andover
(508) 957-5865
Dennis
Albatross
33 Saltmarsh Rd.
E. Dennis
(508) 385-3177
Bluefish
(508) 378-3245
Champion
44 Rt. 28W
Dennis
(508) 398-2266
Dream Chaser
17 Upcountry Rd.
S. Dennis
(508) 394-4427
Kimpa
110 Hillside Dr.
E. Dennis
(508) 385-8186
Skip Skip
46 Cedar Crest Dr.
Bridgewater
(508) 697-0617
Duxbury
Blue Hunter II
(617) 585-9765
Kestrel

(617) 294-8172
Jazz
88 Woodbridge Rd.
Duxbury
(617) 934-5040
Edgartown
Knot II Knight
Box 984
Edgartown
(508) 627-8780
Nisa
Box 1054
Edgartown
(508) 627-8780
Slapshot
(508) 627-8087
The Big Eye
(508) 627-3649
Honker
182 Main Street
Fairhaven
(508) 996-3892
Falmouth
Amethyst II
P.O. Box BB
E. Falmouth
(508) 548-0019
Black Hawk
60 Westwood Dr.
N. Darmouth
(508) 992-2038
Cygnet
Clinton Ave.
Falmouth
(508) 548-6274
East Wind
(508) 457-9811
Escape
P.O. Box 1034
N. Falmouth
(508) 564-5304
Freedom
Box 3478
Pocassett
(508) 563-7419
Lee Marie
(508) 548-9498
Minute Man
227 Clinton Ave.
Falmouth
(508) 548-2626
Sea Fox
70 Lake Leamon Rd.
Falmouth
(508) 540-3309
Stinger

(617) 964-2227
Swordfish
Clinton Ave.
Falmouth
(508) 775-2648
Gloucester
Christina
27 Summer Street
Chelmsford
(508) 256-7482
Island Queen
Main St.
Gloucester
(508) 283-6995
Kerri Lynne
17 Regina Dr.
Chelmsford
(508) 256-4900
Liesure Knot
113 Amherst Street
Granby
(413) 467-3290
Rainbow Chaser
908 Mammoth Rd.
Dracut
(508) 957-5865
The Yankee Fleet
1-800-942-5464
Capt. Bill's Deep Sea Fishing
1-800-339-4253
Reel Treat Charters
(508) 851-9622
Harwich
Arlie M
324 Forrest Beach Rd.
S. Chatham
(508) 432-1145
Booby Hatch
(508) 430-2312
Catherine L.
17 Linda Ave.
Auburn
(508) 394-3869
Fire Fly
16 Shaggy Pine Road
W. Harwich
(508) 432-3089
Golden Eagle
1040 Main St.
S. Harwich
(508) 945-0167
Mooncusser
(508) 432-7514
O'Jay
Buzzards Bay
(508) 759-7969

Sea Joy
(508) 432-0177
Sue Z
Pamela's Way
E. Harwich
(508) 432-4025
Yankee
Harwichport
(508) 432-2520
Hyannis
Fish Hawk
75 Park Ave.
Centerville
(508) 775-3403
Jackpot
137 Lumbert Mill Rd.
Centerville
(508) 428-8825
Rosey S
252 Skunknet Rd.
Centerville
(508) 775-8517
Sea Swan
Ocean St. Dock
Hyannis
(508) 775-7185
Straycat
40 Lovell Rd.
Osterville
(508) 428-8628
Wanderers V
P.O. Box 1292
(617)731-1172
Lynn
Amber Jack
Rt. 1, Harbor Mall
Lynn
(617) 599-9480
Traveler
(617) 598-0260
Marblehead
The Fox
(617) 631-1262
Marshfield
Arminda
69 Central Avenue
Brant Rock
(617) 837-5424
Big Fish II
(617) 536-6737
Big Mac
Marshfield
(617) 837-0308
Brenda Marie
346 Plymouth St.
Holbrook

(617) 767-1635
Cathy Ann
109 Rice Ave.
Rockland
(617) 878-6798
Frosty V
(617) 878-6882
Overtime
(617) 878-2323
Mattapoisett
Sandra Ann
1 Marilane Place
Fairhaven
(508) 994-2214
New Bedford
Captain Leroy
1 Popes Island, Route 6
New Bedford
(508) 992-8907
Just About
257 Popes Island
(508) 996-8682
Let's Go Fishin
Swansea
(508) 672-7177
Newburyport
Aimee Joe II
Amesbury
(508) 388-9116
Barracuda
8 Peters St.
Newburyport
(508) 465-6463
First Alternative
(508) 462-1374
Hilton's Fishing Dock
(508) 465-3885
Oak Bluffs
Banjo
Box 2441
Oak Bluffs
(508) 693-3154
Milton James
Oak Bluffs
(508) 693-1238
Summer's Lease
(508) 693-2880
Orleans
Columbia
(508) 255-0801
Luau
N. Eastham
(508) 255-4527
Nekton
192 Rock Harbor Rd.
(508) 255-1289

Osprey
47 Namskaket Rd.
Orleans
(508) 255-1266
Stunmai
190 Rock Harbor Rd.
(508) 255-0018
White Hunter
E. Orleans
(508) 255-2065
Plymouth
Andy Lynn
Woodbine Dr.
Plymouth
(508) 746-4922
Capt. John
(508) 746-2643
Jeanette Four
17 Sever St.
Plymouth
(508) 746-7538
Salty Lady
(617) 585-8451
Provincetown
Cee J
37C Court St.
(508) 487-2353
Shady Lady
(508) 487-0182
Quincy
Selma K.
170 Burlet Rd.
Quincy
(617) 479-6463
Easy Livin
(508) 546-3323
Salem
Pearl Beverly
(617) 356-2701
Silver Clean
9 Buford Rd.
Peabody
800-498-0955
Clipper Fleet
(508) 465-7495

Family Affair
18 Forest Street
Byfield
(508) 464-9072
North Star II
59 East St.
Ipswich
(508) 783-9407
Sandwich
Excavator
1403 Wachusett St.
Jefferson
(508) 829-4072
Patricia C.
19 Carr Lane
Forestdale
(508) 477-9346
Poke About III
(508) 533-7777
Roamer
Box 1329
Sandwich
(508) 888-7621
Tigger Too
41 Moody Drive
Sandwich
(508) 888-8372
Scituate
Applejack
(617) 545-9643
Ejj
55 Franklin Rd.
Norwell
(617) 878-6731
Half Bass
Randolph
(617) 986-4375
Irish Rover
Scituate
(617) 545-4708
Julin
(617) 545-2283
Katmandu
28 Regatta Rd.
N. Weymouth

(617) 331-7328
Maquipmen
Holbrook
(617) 767-2675
Pisces
Marshfield
(617) 837-2701
Wareham
Neat Lady
Wareham
(508) 295-9402
Wellfleet
Erin H.
(508) 349-9663
Hobo
N. Eastham
(508) 255-6081
Navigator
South Wellfleet
(508) 349-6003
Night Cap
(508) 349-2607
Snooper
Wellfleet
(508) 255-8268
Westport
Jitterbug
(508) 636-3978
Laughing Gull
Westport Point
(508) 636-2730
Outrigger
S. Dartmouth
(508) 636-3851
Rip Dancer
Attleboro
(508) 226-2462
Yarmouth
Beverly Ann
South Yarmouth
(508) 394-6344
Kay
(508) 263-4601

STATE AGENCIES

MAINE

(All area codes 207)
State of Maine—Department of Marine Resources
State House Station #21
Augusta, ME 04333
289-6500

Division I—Bureau of Marine Patrol
21 Vocational Drive
South Portland, ME 04106
799-3380 or 799-7641

Division II—Bureau of Marine Patrol
5 Main Street
Rockland, ME 04841-0387
596-2262 or 596-2263

Division III—Bureau of Marine Patrol
RFD #2
C/O Lamoine State Park
Ellsworth, ME 04605
667-3373

National Marine Fisheries Service
Atlantic Bluefin Tuna Permit
United States Courthouse
156 Federal Street—Room 329
Portland, ME 04101
780-3241

Atlantic Salmon Commission
Regulations & License Information
P.O. Box 1298
Bangor, ME 04402-1298
941-4449

Department of Inland Fisheries and Wildlife
Law & Boat Safety
284 State St., Station 41
Augusta, ME 04333
289-5220

Maine Publicity Bureau
Travel & Tourist Information
97 Winthrop Street
Hallowell, ME 04347
289-5710

NEW HAMPSHIRE

(All area codes 603)
New Hampshire Fish & Game Department
Marine Fisheries Division
37 Concord Ave.
Durham, NH 03824
868-1095

New Hampshire Office of Vacation/Travel
Box 856
Concord, NH 03301
271-2343

New Hampshire Dept. of Safety
Marine Patrol
10 Hazen Drive
Concord, NH 03305
271-2333

MASSACHUSETTS

Massachusetts Division of Marine Fisheries
100 Cambridge Street
Boston, MA 02202
    Boston: (617) 727-3193
    Salem: (508) 745-3107
    Sandwich: (508) 888-1155
    Martha's Vineyard: (508) 693-0060

Division of Law Enforcement
100 Nashua Street
Boston, MA 02114
(617) 727-3190
To report a violation: (617) 727-6308 or (800) 632-8075

Boat Registration
Division of Law Enforcement
100 Nashua Street
Boston, MA 02114
    Boston: (617) 727-3900

Massachusetts Office of Travel and Tourism
100 Cambridge St., 13th Floor
Boston, MA 02202
(617) 727-3201

Nantucket Shoals to Long Island Sound

The inshore water between Cape Cod and New York consists, for the most part, of a series of sounds whose names are derived from the principal islands which mark their seaward boundaries, i.e., Nantucket Island, Martha's Vineyard, Block Island, and Long Island.

Sea-bottom configurations off this area are remarkably different from those to the north. Absent are the deep basins, sheer rock ledges, and broad banks which are common in the Gulf of Maine. Instead, a relatively smooth plain gently slopes from the offshore rim of the sounds out to about the 600-foot contour, a distance from land of 80 miles or more. Even Nantucket Shoals, the series of shifting shoals lying off Nantucket Island, were probably once part of a smooth sandy plain.

About 50,000 years ago a great sheet of glacial ice, originating in the region of Hudson Bay and Labrador, spread southward and covered much of New England. The great accumulation of snow, miles thick over eastern Canada, compressed the bottom layers into ice which, under the influence of gravity, flowed outward from the center of the glacier. This slowly moving amorphous mass of ice had force enough to round off mountains and scour out valleys. The glacier's southernmost extension roughly conformed to a line drawn from Nantucket Island to Martha's Vineyard, to Block Island, thence to Montauk on Long Island, through Ronkonkoma to about Roslyn. After thousands of years, the climate began to warm, causing the ice sheet to melt away gradually, leaving its deposits of sand, gravel, silt, clay, rocks, and boulders to form these areas. After an interval of several thousand years, a cooling period set in, causing the leading edge of the ice sheet to extend southward once more. During the second advance, the edge of the ice extended from Cape Cod along the Elizabeth Islands and the southern coast of Rhode Island to Fishers Island, thence westward along the north shore of Long Island to the point where New York City is now. After holding this position for thousands of years, the ice sheet retreated for a second and final time as the climate again became warmer. Soil, rocks, and boulders carried by the ice were deposited along this second edge to form these peninsulas and islands.

Since deposition of this glacial material, the action of wind, water and waves has worked to shape the land as we know it now. Rocky shores, like those in Narragansett Bay and along Connecticut, erode slowly compared to the sandy beaches of Nantucket Island, Martha's Vineyard, and Block Island. Erosion of the sandy bluffs and cliffs on the eastern side of Nantucket Island, the western end of Martha's Vineyard, and the southern end of Block Island takes place at about 3 feet a year. Montauk Point and the land on Long Island between Port Jefferson and Orient Point are also eroding away by storm-caused waves, but at a slower rate. The eroded sediments when washed into the sea are transported by currents and deposited in other areas. Sandy Point on Block Island, South Beach on Martha's Vineyard, and Smith Point and Great Point on Nantucket are examples of such deposits.

Along the open seacoasts of this section, tides range about 3 feet between high and low water. Nevertheless, owing to the complexities of tides along the protected inshore coast and landward side of the islands, the range varies from only 1½ feet in some areas to over 8 feet in others. For example, the tidal range at Woods Hole is 2 feet while at Cuttyhunk, only 15 miles to the southwest, it is about 4 feet. Near the mouth of Narragansett Bay at Newport it is about 3½ feet, but near the head of the bay at Providence it is 6 feet. At the Race in the eastern end of Long Island Sound, the tide is 2½ feet, but at Eatons Neck in the western end it is 8 feet. As is true along the entire coast, the effect of strong winds in combination with regular tidal action may at times cause the water to rise above or fall below its usual level. The high winds of the September 1938 hurricane coinciding with the peak of a high spring tide caused the water to rise 10 to 20 feet above the ordinary high-tide line.

The climate of the region between southern Cape Cod and New York is moist and cool. From October to March the prevailing winds, usually blowing from 10 to 20 knots over the water, are between west and north. Sometimes northwesterly gales occur, blowing more than 40 knots. From March until June, when the summer wind regime is established, the direction is variable. From June through September prevailing winds are between south and west. As often occurs in summer, hot afternoon air temperatures become reduced by a sea breeze blowing onshore across the cool water. Rarely, however, does this breeze penetrate more than 10 miles inland. Although gales are rare during summer, hurricanes, originating in the tropics, occur occasionally from August through October. Fogs are frequent in late spring and early summer when warm easterly to southwesterly light breezes blow over the still cool water. Though usually lasting only a few hours, they sometimes persist for a week broken only by short periods of clear weather. Winds blowing between west and north dispel fog and bring clear weather.

Fishing has always been important to the inhabitants along the shore of this section. The Indians used weirs made of branches and small trees and nets made of hemp to trap small fishes such as herring, shad, and striped bass. They used harpoons as well as arrows to capture large fish such as sturgeon and mammals such as porpoise and whales. Among the Indians' favorite seafoods were shellfish. Dug throughout the year from along the shores, clams and oysters supplied them meat, and the juices from these shellfish seasoned their soups and breads. During the middle and late 1600's, when most of this area became colonized by Europeans, the Indians shared their knowledge of fishing with the settlers, who quickly learned the necessary skills.

The demand for whale products, primarily whalebone and oil, during the 1600's, 1700's, and early 1800's motivated New Englanders to capture these mammoth animals. From salvaging whales stranded on beaches, the industry expanded to the use of small whale boats, rowed or sailed close to shore, and then to large ocean-going vessels for deep-sea whaling. Whaling ports such as Nantucket, New Bedford, Stonington, New London, and Sag Harbor became known the world over.

During the early days whaling became a status occupation, not just because it was adventurous but because it offered an excellent chance to make a great deal of money. At the same time, however, the inshore fisheries grew and prospered very well. As early as 1750 the fishing grounds of Nantucket Sound, Narragansett Bay, and Gardiners Bay were well known. By the late 1800's over 5,000 men were engaged in fishing in this area. From Montauk Point alone over 35 fishing vessels set sail to catch fishes such as bluefish, striped bass, cod, and weakfish.

The occurrence and movement of fishes within this area are greatly affected by changes in water temperature. While winter and windowpane flounders, tautog, cunner, tomcod, and smelt are year-round inshore residents, most kinds of fishes migrate to and from this area according to seasonal changes of temperature in the spring and fall. Even though the year-round water temperature in depths of 150 feet or more is suitable for cold-water species such as cod, pollock, and several kinds of hake, many of them inhabit nearshore water during winter when temperatures are minimal. Early in March, the surface water begins to warm progressively from offshore and south to inshore and north. As the temperature continues to warm during April, the cold-water visitors begin to move back offshore along the bottom into deeper and cooler water. By May or early June temperate-water species, notably fluke, scup, bluefish, striped bass, and weakfish, which have spent the winter offshore and to the south, begin to migrate here to spend the summer. During August, when the surface water reaches its maximum of about 68° to 73°F, subtropical fishes are occasional visitors. The temperate-water species remain until October or November, when the water cools; then they move offshore and to the south. About the same time cold-water fishes move back into the area to spend the winter.

Estuaries are important as breeding areas for some fishes and nursery areas for many others. Winter flounder, windowpane flounder, tomcod, and smelt as well as baitfishes, such as killifish and silversides, are permanent residents of the estuarine zone. Other baitfish, such as menhaden and mullet, live there only during part of their lives. Even though important anadromous fishes, notably shad, alewife, and blueback herring, spawn in rivers, the sexually mature fish must pass through the estuarine zone on their way upstream to spawn, and later the spawned-out fish and the juveniles must return by the same route on their way to the sea. Juveniles of our only catadromous fish, the eel, either pass through the estuarine zone on their way to fresh water or remain there to develop into adults. At maturity, adult eels move downstream, desert this zone, and swim offshore and south to spawn. Although not spawned in this area, many striped bass migrate here and spend the warm months feeding in the rivers and estuaries, some even staying through the winter. Estuaries are also the homes of shellfish such as oysters, both soft- and hard-shell clams, bay scallops, lobsters, crabs, and shrimps.

Unfortunately, these extraordinarily fertile areas where saltwater and freshwater mix are being continually destroyed through unwise use. Encroachment on estuaries for housing and industrial development conflicts with increasing needs for food and open space. Between 1970 and 1975, for example, nearly 18,000 acres of tidal marshland were destroyed in Massachusetts, Rhode Island, Connecticut, and New York. In addition, dredging and filling destroyed about 7 percent of Massachusetts' 31,000 acres of important shoal-water habitat, 6 percent of Rhode Island's 15,000 acres, 10 percent of Connecticut's 20,000 acres, and 15 percent of New York's 133,000 acres.

Estuaries are treated as convenient dumps for solid and liquid wastes as well as for many other pollutants. Not only is the aquatic life in the immediate dumping sites destroyed, but large portions of surrounding areas are rendered unusable, especially for harvesting shellfish. Thus, the total production from clam flats, scallop beds, and oyster bars has become greatly reduced. The fate of the oyster, which is a permanent estuarine resident, illustrates what has happened to just one resource. During the late 1800's about 3½ million bushels of oysters were harvested yearly from this area. Then, natural bars of oysters occurred at the mouth of the Taunton River in Massachusetts, the Providence River in Rhode Island, and the Poquonock and Thames Rivers in Connecticut. Other grounds were very productive in Connecticut at New Haven Harbor and areas around Saybrook, Clinton, Guilford, Branford, and Norwalk. Indeed, along Connecticut's shoreline the thing most noteworthy was not where oysters grew naturally, but where they did not! Nonetheless, the harvest by 1940 had decreased to about 1½ million bushels even while oystermen used fairly sophisticated techniques of oyster farming. In time, however, even cultivated oysters could not prosper in the polluted water, with the consequence that by the mid-1960's the harvest had dropped to a mere 70,000 bushels, only about one-fiftieth that of the late 1800's. Any hope of restoring such impoverished areas to their former productiveness depends on the effectiveness of pollution-control measures.

An angler in Massachusetts, Rhode Island, Connecticut, or New York does not need a license to fish in salt water. These states, however, have some saltwater regulations. All of them set minimum size limits for striped bass and some states set minimum size limits and seasons for a few other fishes. Either the states or the coastal communities in each state have regulations governing the capture of anadromous fishes. Some communities also have regulations for shellfishing and worm digging, and some require permits for these activities. For a detailed list of state agencies, see the end of this chapter. To obtain copies of fishing and shellfishing regulations, contact the offices listed below:

As we've noted previously, and will continue to stress, fishing regulations are perishable, often changing from year to year. A prudent angler will check for the latest rules before dropping a hook.

- Massachusetts—Massachusetts Division of Marine Fisheries, 100 Cambridge Street, Boston, MA 02202; (617) 727-3193.
- Rhode Island—Division of Fish and Wildlife, Government Center, Tower Hill Rd., Wakefield, RI 02879; (401) 789-3094.
- Connecticut—State of Connecticut, Department of Environmental Protection, Bureau of Fisheries and Wildlife, Marine Fisheries, Waterford, CT; (203) 443-0166.
- New York—New York State Department of Environmental Conservation, Division of Marine Resources, SUNY—Bldg. 40, Stonybrook, NY 11794; (516) 751-7900, ext. 326.

MARTHA'S VINEYARD AND NANTUCKET

About 17 miles south of Cape Cod lies the crescent-shaped island of Nantucket. This sandy, low-relief island is about 13 miles long by 3 miles wide. Now a fishing port and summer resort, Nantucket was the seat of the important whaling industry from about 30 years after its settlement in 1659 until the early 1870's.

LAND CONFIGURATION AND WATER DEPTH

Most of Nantucket is a series of low irregular hills which are partly wooded, the rest covered by grasses and shrubs. The highest elevation, slightly over 100 feet, is at the eastern end. Also at this end of the island, steep sand bluffs, many over 50 feet high, abut the mighty Atlantic Ocean.

The low, sandy islands of Tuckernuck and Muskeget lie to the west of Nantucket. Tuckernuck, the larger of the two, is about 2 miles long by 1½ miles wide. Its

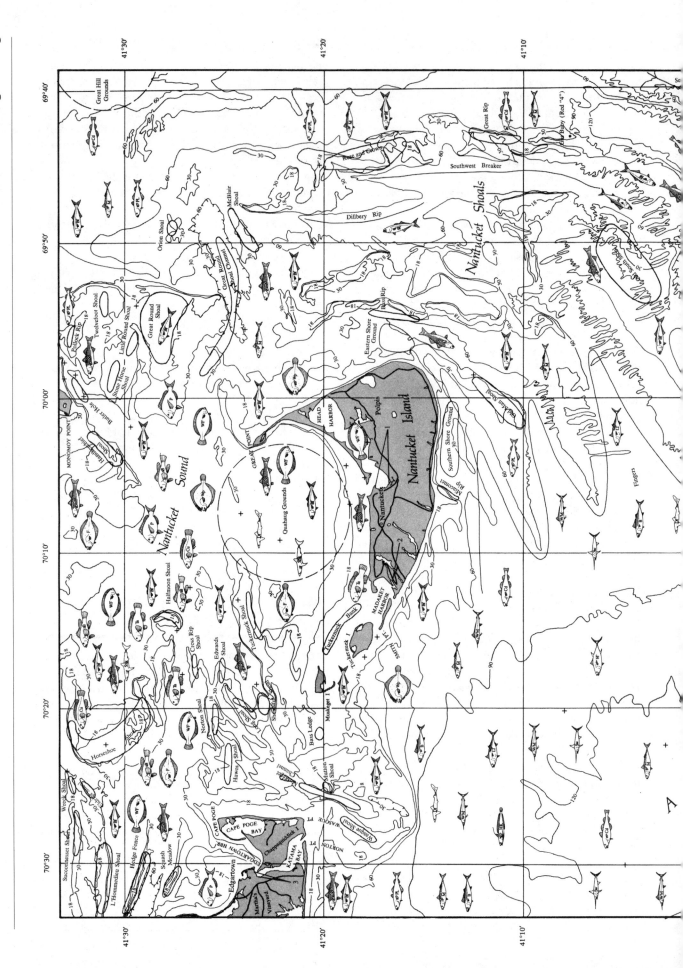

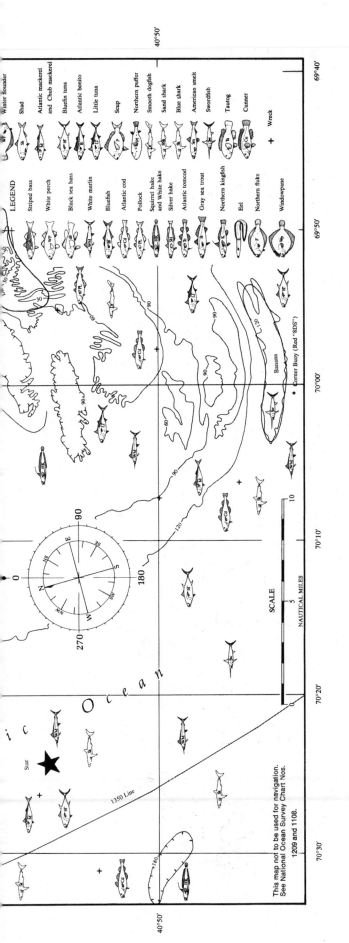

highest point is about 50 feet. Muskeget, 1½ miles long by ½ mile wide, is separated from Tuckernuck by a shallow sand flat, some of which is exposed at low tide. The highest point on Muskeget Island is about 10 feet.

Muskeget Channel is a 6-mile-wide body of water separating Muskeget Island from Chappaquiddick Island. In the past, Chappaquiddick was connected with Martha's Vineyard. Today these two islands are separated by a narrow slue connecting Edgartown Harbor and Katama Bay. Martha's Vineyard, which lies across the slue from Chappaquiddick, is a large, heavily vegetated island, about 15 miles long by 8 miles wide.

Nantucket Shoals is the name given to a series of submerged, shifting sandy shoals which lie off Nantucket Island. These shoals, most of which are only 25 feet under water, extend about 30 miles south of Nantucket and the same distance east. Various shoals still bear the names given to them by fishermen and navigators in the 16th and 17th centuries: Rose and Crown, Old South Shoal, Davis Bank, Davis South Shoal, and Great Rip. Between many of these shallow areas are slues and channels from 60 to 120 feet deep. The extent of their shoalness, their shifting nature, and the strong and erratic currents throughout this area make Nantucket Shoals one of the most dangerous parts along the coast for navigation. An untold number of vessels and human lives have been lost on these shoals, many long before official records were kept.

South and west of Nantucket and Martha's Vineyard, the characteristics of the continental shelf become strikingly different from those of the Gulf of Maine. Offshore banks and enclosed submarine basins give way to a gradual, even slope of the ocean bottom. Fifteen miles south of Chappaquiddick Island the depth is 120 feet; 30 miles out it is 180 feet; about 75 miles out it is 600 feet, a depth marking the limit of the continental shelf.

Nantucket Sound is the body of water lying between the south shore of Cape Cod and Nantucket Island, Chappaquiddick Island, and part of Martha's Vineyard. It is about 25 miles long by 15 miles wide and averages about 35 feet deep. While shoals are numerous and shifting at its eastern end, they become fewer and more stable to the south and west.

FISH AND FISHING

These islands have long been famous for their great inshore sport, especially when it comes to striped bass. Big bass are present from spring through late fall, and can be caught almost anywhere along the islands' sand and rock shores, as well as in the numerous rips that form over sandy shoals washed by powerful tides. Sharing the inshore waters are bluefish and summer migrants like bonito, little tunny, and Spanish mackerel.

Martha's Vineyard's surf-fishery is the stuff of legends. Names like Gay Head, Lobsterville, Menemsha,

Katama, and Squibnocket are synonomous with some of the world's best striper fishing. There's also great action in and around the many island ponds, especially when all kinds of bass food is flushed into the sea on an outgoing tide. Top sport continues all through the summer, when night fishing becomes especially productive in the protected waters of the ponds. Along the ocean, Cape Poge and Wasque Point offer good bluefishing. For boaters, West Chop, East Chop, and Devil's Bridge off Gay Head produce striper and bluefish action through November.

From a boat, anglers can fish famous spots like Old Man Rip, Wasque Shoal, the Middle Grounds, and numerous other shoals, where churning currents boil over shallow sand bottoms, tumbling baitfish and attracting predators. The rips between Nomans Island and Squibnocket Point are particularly fishy. Here you can often watch predators pursuing helpless baitfish through the cresting waves of the rips. Along tide-washed stretches of sandy bottom, such as Dogfish Bar, fluke can be counted on through the summer, and rocky patches and wrecks attract tautog and scup.

Fishing on Nantucket is also fantastic. The waters off Great Point and Smith Point yield blues and bass for both surf- and boat-fishermen, and many fish are taken by plugging or casting flies along the edges of Tuckernuck and Muskeget islands. Fluking is good along the North Shore of Nantucket, and Tom Nevers Rip yields action with everything from bass to bonito.

South of Nantucket lie the undulating, wildly shifting, and very fishy Nantucket Shoals, home to pollock and big codfish throughout the year. In the heat of summer, big stripers can also be caught in these deeper waters, feeding on the abundant shoals of sand eels. Many experts deep-drift live eels for them, or troll with wire line and parachute jigs. For the more experienced boater, or those fishing aboard large charter and party boats, there are the extreme deep-water wrecks of Great South Channel and Georges Bank, where huge "whale cod," along with big hake and pollock, reside throughout the summer.

During the summer months, the 20-fathom line south and west of the islands is where you can find yellowfin tuna, school bluefins, bonito, little tunny, and bluefish during the summer months. White marlin fishing can be excellent at times, especially in places like the Fingers, the Star, the Claw, and the Dump. These same spots are also good for tuna and sharks. Action really picks up when an offshore eddy from the Gulf Stream swings inshore, concentrating baitfish and predators near its edges. Mako, blue, and dusky sharks also provide great summer sport, especially over wrecks and humps on the bottom. Swordfish used to be quite common in these waters during the summer, where they were harpooned on calm days, but overfishing has eliminated this fishery. If you venture far out to the canyons

(Hydrographers, Veatches, or Atlantis) and the Gulf Stream in summer, you can troll or chunk for bluefin, yellowfin, and bigeye tuna. You may even score with tropical gamesters like blue marlin, wahoo, and dolphin (mahimahi).

MARTHA'S VINEYARD TO BEAVERTAIL POINT

LAND CONFIGURATION AND WATER DEPTH

In 1602 Bartholomew Gosnold, sailing in his small ship the *Concord*, came upon a southern New England island which he called Martha's Vineyard. It is believed he named it in honor of his infant daughter and because of the abundance of wild grapes. Martha's Vineyard, locally called "the Vineyard," is a large island which lies about 4 miles south of Cape Cod. It is roughly triangular, being about 8 miles in a north-south direction and 15 miles east-west. The shore is generally hilly and rugged from Vineyard Haven westward, thence southward to Chilmark. Sea cliffs along this section often rise 50 to 100 feet from the sea; one at Gay Head rises nearly 150 feet. The shore eastward of Chilmark thence northward back to Vineyard Haven is, for the most part, composed of low sand dunes. Behind the dunes lies a series of ponds, most of them landlocked but some open to the sea. The highest point on the Vineyard, Prospect Hill, with an elevation of 308 feet, is located just northeast of Menemsha.

One of the interesting geological features of Martha's Vineyard is the 10 miles of smooth, straight beach from Chilmark to Chappaquiddick Island. Many thousands of years ago the coastline along this section was very irregular. At that time the level of the sea was lower than it is now. As the level slowly rose, waves began to erode the cliffs of Nashaquitsa, Waquobsque, and Squibnocket. The eroded sand and other unconsolidated materials were carried eastward along the coast by ocean currents. South Beach, as it is now called, probably originated as an offshore barrier beach which was forced back by wave action until it reached land. In the course of this process, arms of the sea were closed off and became the brackish ponds that we know today. The erosion and transportation of sand go on all the time, so that any opening artificially cut through the beach is usually closed in a few weeks.

Historically, the Vineyard proved to be suitable for farming thanks to its large tracts of fertile soil, which Nantucket lacks. And, although it developed only a small whaling industry of its own, it nevertheless made considerable profit from Nantucket because it provided a base where vessels were fitted and refitted for whaling and commerce. Also, many of the men living on the Vineyard joined the crews of whalers. The Indians, especially those from Chilmark and Gay Head, played an important part in whaling, for they were exceptionally skilled harpooners.

Five miles to the south of Gay Head lies the small, hilly, uninhabited island of Nomans Land. Years ago commercial fishermen lived there, but today it is used as a Navy firing range from November to May. Nomans shore, for the most part, is a series of clay and gravel cliffs 20 to 70 feet high with boulders at the water's edge. The highest point, 110 feet, is near the center of the island.

Vineyard Sound, north of Martha's Vineyard, is a narrow body of water about 4 miles wide by 25 miles long. The bottom is hard, composed mostly of sand and gravel. It is kept clear of silt and mud by the action of 1- to 3-knot currents. Most of the shoals of Vineyard Sound, notably Squash Meadow, Hedge Fence, L'Hommedieu Shoal, and Middle Ground, carry shallow depths of about 5 feet and are composed of hard sand and gravel. Lucas Shoal, however, carries about 10 feet in its shallowest portion and is rocky. During the mid-1800's, these shoals and the surrounding bottom constituted one of the most extensive black sea bass grounds along the New England coast. Now only an occasional sea bass is caught here.

The Elizabeth Islands are made up of a group of 16 small islands, most of which are hilly and partly wooded, the rest covered by grasses and shrubs. Although the highest point is about 175 feet, only a few islands rise over 150 feet above the sea. Cuttyhunk, the southernmost island, is the site of the first attempted English settlement in New England, that of Bartholomew Gosnold in 1602.

The narrow passages between these islands through which boats sail are called Holes. Woods Hole is the major passage from Vineyard Sound to Buzzards Bay. It is also the name of the nearby village, where in some vacant buildings owned by the Lighthouse Board, a predecessor of today's Coast Guard, the first marine fisheries laboratory was established in 1871. The laboratory was equipped with a small yacht on loan from the custom-house at New Bedford and a steam-launch belonging to the navy yard at Boston, collection apparatus borrowed from the Smithsonian Institution, and condemned navy powder-tanks to hold preserved specimens. These buildings and the wharf connected with the buoy station served as temporary quarters until the Fisheries Biological Laboratory and Hatchery were completed in 1883 at the present site of the United States Fishery Laboratory. A block away is the Marine Biological Laboratory, a nonprofit educational institution, which was established in 1888. Diagonally across the street from the Marine Biological Laboratory is the Woods Hole Oceanographic Institution, a privately endowed corporation set up in 1930 to study ocean phenomena.

To the west of Woods Hole is a 200-square-mile body of water known as Buzzards Bay. The shore is irregular, rocky, and indented by bays and rivers. Large rocks and boulders are common and in places extend a considerable distance from shore. The average depth in the lower half of this bay is about 50 feet; the greatest depth of 126 feet is located 2 miles northwest of Cuttyhunk. The bottom of this bay is mostly mud, broken in many places by rocky reefs and boulders.

The shore of southern Massachusetts and Rhode Island is composed of rocky headlands alternating with sandy beaches. Gooseberry Neck, a prominent headland, extends a mile from the mainland, and the rocky shoals of Hen and Chickens and Old Cock extend a mile and a half beyond this. To the west of this headland lie the sandy areas of Horseneck and Goose Wing beaches. Sakonnet Point, and its islets and shoal water which terminate in Schuyler Ledge, is the first major headland in Rhode Island when approaching from the east.

Rhode Island Sound is a basin of water about 30 miles long by 20 miles wide. Its eastern edge is formed by Vineyard Sound, its northern edge by Buzzards Bay and Narragansett Bay, its western edge by Block Island Sound, and its southern edge by a submarine plateau called Cox (also spelled Cox's) Ledge. The deepest part of the basin is 200 feet and is located in the "Mud Hole." The Mud Hole is actually a submarine channel which passes between the East Ground and Cox Ledge. Offshore of Cox Ledge the depth drops from 120 feet to 150 feet in a distance of about a mile. Farther offshore the bottom slopes even more gradually—from 100 feet to 180 feet in 10 miles.

FISH AND FISHING: MARTHA'S VINEYARD TO BEAVERTAIL POINT

Inshore rocks, wrecks, ledges and broken ground draw big tautog (blackfish) in spring along the shores of southeastern Massachusetts and Rhode Island. In fact, many claim this area to be one of the best blackfish grounds on the East Coast. Browns Ledge off the mouth of Buzzards Bay is where you'll find cod and pollock in March and April and tautog in April and May. And they arrive in that order in the late fall. Southwest Ledge is another popular and productive spot for cod in the spring and fall.

Narragansett Bay also offers excellent sport with tautog in March, April, and May when they move inshore to spawn, and again in late fall. The rocks, ledges, and islands off Sakonnet Point and Newport hold tautog in the early spring, although these waters are more legendary for producing big bass.

Blackback or winter flounder become active in muddy bays, marshes, and estuaries along the coast as the water temperatures climb above 40 degrees in March and April. Good action can last until June, when these fish migrate into deeper waters for the summer.

As in Buzzards Bay, every ledge and rip invites exploration, and will likely hold bass and blues of substantial size, even though you may have to fish deep for them at times. Likewise, every boulder, island, point, and creek mouth may have stripers lurking near it from spring through fall. Bluefish usually make their appearance beginning in late May, and roam the inshore waters in large schools through July before moving offshore to spawn. They return in late summer, joined by bonito and little tunny, to feed voraciously before their return trip south. Most years they leave the area by mid-October.

The Sakonnet River is a magnificent striper haunt, and the rocks and islands at its mouth and along "the Boulder Field" on its east bank to Sakonnet Point are particularly famous. The West Rock of Sakonnet Point was once the site of one of the first bass clubs in the country, and in recent years stripers have returned to the wave-pounded rocks and turbulent "holes" surrounding the point. In late summer and fall, schools of menhaden, herring, and other baitfish move into the Sakonnet, where they are fed upon by bonito, blues, and stripers. Moving west, Sachuest Point, Brenton Reef, Cormorant Rock, Cherry Point and the rocky cliffs below the Newport mansions are prime bassing grounds all summer long, and from late summer through the fall host superb action with blues and bonito.

Narragansett Bay also offers prime striper fishing throughout its length, even up around Providence. Menhaden (pogies) schools often push far into the Bay during the summer, pursued by big stripers. Schoolies flood into the Bay by early May, swarming into rivers, creeks, and estuaries. The brackish areas of these systems also provide action with big white perch in March and April. Look for stripers to make their way up the Taunton River in April, providing excellent early-season action in Mt. Hope Bay and the bridges near Fall River. In summer, warm water drives the bass deep during the day, where they hold near structure and drop-offs. Nighttime is when the fish emerge to patrol the shallow tidal flats and rivers.

The Jamestown Bridge is a prime spot for big bass, and many keepers are taken from the swift currents that flow around the abutments. Drifting with bait or chucking bucktail jigs to the pilings can be productive, particularly at night. The strong currents of the West and East passages leading into the Bay provide great action around points, rocks, ledges, wrecks, or any patch of uneven bottom that blocks the flow and provides a sanctuary for gamefish. Two well-known hot spots for bass and blues in the East Passage are the Dumplings and Castle Hill.

48

Summer flounder, or fluke, are another option

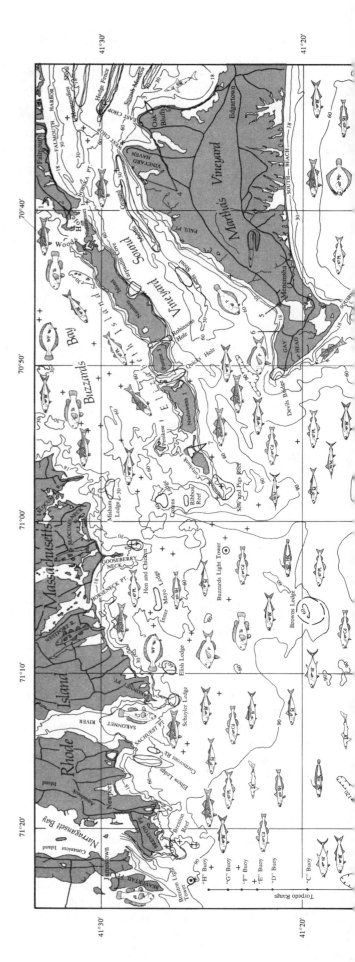

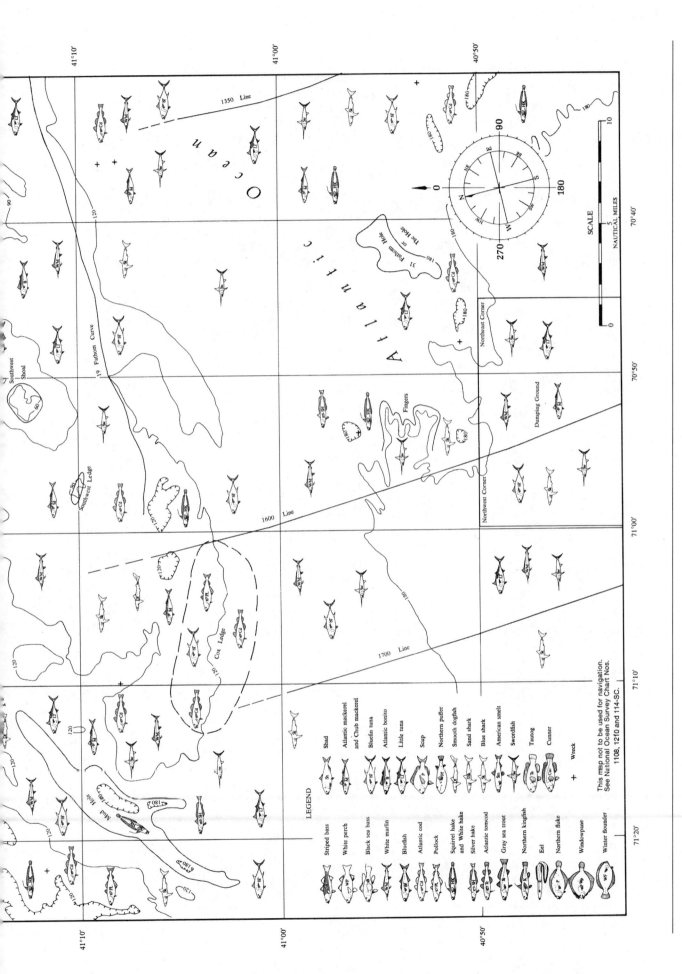

LEGEND

Striped bass	Shad	
White perch	Atlantic mackerel and Chub mackerel	
Black sea bass	Bluefin tuna	
White marlin	Atlantic bonito	
Bluefish	Little tuna	
Atlantic cod	Scup	
Pollock	Northern puffer	
Squirrel hake and White hake	Smooth dogfish	
Silver hake	Sand shark	
Atlantic tomcod	Blue shark	
Gray sea trout	American smelt	
Northern kingfish	Swordfish	
Eel	Tautog	
Northern fluke	Cunner	
Windowpane	+ Wreck	
Winter flounder		

This map not to be used for navigation.
See National Ocean Survey Chart Nos.
1108, 1210 and 114-SC.

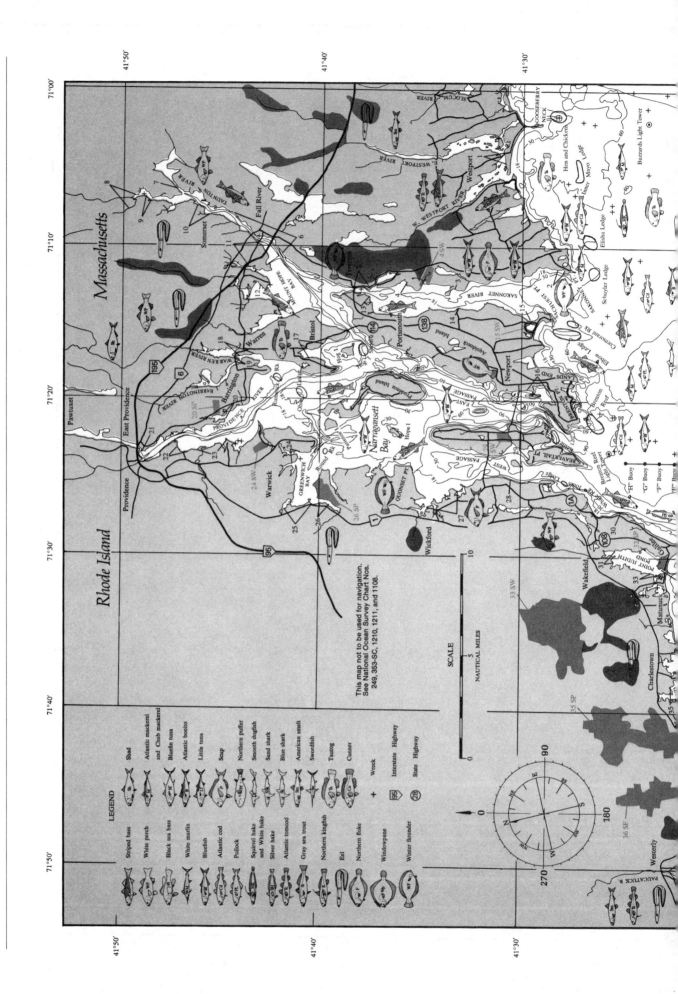

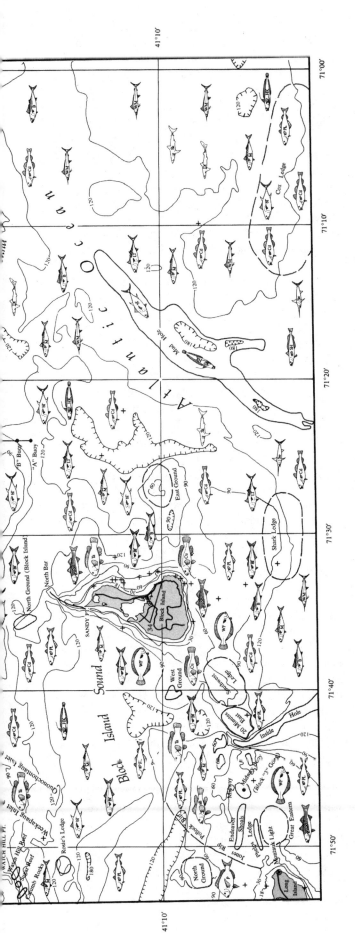

during the warm months. You'll find them on the bottom of sandy shoals and near inlet mouths, and fishing can be great even on bright summer days. Many anglers score well on trolled spinner-and-bait rigs or while drifting pieces of clams or seaworms on spreader bars.

Closer to Point Judith, the Narrow River is an extensive estuary system offering secluded small-boat fishing for white perch and winter flounder in early spring, and striped bass through the summer and fall. It even sees a big run of hefty shad in October.

Moving offshore, cod can be taken over rocky sections of Cox's Ledge, even during summer, although numbers are not what they used to be. The best times for inshore cod are early spring and late fall and winter—if the weather allows a trip. The legendary Mud Hole east of Block Island usually sees a run of giant bluefin tuna every summer, but numbers of these fish are also down, and those fish that do show don't seem to hold in the Hole for long. The Mud Hole is also a prime spot for summer sharking, and many fishermen discover the presence of the giants while fishing for blue sharks in July. These sharks are thick in Rhode Island waters beginning in late June or July and have offered such dependable action in recent years that many have taken to catching them on light gear and fly tackle. The 20-fathom line that skirts the Mud Hole also draws sharks, along with schools of smaller bluefins, bluefish, bonito, and little tunny that come to feed on the plentiful supply of mackerel, whiting, and other baitfish that thrive in these rich, plankton-filled waters.

Beginning in late June and early July, fishermen eye the 20- and 30-fathom lines for migrating schools of school bluefin and yellowfin tuna. These fish then take up residence through the summer and early fall. When they first arrive, the schools can be frustratingly hard to catch, although trolling with squid and mackerel spreader bars seems to work best. Later, when the fish settle down and begin feeding more actively, chunking becomes the preferred method.

GOOSEBERRY NECK TO WATCH HILL POINT

Narragansett Bay is an ancient river valley into which the sea now flows. Extending inland for 20 miles, it contains about one-quarter of the total area of Rhode Island. While exploring the Atlantic coast of the New World in 1524, Giovanni da Verrazzano came upon this bay and remained here for a few weeks. He was delighted by what he described as a "very beautiful port" surrounded by "charming hills with many brooks, which from the height to the sea discharged clear water."

Scattered throughout Narragansett Bay are nearly 20

islands which range in size from a few acres to many thousands of acres. Aquidneck Island, now called Rhode Island, is not only the largest and most important but is also the one from which the name of the state is derived. The surrounding land is characterized by rounded hills, most of them less than 200 feet high. The irregularly shaped shoreline is mostly rocky with boulders and rock ledges extending from shore in many places.

From Point Judith to Watch Hill the shore is low and sandy. Behind the sandy beaches is a series of brackish and saltwater ponds, most of which connect with the sea through narrow inlets called breachways. A short distance offshore of the beaches are scattered boulders, most of which are submerged. Those of Nebraska Shoal, Old Reef, and Watch Hill Reef are excellent fishing spots.

Block Island, an old fishing village that has evolved into a summer resort, lies 8 miles to the south of mainland Rhode Island. To the Indians it was Manisses, which was their tribal name. Verrazzano, as he sailed by it, named it Luisa in honor of his king's mother (later this name was mistakenly changed to Claudia). The first European known to land there was Adrian Block for whom it was named on Dutch sailing maps of the 1600's as Adrian's Eyeland. Eventually it became Block Island.

FISH AND FISHING: GOOSEBERRY NECK TO WATCH HILL POINT

We start at Point Judith, a large commercial fishing port, but one that also serves as an outstanding jumping-off point for recreational fishermen. Action isn't far away, either. In fact, great fishing is available right off the launch ramp in Pt. Judith Pond. Big blackback flounder are caught here in March and April, while striped bass arrive in early to mid April, providing exciting fishing all through the summer, especially at night. This is mostly light-tackle sport with schoolies, but keeper-sized fish visit the ponds, too.

Moving out of the pond, the breachway at Galilee—where currents flow swiftly to and from the open ocean—is a gathering place for big bass and blues that wait for baitfish, shrimp, worms, and eels to be swept out of the pond on an outgoing tide. Then there's the Harbor of Refuge, a huge man-made breakwater of boulders that shelters bait and crustaceans. Tautog lurk around these rocks in early spring and late fall, and fat fluke can be caught during the summer by soaking baits outside the walls of the Refuge. Fluking is great all summer along Rhode Island's extensive beaches. Many score by drifting or slow-trolling with live baits rigged behind spinner blades.

Block Island looms above the Sound to the south. Like Martha's Vineyard and Nantucket, this island is a fisherman's paradise. Striped bass arrive in April, providing action all along the island's rocky shores. In June, the

large bass take up station in the deep water of the famous North Rip, where they fall for eels drifted at night over the lumpy bottom. Boulder fields and rocky outcroppings hold bass tight against the shore, and the numerous nearby rips are where you can find bass, blues, bonito and little tunny all feeding at once, often near the surface.

In the deep water of the Sound itself, big schools of mackerel sweep through in early spring. You'll also find roving bands of blues and other warm-water migrants through the summer. Bluefin tuna may also pass through the Sound on occasion. In fact, giants once stopped to feed on Nebraska Shoal in the 1960's; however, those days of nearshore bluefins are long gone. Nowadays, Nebraska is more reliable for summer flounder, blues and bass.

On the rocky East Grounds east of Block Island, and the West Grounds to the west, you'll find an assortment of bottom fish, everything from cod to tautog. South of Block Island, tuna, bonito, sharks, false albacore, mackerel, and bluefish cruise the 20-fathom line through summer and early fall. Starting in early July, bluefin and yellowfin tuna also show in 20 to 30 fathoms of water. Trolling and chunking around contour lines and bottom structure works through the summer and early fall.

Cod can be caught on various wrecks in 60 to 100 feet of water from March to May, and again in the fall when cool weather brings the fish closer to shore. Cox's Ledge is another prime early-season cod spot, and the rocky bottom will hold fish throughout the summer if you can locate cold pockets of water. For those who seek truly big cod and pollock, party and charter boats out of Pt. Judith make long-range trips to deep wrecks on Georges Bank and Nantucket Shoals.

During calm weather, summer canyon trips to the edge of the continental shelf are another exciting option. These overnight excursions often yield action with such species as bigeye, albacore, bluefin, yellowfin, wahoo, sharks, and even blue marlin on occasion.

Westward from Pt. Judith all the way to Watch Hill is mostly sandy beach broken by pond inlets and small rocky outcroppings. Patches of hard bottom and wrecks hold big tautog and scup in the early spring and again in the fall, but the fish move to deeper water during the warmer months. In April, mackerel pass along the beaches, followed by schoolie bass that usually arrive by mid-month. Schoolie action can be sensational around the breachways and jetties, while mid-May sees the arrival of the larger bass and bluefish. Through the summer, bonito and little tunny can pop up at any time, and fluke can be caught in pockets and contour lines along the sandy bottom.

Four inlets, or breachways, lead to sheltered ponds behind the beach and break up Rhode Island's sandy shore. Like Pt. Judith Pond, these protected waters serve as home to eels, crustaceans, seaworms, baitfish, and juvenile gamefish, providing an ample source of food for bass, blues, and flounder throughout the season. Winter flounder are active in the ponds in late March, April, and May. In and around the narrow breachways leading to and from the ponds, bass and bluefish wait to intercept bait on the ebb tide. You'll find fluke holding on the bottom just outside the inlets for the same reason.

Summer night fishing around the breachways can be productive, especially for striped bass. Daytime fishing during the dog days—when bluefish move offshore and the bass lie low in deeper water—usually involves trolling wire line over stretches of uneven bottom off the beaches or working jigs, eels, and tubes just outside the breachways. Drifting with bottom baits over the same areas can also produce good catches of fluke and scup in summer.

Beginning in late August and running through November, the Rhode Island beaches offer some of the wildest fishing in the Northeast. Huge schools of herring, mackerel, menhaden, squid, silversides, and sand eels attract ravenous schools of bonito, false albacore, bluefish, and stripers preparing for their southward migration. Anglers watch for diving birds, then speed over to cast flies and plugs to the breaking fish. Any day that a south or southwest blow traps bait against the beach can produce nonstop action. By October, summer visitors such as bonito and little tunny have largely left the beaches to the big blues and bass, which often linger right through November. The chilly air of late fall often means action with keeper bass and blues to 20 pounds—the last hurrah before the long winter.

Finally, at the border of Rhode Island and Connecticut, you'll find another fantastic fishy spot: Watch Hill. The rips and rocks off this area produce some of the best striped bass fishing anywhere, and numerous keepers are pulled from here every season. In May, squid arrive in force, only to get caught in the rips and become easy targets for big bass. At this time, surface plugs, poppers and flies can produce outstanding topwater action with big fish. During slower periods, and especially on bright summer days, trolling parachute jigs and umbrella rigs through the rips can pay off.

In summer and early fall, the Watch Hill rips are a superb place to catch little tunny and bonito, as the fish gather to prey on hapless baitfish swept along by the fierce currents. And, of course, bluefish are always a possibility in the late spring and through the fall.

LONG ISLAND SOUND

LAND CONFIGURATION AND WATER DEPTH

Long Island Sound is a semienclosed body of water 90 miles long by 10 miles wide separating Connecticut from Long Island, New York. Its average depth is about 60 feet, its greatest depth 330 feet. Of the two narrow passages into the Sound, the eastern one is the wider and deeper. Excluding the shoal area of Valiant Rock, the depth in the 4 miles between Race Point and Little Gull Island ranges between 50 and 250 feet. Tidal currents flowing through the Race are extremely fast, often reaching velocities of 4 knots. At the opposite end of the sound the western passage is only about half a mile wide and varies in depth from 50 to 100 feet. Here the water from New York Bay flows into the Sound through the East River, which is not a river at all but a channel. At Hell Gate, a constricted area in the East River, the water often flows at 5 knots.

At its eastern end, Long Island divides into two peninsulas, the northern one terminating at Orient Point and the southern one at Montauk Point. Between these peninsulas lies a series of bays and small sounds separated from each other by either islands or land points. The bottom composition along the shores varies considerably from sand and mud to gravel and boulders, depending on the degree of shelter from wave action.

FISH AND FISHING

Although resident species such as tautog, winter flounder, and cunner are common throughout the year, seasonal migrants tend to dominate the fish population—temperate-water species such as bluefish, striped bass, scup, fluke, and weakfish during the warm months and cold-water species such as cod and pollock during the cold months. The young of many warm-water or subtropical species are occasional summer visitors, depending on transport by the Gulf Stream.

Tautog, more often called blackfish, do not migrate extensively. They spend the winter in depths of 90 feet or more, usually in an inactive state. During very cold periods they gather in rocky crevices and holes and become dormant. As the water warms during the spring, they move toward shore into relatively shallow

BURNETT'S MARINA

A Family Oriented Sport Fisherman's Haven

Floating Docks
10, 12, & 15 ft. Wide Slips
Shower
Bait / Tackle / Ice

Come Join Some of the South Shore's Best Fishermen

16 Bayview Ave
Bayshore, NY 11706
(516) 665-9050

This map not to be used for navigation. See National Ocean Survey Chart Nos. 116-SC, 117-SC, 1211, 1212 and 1213.

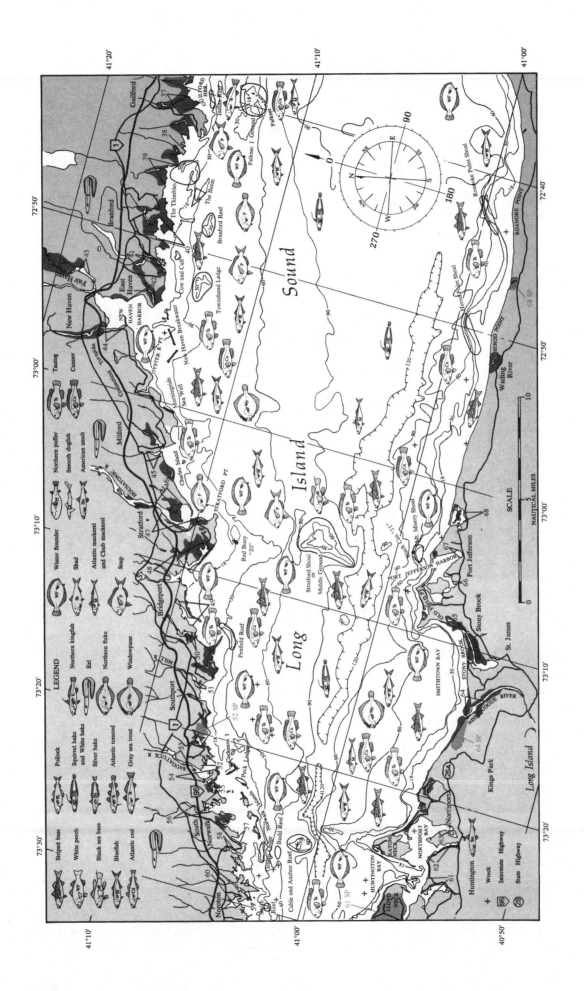

FISH IN COMFORT & SAFETY
STATE OF THE ART ELECTRONICS

LADY GRACE IV

NEW 33 FT. DOWNEASTER 1-6 PASS.

ALL INSHORE & OFFSHORE FISHING
HALF & FULL DAYS-EVES
CHOICE DATES AVAILABLE
FISHING LONG ISLAND WATERS

CAPT. MARIO (516) 842-0237

water where they feed actively throughout the summer. As the water cools during the fall, they move into deep water and become less active as the winter advances. Cunner, also called bergall, are closely related to tautog and follow the same general activity pattern. Although plentiful, because cunner are relatively small fish, rarely reaching over 14 inches long, they are not popular with anglers. Unfortunately, the effectiveness of cunner as bait stealers precludes live-bait-fishing for striped bass until night, when cunner do not feed.

Winter flounder, called blackback in the eastern end of the Sound and flounder in the western end, are one of the most abundant resident species. Their activity pattern differs from that of tautog. During the fall, when tautog move into deep water, flounder move into sheltered bays and estuaries to overwinter and spawn. The peak of spawning takes place from January to March, when they cease feeding. As the water warms in late spring, adults move back into deeper water to feed.

As warm-water migrants arrive during the spring, the species composition of the Sound changes dramatically. Bluefish ranging in size from young stages to adults over 36 inches migrate from as far as Florida. Long Island Sound, especially at the eastern end, seems to be one of the few areas along the East Coast where exceptionally large bluefish occur within casting distance of shore. Striped bass come here from areas as near as the Hudson River and as far away as North Carolina. Scup, fluke, and black sea bass migrate here from their wintering grounds located along the outer edge of the continental shelf between New Jersey and North Carolina. Weakfish and kingfish migrate here from their wintering grounds off Virginia and the Carolinas. During the summers of the 1920's, 1930's, and most of the 1940's, weakfish were abundant throughout this area. Beginning in the late 1940's, they decreased greatly, reaching a low in the mid-1960's. However, there was some evidence that in the late 1960's and early 1970's, the situation was improving, and numbers

did increase in the late 1970's and early 1980's. Recently, however, the weakfish population has once again declined.

Cod and pollock, both cold-water migrants, arrive during the fall and remain throughout the winter. Most of them stay in the eastern end of the Sound near the ocean water inflow. Cod are the first to leave as the water warms, usually in March and April. Pollock remain until about June, then they move offshore into deeper and cooler water. Unlike cod, pollock do not migrate extensively. Instead they seem to remain within the same general area throughout their life.

LONG ISLAND SOUND FISHING TIPS

Blackfish (tautog)
Rocks, pilings, hard bottom jetties, etc.
Late March–early December. Inshore peak: April–June and Sept.–Nov.
Bottom-fishing from shore or anchored boat.
Clams, crabs, worms, mussels, and shrimp.

Black sea bass
Rocks, jetties, pilings, breakwaters, etc.
Mid April–Nov. Peak season: June–August.
Bottom-fishing, drifting, or anchored boat.
Squid, clams, worms, shrimp, cut fish.

Striped bass
Rivers, estuaries, bays, and ocean.
Year round. Peak season: May–June and Sept.–Nov.
Live-lining, casting, jigging, drifting, and trolling.
Eels, menhaden, cut squid and worms. All types of popping, swimming, and diving lures.

Bluefish
Rivers, estuaries, bays, and ocean. Occurs from bottom to surface. Late May–early Nov. Peak season: July–Oct.
Trolling, jigging, drifting, casting, and chumming.
Menhaden, cut fish, eels. All types of jigs, spoons, feathers, tube lures, and plugs.

Snapper bluefish
Inshore, rivers, and estuaries.
Late July–Oct. Peak season: Aug.–Sept.
Casting.
Minnows and small metal spoons.

Weakfish
Ocean, bays, Long Island Sound, estuaries. Favors sandy bottom. May–Oct. Peak Season: Late May–July.
Casting, live-lining, trolling, and jigging.
Worms, shrimp, squid, cutfish. All types of feathers, jigs, bucktails, tubes, spoons, and plugs.

Bonito

Ocean, eastern Long Island Sound.
July–Oct. Peak season: Aug.–Sept.
Trolling, casting, fly casting, and jigging from boat.
Cut fish. All types of feathers, and spoons.

Mackerel

Ocean, Long Island Sound, bays and estuaries.
April–June and Oct.–Nov. Peak Season: May.
Trolling, casting, and jigging.
Cut fish. All types of spoons, spinners, and tube lures.

Fluke (summer flounder)

Left-sided, sharp teeth.
Sand or gravel bottom.
June–Oct. Peak season: July–Sept.
Bottom-fishing, jigging, drifting, and casting.
Squid, snapper bluefish, smelt, cut fish strips, bucktails, and jigs.

Winter flounder

Right-sided, thick lips.
Mud, sand, or gravel bottom.
Year round. Peak season: Mar.–May and Oct.–Dec.
Bottom-fishing, chumming.
Worms, clams, mussels, and squid.

Scup (porgy)

Rocky reefs, pilings, sand, and hard gravel bottoms.
May–Nov. Peak season: July–Sept.
Bottom-fishing.
Worms, shrimp, squid, and clams.

Tomcod

Inshore, rivers, estuaries.
Nov.–Mar.
Bottom-fishing.
Worms, clams, mussels, and cut fish.

Eel

Bays, rivers, estuaries. Active at night.
Apr.–Dec. Peak season: June–Oct.
Bottom-fishing and spearing.
Worms, cut fish.

FISHING REGULATIONS

What follows are abstracts of fishing regulations for Massachusetts, Rhode Island, Connecticut, and New York. This information should be used for general purposes only. Because regulations change frequently, and because the regulations themselves are far more detailed than presented here, all anglers should contact the state agencies listed at the beginning and end of this chapter.

MASSACHUSETTS

Saltwater licenses are not required for sportfishermen in Massachusetts. The sale of fish, however, may require a license from the Division of Marine Fisheries. To obtain an abstract of marine fishing laws or other information concerning the Massachusetts coastal fishery, contact the Division of Marine Fisheries.

Special Regulations: Minimum Size
Atlantic salmon: 15" total length. Fishery closed until further notice.
Cod: 19" total length.
Coho salmon: 15" total length. Mar. 1 to Aug. 31. Limit of two fish per day. No snagging allowed. No size restriction: Sept. 1 to Feb. 28.
Flounders: American dab, 14" total length; Grey sole: 14" total length; Summer flounder, 14" total length; Windowpane, 12" total length; Winter flounder, 12" total length; Yellowtail, 12" total length.
Haddock: 19" total length.
Marlin: Blue, 86" total length; White, 62" total length.
Pollock: no size restriction.
Red drum: 4" total length.
Redfish: 9" total length.
Sailfish: 57" total length.
Scup: 9" total length.
Sea Bass: 12" total length.
Shad: No size restriction. May be taken by hook and line only. No snagging allowed.
Smelt: No size restriction. May be taken by angling only. Closed season March 15 to June 15, inclusive.
Striped Bass: 34" total length. May be taken by hook and line only. Daily limit 1. Possession limit 1.
Sturgeon (Atlantic): 72" total length.
Tautog: 12" total length.

RHODE ISLAND

No license is necessary for saltwater fishing in Rhode Island. However, if an angler wishes to sell his catch, a $25 sportfishing license is necessary and can be obtained from the Rhode Island Department of Environmental Management, Division of Boat Registration and Licenses.

Fishing regulations prohibit the taking of striped bass less than 38" in total minimum length. Out-of-state residents are forbidden to take lobster and also must have a license to shellfish in Rhode Island waters. Quahogs less than 1" width (thickness) may not be kept.

National Marine Fisheries Service regulations forbid taking any tuna under 14 lbs. Between 15 and 115 lbs., four fish per person per day may be taken; 115 to 310 lbs., four fish per boat per day are allowed. Taking giant tuna over 310 lbs. requires a federal license from NMFS. For information, call (617) 281-3600. Vehicles driven on Rhode Island beaches must have a special beach vehicle permit from RIDEM. Driver and vehicle must appear at the Division of Boat Registration and Licenses, 22 Hayes St., Providence.

Minimum Sizes and Possession Limits of Fish

American Plaice (Dab): 14"
Bluefish: 10 per day—no size limit
Blue Marlin[*]: 110" or 200 lbs.
Cod: 19"
Fluke (Summer Flounder): 14"
Haddock: 19"
Pollock: 19"
Sailfish[*]: 76" or 30 lbs.
Striped Bass: 1 per day[**] 38" (no sale)
Tautog (Blackfish): 12"
Weakfish (Squeteague)[**]: 12"
White Flounder (Blackback)[**]: 12"
(Call for current regulations on winter flounder)
White Marlin[*]: 81" or 50 lbs.
Witch Flounder (Gray Sole): 14"
Yellowtail Flounder: 13"

[*] Federal regulations set minimum sizes for billfish.
[**] Regulations may change. Call Division of Enforcement, 277-2284 or Division of Fish & Wildlife, (401) 789-3094.

The Rhode Island Department of Health has issued advisories on the consumption of bluefish and striped bass. Call (401) 277-2833 for more information.

CONNECTICUT

In the marine district, no license is required to fish for finfish recreationally or for personal consumption. However, to sell even one fish, a Commercial Finfish License is required.

Minimum Lengths of Marine Finfish (Total Length)

Fish less than these lengths may not be possessed, regardless of where taken. Any fish less than the minimum length shall, without avoidable injury, be returned immediately to the water from which it was taken.

Scup (porgy): 8 inches
Winter flounder: 10 inches
Tautog (blackfish): 12 inches
Fluke (summer flounder) 14 inches
Yellowtail flounder: 13 inches
Atlantic cod: 19 inches
Haddock: 19 inches
Pollock: 19 inches
Striped bass: 36 inches

Selected Species Restrictions

Atlantic sturgeon

May be taken only from the waters of Long Island Sound. There is a possession limit of three fish per trip or per day, whichever is the longer period of time, and the limit applies to the aggregate of all persons on board the vessel. There is a length limit of 84 inches total length.

Shortnose sturgeon

May not be taken.

Winter flounder

From December 1 through March 31, both dates inclusive, winter flounder shall not be taken by any means from the waters of the Niantic River upstream from the Route 156 bridge in Waterford-East Lyme.

Striped bass

Minimum length of 36 inches, measured from the tip of the snout to the tip of the tail. One fish per angler. Angling gear only; gaffs prohibited. Any striped bass taken contrary to these provisions must immediately, and without avoidable injury, be returned to the waters from which it was taken. The sale of striped bass taken from Connecticut waters is prohibited. Striped bass may not be landed with the head or tail removed. Artificially reared hybrid striped bass (one parent *Morone saxatilis*) less than the minimum length may be possessed and sold if they are properly tagged, if the retailer has documentation attesting to the point of origin in a hatchery or fish farm, and if the retail purchaser has an appropriate receipt.

Bluefish

The sportfishery creel limit for bluefish greater than 12" in total length is 10 fish per angler. Any number of fish less than or equal to 12" may be taken.

NEW YORK

No license is required in the Marine and Coastal District to take fish by angling. The lowest (furthest downstream) dam on any tidal river constitutes the line of demarcation between tidal water (no license required) and inland waters (fresh water license required).

Minimum Size Limits

Striped bass: In the waters of the Marine and Coastal District below the George Washington Bridge, from May 8 through December 15, *one* striped bass per day, of 36 inches in length or longer, may be taken and possessed but not sold. In the water of the Hudson River north of the George Washington Bridge and south of the Federal Dam at Troy, from March 16 through November 30, *one* striped bass per day, of 18 inches in length or longer, may be taken and possessed but not sold.

Fluke: 14" total length.

Atlantic cod: 19" total length.

Yellowtail flounder: 13" total length.

Winter flounder: 11" total length.

Blackfish: 12" total length.

Pollock: 19" total length.

Atlantic sturgeon: 60" total length.

Porgy: No restriction.

Mackerel: No restriction.

Black sea bass: No restriction.

Weakfish: Fish less than 16 inches may not be taken, possessed, transported, bought, sold, or offered for sale. Weakfish taken from Great South Bay or Moriches Bay in May shall not be sold or offered for sale. No person shall take more than 3 weakfish per day from Great South Bay or Moriches Bay during May.

Bluefish: Fish less than 9 inches may not be bought, sold, or offered for sale. There is a 10-fish-per-day possession limit for recreational fishermen.

Red drum: Fish less than 14 inches may not be taken, possessed, transported, bought, sold, or offered for sale. In addition, for recreational fishermen, there is a 2-fish-per-day possession limit for red drum greater than 32 inches.

Tuna: Tuna fishing is managed by the federal Department of Commerce's National Oceanic and Atmospheric Administration (NOAA). Currently three Atlantic tuna are subject to regulations—Atlantic bluefins, bigeyes, and yellowfins. Fishing in the regulated area is authorized for bigeye or yellowfin tuna that weigh seven pounds round weight or more. Bigeye or yellowfin tuna less than seven pounds caught incidentally during authorized fishing may be taken provided the catch does not exceed three percent by weight per trip of all bigeye or yellowfin weighing seven pounds or more. No permit is necessary to fish for these two species. There is no minimum size limit for Atlantic bluefin tuna (ABT), but there are possession and vessel limits which apply to the ABT recreational fishery. Anglers may catch and retain no more than four ABT (other than giant ABT) each day, only one of which may be a medium. No more than four medium ABT may be caught and retained per vessel for vessels having four or more anglers aboard.

Note: Fork length measurement is the sole criterion for determining the size class of ABT. Medium is from 57" to 77". Giant is 77" or more.

Note: It is illegal to remove the tail or fins of any bigeye, yellowfin, or bluefin tuna prior to landing. Each vessel fishing for giant ABT must have on board a valid permit issued by the National Marine Fisheries Service (NMFS). Applications for this permit and complete copies of current regulations may be obtained by request from the National Marine Fisheries Service, Atlantic Tuna Program, Northeast Region, One Blackburn Drive, Gloucester, MA 01930. Telephone (508) 281-9370. Bluefin Tuna regulations are expected to change. Please call NMFS for the latest information.

Note: There is a daily catch limit of one giant ABT per day per vessel. Adjustments to the allowable daily catch limit may be made to provide for maximum use of the quota. After the quota is reached, an angler may fish for ABT under a tag-and-release program. The angler must tag all ABT and release such fish to the sea with a minimum of injury. To participate in this program, an angler must obtain tags, reporting cards, and instruction for their use by writing to Cooperative Gamefish Tagging Program, Southeast Fisheries Center, NMFS, 75 Virginia Beach Drive, Miami, FL 33149-1099.

King of the River

by Barry Gibson

Nobody catches more striped bass in Massachusetts' Danvers River than Joe Karolides. Nobody.

"There he is. There he is. C'mon, c'mon. Ah! Got 'im!"

Joe Karolides pulls the shift lever into neutral and leans back into his fourth hook-up of this beautiful spring morning. A striped bass races to the drop-off and dives for the bottom of the channel, but it's no match for Joe's 20-pound spinning outfit. The fish circles defiantly, yet within seconds it's in the skiff, a wet towel over its head. Joe carefully removes the hook, inserts a bright yellow American Littoral Society

Mike Gibson displays a fine three-pound school striper taken on a seaworm-and-spinner rig in the Danvers River. The fish was one of 18 caught and released that day. (BARRY GIBSON)

spaghetti tag just behind the dorsal fin, and carefully releases the five-pounder. It's the 259th striper he's tagged so far for the year, and the season is just getting underway.

Four guys in a 22-footer bristling with rods and downriggers ease over in our direction. "What did you get him on," one calls over, "a plug?"

Joe responds by shrugging his shoulders and smiling cheerfully in their direction. The anglers scratch their heads and idle back out into mid-channel. "I drive 'em crazy!" he grins, clamping his teeth on his ever-present cigar.

And drive 'em crazy he does. Karolides, in his early 60s and a retired supervisor for New England Telephone, has become a legend in his own time among striped bass fishermen in the Danvers River system on Massachusetts' North Shore, simply because he catches and tags more bass—way more—than anyone else. A dedicated conservationist, he tags from 500 to 1,000 bass a year ranging from two to 40 or more pounds, and releases about the same number of smaller fish under 16 inches untagged. He catches the vast majority of them by quietly trolling in his customized 1971 16-foot aluminum skiff and 25-horse outboard.

Seaworms and Spinners

Contrary to what a lot of people think, however, Joe doesn't pull plugs like everyone else. He trolls a deadly seaworm-and-spinner combination, and he recently agreed to share his secret.

Joe's basic setup consists of a ⅜-ounce keel sinker and four feet of 30-pound mono attached to a three-blade "willow leaf" spinner he has custom made at Joe's Bait Shop in nearby Ipswich. It's rigged with tandem 4/0 hooks crimped together with 50-pound mono. The trick is in hooking the seaworms. "Pin a big one (six inches long or more) through the collar on the front hook," he advises, "so that

it drapes over the rear hook. Then place a smaller worm, the same way, on the back hook. The bass will hit the rear worm first, then go in for another bite. That's when you'll hook him."

The rig itself, though, isn't the only secret. Joe consistently hammers bass in water most striper buffs would consider too shallow, but that's where his seaworm-and-spinner rig really shines. "Most of my bass are taken in two- to 12-feet of water," he says, "but the real magic zone is six to eight feet. Bass move to the edges of the channel and out into the shallows to feed. I don't catch many in the deep water."

Walking the Drop-Off

Joe's strategy? He trolls his rigs about 60 feet back from the boat, at a slow pace that might best be described as a leisurely walk. He likes to work the drop-off, with one rod towing a bait along the edge and the other pulling a rig up on the flat, and he keeps one eye riveted on his LCD fishfinder. When he gets the telltale tap-tap hit he'll methodically swing his rod tip aft to let the bass grab that second mouthful of seaworm, the one with the hook in it. He misses only an occasional fish, but I blew a dozen strikes before I started to get the hang of it.

Stripers can be caught almost anywhere along the edges of this four-river system. The main river, the Danvers, is Coast Guard buoyed up to where it splits three ways into the Crane, Waters and Porter rivers. All four feature unmarked shallow areas, sand and mud bars and rock piles, but they are navigable and fishable from a small outboard boat like Joe's. Don't try this in your 30-foot cruiser.

We caught fish down near the Kernwood Bridge on the Danvers, and as far upriver as the Route 35 causeway on the Crane. We took fish in front of Liberty Marina at the mouth of the Waters, and in the quiet bay behind the Kernwood Golf Course.

Low Tide for Visibility

As for time and tide, Joe's emphatic. "I go weekdays or just early morning on weekends to avoid boat traffic," he says. "Bass can be caught on any stage of the tide, but I like dead low water since I can see all the edges, drop-offs and structure. There's always a few big fish hiding in certain spots." He doesn't say where, and clamps down on his cigar, eyes twinkling. Nobody knows these rivers like he does. Nobody.

Our morning's catch of 18 schoolie bass in the two- to six-pound range was only fair, according to Joe, who routinely tags and releases 30 or more fish per outing. Keeper bass are taken here, primarily in mid-June when the pogies (menhaden) arrive, but otherwise this is mostly a light-tackle catch-and-release fishery. There's also some

Fishing the Danvers River System

Small 14- to 18-foot shallow draft outboard boats are best for fishing this four-river system. Chart #13275 provides a general overview, but this is mostly a "local knowledge" area and boaters are advised to travel slowly and watch the water carefully, especially at low tide.

The handiest public launch ramp is Pope's Landing (take Exit 23S or 22E off Rte. 128) on Harbor Street in Danvers, on the Porter River. It's a double-wide, with plenty of parking. Fee is $5. Nearby bait and tackle stores include:

Joe's Bait Shop, 357 Topsfield Rd., Ipswich (508) 356-4970

ANA Bait & Tackle, 467 Maple St., Danvers (508) 774-2443

J&M Custom Tackle, 11 Water St, Beverly (508) 922-3480

fine topwater plugging (freshwater bass tackle is ideal) and these rivers are perfect for taking stripers on fly.

All in all it was a most enjoyable morning's fishing. The water was glassy calm, the June air was warm and still, and the sky was bright blue. Joe Karolides was the perfect fishing companion, upbeat and entertaining, and he knew exactly where the fish were and how to catch them. And like a true pro at any sport, he sure made it look easy! ■

Fly-Fishing Martha's Vineyard

by Nelson Sigelman

"Baloop!" The sound echoes in the still, dark night as a barely visible ring widens on the surface of the water where a sand eel just disappeared. You're standing on Lobsterville Beach on the north shore of the island. The silhouette of the Elizabeth Islands is just barely visible across the Sound and the wind is southwest, which puts it at your back and slightly to your left. In other words, it's perfect.

It is that spring southwest wind that brings the bait; first the herring, then the mackerel, squid and sand eels that mean bluefish and bass; later in the season it'll be false albacore and bonito, but the sound you just heard, like the last chug of water down a drain, means only one thing—*stripers!*

"Baloop!" There's that sound again. You've walked along the shore, ears and eyes straining, waiting for a sign of fish and now you've found it. A nine-weight floating line is coiled in your shooting basket. You make a 50-foot cast in front, tuck the reel under your

Bob Popovics with a school striper taken on one of his Candy flies. Popovics annually travels to Martha's Vineyard for its excellent fly-fishing opportunities for striped bass, bluefish, and false albacore.

(VIN T. SPARANO)

arm and start stripping the white Lefty's Deceiver in with short pulsing motions—a fishing Morse code sending an unmistakable message of delicious vulnerability.

"Kaploosh!" The impact of the watery explosion is immediate and unmistakable as the striped bass hits the fly. You're on! Welcome to Martha's Vineyard.

Lying just off the elbow of Cape Cod, bordered by Vineyard Sound, Nantucket Sound and the Atlantic Ocean, twenty miles long and nine miles at its widest, the island of Martha's Vineyard is best known as a summertime home for celebrities and as a tourist destination. However, the real attraction for an increasing number of saltwater fly fishermen is the opportunity to hook up with all of the Northeast's premiere gamefish on some of the prettiest beaches and water anywhere in the United States.

Bluefish, striped bass, bonito, false albacore and Spanish mackerel can all be caught in-season by fly rodders from beaches and jetties of the Vineyard. In addition, white marlin, yellowfin tuna, football-size bluefins and shark are all within boat range for anglers with lots of backing on their reels.

Of course, you don't have to venture offshore to watch your backing disappear from your reel. Just hook one of the 12- to 14-pound false albacore that show up in late summer and stay till the first autumn winds and you'll have plenty of opportunity to wish you had another fifty yards on your spool. But that's part of the challenge and excitement of fly-fishing on Martha's Vineyard.

From Cape Poge to Gay Head Light, the island's six towns, each with its distinctive character and varied topography, offer a variety of fishing conditions. There are the deep strong-flowing inlets of Cape Poge gut, Tashmoo and Menemsha; the white sand beaches of Chilmark and Gay Head that face the Atlantic surf; the boulder-strewn ledges of Squibnocket Point, where 19th-century anglers fished from the bass stands of their private clubs by hurling lobster on hand lines; the rocky bar stretching out beneath Cape Poge lighthouse where local angler Kib Bramhall once decided to take a nap, later waking up in time to catch a 42-pound, 13-ounce striper on his fly rod; and the rocky shore of Lobsterville Beach overlooking Vineyard Sound that boasts some of the Island's best all-around fly-fishing.

Winter leaves the island slowly as Vineyarders anxiously await the first signs of spring. For businesses that cater to tourists, that means the first sighting of 300-pound tourists in yellow spandex, eating double-scoop ice cream cones. But the Island's fly fishermen look forward to a much more appealing sight—herring. Once the herring arrive with a panicked expression on their little bullet faces that says, "Man, just let me spawn one more time because I've got some hungry stripers and blues right behind me," the first strike of the season is not far off.

Small schoolies, stripers in the six- to ten-pound range, start showing up off south-facing beaches as early as April. However, the really consistent action doesn't start until early May.

That's when substantial schools of bluefish and striped bass start to reach the Vineyard and a unique Island get-together takes place on the corner of Chappaquiddick Island at Wasque Point. This fabled fishing spot is famous for its tremendous rip and strong current that flows at up to four knots, often building large roiling waves up to five feet just off the beach. With a warm spring southwest wind and a falling westerly tide it is one of the first places fish show in any great numbers, particularly the spring run of bluefish.

When that happens, many familiar island faces, propelled by instinct and experience, show up on the beach. It is an annual spring rite on the Vineyard, born of tide, temperature, wind and winter's fading embrace, a sort of Wasque Point fishermen's block party where many of the fishermen know each other and catch up on the news as they wait for the guests of honor to arrive. Often, it is in the best Vineyard party tradition, late and hungry, that bluefish do finally show up, but when they do, the action is exciting and nonstop.

Slick after slick, the oily sheen on the water that betrays the presence of feeding blues, drifts along the shore as bluefish erupt from the water savagely attacking the surface poppers favored by the surfcasters. The experienced fly fishermen avoid the mayhem right at the point of the rip where shoulder-to-shoulder surfcasters participate in a Wasque minuet, stepping in front of each other as they walk their fish out of the strong current. Instead, fly casters walk up the beach, a hundred yards or so, putting the southwest wind at their back and the bluefish right in front of them.

Lean and hungry from their northerly migration, the spring blues weigh anywhere from four to fourteen pounds, but average about seven. Pound for pound, they fight as hard as most fish you'll hook on a flyrod and attack with a fury that goes beyond hunger—these fish are mean! And that is a good idea to remember when you go to remove your fly. We're not talking trout here. An orthopedic surgeon once told me of a patient who had lost a toe to a bluefish. While that's an interesting lure, you're apt to run out

of them rather quickly.

Typical tackle consists of a nine-weight rod, weight forward floating line, and a shock leader that can be either wire or a minimum of sixty-pound mono. I wouldn't bother casting out any artistic creation you labored over to recreate the facial expressions of a baitfish because once a blue gets a hold of it, it'll look like a T-bone you threw out to a junkyard dog. A white Lefty's Deceiver, a sand eel, or just a clump of white bucktail on a hook will draw a strike, but you may want to use something with epoxy that will hold up.

One piece of equipment you should not forget is a stripping basket. You can find the high-tech models in a catalog, or go for the dish-pan-and-elastic-cord look. Either way, you need to keep your fly line out of the wash where it will only entangle you. The basket also helps to gain extra casting distance and allows a smooth flow of line once you have hooked up.

After the initial excitement of spring blues, most island fly fishermen turn their attention to striped bass. The spring run may start in April but the best action is in June. That is when the bigger fish begin to prowl the waters just off the beach and within easy fly casting distance. The average fish is about fifteen pounds and from twenty-four to thirty-four inches, but larger fish up to forty pounds are not unusual.

A nine-weight rod is perfect, but an eight-weight is adequate. Just make sure you have a reel with two hundred yards of backing on it so you will be able to handle the freight train run of any big fish. In most cases, the main consideration in choosing a heavier rod, like a ten-weight, will be the wind, but you can always find a spot in the lee on Martha's Vineyard. That is not to say that a gale would stop any island fly fisherman if fish are around.

Leader systems are kept pretty simple. A weight forward floating or intermediate line with a leader made up of three feet of 30-pound, three feet of 20-pound and two feet of 15-pound will work just fine. Tie the fly directly to the fifteen-pound as stripers are rarely leader shy.

Flies that tend to imitate sand eels and silversides do well as these have been the most abundant natural bait during the past few years. The sparser they are the better. White or white and yellow in combination tend to be the most effective colors, but size seems to be the more important factor. Some nights, big Lefty's Deceivers will work like a charm (you can never go wrong for long on the Vineyard with a white Deceiver), and on other nights bass will turn away from everything, including live eels, to take small sand-eel imitations no longer than an inch-and-a-half on No. 2 hooks.

And stripers are *the fish* on the Vineyard. Discussed in secretive tones in the island's tackle shops and stalked along the beaches late at night by singular shadowy figures long after the casual plug popper has retreated to the evening's sitcoms, stripers preoccupy most Island fishermen. Sometimes, they take your fly with a delicacy that belies their strength and size, while other times, propelled by their broad-sweeping tail, their strike is a powerful burst of fin and scales.

The larger fish can make you doubt the amount of your backing, the quality of your knots and the force of your drag with their first surging run, and then suddenly, they'll turn and come straight back at you. When that happens, you can't reel in line fast enough and only the fly fisherman with the presence of mind to backpedal up the beach will keep a tight line and maybe the fish. Then, too, they'll rub against the rocks trying to remove the offending hook, or simply catch it just right to pry it open in their powerful jaws. There are many ways for a fly fisherman to lose a big striped bass on Martha's Vineyard, but few fish are more exciting to catch.

And, when you finally slide your first striper of the season up onto the beach, glistening beneath the stars and moon, you'll appreciate just why they have captured the imagination of generations of island fishermen.

Nelson Bryant, a longtime island resident and outdoor writer for *The New York Times*, recalls a time when, during World War II, he was sitting in the fields of Holland after jumping in with the 82nd Airborne. He had just received a letter from his father describing fishing for stripers up to five and six pounds. For a twenty-one-year-

old soldier far from home, fly fishing for stripers was something to look forward to when he returned home.

Another well-known Island fisherman, Kib Bramhall, an artist and former writer for *Saltwater Sportsman*, recalls that the first time he picked up a fly rod on the Vineyard was in the early 1960's. It was a large tarpon rod that he says was "absurdly heavy" and he didn't become interested again until the '70's. There were already a few fly fishermen on the Vineyard, including Nelson Bryant, Bruce Pratt, the former police chief of Edgartown, and a gentleman named Arthur Silva, who Kib calls, "one of the finest fly casters around." He relates, "Those two guys used to catch astounding numbers of bass, at least astounding to me, and at one point a shore-caught fly rod striper was leading in that year's Derby. But what astounded me is that Arthur Silva would go up to the beach in his street shoes and catch stripers on his fly rod without ever getting his feet wet, and therein lies a great lesson."

There are many more expert fly fishermen on the Vineyard these days, and in June many of them can be found at Lobsterville Beach on the Vineyard's north shore, one of the finest beaches in New England to fly fish for stripers. Some nights almost everyone is a fly caster and the only sounds are the gentle rustle of small stones washing up on the beach and the soft "whoosh, whoosh" of fly lines cutting through the night air—and, of course, the heart-stopping crash of striped bass up and down the beach slamming sand eels on the surface of the water.

On one of those nights when the bass seemed particularly fussy one fisherman turned to his companion in frustration and said, "If I'm still here in an hour would you put me in a straitjacket and take me home?" But those are the fun nights, the ones that challenge the fly fisherman and his selection of flies. And no island fisherman loves it more than when he finally solves the puzzle before his friends and can engage in the good-natured kidding that is so much a part of the Vineyard fly-fishing fraternity.

One of the best at the game is Cooper "Coop" Gilkes III. An expert Island fly fisherman, Coop owns a

tackle shop that is adorned with the signed dollar bills of fly fishermen who took his challenge of "first fish caught" or "most fish caught and released."

One June night as stripers swirled and broke sporadically along the beach he kept kidding his fishing buddy, who was doing his best to keep his line off the bottom, about hooking rocks. Coop's friend had brought along an eight-weight rod rigged with a floating line and sink tip, a poor choice for the rocky shallow bottom at Lobsterville at low tide. Coop had already collected a dollar bill for the evening and with every new fish he released, Coop would walk over and tap out his growing count of fish on his friend's shoulder with a hearty laugh.

Stripping in line the beleagured fisherman's fly suddenly stopped not more than ten feet in front of his rod tip on what he once again *assumed* was a rock.

"Damn," escaped his lips as Coop turned to him with a laugh and said to no one in particular, "Look at that, he thinks he's on a rock and he's got a bass." No sooner had he finished the sentence than the striper was already taking out his friend's backing in a surging run. Fifteen minutes later a thirty-pounder was slid up on the beach a couple of hundred yards from where the battle had begun.

June also marks the month of a unique Vineyard tournament. The annual Fly Rod Catch & Release Striped Bass Tournament sponsored by the Martha's Vineyard Rod & Gun Club. Attracting national attention, this tournament awards plaques for the most fish caught and released, as well as the largest in a one-night contest. Anglers are paired off, with an attempt at pairing Islanders with off-Islanders, and partners must fish together and record the other's catch.

As the water warms in July and August the striper fishing often slows down as fish seek deeper, cooler water. The bigger blues still make occasional runs along the beach, but more often than not it's the little snapper blues in the three- to five-pound range that provide shorefront action.

The warmer water also heralds the arrival of bonito and false albacore. These turbocharged fish create a madness all their own that can be dangerous to any Island fly fisherman with a family and job. Throughout August, and sometimes lingering into October, schools of bonito and albies careen from the water, feeding on sand eels, silversides and tinker mackerel. The best fishing is at sunrise but they can be found any time during the daylight hours wherever the bait holds. And in a fish shell game, pursuing fly fishermen try to guess where they'll show up. Edgartown Harbor amidst the white hulled sailboats, Cape Poge Gut crashing along the channel, Menemsha Jetty, and Lobsterville Beach are all great fishing spots where these open-ocean speedsters come within range of a well cast fly.

Ten-pound test tapered leaders give anglers the best chance of overcoming both species' keen eyesight and finicky nature. Flies that imitate sand eels and tinker mackerel work best; green clouser minnows are also effective. Many fishermen try to cast to breaking fish but more fishermen hook up to unseen

ones. Chasing albies and bonito can be an exasperating experience, and the best strategy is to watch their pattern of movement and aim to be at the right place at the right time. Don't be afraid to experiment with your flies because you never know what will be effective or when it will happen.

Dominic Guarino, a fly fisherman from Connecticut, found that out the hard way. Sitting in his boat surrounded by a school of albies refusing any of his offerings, he decided to take a break and put his fly rod down without realizing that the fly, which up to that point hadn't provoked the slightest interest, was hanging over the side. An albie hit it and over the side went his fly rod and reel—an example of very selective feeding.

The first cool winds and shortening days of September set the stage for the annual fall migration and the Vineyard's premier tournament—the annual Martha's Vineyard Striped Bass & Bluefish Derby. This month-long event beginning in September and

ending in October celebrated its 50th anniversary in 1995 and annually attracts more than 2,000 entrants, almost 200 in the fly-rod category. Rich in Vineyard fishing tradition, almost 900 Islanders among the year-round population of 14,000 participate. More than just a fishing contest, it initiates a month when the common language is of wind, tides, and fish. Although the primary focus is on fishing, this tournament has become a grand and unique "fishing reunion," where during the day or under a canopy of stars, new friends are made and old friendships renewed.

For fly fishermen, the Derby is a chance to share techniques, swap flies and take advantage of the heavily feeding schools of fish that can blitz a beach without warning.

In late September the albies are usually the first to go. And depending on the weather the bonito will linger off Menemsha feeding on the heavy concentration of bait well into October. This time of the year also presents

A Vineyard Fisherman's Primer

Never ask prying questions, particularly when it comes to striped bass. Islanders rarely ask someone directly where he caught a fish, but they are very good listeners with acute hearing in tackle shops where they browse and feign total disinterest as they pick up on very bit of information freely given by excited visitors.

The truthfulness of any answer relating to locations and flies diminishes in direct proportion to the size of the fish caught.

All locations are related to Island macro-geographics. This involves referring to locations very broadly: the north shore, the south shore, up-Island, down-Island and Chappy when asked to give specific locations.

Any description of fishing spots is comprised of vague phrases such as "the rock," "the jetty" and "the point," with the assumption that you will know exactly which place is being discussed by the nuance of the conversation. Act like you do even if you don't

and you may find out something.

A fine fishing book and excellent collection of Vineyard fishing stories as told by island fishermen is *Reading the Water* by Robert Post (Globe Pequot), an Island resident who claimed to be a fisherman trapped in the body of a dentist.

How to Get to the Vineyard

Year-round car ferry service is available from Falmouth, Massachusetts, on the Steamship Authority. Reservations are recommended and may be made by calling (508) 477-8600.

There is also a passenger ferry from New Bedford, Massachusetts, that sails from June to October. Call (508) 997-1688.

There is also scheduled air service from Boston and New York. Check with your local travel agent for flights and carriers.

Accommodations

The Martha's Vineyard Chamber of Commerce can supply you with a list of accomodations including inns and hotels. Call (508) 693-0085.

Tackle Shops

All of the Island's tackle shops carry fly-fishing equipment and can make both boat and shore charter arrangements. Many of the Island's beaches are private or have some restrictions and first time visitors should consider a guide to help them get a feel for the Island's fishing spots.

Boat charters average $350 for a half day and $650 for a full day of fishing. The average cost of a shore guide for a four- to six-hour period is $175 for two fishermen.

Coop's Bait & Tackle, (508) 627-3909.

Dick's Bait & Tackle, (508) 693-7669.

Larry's Tackle Shop, (508) 627-5088.

Capt. Porky's Bait & Tackle, (508) 627-7117.

the fly-rodder the chance to battle blues in the teens as these fish can blitz along any of the Island's beaches.

Once again though, it is the striped bass that lure the fishermen. This is the time that the Vineyard's jetties, beaches and inlets present the opportunity for hooking 40- and 50-pounders on the

fly. It may not be easy, but the big fish are there.

Old-timers say that the fishermen leave before the fish. More than one Islander, trying to hold off winter as long as he can, has ventured out, fly rod in hand, during the month of December until slowly and reluctantly,

reels are cleaned, rods stored away; and many of the Island's fly fishermen gather at the Martha's Vineyard Rod & Gun Club for another winter of tying flies, embellishing stories and anticipating the arrival of the next spring on Martha's Vineyard.

∎

Season's Finale

by Capt. John N. Raguso

Long after the last yellowfin, albacore and big eye tuna have left the Northeast canyons for the Gulf Stream's warmer environs, Northeast anglers looking for one more flurry of quality rod-bending before calling it a season can frequently get some attention, in addition to a tasty meal, from an often forgotten audience . . . cooperative schools of cod and pollock.

These bottom dwellers frequent rough patches of the ocean's seabed in 120 to 220 feet of water, in an area stretching a good length of the eastern Atlantic coast, from New Jersey's Cape May to the south, to Georges Bank on the northern perimeter. Although not as glamorous as the pelagic species that visit the Mid-Atlantic coast states during the summer, these boreal, or cold water fish can frequently be caught year-round from the same waters that yielded shark, tuna and billfish in the warmer months. Once the frost is on the pumpkin, they offer the "only show in town."

Catch of the Day

According to Dr. Steven Murawski, chief of the Population Dynamics Branch of the National Marine Fisheries Service in Woods Hole, Massachusetts, the cod stocks that frequent the northeast region are really components of one general population that ranges from Georges Banks down to Delaware Bay. Although each area will have its own schools of smaller (2 to 8 pounds), year-round resident cod, there appears to be an east-to-west

migration of larger fish (10 to 70 pounds and up) from summer to winter. It's been my experience that these transient cod are usually larger than the smallish local fish, as dictated by the perils of the migrations from location to location, when various predators thin-out their ranks. As fall approaches, some of the schools of bacalao that summer in the waters off Georges Banks and Nantucket Shoals eventually make a move west when the New York Bight and Jersey coast waters start to cool off in November and December, leaving again and reversing course for the deeper and cooler waters out east in the late spring.

Cod normally congregate in loosely defined schools, where there may be a lack of consistent sizing among members. Many Atlantic states require minimum sizes for taking cod and pollock (19 inches in New York State for both). The largest recorded cod ever taken was over 211 pounds, but according to the IGFA, the all-tackle rod-and-reel record was a mere 98 pound 12 ounce specimen, caught by an Isles of Shoals, New Hampshire, angler back in June of 1969. The typical fall cod will usually range from 5 to 50 pounds, with a few fish falling on either side of these parameters. Pollock come in a slightly smaller package, the largest fish on record tipping the scales at 70 pounds, with the all-tackle record of 48 pounds, 2 ounces being taken by a Massachusetts angler in September of 1992. The average-sized pollock that you're likely to encounter in the fall will typically range between 10 to 30 pounds.

The Time of the Season

November's chill, combined with the fading daylight hours and dominant northerly winds, will certainly get nearshore water temps going in the right direction to promote the migration of the cod and pollock schools closer towards New England, Long Island and New Jersey ports. While the past few seasons have seen cod and pollock caught continuously throughout the summer on many of the 20 to 30 fathom shipwrecks that dot the New Jersey and Long Island shorelines, November and December will usually bring these fish to within less than an hour's steaming from most New York Bight inlets. It's this time of the year, before the really heavy winter weather patterns set in, that bluewater anglers have one last shot at some quality bottom-fishing before they stow their tackle for the season.

Multiple Challenges

Rather than roaming the temperate waters above the thermocline, like the majority of the migratory pelagic species, cod and pollock seek the lower third of the water table, where temperatures usually range from 35 to 52 degrees. These species normally congregate in similar locations—deepwater ledges, rockpiles, gulleys, shipwrecks, reefs and other submarine structure where smaller baitfish can be found in abundance. Some of the most productive locations in the Northeast for cod and pollock are on the 20 to 30 fathom shipwrecks that dot the

New Jersey and Long Island coastlines, grim reminders of a bustling commerce center and the dark side of two world wars in this century, where German U-Boats wreaked havoc on coastal shipping. The *Virginia, Coimbra, Texas Tower, Bidevind, Bacardi, Suffolk, Arundo, Resor, Varanger,* and other wrecks are among the most popular places to start your search for cod and pollock.

Unlike trolling or drifting in a general area, which can often be productive for tuna, shark and billfish, angling for cod and pollock usually requires positioning your boat over small, pinpoint sections of the ocean bottom in order to maximize your chances for success. Suspend your boat directly over a deep-water wreck that holds fish and you can bail 20-pounders all day long. Miss your mark by as much as 20 to 30 feet, and you might go fishless for an entire day!

A cod or pollock trip usually starts off the night before, preparing the tackle and baits and deciding which wrecks, reefs or bottom might hold fish. Accurate loran-C numbers are like gold to sinker-bouncers, since they hold the key to the venture's ultimate success or failure. The casual bottom-fishing tyros typically punch in the most popular wrecks and reefs, but these get a full-court press from each area's many party, charter, and private boats. Such "published" locales frequently get fished out for periods of time during the peak spring and fall seasons. Having a good list of "secret" numbers that are usually unlisted on the diveboat or fishing charts practically guarantees a successful trip, since these locations will often hold the most fish. Why? Because they get the least amount of fishing pressure, with plenty of quality recovery time between angler visits. Captains have been known to take these numbers to their graves, and there have been numerous lawsuits between charter skippers when these top-secret bread-and-butter hotspot loran numbers are stolen or "borrowed" illegally by competitors.

Once a wreck, or better yet, a group of wrecks has been targeted, the second challenge is to actually find the structure before starting to fish. One of the keys to getting a piece of the action

is to position your boat over a piece of a shipwreck, rockpile, fathom depression, or any other form of submarine structure that will hold bait and eventually attract cod and pollock. A loran-C navigator is a must, as is a high-resolution color CRT or LCG echo sounder and a no-spin compass. The inherent inaccuracy in GPS navigators caused by the Department of Defense's "selective availability" feature which intentionally degrades the satellites' positional signals to plus or minus 100-meter accuracy, just doesn't cut it when you're 50 miles off the beach, trying to find a piece of bottom that may only be 20-feet wide by 30 feet long and comes up only a few feet off the bottom. Differential GPS units hooked up to the primary GPS unit help to bring the accuracy back to the expected plus or minus 10 to 15 meter figures, but many savvy skippers continue to rely on good old-fashioned loran-C to get them back to their favorite bottom structure time after time.

Presuming that the wreck has been found and that the appropriate floats have been deployed to mark the structure's precise location, the third and sometimes ultimate test is to position your vessel over the spot so that it won't repeatedly swing on and off the piece of bottom, causing frustration among your crew as they constantly snag their jigs and hooked baits into the sticky bottom, breaking off their rigs. Sometimes an experienced skipper can hold off the wind and tide with a solo anchor, but this type of precision fishing almost requires the use of twin anchors in a bridle set-up. An interesting compromise is to employ a single hook and then use a grapnel to snag a piece of the structure when directly overhead to prevent any unwanted movement. Just remember that the grapnel's line, typically tied off on the amidships cleat, offers an inviting target for an energetic cod or pollock to wrap your fishing line and break off.

Anchor or Drift?

If the wind and seas are calm enough, it might be possible to drift over the structure you've chosen, if the current isn't running too strong. The advantage

of this tactic is that it allows you to cover different pieces of the wreckage or rockpile, working the various nooks and crannies to find the largest schools of fish. Once (if ever) you hit the mother lode, drop a second marker float as an additional reference point and concentrate your activities on this latest section of the bottom. Make short drifts near the second marker float and be sure not to snag it with your fishing lines, pulling it away from the hot area. As with every plan, there's always a downside, and the major liability of drifting over structure is the enhanced likelihood of dragging your terminal tackle or jig directly into the wreckage, breaking it off. Do this often enough and it begins to become an expensive date. I've seen grown men cry after losing a few of those big-ticket 14-ounce Norwegian jigs into the mangled remains of sunken shipwrecks.

Tackle and Technique

Many old-timers prefer to use stiff, 7½- to 8-foot-long "telephone poles" when sinker-bouncing for bacalao and pollock, but I've always found these cut-down surf rods a bit unwieldy. I can't help but chuckle a bit when I observe them tucking these massive sticks, armed with heavy 4/0 type reels, spooled with 40- or 50-pound mono, under their arms, struggling to pump a decent-sized fish off the bottom, while having the fish lift them off the deck half the time due to poor leverage. The same principle that applies to short sticks for tuna fishing also has some merit when angling for cod. Of course, a tip that's too limber might strain under the influence of 12 to 14 ounces of lead, but there's a happy medium. Six-foot blanks like Penn's stand-up Slammers or their 6- to 7-foot Sabre series rods will do nicely on the cod grounds. Custom rods made from Lamiglass or Seeker blanks can also do nicely. These sticks can perform admirable double duty for bouncing sinkers or jigs, are long enough to be able to cast a bait or jig out and away from the boat, and have plenty of lifting power to pull an over-sized bacala or pollock out of the wreck when a lunker inhales your offering. Match this up to a Penn GLS-

45 or Shimano TLD-20 graphite lever drag reel spooled with 40-pound mono and you've got a lightweight outfit that's ready for action and won't drag you down.

Rigging a baited hook for cod is fairly simple. A classic overhand knot at the end of your line for the sinker (usually from 8 to 12 ounces) and a dropper loop(s) tied 2-to-3 feet above this for a Sproat hook(s) on a 12- to 18-inch leader has caught many a bacalao and pollock on the offshore grounds. Add on a fresh gob of skimmer clam to the end of a 6/0 to 8/0 hook and you're ready to fish. Small, whole squid baits will also work at times as an alternate bait, as will small bergalls and pieces of herring or mackerel. If you want to experiment a bit, try a Virginia hook/crab combination about a foot above the sinker and the skimmer clam offering about three feet up and there's always a chance that a large tautog will find the lower offering to its liking. However, don't be too shocked if a cod takes the crab bait, as I've caught quite a few on these crustaceans. Drop or cast the baited hook(s) down into the structure and keep the rig fairly still on the bottom, taking up most of the slack in the line, and wait for a nice cod to sniff it out. When you feel a good tug on the other end of the line, set the hook with a quick upward lift of the rod tip, give a couple of quick cranks on the reel handle to get the fish up and out of the structure, and let the action begin!

Cod and pollock will also respond readily to jigs worked off the bottom. When employing this method, I like to tie a teaser of some sort about a foot above the 8- to 12-ounce diamond or Vike jig, like a surgical tube tail, rubber worm, soft stick bait or any other wiggly rubber bait that's roughly 6 inches in length. Bright colors like hot orange, pink and lime green have all produced for me in the past. To rig a teaser, attach a hook about 12 inches above the jig via a dropper loop and push the point of the hook through the head of the rubber bait, exposing the barb about halfway down. You can either yo-yo these jigs off the bottom, lifting them up quickly, letting them flutter for 3 to 4 seconds and then dropping them back to the sand, repeating the process; or you can simply reel the jigs 10 to 15 turns slowly off the bottom, dropping them back down and repeating. When jigging, cod will typically be located within a few cranks of the bottom, while pollock, often congregating in dense schools, will frequently be taken 20 to 30 feet above the structure.

In the case of pollock, a.k.a. "Boston blues," you'll quickly learn that these gamesters are not quite as lethargic as their cod cousins, and will readily slam a jig either on the way down to the bottom or when lifting it too far off of the structure. Pollock will swarm above, downtide and off to the side of wrecks and rockpiles, and sometimes can be found halfway up to the surface when chasing schools of squid or herring. There's no mistaking when a pollock hits your lure, as it will slam it aggressively and really pull some drag off of your reel. The same yo-yo or slow-retrieve techniques will work on pollock, but start to yo-yo about 15 turns off the bottom, and try retrieving your jig up to one-third of the way up off the sand before dropping it back and repeating the process.

A Conservation Note

After talking with Dr. Steve Murawski from the NMFS, I learned that the cod stocks are going into a deep decline. I've heard stories of anglers taking 40 to 50 fish at a time when the action is hot, but this type of unrestricted behavior has the potential to be wasteful and contributes to the extended down cycle of the overpressured cod population. Dr. Murawski continued to explain that the cod stocks are at historically low levels and in a word, are in "grim" condition. Popular wrecks can get "fished out" when hit too frequently, and sometimes it takes up to a few weeks to repopulate them during calm weather periods. So, if you're lucky enough to get a calm weather day this fall and hit a good school of fish on one of the wrecks, why not just take what you know you will eat, and return the rest to provide some action for someone else? Be sure to keep a watchful eye on the weather, as the northerly winds can sometimes kick up on short notice, and save a few of these wonderful cod and pollock for our kids. See 'ya out there! ∎

FISHING ACCESS

MASSACHUSETTS

For a listing of ramps, jetties, and piers in Massachusetts, see page 30.

RHODE ISLAND

Town	Public Shore Access
Newport	Zandt Pier, Van Zandt & Washington St.
	Storer Park Pier, Elm St.
	Causeway at Goat Island Piers, etc.
	at Ft. Adams State Park
	Old Stone Pier, Wellington Ave.
	Brenton Pt. State Park, Ocean Drive
Portsmouth	Old Stone Bridge, Point Street
	Railroad Bridge, Riverside Ave.
Tiverton	Nannaquaket Bridge, Nannaquaket Rd.

Town	Public Shore Access
	Old Stone Bridge, Rt. 77
	Railroad Bridge, Riverside Ave.
Little Compton	Sakonnet Harbor Breakwater, Rt. 77
Bristol	State Street Pier, State Street Fishing Pier, Colt State Park
Warwick	Rock Island Fishing Area, Narragansett Parkway Piers & Shore, Rocky Point Amusement Park
North Kensington	Town Dock, Wickford
Narragansett	Monahan's Dock, Ocean Road
	East Wall, West Wall of the Harbor of Refuge
	Breachway to Pt. Judith Pond
South Kingston	Deep hole fishing area, Matunuck Beach Rd.
	Causeway portion of the old Jamestown Bridge has been converted to a fishing pier
Charlestown	Breachway to Charlestown Pond
	Breachway to Quonochontaug Pond
Westerly	Breachway to Winnapaug Pond
	Sandy Pt., Watch Hill

CONNECTICUT

Site Characteristic Legend
R—Boulders, natural rock stuctures
S—Sand, mud, or fine gravel bottom
CH—Channel or drop-off near site
E/R—Site located in estuary or river
M—Man-made structures such as docks, jetties, pilings, etc. are present
$—Seasonal daily fee

Town	Public Shore Access
Branford	Branford Point pier (R, S, CH, E/R, M)
	Branford state launch (S, CH, E/R, M)
Bridgeport	Fairfield town launch and access (R, S, CH, E/R, M)
	Fayerweather Island (R, S, CH, M) $
	Seaside Park (S, M)
	Pleasure Beach Park (S, CH, E/R, M)
Clinton	Clinton town dock and launch (S, CH, E/R, M) $
	Clinton town beach (S, E/R)
East Haven	East Shore Park (S, E,/R)
	Fort Hale Park (S, E/R, M)
	Lighthouse Park and launch (R, S, E/R, M) $
Essex	Essex town launch (S, CH, E/R, M)
Fairfield	Penfield Reef access (R, S, CH)
	Jennings Beach (S)

Town	Public Shore Access
Greenwich	Greenwich town pier (R, S, CH, E/R, M)
	Cos Cob town dock (S, E/R, M)
Groton	I-95 state launch, Groton (R, S, CH, E/R, M)
Guilford	Guilford town marina and launch (S, CH, E/R)
Lyme	Lieutenant River, Rte. 156 bridge, (S, CH, E/R—unsafe to fish from the bridge)
	Great Island state launch (S, CH, E/R)
	Black Hall River, Rte. 156 bridge (S, CH, E/R)—unsafe to fish from the bridge
	Sound View Beach (S,M)
	Four Mile River state launch (S, CH, E/R)
	Rocky Neck State Park (R, S, M) $
Madison	West Wharf (R, S, M) $
	Middle Road (R, S)
	Hammonasset State Park (R, S, M) $
Milford	Devon state launch (R, S, CH, E/R, M)
	Charles Island (Silver Sands State Park) (R, S, M)
	Milford town pier (S, CH, E/R, M)
	Gulf Beach (R, S, CH, E/R, M)
Mystic	I-95 overpass access (S, CH, E/R, M)
	Quiambaug Cove access (S, CH, E/R)
New Haven	Long Wharf (S, E/R)
New London	Ocean Beach Park (R, S) $
	New London town pier (S, CH, E/R, M)
	I-95 state launch, New London (R, S, CH, E/R, M)
Niantic	McCook's Point and Hole-in-the-Wall Beach (R, S, M) $
Noank	Noank town dock (S, CH, E/R, M)
Norwalk	Norwalk town launch (no fishing from ramp)$
	Veterans Memorial Park (S, CH, M)
	Calf Pasture Point (S, M)
Old Saybrook	Cornfield Point (R, S) No parking
Rowayton	Rowayton Town Dock (S, CH, M)
Stamford	Stamford Southfield Park and Launch (S, CH, E/R, M) $
	Cummings Beach Park (S, CH, M) $
	Cove Island Park (R, S, CH, M) $
	Weed Beach (S) town residents only
Stonington	Stonington Town Dock (S, CH, M)
	Barn Island state launch
Stratford	Long Beach (S)
	Short Beach (S)

Town	Public Shore Access
	Stratford town dock and launch (S, CH, E/R, M)
Waterford	Niantic River state launch (no fishing from ramp) $
	Dock Road state launch (R, S, M)
	Harkness Memorial State Park (R, S)$
Westbrook	Westbrook town dock (S, CH, E/R, M)
West Haven	West Shore Beach (S, M)
	Prospect Beach, (S, M)
	Savin Rock, Bradley Point (R, S, M)
	Public Piers at: Palace Street (S, M), Washington Street (S, M), Beach Street (S, M), Morse Park (S), West Haven public beach (S), Sandy Point (S, M)
	West Haven town launch (S, E/R)
Westport	I-95 state launch, Saugatuck River (R, S, CH, E/R)
	Compo Beach (R, S, M) town residents only
	Sherwood Island State Park (R, S) $

NEW YORK (LONG ISLAND)

Town	Public Shore Access
Amagansett	Atlantic Avenue Beach, Atlantic Ave. (Off-season.)
Amityville	Cooper Avenue, Cooper & Riverside Ave.
	Griffing Avenue, Griffing & Riverside Ave.
	Perkins Avenue, Perkins & Riverside Ave.
Atlantic Beach	East Atlantic Beach Park, Clayton Ave.
	Silver Point Park, Park St.
Babylon	Municipal Dock & Marina, Fire Island Ave.
	Baxter Estate Sunset Park, Main St.
Bayville	Centre Island Beach, Centre Island Rd.
Blue Point	Blue Point Ave. Fishing Pier, Blue Point Ave.
Bridgehampton	Scott Cameron Beach, Dune Rd. (Off-season.)
	Surfer's Beach, South of Flying Point Rd. (Off-season.)
Center Moriches	Union Avenue Dock, Union Ave.
Cherry Grove	Cherry Grove Dock, Bayview Walk.
East Hampton	Egypt Beach, Old Beach Ln. (Off-season.)
	Georgica Beach, Apaquogue Rd. (Off-season.)
	Main Beach, Ocean Ave. (Off-season.)
	Wiborg Beach, Highway behind pond. (Off-season.)
East Moriches	Moriches Island Road Dock, Moriches Island Rd.
East Patchogue	Pine Neck Avenue Park, Pine Neck Ave.
Fire Island	Smith Point County Park, Fire Island Beach Rd.
Greenport	Norman Klipp Marine Park, Manhansett Ave. (State Funded.)
	Third & Wiggins St. Water Access, Third and Wiggins St.
Hampton Bays	Dolphin Lane Beach, Dolphin Ln. (Off-season.)
	Ponquogue Beach, Dune Rd. (Off-season.)
	Shinnecock Beach (East), County Park, Dune Rd.
	Shinnecock Beach (West), County Park, Beach Rd.
	Shinnecock Inlet Basin, Dune Rd.
	Tiana Beach, Dune Rd. (Off-season.)
	Triton Lane Beach, Triton Ln. (Off-season.)
Huntington	Halesite Park, East Shore Rd.
Lindenhurst	Venetian Shores Beach, Granada Pkwy.
Long Beach	Magnolia Blvd. Park, Magnolia Blvd.
	Ocean Beach Park, New York Ave.
Mastic	Forge River Marina, Riviera Ave.
Montauk	Kirk Park Beach, South Eagle St. (Off-season.)
	Montauk County Park, Montauk Hwy.
	West Lake Drive, Water Inlet Access, West Lake Dr.
Mount Sinai	Cedar Beach and Marina, Harbor Beach Rd.
Northport	Cow Harbor Park, Woodline Ave.
Northville	Iron Pier Beach, Pier Ave.
Northwest Harbor	Cedar Point County Park, Cedar Point Rd.
Oak Beach	Oak Beach, Ocean Pkwy.
Ocean Beach	Ocean Beach Recreational Area, Hay Walk.
Patchogue	Mascot Dock, Maiden Ln.
	River Avenue Park, River Ave.
	Shore Front Park, Smith St.
Port Jefferson	Port Jefferson Marina & Town Dock, West Broadway
Riverhead	Indian Island County Park, Hubbard Ave.
	Peconic River Park, Peconic Ave.
Sag Harbor	Amherst Road Water Access, Amherst Rd.

	Cove Road Water Access, Cove Rd.
	Fishing Bridge, Redwood Rd.
	Long Dock, Wharf St.
	Notre Dame Road Water Access, Notre Dame Rd.
	Yale Road Water Access, Yale Rd.
Sagaponack	Sagg Beach, Sagaponack Rd. (Off-season.)
Saltaire	Village Beach and Bulkhead, Bay Promenade.
Sea Cliff	Dock Hill Park, Shore Dr. (Oyster Bay.)
	Rum Pt. Shore Rd.
Shinnecock Hills	Shinnecock Canal, County Marina, Old North Rd.
Shirley	Smith Point County Marina, Lombardi Dr.
Smithtown	Landing Avenue Park, Landing Ave.
Southold	Cedar Beach County Park, Cedar Beach Rd.
Stony Brook	Stony Brook Dock, Shore Rd.
Water Mill	Flying Point Beach, Flying Point Rd. (Off-season)
West Hampton Beach	Lashley Pavilion Village Beach, Dune Rd. (Off-season.)
	Rogers Pavilion Village Beach, Beach Ln. (Off-season.)
	Captree State Park
	Caumsett State Park
	Hecksher State Park
	Hither Hills State Park
	Jones Beach State Park
	Montauk Point State Park
	Napeague State Park
	Orient Beach State Park
	Robert Moses State Beach
	Sunken Meadow State Park
	Wildwood State Park

NEW YORK CITY FISHING ACCESS SITES

Town	Public Shore Access
Bronx	Ferry Point Park (East R.)
	Pelham Bay Park (Eastchester Bay)
	Soundview Park (East River.)
Brooklyn	69th St. Pier
	Bensonhurst Park (Gravesend Bay)
	Breezy Point/Ft. Tilden (NPS)
	Canarsie Pier (Natl. Park Service)
	Drier-Offerman Park
	Marine Park (Adjacent Floyd Bennet Field)
	Paeraegat Basin
	Sheepshead Bay
	Steeplechase Pier (Coney Island)
Manhattan	Highbridge Park
	Riverside Park
	Wards Island
Queens	Alley Pond Park (Little Neck Bay)
	Bayside Marina (Little Neck Bay.)
	Little Bay Park (Little Ray-Ft. Totten)
	North Channel B'ways (Jamaica Bay)
Staten Island	Cedar Grove Beach
	Conference House Point (Raritan Bay)
	Ft. Wadsworth (Verrazano Bridge)
	Great Kills (Natl. Park)
	Lemon Creek (Princess Bay)

NEW YORK STATE MARINE ARTIFICIAL FISHING REEFS

Rockaway Beach Artificial Reef
Year developed: 1967
Latitude: 40 32.50
Longitude: 73 50.52
Loran C: 26939.2/43749.6
Dimensions: 2,000 yds. × 1,000 yds.
Depth (ft.): 35–38
Max. relief: 11
Materials: 6,000 tires in 3-tire units; 60 steel buoys; rock; and concrete slabs, piles, culvert, decking and rubble. One tire unit is configured into a 15-tire pyramid.

Atlantic Beach Artificial Reef
Year developed: 1967
Latitude: 40 31.90
Longitude: 73 43.00
Loran C: 26870.6/43734.7
Dimensions: 2,000 yds. × 1,000 yds.
Depth (ft.): 56–63
Max. relief: 13
Materials: 30,000 tires in 3-tire units; 404 auto bodies; 10 Good Humor trucks; 9 barges; the tug *Fran S*; a steel lifeboat; steel crane and boom; and concrete culvert, rubble, abutments, and decking.

McAllister Grounds Artificial Reef
Year developed: 1949
Latitude: 40 32.12
Longitude: 73 39.27
Loran C: 26840.8/43733.6
Dimensions: roughly circular, 200 yds. in diameter
Depth (ft.): 52
Max. relief: 2
Materials: rock, brick, and concrete rubble

Hempstead Town Artificial Reef
Year developed: 1967
Latitude: 40 31.25
Longitude: 73 32.35
Loran C: 26782.5/43715.5

Dimensions: 3,000 yds. × 1,200 yds.
Depth (ft.): 50–72
Max. relief: 15
Materials: eight vessels, a drydock, and concrete rubble

Fire Island Artificial Reef
Year developed: 1962
Latitude: 40 35.75
Longitude: 73 12.60
Loran C: 26633.0/43735.0
Dimensions: 2,025 yds. × 200 yds.
Depth (ft.): 68–73
Max. relief: 10
Materials: 1,500 tires; 10 barges; 2 boat hulls; 2 dry-
    docks; coal waste blocks (experimental);
    rock; and concrete rubble and cesspool rings.

Moriches Anglers Artificial Reef
Year developed: 1968
Latitude: 40 43.50
Longitude: 73 44.66
Loran C: 26431.0/43771.5
Dimensions: 450 yds. × 150 yds.
Depth (ft.): 72
Max. relief: unknown
Materials: two small wooden boats and 600 tires

Shinnecock Artificial Reef
Year developed: 1969
Latitude: 40 47.98
Longitude: 72 28.55
Loran C: 26287.5/43787.5
Dimensions: 450 yds. × 150 yds.
Depth (ft.): 76–85
Max. relief: 20
Materials: 3,000 tires in three-tire units; 3 barges; a tug;
    a wood drydock; a wood oyster boat; a steel
    cruiser; and steel and concrete bridge rubble.

Great South Bay (Kismet) Artificial Reef
Year developed: 1967
Latitude: 40 38.20
Longitude: 73 12.75
Loran C: 26637.3/44757.9
Dimensions: 1,000 yds. × 50 yds.
Depth (ft.): 8
Max. relief: 8
Materials: 4,000 tires in 3- or 4-tire units; two barges;
    24,000 cement blocks; and concrete culvert
    and rubble.

Smithtown Bay Artificial Reef
Year developed: 1976
Latitude: 40 56.00
Longitude: 73 11.10
Loran C: 26667.5/43916.2
Dimensions: 150 yds. × 100 yds.
Depth (ft.): 38–40
Max. relief: 15
Materials: 22,000 tires; 5 barges; 6 steel cylinders.

FISHING OFF LONG ISLAND THROUGH THE YEAR

JANUARY AND FEBRUARY

Few boats, open or charter, operate. Those that do usually sail weekends and holidays only. Cod is the main species sought, although whiting (silver hake), herring, and red hake (ling) will also be caught. Likely ports are Sheepshead Bay (Brooklyn), Freeport, Captree State Park, and Montauk. There is some fishing at Steeplechase Pier (Coney Island) for whiting and herring. In some years, herring may be available to bank and pier fishermen in such areas as the Jones Beach piers, Captree State Park piers, Shinnecock Canal, the jetties at Mount Sinai Harbor and other areas where there is access. Some white perch may be caught at Sunken Meadow State Park and some of the south shore rivers.

MARCH, APRIL, AND MAY

Large winter flounder ("snowshoes") are sought by anglers aboard Montauk-berthed open and charter boats. Winter flounder will provide action through mid-May (even to mid-June in some years) for anglers aboard most of the open and charter boats from other ports, for those using rental boat stations, and for bank and pier anglers. Popular ports for open- and charter-boat anglers include: Babylon, Sheepshead Bay, Freeport, Captree State Park, Greenport, Port Jefferson, and Huntington; rental boat stations may be found at Freeport, Seaford, Amityville, Babylon, Mastic Beach, East Moriches, Hampton Bays, Sag Harbor, Montauk, Mattituck Inlet, New Suffolk, Mt. Sinai Harbor, Port Jefferson, Kings Park, and many other villages along Long Island Sound and the south shore bays. Among the more popular bank and pier fishing areas are the west shore of Little Neck Bay, the banks of the Shinnecock Canal, and the fishing piers at Coney Island, and Captree, Robert Moses, and Jones Beach State Parks.

Some Freeport and Sheepshead Bay open boats seek cod (along with whiting and ling) through mid-April. These boats, along with some of those berthed at Captree State Park, switch to mackerel in mid- or late April and early May. Some other Captree-berthed open boats may switch to weakfish about the same time. Summer flounder (fluke) fishing can start about as early as mid-May for the Captree fleet. Mid- to late May also sees the beginning of scup (porgies) in the Peconics and northern puffer (blowfish) in south shore bays.

Tomcod may add a little variety to winter flounder catches in late March through April for anglers fishing Narrow Bay, Quantuck Bay, the Quogue Canal, and western Tiana Bay on the south shore and in some of

Anglers can easily find schooling bluefish inshore and offshore during early spring. White bucktails and diamond jigs seem to work best. This is also an ideal time to try saltwater fly-fishing. Blues are thick and cooperative. (VIN T. SPARANO)

the harbors of the western Sound. Smelt (although quite scarce in recent years) may show in a few north shore tidal streams in March. White perch will provide some early spring (March-April) action in some of the larger rivers emptying into the south shore bays. The striped bass season starts in May. The south shore beaches and Little Neck Bay are often early "hot spots."

JUNE

Early in the month, anglers fishing from open boats at Montauk will continue to catch cod, pollock, and winter flounder. About mid-month, black sea bass, scup (porgies), and summer flounder (fluke) will become important at Montauk. The charter-boat fleet there begins to work on bluefish and striped bass. Several charter boats from Montauk will fish exclusively for sharks from June through October. Greenport open and charter boats fish for porgies and weakfish, and some large blackfish (tautog) may also be taken. There may be a few bluefish caught out of Port Jefferson late in the month; otherwise boats from that port will concentrate on porgies, blackfish, flounder, and fluke. Anglers fishing from Captree State Park open and charter boats and from rental boats throughout the south shore bays are after fluke (summer flounder) and weakfish. Porgies and weakfish form the bulk of the catches for rental-boat anglers in the Peconics. Anglers fishing from open boats from Freeport and Sheepshead Bay will generally fish offshore and take mixed bags of porgies, black sea bass, blackfish, and fluke. Occasional spurts of bluefish fishing will begin from these ports. Bank- and pier-fishing along the south shore is for fluke, weakfish, blowfish, kingfish, winter flounder, and blackfish. Bluefish, kingfish, and

blowfish will join weakfish and striped bass in the surf fisherman's catches. North shore bank fishermen will be taking a mixed bag of flounder, blackfish, weaks, striped bass, and bluefish. Shark fishing out of several south shore ports begins this month and lasts through October. Blue shark, shortfin mako, and dusky shark will be the most frequently caught sharks.

JULY AND AUGUST

Most anglers aboard Montauk open boats will take home fluke, porgies, and sea bass. Also becoming increasingly popular is the offshore fishery from Montauk and other ports that includes tuna fishing and other canyon fishing. A few boats from Montauk will take their fishermen to Cox's Ledge and Block Island for cod all summer long. Although bluefish will be the main support of charter-boat anglers from all ports, some tuna will be taken by anglers chartering boats from Hampton Bays, Montauk, Freeport, and Sheepshead Bay. Fluke fishing continues throughout the south shore bays. Some good catches of weakfish may be made near Hecksher State Park. Porgies, with kingfish and weakfish, dominate fishing in the Peconics. Anglers fishing aboard the open boats leaving Freeport and Sheepshead Bay will concentrate on bluefish. Anglers on Port Jefferson–based boats will hit good schools of bluefish from time to time now through late September. On days when bluefish are not to be found, fluke, porgies, and blackfish will provide a willing substitute. "Snappers" (young bluefish) will support the bank and pier fishery in August. Surf-fishing on the south shore and bank fishing on the north shore will be similar to the fishing in June. Charter boats from Greenport will concentrate on large bluefish and striped bass through November. Open boats based there will concentrate on fluke, porgies, and weakfish.

SEPTEMBER

Porgy fishing aboard Montauk open boats is usually at its best this month. Striped bass begin to be more frequent in the catches of anglers fishing from charter boats from all ports. Through mid-November big blackfish near Orient Point will be sought by fishermen aboard Greenport- and Orient-berthed boats. Blackfish and bluefish will dominate the catches from other north shore ports. Anglers fishing from Captree will be taking mixed bags of several species.

Blackfish angling becomes good late in the month through November on all the artificial reefs on the south shore. Freeport and Sheepshead Bay anglers will be looking for school tuna in addition to bluefish. "Snapper" fishing is at its best for the bank and pier fishermen during the first half of the month. Striped bass become more common in the surf fishermen's bag.

OCTOBER

Open boat anglers at Montauk may take some porgies, but cod will become the main objective there. Charter-boat anglers from this port should find striped bass fishing at its best. Anglers using the Captree open boats and rental boats throughout all of Long Island will be catching winter flounder, as will bank and pier fishermen. A few bluefish and occasionally large schools of tuna will be good this month at Montauk and along the south shore. North shore bank fishermen will also do well at some spots for stripers.

NOVEMBER

The best fishing will be for codfish at Montauk, winter flounder at Captree and throughout Long Island, and big blackfish and a few cod near Orient Point. Some striped bass will be taken by charter-boat fishermen from all ports. Bank- and pier-fishing for winter flounder should be at or near its best. Surf-fishing will probably taper off about mid-month, though bluefish may surprise with some "blitzes" near Thanksgiving. Freeport and Sheepshead Bay open boats fishing offshore will concentrate on blackfish and sea bass until the cod and whiting come in.

DECEMBER

Cod will be the prime objective of most boat fishermen from all ports. Nearly all fishing will be done on weekends. Some rental boat stations may have a few boats

still in the water for winter flounder fishermen early in the month. Bank fishing is mostly for flounder. Some blackfish may linger through the first week or two of the month. Herring may show in some years. White perch may be found at Sunken Meadow State Park and in some of the south shore rivers.

LAUNCH RAMPS

MASSACHUSETTS

Ramps in Massachusetts are included in a listing of ramps, piers, and jetties beginning on page 30.

RHODE ISLAND

Town	Public Access
Barrington	Haines Memorial Park on Bullocks Cove, off Metropolitan Park Drive. Concrete.
Bristol	Bristol Harbor, State St. Concrete.
	Thames St., foot of Church St. Concrete.
	Bristol Narrows, off Rte. 136.
	Colt State Park, off Hope St.(Rt.114) Concrete.
	Mt. Hope Bay, end of Annawanscutt Dr. Concrete.
Charlestown	Charlestown Breachway. Concrete.
	Quonochontaug Breachway.
	Town Dock Rd. Cement slab.
Cranston	Pawtuxet, Aborn St.
	Pawtuxet, Narragansett Blvd., and Ocean Ave.
East Greenwich	Pole #6, Crompton Ave., Greenwich Cove.
East Providence	Bold Point, off Veteran's Memorial Parkway via Mauran Ave., at the end of Pier Rd. Hard-packed gravel.
	Sabin Point Pk., off Bullock's Pt. Ave., at the end of Shore Rd.
	Beach Rd., off Bullock's Pt. Ave. Hard-packed sand.
	Haines Memorial Pk., off Metropolitan Park Drive.
Jamestown	Fort Getty Memorial area, off Beavertail Rd. Concrete.
	Fort Wetherill. Concrete.
Little Compton	Sakonnet Harbor, Sakonnet Point Rd. Cement.
Middletown	Third Beach Rd. Steel mesh.
Narragansett	Snug Harbor, Jerusalem.
	Galilee, near corner of Galilee Rd.

Newport	and Great Island Rd. Concrete slab. Monahan's Dock. Concrete. Off Washington St., two locations: Elm St. & Poplar St. Kenny's Beach, directly off Ocean Dr. Natural rock and cement. Fort Adams State Park. Concrete.
North Kingston	Wickford, Rte. 1, near fire station. Pleasant St., Wickford. Allen's Harbor
Portsmouth	Sandy Point Rd., off Rte. 138. Con- crete. Stone Bridge, east of junction of Rtes. 138 and 24 on Park Ave. Con- crete. Gull Cove, Rte. 138. Concrete
South Kingston	Snug Harbor, foot of Gooseberry Rd. Narrow River, off Pettaquamscutt Rd., between Middle Bridge Rd. and Bridgetown Rd. Cement Pond Street at the end. Gravel. Marina Park Exit, Rte. 1. Concrete ramps.
Tiverton	Sakonnet River Bridge. At the beach, Rte. 77. Sapowet Point, Rte. 77, to Sapowet Ave. Hard beach with natural slope ramp.
Warwick	Goddard State Park, via U.S. 1 and East Greenwich. Concrete. Longmeadow. Cement ramp.

In May and June, fishermen will score on stripers, such as this keeper bass, in New York–New Jersey waters. This bass took a Hopkins jig. (VIN T. SPARANO)

Conimicut Point, off Shawomet Ave. Cement, Problematic.
Arnold's Neck area, end of Harrop Ave. Cement.
Passeonkquis Cove.Concrete and asphalt.
Warwick Neck on Randall Ave., off Warwick Neck Ave. Hard packed gravel.
Chepiwoxet, off U.S. 1, Alger Ave. Boat sling launching.
Pawtuxet Park, East View St., off Narragansett Parkway.
Warwick Downs, Narragansett Parkway. Dirt roads, ledge just below surface of water at launching site.
Longmeadow. Concrete.

CONNECTICUT

For information on ramps in Connecticut, see Access, page 68.

NEW YORK (LONG ISLAND) LAUNCH RAMPS

Town	Public Access
Amityville	Amityville Village Beach, Bayview Ave.
Atlantic Beach	Silver Point Park, Park St.
Babylon	Village Beach, Fire Island Ave.
Bellport	Bellport Village Dock, Bellport Ln.
Blue Point	Blue Point Ave. Fishing Pier, Blue Point Ave. Corey Creek Park, Corey Ave. Corey Park, Davis Ave.
Center Moriches	Laura Lee Drive Park, Laura Lee Dr.
East Patchogue	Pine Neck Avenue Park, Pine Neck Ave.
Eastport	Seatuck Dock, Seatuck Ave.
Fire Island	Smith Point County Park, Fire Island Beach Rd.
Freeport	Albany Avenue Boat Launch, Albany Ave. (State Funded.)
Great River	Hecksher State Park. Hard-surface ramp. Parking for 100 cars and trailers.
Greenport	Norman Klipp Marine Park, Manhansett Ave. (State Funded.) Stirling Basin Launch Ramp, Sandy Beach Rd. Third & Wiggins St. Water Access, Third and Wiggins St.
Hampton Bays	Shinnecock Bay Dock, Triton Ln. Shinnecock Beach (East), County Park, Dune Rd. Shinnecock Beach (West), County Park, Beach Rd.

Huntington	Mill Dam Boat Ramp & Marina, Mill Dam Rd.
Jamesport	S. Jamesport Beach Marina & Ramp, Peconic Bay Blvd. (State Funded.)
Lawrence	Lawrence Yacht Club, Sage Ave.
Lindenhurst	Venetian Shores Beach, Granada Pkwy.
Mastic	Forge River Marina, Riviera Ave.
Montauk	Montauk County Park, Montauk Hwy.
Mount Sinai	Cedar Beach and Marina, Harbor Beach Rd.
New Suffolk	New Suffolk Town Beach, Jackson St.
Northport	Scudder Park and Beach, Ketcham Place.
Northville	Iron Pier Beach, Pier Ave.
Northwest Harbor	Cedar Point County Park, Cedar Point Rd.
Oak Beach	Oak Beach, Ocean Pkwy.
Patchogue	Sand Spit Park and Beach, Beach St.
Port Jefferson	Port Jefferson Marina & Town Dock, West Broadway.
Riverhead	Indian Island County Park, Hubbard Ave.
	Peconic River Park, Peconic Ave.
Sag Harbor	Marine Park, Bay St.
Shirley	Smith Point County Marina, Lombardi Dr.
Southold	Laughing Waters Launch Ramp, Minnehaha Blvd.
Stony Brook	Stony Brook Dock, Shore Rd.
Westhampton Beach	Westhampton Beach Municipal Marina, Steven's Lane & Library Ave.

FISH RECORDS

MASSACHUSETTS

For Massachusetts records, see page 33; for information on the Massachusetts Saltwater Fishing Derby, see page 34.

RHODE ISLAND

Albacore: 67 lbs. 3 oz.; Block Island; 1990
Sea Bass: 8 lbs. 7¼ oz.; Block Island; 1981
Striped Bass: 70 lbs.; Block Island; 1984
Bluefish: 26 lbs.; 1981
Cod: 71 lbs.; 1965
Summer Flounder: 17 lbs. 8 oz.; Narrow River; 1962
Winter Flounder: 6 lbs. 7 oz.; Galilee; 1990
King Mackerel: 10 lbs. 12 oz.; Watch Hill; 1992

White Marlin: 125 lbs.; South Block Island; 1987
Scup: 5 lbs.; Block Island; 1990
American Shad: 6 lbs. 8 oz.; Runnins River; 1985
Hickory Shad: 2 lbs. 11 oz.; Narrow River; 1989
Blue Shark: 385 lbs. 8 oz.; NW The Dump; 1989
Mako Shark: 718 lbs.; Block Island; 1993
Tiger Shark: 597 lbs.; South Block Island; 1990
White Shark: 2,909 lbs.; Block Island; 1991
Thresher Shark: 448 lbs.; S. Cox Ledge; 1991
Swordfish: 314 lbs.; 1964
Squeteague: 13 lb. 8 oz.; North Jamestown; 1987
Tautog: 21 lbs. 4 oz.; Jamestown; 1954
Trigger Fish: 2 lbs.; Pine Hill; 1991
Bluefin Tuna: 1,142 lbs. 12 oz.; The Dump; 1987

CONNECTICUT

Blackfish: 18 lbs. 6 oz.; Long Island Sound off Black Point; 1988
Black Sea Bass: 4 lbs. 15 oz.; Long Island Sound off Great Captain Rocks; 1989
Bluefin Tuna: 770 lbs. 0 oz.; Block Island Sound; 1990
Bluefish: 24 lbs. 13 oz.; Long Island Sound off Norwalk; 1979
Blue Shark: 268 lbs. 0 oz.; Ryans Horn, south of Montauk Pt.; 1989
Cunner: 2 lbs. 7 oz., Long Island Sound off Groton; 1989
Mako Shark: 650 lbs. 0 oz., Block Island; 1987
Scup (Porgy): 3 lbs. 11 oz.; Long Island Sound off Bridgeport; 1987
Striped Bass: 71 lbs. 0 oz.; Long Island Sound off Norwalk; 1980
Summer Flounder: 14 lbs. 8 oz.; Misquamicut Beach; 1989
Weakfish: 17 lbs. 14 oz.; Long Island Sound off Fayerweather Island, Bridgeport; 1986
White Marlin: 108 lbs. 8 oz.; Block Canyon; 1988
Winter Flounder: 4 lbs. 1 oz.; Block Island Sound; l989
Yellowfin Tuna: 210 lbs. 7 oz.; Block Canyon; 1991

Trophy Fish Awards Program
The "Trophy Fish Awards Program" is not a fishing contest; no prizes will be awarded for the largest fish recorded. However, awards of merit will be issued for qualifying marine species and official saltwater state records can be established. Qualifying catches will be awarded a bronze pin and a certificate of merit for each trophy fish taken. A silver pin will be awarded for the fifth fish of merit from a single angler and a gold pin for the tenth.

In order to qualify for a saltwater award the following minimum weights are required:

Minimum Saltwater Entry Sizes
Striped bass: 45 pounds
Bluefish: 18 pounds
Weakfish: 12 pounds
Blackfish: 10 pounds

Black sea bass: 4 pounds
Atlantic mackerel: 4 pounds
Summer flounder (Fluke): 8 pounds
Winter flounder (Blackback, Flatfish)[*]: 3 pounds
Porgy (Scup): 3 pounds
Cunner: 1.5 pounds
Pollock[*]: 25 pounds
Cod: 40 pounds
Bonito: 8 pounds
Bluefin tuna: 400 pounds
Yellowfin tuna[*]: 150 pounds
Albacore: 35 pounds
Blue shark[*]: 175 pounds
Mako shark: 200 pounds
White marlin[*]: 80 pounds
Blue marlin: 100 pounds
Swordfish: 100 pounds
[*]Photograph suitable to provide positive identification required.

Saltwater entries must be caught from shore in Connecticut or from a boat which leaves from or returns to a Connecticut port or launching area. Other rules are identical to those for freshwater award entries. Rules and affidavit forms can be obtained from the DEP Fisheries Bureau in Hartford 566-2287; Marine Fisheries, Waterford 443-0166; Eastern District Office, Marlborough 295-9523; and Western District Office, Harwinton 566-2375.

NEW YORK

Albacore (Longfin): 69 lbs. 10 oz.; 1988
Black Sea Bass: 9 lbs 0 oz.; 1983
Blackfish: 19 lbs. 0 oz.; 1989
Bluefish: 24 lbs. 8 oz.; 1979
Cod: 85 lbs. 0 oz.; 1984
Dolphin: 52 lbs. 0 oz.; 1985
Flounder (Winter): 7 lbs. 0 oz.; 1986
Fluke[*]: 22 lbs. 7 oz.; 1975
Marlin (Blue): 1,174 lbs. 0 oz.; 1986
Marlin (White): 130 lbs. 0 oz.; 1951
Pollock: 45 lbs. 15 oz.; 1988
Porgy (Scup): 6 lbs. 4 oz.; 1978
Shark (Blue): 393 lbs. 0 oz.; 1979
Shark (Mako): 1,080 lbs. 0 oz.; 1979
Shark (Tiger): 1,087 lbs. 0 oz.; 1986
Shark (White): 3,450 lbs. 0 oz.; 1986
Striped Bass: 76 lbs., 0 oz.; 1981
Swordfish: 492 lbs. 4 oz.; 1959
Tuna (Bigeye): 355 lbs. 0 oz.; 1981
Tuna (Bluefin): 1,071 lbs. 0 oz.; 1977
Tuna (Yellowfin): 239 lbs. 0 oz.; 1978
Weakfish[*]: 19 lbs. 2 oz.; 1984
All-Tackle[*] World Record

New York State Official Weigh Stations

Johnny's Tackle Shop, Montauk
Merrick Tackle, Bellmore
Star Island Yacht Club, Montauk
Causeway Bait & Tackle, Wantagh
Montauk Marine Basin, Montauk
Hudson Point Fishing Station, Freeport
Tuma's Tackle, Montauk
Hook, Line and Sinker, Freeport
Gone Fishing Marina, Montauk
Sea Isle Sport Center, Freeport
Westlake Fishing Lodge, Montauk
Lou's Fishing Station, Freeport
Captain's Cove, Montauk
Kaysee Marine, Freeport
Uihlein's Boat Rentals, Montauk
Scotty's Marina, Point Lookout
Harbor Marina, East Hampton
Ed's Fishing Station, Point Lookout
Bayview Tackle, Sag Harbor
Commodore Fishing Station, Island Park
Noyac Marina, Noyac
Beckmann's Tackle, Lynbrook
Specks's Tackle Shop, Southampton
Skippy's Bait & Tackle, Atlantic Beach
Corr's Fishing Station, Hampton Bays
Cross Bay Marine, Howard Beach
Molnar's Landing, Hampton Bays
Cross Bay Bait & Tackle, Jamaica Bay
Altenkirch and Son, Hampton Bays
Mike's Tackle Shop, Sheepshead Bay
Three Aces Tackle Center, Hampton Bays
Stella Maris Tackle, Sheepshead Bay
L&M Marine, East Moriches
Frank's Sport Center, Brooklyn
Silly Lilly Fishing Station, E. Moriches
Staten Island Bait & Tackle, Staten Is.
Tadsen's Fishing Station, E. Moriches
J.F. Tackle Shop, Staten Island
Las Brisas Fishing Station, E. Moriches
Shooter and Anglers, Queens
Cerullo Bros Fishing Station, E. Moriches
Big B Bait & Tackle, Rosedale
Shoreline Marina, Center Moriches
Cast-A-Way Bait & Tackle, Franklin Sq.
J&J Tackle, Patchogue
John's Gun & Tackle, New Rochelle
J&R Sport Center, Oakdale
Jack's Bait & Tackle, City Island
Peppy's Bait & Tackle, East Islip
Glen Cove Sport Shop, Glen Cove
Smokey's Bait & Tackle, Bay Shore
Four Winds Bait & Tackle, Huntington
Captree Bait & Tackle, Captree
Huntington Prop & Tackle, Huntington
Babylon Fishing Station, Babylon

Greenlawn Sport Shop, Greenlawn
Augie's Bait & Tackle, Babylon
Bowman's Sporting Goods, Northport
Fish Unlimited Taxidermy, Babylon
Caraftis Fishing Station, Port Jefferson
Lock 'N Tackle, West Babylon
Sutler's Bait & Tackle, Port Jefferson
Lindenhurst Bait & Tackle, Lindenhurst
Ralph's Fishing Station, Mount Sinai
Z Crab Tackle, Copiague
Dick's Sporting Goods, Mount Sinai
Bob's Bait & Tackle, Amity Harbor
Capt. Al's Bait & Tackle, Miller Place
Edelman's, Farmingdale
Sportsman's Center, Medford
Comb's Bait & Tackle, Amityville
Warren's Archery & Tackle, Centereach
The Store, Oak Beach
Rocky Point Fishing Stop, Rocky Point
Jones Beach Bait Station, Jones Beach
Landmark Food Shop, Wading River
Wanser's Bait & Tackle, Seaford
Fisherman's Deli, Riverhead
Pop's Fishing Station, Seaford
Warren's Tackle Center, Aquebogue
Capt. Eddie's Fishing Station, Seaford
Capt. Marty's Fishing Sta., New Suffolk
Kim's Reef Marina, Seaford
Port of Egypt, Southold
Nick's Fishing Station, Merrick
A.P. White Bait Shop, Greenport
Garan's Bait & Tackle, Merrick

New York State Angling Award Requirements

Skillful Angling Award

Certificate of Achievement suitable for framing awarded to any angler meeting the minimum weight requirements for category.

State Angling Award

A handsome pin recognizing the outstanding catches of anglers who meet the highest standards established for this award.

State Record Award

Anglers establishing a new state record will receive a State Record Certificate denoting their accomplishments as well as a State Angling Award Pin.

Weight Requirements (in pounds)

Species	Skillful Angling Award	State Angling Award
Black Sea Bass	4	5
Blackfish	10	12
Bluefish	18	20
Codfish	40	50
Dolphin	30	40
Flounder (Winter)	3	4
Fluke	10	12
Marlin (Blue)	500	800
Marlin (White)	80	100
Pollock	35	38
Porgy (Scup)	4	5
Shark (Blue)	300	350
Shark (Mako)	400	500
Shark (White)	500	800
Striped Bass	40	50
Swordfish	300	450
Tuna (Bigeye)	250	300
Tuna (Bluefin)	600	800
Weakfish	12	14

LOCATING PARTY, CHARTER, OR RENTAL BOATS

For the most up-to-date information on party, charter, or rental boats, call the chamber of commerce or the state agency with jurisdiction in the area you are interested in visiting (see state agencies, below).

At the various coastal ports, you will find party boats and crews inspected and licensed by the U.S. Coast Guard to take people on coastal fishing cruises. The vessels are equipped with safety and communications devices, and many have electronic systems for depth recording and fish finding. The crews are experienced and knowledgeable about locating fish, and their guidance will help you have a good catch. A charter boat, which is not inspected or certified, carries up to six people and is hired at a fixed price per boat per day. A headboat carries more (average capacity is 30, but at present some carry as many as 100) and operates on a fixed price per person per day or may be chartered for private groups. We recommend advance reservations for trips on either type of vessel.

In Rhode Island, party "head" boats take 39 to 115 persons for bottom-fishing. Reservations are not required and they operate on a set schedule—usually leaving at 6 A.M. and returning at 2:30 to 3 P.M. Tackle may be rented.

Coast Guard regulations are rigid and are strictly

enforced for boat to be registered. Captains must pass qualifications test.

You can pick up headboats in Galilee/Jerusalem, Sakonnet Point, Westerly, and East Greenwich.

Charter fishing boats require prior reservations, and take a number of passengers. They sail at their passengers' bidding. Bait and tackle are provided free in the charter fee. The boats are also available for cruising the coastline.

You can charter boats from Bristol, Watch Hill, Block Island, Newport, Little Compton, with a heavy number of boats operating from Jerusalem and Point Judith.

In Connecticut, party, charter, and rental boats operate out of Clinton, Groton, Old Saybrook, and Stonington, with larger numbers of boats departing from New London, Noank, and Niantic.

Numerous charter boats operate in New York; for a seasonal account of where to fish, and for what, see Fishing off Long Island Through the Year, page 71.

RHODE ISLAND

(Unless otherwise noted, all area codes 401)
Fly-Fishing
On the Fly, 596-1914
Sea Duce, 783-5912
E. Greenwich
Desiderata, 884-3460
Watch Hill
Billfish, (203) 741-3301
Blue Heron, (203) 535-3387
Kingfisher, 596-6350
Wickford
Razin' Kane, 295-0642

Block Island
G-Willie-Makit, (203) 245-7831
Murmo, 466-2814
Sheila L, 466-5000

Point Judith/Jerusalem
Avenger, 789-0049
Bluefin, 737-7271
Cayenne Cay, 792-3581
C.J., 789-8684
Drifter, 294-6303
Earlybird, 789-7596
The Edge, (617) 678-6720
Hot Pursuit, 738-2427
Hooked Up, (203) 276-0503
Joel L, 364-6291
Karuna, 364-8564
Mako Ii, 294-2603
Misty, 789-6057
Never Enough, (203)653-7842
Noodle Too, 461-1032

Old Salt, 783-4805
Pathfinder, 736-8388
Poseidon, 789-1444
Prowler, 783-8487
Reel Time, 783-0049
Restless, 728-2081
Sakarak, 789-8801
Seven B's V, 789-9250
Sundancer, 423-0195
Tuna Fever, 944-1844
Vycore, (914)471-6611
Wet-N-Wild, 941-5562
White Lightning, 568-2558

Newport
Copasetic, 846-0565
Fishing Off, 849-9642
Sundancer, 423-0195

Little Compton
Sportfisherman, 635-4292

STATE AGENCIES

MASSACHUSETTS

Massachusetts Division Of Marine Fisheries
100 Cambridge Street
Boston, MA 02202
 Boston: (617) 727-3193
 Salem: (508) 745-3107
 Sandwich: (508) 888-1155
 Martha's Vineyard: (508) 693-0060

Division of Law Enforcement
100 Nashua Street
Boston, MA 02114
(617) 727-3190
To report a violation: (617) 727-6308 or 800-632-8075

Boat Registration
Division of Law Enforcement
100 Nashua Street
Boston, MA 02114
(617) 727-3900

Massachusetts Office of Travel and Tourism
100 Cambridge St., 13th Floor
Boston, MA 02202
(617) 727-3201

RHODE ISLAND

Rhode Island Tourism Division
7 Jackson Walkway
Providence, RI 02903
(401) 277-2601

Division Of Boat Registration And Licenses
22 Hayes St.
Providence, RI 02908
(401) 277-6647

Department Of Environmental Management
Division Of Fish And Wildlife
Marine Fisheries Section
Government Center, Tower Hill Road
Wakefield, RI 02879
(401) 789-3094

CONNECTICUT

Connecticut Dept. Of Economic Development
865 Brook St.
Rocky Hill, CT 06067
(203) 258-4200

State of Connecticut
Department of Environmental Protection
Bureau Parks and Forests
Boating Safety Education Section
Public Information, Boating Safety Courses
Certification, Boating Publications
Headquarters: (Old Lyme) (203) 434-8638

Bureau of Operations Mangement
Office of Boating Facilities/Navigation Safety
State Boating Law Administrator, Town Boating
Ordinances, Marker Permits, Access Areas,
Navigation Aids
Headquarters: (Portland) (203) 344-2674

Bureau of Fisheries and Wildlife
Division of Law Enforcement
Marine Fisheries
Waterford (203) 443-0166
Accident Reporting, Boating Regulations
Headquarters: (Old Lyme) (203) 434-0316
Agency Boat Patrols
Western District (Harwinton) 485-0226
Eastern District (Marlborough) 295-9523
Marine District (Old Lyme) 434-0316

United States Coast Guard
Station New London 442-4471
Station New Haven 468-4400

Department of Transportation
Harbor/Harbormaster Information
Bureau of Waterways 443-3856

NEW YORK

New York Department of Economic Development
Tourism Division
99 Washington Ave.
Albany, NY 12245
(518) 474-4116

New York State
Office of Parks, Recreation, Historic Preservation,
Marine & Recreational Vehicles
Empire State Plaza
Albany, NY 12238
(518) 474-0445

New York State Department of Environmental
Conservation
Division of Marine Resources
SUNY—Bldg. 40
Stonybrook, NY 11794
(516) 751-7900, ext. 326

LIVE WIDE!

Go ahead. Step over the line. Say good-bye to the ordinary. LIVE WIDE!

It's the secret to getting more out of life. And more out of fishing than ever before. It comes from having a wide-open, go-for-broke attitude...and from having Humminbird Wide™, the broad line of seven feature-packed fishfinders designed to help you see more, see better, and get information easier, quicker, and in a greater variety of ways than you ever imagined.

Whether you fish every day or once a month–inland or offshore–there's a model that's perfect for you. Wide View™, for example, offers value, versatility, and many of our most advanced features such as a Dual Beam Transducer, Fish Location, ID+, and Structure ID™ on a wide screen with outstanding visibility.

So don't get boxed in by conventional thinking or the limitations of ordinary depth sounders. LIVE WIDE! And Fish Wide Open!

AMERICA IS Hummin'
WITH DEPENDABLE CHEVY TRUCKS

Speed and temperature gauge is optional purchase on this model.

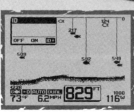

Wide's Menu System is simple to operate. With ID+ turned on, a digital readout of the fish's depth is shown above the fish symbol.

Optional Wide Side shows fish, structure and continuous historical data on both sides of your boat simultaneously, and always displays a digital depth reading.

HUMMINBIRD® WIDE

fish wide open!™

For more information, call 1-800-633-1468.

3

Block Island to Cape May, New Jersey

The section of coast from Montauk Point, Long Island, to Cape May, New Jersey, and seaward out to the edge of the continental shelf, is called the New York Bight. From Montauk Point the shoreline runs westward the entire length of Long Island, a distance of over 100 miles. At about the longitude of New York City, it changes direction sharply and runs southward the entire length of New Jersey, again a distance of over 100 miles.

The eastern end of Long Island marks the beginning of a remarkable estuarine system which extends almost unbroken all the way to Florida. It includes bays, sounds, lagoons, river mouths, tidal streams, and creeks, and extends from the sandy barrier islands which lie between the mainland and the open ocean to the limit of saltwater intrusion—in the Hudson River, for example, nearly 100 miles. New Jersey marks the beginning of a nearly flat, sandy expanse of land, called the coastal plain, which extends southward through Florida and out to the edge of the continental shelf. The sea floor, strikingly uniform for the most part, gently slopes downward at a rate of about 7 feet a mile.

Two channels or canyon systems, one off Block Island and the other off New York City, cut along the sea bottom 100 miles or so from the mainland out to the edge of the continental shelf. These are remnants of ancient river systems which once carried fresh water across what was then dry land. Within 20 miles of land along this section of coast a number of flat-topped, sand-covered hills, commonly called banks, rise as much as 50 feet above the surrounding floor. These banks, as well as the ancient river channels, are favorite gathering places for fishes.

Along the open seacoast of the New York Bight, high and low tides occur twice each day. But owing to the shape of the coastline—an inverted V—the tidal range (i.e., difference in water level between high and low tide) varies. It is highest at the head of the V, the vicinity of New York City, where it is about 5 feet. From there eastward to Montauk and Block Island the range gradually decreases to about 3 feet, southward to Cape May to 4 feet. Tidal ranges in the bays vary from a few inches to a few feet, the one at Jamaica Bay, Long Island, at 5½ feet, being the greatest within the entire New York Bight. Usually large coastal rivers have complicated tidal patterns. At the mouth of the Hudson River the tides range about 5 feet. From there to West Point, 60 miles upriver, they drop progressively to about 3 feet. From West Point upriver all the way to the Troy Dam, 120 miles from the river's mouth, they increase progressively again to a maximum of about 5 feet.

The New York Bight is characterized by two principal seasons, 6 months of warm weather and 4 months of cold, separated by brief fall and spring transitional periods. From May to October, the warm period, the weather usually remains unchanged for several weeks at a time, the prevailing southerly and southwesterly winds keeping the temperature uniformly warm and the humidity high. However, since in summer the air over the sea averages 5°F lower than over land, a change to an easterly wind causes a sharp change in the coastal temperature. This brings relief during hot July and August afternoons when breezes, moving across the cool water, blow in from the sea. These, however, seldom penetrate more than a mile inland. Sometimes, especially in late spring and early summer, the warm, moist air brought northward by the southwesterlies is cooled to form fog. This often sets in without warning and may last for several days, sometimes even a week or more. Even though hurricanes are uncommon, they have been recorded in every month from May through December, being most frequent and severe during August, September, and October. During the fall there is a gradual transition from the high temperatures and mild breezes of summer to the low temperatures and blustery winds announcing the advent of winter. From December to March, the cold period, the weather is variable and marked by frequent shifts in the prevailing northwesterly winds and rapid changes of temperature. The northwesterlies usually blow between 10 and 20 knots, but often increase to about 40 knots as large cold fronts push down from the north. Often while these cold fronts are moving through this area the Intracoastal Waterway and many of the bays ice over. Usually the most devastating northeast storms strike during the cold period, bringing snow or freezing rain. Southerly and southwesterly winds, blowing across the sea with air temperatures 6°F higher than those on land, moderate the weather. During spring, a time of transition, the weather is at first more variable than in winter as air masses change rapidly. With the approach of summer, however, it gradually becomes more stable and warmer.

Migratory fishes tend to gather in areas where temperature and food supply are favorable to their particular needs, and to remain there as long as those conditions persist. Thanks to the wide range of environmental features in the middle Atlantic section a remarkable diversity of sea life gathers here during the course of a year, including boreal, oceanic, tropical, and temperate-water fishes.

All of these fishes are here at the same time during the warmer months. What makes such a diversity possible at that season is the temperature structure of the water, the most striking feature of which is an enormous mass of cool bottom water extending from about Montauk, Long Island, to just south of Delaware Bay. Oceanographers explain this mass as leftover winter water, for it was chilled during the preceding winter and remained cold even after the spring warming of the surface. It is called the Middle Atlantic Cold Cell. Its shape is roughly that of a triangle, of which the vertex is some 6 to 10 miles off Asbury Park, New Jersey; the northern

point is about 20 miles off Montauk; and the southern point is about 45 miles off Delaware Bay.

The summer temperature in the Middle Atlantic Cold Cell ranges from about 45° to 50°F. Boreal or cold-water fishes that can tolerate such cool water inhabit the bottom here. A few of them which are familiar on the New England banks, such as cod and pollock, are permanent residents in this region rather than casual visitors, and probably belong to southern races of their respective species. They are generally sparsely distributed, tending to concentrate around sharp irregularities on the sea floor such as wrecks. In midautumn they begin moving southward about the same time as their northern relatives migrate into the area for the winter. These groups seldom go south of Cape Hatteras or east or north of Nantucket Shoals off Cape Cod.

Meanwhile, the water temperature at the surface overlying the area of the cold cell is 70° to 75°F, and it remains fairly even down to a depth of about 30 to 50 feet. Between this surface layer and the cold cell the temperature generally drops about 10°F or more in just a short distance. This water layer of rapidly changing temperature is called the thermocline.

Oceanic fishes such as the tunas (bluefin, yellowfin, bigeye, skipjack, and albacore), bonito, mackerel, white and blue marlin, mako shark, dolphin, and other species that are independent of the bottom roam in the surface layer throughout the summer. Many of these tend to concentrate just above the thermocline where they find an abundance of food, particularly along the slopes of the canyons.

It is on the landward side of the cold cell, in the shallow water near the shore and in the estuaries, where the greatest concentration of fishes gathers. These species migrate in response to seasonally changing temperatures, their migratory habits varying with species, size, and, in some instances, sex. Bluefish, fluke, sea bass, blackfish, scup, striped bass, and sea trout (locally called weakfish) make up about a third of the total anglers' catch. By far the most abundant of temperate-water migratory fishes visiting here, the menhaden, is not a food or gamefish but has great economic value for manufacture into meal and oil and for bait.

On the ocean side of the cold cell, as we approach the edge of the continental shelf and continue over its slope, we find at the bottom still another assemblage of fishes including many strange and grotesque forms. Although there are many of the same species of boreal fishes that occur in the cold cell, these tend to be much larger. Cod 70 to 80 pounds, white hake 40 to 50 pounds, and pollock 30 to 40 pounds are fairly common so that an angler has a reasonable chance to catch one of these giants.

Thus, from spring into fall, an angler in a seaworthy boat has at his disposal a wide range of fishes—boreal, oceanic, and temperate-water groups. By winter, though the last two of these have left, there are more boreals which have come down from the north.

Many of the fishes now caught off this section of coast were unknown to the natives, for they only fished along the shore with primitive gear. The fishes they found, however, were apparently abundant and they used what they caught to feed themselves as well as to fertilize the soil. Striped bass, shad, sturgeon, eels, and flounders, as well as shellfish, were used for food. Menhaden, an oily fish belonging to the herring family, were put in the soil when planting corn. Indeed, the word menhaden is a modification of an Indian one meaning "that which enriches the earth" or "fertilizer."

FISHING THE METROPOLITAN AREA

The Metropolitan New York region stretches well into Connecticut and down the Jersey Shore and offers some of the world's finest saltwater fishing. There are few other such populated areas that can boast of excellent fishing within easy reach of millions of anglers—and even very few remote areas are blessed with fisheries as abundant and diverse.

It may not be like it was a century ago but, considering the impact of a huge population and the depredations of commercial fishing, there is still very high-quality sportfishing in the Metropolitan New York–New Jersey area for everything from bottom fish to exotic big-gamefish.

What the area has going for it that many others lack is the huge continental shelf between New Jersey and New York. It may be inconvenient for big-gamefishermen to have to run 80 to 90 miles offshore to fish the canyons, but that broad continental shelf attracts vast quantities of bait and predators that aren't available in areas with narrow shelves. Add to that the lengthy "fish traps" known as Long Island and Block Island sounds, and you have a world-class fishery.

Connecticut anglers fish primarily in the sounds and the many rivers and bays emptying into them, though many skippers run offshore past Block Island or Montauk to seek tunas and billfish. New Yorkers have a choice of fishing in the sounds and bays along the north shore of Long Island, or the bays, barrier beaches and offshore grounds of the south shore. The brownish waters of the Hudson River may not look inviting, but they have been cleaned up considerably during the last two decades and maintain a large spawning population of striped bass plus fine fishing for bluefish just a stone's throw from Manhattan's skyscrapers.

New Jersey may be small, but it provides myriad saltwater fishing opportunities in five saltwater regions. At the northern end is the Hudson River-Raritan Bay section. Heading south, the coastline can be divided into three areas, with the northern portion extending from Sandy Hook to Barnegat Inlet being fished pri-

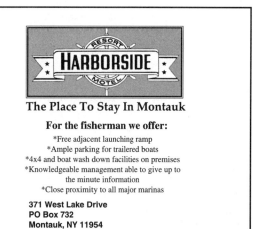

HARBORSIDE
RESORT MOTEL

The Place To Stay In Montauk

For the fisherman we offer:

*Free adjacent launching ramp
*Ample parking for trailered boats
*4x4 and boat wash down facilities on premises
*Knowledgeable management able to give up to the minute information
*Close proximity to all major marinas

**371 West Lake Drive
PO Box 732
Montauk, NY 11954**

marily by anglers from North Jersey, while the central Shore from Barnegat Inlet to Atlantic City and the southern from Atlantic City to Cape May are playgrounds for South Jersey and Pennsylvania fishermen. Finally, there's Delaware Bay, which is covered on page 132.

The prime inshore species through the region are striped bass, bluefish, fluke, winter flounder, blackfish, weakfish, sea bass, porgies, little tunny, bonito, ling and whiting. Offshore targets are bluefin, yellowfin, bigeye and albacore tuna, blue and white marlin, sharks, dolphin, cod and pollock.

The region is just long enough that a few species are common only in certain areas. The burly black drum can be heard drumming beneath the surface on a regular basis in Delaware Bay each spring, while only a few are caught along the Jersey coast and almost none north of Great Bay—though that species was common in Long Island bays a century ago.

Indeed, a number of species have virtually disappeared from the Metropolitan area over the years. The sheepshead was once so common that the famous N.Y.C. party-boat port was called Sheepshead Bay, but that species is rarely encountered north of Virginia any longer. Large red drum, then called channel bass, were an important species for surfcasters on New Jersey's Long Beach Island during the early portion of the century, but the big fish disappeared decades ago, and the capture of an occasional puppy drum in the fall is now considered newsworthy.

As short as the land mass is, there's some variation in fish names from one end to the other. Blackfish is the common Metropolitan name for the species properly known as tautog. The proper name becomes more commonly used in eastern Connecticut, and from South Jersey through Virginia. However, some South Jersey fishermen refer to tautog as slippery bass.

Winter flounders are simply "flounders"—except in Cape May County and the rest of Delaware Bay, where that name is applied to the summer flounder—or fluke, as it's known to the rest of the region. Porgies become known by their proper name, scup, in eastern Connecticut. Little tunny are abused throughout the region by being called false albacore or simply "albacore," which confuses that great-fighting but poor-eating gamefish with the "true" albacore caught in the canyons.

In addition to the species common to the region, many semitropical visitors may be encountered during late summer—especially in the ocean. Spanish mackerel have become a regular summer visitor in recent years, and king mackerel aren't uncommon as far north along the Jersey coast as Barnegat Ridge. Triggerfish often surprise anglers bottom-fishing for blackfish and sea bass, and a few cobia are caught each summer. Very few tarpon catches have been recorded, but several have been removed from fish traps in Long Island Sound.

Saltwater fishing is a year-round sport throughout the region, even if there is very limited activity in February. There can be some very good offshore bottom-fishing plus loads of mackerel in January if temperatures don't fall too fast, and spring flounder fishing in bays and rivers traditionally starts around St. Patrick's Day, though catches are usualy made even before then. From April into December there's a good variety of fishing in every section. Indeed, some of the best occurs during the fall migrations, and most anglers now know enough not to hang up their rods at the end of summer.

An angler in New York and New Jersey does not need a license to fish or crab in salt water. These states, however, have some saltwater regulations and size limits. To obtain copies of fishing and shellfishing regulations, contact the following:

As we've noted previously, and continue to stress, fishing regulations are perishable, often changing from year to year. A prudent angler will check for the latest rules before dropping a hook.

- New York—Department of Environmental Conservation, Division of Marine Resources, SUNY—Bldg. 40, Stonybrook, NY 11794; (516) 751-7900, ext. 326
- New Jersey—Division of Fish, Game and Wildlife, Mail: CN 400, Trenton, NJ 08625; Office: 501 E. State St., Station Plaza 5 (3rd floor); License Information: (609) 292-2966 or 9590

BLOCK ISLAND TO SHINNECOCK BAY

LAND CONFIGURATION AND WATER DEPTH

When Long Island was formed by glacial deposits of soil and rocks many thousands of years ago, its outer coastline was very irregular. The level of the surrounding sea was lower than it is now, but as the glaciers gradually melted, they released an enormous volume of water into the sea, causing its level to rise. As the old shore became inundated and eroded by wave action, currents

The most complete book ever written about our oldest and most popular game fish.....

The Striped Bass

By Nick Karas

Packed into nearly 500 pages is all you'll ever need to know about catching striped bass, from their biology to where to find them and the tackle and gear you'll need to catch them, and illustrated with 180 photographs, drawings and charts. Nick Karas, outdoors columnist for NY Newsday, has chased them for more than 35 years in every state and province where they swim, in both fresh- and saltwater.

"The definitive book on striped bass."....Al Ristori
For anyone who really wants to know the striped bass, this is the book.".......John Cole

Send check/MO for $40.36 (book $35, NYS Tax $2.96, postage/handling $2.40) to: KARMAPCO, PO Box 194, St. James, NY 11780.

carried the sediments westward and deposited them along the coast. During the slow course of erosion and deposition which still continues, the original embayments were closed off, becoming brackish or, sometimes, freshwater ponds. From time to time, however, these have become joined again with the sea as storm-caused waves washed away small sections of the beach to form inlets, which lasted awhile, only to be closed once more by the current-carried sand. Such an opening was cut through the barrier beach to Shinnecock Bay by the 1938 hurricane. This one is likely to remain permanent, for man-made rock jetties have been built there to keep it open.

A narrow neck of land separated Shinnecock Bay from Great Peconic Bay for many thousands of years until the early 1890's, when a man-made canal provided a passage between them. Like Long Island Sound, the Peconic Bays are sheltered by the land and therefore are not subjected to the heavy wave action that affects the exposed south shore beaches. Nonetheless, the environment of the Peconic Bays and the fishes which inhabit them are more characteristic of south shore beaches than of those on Long Island Sound.

Except for Block Channel, a remnant of an ancient river valley, the sea bottom off the southeast coast of Long Island is a gently sloping sandy plain, descending in 4 miles to 90 feet, in 15 miles to 150 feet, and in 60 miles to 300 feet. It is in striking contrast to the topography of the land, where in 2 miles from the ocean beach the elevation gradually rises to 90 feet, in 3 miles to 150 feet, and in 4 miles to 280 feet, its highest point.

FISH AND FISHING

The many kinds of fishes inhabiting the water around eastern Long Island make this area extremely popular for angling. Winter flounder, a resident fish important to bay anglers, grows to a larger size in the Peconic Bays-Gardiners Bay complex than in any other Long Island bay. The name "winter flounder" is derived from the adult flounder's habit of moving into shallow water during cold months and back into deeper water during warm ones. Although most of the adults follow this pattern, some of them, as well as many young ones, remain in these bays year-round. It is only when they cease feeding during peak spawning time that anglers have difficulty catching them.

The habits of tautog or blackfish, another resident species, differ from those of flounder. A fish much smaller than the tautog but in the same family and of similar habits is the cunner or bergall. These fish spend the winter in depths of 90 feet or more, their activity lessening as the water becomes colder. During very cold periods they gather in rocky crevices and wrecks and become dormant. As the water warms during the spring, they become active and move towards shore

into relatively shallow water where they feed throughout the summer. As the water cools during the fall, they move back into deep water and become less active as the winter advances.

During May, as many adult winter flounder are moving offshore, porgies, more properly called scup, begin to migrate inshore after spending winter along the edge of the continental shelf. The larger ones usually are the first to arrive, followed in a week or two by smaller ones. Scup remain here throughout the summer and into mid-fall, then migrate back offshore into deep water to spend the winter. Generally the large ones are the last to leave during the fall. Scup now provide the largest catch of gamefish in this area.

The Peconic Bays-Gardiners Bay complex is the most important northern population center of weakfish (in sections of the coast outside this area, usually called gray sea trout). From the early 1880's to the late 1940's gray sea trout were very abundant in these bays. During the 1930's anglers caught more of them than any other species. Nevertheless, beginning in the late 1940's, their numbers decreased greatly, reaching a low in the mid-1960's. There is now enough evidence of a recovery to offer hope that this excellent gamefish is returning to its former abundance.

Black sea bass and summer flounder or fluke, like scup, migrate here from their wintering grounds along the outer edge of the continental shelf between New Jersey and North Carolina.

Bluefish, ranging in size from young stages to adults of over 3 feet, migrate here each year. The eastern end of Long Island seems to be one of the few areas along the east coast where exceptionally large bluefish occur within casting distance of shore. Striped bass, more coastal in habit than bluefish, are also abundant around the eastern end of Long Island, especially Montauk Point. They spawn in waters from the Hudson River to Chesapeake Bay. Although some overwinter in Long Island estuaries, most return in the fall to their home rivers or along nearby ocean beaches.

Even though cod and pollock live year-round in the cold bottom water offshore, many come inshore to spend the winter. Arriving during fall they move into shallow water, some right to the beaches, though they retreat into greater depths when the water temperature drops to near freezing. Cod are the first to leave the inshore areas as the water warms, usually in March and April. Pollock remain until about June, when they move offshore back into deeper and cooler water. The eastern end of Long Island is the southernmost point on our Atlantic coast where large numbers of adult pollock are found inshore each year.

The presence of large pelagic fishes, such as blue and mako sharks, white marlin, bluefin tuna, and swordfish, make this an excellent area for big-gamefishing. Although these fishes come close to shore in the

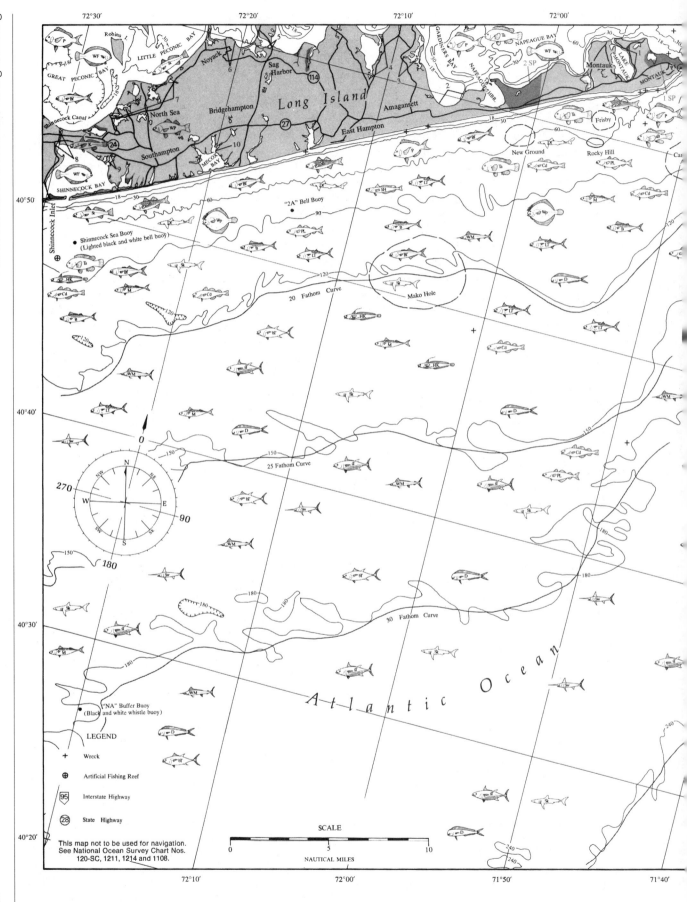

LEGEND

+   Wreck

⊕   Artificial Fishing Reef

95   Interstate Highway

28   State Highway

This map not to be used for navigation.
See National Ocean Survey Chart Nos.
120-SC, 1211, 1214 and 1108.

SCALE

0   5   10

NAUTICAL MILES

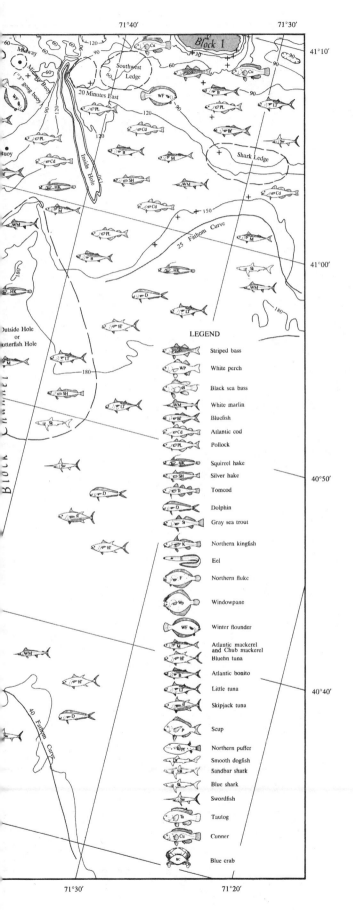

LEGEND

- Striped bass
- White perch
- Black sea bass
- White marlin
- Bluefish
- Atlantic cod
- Pollock
- Squirrel hake
- Silver hake
- Tomcod
- Dolphin
- Gray sea trout
- Northern kingfish
- Eel
- Northern fluke
- Windowpane
- Winter flounder
- Atlantic mackerel and Chub mackerel
- Bluefin tuna
- Atlantic bonito
- Little tuna
- Skipjack tuna
- Scup
- Northern puffer
- Smooth dogfish
- Sandbar shark
- Blue shark
- Swordfish
- Tautog
- Cunner
- Blue crab

warm surface water brought here during periods of prevailing southeast winds, many concentrate between the 300- and 600-foot bottom contours, especially when prevailing northeast winds keep the warm surface water away from land.

SHINNECOCK BAY TO SOUTH OYSTER BAY

LAND CONFIGURATION AND WATER DEPTH

Along this stretch of coast, a series of shallow saltwater and brackish bays varying in widths from a few hundred feet in some places to 5 miles in others lies behind the nearly straight ocean beaches. Quite unlike the deep open bays of New England, these are shallow lagoons, separated from the open sea by long sand bars, called barrier beaches, which nearly parallel the main shore. Connecting these bays with the sea is one large opening, Fire Island Inlet, and two smaller ones, Moriches and Shinnecock Inlets.

Inlets are cut through the barrier beaches on the south shore of Long Island from time to time by storm-caused waves. These inlets last awhile, and then become closed by accumulating sand. New openings are generally formed westward of the site of old ones. Because inlets are important for the passage of both fish and boats, people work to keep them open by dredging them continually and by building jetties. Once marine and estuarine organisms, such as saltwater fishes, clams, and oysters, become established in these bays, their dependence upon the interchange of sea water with bay water continues throughout their lives. When inlets close, these organisms become entrapped and die either when the water gets cold or when it becomes fresh due to the influx from streams emptying into the bays. An example of this occurred in Shinnecock Bay during the 1800's. For many years this bay had an inlet, but in October of 1880 current-carried sand closed it. As a result bluefish, weakfish, porgies, and menhaden were among the many thousands of trapped fishes inside that died from the cold water as winter approached. In the following years the water became progressively so brackish that it would not support a marketable crop of oysters or clams. Indeed, it was the desire to restore the bay's fish and shellfish that prompted the digging of the Shinnecock Canal to Great Peconic Bay in the early 1890's.

Great South Bay, the largest on Long Island, lies behind the 25-mile-long barrier beach called Great South Beach or Fire Island. It is traditional in this area to speak of the ocean side of the bay as "the beach" and of the land side as "the shore." Unlike the nearly straight beach, the shore is scalloped with sandy beaches and

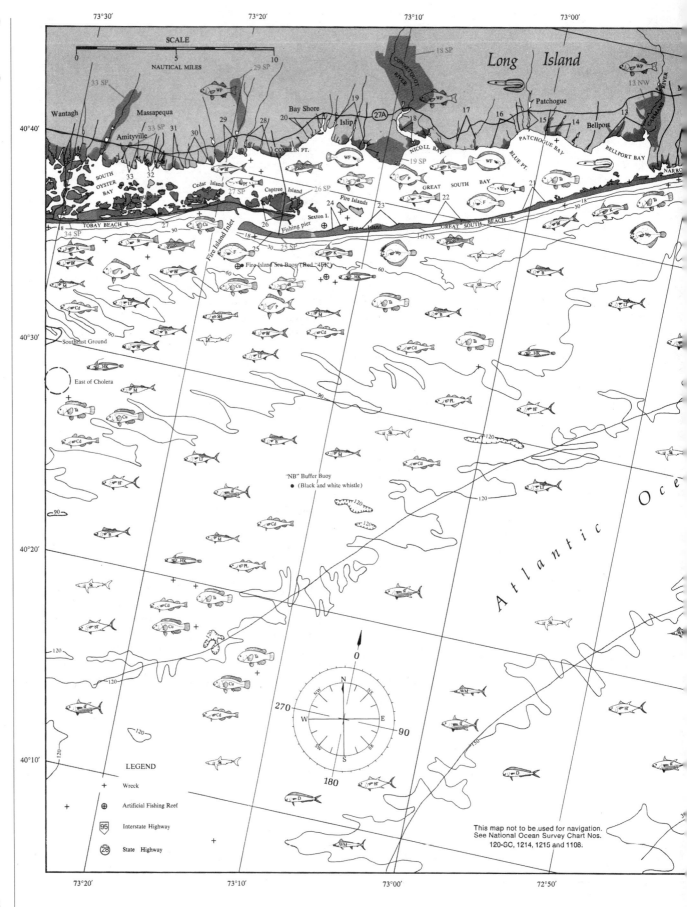

SCALE

0   5   10
NAUTICAL MILES

Long Island

Wantagh
Massapequa
Amityville
Bay Shore
Islip
Patchogue
Bellport

SOUTH OYSTER BAY
CONKLIN PT.
Cedar Island
Captree Island
Fire Islands
PATCHOGUE BAY
BELLPORT BAY
GREAT SOUTH BAY
BLUE PT.

TOBAY BEACH
Fishing pier
Fire Island
GREAT SOUTH BEACH

Fire Island Inlet
Sexton I.
Fire Island Sea Buoy (Red "4FI")

Southeast Ground

East of Cholera

"NB" Buffer Buoy
● (Black and white whistle)

Atlantic Ocean

0

N
NW   NE
270 W   E 90
SW   SE
S
180

LEGEND

+   Wreck

⊕   Artificial Fishing Reef

95   Interstate Highway

28   State Highway

This map not to be used for navigation.
See National Ocean Survey Chart Nos.
120-SC, 1214, 1215 and 1108.

88

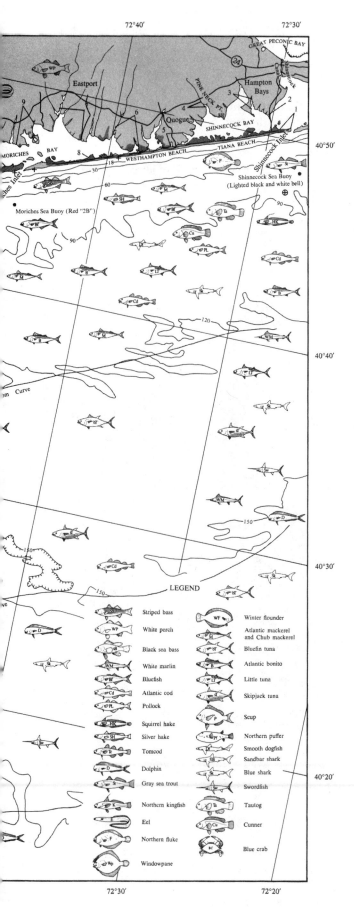

saltmarsh sod banks. Lobelike land formations, called necks, project into the bay and terminate in points. The most notable of these is Blue Point where formerly great quantities of the famous "Blue Point" oysters were dredged and tonged. These necks are interspersed by coves, harbors, and small bays into which flow many creeks and small rivers.

Offshore of Great South Beach the gently sloping sandy sea bottom descends in 5 miles to 90 feet, in 20 miles to 150 feet, and in 65 miles to 300 feet. Between 80 and 100 miles from shore lies the 600-foot bottom contour marking the edge of the continental shelf.

FISH AND FISHING

Of the many kinds of fishes inhabiting Great South Bay each year, winter flounder and fluke are among the most important to anglers. During some seasons within the last 15 years, these two fish made up as much as 90 percent of the anglers' catch. Even though many winter flounder are year-round residents and as such must withstand the cold of winter and heat of summer, their abundance seems to have remained about the same for at least the last 35 years. Each year about a quarter million anglers catch nearly one and a half million winter flounder in this bay. Until 1959 they also caught about the same number of fluke, a summer visiting flatfish averaging three times as heavy as winter flounder. Since then, however, the catch of fluke has declined.

With stocks of cod at near-record lows, anglers in the Metropolitan area are facing a tough search for the winter king. However, there were some indications during the fall of 1994 that there may be more school cod in the southerly extreme of the cod's range than would be expected when the stocks are so low.

Very cold water temperatures created by the severe winter of 1994 dropped the bottom water temperatures into the mid-thirties off the North Jersey Shore, and there was little improvement through the spring and well into the summer. As a result, bottom-fishing for sea bass and blackfish over inshore wrecks was very poor until those bottom temperatures moderated by late summer. However, the one positive effect of that cold bottom water is that it seems to hold school cod in areas they don't normally inhabit after the spring.

Skippers struggling to catch ling (red hake) from wrecks as shallow as 60 feet often caught cod, and those fish were taken with regularity throughout the summer from the deeper Mud Hole wrecks. Early fall may be the least likely time to catch cod in inshore areas (even off Montauk), but Capt. Don Hager Jr. was amazed at the numbers he found in 1994 after switching from fluke to ling fishing with his *Sea Fox* out of Atlantic Highlands, New Jersey.

Wrecks in 100 to 140 feet along the edge of the very northern end of the Mud Hole, not far from New York

City, produced surprising quantities of cod as well as the targeted ling. In seven days in early October, Hager counted 138 legal (19-inch) cod ranging up to 17¼ pounds—with pool winners in the teens every day. That was better codfishing by accident than some boats had the previous winter by design. Such an abundance at an odd time of year could indicate a concentration of cod that may not be migrating north in the spring and could provide better winter fishing than the overall picture would indicate.

Capt. Joe Bogan is one of the few New Jersey party-boat skippers who have stayed with cod every winter regardless of how tough the fishing became. Bogan's *Jamaica II* runs for cod out of Brielle on Wednesdays, Saturdays, Sundays, and some holidays from late November into early spring. During a

marathon Mud Hole ling trip on October 21, 1994, there were about 50 cod caught as anglers concentrated on red hake. That turned out to be a preview of the 1995 winter season, which produced fair numbers of school cod on almost every wreck trip, but very few large fish. It may not have been great, but compared with some of the reports from New England, anglers in the Metropolitan New York area had nothing to kick about.

Back in the "good old days" of Jersey codfishing, it was possible to catch plenty of school cod during the winter on the clam beds. Anglers along the south shore of Long Island also used to open their cod season on open bottom before switching to wrecks, but cracking clams in such areas these days rarely produces anything

(continued on page 92)

A true heavyweight cod from the waters off Montauk, New York. (AL RISTORI)

School cod are often caught during the fall with other species such as sea bass and bluefish. The fisherman is the late Bill Backus, a New Jersey outdoor writer who pioneered saltwater fishing in his state's waters. (AL RISTORI)

Where are they biting?

Subscribe to
The Fisherman and find out!

Only *The Fisherman,* America's premier weekly fishing magazine, can tell you. Up-to-the-minute saltwater reports cover all major coastal fishing centers, pinpointing the action along the beaches on the inshore ridges, wrecks and off-shore in the canyons. A complete reports section for fresh-water enthusiasts tells you where the bass are hitting best, which flies the trout are rising to and provides catch reports from the lakes, streams and rivers in your area.

Reports this current are worth the subscription price alone, but that's not all you get in each big weekly issue of *The Fisherman.* More how-to and where-to articles than any other publication in the country! Written by outdoor writers and the top local fishermen in your fishing area, they instruct you in all phases of fishing from the basics to the latest techniques catching fish "right now!"

But there's even more! Product reviews on electronics, tackle and accessories to help you spend your hard earned dollars more wisely, tournament coverage, tide tables, club information and environmental and conservation news. Haven't you gone without this valuable information long enough? *Subscribe today and save $20 off the news-stand price!*

Five Regional Editions

☐ New England   ☐ Long Island, Metro NY
☐ New Jersey,   ☐ Mid Atlantic
   Delaware Bay   ☐ Florida

Name _____
Address _____
City _____
State _____ Zip _____

☐ 1 Year, 50 Issues $25.00
☐ 2 Years,100 Issues $48.00

Check One: ☐ New ☐ Renewal ☐ Gift
                  ☐ Payment Enclosed ☐ Bill Me Later

Charge To My: ☐ Visa ☐ MasterCard

Account # _____
            Exp Date _____

Please Allow 6-8 Weeks For First Issue!
Send Check or Money Order To:

The Fisherman
14 Ramsey Road, Shirley, NY 11967

91

other than spiny dogfish. Codfishing has become almost exclusively a wreck-fishing proposition from Fire Island to Barnegat, though anglers fishing out of Montauk still find good action on rough bottoms such as the Cartwright Grounds.

One of the advantages of wreck-fishing before the water gets very cold is that the worst of the dogfish plague can be avoided by staying on top of the wreck. Swing off a bit and the dogfish will be on you like locusts. Bergalls (cunners) will often make mincemeat of clam baits on a wreck, but if they're around, cod will eventually beat the burglars to the baits. When the bergall problem is bad, it's helpful to have some conch for bait. Even after being beaten with a wooden mallet, conch is tough enough on the hook to withstand bergalls. It's not as attractive a bait for cod as a juicy skimmer clam—though it's a lot more likely to get hit than a bare hook. Try running a healthy piece of conch on the hook before adding a half-clam.

Cod are quite active when they first arrive but become somewhat lethargic during the depths of winter. Montauk skippers used to load up with school cod off Block Island by diamong jigging them when the fish first arrived and were feeding on sand eels in shallow waters. It's also possible to jig cod well into the winter when there's live bait (particularly herring and squid) around wrecks, but bait is usually the best bet. Furthermore, as bottom waters get colder it's best to let the bait lie on the bottom rather than moving it up and down. When bergalls aren't a problem, some pros tie their rod to the rail and leave enough slack to make up for the swell—only returning occasionally to see if a cod has swallowed the bait.

The first wrecks to produce are usually in the 90- to 100-foot range, while those down to 140 feet tend to be better in mid-winter. Fortunately, the Metropolitan area is loaded with wrecks after two wars and decades of accidents in the shipping lanes. Yet, even with all those wrecks it's often difficult to find one without a boat on it during a pleasant winter weekend. Party boats fish the wrecks constantly during the winter, and one of the big factors in this sport is picking one which hasn't been pounded recently.

The movement of cod isn't great once the waters cool, and it takes time for wrecks to fill in. If boats are on them almost every day it's unlikely that you'll do well. One of the best times to fish wrecks in the winter is after a period of bad weather, which keeps even party boats in port. It may take a day for the bottom to settle, but the best wrecks should then have a new charge of cod ready to feed.

For private boaters, small wrecks are often the key to success as party boats may avoid those which can't provide action around the boat. Smaller boats also have an advantage in that the skipper can "wiggle" around the wreck and often squeeze out enough fish to satisfy a few anglers rather than having to continually move to other wrecks. That's easiest to do by putting out two anchors but can also be accomplished with one anchor on fairly calm days by adjusting the length of the anchor line and cleating it off at various points around the boat in order to cover every nook and cranny of the wreck. If the dogfish aren't too bad (and they do tend to move off as the waters cool), it's also advisable to try drifting alongside the wreck, as cod will sometimes lie on the sand.

A look at scientific reports on the cod stocks is almost enough to turn off even the most ardent winter angler, but that strange fall abundance of school cod in 1994 may well indicate that the Metropolitan area will have some decent fishing for years to come even as entire areas are closed to the north. Large cod certainly won't be as abundant on offshore wrecks as they were a couple of decades ago, but there are always a few around to keep the sport interesting, and party boats usually hit a few bonanza days with the cows every winter.

With warm, well-ventilated cabins and heated rails, party-boat codfishing is no longer a sport just for the rugged. Pick a day without a bad wind forecast, dress warmly, and enjoy a day at sea when most anglers are just sitting and wishing.

Party boats, and a few charter boats, sail for cod throughout the winter out of Captree, Freeport, Point Lookout and Sheepshead Bay, N.Y., plus Belmar and Brielle, N.J. Some fish daily, while others only run on certain days. Montauk used to have a large winter cod fleet, but party boat trips are now often limited to weekends.

LLOYD NECK TO ELBERON

LAND CONFIGURATION AND WATER DEPTH

The low-lying rocky and gravelly shores along the western end of Long Island Sound are indented by bays, harbors, and coves. Most of these indentations are estuaries which open into the Sound, usually with a transition to marshes toward their heads, where streams of fresh water enter. Depths in the Sound decrease from about 140 feet off Lloyd Neck to 50 feet off Throgs Neck, the mouth of the East River. Not a river at all but a narrow channel, the East River holds depths of 40 feet or more for its entire length. At Hell Gate, a constricted area in this channel, the twice-daily high and low tides cause the water to flow at 5 knots or more. This is among the fastest tidal currents along the entire eastern coast of the United States.

For 22 miles between Fort Lee, New Jersey, and Haverstraw, New York, the Hudson River flows through a defile whose western side consists of a precipitous rocky cliff, the Palisades, and whose eastern side consists of steeply sloping hills. Rising in some places over 500 feet straight up from the water's edge, the Palisades' columnar-structured rock cliff of basalt is indeed a spectacular geological formation. The Indians called the Palisades "weehawken," a word describing the fact that the columns of rock resembled rows of trees.

From Upper Bay to about the New Jersey–New York boundary, the Hudson is narrow and deep, being a half to three-quarters of a mile wide and 30 to 50 feet deep. The original beauty of this shoreline is now blemished by hundreds of tumbledown piers and derelict barges hard aground. Northward of there the Hudson widens to over 3 miles in the area of Tappan Zee, Croton Bay, and Haverstraw Bay. Along this stretch, extensive shallow areas, called flats, lie on either side of the 30-foot-deep channel. Large rocks, placed to support railroad tracks, extend into the river in many places along these shores. At the head of Haverstraw Bay in the vicinity of Stony Point the channel deepens again. Northward of here in about a 10-mile stretch many spots are over 100 feet deep, the deepest one at 216 feet, located near West Point at a bend in the river called Worlds End. Throughout the lower portion of the Hudson River, the bottom is characterized by dark-gray mucky clay. Some bars and beaches consist of fine gray sand, a few others of relic oyster shells. Scattered about the bottoms are rocky reefs and boulders and also sunken wrecks.

The 50-mile stretch from the tip of New York City to Verplanck, often referred to as the Lower Hudson, is actually an estuary. The early Dutch settlers realized the saltiness of the Groote or Noort (Hudson) Rivier and distinguished it from the Versche or Fresh Rivier, now called the Connecticut River. Haverstraw Bay, located just south of Verplanck, has fauna and flora that are dominantly marine, including saltwater fishes (bluefish, jack crevalle, bay anchovy, and white mullet), barnacles, crabs, oysters, jellyfish, marine crustaceans and worms, and also seaweeds and saltmarsh grasses. In summer and fall, when freshwater runoff is low, marine organisms predominate 20 miles farther north to Newburgh-Beacon, especially in the channel, where salinities are highest. During times of drought, brackish water extends all the way to Poughkeepsie, permitting marine and estuarine organisms to extend nearly 100 miles inland from New York City in this arm of the sea. Under normal flow conditions aquatic organisms above Poughkeepsie are typically freshwater forms.

Another feature of the Lower Hudson indicative of the sea is its tides. Because the surface elevation of the river is the same for the 150 miles from New York City to Troy, the water level rises and falls twice each day in response to celestial caused tides. During high tide, at times raising the water level 5 feet or more, the Hudson flows "upstream" or north about a knot for 6 hours. Upon ebbing, it flows "downstream" or south at about 1½ knots for the same length of time until the next flood tide. Thus, a block of wood thrown off the Tappan Zee Bridge at the start of flood tide would float first upstream for about 6 miles, then downstream for 9 miles on the ebb. During a tidal cycle of 12 hours the block would cover a total distance of 15 miles but would only be about 3 miles closer to the sea. At this rate it would take 5 days for it to reach the Verrazzano Bridge at the Narrows.

Big, brawny party boats, such as the White Star *out of Barnegat Light, fish nearly year-round in the offshore waters of New York and New Jersey, following the seasons and the fish.* (VIN T. SPARANO)

From the Narrows southward and westward to New Jersey, the mouth of the Hudson estuary is a triangular-shaped bay which the early settlers called Godyns Bay, after Samuel Godyn, one of the supporters of Henry Hudson's expedition. Later, during part of the 1700's and most of the 1800's, it was called New York Bay. Maps today show this 60-square-mile body of water fancifully separated into Lower, Raritan, and Sandy Hook Bays. Low-lying sandy beaches form the bronze-colored shores. The land a short distance behind these shores seldom rises over 100 feet. Elevations of about 300 feet are reached in just two places—the northern end of Staten Island and the Highlands of Navesink in New Jersey. The Highlands is usually the first land sighted when sailing northwest into New York Harbor from offshore. Except for the five major ship channels, which are dredged to 30 feet, depths rarely exceed 25 feet in Godyns Bay. Separating Staten Island from New Jersey are two narrow channels called the Arthur Kill and the Kill Van Kull. "Kill," incidentally, is the Dutch word for channel, creek, or stream. The shallow areas on either side of these channels, as well as the adjoining wetlands, called meadows, are lined with hundreds of relic barges and boats, some partially submerged and others floating, which have been abandoned by their owners. Flowing into the Arthur Kill and Kill Van Kull is the water from Newark Bay, which in turn is fed by the Passaic and Hackensack Rivers. In these rivers and kills as well as in shallow Newark Bay, the water oscillates according to tidal currents with a slight net movement towards the sea.

Low, sandy barrier beaches abut the Atlantic Ocean along the south shore of Long Island and along New Jersey. Built by the deposition of marine sediments, south shore beaches owe their existence to westward-flowing currents carrying material eroded from Long Island's eastern end. Inlets that cut through the beaches usually extend a little farther to the west each year as deposits accumulate. In the last 125 years Rockaway Inlet and East Rockaway Inlet have both moved 4 miles to the west. Along the New Jersey shore, sediments are carried northward by prevailing currents. Sandy Hook has actually increased by more than a mile during the last 200 years.

Unlike the plain sand beaches east of Jones Inlet, those of Long Beach, Atlantic Beach, and Rockaway Beach on Long Island, and from Sandy Hook south to Asbury Park along New Jersey are intensively jettied or groined. Built of rock or creosoted wood, most of the jetties extend a few hundred feet into the ocean. Behind the barrier beaches lie shallow embayments consisting of both open waters and marshes. Examples of this are South Oyster Bay, Hempstead Bay, and Jamaica Bay on Long Island and the Navesink and Shrewsbury Rivers in New Jersey. These extremely nutrient-rich areas extend inland 1 to 6 miles before they give way to drylands.

Off Long Island the sandy bottom gently slopes

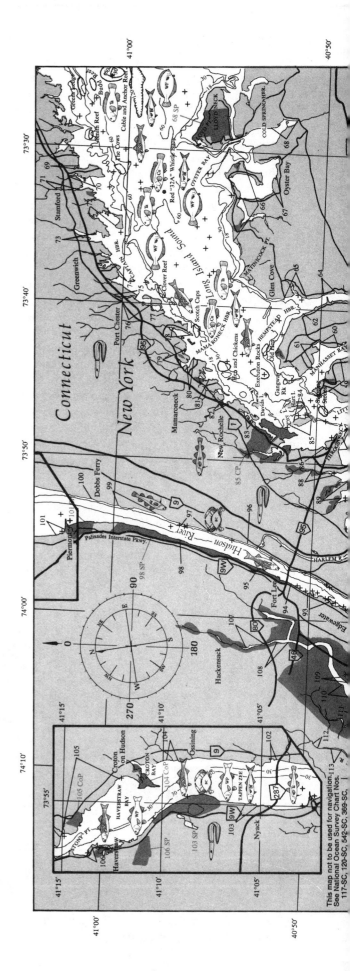

SCALE

NAUTICAL MILES

down from shore to 90 feet in 10 to 15 miles. Off Sandy Hook it reaches that depth in only 6 miles, and then, within a mile or two farther, drops to over 200 feet. This naturally occurring depression, called the Hudson Gorge or Hudson Channel, can be easily traced 100 miles across the entire continental shelf. An extension of the Hudson River, this gorge was carved out many thousands of years ago during glacial times. Its head is first discernible at an area fishermen call the Mud Hole. Particles of silt, clay, and mud brought down by the Hudson settle out and collect in this deep depression, hence the name. The Hudson Gorge is bounded on either side by the great plateau of the continental shelf.

FISHING GROUNDS

The various fishing grounds adjacent to the New York metropolitan area are among the most intensively fished in the world. Since first fishing these waters, people have found that fish tend to concentrate more consistently in some areas than in others. Many of these areas, which fishermen call spots, banks, or grounds, are characterized by outcrops of rocks and large boulders which interrupt the otherwise smooth sandy bottom. The irregular shapes of rocks provide not only convenient hiding places for many fishes but also a suitable substrate for the attachment of sessile food organisms such as mussels, barnacles, and tube-building worms.

Such grounds as Shrewsbury Rocks, 17 Fathom Bank, Cholera Bank, Southeast Ground, and the Stone Pile are part of a naturally occurring, horseshoe-shaped, rocky submarine reef that extends from the Shrewsbury River in New Jersey to about East Rockaway Inlet on Long Island. Much of this reef remains covered by sand with only scattered protruding portions. Other rocky areas such as Southwest Ground, Scotland Ridge, Lump or Sea Gull Bank, New Grounds, Subway Rocks, Lightship Ridge, and the Tin Can Grounds are old dumping grounds for excavated materials, building rubble, and garbage, of which only the insoluble material remains.

The hulls of hundreds of vessels—many broken, twisted, and smashed—and the cargoes they carried are equally effective in providing shelter for fishes and attachment surfaces for food organisms. Wooden ribs, the skeletons of old schooners and square riggers, still lie on the bottom. From 1839 to 1848, over 300 vessels were wrecked along the shores of New York and New Jersey. Steel hulls deteriorate more slowly than wooden ones, and a great many have gone down in these waters, especially during World Wars I and II when shipping was unusually heavy and enemy submarines were active. Over 10 torpedoed ships sank within a mile of New Jersey's beaches during World War II alone. Even now hardly a year goes by without a tug, barge, or ship going down because of storm, fog, or man's carelessness.

The attraction of fish to these wrecks and rock outcrops has inspired biologists from state and federal governments as well as cooperating sportfishing groups to establish artificial reefs. Fishes that inhabit reefs have a strong sense of territoriality, and since the total area of natural and accidental reefs is limited, it follows that by providing more living space, new reefs increase the population potential of fishes. Even species that do not inhabit reefs benefit from them by feeding on the resident reef fishes. The artificial reef 3 miles off Atlantic Beach, Long Island, is one of the largest along the eastern coast. It now consists of over 30,000 automobile tires, 500 tons of concrete culvert, 400 junk automobiles and trucks, and 8 large barges, and its size continues to increase with the addition of more material.

Some of the fishing grounds, famous for certain species, have in recent years undergone name changes. An example of this is the bluefish grounds off New Jersey. From at least the early 1600's to the mid-1700's, bluefish were plentiful along our coast. Then they disappeared, presumably from natural causes, and were not seen again for about 70 years. When they did reappear, no one knew what they were. Soon, however, people welcomed them, and fishing smacks, many of them equipped with livewells, were sailing out from Fulton Fish Market about 25 miles south to grounds where bluefish often congregated. The largest of these grounds, called Fishing Bank, covers the offshore side of the areas anglers now call Shrewsbury Rocks, Long Branch Ground, West End or Elberon Ground, and England Bank. Another old bluefish ground, Rocky Spots in the Channel, is now called 17 Fathom Bank, and Rocky Ground is now called The Farms.

Before the early 1800's boats rarely had to go outside the range of Sandy Hook Light to catch sea bass, a favorite fish then in great abundance. As fishing pressure in Lower Bay and along the shore increased, the yield followed the usual course of overexploitation. The catch per fisherman, and eventually the total catch, decreased so that fishermen were forced to go offshore to seek concentrations of fish. By randomly searching they slowly discovered the various grounds where fish congregate. One of the better grounds was found in 1832 when a boat dropped anchor on a rocky spot that proved to abound with large sea bass. The captain quickly signaled other boats to share his good fortune. Because it was such a good ground, the fishermen decided to give it a name, and because it was the time of a great cholera epidemic, they called it Cholera Bank. Although the original location of this ground lies about 17 miles east of Sandy Hook, boat captains now refer to another part of the reef, 5 miles to the northeast, as Cholera Bank. Located on the same submarine reef are two grounds west of Cholera, Middle Ground and Angler Bank, and one to the east, appropriately called East of Cholera. Since these grounds are defined as being located so far west or east of Cholera Bank, their positions change when Cholera Bank's does.

Ever since making a comeback during the late-1950's, bluefish have been the most important gamefish in the Metropolitan area. Blues provide everything an angler could want in a gamefish—they bite readily, fight hard, jump and are good eating. Unfortunately, their very abundance during peak years of the current cycle led many to downgrade bluefish as they interfered with catching other species such as striped bass and weakfish.

Now that we're in a period of declining bluefish populations, that attitude may change. While blues remain incredibly abundant during the spring migration through the Metropolitan area, summer fishing has tended to become spotty—and the fall migrations have been poor. Whether this indicates that another cycle is coming to an end or that it's just a matter of a few poor spawning years combined with too much fishing pressure is a matter of speculation. What we do know is that it would be a very big shock to present-day anglers to be left with virtually no adult bluefish as was once the case.

When populations become scarcer, they tend to contract in range. That likelihood will leave the Metropolitan area in relatively good shape since catch statistics have long indicated that a large proportion of the catch is taken here. Large party- and charter-boat fleets from the south shore of Long Island and along the northern portion of the Jersey Shore rely heavily on day and night bluefishing throughout the long season from May to October or even November.

Blues arrive right behind the spring mackerel run, when surface water temperatures go over 50 degrees. The first few could be caught at Cape May by the third week in April, but party boats there don't start night-chumming until the end of the month. Blues may also appear at inlets up to Manasquan by the end of April or the first week in May, and they tend to flood into the warmer waters of Great, Barnegat and Raritan bays almost immediately. Indeed, the Shrewsbury and Navesink rivers often get a shot of big blues before Raritan Bay gets hot.

That action quickly spreads to the south shore of Long Island, but eastern areas take a bit longer to heat up. Gardiners Island is one of the first northern areas to get a run of blues, and they soon spread into Peconic Bay and finally into the cooler waters of Long Island Sound—where the best fishing doesn't occur until June.

The fall fishery works in the opposite direction, with the Sound emptying out as those schools swarm past Montauk Point along with others moving south from New England. Bluefish tend to follow the coast as their journey takes them to areas south of Hatteras or offshore.

While spring fishing for blues has been excellent the last few years, there's been a substantial fall-off during

Big catamaran-hulled Miss Barnegat Light *is exceptionally fast and stable in heavy seas. Like many New Jersey and New York party boats,* Miss Barnegat Light *fishes daily during warm-weather months for a variety of fish.* (VIN T. SPARANO)

the summer—and the fall fishery has been a big disappointment. There is some indication that large bluefish have been migrating farther offshore, as deepwater wrecks are often covered with them in November and December. Most blues leave easterly areas during November, but it's not unusual to catch them in early December along the Jersey Shore.

Metro party- and charter-boat bluefishing has traditionally been a chumming fishery. Ground mossbunker is ladled over by party boats, while charter and private boats generally hang a frozen bucket of chum over the side and let it thaw gradually to form a slick. Some chunks may be added to the slick, and anglers drift their lines out with chunks of bunker, mackerel, butterfish or almost any other available fish. Chumming can be done from anchor or on the drift, with drifting being more popular in open areas and anchoring most common on lumps, ridges, and rough bottoms. Weights aren't used on the lines except when split-shot is needed during strong currents.

Tackle requirements for chumming vary with the size of the fish and conditions. Light spinning or bait-casting gear is ideal, but not practical in a party-boat situation. Boat rods with small conventional reels filled with 20- to 30-pound mono are fine on party boats where heavier tackle enables anglers to keep tangles to a minimum and permits swinging smaller blues aboard without being gaffed.

When sand eels were abundant from the 1970's well into the 1980's, diamond jigs were very effective on bluefish and party boats often got away from using chum or bait altogether. Skippers simply chased birds working over feeding bluefish or spotted readings on graph recorders before anglers dropped jigs to the choppers. That situation has changed greatly in the last few years as sand eels have all but disappeared in many areas and diminished greatly even in their more natural

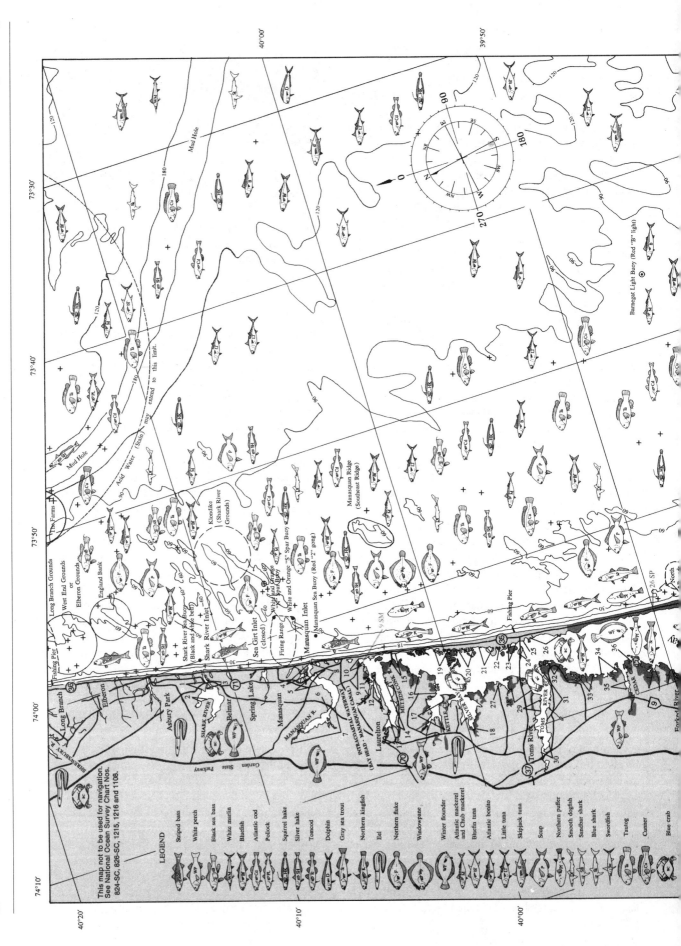

This map not to be used for navigation.
See National Ocean Survey Chart Nos.
824-SC, 826-SC, 1215, 1216 and 1108.

LEGEND

Striped bass
White perch
Black sea bass
White marlin
Bluefish
Atlantic cod
Pollock
Squirrel hake
Silver hake
Tomcod
Dolphin
Grey sea trout
Northern kingfish
Eel
Northern fluke
Windowpane
Winter flounder
Atlantic mackerel
and Chub mackerel
Bluefin tuna
Atlantic bonito
Little tuna
Skipjack tuna
Scup
Northern puffer
Smooth dogfish
Sandbar shark
Blue shark
Swordfish
Tautog
Cunner
Blue crab

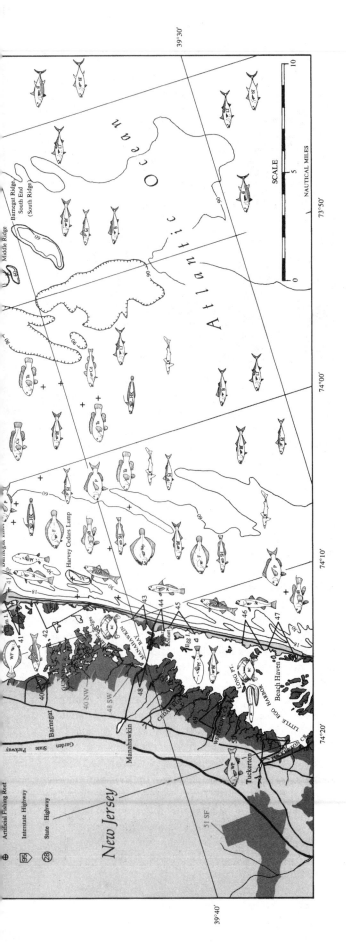

settings toward the east. Jigs are still very effective at times but just can't compete with bait most days.

Trolling is a standard technique that never goes out of style. Most blues caught off Montauk and in Block Island and Long Island sounds are taken in that fashion. When Capt. Gus Pitts developed the umbrella rig for Montauk striped bass, it turned out to work even better on the bluefish that were feeding on sand eels. With the change in baitfish, umbrella rigs aren't quite as good as they used to be but are still among the best lures. Blues will hit just about anything at times, including lead-head jigs, small spoons and tubes.

Early-season bluefishing is a surface fishery, as the blues move inshore and stay in the warmest surface waters. Trolling Bombers and other small plugs is effective at that time, as is casting those lures to blues finning on the surface. As the water column warms the blues go deeper and it's necessary to switch to downriggers, wire line or planers in order to hook them in quantity.

Bait-fishing is popular in many areas to the east as drail rigs with half or whole herring, ling, whiting, bunkers, etc. are fished near the bottom at The Race, Cartwright Grounds, and other rough bottom spots by boats from eastern Long Island and Connecticut. This technique works best in the summer and fall, and is also utilized to some extent at Metro deep water areas such as The Farms and 17 Fathoms. Live baits, such as bergalls and sea bass caught on the spot, are a prime bluefish attraction.

ELBERON TO BEACH HAVEN

LAND CONFIGURATION AND WATER DEPTH

The shoreline from Long Branch to Manasquan Inlet is low country, typical of the Atlantic Coastal Plain. The land within a mile or so of the beach usually rises between 20 and 40 feet—exceeding 100 feet in only three localities. Interrupting the otherwise straight, sandy shoreline are a few small freshwater streams that flow into the sea. The largest and most important of these is Shark River. Dredged to 4½ feet in the channel, it is the only small-boat haven in the 25 miles between Sandy Hook and Manasquan. The narrow inlet at the mouth of the river tends to shoal with sand and is kept open by periodic dredging. Where once only sand beaches and dunes lined this stretch of coast, it is now lined with small jetties.

Manasquan Inlet, the next break in the shoreline, is the northernmost point of the Intracoastal Waterway which continues on to Key West, Florida. Manasquan River and Inlet derive their names from the

Shorebound fishermen have a choice of numerous jetties, where bluefish, stripers, and fluke are always within range. The best jetties range from Sandy Hook south to Barnegat Inlet. This angler fights a bluefish from the south jetty at Barnegat Inlet. (VIN T. SPARANO)

Local Toms River expert Pete McLain, at the wheel, found this keeper striper for Dennis Phillips. The bass hit a surface plug cast into pockets along a jetty. (VIN T. SPARANO)

Indian word "Manatahsquawhan," meaning "Stream of the Island for Squaws." During summer and fall months, when various tribes journeyed to the coast, the women and children camped there to gather shellfish and beach plums while the men fished and hunted nearby.

South of Manasquan Inlet, a series of sandy barrier beaches stretches out in front of the mainland and intercepts the sea. Behind these beaches are protected shallow estuaries, the longest one being Barnegat Bay, whose name is a corruption of the Dutch "Barende-gat," meaning "Breakers Inlet." Barnegat Bay has three openings—Little Egg Inlet and Barnegat Inlet, which were both formed by nature, and Bay Head-Manasquan Canal, which was man-made in 1925. Once there was another one, Cranberry Inlet, that had been cut through the beach by a storm in 1750. It was sufficiently wide and deep to provide safe passage for large square-rigged sailing vessels. Unfortunately, current-carried sand finally closed it off in 1812.

FISH AND FISHING

All marine fishes undergo periodic fluctuations in abundance, and striped bass are no exception. Judging from early 19th-century accounts, stripers and their close relative, white perch, occurred at the northern end of Barnegat Bay, especially about the Metedeconk River, in such large numbers as to keep nearly 200 men busy fishing for them. Fishermen sometimes took 15,000 to 20,000 pounds in a day, once even 80,000 pounds in a

single catch. In 1880, the first year in which fishing statistics were recorded, the total catch on the Metedeconk was over half a million pounds. During the first third of the 1900's, however, the abundance of stripers all along the middle Atlantic coast declined. After reaching a low point about 1933 they staged a remarkable recovery and have fluctuated ever since. Among all our coastal fishes, the striper appears to be the most resilient.

Here, as along all the ocean beaches of the middle Atlantic states, scup, northern fluke, sea bass, tautog, bluefish, bonito, and tunas are important summer fishes. But as these temperate- and warm-water species are migrating to their wintering grounds offshore or to the south, cold-water or boreal species, like the cod and its relatives, the silver hake, squirrel hake, and white hake, take their place.

People tend to associate cod with the North Atlantic banks of New England and Canada, as well as the cold waters of Iceland, Greenland, and northern Europe. To them, the catching of cod off New Jersey and even southward as far as North Carolina comes as a surprise. But actually cod are only to be expected, for the bottom-water temperature off this stretch of coast falls within their limits of tolerance—the year round off the coast of New Jersey and during the winter and spring farther south.

Bluefish have been the most important species in the Metropolitan area for decades, but the striped bass is the species most desired by inshore anglers. That applied to the years of great scarcity during the 1980's and is even truer now that stripers are making a big comeback after years of protection under plans devised by the Atlantic States Marine Fisheries Commission and backed by federal law.

Excellent striper fishing is available throughout the region, but it tends to get better to the north and east. Montauk has long been justly famous for quantities of large stripers, and the western end of Long Island Sound is hard to beat for the volume of schoolies due to its proximity to the spawning areas of the Hudson River.

Though most anglers think in terms of the migratory run of stripers, there is fishing available for that species throughout the year within the Metropolitan area. December is often the best month for stripers along the Jersey Shore, and power-plant hot-water discharges maintain winter fisheries at Northport on Long Island's north shore and in Connecticut's Thames River. The Thames winter fishery used to be so good that some local fishermen made a living catching bass for the market before the species was made a gamefish in Connecticut.

New Jersey, where stripers have also been accorded gamefish status, gets the first of the Chesapeake migratory run. A few decades ago there were good catches of schoolies on seaworms fished in the surf during March, but it's rarely worth looking for them before April these days. A new fishery has been developed during April in the Cape May Rips, where party and charter boats drift jigs across the sandy rips to catch mostly school bass.

Stripers start spreading into all areas along the Jer-sey Shore and the south shore of Long Island during April, with the Chesapeake fish being joined by those leaving the Hudson River. The Hudson fishery comes alive at that time and should be hot into mid-May. The river was once known almost exclusively for the quantities of small bass that could be caught on worms, jigs, and small plugs. However, some super-size stripers have been boated the last couple of years. The early action centers around Croton-on-Hudson but is also good quite a bit upriver from there. Trolling large plugs is an effective means of catching larger bass.

Lots of schoolies are also available in the western end of Long Island Sound during April, as many of the Hudson fish migrate out through the East River. The Greenwich, Connecticut, area offers excellent habitat for those early bass, and flyrodders score heavily in the shallow waters.

Stripers are available throughout the region by May, and fishing continues into November. Spring and fall migrations provide the fastest action, but it's possible to do very well during the summer with special techiques such as using live bunkers off ocean jetty tips and along rocky Long Island shorelines, bunker chunking off Sandy Hook, clam belly chumming in South Shore bays and inlets, and live eels at night in the Montauk Rips, Plum Gut, The Sluiceway and The Race.

The fall migration usually provides the best action of the year as hungry bass chase schools of bait to the

Robbie's Marine Service

Mercruiser   Yanmar Diesel

Factory Authorized Sales and Service
Factory Trained Certified Technicians

*Electrical Repairs * Sales and Installation of Electronics
*Haul-Outs * Spring Recommission *Winterizations
*Shrink Wrapping * Repowers *Rewiring
*O/B motor Installations

405 Broadway Ave. Barnegat Light, N.J. 08006
Phone: 609-494-4801

The Only Logical Choice

MARINE PARTS AND ACCESSORIES

south. When schools are located under flocks of diving birds, it's possible to catch one after another of varying sizes on diamond jigs, lead-head jigs, tiger tails, nordic eels and other weighted lures. Poppers are more fun but are hard to work when there are so many birds around.

Trolling with wire line is the most dependable technique. Umbrella rigs, lead-head jigs, long tubes and bunker spoons are most commonly trolled during the day, while large plugs and artificial eels are popular at night, when larger bass tend to hit. Trolling accounted for the vast majority of bass caught at Montauk until recently when almost the entire charter fleet switched to fishing bunker chunks at anchor in the rips in October and November.

Anglers trolling open bottom off the sand beaches of western Long Island and northern New Jersey target big bass by using huge bunker spoons, and that fishery can continue into early December. The Cape May Rips provide a last shot at the Chesapeake and Delaware Bay stocks as they head into wintering areas. Rather than employing the jigs used in April, anglers fish live eels and often catch great numbers of bass while making short drifts through the rips.

Stripers can be caught in so many inshore areas and by so many techniques that it's little wonder they're so popular with Metropolitan anglers. Even in downtown Manhattan it's possible to catch schoolies off the piers at night or by fishing lures or bait off such obvious locations as Ellis Island and the Statue of Liberty.

BEACH HAVEN INLET TO CAPE MAY

LAND CONFIGURATION AND WATER DEPTH

From Beach Haven Inlet to Cape May the shoreline is formed by a number of low-lying, sandy barrier islands that vary from 3 to 7 miles in length and from a few hundred yards to 1½ miles in width. They are separated from each other by shoals and inlets and from the mainland by a network of saltmarshes and shallow estuaries which is usually several miles wide. By tradition the irregularly shaped saltmarshes are called meadows or sedges and the large patches of open estuarine water, bays and sounds. When viewed from a high-flying airplane, narrow interconnecting waterways, often called thoroughfares, form a kind of lattice work. Along this stretch of coast there are only two places where sizable rivers join and flow to the sea. One, the Mullica River and its important tributaries, Wading and Bass Rivers, flows into Great Bay. The other, Great Egg Harbor River, is joined by the Middle and Tuckahoe Rivers near its mouth before flowing into Great Egg Harbor Bay.

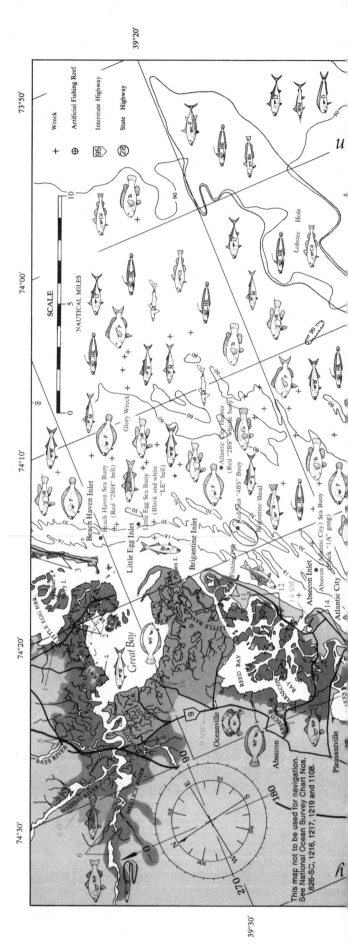

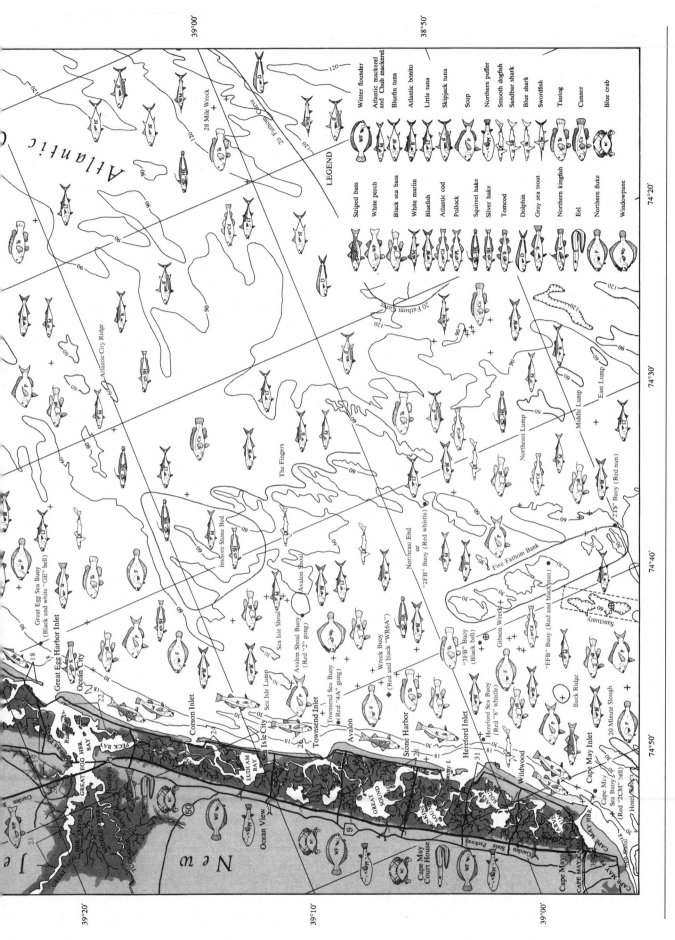

LEGEND

Winter flounder	Striped bass
Atlantic mackerel and Chub mackerel	White perch
Bluefin tuna	Black sea bass
Atlantic bonito	White marlin
Little tuna	Bluefish
Skipjack tuna	Atlantic cod
Scup	Pollock
Northern puffer	Squirrel hake
Smooth dogfish	Silver hake
Sandbar shark	Tomcod
Blue shark	Dolphin
Swordfish	Gray sea trout
Tautog	Northern kingfish
Cunner	Eel
Blue crab	Northern fluke
	Windowpane

Off this section of New Jersey, the sea bottom slopes downward at a moderate rate to a depth of 35 feet about a mile offshore. From there to about the 300-foot bottom contour, located 60 miles farther offshore, the descent is very gradual. For the most part the bottom over this part of the continental shelf is virtually a level sandy plateau, interrupted by scattered shoals, the most famous and extensive of which is Five Fathom Bank. This series of gullies and sand mounds, some of which rise to within 17 feet of the surface, has been an excellent fishing ground for nearly 300 years.

FISH AND FISHING

As the cold, strong northwest winds of winter subside and the weather becomes milder, ocean temperatures begin to rise. When the water over the inner third of the continental shelf reaches about 45° or 46°F, sometime early in April, Atlantic mackerel usually arrive inshore. After overwintering at mid-depths in the warm band of water overlying the outer edge of the continental shelf, they migrate inshore and begin feeding on the profusion of zooplankton, primarily copepods.

Within the western North Atlantic there are two groups of Atlantic mackerel, northern and southern, which together have a range from Newfoundland to North Carolina. They have different wintering and summering areas and different routes to reach them. The southern group, which occurs off this stretch of coast, comes in from offshore towards New Jersey during spring, beginning to spawn en route over the continental shelf. The spawning is heaviest, however, off New Jersey and Long Island where the adults pause for a month or so before passing eastward to Nantucket Shoals and eventually, about midsummer, into the western part of the Gulf of Maine.

Unlike the adults, juvenile mackerel spawned off New Jersey remain through the summer, apparently in or near the area where they were hatched. We know this because tuna and other large pelagic fishes caught off Cape May, Atlantic City, and Beach Haven are often gorged with mackerel 2 to 6 inches long.

While bluefish and striped bass are the glamour fish in the Metropolitan area, blackfishing is very popular with a great many anglers who not only enjoy the challange but also the great eating.

Tautog (as blackfish are known outside the Metropolitan area) move very little throughout their lives, and each area has a separate population with little observable interchange. Though very prolific, they've been hard hit by a sharp increase in commercial fishing. Nevertheless, when water temperatures and currents are right it's still possible to make large catches of this fine sport and food fish. Blackfish live only on rough bottoms and follow an inshore-offshore pattern. Adults winter in the warmer depths and become relatively inactive after January before moving inshore during April and ending up in very shallow waters by May and June. They then become fairly inactive again during the summer before feeding heavily throughout the fall as the movement offshore commences.

Crabs are the usual baits for blackfish, though soft baits such as clams and worms are often preferred early in the spring when the fish are reputed to have "soft mouths" and, most importantly, bergalls still haven't become active. Bergalls, members of the wrasse family, are small cousins to the tautog, and they eat soft baits so quickly that it's often almost impossible to fish through them after the waters warm a bit. They'll also work on crabs, but it takes a bit longer and gives blacks a chance to look over the bait.

Since rough bottom is the key to this fishery it's not surprising that only certain portions of the region have exceptional blackfishing. The entire length of rocky Long Island Sound is ideal tautog habitat, and the list of good areas on both sides of the Sound is endless. Eaton's Neck at Huntington, Long Island has long been famed for its volume of blackfish, and Orient Point at the end of Long Island's North Fork is justly famous for the big blacks it produces—especially in the fall. From there you can fish Plum Gut, Plum Island and Great Gull Island waters. The many reefs along the Connecticut shoreline, such as Cockenoe off Norwalk and Bartlett's off Waterford, provide excellent blackfishing. However, there are so many small spots which provide blackfish habitat in the Sound that anyone with a fishfinder can look around and often locate his own honey hole. Check out areas where you see lobster pots, as those critters utilize similar habitat.

Blackfishermen in the New Haven area don't even need fishfinders to work one of the best spots in the Sound. New Haven Harbor is protected by three large breakwaters which provide shelter for great quantities of tautog. Boaters usually anchor with a grapple from the bow into the rocks and hold themselves off with a stern anchor. This fishery is best on calm days or in northerly winds. A $14\frac{3}{16}$-pounder was caught there recently.

Montauk is surrounded by rocky areas that hold plenty of blackfish. The outer portions of Shagwong Reef and Cerebus Shoals are good local areas, but the best late fall fishing occurs over toward Block Island at Southwest Ledge where 5- to 8-pounders are often caught in quantity around slack water. Strong currents, especially during the new and full moon, make it impractical to fish Southwest Ledge at times, so time your trip for two hours before and after the slack.

The generally sandy south shore of Long Island isn't prime blackfishing country, but you'll find plenty of those fish on inshore wrecks, at inlet jetties and around bridge pilings. Some of the most productive wrecks along the beach from Fire Island to Jones inlets, such as the Rota and Tea, are so shallow they can be seen on calm, clear days.

The North Jersey coast is once again prime blackfish territory as there are many rocky areas from Sea Bright to Deal plus loads of wrecks and great deep-water wintering habitat at 17 Fathoms and the Farms. Shrewsbury Rocks has long been famed as a shallow-water blackfishing ground, and the Rattlesnake just offshore of it holds blacks in its 60-foot depths into December or even January if the waters don't cool too fast. Though tautog aren't supposed to be active in such cold waters, winter water temperatures in the mid-40's are fine for the 17 Fathoms fishery, which features lots of 5- to 10-pounders.

Jetties along the North Jersey coast are also very good for shore fishermen, while others fish the rocks at Shark River, Manasquan and Barnegat inlets. Wrecks in 90-foot depths off Barnegat Inlet produce the largest blackfish in North Jersey waters early each spring. Tautog of 10 to 16 pounds are relatively common catches, and most are caught on skimmer clam because there are few bergalls on those wrecks.

South Jersey is sandy and not ideal for tautog, but there is some fine wreck-fishing and the slightly warmer water temperatures provide a longer growing season, which results in some large specimens of this long-lived but very slow growing species. The world record of 21-pound, 6-ounce tautog taken by R.N. Sheafer off Cape May on June 12, 1954, lasted for decades before even larger blacks were discovered on wrecks off Virginia a few years ago.

Techniques for blackfish vary little throughout the region. Except for the early spring fishing, it's basically a matter of getting a half or whole green crab (blue-claw and calico crabs are often substituted in South Jersey) or a fiddler crab to bottom and waiting for the nibbling with the protruding front teeth that characterizes a blackfish bite. After that there's a more solid pull as the bait goes back to the crusher teeth in the throat before the shells (and your hook) are spit out. The strike must be at the precise moment the bait is in the mouth or you'll come up with an empty hook. That's what makes blackfishing such a challenge and results in a few anglers scoring big while others only watch. With large tautog, the next challenge is to get them out of the rocks or wreck right away before they break you off.

Anglers who don't have their own boats can sail with the many party- and charter-boat skippers who specialize in blackfishing. Be sure to check ads in newspapers and weekly fishing magazines in order to be sure the skipper carries crabs and will be sticking with blackfish rather than splitting time with other species.

FISHING REGULATIONS

What follows are abstracts of fishing regulations for New York and New Jersey. This information should be used for general purposes only. Because regulations change frequently, and because the regulations themselves are far more detailed than presented here, all anglers should contact the state agencies listed at the beginning and end of this chapter.

NEW YORK

A synopsis of New York fishing regulations, including tournament information and special angling programs, begins on page 58.

NEW JERSEY

Resource Information
Anyone who takes fishes may be required to provide information on the species, number, weight, or other information pertinent to management of resources.

Methods of Fishing
No person may take, catch, kill, or attempt to take, catch, or kill any fish within New Jersey waters by any means except in the manner commonly known as angling with handline or rod and line unless specifically provided for by statute or regulation.

Spear Fishing
Spear fishing can be conducted by means of a spear, harpoon, or other missile while completely submerged in New Jersey waters for any species. The use of spears, gigs, gaffs, or other penetrating devices for lobstering is prohibited.

Convictions
Any person who violates any rule, regulation, or provision of the Marine Fisheries Act runs the risk of having his license revoked.

Weakfish
The possession and size limit for weakfish is 14 fish, at least 14 inches in length.

Summer Flounder (Fluke) and Winter Flounder
The minimum size limit for winter flounder is 10 inches.

The open season is March 1 through May 31 and Sept. 15 through December 31.

The possession and size limit for summer flounder is 8 fish, at least 14 inches.

(continued on page 107)

Now, Which Way is That Hot Spot?

Magellan GPS 2000 gets you there and back again.

For more information on the ultimate personal satellite navigator, contact Magellan at 1-800-707-5221.

MAGELLAN

WE BRING GPS DOWN TO EARTH.

Striped Bass

It is illegal to take, catch, or kill any striped bass from or in any New Jersey marine waters using any kind of net, or by any methods other than by angling with a hook and line, or by spear fishing.

It is illegal to possess any striped bass, or parts of a striped bass from which the head and/or tail has been removed (other than while in preparation or being served as food), which are less than the legal minimum size.

Harvest and possession of striped bass from federal waters (outside 3 miles) is prohibited.

Closed Seasons

All waters except the Atlantic Ocean, January 1 through February 28.

Delaware River and tributaries between Trenton Falls and the boundary between New Jersey and Delaware, April 1 through May 31.

The legal size and possession limit for striped bass is 2 fish, either striped bass or hybrid bass, NOT OF EACH, 28 inches in length.

Trophy Fish Program

Fishermen may possess one additional striped bass per day under the Striped Bass Trophy Fish Program subject to the following:

1. The fisherman must apply for and receive a fish-possession tag in advance of attempting to take a trophy fish.
2. The striped bass taken under this program must not be less than 38 inches total length.
3. The fisherman must comply with all aspects of the regulations. Copies of the regulation are provided with the fish-possession tag.

The Striped Bass Trophy Program does NOT apply to the Delaware River and Bay, and their tributaries, where the daily possession limit is one fish of at least 36 inches total length.

Hybrid Striped Bass

It is illegal to possess any hybrid striped bass from which the head, tail, or skin has been removed except immediately prior to preparation or serving as food. The minimum possession size is 16 inches, 2 fish per day.

Short-Nosed Sturgeon

No open season on this endangered species. It is illegal to possess a short-nosed sturgeon, or any part of one.

Baitfish

No license is required for the taking of baitfish for personal use with the following gear:

1. Dip nets 24 inches or less in diameter for the taking of herring for live bait.
2. Bait seines 50 feet long or less.
3. Cast nets 20 feet or less in diameter.
4. Lift or umbrella nets four feet square or less.
5. Not more than five killipots for taking killifish for bait.

Fish taken in this manner may not be sold or used for barter except by individuals possessing a commercial bait net license.

New Jersey 1995–96 Fishing Seasons and Bag Limits

Summer flounder, no closed season, 14", 8 per day
Winter flounder, March 1-May31, Sept. 15-Dec. 31, 10", no limit
Bluefish, no closed season, no minimum size, 10 per day
Weakfish, no closed season, 14", 14 per day
Red Drum, no closed season, 18", 5 per day, only 1 over 27"
Atlantic sturgeon, **NO OPEN SEASON**
Tautog, no closed season, 12", no limit
Cod, no closed season, 19", no limit
Pollock, no closed season, 19", no limit
Haddock, no closed season, 19", no limit
Cobia, no closed season, 37", 2 per day
Spanish mackerel, no closed season, 14", 10 per day
King mackerel, no closed season, 23", 5 per day
Striped bass, see text above, 2 per day

New Jersey's Big-Gamefisheries

by Bill Figley

During the warm months, a wide variety of big-gamefishes—marlin, tuna, swordfish, dolphin, wahoo, and sharks—migrate northward and inshore into New Jersey's ocean waters and become available to sportfishermen. Since 1981, the Marine Fisheries Administration has conducted a survey of New Jersey's recreational big-gamefisheries. The purpose of this survey is to systematically collect information—on the participation, effort, harvest, and economic value of these fisheries—needed to properly manage highly migratory species and uphold the interests of sportfishermen. The following is an analysis and summary of big-gamefishing trips from past fishing seasons.

Both marlin and tuna fishing in the canyons and shark fishing are relatively new fisheries in New Jersey, not gaining wide popularity until the early 1970's. Now, they are growing quickly, with the marlin and tuna fishery experiencing an 8 percent growth rate in the number of boats participating annually and the shark fishery expanding almost 15 percent yearly. The number of shark, marlin, and tuna tournaments

held each summer has also increased sharply in recent years.

While participation has shown a steady upward trend, fishing effort, measured by the number of trips, has fluctuated widely from year to year, seemingly in response to weather conditions and fishing success. Bad weather, of course, cancels trips, and when fishing is poor, anglers are unwilling to take the long and expensive runs to offshore fishing grounds. Marlin and tuna fishing efforts have fluctuated between 4,000 and 7,000 fishing trips per season, while shark fishing ranged between 3,000 and 6,000 trips. However, the continued increase in numbers of boats involved in these fisheries does create the potential for an upswing in fishing pressure on the highly migratory offshore fish stocks.

Catch

Catch statistics for this survey are based on data collected from 4,625 marlin and tuna and 1,734 shark fishing trips. The total catch of all species in the marlin and tuna fishery has fluctuated widely

during the seven-year survey, from a low of 12,000 fish to a high of over 40,000. Likewise, the shark fishery has shown wide annual fluctuations, from a high of almost 9,000 sharks to a low of 3,000. While some of this variation can be explained by changes in fishing effort, oceanic conditions and fish distribution probably have a much greater effect on catches. Offshore pelagic fishes, such as billfish, tuna, and sharks, are highly migratory and mobile species which may travel hundreds of miles in search of ideal living conditions—preferred water temperature and clarity and baitfish abundance. The big-gamefishes will concentrate in areas where conditions and food are favorable to their needs, leaving scattered and small numbers of fish in less favorable areas. Unfortunately, these fast swimming, pelagic fish have much greater range than the fishermen chasing them. When fish are schooled north of Block Canyon or south of Washington Canyon, they are out of reach of New Jersey anglers. And often, they stay in these locations for weeks or even for an entire fishing season. Therefore, a drastic decline or increase from one year to the next in the catch rate of a pelagic species in a particular area does not necessarily reflect the species' overall coastwide population level. What is needed to accurately assess trends in pelagic fish populations is long-term data collected from all the states within the fish's range. This information is now being collected along much of the eastern seaboard.

Another factor that can influence catch rates is the development of new fishing techniques. The advent of chunking in 1985 led to an immediate and sharp increase in the catch rate of tuna, particularly yellowfin. The advantage of chunking is that it draws fish up from depths beyond the sight of trolled lures.

Marlin and Tuna Distribution

The compilation of seven years of catch data indicates that many offshore pelagic species exhibit a geographical

The Jersey Devil *is a typical New Jersey party boat geared, as its sign indicates, to fish for a variety of inshore and offshore species. The* Jersey Devil *sails from Barnegat Inlet.* (VIN T. SPARANO)

preference even along New Jersey's short coastline. Yellowfin, bigeye, and albacore catch rates are much higher in the northern canyons, perhaps because of these tunas' preferences for cooler waters. In contrast, white marlin and to a lesser degree blue marlin, appear to be more abundant in the southern canyons. Swordfish, dolphin, and wahoo do not exhibit any clear-cut north-south preferences. These distributional patterns, long-term averages and temporary distributions, for a few weeks or even an entire season, may be quite different.

Releasing Fish

New Jersey sportfishermen are concerned about the possibility of overfishing sharks, because of their slow growth rates, late ages of maturity, and low reproductive potentials. The mako shark, in particular, has been subjected to intense sport- and commercial fishing pressure, and because of its tasty flesh, only about 28 percent are released alive by anglers. The other

shark species show much higher release rates, between 65 and 83 percent. Tournaments are encouraging conservation of sharks by adopting minimum entry weights and by basing awards on the largest shark rather than on aggregate weights. If you are a serious shark fisherman and would like to tag and release sharks, contact:

National Marine Fisheries Service
Northeast Fishing Center
Narragansett, RI 02882

About 56 percent of the white marlin and 43 percent of the blue marlin are released alive. There are no longer any marlin kill tournaments in New Jersey. Many tournaments are release only, while others maintain a high minimum entry size to reduce the number of billfish that are killed. At present, very few tuna and swordfish are released by sportfishermen.

Surface Water Temperature

Each species of shark is physiologically adapted to a particular range of water

temperature. Of New Jersey's recreational shark species, the blue shark is the most tolerant of cool water temperatures. Blue sharks are already moving north and offshore by the time New Jersey's shark fishing season gets started. The mako shark has a wide temperature range and provides good catch rates in surface temperatures between 57° and 77°F. Sandbar and dusky shark catches peak at water temperatures near 70°F while tiger and hammerhead sharks appear to favor waters in the mid- and upper 70's.

Weights

The decline in the average weight of a species can signal an overfishing problem. With the exception of bigeye tuna, none of the other tuna species, white marlin, or mako shark exhibited any noticeable downward trend in average weight over the survey. ■

Fluke—the Crowd Pleasers

by Al Ristori

They may not be the greatest of gamefish, but the lowly fluke could hardly be any more popular with the great majority of casual saltwater fishermen in the Metropolitan region, as well as with many real pros who enjoy the challange of catching them consistently.

The eating quality of the summer flounder is its greatest asset, but there's also the possiblity of catching a big one. While the vast majority of fluke are removed from the fishery by hard fishing and natural mortality within their first three years, a few survive much longer. Jumbos of 5 to 8 pounds aren't all that uncommon, but the real fluke pro will only accord the doormat name to one weighing at least 10 pounds.

Compared to their cousin the winter flounder, fluke are relatively thin

and much more active predators who use their teeth to nail smaller fish and squid. They can be quite fast over a short distance and will attack lures readily when they're living in shallow waters.

Fluke are universally distributed throughout the inshore waters of the region. They winter offshore on the edge of the continental shelf and are subject to great pressure when they're concentrated in that area. Those who escape start migrating inshore and arrive in quantity during May. The 14-inch limit was started in New York decades ago as a means of maintaining the Great South Bay fishery, since New York marine biologists determined that most of what the area receives in fluke for the season arrives in the spring. By throwing back smaller fluke in the

spring anglers will have another shot at these fast-growing fish later in the summer. In more recent years the 14-inch limit has been spread along the coast by the Atlantic States Marine Fisheries Commission (ASMFC) in order to ensure that the population spawns at least once before being harvested.

While large fluke were common years ago, the vast majority of the catch these days involves shorts plus lots of 14- to 16-inch fish. Fluke up to 20 inches are common, but anything over 4 pounds is considered noteworthy and even 6-pounders are hard to come by. Only a few real doormats are boated from New Jersey through the south shore of Long Island each year, but there's a much better chance of catching such fluke in Montauk waters.

The Montauk Rips and Shagwong

Fluke will attack when they're living in shallow waters.

Reef produce good quantities of fluke and some nice sizes throughout the summer, but doormats are rare until the period from mid-August through September when there's a good shot at a trophy on the mussel-covered bottoms south of the Point in about 60 feet of water. Currents are strong, and rough bottom plus the placement of lobster pots in the area makes for lots of lost rigs if you're not careful in setting up drifts. The dinky little sinkers fluke fishermen generally employ are of little use in this fishery, and it's often necessary to utilize from 8 to 16 ounces in order to tend bottom. Double-hooked whole small squid are good baits as are strip baits from fluke, sea robins or dogfish. Smelt can be combined with long squid strips for another big fluke attractor.

One year during the 1970's, fluke pros Judd York and the late Frank Lovello caught over 60 doormats before they stopped counting. That was around the time (September 15, 1975) when Capt. Charlie Nappi caught his world record 22-pound, 7-ounce fluke on a live snapper bluefish (an ideal bait around slack water). Don't expect sizes or quantities like that any more, but the good shot at a doormat is still there if you're willing to suffer the losses incurred in drifting the rough bottoms which jumbo fluke prefer. The same thing applies to rough bottom areas off the North Jersey coast such as Long Branch, Deal and Elberon. Working baits around wrecks is another good way of isolating big fluke, particularly from late summer into early fall as they move offshore.

Gardiners Bay is another area noted for doormats as well as for large quantities of average-size fluke. Long Island Sound wasn't considered prime fluking country when I was a kid, but some pretty good fishing is available in many areas throughout the Sound each summer.

Killies are the most common bait for fluke in bays and rivers, and they'll also do the job in the ocean, though spearing and sand eels are often more popular off the beaches. Squid strips are frequently added to all of those baits for added attraction. Drifting on bottom with long leaders is the common method, and the English-style hook has become most popular in recent years as it hooks well and isn't as readily swallowed by shorts.

Fish on the ocean side are rarely in deep water, but they will move in and out depending on water temperatures and currents. At times you may have to fish practically up to the outer bar, while under other conditions the fish could be located in 40- to 50-foot depths. Fluke like movement, and when there's little drift it's best to cast your bait and move it or power drift with the engines. Successful shore fishermen cast and retrieve slowly rather than letting their bait sit in one spot. Jigs can be effective when tipped with squid.

The one exception to normal fluking which proved very successful for me when I was a youngster involved chumming for fluke at anchor on Farm Shoals inside Fire Island Inlet. The largest catches of average-size fluke I ever made were taken in that fashion from just a few feet of water on live killies next to a chum pot full of frozen ground bunker.

Fluking has become the most popular summer party-boat sport despite bag limits of 8 in New Jersey and 6 in New York. Be sure to keep up with the fluke regulations, which may change every year in response to varying estimates of stock. There was a real population crash a few years ago, but the last several years have produced decent, though hardly "old-fashioned," angling. ∎

Sharks: Blue Water Action

by Pete Barrett

"We look for structure," Rich told our charter as he pointed to the depth finder. "Here's the cliff," he announced as the bottom line began to fall off in a steep slope. Our drift was about to take us across a steep drop-off at a spot known as Monster Ledge, an offshore location famous for big mako sharks. The steady rhythm of the waves lapping the side of the hull was suddenly shattered by the harsh screeching of the click on the Penn International reel. Rich yanked the rod from the gunwale rod holder and in one motion shoved the rod butt into the gimbal belt while his right hand pushed the clicker button to the off position.

Pointing the rod tip toward the fish, he kept slight thumb pressure on the spool to avoid a backlash. "He's not stopping! This one has the bait and he's heading south." Rich slid the drag lever to the strike position, and as the line came tight, yanked back hard on the rod, lifting the tip three times to set the hook in the shark's belly.

Two hundred fifty pounds of ticked-off mako shark skyrocketed from the blue waters, cartwheeling at the top of the jump then tumbling back into the water in a crashing shower of spray. It looked like a bomb had gone off, and the battle had just begun.

For the next half hour that mako gave us an aerial display few other fish, even the vaunted billfish, could match. Three times the bright cobalt-and-silver fish cleared the water in wild, twisting leaps. Four more times the great fish broke the water's surface, shoulders clear, head shaking violently left to right, throwing sheets of water in the air.

A nasty fish, but he was finally within boating range. I prepared the flying gaff. My buddy Matt grabbed the leader and eased the fish close to the starboard stern quarter for a clear shot with the gaff. I pulled hard, setting the big hook into the mako's back just aft of the dorsal fin. "Loosen the drag! Watch the gaff line! Haul back on that

rope!" Orders were yelled at fever pitch as the angry mako thrashed at the stern, drenching everyone in the cockpit with water.

Twisting and shaking almost out of control, the beautiful mako was soon tail-roped and left to hang from a tower leg, safe from damaging the boat or the crew with his wicked set of dentures. This fish was finally ours.

For decades many sport anglers

looked down their noses at sharks as something less than a true sport fish. Thankfully that has changed, and many sharks are appreciated for their own special challenges. At the top of the ladder is the high-flying mako shark, followed by a host of other sharks from huge tiger sharks to weird-looking hammerheads. An aura of danger surrounds them all, backed by tough fights and great sport.

The strange-looking hammerhead—as with other sharks, danger, tough fights, and great sport.

Sharks are found all along the Atlantic Coast, and many species are found in coastal bays. I've had the pleasure of catching them from the Mid-Atlantic Bight out to the Hudson Canyon and on down the coast to the Florida Keys. The trick to finding them consistently is to look for the best structure. While most sharking can be done within 15 miles of the beach, the choice sharking grounds in the mid-Atlantic are found along the 20- to 40-fathom curves. Anyplace along the coast where there is irregular bottom—deep sloughs, sharp drop-offs, and ridges—is sure to be a potential hangout for sharks. These structures are clearly shown on the NOAA navigation charts sold in most marinas. To make them stand out better on the charts, trace the contour lines with colored magic markers so the line jumps off the chart, giving away all the good spots.

Water temperature can be critical when hunting for sharks. From Cape Cod to Hatteras the season gets underway as the winter coastal waters rise to the high-50-degree range and blue sharks are the target. Mako fishing gets underway when water temperatures reach the 60-degree range. Once the temperature hits the low 70's, shark fishermen look for dusky, tiger and hammerhead sharks. The season lasts from May to October in the northeast, and runs all year in southern waters.

Fifty- and 80-pound-class tackle will handle most any shark, but since most sharks will range in weight from 75 to 200 pounds, 20- and 30-pound-class tackle is a better choice. I keep several outfits rigged and ready on my charter boat, the *Linda B*, to suit the size fish we expect on any given day. For light-tackle fishing, which we prefer for maximum sport, the 20-pound outfits are ideal, and we've taken sharks over the 300-pound mark on this class tackle.

Our standard tackle is a 4/0 reel loaded with 30- or 40-pound-test mono to handle sharks up to 400 pounds. Our heavy-duty tackle for tournaments and huge tiger sharks is a 9/0 reel loaded with 50- or 80-pound-test line.

Shark teeth are razor sharp and some sharks, like the mako, have teeth that protrude in a hundred and one

angles; wire leaders are essential. The International Gamefish Association rules allow 15 feet of wire leader to be used with 50-pound-test lines and 30 feet for heavier lines. Leaders this long not only protect line from sharp teeth but also from the highly abrasive, sandpaper skin of sharks. Wire leaders can be made of either braided or single-strand stainless wire. Both have their good and bad points. Braided wire leaders are more flexible and handle well when leadering in a fish. Most important, they don't break easily if the leader gets tail-wrapped as a fish flips at the top of its leap. Constructing braided leaders, however, requires special cutting and crimping tools. These leaders also have larger diameters than single-strand wire leaders, and this makes them more obvious in the water. They could possibly spook some sharks.

Coffee-colored single-strand wire leaders are preferred by many sharkers, but their main drawback is that the leader breaks so easily when kinked on a jumping fish. Use haywire twists to form the loops on which hooks and swivels are attached.

Sharks like to have a ready supply of food close at hand and will follow schools of mackerel, whiting, ling, cod, pollock, small tunas, kingfish, and smaller billfish. If you find schools of baitfish, chances are sharks will be nearby.

The basic strategy for shark fishing from Massachusetts to Hatteras is to drift and chum using three rods and three baits. The lines are set so the baits drift at different depths and distances from the boat to take advantage of as much of the chum slick as possible.

One bait is set out about 200 feet from the boat with the bait suspended off a float at 120 feet. A second bait is set down 75 feet and is about 125 feet from the boat. A third bait is dropped with no float only 30 feet from the boat. The floats quickly break when a shark takes the bait, so the shark feels no resistance as he runs off with his meal. Reels are left in free spool with the click on.

Mossbunker, mackerel, bonito, whiting, skipjack, butterfish, blue runners and jacks make the best chum, but almost any chopped-up fish will do. Drifting allows anglers to cover a wider

range of water, thereby increasing the chances of finding sharks. The chum slick becomes most effective as it lengthens during a long drift. When it stretches out for several miles, the slick can attract sharks from great distances.

Chum is traditionally ladled in a steady succession of small scoopfuls. As one scoop of chum settles in the water and floats out of view, another scoop is ladled into the water. The process can get messy, but it is effective. A simpler, automatic chumming system can be devised by using a plastic storage box like the kind that are sold in department stores and resemble milk shipping crates. Two lengths of line tied to opposite sides of the box form two crisscrossing loops. Tie another line about six feet long to these loops so the box balances from this line. Place a bucket of frozen chum upside down in the box, swing the works overboard, and secure it to a cleat. The natural rocking action of the boat will suck small amounts of chum from the bucket in a steady stream. The amount of chum going out can be increased or decreased simply by raising or lowering the chum bucket.

Since sharks have a reputation for eating practically anything that swims, it is hard to imagine a bait that won't attract them, but whole squid, mackerel, bunker, whiting, bonito, skipjack, false albacore, jacks, and school-sized bluefish are generally considered to be among the best baits. All of these baits can be fished either whole or as fillets. Whole baits are rigged with the hook under the chin or with the hook seated in the vent and belly. The best hooks are the Mustad #7699, with an offset to the point for guaranteed hook ups. Sizes 8/0 to 12/0 are preferred.

When fillets are used, trim the forward end to a taper so the bait won't spin. Splitting the narrow end makes the bait flutter more in the water. Place fillets on the hook skin-side to skin-side so the flesh is exposed. My own preference in baits is to use fillets and smallish (8/0 or 9/0) hooks. Because a mako chews on a whole bait it's possible the hook can get buried inside the bait itself, preventing a solid hookup. With a fillet the hook-up ratio is much higher, and fewer fish are lost at the strike while setting the hook.

Both rigging methods allow the bait to move naturally, tantalizingly in the chum slick. It is important to check the bait frequently to be sure it does not spin or appear unnatural in the water as the boat drifts. Fillet baits wash out and lose their smell, so it's a good idea to change them every half hour or so. This movement of the baits can also get a mako into a feeding mood as he sees food moving in the slick.

The starting position of the drift is all important. Check the wind and current, then pick an area with good structure and start on the upwind side so the drift takes the boat over the structure. To be assured of getting a drift to start at exactly the right spot a loran receiver is vital. If the drift takes the boat over flat bottom the only guarantee will be for lots of storytelling, but probably not much sharking. Look for the up and down bottom structure.

Sharks can pick up vibrations from great distances. Sometimes they can be attracted to a boat by the sounds created by tilting and lowering the tilt-and-trim controls of an outboard motor, by switching a baitwell pump on and off, by pounding the sides of the boat with a fist, or by just splashing water. Some sharks show their dorsal fins as they glide through the slick and approach the boat, others may swim deep and take a bait in such a way that the angler is unaware of it until he sees the float moving off.

Each shark reacts differently when the hook stabs home. Some take off in long runs, often circling the boat. Others head for the bottom or take off like a rocket, ripping off yards of line, then leaping high into the air. Whatever the shark chooses to do, the battle is usually memorable, and few sharks ever come to the boat without a good fight.

The moment of truth arrives when the fish is about to be leadered. It takes nerve to look into the black eye of a big mako or tiger and get within a few feet of these awesome fish. Once the flying gaff is placed in the fish, all hell breaks loose.

I like to get the gaff behind the dorsal fin to partially immobilize the tail, preventing the fish from joining you in the boat. I had one small mako that was gaffed in the head make a half-hearted leap and land on top of the gunwale only inches from taking a bite out of a buddy's leg.

Small sharks and any shark not intended for the dinner table should be tagged and released.

Sharks are great sport and are within range of most coastal sportfishermen. I've taken 500-pound fish only 15 miles from the beach in a small boat. With a 23-foot boat and 100 gallons of fuel, the chance to catch some truly big fish is within the reach of thousands of coastal fishermen. The challenge and enjoyment are high and the light-tackle sport is tremendous. ∎

Jersey's Intracoastal Bass

by Dusty Rhodes

Is the prospect of taking a wave or two over a set of waders too high a price to pay for striper action? Not to fret. Not all linesider action erupts at the Jersey shore, and river angling can be just as hot. Here are some of the best spots.

Navesink River

Anglers drift seaworms and liveline bunker at the Oceanic, Highlands and the Sea Bright/Rumson bridges for impressive catches. But those are sea-run fish, whereas in the upper Navesink swim year-round stripers from the almost 150,000 stocked in 1984. A non-migratory Brookneal strain, Navesink linesiders prowl the estuary from the Hockhockson Brook to and into the Shrewsbury River but do not migrate into the Atlantic.

Work the banks and structure of the Hockhockson Brook and Swimming River, which eventually flow into the Navesink. Don't miss the spillway below the Shadow Lake dam, a noted mecca for spring herring, because you can bet the farm and the dog the stripers won't.

Also check the railroad bridge or the Route 35 bridge to the west. Give Marine Park a try, and if you have a small boat work both shorelines from there to the Oceanic Bridge in Rumson. The mouths of McClees and Claypit creeks merit additional attention during early stages of the outflow. Add to your list the sedge banks, sluiceways and deep cuts characterizing the shoreline from the Oceanic Bridge to the river's union with the Shrewsbury, and the stretch from the twin-river junction to the icebreaker by Schupps Landing.

Mullica River

A hot spot for spring surf-casters, the Mullica River's prime access is Graveling Point where the big flow enters Great Bay. Mussel beds stretching bayward for a good 100 yards attract early run linesiders and holdovers. Use bloodworms, especially when incoming tide coincides with dawn or dusk. Fishing's best with a southeasterly wind in your face, which puts fish at your feet.

Upriver shoreline access is available at Clarks Landing across from Hog Island. From a boat, try Swan Bay, upriver a bit and along the opposite shoreline from Collins Cove, and ply the mouths of feeder creeks as well as the small creeks flowing into the Wading and Bass rivers which merge with the Mullica. And don't neglect steep sedge banks and grassy ditches.

Great Egg Harbor River

The Great Egg must be fished with the Middle and Tuckahoe rivers, although the Great Egg holds most of the fish.

113

Dusty Rhodes with a sedge-bank striper caught along Gravelly Point. Light tackle and bloodworms work during early spring. As water warms, fishermen switch to lures. (DUSTY RHODES)

Action begins in late March and is usually in gear by April. It continues throughout the summer with holdover fish, but early stripers up to 46 pounds have been taken off Beesley's Point where the mouths of the rivers meet.

Gravelly Point, about three or four miles up the Great Egg, is a prime spot for boaters and shoreline casters. But don't overlook feeder creeks; any might harbor spawning cows. Expect increasing boat traffic to push spring linesiders off the Great Egg River and onto the less traveled companion flows, and fish accordingly. You'll find holdover fish running with the area's considerable white perch population. Small stripers actually provide a summer-long fishery and favor deep holes just off shelves or flats at creek bends.

Lower Delaware River/Cohansey/Maurice

On the basis of fish numbers alone, the Delaware River is the queen of river striper action. Cows weighing more than 69 pounds have been hoisted from her depths, and schoolies are caught as far north as the Water Gap.

March to May are the prime spring months along the lower stretches from the River's mouth to the Tacony Palmyra Bridge, where numbers of larger fish begin to thin. However, if 1994 regs remain in place, it's release-only fishing from January 1 through April 30. Concentrations run from the

Betsy Ross Bridge to Peapatch Island. Expect to find early fish along sandy bars and beaches in the Penns Grove area.

And during a four-week spawning period cows move into shallows, along flats and at creek mouths like the Mantua, Salem, Raccoon, Rancocas and Pennsuaken. Otherwise, fish the deeper channels by livelining white perch, herring and shad, or the top bait, bloodworm.

Aim your search along 15- to 40-foot drop-offs, at eddies and bridge abutments like those at the Delaware Memorial, Commodore Barry, Betsy Ross and Walt Whitman. The Tinicum Island shoals behind the Philadelphia International Airport present about 100 to 200 yards of rock-strewn bottom which holds bass for those who can find and negotiate the spot.

Also try nearby rivers like the Cohansey and Maurice. Islands, bridge abutments, old pies, docks and pilings abound along the Cohansey. Some of the best action along the Maurice occurs from the Fowser Street ramp to the Route 49 bridge in Millville. But don't neglect Union Lake Dam, the Maurice's headwaters, where herring hold all summer. ■

Bottom Bonus

by Al Ristori

Sea bass and porgies (scup) provide fine bottom-fishing in inshore areas throughout the region from May to November, and can even be caught year-round by following the migration offshore in the winter. Both are good sport and food fish, and the sea bass, which has long been recognized as a gamefish by the IGFA, may well be the finest eating fish in northern waters. The succulent white meat makes it a favorite with Chinese restaurants.

Some of the best sea bass fishing occurs each winter during 80-mile wreck trips run by such party boats as the *Jamaica* from Brielle, N.J. By winter, the sea bass at that time are almost all

good-sized fish, and many are real jumbos ranging from 4 to 8 pounds. Of course the sport isn't the same in 200-foot depths, but it's the surest shot at catching a jumbo sea bass. Very large porgies are often present on the same wrecks.

Sea bass up to jumbo size migrate inshore during the spring, and the best fishing for them, on wrecks from 60 to 120 feet, occurs right after they arrive in late-April or early-May. Their numbers are quickly reduced and fishing generally drops off in June. Another surge of sea bass often shows in August or certainly by early fall, moving into rocky areas not far off the beach.

As they move back offshore, some of the largest of the year will be caught on medium-depth wrecks. The Submarine Wreck off Montauk has produced many jumbos in the fall.

Sea bass have big mouths and are easily caught even when anglers are seeking much heavier species, such as cod, with large hooks. On the other hand, even big porgies have small mouths, and few get stuck with hooks designed for heavyweights. Though often very abundant, porgies are only caught in large quantities by those who fish for them with the proper tackle and techniques.

Porgies were once super-abundant

throughout the region, but the discovery by trawlers of offshore wintering grounds along the continental shelf plus intensive netting inshore combined to deplete the species along the New Jersey coast and off southern Long Island. Those areas now get mostly a fall migratory run of hand-size porgies with relatively few running over a pound.

On the other hand, excellent porgy fishing can still be found off Montauk, in Gardiner's Bay, in Lord's Passage off Stonington, Connecticut, and around Block Island. Long Island Sound frequently has good quantities of sand porgies during the summer, though larger fish can be caught in various areas such as off Port Jefferson. The once great spring spawning run into Peconic Bay doesn't amount to much anymore.

Porgy fishing in the Montauk Rips can be so good at times that a few fishermen make a June-to-October living by catching them on rod and reel for the market. They chum with frozen ground clams placed in a weighted chum pot and bait with tiny pieces of clam or squid on small hooks and often catch hundreds in a day. Many of the eastern porgies are in the 1- to 2-pound class and are fairly common up to 3½ pounds. A few to 5 pounds may be encountered off Block Island in the fall.

Sand porgies are the young of the species and those 6-inch fish provide some fun in shallow, protected waters for kids and even some adults who like to fry them up whole. Long Island Sound bays and Peconic Bay are good areas for summer sand porgies, and they're also encountered at times in South Shore bays. Along the North Jersey coast there are often good quantities during late summer in the Point Pleasant Canal and in Manasquan River at the Rt. 70 Bridge. Anglers should be aware that the Mid-Atlantic Fishery Management Council has proposed a Scup Management Plan which would place a 7-inch minimum on porgies from New Jersey south and 8 inches north of there.

∎

Tog Hole Heaven

by Dusty Rhodes

"They sleep at night," he confided, eyes atwinkle. I knew instinctively that it wasn't the first time marine biologist Kevin Schick had revealed this news about tog (blackfish). Pausing to gauge my reaction before resuming his narrative, Schick warmed to the telling.

"They lose their orientation at night, and during dives I've found tog dozing upside down, almost paralyzed by my light. I've actually been able to swim close and touch them before they exploded in a frenzy."

The twinkle again, and more close scrutiny for my reaction. Did I seem that gullible, I wondered? No matter. If the price of firsthand information about backwater togging was being kidded a little, I was ready to pay the piper. After all, I had asked for the dance.

That episode, played out on a Great Bay sedge bank at the end of Tuckerton Neck, occurred 10 years ago. Although I never have been able to verify that startling news about tog slumber, everything else Schick revealed about those leathery denizens of rocky terrain has proven true. As far as I'm concerned, tog sleep upside down.

But this isn't a tale about tog sleep habits. Rather, it's about the availability of tog for small-boat anglers, access that is too often overlooked.

Despite their reputation for lurking around rocky structure, tog are not strangers to the mussel-encrusted banks of backwater islands and shoreline which characterize New Jersey's bays. Also, green crabs, skulking about in burrows carved into the soft, muddy earth of those banks, draw tog like a magnet.

Representative of many of the shoreline spots frequented by tog, Tuckerton Neck offers about 500 feet of prime mussel encrusted bank for both foot anglers and those working from boats. A key feature of the Neck's point—and something essential when probing other sedge banks—is deep water. Running from 15 to 20 feet almost at the edge, the depth goes to 35 feet just a scant 50 feet from shore (the channel, which runs to a depth of 60 feet and more, passes very close to the shoreline at the Neck). More than just deep, the underwater topography is characterized by a series of mussel holding ledges which slope from sedge bank to channel bottom. Tip: Any sedge bank with similar characteristics

in back bays is worth exploring for tog possibilities. Some locations which come to mind are found behind Brigantine as well as along deep cuts in lower Little Egg Harbor.

As with any angling pursuit, timing is critical. Low or dropping water benefits shoreline fishing because anglers are then able to get closer to the edge and don't have to flip their lines out so far. At high tide, by contrast, banks are often awash, especially during moon tides, and it's difficult to drop an offering in the right spot. Boat anglers have more flexibility, anchoring over whatever depth they choose.

Also consider seasonal timing. Tog will linger on the mussel beds all summer, but seem reluctant to take bait when the water is warm. April through early June are prime months, therefore, with action picking up again in September and lasting until bay water cools below their tolerance point. Consider a bonus any togging after October (possibly to mid-November during relatively warm falls).

Best baits are fiddler, green and calico crabs, with clams also producing strikes during the spring. Enterprising fishermen can gather fiddlers in the marshes adjacent to Tuckerton Neck and similar land structures throughout South Jersey's bays. If you've the nerve for it and don't mind poking your hand into places where your eyes can't follow, you can also glean green crabs from the underwater burrows along the edge of sedge banks. And those who fish from boats can find calicos by digging at the ends of bay sand bars during low tide. If you have access to beach jetties prior to your back-bay tog tug, rake them at the foot of the rocks during low water.

Quarter the baits and impale the pieces on Virginia or beak hooks (1/0 will do nicely). Present the fare via conventional tackle, which is more aptly suited than spinning gear for hoisting tog from deep water. Twenty-pound line is sufficient since you won't have to tangle with the rocky terrain of jetties or open-water wrecks where much togging goes on. However, don't

expect to avoid bottom hangups altogether. Although you won't have the fouling common to jetty and wreck togging, a mussel bottom strewn with assorted debris can play havoc every now and again.

I also suggest a graphite rod in the 3 to 4-ounce range to ensure that you'll be able to handle the sinker weight needed when the current runs hard. The graphite, of course, is to provide the sensitivity needed to time the hookset. Togging isn't so much about finding the fish as it is about hooking them. Adept bait stealers, crafty togs can stomach a goodly amount of chow while dogging the jab of a hook. The idea is to avoid striking at the first nibble while at the same time not tarrying so long that your trip results in feeding wildlife rather than catching fish.

Perhaps the advice offered me by an old togger will put the issue into perspective: "Wait for the third nibble,"

he cautioned, "and hit him hard right after the second tug!"

Before I put a wrap on this tog narrative, allow me to suggest a change of venue of sorts. Besides sedge banks, New Jersey's back bays are blessed with bridges, the footings of which are also home to tog. If you've a boat, anchoring adjacent to pilings (remember to check regulations) and applying the aforementioned techniques can also yield worthwhile results. The bottom line is that if you know where to look and when, backwater togging can be every bit as productive as jetty or even wreck angling. Although bays won't produce the larger specimens common to outside fishing, the backwaters are worth a shot for the small-boater or foot angler.

Just be sure to check the regulations concerning minimum size, which at the start of 1995 was 12 inches with a larger minimum on the horizon. ∎

FISHING ACCESS

A listing of a fishing access for Long Island and New York City, and a listing of New York State artificial reefs begins on page 70.

A listing of launch ramps on Long Island begins on page 74.

NEW JERSEY COASTAL BOAT-LAUNCHING SITES

Town	Public Shore Access
Passaic River	Nutley Municipal Ramp. Park Avenue, Nutley, N.J. Concrete ramp. Permit required. Phone: 201-284-4955. Chart 12337. Kearney Municipal Ramp. E.J. Vincent Waterfront Park, Bergen Avenue and Afton Street, Kearny, N.J. Concrete ramp. Permit required. Phone: 201-991-2700. Chart 12327.
Hackensack River	Sky Harbor Marina. Out Water Lane, Carlstadt, N.J. Concrete ramp. Fee per launch. Phone: 201-933-8270. Chart 12337.
Hudson River/ New York Harbor	Hazard's Ramp, Palisades Interstate Park, Englewood Cliffs, N.J. Concrete ramp. Daily

Arthur Kill

Raritan River

or seasonal fee. Phone: 201-768-1360. Chart 12345.
Liberty State Park, Jersey City, N.J. Cement ramps. Daily permit required. Phone: 201-547-5000/ 4757. Chart 12327.
Elizabeth Municipal Ramp. Front Street, Elizabeth, N.J. Concrete ramp. Fee per launch. Phone: 201-820-4033. Chart 12327.
Sewaren Marine Basin. Cliff Road, Sewaren, N.J. Concrete ramp. Fee per launch. Phone: 201-636-3917. Chart 123237.
Sewaren Municipal Ramp. Cliff Road and Ferry Street, Sewaren N.J. Blacktop ramp. No charge. Phone: 201-534-4500. Chart 12327.
Highland Park Municipal Ramp. Foot of South Second Street, Highland Park, N.J. Concrete ramp. No charge. Phone: 201-572-3400 or 201-745-2630. Chart 12332.
Edison Municipal Ramp. Meadow Road, Edison, N.J. Concrete ramp. Permit required. Phone: 201-287-0900. Chart 12332.

Matawan Creek/ Keyport Harbor

Sayreville Municipal Ramp. River Road, Sayreville, N.J. Concrete and asphalt ramp. Parking by permit. Phone: 201-826-0290. Chart 12332.

Perth Amboy Municipal Ramp. Second Street, Perth Amboy, N.J. Concrete ramp. Permit required. Phone: 201-826-0290. Charts 12327/12332.

South Amboy Boat Club. Foot of George Street, South Amboy, N.J. Dirt and concrete ramp. Daily fee or seasonal permit. Phone: 201-727-0657. Chart 12327.

Browns Point Marina. West Front Street, Keyport, N.J. Concrete ramp. Fee per launch. Phone: 201-264-7176. Chart 12327.

Twin Towers Marina. Amboy Road, Cliffwood, N.J. Concrete ramp. Fee per launch. Phone: 201-566-3163. Chart 12327.

Keyport Marine Basin. West Front Street, Keyport, N.J. Concrete ramp. Fee per launch. Phone: 201-264-9421. Chart 12327.

Olsen Boat Works. East Front Street, Keyport, N.J. Concrete ramp. Fee per launch. Phone: 201-264-4198. Chart 12327.

Keyport Municipal Ramp. American Legion Drive and Lower Broad Street, Keyport, N.J. Concrete ramp. Permit required. Phone 201-739-3900. Chart 12327.

Raritan Bay

Leonardo State Marina. Concord Avenue, Leonardo, N.J. Surfaced ramp. Fee per launch. Phone: 201-291-1333. Charts 12327/12324.

Atlantic Highlands Municipal Marina. Foot of First Avenue, Atlantic Highlands, N.J. Concrete ramp. Fee per launch. Phone: 201-291-1670. Charts 12327/12324.

Sandy Hook Bay/Brooks Marina. Ocean Avenue, Shrewsbury River Sea Bright, N.J. Surfaced ramp. Fee per launch. Phone: 201-747-8297. Chart 12324.

Navesink River

Fair Haven Municipal Ramp. Batten Road, Fair Haven, N.J. Surfaced ramp. Fee per launch. Phone: 201-747-8297. Chart 12324.

Red Bank Municipal Ramp. Department of Parks and Recreation, Washington Street, Red Bank, N.J. Paved ramp for craft to 21 feet. No charge, limited parking. Phone: 201-530-2740/2782. Chart 12324.

Sea Land Marina. West Front Street, Red Bank, N.J. Asphalt ramp. Fee per launch. Phone: 201-741-5753. Chart 12324.

Chris's River Plaza Marina. West Front Street, Red Bank, N.J. Concrete ramp. Fee per launch. Phone: 201-741-9676. Chart 12324.

Shrewsbury River

Monmouth Beach Municipal River Ramp. West Street, Monmouth Beach, N.J. Asphalt ramp. No charge, limited parking. Phone: 201-229-2204. Chart 12324.

Pleasure Bay

Long Branch Municipal Ramp. River Lane, Long Branch, N.J. Asphalt ramp. No charge. Phone: 201-222-7000. Chart 12324.

Atlantic Ocean

Monmouth Beach Ocean Boat Launch. Route 36/Ocean Avenue, Monmouth Beach, N.J. Ocean launch, small boats only. No charge. Phone: 201-229-2204. Chart 12324.

Long Branch Ocean Boat Launch. Seven Presidents Park, Ocean Avenue. Sand beach ocean launch site, small boats only. No charge. Phone: 201-222-7000.

Shark River

Bry's Marine. Highway 35, Neptune, N.J. Concrete ramp. Daily or seasonal fee. Phone: 201-775-7364. Chart 12324.

Shark River Hills Marina. Riverside Drive, Neptune, N.J. Concrete ramp. Fee per launch. Phone: 201-775-7400. Chart 12324.

Belmar Marine Basin. Highway 35, Belmar, N.J. Concrete ramp. Fee per launch. Phone: 201-681-2266. Chart 12324.

Manasquan River

Dyna-Marine. Brielle Road, Manasquan, N.J. Concrete ramp. Fee per launch. Phone: 201-223-4277. Chart 12324.

River Watch Marina. Ridge Road, Brick Town, N.J. Concrete ramp. Fee per launch. Phone: 201-458-2016. Chart 12324.

Beaverdam Creek	Starck's Landing, Princeton and Beaverdam Roads, Brick Town, N.J. Wood ramp. Fee per launch. Phone: 201-892-7558. Chart 12324.
	Sherman's Boat Basin. Princeton Avenue, Brick Town, N.J. Concrete ramp. Fee per launch. Phone: 201-295-0103. Chart 12324.
Metedeconk River	Green Cove Marina. Division Street, Brick Town, N.J. Concrete ramp. Fee per launch. Phone: 201-840-9090. Chart 12324.
	Johnson Boat Basin. Route 70. Brick Town, N.J. Wood ramp. Fee per launch. Phone: 201-840-9530. Chart 12324.
	Huppert Marina. Route 70, Brick Town, N.J. Wood ramp. Daily or seasonal fee. Phone: 201-840-1100. Chart 12324.
Kettle Creek	Shore Acre's Yacht Club. Drum Point Road, Brick Town, N.J. Wood ramp. Daily or seasonal fee. Phone: 201-477-3736. Chart 12324.
	Kettle Creek Marina. Kettle Creek Road, Silverton, Toms River, N.J. Concrete ramp. Fee per launch. Phone: 201-255-5890. Chart 12324.
Toms River	Toms River Municipal Ramp. Riverside Drive, Toms River, N.J. Concrete ramp. No charge. Phone: 201-341-1000. Chart 12324.
	Island Heights Municipal Ramp. Lake Drive, Island Heights, N.J. Paved ramp. No charge. Phone: 201-270-6415. Chart 12324.
	Toms River Municipal Ramp. Garfinkle Park, Toms River, N.J. Concrete ramp. Limited clearance under bridges to east of ramp. No charge. Phone: 201-341-1000. Chart 12324.
	Ocean Gate Yacht Basin. Bay View Avenue, Ocean Gate, N.J. Concrete ramp. Fee per launch. Phone: 201-269-2565. Chart 12324.
Barnegat Bay	Point Pleasant Municipal Ramp. Foot of Bay Avenue, Point Pleasant, N.J. Concrete ramp. No charge. Phone: 201-892-3434. Chart 12324.
	Baywood Marina. Pilot Drive, Brick Town, N.J. Concrete ramp. Fee per launch. Phone:

201-477-3322. Chart 12324.

Chadwick Island Marina. Strickland Boulevard, Normandy Beach, N.J. Concrete ramp. Fee per launch. Phone: 201-793-7227. Chart 12324.

Ocean Beach Marina. Route 35 South, Lavallette, N.J. Concrete ramp. Fee per launch. Phone: 201-793-7460. Chart 12324.

Lavallette Municipal Ramps. Bay Boulevard, Lavallette, N.J. Concrete ramps. Parking permit required. Phone: 201-793-5114. Chart 12324.

Bayside Marina. Bayside Terrace, Seaside Heights, N.J. Concrete ramp. Fee per launch. Phone: 201-793-8554. Chart 12324.

Seaside Heights Municipal Ramp. Bayview Avenue, Seaside Heights, N.J. Concrete ramp. No charge. Phone: 201-793-9100. Chart 12324.

Pelican Harbor Marina. Route 37 East, Seaside Heights, N.J. Concrete ramp. Fee per launch. Phone: 201-793-1700. Chart 12324.

East Dover Marina. Fischer Boulevard, Toms River, N.J. Concrete ramp. Fee per launch. Sunnyside Boats. M Street and Bay Avenue, Seaside Park, N.J. Concrete ramp. Fee per launch. Phone: 201-793-0857. Chart 12324.

Seaside Park Municipal Ramp. Bayview Avenue and 13th Street, Seaside Park, N.J. Concrete ramp. Permit required. Phone: 201-793-0234.

Red Top Boats Marina. 29th Avenue at the Bay, South Seaside Park, N.J. Concrete ramp. Fee per launch. Phone 201-793-0507. Chart 12324.

Wheel House Marina. Bayview & 24th Avenue, South Seaside Park, N.J. Concrete ramp. Fee per launch. Phone: 201-793-3296. Chart 12324.

Good Luck Point Marina. Good Luck Drive, Ocean Gate, N.J. Concrete ramp. Fee per launch. Phone: 201-269-3700. Chart 12324.

Becker's Boat Basin. Bayview Avenue, Ocean Gate, N.J. Wood ramp. Fee per launch. Phone:

201-269-3723. Chart 12324.
Rinderer's Marine. Sloop Creek Road, Bayville, N.J. Dirt ramp. Fee per launch. Phone: 201-269-9494. Chart 12324.
Whitey's Landing. Butler Boulevard, Bayville, N.J. Concrete ramp. Fee per launch. Phone: 201-269-1186. Chart 12324.
Downe's Fishing Camp. Brennan Concourse, Bayville, N.J. Concrete ramp. Fee per launch. Phone: 201-269-0137. Chart 12324.
Trixie's Landing. Brennan Concourse, Bayville, N.J. Concrete ramp. Fee per launch. Phone: 201-269-5853. Chart 12324.
Waretown Fishing Station. Bryant Road, Waretown, N.J. Concrete ramp. Fee per launch. Phone: 609-693-2813. Chart 12324.
Mac's Dock. Oregon Avenue, Waretown, N.J. Concrete ramp. Fee per launch. Phone: 609-693-4443. Chart 12324.
Sanborn Marine Center. Baltic Avenue, Waretown, N.J. Concrete ramp. Fee per launch. Phone: 609-693-3184. Chart 12324.
Barnegat Municipal Ramp. Bay Avenue and 10th Street, Barnegat, N.J. Concrete ramp. Daily fee or seasonal permit. Phone: 609-698-6658. Chart 12324.
East Bay Marina. East Bay Avenue, Barnegat, N.J. Asphalt ramp. Fee per launch. Phone: 609-698-3746. Chart 12324.
Barnegat Light Municipal Ramp. Bayview Avenue and 10th Street, Barnegat Light, N.J. Asphalt ramp. Daily or seasonal permit. Phone: 609-494-2343. Chart 12324.

Cedar Creek
Up The Creek Marina. Harbor Inn Road, Bayville, N.J. Concrete ramp. Fee per launch. Phone: 201-269-6469. Chart 12324.
Cedar Creek Marina. Harbor Inn Road, Bayville, N.J. Concrete ramp. Fee per launch. Phone: 201-269-1351. Chart 12324.

Laurel Harbor
Laurel Harbor Marina. Laurel Boulevard, Lanoka Harbor, N.J. Concrete ramp. Fee per launch. Phone: 609-693-6111. Chart 12324.

Forked River
Southwind Marina. Lacey Road, Forked River, N.J. Concrete ramp. Fee per launch. Phone: 609-693-6288. Chart 12324.
Townsend's Marina. East Lacey Road, Forked River, N.J. Concrete ramp. Fee per launch. Phone: 609-693-6100. Chart 12324.
Bara Marina. Marine Plaza South, Forked River, N.J. Concrete ramp. Fee per launch. Phone: 609-693-2748. Chart 12324.
Rick's Marina. Marine Plaza, Forked River, N.J. Concrete ramp. Fee per launch. Phone: 609-693-2134. Chart 12324.

Waretown Creek
Long Quay Marina. Main Street, Waretown, N.J. Concrete ramp. Fee per launch. Phone: 609-693-9444. Chart 12324.

Manahawkin Bay
Surf City Municipal Ramp. Division Street and Bay Avenue, Surf City, N.J. Concrete ramp. Permit required. Phone: 609-494-3064. Chart 12324.
Margo's Inn Marina. Route 72 West at Causeway, Manahawkin, N.J. Concrete ramp. Phone: 609-597-8909. Chart 12324.
Causeway Rentals. Route 72 Causeway, Ship Bottom, N.J. Concrete ramp. Fee per launch. Phone: 609-494-1371. Chart 12324.
Duck Inn & Marina. Route 72 West at Causeway. Ship Bottom, N.J. Concrete ramp. Fee per launch. Phone: 609-494-9010/9100. Chart 12324.
Ship Bottom Municipal Ramp. Foot of 10th Street, Ship Bottom, N.J. Concrete ramps. Daily fee or seasonal permit. Phone: 609-494-9819. Chart 12324.

Little Egg Harbor
Hagler's Marina. Long Beach and Tributaries Boulevard, Brant Beach, N.J. Surfaced ramp. Fee per launch. Phone: 609-494-4509. Chart 12324.
Cedar Run Municipal Ramp. Cedar Run/Dock Road, Cedar Run, N.J. Concrete ramp. No charge. Phone: 609-597-1061. Chart 12324.
West Creek Municipal Ramp. Dock Street, West Creek, N.J. Concrete ramp. No charge. Phone: 609-597-1061. Chart 12324.

Mariner's Landing. Dock Road, West Creek, N.J. Concrete ramp. Fee per launch. Phone: 609-296-3040. Chart 12324.

Little Egg Harbor Township/ Parkertown Municipal Ramp. Brook Street, Parkertown, N.J. Asphalt ramp. Permit required. Phone: 609-296-7241. Chart 12324.

Beach Haven Municipal Ramp. Foot of 9th Street, Beach Haven, N.J. Concrete ramp. Daily fee, weekly or seasonal permit. Phone: 609-492-0111. Chart 12316.

Captain Speck's U-Drive Boats, Parker Avenue & South Green Streets, Tuckerton, N.J. Concrete ramp. Fee per launch. Phone: 609-296-2529. Chart 12316.

Ace's Place. Parker Avenue, Tuckerton Beach, N.J. Wood ramp. Fee per launch. Phone: 609-296-2979. Chart 12316.

Mac-Hoeh's. Great Bay Boulevard, Tuckerton, N.J. Concrete ramp. Fee per launch. Phone: 609-296-1888. Chart 12316.

Tuckerton Creek

Magley's G.E.B. Marina. South Green Street, Tuckerton, N.J. Concrete ramp. Fee per launch. Phone: 201-892-6698. Chart 12316.

Skinner's Marina. Bartlett Avenue. Tuckerton, N.J. Concrete ramp. Fee per launch. Phone: 609-296-3051. Chart 12316.

Great Bay and Tributaries

Capt. Mike's U-Drive Boats. Great Bay Boulevard. Tuckerton, N.J. Concrete ramp. Fee per launch. Phone: 609-296-4406. Chart 12316.

Rand's Boats. Great Bay Boulevard, Tuckerton, N.J. Concrete ramp. Fee per launch. Phone: 609-296-4457. Chart 21316.

Munro's Marina. East Anchor Drive, Mystic Island, N.J. Cement and wood ramp. Fee per launch. Phone: 609-296-8202.

Mystic Island Marina. Radio Road and Bayview Avenue, Mystic Island, Tuckerton, N.J. Concrete ramp. Fee per launch. Phone: 609-296-2567. Chart 12316.

Great Bay Marina. Radio Road,

Tuckerton, N.J. Cement and wood ramp. Fee per launch. Phone: 609-296-2392. Chart 12316.

Oyster Creek Municipal Ramp. Foot of Scott Landing Road, Leeds Point, N.J. Steel mat ramp. No charge. Phone: 609-652-9871. Chart 12316.

Bass River

Bass River Municipal Ramp. Amosas Landing Road, Bass River Township, N.J. Concrete ramp. No charge. Phone: 609-292-1666. Chart 12316.

Mullica River

Chestnut Neck Boat Yard. Route 9, Port Republic, N.J. Concrete ramp. Fee per launch. Phone: 609-652-1119. Chart 12316.

Crowley Landing. Route 452, Green Bank, N.J. Concrete ramp. No charge. Phone: 609-965-1410. Chart 12316.

Fork's Landing. R.D. #1 Sweetwater, Hammonton, N.J. Concrete ramp. Fee per launch. Phone: 609-561-4337. Chart 12316.

Cavileer's Clam House. River Road, Lower Bank, N.J. Concrete ramp. Fee per launch. Phone: 609-965-3531. Chart 12316.

Mott Creek

J.B. Docks. East Mott Creek Road, Absecon, N.J. Concrete ramp. Fee per launch. Phone: 609-652-7843. Chart 12316.

Mott Creek Inn. East Mott Creek Road, Absecon, N.J. Concrete ramp. Fee per launch. Phone: 609-652-1444. Chart 12316.

Bonita Tideway/ Wading Thorofare

Brigantine Municipal Ramp. 6th Street South and Bayshore Avenue, Brigantine, N.J. Concrete ramp. No charge. Phone: 609-266-7600. Chart 12316.

Absecon Creek

Absecon Municipal Ramp. East Faunce Landing Road, Absecon, N.J. Cement ramp. No charge. Phone: 609-641-0663. Chart 12316.

Lakes Bay and Thorofares

Pleasantville Municipal Marina. Bayview Avenue, Pleasantville, N.J. Wooden ramp; larger boats may have problems. No charge. Phone: 609-646-6045. Chart 12316.

Linwood Municipal Ramp. Seaview Avenue, Linwood, N.J. Dirt ramp; larger boats may have problems. No charge. Phone:

609-927-4108. Chart 12316.

Atlantic City Municipal Ramp. Bader Field, Albany Avenue, Atlantic City, N.J. Concrete ramp, smaller boats only. No charge. Phone: 609-347-5421. Chart 12316.

Ventnor Municipal Boat Launch. Ski Beach, Dorsett Avenue, Ventnor, N.J. Sand beach launch site, small boats only. No charge. Phone: 609-823-7904. Chart 12316.

Hackney's Boat Yard. Margate Bridge Road, Northfield, N.J. Concrete ramp. Daily fee or seasonal permit. Phone: 609-641-1379. Chart 12316.

Angler's Roost. Amhurst Avenue, Margate, N.J. Concrete ramp. Fee per launch. Phone: 609-822-2272. Chart 12316.

Great Egg Harbor Bay
Bay Shores II. Bay Avenue, Somers Point, N.J. Concrete ramp. Fee per launch. Phone: 609-653-6772. Chart 12316.

Smith's Marina. Bay Avenue, Somers Point, N.J. Concrete ramp. Fee per launch. Phone: 609-927-7322. Chart 12316.

Somers Point Municipal Ramp. J.F. Kennedy Park, Broadway Road, Somers Point, N.J. Asphalt ramp. Daily fee or seasonal permit. Phone: 609-927-2951. Chart 12316.

Beesley's Point Municipal Ramp. Harbor Road, Beesley's Point, N.J. Paved ramp. No charge. Phone: 609-628-2011. Chart 12316.

Great Egg Harbor River
Meadowview Marina. Thompson Lane, Mays Landing, N.J. Concrete ramp. Fee per launch. Phone: 609-927-3627. Chart 12316.

Shady River Marina. Somers Point Road, Mays Landing, N.J. Asphalt ramp. Fee per launch. Phone: 609-625-9428. Chart 12316.

Spoony's Marina. River Drive at Great Egg Harbor River, Mays Landing, N.J. Concrete ramp. Fee per launch. Phone: 609-625-3141. Chart 12316.

Peck Bay and Beach Thorofares
Ocean City Municipal Ramp. Tennessee Avenue, Ocean City, N.J. Concrete ramp. Daily fee or seasonal permit. Phone: 609-399-6111. Chart 12316.

Ocean City Municipal Ramp. 34th Street, Ocean City, N.J. Concrete ramp. Daily fee or seasonal permit. Phone: 609-399-6111. Chart 12316.

Corson's Inlet
Corson's Inlet State Park. Corson's Inlet. Ocean Drive, Ocean City, N.J. Cement ramp. No charge. Phone: 609-861-2404. Chart 12316.

Flat Creek
Strathmere Municipal Ramp. At the Bay, Strathmere, N.J. Asphalt ramp. No charge. Phone: 609-628-2011 or 609-390-1523. Chart 12316.

Ludlam Bay and Sea Isle City
Municipal Ramp. Ludlam Thoroghfare, 42nd Street and Back Bay, Sea Isle City, N.J. Paved ramp. No charge. Phone: 609-263-4461. Chart 12316.

Great Sound and Thorofares
Avalon Bay Park. Ocean Drive and 54th Street, Avalon, N.J. Concrete ramp. Fee per launch. Phone: 609-967-8200. Chart 12316.

Stone Harbor Municipal Marina. Foot of 81st Street, Stone Harbor, N.J. Concrete ramp. No charge. Phone: 609-368-5102. Chart 12316.

Hereford Inlet/ Beach Creek
Wildwood Municipal Ramp. Foot of 5th Street, Wildwood, N.J. Concrete ramps. No charge. Phone: 609-522-2444. Chart 12316.

Cape May Harbor
Hinch Marina. Ocean Drive, Cape May, N.J. Concrete ramps. Fee per launch. Phone: 609-884-7289. Charts 12316/12304.

Bree Zee Lee Yacht Basin. Ocean Drive, Lower Township, Cape May, N.J. Concrete ramps. Fee per launch. Phone: 609-884-4849. Charts 12316/12304.

McNeill's Marina. Ocean Drive, Cape May, N.J. Concrete ramp. Fee per launch. Phone: 609-884-1795. Charts 12316/12304.

Cape May Marine. Cape Island Creek, Cape May, N.J. Concrete ramp. Fee per launch. Phone: 609-884-0262. Charts 12316/12304.

Maurice River
Ebb Tide Marina. Matts Landing Road, Heislerville, N.J. Concrete ramp. Fee per launch. Phone: 609-785-2402/628-2608. Chart 12304.

Cossaboon Marina. Matts Landing Road, Heislerville, N.J. Con-

crete ramp. Fee per launch. Phone: 609-785-0101. Chart 12304.
Berry's Driftwood Marina. Maurice River Road, Matts Landing, N.J. Concrete ramp. Fee per launch. Phone: 609-785-9825. Chart 12304.
Anchor Marina. Matts Landing Road, Matts Landing, N.J. Concrete ramp. Fee per launch. Phone: 609-785-9899. Chart 12304.
Four Star Marina. River and Menhaden Roads, Leesburg, N.J. Concrete ramp. Fee per launch. Phone: 609-785-1273. Chart 12304.
Millville Municipal Ramp. Fowser Road, Millville, N.J. Cement ramp. Permit required. Phone: 609-825-7269.
King's Marina. Landing Road, Port Norris, N.J. Concrete ramp. Fee per launch. Phone: 609-785-2424. Chart 12304.
Port Norris Marina. Ogden Road, Port Norris, N.J. Asphalt ramp. Fee per launch. Phone: 609-785-1205. Chart 12304.

Dividing Creek Dividing Creek Marina. Route 553, Dividing Creek, N.J. Shell and wood ramp. Fee per launch. Phone: 609-785-2338. Chart 12304.

Delaware Bay Double "A" Marina. Public Road, Fortescue, N.J. Concrete ramp. Fee per launch. Phone: 609-447-3014. Chart 12304.
Gandy's Beach Marina. Gandy's Beach, Newport, N.J. Concrete ramp. Fee per launch. Phone: 609-447-3002. Chart 12304.

Nantuxent Creek Money Island Marina. Money Island, Newport, N.J. Concrete ramp. Fee per launch. Phone: 609-447-4103. Chart 12304.
Newport Landing Marina. Landing Road, Newport, N.J. Concrete ramp. Fee per launch. Phone: 609-447-4413 or 609-455-2897. Chart 12304.

Back Creek Husted's Landing. Back Creek, Rockville Road, Bridgeton, N.J. Concrete ramp. Fee per launch. Phone: 609-451-6195. Chart 12304.

Cohansey River Bridgeton City Municipal Ramp. Cohansey Riverfront Park, Highway 49 and Washington Street, West Park Drive,

Bridgeton, N.J. Concrete ramp. No charge. Phone: 609-455-3230. Chart 12304.
Fairton Marina. Main Street, Fairton, N.J. Concrete ramp. Fee per launch. Phone: 609-451-3220. Chart 12304.
Greenwich Boat Works. Greenwich, N.J. Concrete ramp. Fee per launch. Phone: 609-451-7777. Chart 12304.
Hancocks Harbor. Bacons Neck Road, Bridgeton, N.J. Concrete ramp. Fee per launch or seasonal permit. Phone: 609-455-2610. Chart 12304.

Salem River Penns Salem Marina. Highway 49, Tilbury Road, Salem, N.J. Concrete ramp. Fee per launch. Phone: 609-935-2628. Chart 12311.

Delaware River Pennsville Municipal Ramp. Riviera Drive, Pennsville, N.J. Concrete ramp. No charge. Phone: 609-678-6777. Chart 12311.

Racoon Creek Bridgeport Boat Yard. Old Ferry Road, Route 324, Bridgeport, N.J. Concrete ramp. Fee per launch. Phone: 609-467-1716. Chart 12312.

Big Timber Creek Joe's Marina. Creek Road, Bellmar, N.J. Concrete ramp. Fee per launch. Phone: 609-931-6498. Chart 12312.

Back Channel-Delaware River Pyne Point Marine, North 7th Street, Camden, N.J. Concrete ramp. Fee per launch. Phone: 609-966-1352. Chart 12312.

Rancocas Creek Art's Rancocas Marina. Laycock and Harrisons Streets, Riverside, N.J. Concrete ramp. Fee per launch. Phone: 609-461-6238. Chart 12314.
Big "D" Valley Marina. Route 130 Rancocas Creek, Willingboro Township, N.J. Concrete ramp. Fee per launch. Phone: 609-461-3550. Chart 12314.
Eble's Marina. Creek Road, Delanco, N.J. Concrete ramp. Fee per launch. Phone: 609-461-3835. Chart 12314.
Ren-Del Marina. Rancocas Avenue, Delanco, N.J. Concrete ramp. Fee per launch. Phone: 609-461-5094. Chart 12314.

Delaware River/ Assiscunk Creek Burlington City Municipal Ramp. East Pearl Street, Burlington, N.J. Concrete ramp. Daily fee or seasonal permit.

Phone: 609-386-4070
Curtin Marina. East Pearl Street, Burlington, N.J. Concrete ramp. Fee per launch. Phone: 609-386-4657. Chart 12314.

Delaware River Florence Municipal Ramp. Front and Broad Streets, Florence, N.J. Concrete ramp. Permit required. Phone: 609-499-2525/3131. Chart 12314.
Bordentown Municipal Ramp. Bordentown City Park, Park Street, Bordentown, N.J. Steel mat ramp. Permit required. Phone: 609-298-9027. Chart 12314.
Ross Marine Service. Lamberton Road, Trenton, N.J. Concrete ramp. No charge. Phone: 609-393-2546. Chart 12314.
Mercer County Boat Ramp. Lamberton Road, Trenton, N.J. Concrete ramp. No charge. Phone: 609-982-6545. Chart 12314.

NEW JERSEY FISHING-ACCESS FACILITIES BY TOWN

The following is an alphabetical listing by town of the fishing-access facilities available along the New Jersey coast and in Delaware Bay, describing the general facilities offered in each town, including bay piers, ocean piers, jetties, surf- and bank-fishing areas, and beach buggy use. Also listed are the specific sites of boat-launching ramps, boat rentals, and party- and charter-boat fishing.

Many of the fishing piers listed are commercially operated and charge a fee. Jetties are located all along the eastern seaboard; those listed are the more popular ones. With the exceptions of Island Beach State Park, Hogate, and part of Brigantine, beach buggy-use is seasonal. In most areas, a permit and a specialized vehicle are required.

Most of the boat-launching ramps listed charge a fee. Launching at low tide may be difficult at a few of the ramps. A wide variety of fishing boats are available for rental, including rowboats, garveys, and open skiffs, with or without motors. In most cases, rental boat use is restricted to bays and rivers.

For deep-sea fishermen, New Jersey has over 100 party and 200 charter boats. Party or headboats handle large groups of fishermen who pay as they board. These boats are available for full-day, half-day, and night fishing. Bait is provided; rods and tackle can be rented. Charter boats cater to small groups, usually six or fewer, who must reserve their trip in advance. All bait and tackle are provided by the boat.

Town	Public Shore Access
Absecon	Public Ramp, Faunce Landing Road
Asbury Park	Ocean Piers—Jetties—Surf
Atlantic City	Ocean Piers—Jetties—Surf—Bank
	Public Ramp, Boulevard Avenue
	Public Ramp, Bader Field, Albany Avenue
	Farley State Marina, Party, Charter
Atlantic Highlands	Bay Piers; Atlantic Highlands Marina, First Street, Ramp, Party, Charter
	Frank's Boats, First Avenue, Rental
Avalon	Public Ramp
Barnegat	Public Ramp, Ramp and Rental
	East Bay Marina, East Bay Avenue, Ramp and Rental
	Frank's Dockage, East Bay Avenue, Rental
	Barnegat Boat Basin, East Bay Avenue, Rental
Barnegat Light	Bay Piers—Jetties—Surf—Bank
	Public Ramp, Bay Avenue and 10th Street
	Henry's Boat Rentals, 7th and Bay Avenues, Rental
	Bobbie's Boat Rental, 7th and Bay Avenues, Rental
	Ed's Boat Rentals, 9th Street, Rental
	Myer's Yacht Basin, 6th Street, Party, Charter
	Bayview Marina, Bay Avenue Party, Charter
	Fisherman's Marina, Bay Avenue, Party, Charter
	Barnegat Light Yacht Basin, Bay Avenue, Party, Charter
Bass River	Public Ramp
Bayville	Harbor Light Marina, Sloop Creek Road, Ramp and Rental
	Moby Dick's Landing, Berkley Shores, Rental
	Downes Fishing Camp, Brennan Concourse, Ramp and Rental
	Whitey's Boats, Butler Boulevard, Rental
	Cedar Creek Marina, Harbor Inn Road, Ramp
Beach Haven	Surf—Beach Buggy; Public Ramp
	Sportsman's Dock, 20th Street and Bay Avenue, Rental
	Polly's Rowboats, Dock Road and Center Street, Rental
	George's Dock, Center Street, Rental Party
	Schoenberg's Dock, Engleside Avenue, Party

123

Belmar	Bay Piers—Ocean Piers—Jetties—Surf—Bank		Roseman's Boatyard, Schellinger's Landing, Charter
	Public Ramp, Highway 35		South Jersey Fishing Center, Route 9, Charter
	Belmar Marine Basin, Highway 35, Rental, Party, Charter	Cliffwood	Wagner's Ramp, Amboy Road
	Bidwell's Ditch	Forked River	Captain Richie's, East Lacey Road, Ramp and Rental
	John F. Gant Marina, Ramp		Forked River Marine Mart, Marine Plaza, Ramp and Rental
	Capt. Walt's Landing, Ramp		The Houseboat, Lacey Road, Rental
Brant Beach	Surf—Beach Buggy		
	Sickinger's Marina, 4114 Boulevard, Ramp		Bara Marina, Lakeside Drive, Ramp
Bricktown	Sportsman's Island, Riverside Drive, Ramp		Forked River State Marina, Marine Plaza, Party
	Green Cove Marina, Division Street, Ramp		Captain's Inn Dock, Lacey Road, Charter
	Meadow's Marina, Ridge Road, Ramp, Bank	Fortescue	Anderson's and Hopely's, Rental
Brielle	McCarthy's Marina, Route 70, Ramp		The Captain's Association, Party, Charter
	Brielle Anchorage, Green Avenue, Charter		Double A Marina, Ramp
	Hoffman's Anchorage, Green Avenue, Charter	Galloway	Higbee's Marina, Ramp
	Brielle Marine Basin, Green Avenue, Charter		Oyster Creek, Moss Mill Road, Ramp, Charter
	Captain Sam Good's Place, Green Avenue, Charter		Motts Creek Dock, Motts Creek Road, Ramp
	Cline's Anchorage, Union Lane, Charter		Scott's Landing, Scott's Landing Road, Ramp
	Brielle Yacht Basin, Ashley Avenue, Charter	Hancock's Bridge	Alpha Yacht Club, Ramp
	Bogan's Brielle Basin, Ashley Avenue, Party, Charter	Harvey Cedars	Houghton's Rowboats, 83rd Street and Bay, Rental
Brigantine	Municipal Ramp, Ocean Piers, Bay Piers—Jetties—Surf—Bank—Beach Buggy		Harvey Cedars Marina, 683 Long Beach
	Young's Dock, East Shore Drive, Ramp and Rental	Heislerville	Matt's Landing, Ramp
	George's Dock, East Shore Drive, Rental		Mud Flat Marina, Ramp
	Bayshore Marina, Rental	Highlands	Johnny's Landing, Shrewsbury Avenue, Rental
	Jim's Boats, East Shore Drive, Rental		Henjo Dock, Shrewsbury Avenue, Rental
	Viking Marina, West Shore Drive, Rental		Jim's Boats, Rental
	Arby's Boat Dock, 13th Street, Rental		Kesgal Snub Harbor, Washington Avenue, Charter
Canton	Mad Horse Creek Wildlife Management Area, Ramp		Highlands Marina, Bay Avenue, Charter
Cape May	Jetties—Surf—Bank		Bahr's Pier Seven, Party Boats, Charter
	Miss Chris Fishing Center, Wilson Avenue, Party, Charter	Island Beach State Park	Jetties—Surf—Beach Buggy
	Pharo's Marina, Cape Island Creek, Ramp	Island Heights	Island Heights Marina, Ramp
	Bree-Zee-Lee Marina, Ocean Drive, Ramp		Public Ramp
	McDuell's Marina, Ocean Drive, Ramp	Jersey City	Liberty State Park, Ramp
	Hinch's Marina, Ocean Drive, Ramp	Keyport	Bay Piers
			Public Ramp
	Utsch's Marina, Harbor, Charter		Keyport Marine Basin, Front Street, Ramp, Rental
			Snug Harbor Marina, Route 35, Ramp
			Olsen Boat Works, Front Street, Ramp
		Lavallette	Beach Buggy
			Campbell's Boat Basin, Bay

	Boulevard, Rental	Oceangate	Street and Bay Avenue, Rental
	Ocean Beach Marina, New Brunswick Avenue, Ramp		Good Luck Point, Ramp and Rental
Linwood	Public Ramp, Seaview Avenue		Norm's Marina, Bayview Avenue, Ramp
Long Branch	Ocean Piers—Jetties—Surf—Bank		Beckor's Marina, Bayview Avenue, Ramp and Rental
Manahawkin	Causeway Rentals, Ramp and Rental		Cerreta's Marina, Chelsea Avenue, Ramp
	Margo's Marina, Causeway, Ramp	Ortley Beach	Yachtsman's Anchorage, 6th Avenue and Bay Blvd., Ramp and Rental
	Butch's Boats, First Street, Rental		
Manasquan	Jetties—Surf—Bank	Parkertown	Public Ramp, Brook Street
	Seaway Marina, Brielle Road, Ramp	Perth Amboy	Municipal Boat Basin, Party
		Pleasantville	Public Ramp, Bayview Avenue
	Christiana Boat Basin, East Main Street, Ramp	Point Pleasant	Party Boats, Channel Drive
	Jim Blair's Rowboat Rentals		Pt. Pleasant Marine Basin, Charters
Mantoloking	Traders Cove Marina, Ramp		Broadway Basin, Broadway Bridge, Party
	Pleasure Cove, Inc., Mantoloking Road, Rental		Ken's Landing, Broadway Avenue, Party
	Winter Yacht Basin, Route 528, Ramp and Rental		Inlet Basin, Party, Charter
Margate	Scott's Dock, Rental	Port Monmouth	Port Monmouth Marina, Port Monmouth Road, Ramp
	Capt. Andy's Fishing Fleet	Port Republic	Chestnut Neck Boat Yard, Route 9, Ramp and Rental
Marmora	All Seasons Marina, 34th Street, Ramp	Red Bank	Pubic Ramp, Washington Ramp
Matts Landing	Driftwood Marina, Maurice River Road, Ramp		Sealand Boat Livery, Front Street, Rental
	Bailey's Marina, River Road, Rental	Rumson	Municipal Ramp, Avenue of Two Rivers
	Anchor Marina, River Road, Party		Oceanic Marina, Washington Ave., Rental
Mays Landing	Shady River Marina, Ramp	Salem	Marlboro Marina, Inc., Ramp and Rental
	Spoony's Marina, River Drive, Ramp	Sea Bright	Jetties—Surf—Bank—Beach Buggy
Metedeconk	Stark's Landing, Princeton and Beaverdam Roads, Ramp		Trade Wind Marina, Ocean Avenue, Ramp
Middletown	River Plaza Marina, Ramp and Rental		Surfside Marina, Ocean Avenue, Ramp
Millville	Public Ramp, Fowser Road, Menantico Creek, Ramp		Mihm's Nauvoo Marina, Ocean Avenue, Ramp
	Manamuskin Creek, Ramp, Holiday Beach, Rental	Sea Isle City	Beach Buggy
Neptune	Shark River Hills Marina, Riverside Drive, Ramp		Public Ramp, 42nd Street
	McGreevey's Realty, Trenton Avenue, Ramp		Party Boat Marina, 44th Street, Party
Newport	Hollywood Beach, Hollywood Beach Road, Rental	Seaside Heights	Ocean Piers—Bay Piers—Beach Buggy
	Beaver Dam Boat Rentals, Beaver Dam Road, Rental		Public Ramp, Bayview Avenue
Normandy Beach	Normandy Beach Marina, Route 35, Ramp		Beacon Light Boats, Dupong and Bay Front, Rental
	Chadwick Marina, Strickland Boulevard, Ramp and Rental		Bayside Marina, Bayview Terrace, Ramp and Rental
Ocean City	Ocean Piers—Bank—Surf—Beach Buggy	Seaside Park	Public Ramp, 13th Street and Bayview Avenue
	Speed and Ski, Boat Rentals		Sunnyside Boats, M Street and Bay Avenue, Rental
	Public Ramp		Red Top Boats, 20th Street, Ramp
	Harbor House Marina, 2nd		

	Wheelhouse Boats, Bayview and 24th Streets, Ramp and Rental
Sewaren	Sewaren Marine Basin, Ramp
	Cliff Road Marina, Charter
Ship Bottom	Beach Buggy
	Public Ramp, Route 72
Somers Point	Bank
	Smith's Pier, Bay Avenue, Ramp and Rental
	Corlettes Marina, Bay Avenue, Rental
	Gateway Marina, Route 559, Rental
	Kennedy's Park, Ramp
	Dick's Dock, Rental
Stone Harbor	Surf—Bank—Beach Buggy
	Public Ramp
Surf City	Jetties—Surf—Beach Buggy
Toms River	Public Ramp, Riverside Drive
	East Dover Marina, Fisher Boulevard, Ramp
	Bay Bridge Marina, Route 37, Rental
	Cedarmar Marina, Ramp
	Shelter Cove Marina, Shelter Cove, Ramp
Tuckahoe	Tuckahoe Wildlife Management Area, Ramp
	Beesley Point, Public Ramp
Tuckerton	Bank
	Captain's Speck's, Parker Avenue and Green Street, Ramp and Rental
	Tuckerton Marina, Green Street, Ramp
	Ray's Boat Rental, S. Green Street, Ramp
	Cedar Harbor Marina, Great Bay Boulevard, Ramp
	Ace's Place, 115 Parker Avenue, Rental, Ramp
	Skinner's Marina, Barlett Avenue, Rental
	Rand's Marina, Great Bay Boulevard, Ramp and Rental
	Great Bay Marina, Radio Road, Ramp
	Captain Mike's, Great Bay Boulevard, Ramp and Rental
	Mystic Islands Marina, Mystic Island, Ramp
Ventnor	Ocean Piers
	Public Ramp
Waretown	Holiday Harbor, Lighthouse Drive, Ramp
	Waretown Fishing Station, Bay Street, Rental
	Sanborn's Anchorage, Baltic Avenue, Ramp
	Carl's Boat Service, Bay Avenue,

	Rental
	Mac's Dock, Oregon Avenue, Ramp and Rental
	Liberty Harbor Marina, Washington Avenue, Rental
West Creek	Public Ramp, Bay Avenue
	Burton's Boats, Landing Road, Rental
Wildwood	Surf—Bank—Bay Piers
	Public Ramp, 5th Street
	Dad's Place, Hereford Inlet Br., Rental
	Otten's Harbor, David Avenue, Party
	Wildwood Yacht Basin, Rio Grande Ave., Charter
	Starlight Party Boats, Blakes Dock
	Royal Flush Fleet, Park Blvd., Party

FISH RECORDS

NEW YORK

New York State fish records, official weigh stations, and information on New York State angling requirements begin on page 76.

NEW JERSEY

Amberjack, greater: 85 lbs. 0 oz.; off Cape May; 1993
Barracuda: 27 lbs. 8 oz.; off Cape May; 1991
Bass, black sea: 8 lbs. 2 oz.; Inshore Wreck; 1992
Bass, black sea: 8 lbs. 2 oz.; Off Pt. Pleasant; 1995
Bass, striped*: 78 lbs. 8 oz.; Atlantic City; 1982
Blowfish (puffer): 1 lb. 14 oz.; Delaware Bay; 1987
Bluefish: 24 lbs. ¼ oz.; Atlantic City; 1985
Bonito (Atlantic): 13 lbs. 8 oz.; off Sandy Hook; 1945
Cobia: 83 lbs. 0 oz.; off Cape May; 1985
Cod: 81 lbs. 0 oz.; off Brielle; 1967
Croaker, Atlantic: 5 lbs. 8 oz.; Delaware Bay; 1981
Cunner: 1 lb. 10 oz.; Offshore Wreck; 1993
Dogfish, smooth*: 17 lbs. 13 oz.; Great Bay; 1988
Dogfish, spiny: 15 lbs. 12 oz.; off Cape May; 1990
Dolphin: 63 lbs. 3 oz.; Baltimore Canyon; 1974
Drum, black: 105 lbs. 0 oz.; Slaughters Beach; 1995
Drum, red: 55 lbs. 0 oz.; Great Bay; 1985
Eel, American: 9 lbs. 12½ oz.; Atlantic City; 1988
Fluke: 19 lbs. 12 oz.; off Cape May; 1953
Flounder, winter: 5 lbs. 11 oz.; Barnegat Light; 1992
Hake, white: 41 lbs. 7 oz.; off Barnegat Light; 1989
Kingfish, northern: 2 lbs. 3 oz.; Barnegat Light; 1993
Ling (red hake): 8 lbs. 12 oz.; Belmar; 1990

Mackerel, Atlantic: 4 lbs. 1 oz.; Manasquan Ridge; 1983
Mackerel, king: 29 lbs. 0 oz.; off Beach Haven; 1987
Mackerel, Spanish: 9 lbs. 12 oz.; off Cape May; 1990
Marlin, blue: 1,046 lbs.; Hudson Canyon; 1986
Marlin, white: 137 lbs. 8 oz.; Hudson Canyon; 1980
Perch, white: 2 lbs. 9 oz.; Mullica River; 1995
Pollock*: 46 lbs. 7 oz.; off Brielle; 1975
Porgy: 5 lbs. 14 oz.; Delaware Bay; 1976
Sailfish: 41 lbs. 0 oz.; Wilmington Canyon; 1984
Seatrout, spotted: 11 lbs. 2 oz.; Hogate surf; 1974
Shad, American: 7 lbs. 0 oz.; Great Bay; 1967
Shark, blue: 341 lbs. 0 oz.; Wilmington Canyon; 1984
Shark, dusky: 530 lbs. 0 oz.; off Great Egg inlet; 1987
Shark, hammerhead: 365 lbs. 0 oz.; Mud Hole; 1985
Shark, sandbar: 168 lbs. 8 oz.; Little Egg inlet; 1987
Shark, sand tiger: 246 lbs. 0 oz.; Delaware Bay; 1989
Shark, s-fin mako: 856 lbs. 0 oz.; Wilmington Can.; 1994
Shark, thresher: 583 lbs. 0 oz.; Mud Hole; 1980
Shark, tiger: 880 lbs. 0 oz.; off Cape May; 1988
Shark, white: 759 lbs. 0 oz.; off Point Pleasant; 1988
Sheepshead: 14 lbs. 1 oz.; Great Egg Inlet; 1995
Spearfish, longbill: 42 lbs. 0 oz.; Poorman's Canyon; 1989
Stargazer, northern: 10 lbs. 4 oz.; off Shark River; 1988
Striped Bass: 78 lbs. 8 oz.; Atlantic City; 1982
Striped Bass Hybrid: 12 lbs. 7 oz.; Cape May Rips; 1993
Swordfish: 530 lbs. 0 oz.; Wilmington Canyon; 1964
Tarpon: 53 lbs. 0 oz.; off Sea Bright; 1982
Tautog: 21 lbs. 8 oz.; off Cape May; 1987
Tuna, albacore: 77 lbs. 15 oz.; Spencer Canyon; 1984
Tuna, big-eye: 364 lbs. 14 oz.; Hudson Canyon; 1984
Tuna, bluefin: 1,030 lbs. 6 oz.; off Point Pleasant; 1981
Tuna, skipjack: 13 lbs. 2 oz.; Wilmington Canyon; 1993
Tuna, yellowfin: 290 lbs. 0 oz.; Hudson Canyon; 1980
Tunny, little: 24 lbs. 15 oz.; off Sea Bright; 1977
Wahoo: 123 lbs. 12 oz.; 28 Mile Wreck; 1992
Weakfish: 18 lbs. 8 oz.; Delaware Bay; 1986
* Certified by the IGFA as a world record

For information concerning the New Jersey Record Fish or Skillful Angler programs, contact the New Jersey Division of Fish, Game, and Wildlife, CN 400, Trenton, NJ 08625-0400; (609) 633-7768.

Skillful Angler Awards Program

Dissapointed that the "big one" you reeled in wasn't quite big enough to make a state record? Well, don't despair because there exists a special awards program sponsored by the N.J. Division of Fish, Game and Wildlife designed for anglers in this situation.

The Skillful Angler Awards Program is for individuals who fish for both marine and freshwater species. There is a minimum weight requirement, and those whose applications qualify will receive a signed certificate recognizing the achievevement along with a special bronze pin. An awards presentation is held yearly to honor the anglers who catch the largest fish in each category.

This is a great opportunity for anyone who enjoys the sport of fishing. For a brochure write to the New Jersey Division of Fish, Game and Wildlife, CN 400, Trenton, New Jersey, 08625-0400, Attn: Skillful Angler Program.

Minimum weight requirements for the program are as follows:

Black Sea Bass	4 lbs.
Striped Bass	40 lbs.
Black Drum	70 lbs.
Bluefish	18 lbs.
Cod	30 lbs.
Dolphin	30 lbs.
Winter Flounder	2 lbs.
Fluke	8 lbs.
Kingfish	1 lb.
Blue Marlin	400 lbs.
White Marlin	60 lbs
Pollock	25 lbs.
Mako Shark	250 lbs.
Tautog	8 lbs.
Albacore Tuna	50 lbs.
Big Eye Tuna	200 lbs.
Bluefin Tuna	500 lbs.
Yellowfin Tuna	120 lbs.
Tuna (other)	250 lbs.
Weakfish	10 lbs.

LOCATING PARTY, CHARTER, OR RENTAL BOATS

For the most up-to-date information on party, charter, or rental boats, call the chamber of commerce or the state agency with jurisdiction in the area you are interested in visiting (see State Agencies, below).

NEW YORK

Numerous charter boats operate in New York; for a seasonal account of where to fish, and for what, see Fishing off Long Island Through the Year, page 71.

NEW JERSEY

Whether you're a novice or seasoned angler, diver or sightseer, New Jersey party and charter boats offer year-round adventure on the state's bay and ocean waters. Party and charter boats let you take advantage of the skill and knowledge of experienced captains and benefits of well-equipped vessels at a reasonable cost. All party and charter boats are inspected and licensed by the U.S. Coast Guard for the passenger's safety; all captains are qualified and licensed.

New Jersey's extensive fleet consists of about 100 party and over 300 charter boats which are docked in ports at all the major ocean inlets and bays. The basic difference between the two types of boats is that passengers on a party or headboat pay individually as they board on a first come basis until the boat is filled, while a charter boat must be reserved in advance by a group of passengers.

Party boats are large vessels, ranging from 60 to over 100 feet in length, and carry anywhere from 20 to 150 passengers. They provide anglers with the ability to go fishing at almost anytime with no advance planning, allowing them to go when the fish are running. Party boats sail on a daily schedule for designated species. Bait is provided and rods, reels, and tackle may be rented onboard. Cold soda and beer are available; some boats even have snack bars that prepare hot food. The cost of the trip depends on the type of fishing or activity; for example, bluefishing, which usually requires a long run and large amounts of chum and bait, is slightly more expensive than inshore wreck- or bottom-fishing. Children's fares are usually discounted.

Most ports have several party boats, offering a variety of different types of fishing. There are full, half, and three-quarter day, morning, afternoon, evening, and night trips available. Some party boats feature special long-distance trips for tuna, cod, or whale watching. Such trips usually require advanced reservations.

Some tips for fishing on party boats:

Read the fishing reports in the newspaper to find out which species are abundant. Listen to the marine weather forecast the night before a trip. If the forecast is unfavorable, go another day. Arrive at the dock early, especially on weekends, to secure a place on the boat. Take plenty of warm clothes; even during the summer, it can be cold on the water. Take something to hold your catch, preferably a cooler with ice.

Charter boats are typically smaller, between 25 and 60 feet in length. While most charter boats carry a maximum of 6 to 8 anglers, others carry much larger groups. Many party boats can also be reserved for large group charters. The primary advantage of a charter is that you can reserve the entire boat for a selected group. Charters should be arranged well in advance, up to 6 months ahead of time. Decisions that should be made prior to contacting a charter captain include:

- size of your group
- type (age and experience) of people in group
- port of departure
- approximate date and time
- type (method, species) of fishing or activity

Charter captains require an advanced deposit. The trip fee varies considerably, depending upon the length of the trip and fuel and bait expenses. All bait and tackle is supplied on charter boats. Some boats will arrange to cater food if requested. (Unless indicated, all area codes 609.)

Party Boats

Ocean City
Buccaneer, 398-0424
Challenger, 399-5011

Sea Isle City
Capt. Robbins, 263-2020
Starfish, 263-3800

Avalon
Miss Avalon II, 967-7455

Stone Harbor
Capt. Cramer, 368-1548

Wildwood
Adventurer II, 729-7777
Rainbow, 522-0881
Sea Raider, 522-1032

Wildwood Crest
Royal Flush, 522-1395
Star Light, 729-7776

Cape May
Miss Cape May, 886-9176
Miss Chris, 884-3939
Nada Jane, 884-0909
Porgy III, 465-3840
Sea Star, 884-4671

Charters

Ocean City
Maine Lady, 390-3894
Our Thor III, 399-2344
School's Out, 399-1724

Sea Isle City
Jeanne B, 263-6226
Mumbo Jumbo, 263-9550
Patricia M., 263-8174

Avalon
Artifishal, 967-4644
Chopper II, 465-1532
Delta Dawn, 263-9447
Escapade, 861-5951
Executive Blues, 967-3402
Fast Pace, 861-4501
Gin & Tomic, 368-3736
Highliner, 624-9277
Marlyn II, (215)343-2785

Stone Harbor
Jolle G, 368-1141

Wildwood
Bounty, 729-3550
Krazy K., 729-1614
Lady Margaret, 886-6540
Miss Doris, 853-2980
Zebulin, 522-0900

Wildwood Crest
Capt. Carleson 522-0177
Pain Killer, 522-1314
Star Gazer, 884-1556
Allison, 884-6262
Billy Bones, 886-1089
Bobbi Lynne, 884-8031
Budoris, 468-1162
Bugs Ahoy, 794-3459
Capt's Lady, 884-0317

Cape May
Chillin Out, 729-9269
Corner Kick III, 423-5088
Current Affair, 884-0404
Down Deep, 654-6188
Fin Addict, 456-4625
Fish Hawk, 456-2176
Hammer, 884-1337
In Law, 848-0318
Intruder, (215)494-0174
Jo-Ed IV, 522-4212
Jumpin' Joe, 884-5057
Mako Man, 861-2413
Miss Behavin', 898-1661
Nomad Too, 435-4271
Pilot House, 884-3449
Rambunctious, 829-1813
Slammer, 299-5728
Thriller, 884-2051
Gallant Lady, 884-7754
Huntress, 884-1227
Michael D, 884-6093
Morning Star, 898-1303
Noreaster II, 898-0301
Outward Bounds, (215) 489-1534
Sandi Pearl, 785-2836
Sonny's Toy, 886-0970

STATE AGENCIES

NEW YORK

New York Department of Economic Development
Tourism Division
99 Washington Ave.
Albany, NY 12245
(518) 474-4116

New York State Office of Parks, Recreation, Historic
Preservation, Marine & Recreational Vehicles
Empire State Plaza
Albany, NY 12238
(518) 474-0445

New York State Department of Environmental
Conservation
Division of Marine Resources
SUNY—Bldg. 40
Stonybrook, NY 11794
(516) 751-7900, ext. 326

NEW JERSEY

New Jersey Department of Tourism
20 West State St.
Trenton, NJ 08625-0826
(609) 292-2470

New Jersey State Police
Marine Law Enforcement Bureau
Box 7068
West Trenton, NJ 08628-0068
(609) 882-2000, ext. 2530

New Jersey Division of Fish, Game and Wildlife
Mail: CN 400
Trenton, NJ 08625
Office: 501 E. State St.
Station Plaza 5 (3rd Floor)
License Information: (609) 292-2966 or 9590
Bureau of Law Enforcement: (609) 292-9430
Marine Fisheries Administration: (609) 292-2083

Atlantic City Station
1200 N. Rhode Island Ave.
Atlantic City, NJ 08401
(609) 441-3586

Bivalve Station
c/o Port Norris SP Station
RD 1, Haleyville/Mauricetown Rd.
Port Norris, NJ 08349
(609) 785-1839

Burlington Station
601 Pearl St.
Burlington Station, NJ 08016
(609) 387-1221

Monmouth County Detachment
c/o Marine Law Enforcement Bureau
Box 7068
West Trenton, NJ 08628-0068
(908) 842-5171

Newark Bay Station
Building 400
Corbin Street
Port Newark, NJ 07114
(201)578-8173

North Wildwood Station
Central Ave.
North Wildwood, NJ 08260
(609) 522-0343

Ocean Station
Route 9 and Cox Ave.
West Creek, NJ 08092
(609) 296-5807

Point Pleasant Station
2001 Loveland Place
Point Pleasant NJ 08742
(908) 899-5050

4

Delaware Bay to False Cape, Virginia

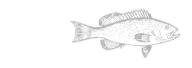

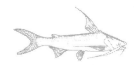

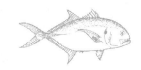

From Cape May, New Jersey, to False Cape, Virginia, the shoreline configuration, estuaries, sea floor, and marine life are generally typical of the large concavity of the coast called the Middle Atlantic Bight, which extends all the way from Cape Cod, Massachusetts, to Cape Hatteras, North Carolina.

Along the open sea coast of this section the tides occur twice each day, ranging from 3½ to 4½ feet between high and low water. In the bays behind the nearly straight, sandy beaches and barriers from Cape Henlopen at the mouth of Delaware Bay to Chincoteague Inlet in Virginia, the tides range between ½ and 2 feet, and south of Chincoteague along Virginia's eastern shore bays, they range about 4½ feet. The nearly freshwater bays south of Virginia Beach, Virginia, are so far removed from the influence of the sea that there are no detectable tides in them, but strong winds from the north, east, or west can cause high or low water levels.

Along this section of coast summers are relatively long and winters short. From about May to October or early November, the weather is warm, the humidity high, and the winds gentle. The prevailing southerly or southwesterly winds bring the warm, moist air from the Gulf of Mexico and the weather usually remains fairly uniform for several weeks at a time. In July, the hottest month, the air temperatures along the coast often rise above 90°F, sometimes to 100°F. They are 5° to 10°F cooler over the sea, moderated by surface-water temperatures that rarely exceed 80°F. During the summer, clear skies persist about three-quarters of the time. Showers and thunderstorms are most frequent over the coast during late afternoon and over the open water at night. Gale-force winds, though infrequent, sometimes accompany thunderstorms. When they do, they can cause serious trouble to small-boatmen caught in unprotected waters. Fogs, which occur occasionally, are usually light and burn off by noon. Fall is a brief period consisting of the few weeks after summer in which the warm, gentle southerlies gradually become more variable, then shift to the northwest, and become progressively stronger and colder. Winter, a time of unstable weather, is marked by rapidly changing air masses. As each air mass passes over the area, the usual condition of raw overcast days is interrupted by brief periods of strong, gusty winds followed by a few clear, crisp days, usually followed by periods of rain, freezing rain, or snow. Rarely does the temperature drop to 0°F and it goes below freezing only about 40 days a year. Winds are strongest during winter, especially in March. Spring is like the fall with the pattern reversed, the weather gradually merging into the summer regime.

The seasonal weather pattern is the principal agent controlling the temperature of the sea, which in turn affects the distribution of the 150 to 200 species of fishes in this area. Although some of the species are residents, most of them are seasonal migrants. Many arrive in late spring or early summer as the water warms and remain until it cools during fall. A few others arrive late in the summer and remain a few months while surface-water temperatures are at their maximum for the year. Still others arrive late in the fall as the water becomes cold and stay until it warms during the spring. In all instances, however, their arrivals, sojourns, and departures are governed to a large degree by the temperature of the water.

During March and April, as the cold winter water begins to warm slightly, large schools of Atlantic mackerel appear along the shore from offshore and southward of here. The various schools remain a few weeks before moving northward. Cod, pollock, silver hake, squirrel hake, and other cold-water fishes which had moved into this area from offshore or the north during early winter are still here. Because the bottom water offshore continues to be cold into August or even early September, some of these cold-water fishes remain until summer, especially on the offshore wrecks. With the increasing sunlight and moderate air temperatures of spring, the water near shore, as well as that offshore, warms down to a depth of 30 to 40 feet. Then the cold-water fishes move out into deeper water offshore or northward, as warm-water migrants move in. Bluefish, black sea bass, scup, summer flounder, gray sea trout (called weakfish in Delaware Bay and north), spot, silver perch, and others are here by May or early June from southward and offshore. As the water warms even more during early summer, many oceanic and pelagic fishes arrive—bluefin tuna, Atlantic bonito, skipjack tuna, Spanish mackerel, king mackerel, yellowfin tuna, dolphin, and little tuna. From midsummer to early fall, when the temperatures of nearshore and surface water are warmest, we find a few tropical fishes such as tarpon, pompano, barracuda, triggerfish, and crevalle jacks. As the water cools in the fall, the warm-water migrants return southward or offshore to spend the winter. About this time the cold-water migrants move into the area to spend the winter.

When the first Europeans arrived in this area during the late 1500's and early 1600's, the native seaside inhabitants lived by hunting and fishing and by growing a few crops. Usually it was the men who shot or snared the game and speared or netted the fish. The women and children treaded the shallow bays for oysters, clams, and mussels, and tended the gardens. Although the Indians were very proficient at capturing any seafood they needed, the European settlers apparently paid little attention to fishing or shellfishing. Although many of the farmers living near the coast caught fish for themselves or to sell, especially during the spring, agriculture was the predominant occupation throughout the colonial period. Indeed, the growth of commercial fishing was greatly retarded by the section of the Navigation Act instituted by the English to forbid Maryland, Vir-

ginia, and the other southern colonies from importing salt except from England or their sister colonies to the north, at double the usual cost. Since salt was so necessary in preserving fish to be sold in distant markets, this provision of the law was designed to discourage fishing in favor of agriculture. It was not until the early 1800's that fishing gained in importance as a commercial occupation. Some of the people became full-time fishermen, though most who fished commercially did so only during those seasons when their principal work permitted them the time. Oystering and clamming were pursued throughout the year; crabbing during the summer months. The netting of shad and sturgeon during the spring by hundreds of fishermen living along the Delaware Bay was profitable. Beach seining and the setting of pound nets for spot, gray sea trout, bluefish, and menhaden along the eastern shore of Delaware, Maryland, and Virginia during the summer provided the fishermen with an additional source of income. And the netting of striped bass and white perch in the rivers and bays during winter provided income to both the commercial fishermen and farmers whose principal work was over for the year. Fishing offshore was pursued mostly by men out of New Jersey, New York, and Philadelphia sailing in vessels called smacks and pungies. Until the early 1930's most of the offshore grounds lay less than 15 miles off the coast. With the discovery in the early 1930's of the wintering grounds of scup, flounder, and black sea bass, some 20 to 80 miles off this section of coast, the commercial fishery rapidly expanded to the use of large motorized trawling vessels which could stay at sea for a week or more.

Fishing for pleasure with hook and line was carried on throughout this area from the days of the first settlers. If the people living near the shore had spare time, they would fish from the various landings or from small boats. During the 1800's as summer resorts in Cape May, New Jersey, Ocean City, Maryland, and Hampton, Virginia, became popular, pleasure fishing increased in importance.

At first many species were so abundant that market fishermen had no trouble catching as much as they needed. Their only problem was the limited quantity the local market could absorb. The cost of packing the excess fish and shipping them to the large markets of New York City, Philadelphia, or Washington, D.C., barely allowed for any profit. Anglers often enjoyed such good fishing that they had a great deal of difficulty in disposing of their catch and threw many away. However, as in other areas along our coast, a decline in the abundance of a number of species became evident. The seemingly inexhaustible native oysters in Delaware Bay began to be depleted by overharvest and other abuses during the early 1800's. At one time these oysters grew over extensive areas of the bay, from the tidal sedge creeks and flats to the deep ship channel. Even with refined culture methods used during the early 1900's, the annual harvest fell from an average of 640 million oysters to less than 90 million, a decline of 85 percent. The advancement of the destructive oyster drill upstream to the natural seed beds, a plague of mudworms whose colonies grow on the oysters and ultimately smother them, and a protozoan epidemic contributed to this decline. In addition, foreign substances carried into the bay from the surrounding land gradually fouled the water and apparently reduced the chlorophyll production of estuarine and marine plants. The decline and perhaps even the extinction of other fisheries in this area can generally be attributed directly or indirectly to man. During the 1800's, Delaware Bay and River provided important spawning and nursery areas for striped bass, which at that time occurred throughout the bay and upstream to the headwaters of the Delaware River. By the early 1900's a decrease in the number of large fish was reported. By the mid-1950's, because of industrial and domestic pollution, striped bass became conspicuously absent from the stretch of river above Wilmington, Delaware. Striped bass, despite the pollution, have now established a spawning stock in the river mud, and shad, also severely depleted at one time, now run all the way up into New York.

Estuaries are important spawning and nursery areas for many other species besides striped bass and shad. White perch, winter flounder, windowpane flounder, and shortnose sturgeon, as well as bait species such as killifish and silversides, often spend most of their lives in the estuaries. Other important bait fishes, notably menhaden, mullet, and anchovies, live and depend on estuaries during parts of their lives. The alewife and blueback herring, like the shad, spawn in the rivers, and the sexually mature fish as well as the juveniles must pass through the estuary on their way to the sea. Juveniles of our only catadromous fish, the eel, either pass through the estuary on their way to fresh water or remain there to develop into adults. At maturity, adult eels desert this area, move downstream, and swim offshore and south to spawn. Estuaries are the habitat not only for oysters but for other shellfish such as blue crabs, soft- and hard-shell clams, and bay scallops.

Unfortunately, these extraordinarily fertile areas where saltwater and freshwater mix are being continually ravaged through unwise use. Encroachment on estuaries for housing and industrial development conflicts with increasing needs for food and open space.

An angler in New Jersey or Delaware does not need a license to fish or crab in salt or brackish water, though Maryland and Virginia now require a license for Chesapeake Bay. As we've noted previously, fishing regulations are relatively perishable, often changing yearly. All of these states regulate striped bass fishing. New Jersey has a minimum size limit, daily catch limit and season along its seacoast; and a minimum and maximum size

limit in Delaware Bay. Both Maryland and Virginia have minimum and maximum size limits and seasons on striped bass. These two states also have minimum size limits for a few other fishes. Virginia has a daily catch limit for large red drum. Each of the states has regulations governing the digging of clams and the capturing of anadromous fishes. Also, they have minimum size limits for both the hard and the soft stages of blue crabs; Maryland prohibits keeping egg-bearing females, though Virginia has no such prohibition. To obtain copies of the fishing and shellfishing regulations, contact the following:

- New Jersey—New Jersey Division of Fish, Game and Wildlife, CN 400, Trenton, NJ 08625; license information: 609-292-2966 or 9590
- Delaware—Delaware Division of Fish and Wildlife, P.O. Box 1401, 89 Kings Highway, Dover, DE 19903; fisheries section, (302) 739-3441
- Maryland—Maryland Department of Natural Resources, Tidewater Administration, Tawes State Office Building, Annapolis, MD 21401; (301) 974-3765, (410) 974-3558
- Virginia—Marine Resources Commission, P. O. Box 756, 2600 Washington Avenue, Newport News, VA 23607-0756.

DELAWARE BAY

Delaware Bay is a large deltoid estuary indenting the coastline between New Jersey and Delaware. Each day an average of nearly 13 billion gallons of fresh water flows into it, mostly from the Delaware River; and each day over 1,000 billion gallons of seawater moves in with the tide and mixes with the fresh. Under normal river-flow conditions a trace of brackishness can be detected as far as Wilmington, 65 miles from the entrance of the Bay, though during droughts it may extend beyond Philadelphia, about 100 miles from the entrance.

LAND CONFIGURATION AND WATER DEPTH

The land within a few miles of Delaware Bay is low and flat, most of it rising less than 20 feet above sea level. Except for a couple of places where dry land runs to the water's edge or dredged material has been heaped up to form land artificially, saltmarshes border the entire shoreline. These saltmarshes vary in area, some merely fringing the edge of the Bay, others extending inland for miles along tributary streams, encompassing thousands of acres. The dozen or so rivers and hundreds of winding creeks that flow into Delaware Bay are surprisingly deep in relation to their width. Many of the rivers carry depths of 15 feet, some even more, for considerable distances upstream. Years ago when sailing vessels were the principal means of transporting goods, coastal schooners sailed up and down the Maurice River to Port Elizabeth and the Cohansey River to Fairton and Bridgeton in New Jersey, and the Murderkill River to Frederica and the Mispillion River to Milford in Delaware. Even most of the creeks that are barely wide enough for the gunnels of a bateau to fit from bank to bank are deep enough to float this flat-bottomed boat with a raked bow and stern and flared sides so familiar to this section of the country.

From shore out to about the 18-foot contour the bottom slopes downward very gradually. This gradualness becomes evident during an ebb tide, especially along the New Jersey shore when the water drains down exposing miles of sand and mud flats. Beyond the 18-foot contour in the upper half of Delaware Bay the bottom slopes rather steeply to the 40-foot main ship channel located in the middle of the Bay. In the lower half of Delaware Bay, fingerlike projections of deep water extend upriver on both sides of the main ship channel. Fishermen call them sloughs or channels, and have given them picturesque names—Four Fathom Slough, Deep Brandywine Slough, Egypt Bottom, and Blake Channel. Separating these deep depressions are sandy shoals, some rising to a within foot or so of the surface. Early in the spring, fish enter Delaware Bay usually moving along the floor of the sloughs where the water is warmer than at the surface. Later, as the surface water warms, many of them move out of the deep sloughs into shallower water. Then, during summer when it becomes too warm there, they move back into the sloughs. Knowledgeable anglers, of course, shift their activities accordingly.

FISH AND FISHING: DELAWARE BAY

From the nadir of man's abuse the Delaware River and Bay have gone to the pinnacle of man's progress to reverse the effects of pollution and overfishing. As late as the 1960's no fish could migrate up the Delaware due to the pollution block between Wilmington, Delaware, and Trenton, New Jersey. Today striped bass breed in these waters and American shad run all the way to the headwaters in New York.

Considering the condition of the Delaware River it is surprising that fishing in the Delaware Bay was not only possible but productive during the 1950's and 1960's. Croaker, known locally as hardheads, provided most of the action with the occasional weakfish, called trout or sea trout in Delaware, taken by lucky anglers.

During the past 30 years we have seen the croaker all but disappear. Weakfish runs were so strong it seemed impossible they would ever end, but they did. And now the croaker are back, along with some of the

best striped bass fishing anyone can remember. Change is the only constant in saltwater fishing.

The upper portion of the Delaware Bay is a brackish estuary where catfish, perch and carp may be taken in the spring only to be replaced by blues and weakfish during the summer. Rockfish can be taken throughout the year, but size and bag limits prevent most of these fish from seeing the inside of a cooler.

The Reedy Point Jetty at the mouth of the Chesapeake and Delaware Canal is a good location for shore-based anglers. A boat ramp and additional shore-fishing opportunities are provided at St. Augustine, about six miles south of the canal on Route 9.

Peeler crab and bloodworms are the most popular baits for just about anything that swims in this part of the bay. Artificials are seldom employed, and even when a bucktail is used there will be a small piece of peeler crab on the hook.

The bottom between Woodland Beach and Port Mahon is covered with oyster beds that attract trout, croaker and blues on high tides. The same fish will work along the edge of the shipping channel during low water. The shallow areas close to shore are ideal for small-boat anglers willing to get out early or stay late, as fish seem more active here when the sun is low.

The town of Fortescue on the New Jersey side of the bay provides headboats, charter boats, small-boat rentals and launch ramps for private boats. This has been a sportfishing center for many years and you will find plenty of fish-producing structure within a short distance.

The Triangle Stakes lie within rowing distance of Fortescue and some anglers still fish the area in self-propelled boats. Ben Davis Shoal to the north and the Cross Ledge to the south also hold trout, flounder and bluefish. The Egg Island Flats produce big black drum in the spring for those who are willing to soak clam baits on the bottom.

Bowers Beach, Delaware, is the largest fishing facility on the Delaware side where headboat and charter boats have been plying the bay for more than fifty years. The Miah Maull Shoal is a favorite of local anglers but a quick check of your chart will reveal a considerable amount of other good bottom structure a short distance from the entrance buoy. The oyster grounds that lie between Hawknest Shoal and Cedarbush Hole can be good during the summer especially on flood tides late in the day.

The Cedar Creek boat ramp at Mispillion is one of the most popular in Delaware. The line of boats and tow vehicles stretched for miles in the spring when huge weakfish came into the bay, and even though the big trout come no more, the fishing is still good enough to attract anglers from far and wide.

Small boaters can head south out of Mispillion Inlet to the Coral Beds off the southern end of Slaughter

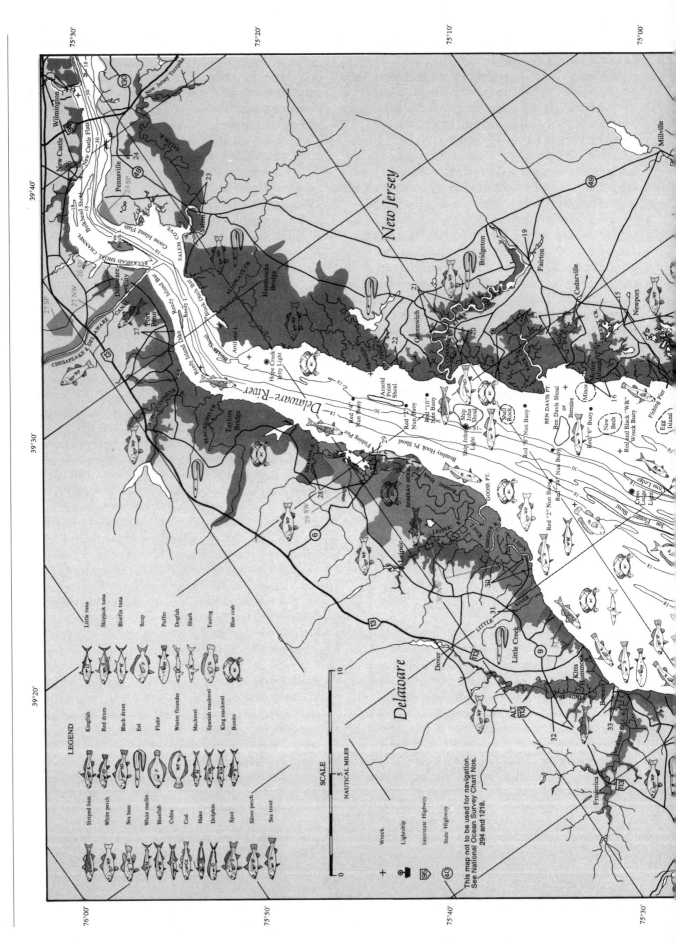

LEGEND

Striped bass	Kingfish	Little tuna
White perch	Red drum	Skipjack tuna
Sea bass	Black drum	Bluefin tuna
White marlin	Eel	Scup
Bluefish	Fluke	Puffer
Cobia	Winter flounder	Dogfish
Cod	Mackerel	Shark
Hake	Spanish mackerel	Tautog
Dolphin	King mackerel	Blue crab
Spot	Bonito	
Silver perch		
Sea trout		

SCALE

NAUTICAL MILES

0   5   10

Wreck
Lightship
Interstate Highway
State Highway

This map not to be used for navigation. See National Ocean Survey Chart Nos. 294 and 1218.

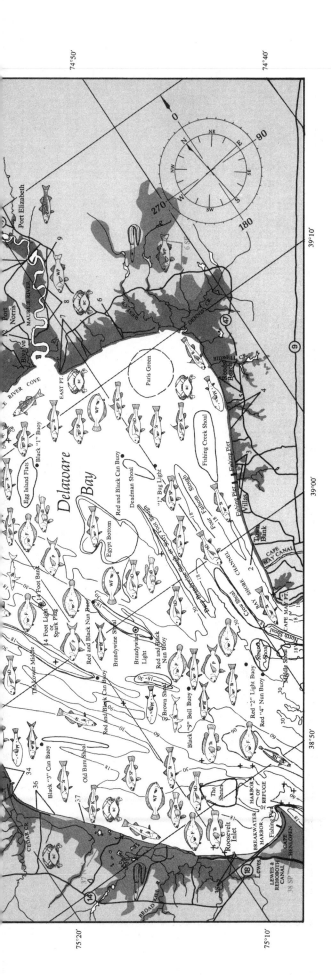

Beach. These beds are not made from the type of coral found in the tropics but by a type of seaworm that builds up mounds of mud on the bottom and finds this particular area to its liking. The food chain builds up from there and ends with croaker, trout and flounder.

The A Buoy sits at the top of Broadkill Slough and just west of Bare Shoal. The drop from the shoal to the slough is over 20 feet and provides good structure for catching trout, blues, flounder and black drum.

Further to the east is the Anchorage with water depths of 100 feet or more. Fishing here can be difficult on a running tide but some of the biggest flounder and trout are taken from these depths every year.

Brown Shoal has always been a good location for a variety of fish and now the State of Delaware has added an artificial-reef site. This structure should attract tog, sea bass and other bottom fish that will join the trout, blues and flounder.

Brandywine Shoal may be the most famous fishing spot in Delaware Bay. It received most of its reputation during the 1980's when big trout were caught there in numbers that today seem almost impossible. The trout may be smaller but they still come here in the spring and summer to join flounder, blues and croaker.

The technique for fishing Brandywine and all the other shoals in the Delaware Bay is to drift while soaking peeler crab, squid, live minnows or cut fresh bait along the bottom. Bucktails, usually tipped with bait or with some type of rubber tail, are cast or simply drifted along with the bait if weakfish are the main target.

Some anglers will anchor on the oyster beds and fish the same baits. This practice is more popular in the northern portion of the bay.

The town of Lewes lies at the mouth of the bay and offers ocean-fishing as well as bay fishing opportunities. Several headboats sail from here, along with a large charter boat fleet. The boat ramp is well used in the spring and summer but is a relatively new facility, and traffic is seldom a problem.

Good fishing is available close to the ramp, as flounder are frequently taken from boats drifting in the canal that runs through town. The jetty that protects Roosevelt Inlet holds good numbers of trout and flounder, but it takes time to find the most productive spots along the submerged structure. Bucktails and live bait work well here but expect to donate a fair amount of tackle to the jetty.

There are several other jetties within sight of Roosevelt Inlet and all hold fish. The most productive method for working this structure is casting bucktails to the rocks. Drifting live bait close to the edge of the jetty is also productive and both methods will draw strikes from weakfish, blues and flounder.

In the spring and fall tog become the favorite target of anglers who anchor close to the rocks and fish crab baits on the bottom. This is a tricky procedure and inexperienced boaters would be well advised to book a charter to learn the technique.

The recovery of striped bass has created a new fall fishery out of Lewes. Good numbers of big stripers are taken by anglers drifting live eels or bucktails over the shoals at the mouth of the bay. The area off Breakwater Light has been particularly good for this style of fishing.

To the north of Lewes is the Shears and the Haystacks. The Shears is actually a shoal and the Haystacks or Ice Breakers sit on its southern end. The Haystacks are a series of rock piles that hold everything from trout to tog. The Shears attract blues, trout and flounder with some of the best action at the drop-off to 20 feet just south of the Haystacks.

CAPE MAY TO SINEPUXENT BAY

LAND CONFIGURATION AND WATER DEPTH

The land along this stretch of coast is sandy and low, the highest elevations within 3 miles of the shore being the crests of sand dunes rising up behind the ocean beaches. From Cape Henlopen, the shore runs nearly due south about 20 miles to Fenwick Island; from there it curves back slightly and runs southwestward past Ocean City, Maryland, to the southern end of Assateague Island.

Along most of this section the mainland is indented with bays and separated from the sea by long, narrow, barrier beaches. The bays receive fresh water on their mainland side from scores of twisting, winding streams and creeks, and salt water from the sea through inlets, which are narrow openings in the barrier beach. The bays are connected to each other by a shallow waterway, most of it natural, but part of it dug out artificially.

A series of shoals interspersed with depressions forms a corrugating pattern running more or less parallel to the coast between Cape May and the mouth of Chesapeake Bay. The amplitude of the corrugations reaches its maximum off Ocean City, Maryland. Depths on the shoals range from as shallow as 15 feet on Little Gull and Great Gull Banks, which lie near shore, to 70 feet on the Jack Spot, which is over 20 miles offshore. Fishes, especially pelagic species, seem to congregate around these shoals, of which the Jack Spot is particularly famous. The depressions between the various shoals are usually twice as deep as the shoals. The corrugations extend, though with diminishing amplitude, clear across the continental shelf.

Between the shoals off Cape May and Cape Henlopen a deep gorge bisects the corrugated pattern of shoals and depressions. This is a remnant of the ancient

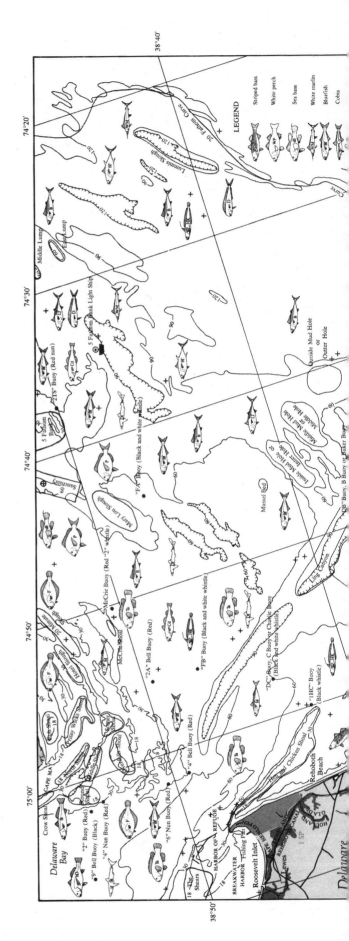

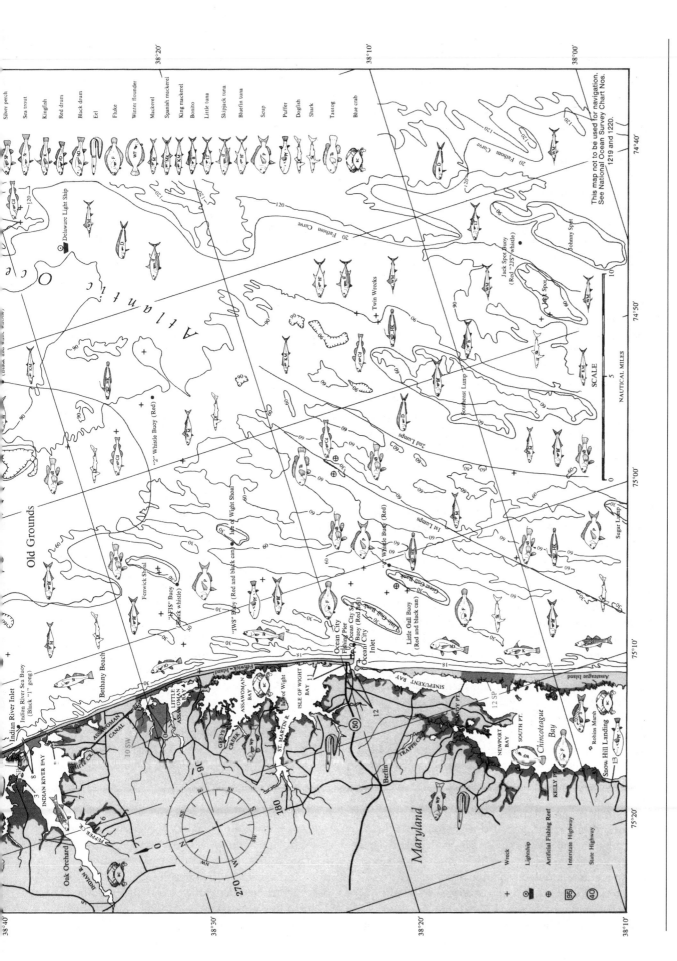

Delaware River Channel which thousands of years ago cut across the continental shelf. Unlike the Hudson Channel it cannot be followed entirely across the shelf, since only its inshore half being still discernible. Located near the head of Delaware Channel is Ling Canyon, a fishing ground abounding in ling (squirrel hake). This is not actually a canyon at all but simply a trough near shore, 100 feet deep by 10 miles long, facetiously named by local fishermen during the 1960's to parody the extravagant radio reports of fishing success around Wilmington and Baltimore Canyons. It became a standing joke among captains to call each other repeatedly on their radios reporting they are sailing off to fish around Ling Canyon, and the name has stuck.

Shoreline Changes

During the early 1600's, when Cornelius May and David De Vries sailed into the mouth of Delaware Bay, Cape Cornelius (as Cape Henlopen was then called) was just a small, blunt patch of land, not the elongated deposit of sand it is today. Cape Henlopen Lighthouse, a seven-story brick structure built in the late 1760's, was situated on a knoll 50 feet high, a quarter mile from the sea. About a century and a half later, in spite of repeated attempts to save it, waves undermined the foundation and the lighthouse fell into the sea. When the March 1962 storm cut away great portions of Delaware's beaches, tree stumps were uncovered out to 900 feet from the existing shoreline. Carbon-14 dating of these stumps revealed that about 300 years ago a pine forest grew on high ground that has since become surf-pounded shore.

The loss of many beaches and the building of new ones along Delaware and Maryland, as well as the rest of the Atlantic coast, have been going on a very long time. When this section of North America was formed many thousands of years ago by deposits of gravel, sand, and silt eroded from interior rock formations, its ancient shoreline was more irregular and the level of the sea was considerably lower than they are now. As the world's large glaciers gradually melted, they released into the sea an enormous volume of water, causing its level to rise, inundating the old shore. Forces that always affect shorelines shaped the new one: waves eroded the old shore, and longshore currents redistributed the sediments. Along this stretch of coast two main longshore currents now flow in opposite directions from Fenwick Island opposite Little Assawoman Bay, one northward and the other southward. The processes of erosion and redistribution, which continue all the time, tend to smooth and straighten the shoreline. They close off embayments, turning them into brackish water and sometimes into freshwater ponds, only later to reopen them as storm-caused waves wash away sections of the beach to form inlets. The inlets last awhile, only again to be closed by current-carried sand. Thus, Indian

River, which was connected to the sea through most of the 1800's, closed and reopened repeatedly during the early 1900's according to the direction and severity of storms. In 1925 it became completely closed and remained so until local people dug it open in 1929. Within a year it closed again. Between 1930 and 1939 it opened and closed at least five more times before it was dredged and jettied.

FISH AND FISHING: CAPE MAY TO SINEPUXENT BAY

The oceanfront, barrier islands and shallow bays along this section of the coast have attracted millions of people from the large inland cities looking for relief not only from the summer heat but from the noise and congestion associated with urban life. Unfortunately they have brought these same problems with them, turning once sleepy summer towns into crowded cities. This same overcrowding also affects the waterways, and serious anglers fish early and late in the day to avoid the many other user groups.

Cape May is not quite as crowded as some other New Jersey seaside towns but it does receive a fair number of tourists during the summer. Fortunately there are also many fishing opportunities, so overcrowding is seldom a problem.

The jetties that line the oceanfront provide excellent fishing platforms for the shore-based angler. You must fish between dusk and first light to avoid problems with bathers, surfers and other non-angler types but this is true almost anywhere along the coast.

Weakfish, striped bass and blues are the primary targets for most jetty jockeys. Casting bucktails or swimming plugs around the rocks will take any of these three fish. Those who work bloodworms, squid, cut bait or crab in the surf or from the rocks, can expect whiting, flounder, croaker, sea bass and, during cold weather, the occasional tog.

Boaters have much to chose from out of Cape May. The Cape May Canal cuts the southeast tip off of the cape and provides easy access to either the Delaware Bay or the Atlantic Ocean. Brandywine Light is a favorite destination for bay fishermen while ocean anglers may fish anywhere from Overfall Shoals at the mouth of the bay to the 100-fathom line and beyond. Drifting along the Intracoastal Waterway behind the barrier islands is a good method for small boaters who would like to catch flounder, weakfish or small blues.

Cape May does have a fleet of charter and headboats as well as launch ramps for private boats. In addition to the many hotels and motels there are several campgrounds that cater to the traveling angler.

The next opening to the ocean south of Cape May is Indian River Inlet, Delaware, where the waters of Indian River and Rehoboth Bay rush in and out, creating one of the more dangerous inlets on the east coast.

There is plenty of sheltered water in Rehoboth Bay and the Indian River and pontoon boats are a favorite fishing platform. Drifting is the approved method for catching flounder, weakfish and small blues, with live minnows the most popular bait.

Massey's Ditch between the two main bodies of water is a good location for flounder. The best fishing occurs at either end of the ditch, where flounder wait to ambush bait moving out on the tide.

A channel that runs behind South Shore Marina and the flats between Holts Landing and Quillen's Point are also good for flounder. Jetty jockeys cast bucktails and plugs for striped bass, weakfish and blues from either side of Indian River Inlet. Surf-casters work the beach for bottom fish such as whiting, flounder and weakfish.

Boaters who travel through the inlet find a wide variety of fishing opportunities. The inshore waters hold blues, trout, croaker, sea bass, tog, false albacore and sharks. Trolling with plugs and spoons works well for blues and false albacore, while bottom-fishing with fresh or live bait is the best method for the other species.

Hen and Chicken Shoal, the rough bottom around the DB Buoy, and the Old Grounds between DA Buoy and the D Buoy are good bottom-fishing locations. Trolling is good in these same locations and once you move past the D Buoy, it is the primary method for catching large pelagic fish.

Offshore fishing for tuna, marlin, dolphin and wahoo begins at the 20-Fathom Fingers and continues out as far as your fuel capacity will take you. Dragging dead baits such as ballyhoo, mullet and squid will catch all of these fish but more and more offshore fishermen are setting artificials in their spread.

There are several boat ramps with access to Indian River Inlet, the closest being at the state-owned marina on the north side. Holts Landing State Park is one of several boat ramps leading to Indian River Bay. Campgrounds are plentiful in the area, but motels are more numerous in the resort towns of Rehoboth and Dewey Beach.

Ocean City Inlet is the next outlet to the south. This is home to the largest white marlin tournament in the world, and the city bills itself as the White Marlin Capital. A large fleet of big charter boats runs from here during the summer fishing the canyons for not only white marlin but blue marlin, wahoo, dolphin and tuna. Headboats also run out of Ocean City with at least one, the *Ocean City Princess*, offering overnight trips to the canyons.

Closer to shore, the Fenwick Shoal and the Lumps offer a wide variety of bottom fish along with some big blues, false albacore, bonita, king mackerel and Spanish mackerel. Trolling with spoons and plugs remains the top method for most of the pelagics but live bait is becoming more popular especially for king mackerel. Chunking for bluefin tuna has been good at the Hot Dog and Jackspot during the summer.

Flounder fishing is the prime activity for anglers in Isle of Wight and Sinepuxent Bays. Drifting with live minnows along channel edges on low tides or over flats on the flood remains the most productive technique. The Route 50 Bridge and the fishing pier provide access for shore fishermen while surf-fishing is very popular along the oceanfront. Assateague Island offers a long unspoiled beach that is very popular with surf-casters.

There is seldom a shortage of accommodations in Ocean City except on holiday weekends. Camping is available on Assateague Island and at several locations near the city. Public and private boat ramps can be found throughout the area, with the West Ocean City Ramp one of the better facilities.

CHINCOTEAGUE BAY TO QUINBY INLET

LAND CONFIGURATION AND WATER DEPTH

The mainland along this section of coast is composed of gently rolling hills, most of which are 20 to 40 feet above sea level. Upon nearing the brackish water bays, the land gradually levels to a low plain. Here, many small streams of fresh water broaden out, their shores reticulated by marshes which gradually merge from fresh water to salt as they eventually fall under the influence of tidal water.

In the northern part of this section, Chincoteague Bay separates the mainland from the barrier island called Assateague. Chincoteague Bay is about 20 miles long by 4 miles wide and averages 5 feet deep. The bay side of Assateague Island, like the mainland shore, is uneven, fringed along its whole length by a saltmarsh. The sea side of Assateague Island is nearly straight. During various times in the past, storms have cut inlets through this sandy barrier island in at least 10 places, sometimes several simultaneously. Today, however, owing to artificial stabilization of the dunes, the island extends unbroken from Ocean City Inlet south to Chincoteague Inlet, a distance of over 30 miles.

The southern part of this section, below Chincoteague Inlet, is characterized by a series of bays separated by broad saltmarshes. These bays are connected by a system of narrow, meandering waterways called passages, narrows, and creeks. Most of these passages average 6 to 10 feet deep, though some carry depths as much as 30 feet. At low tide very large areas of muddy bottoms in the bays become completely exposed while

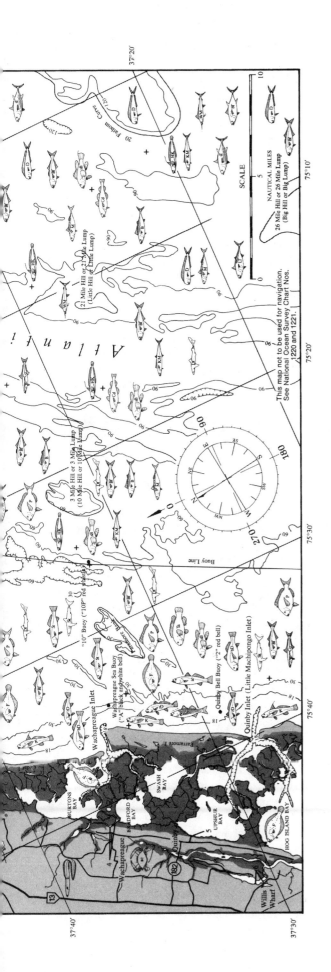

the remaining areas are covered with water as deep as 2 feet. The tidal mud flats and the submerged parts of the bays are drained by deep channels branching into still deeper trunk channels, some of which carry depths of over 45 feet. Two or more of these trunk channels join at an inlet through the barrier beach. The effect of the numerous inlets is to divide the barrier beach into over a dozen islands ranging in size from a few square rods to several thousand acres.

The sea floor off this section, composed mostly of sand, slopes away from land at a rate of about 10 feet a mile for the first 5 miles and about half that rate for the next 30 miles. The corrugations of shoals and depressions described in the previous section continue to parallel the coast. They are most prominent close to Ocean City, Maryland, and progressively less so southward. The line of shoals closest to the beach can be followed along First Lumps, Ship Shoal, and Paramore Bank; the next line along the Second Lumps, Winter Quarter Shoal, Blackfish Bank, and the 3 Mile Lump; and the third and least prominent line along the Jack Spot and Johnny Spot to the 21 Mile Hill and 26 Mile Hill. All these shoals act as congregating places for fishes, especially pelagic species.

FISH AND FISHING: CHINCOTEAGUE BAY TO QUINBY INLET

The Barrier Islands off the coast of Virginia are the longest stretch of undeveloped beach along the Atlantic Coast. The Nature Conservancy purchased many of these islands, while state or federal agencies hold title to the rest. This partnership has protected the land from development and the water from the loss of quality that always follows such development.

Chincoteague is the largest town along the coast, with numerous motels, restaurants and tourist attractions. A fair-size fleet of charter and headboats runs out of here and there are several boat-rental facilities. Surf-fishing is possible on nearby Assateague Island, but you do need a federal permit to drive on the beach.

Inshore fishing is very popular here, with flounder the main target. A quick check of your chart will reveal numerous channels between shallow bays or along marshes. These channels hold flounder all year but the best action on large fish occurs in the spring. Live minnows are the best bait but frozen shiners, squid, cut fresh fish and bucktails will also tempt the local flatfish.

During the summer the best flounder fishing will be found near the inlet, where cooler water will move in from the ocean. In addition to the flounder anglers will also take weakfish, whiting, small blues, croaker and spot.

Bigger blues, false albacore, king mackerel and Spanish mackerel are taken by anglers who troll plugs and spoons around bottom structure such as Winter Quarter Shoal. In the winter wreck fishing for sea bass and tog is very good, but quite often the weather is very bad.

Offshore fishing takes place all along the 100-fathom line from Baltimore to Norfolk Canyon. The best of this action is in late summer or early fall.

Although the inlets from Chincoteague down to Wachapreague are served by public boat ramps, the inlets are uncharted. Fishing can be good all along this section of beach but only from a shallow-draft boat with an experienced guide at the helm.

Flounder are the lifeblood of Wachapreague, and every business in town depends on flounder fishermen to keep afloat. You will find several charter boats that specialize in flounder fishing or you can rent a small boat to try fishing on your own. A new public ramp and a private ramp at Wachapreague Marina provide access for trailer boats.

In the spring, look for flounder in Wachapreague Channel but in the summer you will find them closer to the inlet. A deep hole behind the Parramore Island Coast Guard Station is a favored location on incoming tides.

Bluefin tuna used to provide exciting action at the 26 and 21 Mile Hills during June and July, but a decline in their population has made this fishery difficult at best. Fortunately a technique new to Virginia but long common elsewhere has proved productive. Chunking with cut-up butterfish on or near the hills during August and September has put new life in the bluefin fishery. The fish are bigger, some weighing more than 100 pounds, but not nearly as numerous as they once were.

The Norfolk Canyon lies about 40 miles from Wachapreague Inlet and draws many of the local offshore fishermen. In recent years dolphin have provided most of the action, but marlin, tuna and wahoo are taken on a regular basis.

The town of Quinby may be small but the nearby fishing is as good as anywhere along the Virginia coast. And while a public boat ramp with plenty of parking space allows private boaters easy access, navigating out to Quinby Inlet can be a difficult task. The channel is well marked but any deviation from the correct course can leave you high and dry.

The same flounder baits and techniques that work elsewhere are effective here. My favorite is a live minnow and a strip of squid on a wide-gap hook dressed with a bit of bucktail. My favorite fishing spot is the channel behind Hog Island out to the ocean end of Quinby Inlet.

GREAT MACHIPONGO INLET TO FALSE CAPE

LAND CONFIGURATION AND WATER DEPTH

The mainland along this entire section of coast is uniformly low and sandy. North of Chesapeake Bay's entrance, that is, from Hog Island on Virginia's eastern shore to Fisherman Island, just below Cape Charles, the coast is characterized by broad bays and saltmarshes which are separated from the open sea by about a dozen closely spaced barrier islands. This complex of bays and saltmarshes is a continuation of the one described in the previous section.

The evenness of the coast south of Cape Henry is in sharp contrast to the irregularity of that to the north. Rudee Inlet is now the only opening through the barrier beach for 75 miles from Cape Henry to Bodie Island, North Carolina. Even this narrow break in the shoreline would fill with drifting sand were it not constantly dredged. A succession of inlets once connected the sea with a series of bays which lie behind the barrier beach just south of Virginia Beach, but the last inlet was closed in the late 1820's by drifting sand. Even after the inlets closed, however, the lowness of the newly formed sand dunes permitted the sea intermittently to wash over the barrier beach. In the late 1930's the dunes were artificially built up to prevent the influx of salt water. Since then the fresh water flowing into these bays has nearly purged them of their salt content, so that the water in North Bay, Shipps Bay, and Back Bay is now nearly fresh.

Separating these two different forms of coast is the mouth of the Chesapeake Bay. Through the 10-mile gap between Cape Charles and Cape Henry flows the tidal water of the largest estuary along the east coast of the United States. Twice each day during the flood tide, about 1,600 billion gallons of sea water flow up the Bay past the Capes; and twice each day during the ebb tide, about 1,620 billion gallons of Bay water flow past the Capes to the sea. The difference in volume between the two tides, about 20 billion gallons, is half the average daily amount of fresh water running into the Bay from myriad streams, creeks, and rivers.

The configuration of the bottom at the mouth of the Chesapeake Bay bears some similarity to that of the adjacent coasts. The northern side is a submerged continuation of the barrier islands, being composed mostly of sandy shoals. The depths of the shoals, which range from a foot to 30 feet, average about 20 feet. In about the middle of the mouth lies the Chesapeake Channel. It is about 2 miles wide by 50 feet deep. To the south is another sandy but smaller shoal area called Tail of the Horseshoe, and beyond this is Thimble Shoal Channel.

This channel, now maintained by dredging to about 40 feet deep, is actually the continuation of the James River. From Thimble Shoal Channel the muddy bottom rises to Cape Henry, located on the southern side of the Bay.

The sea floor off this section of coast is mostly sandy and slopes away from land at a rate of about 4 feet a mile for 50 miles. Over the next 10 miles the slope increases tenfold, reaching a depth of 600 feet, the edge of the continental shelf. The corrugated pattern of shoals and depressions roughly paralleling the coast from Cape May, New Jersey, ends off Cape Henry in the areas known as the Inshore Southeast Lumps and the Offshore Southeast Lumps. Depths on the shoal part of the Lumps range from 45 to 60 feet while depressions range from 75 to 80 feet. These corrugations, like the others along the coast, are congregating places for fishes; and since the corrugations are closely spaced and extend over 300 square miles, this is an especially good fishing ground for both pelagic and bottom-dwelling species.

NATURAL HISTORY

An open sandy coast like this stretch is highly dynamic. The loosely packed sediments which form the land are especially vulnerable to waves and winds which continually act upon them—eroding, transporting, and depositing. Sometimes these processes act so rapidly that during a single storm we can actually watch them operate. In a day or two, sometimes even within hours, inlets hundreds of feet wide may be cut through barrier beaches; vegetation-covered dunes may be leveled; or sand spits or small islands may be formed where a fathom or two of water had been just before. More common, subtle changes proceed so slowly they are scarcely noticed, though they are extremely important.

One such change is the development of saltmarshes, the flat land and communities of plants that usually border estuaries and are periodically covered by the tide. Saltmarshes along this stretch of coast exist in delicate balance between the rising level of the sea and the accumulation of sediments. Along Virginia, Maryland, and Delaware the level of the sea is rising an average of about one-quarter of an inch each year. This rise in water level would eventually cause the shallow bays to deepen were it not for natural compensating processes. Sediments are carried, more or less continuously, into the bays from the land by runoff; and they are carried occasionally into the bays by overwash from the sea during severe storms. A few of these sediments are returned through the inlets by tidal currents to the sea, but most of them remain in the bays, some settling out on the bottom, but more being trapped among the stems and rhizomes of marsh grasses that grow along the shore. These grasses, called cordgrasses, are among the few flowering plants able to withstand periodic sub-

mergence in salt water. Sediments which gradually accumulate around the cordgrasses afford conditions suitable for other varieties of plants to become established, and with the advent of more plants the accretion rate of the newly formed land increases. Through a succession of plants, starting with those of the saltmarsh and usually ending with those of the forest, newly distributed sediments are held by the roots and slowly but continually aid in building up the land. It seems that under natural conditions the loss of sandy beaches along the coast caused by the rising sea level is countered by sediments accumulating in the estuaries. Whatever happens to them in the foreseeable future will be the consequence of man's intervention in the coastal processes.

FISH AND FISHING: GREAT MACHIPONGO INLET TO FALSE CAPE

The boat ramp at Willis Wharf is the best location to put over if you wish to fish the Great Machipongo Inlet. This is a deep, wide channel that ends at one of the more navigable inlets. Unfortunately there are no recreational fishing facilities at Willis Wharf, so most of the traffic is from commercial fishermen.

Flounder are available along the channel edge and at the inlet. Surf-fishing for red drum can be productive on Cobb and Hog islands during the spring and fall, and good runs of gray trout show up along the oceanfront in September and October.

Sand Shoal Channel and Sand Shoal Inlet are the last charted passages to the sea before the mouth of the Chesapeake Bay. The town of Oyster has a very good boat ramp but no charter boats, headboats or tackle shops.

The 224 Day Marker at the junction of Sand Shoal Channel and Eckichy Channel is one of the better fishing locations in this area. Expect to catch flounder, weakfish, blues and just about any bottom fish you might find in Virginia water.

Trolling close to the beach can be very good in the summer when Spanish mackerel become abundant. Weakfish show up at the inlet during the fall, when you may also find a few big rockfish especially in November.

New Inlet, Ship Shoal Inlet, Little Inlet and Smith Inlet are unmarked and can be dangerous especially for boaters unfamiliar with the area. With the exception of the Intercoastal Waterway there are no marked channels behind any of the barrier islands, and these areas should only be explored on a rising tide.

The final stop on our trip down the Virginia Coast is Rudee Inlet out of Virginia Beach. In sharp contrast to the Eastern Shore, Virginia Beach is the largest resort city in the world, with no shortage of accommodations or other facilities.

The charter fleet out of Rudee is small, but there are

several headboats here providing relatively inexpensive trips to near-shore fishing hot spots. A new boat ramp at Owls Creek can handle any craft you can put on a trailer.

The numerous wrecks and shoals close to Rudee Inlet are good locations for sea bass, tog, big bluefish, Spanish mackerel, king mackerel and false albacore. Some very big kings are taken in the fall within a mile of the beach by live-bait fishermen.

A fishing pier at 14th Street and another at Little Island Park in Sandbridge offer good action on bottom fish as well as blues and mackerel. Surf-fishing is possible anywhere along the beach but you may find competition from surfers and swimmers in some locations.

Offshore fishing is good from June to October, with the Cigar a favorite location. This seamount lies about 60 miles southeast of the inlet where you can find marlin, tuna, wahoo and dolphin.

A little closer to shore there are artificial reefs at the Chesapeake Light Tower and the Triangle Wrecks. During the colder months good numbers of big tog and sea bass are caught here, while amberjack, dolphin, big blues and sharks show up when the water is warm.

FISHING BY SEASON IN VIRGINIA

OFFSHORE

The thrill of seeing a "tailwalking" marlin at the end of a fishing line draws thousands of fishermen to the coast of Virginia every year. Waters of offshore canyons and along the 100 Fathom Curve off Virginia offer some of the finest white marlin fishing on the East Coast from July through September, peaking during the latter half of August and throughout September. A good blue marlin fishery has also developed in recent years.

The waters at the edge of the Gulf Stream harbor good numbers of yellowfin tuna, dolphin, and wahoo, all of which are noted for their excellent table qualities as well as their fight at the end of a line. All three are summertime visitors, although yellowfins arrive earlier (generally in May) and stay later (well into October).

The migratory route of bluefin tuna lies close to the Virginia coast, and schools of bluefin begin to appear during the first week of June. The bluefins seem to favor depths of 15 to 20 fathoms, which keeps good numbers of fish within 30 miles of the coast and makes them the most popular offshore pursuit. The best fishing occurs over underwater seamounts, lumps, and holes, most notably the 26-Mile Hill off the Eastern Shore and the Southeast Lumps off Virginia Beach. Many years, bluefin remain abundant until the end of July. The

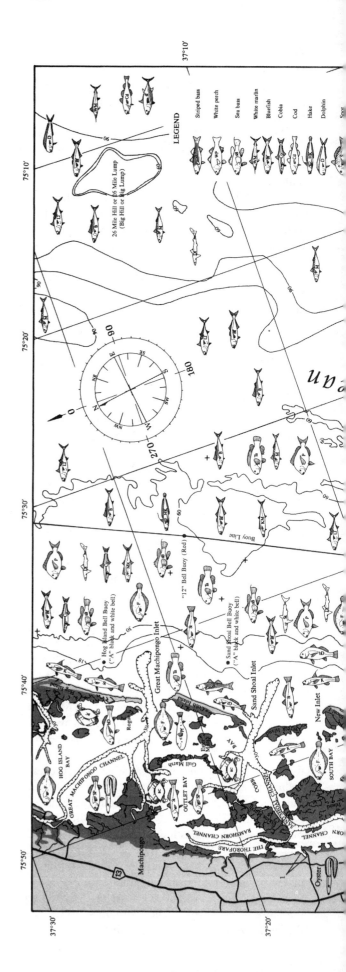

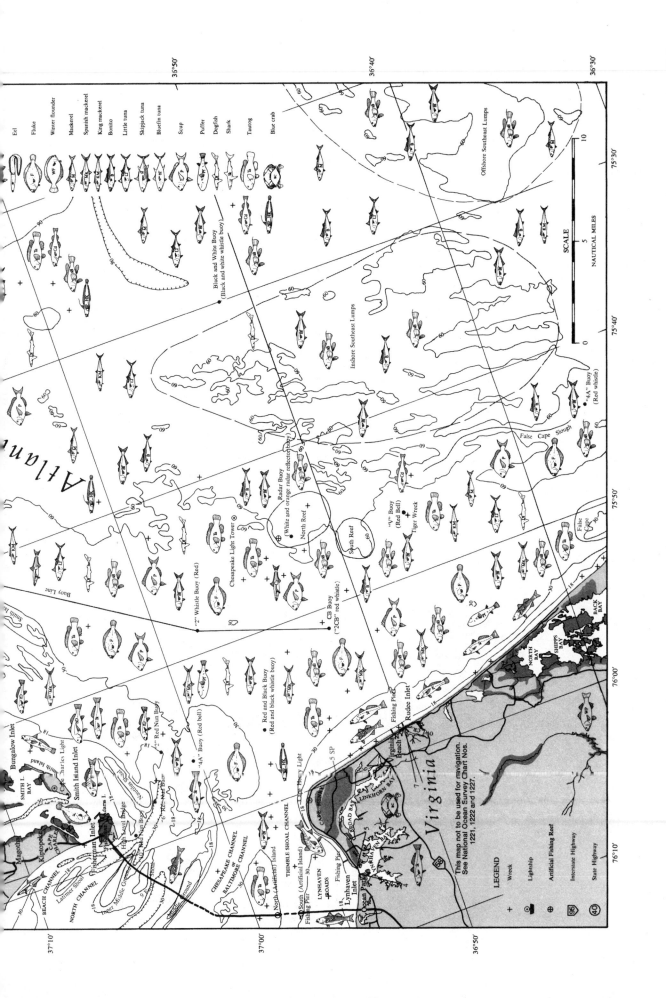

same waters produce good numbers of little tunny (false albacore), king mackerel, bluefish, and bonito.

COASTAL WATERS

The waters within 25 miles of Virginia's ocean beaches harbor gamefish during most months of the year. Bluefish are the first to arrive each spring and the last to leave each fall. Vast schools of blues weighing up to 20 pounds appear in early April, remaining well into June before departing for the northeast. They reappear in October, remaining into early December before heading south for the winter. Blues can be found almost anywhere off the Virginia coast, from just outside the ocean breakers to 30 miles offshore. However, some areas, such as Chesapeake Light Tower, and over many coastal wrecks and submerged seamounts and lumps, are consistent producers. Little tunny (false albacore) are found in the same waters.

Amberjack are Virginia's summertime superstars, appearing around most wrecks and towers and a few buoys, ranging from five to 25 miles offshore. Virginia's jacks are large, averaging 35 to 55 pounds, and a tougher fish is hard to find.

Another delightful summer visitor is the Spanish mackerel. Schools of Spanish appear in May and remain into September around many ocean inlets, the mouth of the Chesapeake Bay, and around drop-offs and channels in the nearshore waters. These mackerels average one to three pounds, and plenty of bluefish of similar size frequent the same areas.

King mackerel and cobia create loads of excitement when they migrate through the coastal zone. The hottest action occurs from August through October as the fish begin to move south in schools, although some good catches are registered throughout the summer months.

An active artificial-reef program and a bottom littered with the sunken hulks torpedoed by the German navy's U-boats create the best bottom-fishing for tautog and sea bass along the east coast. Tautog inhabit coastal structures year round, although they can be hard to catch when the water temperatures fall below 42 degrees. Sea bass are plentiful in all months except January, February, and March, when they migrate to the edge of the Continental Shelf.

EASTERN SHORE FISHING

Visiting the Eastern Shore is like stepping back in time. Rustic fishing villages, farms, and forests provide plenty of solitude. Myriad creeks, bays, and sounds harbor some of Virginia's premier fishing opportunities.

The flounder is the undisputed king of the Eastern Shore's seaside. They are abundant from April through September in virtually every inlet and bay behind the Barrier Islands. Seaside waters also produce lots of gray trout (weakfish), black drum, red drum, bluefish, croaker, kingfish, spot, and Virginia's only viable tarpon fishery. The fall run of gray trout just off the Barrier Island inlets is one of the area's most overlooked opportunities, and sharkers have discovered a splendid fishery for big fish in most Barrier Island inlets.

The Barrier Islands along the peninsula's seaside

Chumming the channels with grass shrimp is one of the most productive ways to catch weakfish. This angler holds up a couple of six-pounders taken close to sod banks.
(VIN T. SPARANO)

Eastern Shore flounder are plentiful from April to September in all inshore waters, especially inlets.
(JOHN E. PHILLIPS)

offer some of the best surf-fishing on the East Coast. With few exceptions, the islands remain in a completely natural state—no people, no development, and no access roads. Surf fishermen must take a boat through the "back country" to reach the islands, anchor their craft behind the islands, and walk across to the beaches.

The trip is worth it! Spring and fall runs of red drum, averaging 35 to 50 pounds, and big and small bluefish, gray trout, flounder, kingfish, croaker, and spot roam along the beaches in astonishing numbers. Most of these islands are owned by The Nature Conservancy and are open for day visits by the public for fishing, hiking, and birdwatching.

Assateague, a 28-square-mile island, is the northernmost Barrier Island, and is part of the National Seashore system operated by the National Park Service. A causeway provides access for surf-fishermen, who can park at numerous areas along a road which runs behind oceanfront dunes.

The creeks along the bayside of the Eastern Shore peninsula harbor the best speckled trout fishing in Virginia. The biggest fish are usually caught in May and June.

The bayside run of huge black drum off Cape Charles is famous among East Coast anglers, and the fall fishery for red drum is beginning to receive some much-deserved recognition. Cobia weighing up to 100 pounds roam the southern bayside, particularly the area from the Cabbage Patch to the High Level Bridge of the Chesapeake Bay Bridge Tunnel. Gray trout, bluefish, flounder, croaker, and spot are available seasonally off most bayside ports.

FISHING REGULATIONS

As we've noted previously, fishing regulations change frequently. What follows are abstracts of fishing regulations for New Jersey, Delaware, Maryland, and Virginia. This information should be used for general purposes only. Because regulations change, and because the regulations themselves are far more detailed than presented here, all anglers should contact the state agencies listed at the beginning and end of this chapter.

NEW JERSEY

Fishing regulations for New Jersey begin on page 105.

DELAWARE

An angler may take gamefish from Delaware tidal waters without being licensed but only with a hook and line. Each gamefish fisherman is limited to two fishing rods or handlines provided each has no more than three hooks or three separate lures with hooks.

Fish Length Limits in Tidal Waters

For conservation reasons, certain fishes have minimum and maximum length limits to protect females long enough for them to spawn at least once or to maximize the yields in weight per recruit.

No one is permitted to possess any species of fish that measures less than the minimum length. The total length of a fish is measured from the tip of the snout to the tip of the tail. Minimum length limits for foodfish in tidal waters are as follows:

Atlantic croaker: 8 inches
Atlantic sturgeon: 54 inches
Summer flounder: 14 inches
Striped bass: 28 inches
Tautog: 12 inches
Swordfish: 31 inches
Sailfish: 57 inches
White marlin: 62 inches
Blue marlin: 86 inches
Weakfish: 13 inches
Spotted sea trout: 12 inches
Red drum: 14 inches

No one may possess any undersized finfish. Possession limits apply at or between the place a fish is caught and a person's personal abode or temporary or transient place of lodging. Permits may be obtained from the Fish and Wildlife Director, to possess undersized or more than a daily creel limit of any finfish for aquacultural purposes or artificial propagation.

Creel Limits

The maximum number of a species of finfish permitted in a recreational fisherman's possession is as follows:

Weakfish: 10/day
Summer flounder: 6/day
Bluefish: 10/day
Striped bass: 1/day
Tautog: 10/day
Spanish mackerel: 10/day
Red drum: 2 greater than 32 inches/day

The creel limit for tautog applies to all categories of recreational fishermen. Creel limits may be commingled in a container provided that all fishermen are present, whether onshore or on a boat.

Seasons

A closed recreational fishing season for summer flounder begins October 1 and ends on May 14.

Striped Bass

Except during the striped bass spawning season, April 1 through May 31, recreational anglers may take and possess no more than one striped bass a day that measures more than 28 inches at any time. During the spawning season, the Nanticoke River, the C&D Canal, and the Delaware River to the north of the southernmost jetty at the C&D Canal entrance and all their tributaries are closed to fishing.

A commercially licensed fisherman is only permitted to take his or her share of the state's allocation of striped bass during a specific fishing season starting on March 1 and ending at 4:00 p.m. on April 30. Consult the Division of Fish and Wildlife for commercial fishing requirements.

The penalty for anyone illegally taking striped bass ranges from $100 to $500 for each fish.

Billfish

The U.S. recreational billfish fishery currently releases approximately 50 percent of its catch. However, to ensure that most billfishes are released so that they may remain available to the recreational fishery, minimum size limits are imposed for each species (except spearfish). Size limits are based on weight, but are expressed in lower jaw fork length. The minimum sizes are 57 inches (30 pounds) for sailfish, 62 inches (50 pounds) for white marlin, and 86 inches (200 pounds) for blue marlin, and are intended to reduce angler retention by 30 percent, 50 percent, and 50 percent, respectively. This measure allows competitive fishing tournaments and retention of trophy-size fish to continue while significantly reducing one source of billfish mortality.

The minimum size limit for swordfish is 31 inches measured from the tip of the lower jaw to the fork of the tail or 41 pounds dressed weight. It is illegal to sell recreationally caught swordfish and recreational swordfishing is restricted to hook and line.

Bluefish

The bluefish-management plan has been approved by the Atlantic States Marine Fishery Commission (ASMFC) and the Mid-Atlantic Fisheries Management Council(MAFMC). Regulations in effect for bluefish include the following:

- a daily possession limit of 10 for recreational fishermen in state and federal waters.
- bluefish caught from party and charter boats may be commingled with other bluefish aboard the vessel.

Atlantic Bluefin Tuna

Atlantic bluefin tuna regulations are currently under review and will change. Federal regulations differ according to the size category of tuna for which you are fishing and the type of gear you are using. The following regulations apply to those using a hand-held rod and reel or handline. Other mechanical devices are prohibited.

Giant bluefin anglers must obtain a valid Federal Fisheries Permit in the General Category for their vessel. The General Category fishery opens June 1 each

year and closes on December 31 or when the annual quota has been harvested. Vessels permitted in the General Category start with a daily limit of one giant Atlantic bluefin tuna per day per vessel. Around September 1 the daily catch limit may be raised to a maximum of three giants per day per vessel. Notices of closures and catch-rate adjustments are sent to all permit holders.

Medium or school bluefin anglers are not required to obtain a Federal Fisheries Permit, although many do on the chance they may catch a giant. All medium and school bluefin harvested by anglers are counted toward the Angling Category. The Angling Category fishery opens January 1 each year and closes on December 31, or when the annual quota has been harvested. The daily catch limit for this category is four per angler per day, only one of which may be a medium. In addition, no more than four mediums may be retained per vessel, even if there are more than four anglers on board.

Anglers may sell their bluefin or keep it for personal consumption. However, it is illegal to sell any size Atlantic bluefin tuna to other than a licensed dealer. Anglers who choose not to sell a giant or medium bluefin to a dealer immediately upon off-loading must call the nearest NMFS Enforcement office for inspection and tagging.

It is illegal to remove the tail or fins from any size bluefin prior to landing. However, the head may be removed.

Tautog

Fishery closed from April 1 to June 30 to protect spawning fish. Free-diving spearfishermen are granted an exception.

MARYLAND (TIDEWATER REGULATIONS)

Bass (Largemouth and Smallmouth)
No closed season—12" minimum size; from March 1 through June 15—15" minimum size
Creel limit: 5 in aggregate

Bluefish
No closed season—8" minimum size
Creel limit: None

Butterfish
No closed season—6" minimum size
Creel limit: None

Catfish
No closed season—10" minimum size
Creel limit: None (except bullheads)

Channel Bass
Minimum size 14"
Creel limit: 2 over 32" per day per person

Flounder

Season—Chesapeake Bay, June 1 to October 30. Tidal waters of Atlantic Ocean, seaside bays and tributaries, May 15 to September 30—14" minimum size

Creel limit: 10 per day.

Hardhead (Croaker)

No closed season—19" minimum size
Creel limit: 20 per person per day.

Pike (Chain Pickerel)

Closed season—March 15 to April 30
Creel limit: 10 in aggregate 14" minimum size

Shad (Hickory-White)

Closed Season—emergency regulations

Spotted Seatrout

No closed season—12" minimum

Striped Bass

Closed, limited fishery

Sturgeon

No closed season—25 pounds minimum
Creel limit: None

Walleye Pike

No closed season—10" minimum size

Weakfish (Seatrout)

No closed season—10" minimum size
Creel limit: None

White Perch

No closed season—No minimum size if caught by hook and line

Creel limit: None

Yellow Perch

No closed season—From February 1 through March 15 (single barbless hooks in open watersheds)
Creel limit—5 per person per day, 8½" minimum size
Areas closed to the taking or possession of yellow perch—Chester, Choptank, Magothy, Miles, Nanticoke, Patapsco, Severn, South, West, 9" minimum: Petuxent, Wye and Choptank Rivers.

Blue Claw Crab

License Requirements: none. Crabbing is permitted April 1 through December 31; 5:30 A.M. to sunset on rivers, 5:30 A.M. to 5:00 P.M. in the Cheasapeake Bay, 24 hours a day from rocks, piers, bridges, and shore.

The daily limit is one bushel per person, two bushels per boat regardless of the number of persons on a boat.

The permitted gear is: Handlines (any number). Ten-per-person limit on collapsible traps or rings except when crabbing from a boat when the limit is 25 traps or rings per boat; cannot be set less than 100' to a trot line, dipnets, 1000' of trotline per person not more than 2 separate 1000' trotlines per boat. Seines up to 50' in length; seines that cannot be pulled onshore must be emptied in water.

Landowners may set up to two commercial pots, with name and address on a sign, from their piers not more than 100 yards from shore. Set crab pots with a 2⁵⁄₁₆ cull ring in upper chamber.

Chesapeake Bay Sportfishing License

No person may fish for finfish in the Chesapeake Bay and its tributaries up to the tidal boundaries without first obtaining a Chesapeake Bay sportfishing license, fee $5.

This license is valid from January 1 through December 31.

Fishing for finfish without a license in the Chesapeake Bay and tributaries is permitted for anyone:

1. 65 years of age or older
2. under than 16 years of age
3. possessing a valid commercial Tidal Fish License
4. fishing from private property as an owner, family member of an owner, or a non-paying guest of an owner
5. fishing a hook and line (rod and reel) from a public bridge or pier which has been designated by the Department as a free fishing area
6. possessing a valid Chesapeake Bay Sport Fishing License issued by the State of Virginia
7. fishing from a licensed charterboat
8. fishing Maryland's Atlantic Ocean and coastal bays
9. fishing the Potomac River's tidal waters or
10. who is a Maryland resident on active duty with the Armed Forces, or on leave with official leave orders.

A license will be required for Maryland's tributaries of the Potomac River. (Maryland's tidal boundary extends to the northwest quadrant boundary lines of the District of Columbia, approximately 0.5 miles upriver from Chain Bridge.)

License Requirements

A person who holds a valid Maryland Fresh Fishing License (persons 65 or older are exempt): $2.50

Special license for a boat, not for hire, to fish the tidal waters of the Chesapeake Bay and tributaries: $25.00

1. Owner or owners purchasing this $25 special license will be issued a personal $5 Chesapeake Bay Sport Fishing License for an individual's use.
2. Guests of special licensed boats will not be required to have a Chesapeake Bay Sport Fishing License.
3. The license sticker is non-transferable. Three consecutive days Chesapeake Bay Sport Fishing License: $2.00

It is unlawful:

(a) for a person to take (or attempt to catch), possess, sell, offer for sale, deliver, carry, or ship any striped bass (*Morone saxatilis*). For the purpose of this regulation any hybrid of striped bass is deemed to be the species striped bass.

(b) to have in one's possession aboard any boat on the tidal waters of Maryland more than fifteen pounds of any fish cut up upon which a size or weight limit is prescribed by law or regulations.

(c) for a person to set or fish a gill net within 1,200 feet of any pier that supports either span of the William Preston Lane Jr. Memorial Bridge between May 1 and October 31, inclusive.

(d) for a person to fish within 1,200 feet of any pier that supports either span of the William Preston Lane Jr. Memorial Bridge if that person:

 1. holds a commercial hook-and-line
 2. uses a treble hook that is not an intrinsic part of a floating lure.

(e) to catch pike or pickerel from March 15 to April 30 in the tidal waters of Maryland. (There is no closed season for pike or pickerel in Maryland's fresh waters.)

(f) to have in one's possession American shad or hickory shad.

It is unlawful to:

(a) take or shoot with a speargun and spear in Maryland's tidal waters between June 15 and December 31 carp, garfish, skate, bull fish, shark, oyster toads, swelling toads (blowfish). American eel, sea lamprey, stingrays or other ray fish may be taken or shot with speargun and spear at any time.

(b) snag or use bow and arrows to obtain carp, garfish, skate, bull fish, shark, oyster toads, swelling toads (blowfish), stingrays or other ray fish only.

(c) use a seine up to 50 feet in length and five feet wide to obtain bait minnows.

(d) use eel pots or fish pots in most areas (except in buoy crab pot free channels).

(e) use a cast net in Chesapeake Bay and tributaries where nets are permitted.

(f) keep any size white perch if caught by hook and line (rod and reel).

Maryland's Tidal Water Designated Free Fishing Areas

North East:	North East Community Park at mouth of North East Creek.
Chestertown:	Maryland Route 213 Bridge over Chester River.
Cambridge:	Long Wharf, south end of city-owned bulkhead near Municipal Yacht Basin.
Charlestown:	Stone wharf at Conestoga and Water Streets.
Denton:	Crouse Memorial Park Pier north of Maryland Route 404 Bridge.
Sharptown:	Pier and town dock off Ferry Street on the Nanticoke River.
Salisbury:	City-owned bulkhead between Mill Street and Division Street.
Snow Hill:	Byrd Park, Sturgis Park, and city bulkhead next to municipal parking lot. Porter's Crossing Road Bridge west of U.S. Route 113.
Pocomoke City:	City docks from Laurel Street boat ramp to U.S. Route 13 overpass and Winter Quarter dock on Pocomoke River. County-owned dock at Cedar Hall Landing near western terminus of Route 371 on Pocomoke River.
Havre De Grace:	Tydings Memorial Park within designated area, and pier at end of Congress Street.
Baltimore County:	Canton Recreational Pier at Boston Street, Hull Street Recreational Pier, and Middle Branch Park from fishing pier south of the Hanover-Potee Street Bridges, to Hanover Street Bridge over Middle Branch.
Annapolis:	Maryland Route 450 Bridge over Severn River.
Worton:	Bridge No. K-004 over Still Pond Creek on Still Pond Creek Road near Chestertown.
Tyaskin Park:	County-owned park on Wetipquin Creek west of Route 349 at Tyaskin.
Friendship Landing:	County-owned pier and property adjacent to the pier off Friendship Landing Road southeast of Ironsides Riverside Road (Route 425) on Nanjemoy Creek.

VIRGINIA

Virginia requires a license to fish the Chesapeake Bay and its tributaries. This does not include the seaside of the eastern shore or Virginia Beach. Any angler between 16 and 65, including anyone fishing on a licensed charter boat, headboat, fishing pier, rental boat, or private boat, must obtain a license. All the following restrictions are subject to change. For the latest information, call the Virginia Marine Resources Commission in Newport News at 804-247-2247. The VMRC monitors VHF Channel 17. The "hotline" number to report violations is 1-800-541-4646.

Regulations for black drum, cobia, gray trout (weakfish), red drum, summer flounder, and speckled trout have been under review; check for the latest limits and restrictions.

Species

Limits listed for each species are minimum size (total length).

Amberjack (Rudder Jack, Rudder Fish): 32"; All fishermen are limited to 2 amberjack per person per day.

Black Drum (Drumfish): 15"; 1 per person. Any person buying, or catching and selling, black drum is required to obtain a Commercial Harvest Permit from the VMRC.

Bluefish: None; Hook-and-line fishermen are limited to 10 bluefish per person per day.

Cobia: 37"; All fishermen are limited to 2 cobia per person per day.

Gray Trout (Weakfish): 12"; 4 per day.

King Mackerel: 14"; Hook-and-line fishermen are limited to 5 king mackerel per person per day.

Red Drum (Redfish, Channel Bass): 18"; No more than 1 fish over 27" allowed daily for any person, firm, or corporation.

Speckled Trout (Spotted Seatrout): 14"; 10 per day.

Shad (American Shad): It is illegal to catch American shad in Virginia tidal waters, except during the announced open season.

Sharks (All species, excluding dogfish): None; Hook and line fishermen are limited to 1 shark per person per day.

Spanish Mackerel: 14"; Hook-and-line fishermen are limited to 10 Spanish mackerel per person per day.

Striped Bass (Rockfish, Rock, Striper): Bay season (spring), May 16-June 15, minimum size 18", maximum size 28", 2 per day. Bay season (fall), Oct. 17-Dec. 31, minimum size 18", 2 per day. Potomac tributaries season, Sept. 16-Dec. 17, minimum size 18", 2 per day. Coastal season, May 16-Dec. 31, minimum size 28", 2 per day.

Sturgeon: It is illegal to catch or possess any sturgeon in Virginia. Short-nosed sturgeon is an endangered species and is protected by federal law.

Summer Flounder (Fluke): 14"; Hook and line fishermen may keep up to 8 flounder per person per day.

Maryland's Offshore Fishing Bonanza

by Gary Diamond

There's nothing more exciting to an offshore angler than seeing the ocean erupt as a huge fish explodes beneath a fast-moving lure. In the blink of an eye, your line pops from the outrigger clip, the rod bucks and the screaming sound of your reel's drag overpowers the boat's roaring engines. Line seems to evaporate from the reel, while off in the distance 150 pounds of finned fury makes its bid for freedom.

At the end an hour-long, arm-wrenching, back-breaking battle, you'll begin to wonder who's winning—you or the fish. Inch by inch, this denizen of the deep is reluctantly winched closer to the boat until a flash of blue is sighted beneath the ocean's azure surface. Seconds later, the mate grabs the heavy monofilament leader and attempts to lead the huge bluefin tuna closer to the boat. However, instead of impaling

the fish on a flying gaff, the mate carefully inserts a brightly colored tag in its back, gently removes the hook and allows this gallant warrior to swim off.

"For a while there, I thought we hooked up with a big blue marlin that didn't want to jump," said Captain Eric Blanks, skipper of a 40-foot charter boat operating from Ocean City, Maryland. "The fish stayed on top, which is unusual for bluefins, but stranger things have happened out here, especially late in the day. Last week we had a half-dozen white marlin chasing our squid teasers but they refused to take a lure. Then a school of yellowfin tuna moved in with the marlin and every rod went off. You just never know," added Blanks.

On this particular offshore trip, Blanks stopped at The Jack Spot, a vast mound on the ocean's floor located 25 miles south of Ocean City's Inlet. He anchored the boat, chunked with butterfish and within an hour caught a limit of bluefin tuna ranging from 35 to 50 pounds. Because of its size, the bluefin tagged later that day could have been kept. However, before leaving the dock, everyone onboard agreed to keep only one tuna per person, regardless of size.

Blanks, like most offshore charter captains, is making a concerted effort to preserve the remaining bluefin tuna stocks.

A recent ruling from the National Marine Fisheries Service (NMFS) requires all boats, including private recreational vessels, to first procure a special permit to catch and keep bluefin tuna. Permit applications are available from the National Marine Fisheries Service, Northeast Region,

One Blackburn Drive, Gloucester, MA 01930. Currently, there is no charge for permits issued to private boats, though an administrative fee will likely be imposed in the future.

The main reason behind issuing permits for private recreational boats is to monitor the bluefin tuna harvest, and document the economic importance of recreational tuna fishing. Both are integral parts of the complete fisheries management plan.

Charter captains and individual recreational anglers alike began voluntarily imposing limits on both tuna and billfish several years ago to protect these fisheries for future generations. In fact, some anglers limit themselves to one fish per boat, tagging all subsequent catches so scientists can obtain much needed migratory information. Tags are available by writing to the National Marine Fisheries Service (NMFS), Southeast Fisheries Center, 75 VA Beach Drive, Miami, FL 33149-1003.

Although the only catch limitation on yellowfin tuna is an 8-pound minimum size, a spokesman for NMFS said stock assessments of the species are now underway and there may be future restrictions for both recreational and commercial fishermen. This would include a commercial harvest cap, increase in minimum size and possibly a recreational bag limit.

Unlike tuna, billfish fishing is strictly a catch-and-release sport. Some marina operators will not allow charter or private boats running from their facility to kill a billfish for any reason. In at least one instance at Ocean City, when it was discovered that an angler kept a billfish, the marina owner politely asked that person to "leave and don't come back."

The angler tried to defend his position, claiming he only killed the marlin to have it mounted. However, anyone wishing to have a mounted billfish needs only to measure the length of his catch, then release it. The measurement can be taken to a reputable taxidermy studio where a lifelike fiberglass reproduction can be ordered. Anglers can select a variety of poses such as: left turn-leaping, right turn, or if display space is a problem, a miniature replica, all without killing the fish.

Gary Diamond with a tuna taken by chunking with butterfish off Ocean City. (GARY DIAMOND)

Light Tackle—Big Fish

There are several methods of catching tuna, marlin and other pelagic species of fish. However, catch-and-release fishing has really popularized light tackle. Some anglers have even taken up the challenge of landing billfish and tuna with a fly rod, a feat that requires stamina, unsurpassed angling skills, specialized tackle and lots of pure, dumb luck.

When fishing offshore, light tackle is a relative term, especially when you consider many bluewater buffs still use IGFA 80- to 130-pound gear to land a

45- to 65-pound tuna. The same fish can be whipped on a lightweight stand-up outfit that's IGFA rated at 30 to 50 pounds and a matching, 4/0, conventional reel, loaded 25- to 30-pound monofilament line. The same rig can also be used to land 50- to 75-pound white marlin, 100-pound-plus blue marlin, big bull dolphin, lightning fast wahoo and submarine sized sharks.

The key to successful light-tackle fishing is patience, and lots of it. When a big tuna slams your lure or bait, it takes off like a shot, running straight for the bottom regardless of water depth. Most of the time, the distance is less than 200 yards. All you have to do is get its undivided attention by setting the hook and applying all the power you can without breaking the rod. This normally amounts to 15 or 20 pounds of pressure at the rod tip, even with stand-up gear.

Granted, you may be built like a Washington Redskins linebacker, but applying more than 15 pounds of pressure to a fish for more than 10 minutes takes a person who's in fantastic physical condition. Still not convinced? Fill a five-gallon plastic bucket half full of water and try to lift it with your most powerful fishing rod. If you're lucky enough to get it off the ground, try holding it up for 10 minutes. Ten minutes is a long time when you're battling any species of fish; it's an eternity when the fish is half your weight and refuses to cooperate.

Keep up the pressure and eventually, your reluctant quarry will turn toward the boat. At this point, it's imperative to pump the rod as hard and fast as possible, keeping the fish moving in the right direction. If you relax, even for a few seconds, the fish will take a breather and suddenly strip hundred yards of line from the reel before you know what happened.

Fortunately, most billfish are not nearly as difficult to land as tuna of the same size. Sure, they hit like a freight train and go berserk at the end of your line, but if they jump repeatedly, they'll soon become exhausted, and relatively easy to land. However, if a marlin refuses to jump, you're in for a long day.

Trolling versus Chunking

There are two schools of thought when it comes to which method is more productive for catching tuna and marlin.

Trolling allows the angler to cover a vast area with an array of lures and rigged natural baits, a technique that often pays off when fish are scattered and tough to locate. However, once the fish are located, trolling requires additional angling skills such as knowing the correct speed, trolling patterns and keeping a sharp eye on the baits to make sure they're not tangled and appear natural. If any one of these factors is overlooked, you'll likely spend lots of time fishing, but little if any time actually landing fish.

Chunking, on the other hand, is a relaxing but exciting method of attracting fish. Essentially, the angler positions his boat over a specific type of bottom structure, anchors, cuts several butterfish into small morsels and tosses them overboard one at a time, creating a chum slick. A whole butterfish is then rigged on a 4/0 to 6/0 hook concealed in its stomach. The bait is then lowered over the side and line is fed out until the butterfish is approximately 50 to 100 feet astern of the boat.

If the fish are schooled heavily over the structure, you'll often see them swarming in your chum slick, waiting for that next morsel to hit the water. When your rigged butterfish is tossed in the slick, it's like rolling a wine bottle through a jail cell, attracting immediate and undivided attention. Once the bait is picked up, set the hook and dig in for a lengthy battle.

Locating the Fish

Most species of fish, even those found far offshore, can be found suspended over or near some type of bottom structure. Large, deepwater wrecks, lumps, troughs and abrupt changes in bottom contour attract a variety of small fish seeking refuge from predators. Consequently, anyplace you find baitfish, gamefish will be somewhere in the same vicinity. Therefore, if you're planning a trip in your own boat, it's a good idea to carefully examine your charts and mark the coordinates of several fishy looking areas before leaving the dock. If you're fishing with a charter captain, he'll know where the fish were yesterday and with luck, they'll be at the same location today.

Although most pelagic species are found 45 to 60 miles offshore, there are times when the fish migrate much closer to the beach. This especially holds true after a prolonged breeze from an easterly direction, a condition that causes inshore waters to become extremely clear and warm. Some of these locations are well within the range of mid-sized, trailer, outboard-powered boats with sufficient fuel capacities to run just 100 miles round trip.

Jack Spot

Just 24 nautical miles southeast of Ocean City lies a vast uprising known as the Jack Spot. Situated at loran-C coordinates 26965.0/42160.0, the Jack Spot is quite easy to find—it's marked with a large buoy. Depths over the lump are just 8 fathoms, while the surrounding area drops off to nearly 17 fathoms. Thousands of big bluefin tuna were taken here during the 1993 season, most of which were caught by chunking. In fact, it was estimated that a truckload of butterfish was transported by more than 100 fishing boats to the Jack Spot nearly every day.

Mixed with the tuna were large numbers of king mackerel, most in the 25- to 30-pound range. The kings hit the butterfish baits like a freight train, but their extremely sharp teeth easily severed the heavy monofilament leaders. Consequently, only one or two kings were landed on each boat, despite multiple hookups.

The huge volume of butterfish also attracted several mammoth sharks, some tipping the scales at more than 300 pounds. Most of the sharks were tagged and released, however, a few outsized makos were brought back to Lewes, Indian River and Ocean City. In addition to sharks, good numbers of bull dolphin were also attracted to the chum slicks. When conditions were right, dolphin ranging from 8 to 25 pounds swarmed over the structure, hitting nearly everything that fell in the water. Tuna anglers took advantage of the situation by casting small bucktails trimmed with chunks of butterfish with light spinning gear. The action was incredible.

Hot Dog 26810.0/42230/0

While half the world converged on the Jack Spot, a few anglers tried their luck at the Hot Dog, roughly 20 nautical miles to the east. This particular piece of underwater real-estate held good numbers of white marlin throughout most of the summer, many of which were estimated in the 80 to 90 pound category. Anglers trolling Green Machines, rigged ballyhoo and rigged mullet tagged and released several marlin, dolphin, tuna and even a few wahoo at this 18-fathom lump.

Baltimore Canyon
26650.0/42230.0

Baltimore Canyon marks the edge of the Continental Shelf with depths plummeting to nearly 700 fathoms where a long finger projects westward. A mile inshore, the bottom rises to 150 fathoms. It's here where warm Gulf currents mix with chilly coastal waters. The temperature gradient may only be a few degrees in mid-summer, but that's all it takes to produce the right conditions for blue and white marlin. Knowledgeable anglers keep a close eye on their surface temperature gauge when fishing this particular location, following warm-water eddies and trolling over them with a criss-cross pattern. The action out here is not fast and furious, but when a 500-plus-pound blue marlin moves in for the kill, it's a sight you'll never forget.

Besides excellent marlin fishing, anglers found large numbers of wahoo, several huge dolphin and a few bigeye tuna that topped the 300-pound mark.

Washington Canyon
26800.0/41760.0

It's nearly a 65-nautical-mile run from Ocean City Inlet to Washington Canyon. But, on a calm day, the trip can be an adventure. During the three-hour journey, anglers can expect to see schools of playful porpoise darting in front of the boat, flying fish skitter over the waves for incredible distances, mammoth sea turtles and if Sargasso grass is encountered, swarms of bull dolphin.

Just inshore of the canyon, commercial lobster fishermen set their traps in depths of 50 to 60 fathoms, tethering the heavy wire traps to large, red floats. Lurking in the shadow of these buoys are swarms of mid sized dolphin and triggerfish. Both provide lots of action on light tackle and make excellent table fare.

A few miles farther east, the canyon's edge becomes apparent, as depths plummet to more than 600 fathoms and the water changes color from hues of green to deep blue. Most of the action takes place along this edge, where water temperatures may

climb to the mid 80's in early August, while inshore waters average 68 to 72 degrees. Huge blue marlin, white marlin, wahoo, bull dolphin and an occasional sailfish inhabit these waters throughout the summer months. It's a great location to troll large, rigged baits or outsized artificials intended for only the largest fish.

One productive offshore fishing

excursion is usually all it takes to make you a bluewater fishing fanatic. It's an addictive sport that challenges your angling skills to the ultimate, and requires more physical strength and stamina than you can imagine.

However, to preserve this fishery for future generations, we must protect this valuable resource today. Conservation is everyone's responsibility. ■

Delaware Rockin'

by Eric B. Burnley

The recovery of striped bass along the East Coast has been remarkable and nowhere more so than in Delaware. I grew up along the Delaware River during the 1940's and 1950's, and it was so polluted with chemicals and human waste that no aquatic life existed from Wilmington north to Trenton, New Jersey.

The first breakthrough came in the 1960's when shad made it as far as the Brandywine River, but by the 1970's the pollution barrier was gone and the shad continued their journey on up to New York. During this same time we saw striped bass in the river, but as the coastal population declined so did the Delaware River stock. Conversely as the management plan for the recovery of striped bass began to work, more and more stripers began to show up in the Delaware River and its tributaries. Some of these fish may have come from the Chesapeake Bay through the Chesapeake and Delaware Canal while others came through the Delaware Bay from the ocean. Today the once polluted Delaware River in back of my old house in Claymont is considered a spawning area for striped bass.

All of this progress has been great for the fish, and now the fishermen will be able to enjoy some exciting action in Delaware waters. Rockfish can be taken along the coast from Claymont to Fenwick Island, but some locations are more productive than others.

If there is one place in Delaware where you can expect to catch a rock-

This striped bass was taken from Indian River Inlet, where fishermen can catch stripers nearly year-round. An incoming tide is best during spring and summer, but a falling tide is more productive in autumn.
(ERIC B. BURNLEY)

fish any time of the year it would be Indian River Inlet. Most of the fish taken here fall for bait or lures fished from the jetties, but boaters can also find action. The biggest problem with the inlet is the number of anglers who attempt to work the area. Boaters should stay out of casting range of those on the jetty or risk a bucktail or sinker bouncing off the gelcoat or through the windshield.

The deep slough running west from the entrance to North Side Marina is a good place to drift a buck-

tail or live eel. The rip that makes up by the west end of the campground on the south side of the inlet and the sea wall protecting the Coast Guard Station on the north side can produce rockfish on a moving tide.

Tide and current controls all fishing activity at Indian River Inlet. Striped bass seldom feed on slack water, preferring to lie in the lee of an eddy or rip and pick off the bait as it tumbles by in the current. The most productive time to fish Indian River Inlet is two hours before slack water, which usually occurs 1½ to 2 hours following the change of tide. I prefer incoming water in the spring and summer, but I like a falling tide in the fall. I really believe the fish have no preference and will feed whenever the opportunity presents itself.

During the past few years an increasing number of rockfish have been taken in the Lewes area. Casters working along the Outer Wall and at the Haystacks will find good action, but the most productive method seems to be drifting with live eels or bucktails over nearby shoals.

Joe Morris who owns Lewes Harbour Marina and fishes the area for rockfish at every opportunity, described the standard live-eel rig. (See pages 241 and 243 for more details.) He begins with a three- to four-foot piece of 30- to 40-pound leader snelled to a 4/0 to 7/0 live bait hook. An inline sinker of 1 to 4 ounces is used to carry the eel down to the rockfish. He uses as light a sinker as possible but makes sure the eel is working on the bottom.

A black ball-bearing snap swivel connects the line to the sinker with a perfection loop in the leader, a convenient way to attach it to your weight. The ball-bearing swivel prevents line twist while the perfection loop makes changing leaders easier.

Live eels can be a problem to deal with especially when you are trying to impale them on a hook. If you put a mixture of half ice and water in the bottom of a small cooler and store your eels in this mixture, they will be less likely to squirm away. A damp rag will keep the slime off of your hands and help you hold the slippery critter.

There are three basic methods for hooking a live eel: through the lips, through the eyes, and in the mouth and out of one eye. I prefer putting the hook through the lips or eyes as this makes for a more normal presentation since the bait pulls straight through the water.

A conventional reel spooled with twenty- to thirty-pound line and mounted on a medium action rod will work well when drifting live eels. Due to its lower water resistance, the lighter line will allow you to work the bottom with less weight. The new braided lines, such as Stren Kevlar, may be ideal for this type of fishing because they have very little drag in the water and are much more sensitive than nylon monofilament.

When live eels are not available, several lures prove quite productive. The Hopkins Shorty in the 2- to 3-ounce sizes, white bucktails and the parachute lures have worked well.

Lures and baits are worked in the same manner. The drift begins uptide of the shoal and proceeds with the current across the structure. As you begin to drift off the down tide side, allow your offering to maintain contact with the bottom by slowly spooling off of your reel and controlling the descent with your thumb.

A bass will pick up an eel and move off a bit before turning to swallow its victim head first. You must feed the fish some line with minimum pressure on the reel until you feel him stop then start off again. At this point crank out all the slack before setting the hook. No hesitation is required when using a bucktail or other type of artificial, and you should clamp down hard with your thumb on the spool, set the hook, engage the reel and start cranking.

This type of fishing is most productive during a strong current. Joe recommends working the northeast corner of the Outer Wall on the flood, Hen and Chicken Shoal on the first of the ebb tide, and then the 8B Buoy when the ebb is running hard.

The striped bass may be fully recovered but it will only remain in good supply if we continue conservation measures. Take care when releasing small fish and use barbless hooks whenever possible. Let's be careful and protect the future striped bass fishery. ■

FISHING ACCESS

NEW JERSEY

For a listing of New Jersey coastal boat launching sites, see page 116.

For a listing of New Jersey fishing access facilities by town, see page 123.

DELAWARE TIDAL FISHING ACCESS AREAS

Area/Location	Comments
Assawoman Wildlife Area/ Little Assawoman Bay	2 ramps, 2 piers, parking capacity: 20.
Augustine Beach/ Delaware River	1 ramp, 1 pier, parking capacity: 100
Bowers Beach/ Delaware Bay	5 ramps, no piers, parking capacity: 200
Canal Wildlife Area/C&D Canal	no ramps, 4 piers, parking along road
Cedar Creek/ Delaware Bay	8 ramps, no piers, parking capacity: 150
Collins Beach/ Delaware	3 ramps, 1 pier, parking capacity: 120
Lewes/ Delaware Bay	3 ramps, no piers, parking capacity: 75
Milton/Broadkill River	1 ramp, piers pending, parking capacity: 10
Phillips Landing/ Nanticoke River	3 ramps, no piers, parking capacity: 50
Port Mahon/ Delaware Bay	3 ramps, 1 pier, parking capacity: 75
Rosedale Beach/ Indian River	2 ramps, 1 pier, parking capacity: 75
St. Jones/ St. Jones River	1 ramp, 1 pier, parking capacity: 10
Woodland Beach/ Delaware River	1 ramp, 1 pier, parking capacity: 50
Edward R. Kock/ Broad Creek	no ramps, no piers, parking capacity: 10
Odessa/Appo- quinimink Creek	1 ramp, no piers, parking capacity: 2

All motor boats launched from tidal access areas administered by the Division of Fish and Wildlife must be registered in Delaware or have a valid ramp certificate. Ramp certificates cost $35.00 and are available from the Division of Fish and Wildlife or its authorized agents.

MARYLAND LAUNCH RAMPS

The following list contains only those ramps in Worcester County, which has Atlantic Ocean access. For a list of ramps in counties with access to the Chesapeake Bay and its tributaries, see page 181.

Worcester County
- Byrd Park (Pocomoke River). Snow Hill, off Market Street.
- Cedarhall Wharf (Pocomoke River). End of Cedarhall Road off Rte. 371.
- West Ocean City (Fisherman's Marina). On North Harbor Road.
- George Island Landing (Parker Bay Chincoteague). Below Stockton end of Rte. 366.
- Gum Landing (Isle of Wight Bay/Turville Creek). On Gum Point Road in Taylorville.
- Mason Landing (Massey Creek/Newport Bay). Off Rte. 113 and Langmaid Road at end of Mason Landing Road.
- Snow Hill Public Landing (Chincoteague Bay). End of Rte. 365.
- South Point (Sinepuxent Bay). End of South Point Road off Rte. 611 on Lower Sinepuxent Neck.
- Taylor's Landing (Chincoteague/Johnson Bay). East of Girdletree off Rte. 12 end of Taylor's Landing Road.
- Shell Mill Landing—St. Martin's Landing (Assawoman Bay/St. Martin's River). End of Daye Road off St. Martin's Landing Neck Road, south of Bishopville.
- Pocomoke River State Park—Shad Landing Area (Pocomoke River). Four miles south of Snow Hill on U.S. Rte. 113.
- Winter Quarters (Pocomoke River). Off Rte. 13, at end of Winter Quarters Drive.
- Pocomoke River State Park—Milbourne Landing Area (Pocomoke River). Rte. 354 near Pocomoke City.
- Assateague Island (Sinepuxent Bay). At Verrazano Bridge northwest side of Rte. 611.

Note: Ramp admission fee may be required by county.

VIRGINIA FISHING PIERS

(All telephone area codes are 804.)

Norfolk/Virginia Beach
Chesapeake Bay Bridge-Tunnel
- Sea Gull Fishing Pier (464-4641)

Norfolk
- Harrison's Boat House & Fishing Pier (587-9630)
- Wolloughby Bay Fishing Pier (588-2663)

Virginia Beach
- Lynnhaven Inlet Fishing Pier (481-7071)
- Virginia Beach Fishing Pier (428-2333)
- Sandbridge Fishing Pier (426-7200)

Lower Peninsula

Hampton
- Buckroe Beach Fishing Pier (851-9146)
- Grandview Fishing Pier (851-2811)

Newport News
- James River Fishing Pier, James River Bridge (247-0364)

BOAT LAUNCH RAMPS

The following list contains only those ramps in areas with ocean access. For a listing of Tidewater and Chesapeake Bay ramps, see page 181.

Eastern Shore Seaside (Accomac County)

Greenbackville
- Greenbackville Harbor

Chincoteague
- Chincoteague Town Dock and Ramp
- Queen Sound Landing
- Chincoteague Memorial Park
- Deep Hole Ramp

Atlantic
- Wishart Point Landing

Mappsville
- Old NASA Dock (Assawoman Creek)

Bloxom
- Kegotank Landing
- Dix's Gargatha Landing

Accomac
- Parker's Creek Landing
- Folly Creek Landing

Quinby
- Quinby Harbor Landing

Willis Wharf
- Willis Wharf Boat Ramp and Dock (Machipongo River)

Nassawadox
- Red Bank Boat Ramp (Red Bank Creek)

Oyster
- Oyster Public Harbor

New Church
- Pitts Creek Launching Ramp

Saxis
- Shad Landing

- Saxis Landing
- Messongo Creek Landing
- The Hammocks
- Cattail Creek

Bloxom
- Muddy Creek Ramp
- Guard Shore Launching Ramp
- Guilford Creek Landing
- Young Creek Landing

Onacock
- Onacock Town Landing
- Schooner Bay Landing (Deep Creek)
- South Chesconessex Landing
- Poplar Cove Wharf

Pungoteague
- Harborton Landing
- Hacks Neck Landing

FISH RECORDS

NEW JERSEY

For New Jersey record fish, see page 126.

DELAWARE

Atlantic Mackerel: 3 lbs. 6 oz.; Atlantic Ocean; 1989
Black Drum: 115 lbs.; Delaware Bay; 1978
Mako: 942.5; 1992
Blue Marlin: 820 lbs.; Poormans Canyon; 1986
Bluefish: 21 lbs. 15 oz.; Rehoboth Beach; 1980
Channel Bass: 75 lbs.; area unspecified; 1976
Cod: 44 lbs.; Five Fathoms Bank; 1975
Dolphin: 49 lbs.; Atlantic Ocean; 1987
False Albacore: 17 lbs. 9 oz.; 30 Fathom Line; 1980
Flounder: 17 lbs. 15 oz.; Indian River Inlet; 1974
Kingfish: 4 lbs.; Bethany Beach; 1973
Porgy: 5 lbs. 5 oz.; area unspecified; 1979
Sea Bass: 7 lbs., 6 oz.: Fenwick Shoal; 1988
Sea Trout: 19 lbs. 2 oz.; Delaware Bay; 1989
Shark: 825 lbs.; Atlantic Ocean, 1981
Tautog: 18 lbs.; Delaware Bay; 1987
Tuna: 322 lbs., 12 oz.; Baltimore Canyon; 1983
White Marlin: 120 lbs.; Baltimore Canyon; 1972
King Mackerel; 48 lbs. 9 oz. 1992
Wahoo; 94 lbs. 1986
Atlantic Croaker; 5 lbs. 3.5 oz. 1980
Swordfish; 276 lbs. 12 oz. 1978
Striped Bass; 51 lbs. 8 oz. 1978

Fishing Tournaments

Fishing tournaments are becoming very popular with some anglers. They started years ago as promotional programs to gain anglers' attention and support and to foster better conservation of fishery resources. Some tournaments have developed into highly competitive events because of the very lucrative prizes and publicity for the winners.

The only tournament the Division of Fish and Wildlife sponsors and endorses is the Delaware Sportfishing Tournament to recognize those anglers who catch certain species above a minimum weight from either salt water or fresh water.

Rules for Delaware Sportfishing Tournament

1. The tournament is open to the public. There is no entry fee. Charter boat captains are eligible. Weighmasters are eligible provided their fish is weighed in at a weighing station other than their own.
2. All fish entered in the tournament, except those caught beyond the three-mile limit in the Atlantic Ocean, must be caught within the boundaries of the State of Delaware. Any fish caught outside the three-mile territorial sea must be landed in a vessel leaving from and returning to a Delaware port.
3. All fish entered in the tournament must be caught in a sporting manner with hook and line. No other person may touch the rod or line until the fish is brought to gaff or net or, in the case of fishing from a boat, until the leader is brought within the grasp of the mate.
4. All fish entered in the tournament must be weighed at an official Delaware Sport Fishing Tournament Weigh Station.
5. All fish entered in the tournament must meet the minimum weight requirements as set for that year's tournament.
6. All scales used to weigh in fish must be certified yearly by the Delaware Division of Weights and Measures (Department of Agriculture).
7. No smallmouth bass from Kent or Sussex County will be recognized unless qualified personnel from the Division of Fish and Wildlife examine and approve the catch.
8. No fish will be recognized as a state record unless qualified personnel from the Division of Fish and Wildlife approve the catch. In case no Division of Fish and Wildlife personnel are available at the time of the weigh-in, the angler must save the entire fish for examination and approval at the earliest time convenient for the Division of Fish and Wildlife.
9. In the case of a tie for the largest fish of the year or a new state record, both fish will be recognized.

10. To replace a record for a fish weighing less than 25 pounds, the replacement must weigh at least 2 ounces more than the existing record. To replace a record for a fish weighing 25 pounds or more, the replacement must weigh at least one-half of 1 per-cent more than the existing record. Example: at 100 pounds, the additional weight required would be 8 ounces. Any catch that exceeds the existing record by less than the amount required to defeat the record will be considered a tie.

11. The Tournament Director reserves the right to dis-qualify any entry.

12. All entry forms must be legibly and completely filled out by the weighmaster and the signed forms should be mailed in by the angler.

13. The tournament runs from January 1 through De-cember 31. No entry forms for the previous tourna-ment year will be accepted after 4:30 P.M. January 31.

14. Only one citation per species of fish will be issued to any individual during the tournament year. In the event an individual catches a larger fish than the one for which he originally was issued a citation, a new citation will be issued for the larger fish if the indi-vidual returns the older citation.

15. Only one saltwater award and one freshwater award will be issued to any one individual during the tour-nament year.

16. Special citations may be issued upon approval of the Tournament Director for unusual catches or for atypical fishermen (young children, handicapped, etc.). If the weigh station feels the catch is unusual, an entry form should be submitted for approval.

17. The Master Fisherman Award will be given to the fisherman who, in the opinion of the Tournament Director, has made the outstanding catch or catches during the tournament year. All decisions will be final after 4:30 P.M. on January 31.

18. The Tournament Director reserves the right to dis-qualify any weigh station where the tournament rules are not observed.

19. The State of Delaware assumes no responsibility in the certification of a catch for consideration by the International Gamefish Association or any record-keeping body other than the Delaware Sport Fishing Tournament. If an angler wishes to qualify his catch for consideration in some other tournament, it his responsibility to ensure that his catch and weigh-in meet the appropriate criteria. The Delaware Sport-fishing Tournament makes no distinction based on the line class or sex of the angler or fly versus con-ventional fishing gear.

Minimum Qualifying Weights (pounds), Saltwater Division

White marlin: any*
Blue marlin: any*
Seabass: 2
Seatrout: 11
Shark (except Mako): 100; Mako: 50
Porgy: 2
Tuna: 50
Kingfish: 1
Black drum: 50
Atlantic mackerel: 2
Channel bass: 30
King mackerel:10
Cod: 20
Wahoo: 20
Dolphin: 15
Atlantic croaker: 3
False albacore: 12
Swordfish: any
Bluefish: 14
True albacore: 30
Flounder: 7
Tautog: 7
Striped bass: 20

* Citations for marlin are awarded only for releases or for those fish landed for taxidermy.

Live Release Awards

The Division of Fish and Wildlife is providing recogni-tion patches to anglers who catch and release alive species that exceed the minimum lengths specified below. To qualify, the angler must make the catch in Delaware waters or off Delaware's Atlantic coastline. The eligible species must be measured from the tip of the tail to the tip of the jaw (straight-line measurement) and this mea-surement must be verified by a witness who then signs the entry form. Any fish so measured shall be released immediately. Fish kept alive or dead and brought to a weigh station shall be weighed for entry in the Sportfish-ing Tournament using certified scales but will not be eli-gible for a live release award. Billfish released are eligible for either the live release award or the Sport Fishing Tournament Award, whichever the angler chooses.

No angler will be issued more than one live-release award patch per year, although he or she may apply for and receive any number of live-release citations.

Applications for live-release-awards may be picked up at any Sport Fishing Tournament weigh station and must be mailed to the Division of Fish and Wildlife within 30 days after the catch. The entry form for a live-release must contain the signature of the angler and the signature of a witness to both the measurement and live release of the fish. No fish entered for a live-release award will be eligible for consideration as a state-record fish. All potential state-record fish must be weighed at a certified weigh station.

Minimum Qualifying Lengths for
Saltwater Live-Release Awards

White marlin: any
Blue marlin: any
Shark (excluding mako): 66
Tuna: 46
Black drum: 45
Channel bass: 45
Cod: 36
Dolphin: 41
False albacore: 26
Bluefish: 33
Flounder: 25
Tautog: 25
Seabass: 15
Seatrout: 33
Porgy: 14
Kingfish: 13
Atlantic mackerel: 17
King mackerel: 36
Wahoo: 50
Atlantic croaker: 19
Swordfish: any
True albacore: 32
Mako shark: 66
Striped bass: 37

MARYLAND (ATLANTIC DIVISION)

White marlin: 135 lbs.; Poor Man's Canyon; 1980
Blue marlin: 870 lbs.; Washington Canyon; 1983
Black drum: 79 lbs.; Bassgrounds; 1985
Tuna: 625 lbs.; 45 miles east of Ocean City; 1975
Shark: 1,210 lbs.; 20 Fathom Lines; 1983
Striped bass: 45 lbs.; Assateague Island; 1975
Dolphin: 67 lbs. 8 oz.; off Ocean City; 1985
Mako shark: 766 lbs.; 1984
Bluefish: 23 lbs. 8 oz.; Assateague Island; 1974
Flounder: 17 lbs.; Assateague Island; 1974
Tautog: 19 lbs. 8 oz.; Jackspot; 1980
Seabass: 8 lbs.; Jackspot; 1978
Spotted seatrout: 13 lbs.; Sinepuxet Bay; 1973
Weakfish: 16 lbs.; Ocean City Inlet; 1976
Porgy: 6 lbs. 3 oz.; Fenwick Shoal; 1966
Kingfish: 2 lbs. 8 oz.; Assateague Island; 1975
Wahoo: 107 lbs.; 15 Fathom Line; 1976
Channel bass: 70 lbs.; Assateague Island; 1977
False albacore: 20 lbs. 8 oz.; Washington Canyon; 1984
King mackerel: 45 lbs.; Big Gull; 1985

VIRGINIA

Albacore: 68 lbs.; Norfolk Canyon; 1992
Amberjack: 118 lbs.; Chesapeake Light Tower; 1986
Barracuda: 27 lbs. 8 oz.; Triangle Wrecks; 1993
Bluefish: 25 lbs., 4 oz.; Bluefish Rock; 1986

Cobia: 103 lbs., 8 oz.; Mobjack Bay; 1980
Cod, Atlantic: 35 lbs.; Off Wachapreague; 1969
Crevalle jack: 35 lbs.; Chesapeake Light Tower; 1993
Dolphin: 71 lbs., 8 oz.; Off Virginia Beach; 1991
Drum
    Black: 111 lbs.; Cape Charles; 1973
    Red: 85 lbs. 4 oz.; Wreck Island; 1981
False albacore: 25 lbs. 4 oz.; Off Virginia Capes; 1964
Flounder: 17 lbs. 8 oz.; Baltimore Channel; 1971
Mackerel (Spanish): 9 lbs. 13 oz.; Va. Beach; 1993
Mackerel (King): 51 lbs. 3 oz.; Off Virginia Beach; 1991
Marlin
    Blue: 1,093 lbs. 12 oz.; Norfolk Canyon; 1978
    White: 131 lbs. 10 oz.; Off Virginia Beach; 1978
Porgy: 5 lbs. 5 oz.; Off Chincoteague; 1978
Sailfish: 68 lbs. 8 oz.; Off Virginia Beach; 1977
Seabass (Tie); 9 lbs. 8 oz.; Off Virginia Beach; 1990
Seabass (Tie); 9 lbs. 8 oz.; Off Virginia Beach; 1987
Shark
    Bigeye Thresher: 149 lbs.; The Cigar; 1992
    Blacktip: 76 lbs. 10 oz.; Off Virginia Beach; 1988
    Blue: 266 lbs.; The Cigar; 1987
    Bull: 256 lbs.; V-Buoy; 1982
    Dusky: 673 lbs.; S.E. Lumps; 1982
    Hammerhead (Great): 430 lbs.; S.E. Lumps; 1984
    Hammerhead (Scalloped): 245 lbs.; The Cigar; 1977
    Hammerhead (Smooth): 272 lbs.; Off Virginia
        Beach; 1988;
    Lemon: 312 lbs. 12 oz.; Sandbridge; 1976
    Mako: 728 lbs.; Chesapeake Light Tower; 1983
    Sandbar: 213 lbs.; Triangle Wrecks; 1986
    Sand Tiger: 339 lbs.; Cape Charles; 1983
    Spinner: 129 lbs. 8 oz.; Off Chincoteague; 1991
    Thresher: 115 lbs. 4 oz.; Off Virginia Beach; 1980
    Tiger: 1,099 lbs. 12 oz.; S.E. Lumps; 1981
    White: 131 lbs.; S.E. Lumps; 1981
Sheepshead: 19 lbs.; Chesapeake Bay Bridge-Tunnel;
    1979
Spadefish: 13 lbs.; The Cell (Chesapeake Bay); 1988
Striped Bass: 61 lbs.; Mattapoini River; 1981
Swordfish; 381 lbs., 8 oz.; Norfolk Canyon; 1978
Tarpon: 130 lbs.; Off Oyster; 1975
Tautog: 24 lbs.; Off Wachapeague; 1987
Tuna
    Bigeye: 275 lbs.; Norfolk Canyon; 1993
    Bluefin: 344 lbs.; Off Virginia Beach; 1995
    Skipjack: 22 lbs.; 11oz.; The Cigar; 1995
    Yellowfin: 203 lbs. 12 oz.; Norfolk Canyon; 1981
Wahoo: 97 lbs.; Off Virginia Beach; 1975

Tournaments

The Virginia Saltwater Fishing Tournament, inaugurated in 1958, awards wall plaques to all anglers catching fish meeting established minimum weights. There are no entry fees or registration requirements. Fish must be caught with a rod and reel in a sportsmanlike manner and weighed at one of the almost 100 designated weigh stations. Awards programs are also sponsored for the catch-and-release of certain species of fish and for the Junior Angler Awards (for children under 16). For more information, contact the Virginia Saltwater Fishing Tournament, 968 Oriole Drive, South, Suite 102, Virginia Beach, VA 23451, telephone 804-491-5160.

LOCATING PARTY, CHARTER, OR RENTAL BOATS

For the most up-to-date information on party, charter, or rental boats, call the chamber of commerce or the state agency with jurisdiction in the area you are interested in visiting (see State Agencies, below).

NEW JERSEY

For a discussion of party and charter boat services in New Jersey, see page 127.

DELAWARE

Charter and headboat services are available at both private and public docks (including the Indian River Marina in Delaware Seashore State Park) from Delaware City on the bay to Indian River Inlet on the Atlantic Ocean. The towns of Bowers Beach, Slaughter Beach, and Lewes also maintain active fleets to get anglers to the fishing action. Check with local docks and marinas in these locations for information on prices and departure times. All boats are operated by Coast Guard-licensed captains.

VIRGINIA

All charters are area code 804, unless otherside noted.

Eastern Shore
Cape Charles
Buccaneer, 331-4400
Miss Denise, 678-5851
Beverly Elizabeth, 331-4910
El Pescadore, 331-1554
Pretty Lady, 331-2058
Cheriton
Miss Jenifer, 331-4746
Chincoteague
Betty J., 336-6865
Proud Mary, 336-5931
Reel Sport, 336-1353
Enforcer, 336-5188
Patty Wagon, 336-1459
Marshell, 336-1939

Two-Aces, 336-3565
Fish Tales, 336-FISH
Cincoteague View, 336-3409
Oyster
Little Bit, 331-2111
Willis Wharf
Safari, 442-7915
Quinby
Kelly Marie, 665-5011
Ron-Jo, 442-9324
Wachapreague
Trashman, 1-800-33-CATCH
Stoney, 787-3824
Are-Star, 787-8052
Bonnie Sue, 787-2467

Canyon Lady, 787-3272
Sea Bird, 787-1040
VimanJo, 787-3341
Sea Fox, 787-4576
Abbsuloot, 787-1125
Janie Mac, (410) 643-6310
Crack of Dawn, 787-4110
Onancock
Fish n' Fit, 787-3399

Norfolk/Virginia Beach
Little Creek
Four Winds, 464-4680
Faith, 583-8502
Screaming Eagle, 627-2598
Sea Hunter II, 919-473-3236
Capt. Alex, 588-2733
Lynn Haven Inlet
Big Time, 496-7388
Sea Horse, 481-1726
Sea Wray, 481-3513
Outriggers, 481-3513
Green Eyes, 481-4424
Mary M., 460-1470
Beverly B., 481-4545
Ebb Tide, 430-1903
Rudee Inlet
Relentless, 497-6377
K-2, 422-2999
High Hopes, 428-2111
Virginia Beach Fishing Center, 491-8000
Willoughby
Harrison's Boat House and Fishing Pier, 588-9968

Lower Peninsula
Hampton
Dandy Haven Marina, 851-5451
Miss Charlie, 723-0998
Sandra, 868-6968
Bay Fisher, 930-8768
Poquoson
Wendana, 868-7195

Middle Peninsula
Deltaville
John Boy, 758-2009
Hungry Pelican, 776-7728
Rogue, 758-4535
Ann Martin, 776-7261
Dawn II, 776-9885
Buddy Lee, 288-4245

Sweet Pea, 776-7804
Dew Drop, 226-9506
Captain Bill, 932-4081
Reel Joy, 776-6855
Miss Ruth, 776-9661
Bay Lady, 776-9748
Capt. Q, 776-9684
Patty Lee, 776-9394
Myrtle M., 776-7757
Gloucester Point
Erin Kay, 642-5096
Grey's Point
Locklies Marina, 758-2871
Yorktown
Miss Yorktown, 879-8276

Northern Neck
Colonial Beach
Big Dipper, 224-0896
Harryhogan Point
Subeck, 472-2358
Sweet Thing, 800-622-2173
Kilmarnock
Gypsy, 435-2919
Lewisetta
Miss Pam, 529-6450
Willie B. II, 529-6819
Bay Quest, 529-6725
Reedville
Robin Sue, 798-5183
Red Osprey, 703-691-1436
Dudley, 453-3568
Mystic Lady, 453-3643
Little Gull, 453-3413
Hiawatha, 453-5852
20th Century, 529-6622
Virginia Breeze II, 443-4612
Skil Saw I, 453-7644
Jimmick Jr. III, 580-7744
Big Foot, 703-670-8364
Betty Jane, 580-5904
Challenger II, 453-3545
Kel-Lee-Lyn, 453-5283
Liquid Assets, 580-7292
Smith Point
Kitt II, 453-3251
Sunrise, 453-4639
Miss Tasha, 453-6206
Blu-Rok, 633-6045
Southern Belle, 453-4928
Ranger II, 703-360-2587
Midnight Sun, 224-7082
Miss Lizabeth, 453-4077

For more information on charter boats, contact the Virginia Charterboat Association, P.O. Box 459, Deltaville, VA 23043, telephone 804-776-9850.

STATE AGENCIES

NEW JERSEY

New Jersey Department of Tourism
20 West State St.
Trenton, NJ 08625-0826
(609) 292-2470

New Jersey State Police
Marine Law Enforcement Bureau
Box 7068
West Trenton, NJ 08628-0068
(609) 882-2000, ext. 2530

New Jersey Division of Fish, Game and Wildlife
Mail: CN 400
Trenton, NJ 08625
501 E. State St.
Station Plaza 5 (3rd floor)
License Information: (609) 292-2966 or 9590
Bureau of Law Enforcement: (609) 292-9430
Marine Fisheries Administration: (609) 292-2083

DELAWARE

Delaware Office of Tourism and Development
99 King's Highway, Room 1401
Dover, DE 19903
(302) 739-4271

Delaware Division of Fish and Wildlife
P.O. Box 1401, 89 Kings Highway
Dover, DE 19903
Boat Registration: (302) 739-3498
Fisheries Section: (302) 739-3441
Enforcement Section/Administration: (302) 739-3440

MARYLAND

Maryland Office of Tourism and Development
217 East Redwood St.
Baltimore, MD 21202
(301) 336-6611

The Maryland Department of Natural Resources
Tidewater Administration
Tawes State Office Building
Annapolis, MD 21401
(410) 974-3765
(410) 974-3558

VIRGINIA

Virginia Marine Resources Commission Offices
Main Office
2600 Washington Ave.
P.O. Box 756
Newport News, VA 23607
(804) 247-2200

499 Menchville Road
Newport News, VA 23062
(804) 877-1181

30 Jefferson Avenue
Newport News, VA 23707
(804) 247-2265

Tidemill Professional Center
Gloucester Point, VA 23063
(804) 642-2640

P.O. Box 166
Lancaster, VA 22503 (on Route 3)
(804) 462-7200

P.O. Box 117
Heathsville, VA 22473 (on Route 360)
(804) 580-2901

5

Chesapeake Bay

With the melting of the great ice sheets that covered much of the northern and southern hemispheres some 12,000 years ago, an enormous volume of water gradually became liberated, causing the sea level to rise all over the world and to flood lowlands, including coastal valleys. It was during this period of flooding that the estuaries of the Atlantic Coast were formed, much as we know them today. The largest of these, in fact the largest in the United States, is Chesapeake Bay. It covers ground that was a valley through which the Susquehanna River once flowed to the sea when the shore was about 70 miles farther to the east than it is now.

Chesapeake Bay is about 160 miles long from Cape Henry to the Susquehanna River mouth and averages about 10 miles wide. Its main axis runs in a north-south direction, roughly parallel to the seacoast. The tidal shoreline of the Bay measures about 4,600 miles, of which 3,400 miles are in Maryland and 1,200 in Virginia. The shoreline of the Bay with its tributaries measures about 8,100 miles, being almost equally divided between both states. The surface area of this vast estuary with its myriad tributaries is about 4,400 square miles.

Chesapeake Bay lies entirely within the coastal plain—a low, nearly flat, sandy expanse of land. Beneath the plain in this region lies a thick sedimentary formation composed mostly of unconsolidated beds of silts, clays, sands, and gravels. Homogeneous gray or black muds form the floor of the main channel of the Bay. This channel was the deepest part of the Susquehanna Valley and now has the greatest deposits of sediment. Broad shoals and extensive flats occur in the Bay about a third of the way up from its mouth, around Tangier, Smith, South Marsh, and Bloodsworth Islands, and at the head of the Bay where the Susquehanna River empties.

Both shores of Chesapeake Bay are deeply and irregularly incised by embayments and streams of various sizes. No fewer than 19 principal rivers and 400 lesser rivers and creeks are tributaries to Chesapeake Bay. The western shore rivers are the largest. Three of them, the Susquehanna, Potomac, and James, contribute 80% of the total fresh water flowing into the Bay. Although the eastern shore rivers are relatively small, nearly all are navigable by small craft, the largest and best known of them being the Choptank. The eastern shore rivers flow through low, flat country, draining rich farm and forest land. Vast marshes renowned for the great numbers of waterfowl which inhabit them during autumn and winter are especially characteristic of the eastern shore. But the western shore, too, has large expanses of wetlands, as anyone who has ever boated the upper Patuxent River, for example, can testify. For the most part, the western shore is a series of nearly flat peninsulas which gradually rise to rolling uplands. To the north and farther into the interior along the western shore, the land rises in an irregular pattern of progressively higher hills until it reaches the principal range of the Appalachian Mountains.

The mean depth of Chesapeake Bay is less than 30 feet; that of the entire system including tributaries to the farthest extreme of tidal influence is about 20 feet. There are, however, deep holes or troughs which have not yet been filled by sediments. The deepest of these, 174 feet, is located 10 miles southeast of Annapolis, Maryland, in a narrow part of the Bay off Bloody Point Bar.

Like the open sea along the eastern coast, high and low tides occur twice daily in Chesapeake Bay. The tidal range, about 3 feet at the mouth, gradually decreases to 1½ feet in the center of the Bay, then to a foot at the Annapolis Bridge. From there to the head of the Bay near Havre de Grace, it increases to 2 feet. The highest tides are associated with periods of high winds which in turn generate high waves. Since these winds are usually westerly or northwesterly, the wave heights tend to be highest on the eastern shore of the mainland and on the northern and western shores of the islands in the Bay. Consequently, these are the most seriously eroded shores. A 1949 study estimated that the mainland had lost 17,000 acres over an 89-year period. About two-thirds of this loss was from the eastern shore. Islands in the Bay had lost some 7,600 acres. Another study has shown the entire area surrounding Chesapeake Bay to be sinking at an average rate of one eighth of an inch a year.

Although the climate of this region is generally mild, it varies considerably with geographic location because of Chesapeake Bay's great length, which extends over nearly three degrees of latitude. At the Bay's mouth the climate is tempered greatly by the sea, while as the Bay extends farther inland, it becomes increasingly influenced by the more severe continental weather. The general pattern, however, is that summers are relatively long and winters short. From about May to October the weather is warm, the humidity high, and the winds gentle. The prevailing southerly or south-westerly winds bring warm, moist air, and the weather usually remains fairly uniform for weeks at a time. During this period, however, there are frequent showers and thunderstorms, some accompanied by gale-force winds which cause serious trouble to small-boatmen caught in unprotected water. July is the warmest month, when air temperatures most often rise to 95°F, sometimes to over 100°F, along the shores of the Bay, especially in the upper sections. Over the water of the Bay, however, the air is 5° to 10°F cooler, and still cooler near the sea.

Fall is a brief period lasting only a month and a half or so, when the warm, gentle southerlies gradually give way to more variable winds. Northwest winds gradually become dominant and progressively stronger and colder. Winter, which lasts from mid-December to March, is a time of unstable weather marked by rapidly changing air masses. As each air mass passes over the area, the usual condition of raw, overcast days is interrupted by brief periods of strong, gusty winds followed by a few clear, crisp days, which in turn are usually followed by periods of rain, freezing rain, or snow. Near the mouth of Chesapeake Bay the temperature drops to freezing only briefly at times, while during most years the tributaries and parts of the upper Bay become frozen solid for weeks at a time. Spring is like fall with the pattern reversed. Warm spells, sometimes with abundant rain, alternate with cool, dry weather. By late April the weather has gradually merged into the summer regime.

Average surface-water temperatures in the Bay range from 80° to 82°F in summer, 55° to 60°F in the fall, 34° to 40°F in the winter, and 54° to 57°F in the spring. The deepest parts of the Bay seasonally provide some refuge to fishes during periods of extreme heat or cold, for temperatures there run 1° to 3°F warmer than at the surface in winter, and 1½° to 2½°F cooler in the summer. The salinity of the surface water in the winter ranges from more than 27 parts per thousand at the mouth of the Bay to less than 3 parts per thousand at its head. In the spring the salinity runs about 2 parts per thousand less on the average than in the winter, and in the fall when it is most concentrated, 2 to 6 parts per thousand higher. At any given latitude the water is saltier on the eastern shore than directly opposite on the western shore. This is caused mostly by the rotation of the earth but also by the greater runoff of fresh water from the western shore. In the deepest parts of the Bay, the salinity is higher by 6 to 8 parts per thousand than at the surface.

More than 200 species of fishes have been reported in Chesapeake Bay. About a quarter of these inhabit fresh or brackish water, the rest being more or less limited to water of a salinity greater than 12 parts per thousand. Because of the peculiarity of the salinity pattern, sea fishes tend to go farther north in the Bay along the eastern shore and to be more numerous there than along the western shore. Their numbers diminish northward beyond the southern end of Kent Island on the eastern side of Chesapeake Bay and Herring Bay on the western side. But tolerance ranges of salinity, like those of temperature, vary from one species to another, and for any given species, from one age to another. Younger fish tend to tolerate, if not require, fresher water than do older ones. This has the advantage of protecting the very young from their carnivorous and undiscriminating parents as well as from the adults of other species. A major cause of irregular fish distribution in the Chesapeake Bay is variation in precipitation, which affects the salinity. During the drought conditions which existed in the early 1960's, Atlantic bonito and king mackerel were caught as far up the Bay as Baltimore, while during years of normal precipitation these two fishes are usually not found beyond about Tangier Island. Hence, no hard and fast rules can be laid down as to how near the head of the Bay a saltwater fish may be taken during an abnormal year.

Most of the sea fishes and certain of the anadromous ones, shad for example, are seasonal migrants, arriving in Chesapeake Bay during the spring and leaving in the fall. A few species, however, reside in the Bay year-round. Fish have various ways of surviving the winter. Some (e.g., eels) descend into deeper water in the Bay and hibernate; others (e.g., northern fluke, scup, black sea bass, spot, Atlantic croaker) move out of the Bay to varying distances offshore, going even as far as the edge of the continental shelf; others (e.g., bluefish, gray sea trout) travel southward along the continental shelf to areas where temperature, food supply, and the amenities of habitat satisfy their specific needs.

Chesapeake Bay marks the geographic limit of the ranges for about a dozen typically northern fishes, such as yellowtail flounder, squirrel hake, cunner, and 25 or so southern ones, like tongue sole, horse-eye jack, southern kingfish, sand drum. Among northern fishes that are rare south of Chesapeake Bay is the winter flounder; among southern fishes rare north of Chesapeake is the pompano.

Fewer than half a dozen species are found in Chesapeake Bay and nowhere else. Fishes that are more abundant in the Bay than in other sections of the Atlantic coast are alewife, striped bass, and white perch. Those which anglers report catching most often in the Bay are white perch, striped bass, and bluefish, in that order.

Since 1880, the earliest year for which there are any statistics, the commercial catch of food fish (i.e., excluding menhaden) and shellfish in Chesapeake Bay has fluctuated over a wide range. The composition of the catch, however, has changed with the highs and lows in the abundance of the various species.

The Atlantic croaker and the gray sea trout both rose to unprecedented prominence early in this century, reached peaks of production in the 1940's and then dropped sharply to comparatively low levels. The shad, following a cycle of high abundance between 1888 and 1909, declined to a lower level about which it has fluctuated ever since. The striped bass was relatively unimportant until after the 1930's. The dramatic rise in recreational fishing about that time gave very great prominence to this species. The most abundant fish in the Bay and the object of the largest fishery, menhaden, is used only for manufacture into oil which is used for a variety of purposes and into meal which is a valuable component of animal feeds. Chesapeake Bay is particularly important to the young of this species as a nursery ground.

Among all the food fishes and shellfish in Chesapeake Bay, the blue crab has consistently provided the largest commercial production for at least 65 years with

only short-term ups and downs. The annual catch, which gives a rough idea of abundance, has wavered since 1930 between about 30 and 97 million pounds. In about half of the years over this period, it has been above 60 million pounds. There is no indication of a declining abundance; indeed, this seems to be a remarkably hardy, resilient species.

Long-term depressions of fish populations, such as have affected the sea trout and croaker, result partly from natural vagaries of environment, but also to a considerable extent from man's activities, of which the most serious are overfishing and damage to nursery grounds in the estuaries. Sea sturgeon is an example of a once valuable seafood that has been depleted to a point of doubtful recovery by overfishing. Sturgeon come in from the sea as early as April and run great distances up tributary streams to clean, swift-flowing water to spawn. There are so few of them now that it is hard to imagine how abundant they must have been when the first Europeans came. Without sturgeon it seems doubtful that Captain John Smith's company could have survived. An account written in 1760 tells of "sturgeons in Chesapeake Bay being of such prodigious numbers that within the space of two miles only, some gentlemen in canoes caught about 600 with hooks." At first the supply was more than the market could bear. Indeed, more were caught by fishermen during the shad and herring runs than could be sold. As a consequence they were considered pests to be destroyed. Nevertheless, their value gradually became apparent in Chesapeake Bay as the demand rose for their eggs, from which caviar was prepared, and for their meat, which was smoked. Large and rather sluggish, sea sturgeon were easily captured in great numbers, and having a slow rate of growth, quickly became overfished so that fewer and fewer were caught each succeeding year. It is unlikely that the sea sturgeon will ever again approach its former abundance. Indeed, its very existence as a species is threatened.

Overfishing of sturgeon, as with other species of fishes, could have been corrected by regulating fishing rates and the sizes of fish taken, so as to achieve, on the average, the highest sustained annual catch. Such regulation, however, would have to have been done species by species, and because almost all of the sea fishes migrate along the coast and the distances over which they travel increase with age, rational management of fishing would have required interstate coordination. While this has been achieved, some conservationists feel that this interstate coordination has yet to work for the benefit of the fish.

Damage to nursery grounds has accelerated greatly during the last two decades because of increasing and often conflicting demands placed on Chesapeake Bay. Since tidal marshes, with their myriad winding and branching waterways and shoal areas are the most important nurseries for a great majority of the marine and estuarine fishes living in the Bay, any loss of these areas will contribute significantly to a decline in those fishes' abundance. Housing and industrial development are the most serious causes of such loss. In the 15 years between 1954 and 1969, a total of 33,000 acres of tidal marshland was destroyed in Maryland and Virginia. At the same time dredging and filling destroyed another 4,000 acres of important shoal-water habitat. Ironically, the damage to nursery areas in the Bay from man's various activities could have been avoided with proper land-use planning. It is not too late to save what remains, but any hope of doing so depends upon timely effective action.

The decline in abundance of Chesapeake Bay oysters is to some extent one of the side effects of deforestation, for as the European settlers cleared away the dense, primeval woods to open up the country for cultivation, they liberated the soil to the creeks and rivers and thence to the Bay. Oyster beds on which the silt accumulated gradually became buried and eventually lost. Other causes contributed even more to the decline: deterioration of public oyster beds resulting from bad harvesting methods; pollution by sewage, which makes oysters unusable; industrial wastes, which affect the health and quality of the oysters; and uncontrolled oyster enemies such as parasitic protozoa and fungi, boring snails and clams, small crabs, etc. Although production could be improved by sophisticated oyster-farming on privately leased grounds, the majority of oystermen resist giving up their way of working, handed down from the past.

An angler in Virginia and Maryland needs a license to fish or crab in the Chesapeake Bay. As we've noted previously, fishing regulations are relatively perishable, often changing yearly. Maryland and Virginia regulate striped bass fishing, with minimum and maximum size limits, and seasons on striped bass. These two states also have minimum size limits for a few other fishes. Virginia has a daily catch limit for large red drum. Both states have regulations governing the digging of clams and the capturing of anadromous fishes. Also, they have minimum size limits for both the hard and the soft stages of blue crabs; Maryland prohibits keeping egg-bearing females, though Virginia has no such prohibition. To obtain copies of the fishing and shellfishing regulations, contact the following:

- Maryland Department of Natural Resources, Tidewater Administration, Tawes State Office Building, Annapolis, MD 21401; (410) 974-3765; (410) 974-3558
- Virginia Marine Resources Commission, P. O. Box 756, 2600 Washington Avenue, Newport News, VA 23607-0756.

CAPE HENRY TO WOLF TRAP LIGHT

LAND CONFIGURATION AND WATER DEPTH

Two mainland points mark the ocean entrance to Chesapeake Bay—Cape Charles to the north and Cape Henry to the south. Cape Charles, located about a mile north of Fisherman Island, is a low, sandy spit. The most prominent feature seen from a vessel sailing into Chesapeake Bay along the eastern side is the 4 miles of sandy cliffs at Kiptopeke Beach rising up to 60 feet. A dozen miles to the west, across the mouth of the Bay, lies Cape Henry. It is distinguished by a prominent range of relic sand dunes rising 40 to 80 feet, the highest of which are about a mile back from the shore. Jutting 163 feet above the beach near the turn of the cape is the modern, functioning Cape Henry Light. Several hundred feet south of this black and white structure stands an abandoned gray lighthouse built in 1791.

Today most people cross the mouth of the Chesapeake Bay not by boat but by car via the Chesapeake Bay Bridge and Tunnel. This is an impressive 21-mile long structure of causeways, bridges, and artificial rock and cement islands connected by two tunnels, each a mile long. The tunnels are buried under the two principal passages—Thimble Shoal Channel and Chesapeake Channel—which lead from the Bay to the sea. North Channel, a passage smaller than the other two, skirts Fisherman Island and is crossed by a fixed bridge 75 feet high. Because it is the highest part of the Bay Bridge and Tunnel and can be seen for a considerable distance, fishermen call it High Level Bridge. The riprap forming the artificial islands, as well as thousands of concrete columns, are centers about which a rich variety of aquatic life concentrates. The passage of tides causes eddies to form on the lee sides of the columns and islands, with resulting local concentrations of plankton. Encrusting organisms such as barnacles and mussels, which feed on the plankton, and algae have formed a thick growth on the concrete and stones, providing habitat for communities of free-living invertebrates. And of course fishes gather about these structures to feed on the accumulations of organisms. At night the lights along the Bay Bridge and Tunnel intensify the effect, for they attract swarms of actively swimming small organisms, and these in turn attract the larger fishes which anglers seek.

Tidal currents, freshets, and wind-driven currents act together to distribute sediments and shape the bottom. The strong tidal currents at the mouth of the Chesapeake Bay have created a series of alternating shoals and channels running nearly parallel to the shoreline and continuing with diminishing amplitude 15 miles up the Bay.

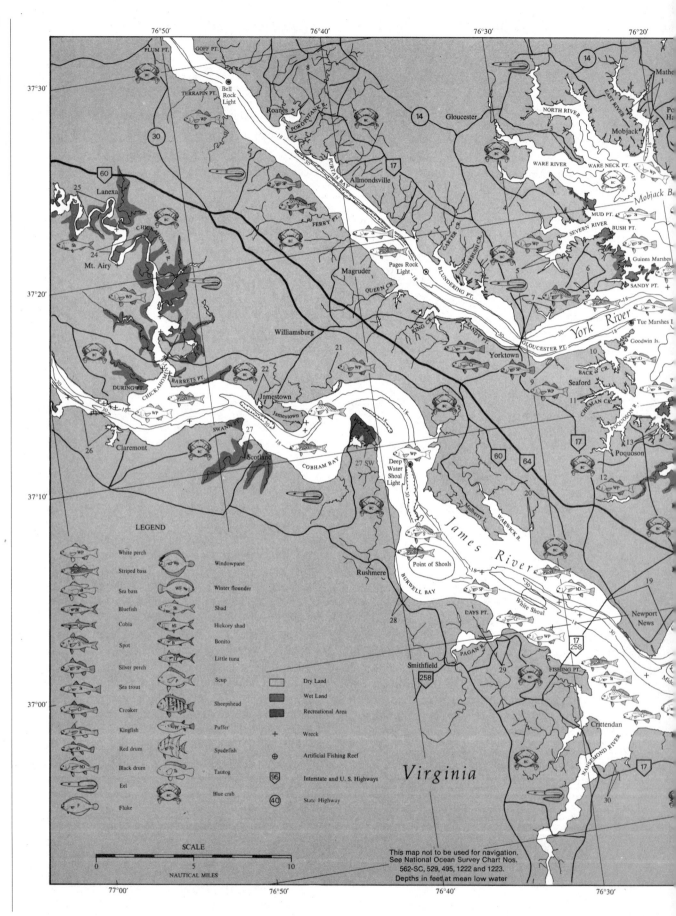

LEGEND

White perch		Windowpane	
Striped bass		Winter flounder	
Sea bass		Shad	
Bluefish		Hickory shad	
Cobia		Bonito	
Spot		Little tuna	
Silver perch		Scup	
Sea trout		Sheepshead	
Croaker		Puffer	
Kingfish		Spadefish	
Red drum		Tautog	
Black drum		Blue crab	
Eel			
Fluke			

Dry Land
Wet Land
Recreational Area
+ Wreck
⊕ Artificial Fishing Reef
95 Interstate and U. S. Highways
40 State Highway

SCALE

0   5   10

NAUTICAL MILES

This map not to be used for navigation.
See National Ocean Survey Chart Nos.
562-SC, 529, 495, 1222 and 1223.
Depths in feet at mean low water

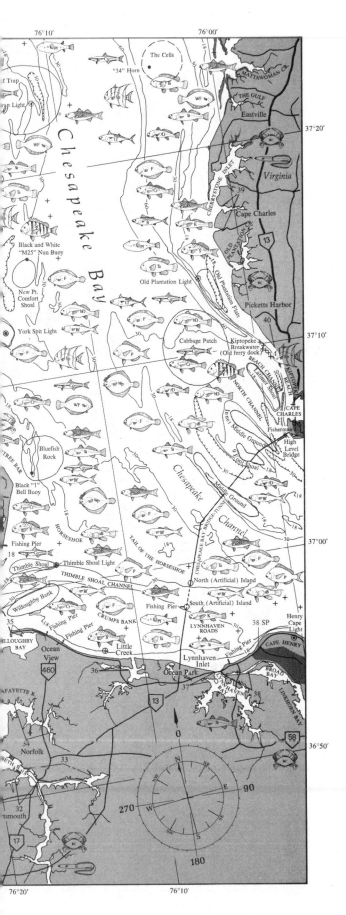

FISH AND FISHING: CAPE HENRY TO STINGRAY POINT

Captain John Smith was one of the first Europeans to enter the Chesapeake Bay, and he is credited with naming Cape Henry for the king's son and Stingray Point after the critter he stepped on that almost killed him. The good captain was also a good fisherman who reported back to his friends in England that the fish were so numerous you could walk over the water on their backs and never get your feet wet. Even if he exaggerated just a bit you can still imagine how many fish there must have been in the bay before man and machine altered the landscape.

Today much progress has been made to correct the excesses of the past, and while fishing in the bay may not be quite as good as Captain Smith described, you can go out with reasonable expectations of catching enough to make the trip worthwhile.

One species that has made a strong showing in recent years is the Spanish mackerel, and the tide rips at Cape Henry are a prime location for catching them. A small spoon trolled at 4 to 6 knots is the best method but casting spoons or flies will also work if the fish are tightly schooled.

The rips off Cape Charles will produce Spanish mackerel in the summer and striped bass in the winter. Bottom-fishing in both locations can be good for weakfish and croaker with the best action late in the summer.

As you enter the Chesapeake Bay you will be greeted by a 21-mile-long bridge tunnel that attracts just about every type of saltwater fish found along the east coast. Trolling with a variety of lures will attract most species, but casting plugs or bucktails around the rock islands that support the two tunnels is great light-tackle sport. Over the course of a season you can expect to catch cobia, black drum, striped bass, weakfish, speckled trout, bluefish and false albacore. Bottom-fishing is also good for flounder, spot and croaker.

Access to this great fishing is found at Lynnhaven Inlet and Little Creek. Only a few charter boats work out of these ports but several headboats sail out of Lynnhaven. Boat ramps are found at both locations. The new Kiptopeke State Park on the Eastern Shore has a ramp but it will not accommodate large boats. The town of Cape Charles does have a good ramp as well as several charter boats.

Moving up the bay we find Hampton Roads on the western shore. A bridge tunnel crosses this busy waterway, and it too holds a wide variety of fish. A sizable headboat fleet sails out of Willoughby Spit, and a boat ramp is also located close by.

Over on the Eastern Shore there are several creeks that empty into the bay. These shallow tributaries are a favorite of the speckled trout anglers who work plugs and jigs at Hungers, the Gulf, Nassawadox and Onancock Creeks from August through October.

Mobjack Bay and the rivers that feed it provide good speckled trout fishing in the spring with fresh peeler crab the top bait. Later in the year plugs and jigs do the trick but those who go after really big trout employ live pin fish.

Although launch ramps are available at or near to all of these fishing spots, charter or headboats do not work these waters. There are several piers along the western shore but only one at Kiptopeke State Park on the Eastern Shore.

WOLF TRAP LIGHT TO BLOODSWORTH ISLAND

LAND CONFIGURATION AND WATER DEPTH

In this section both shores of Chesapeake Bay are exceptionally incised by a profusion of rivers, streams, creeks, and small bays. They differ, however, in the character of the land. The Eastern Shore is nearly all flat and low, rarely rising as high as 20 feet, and is broadly bordered by saltmarshes. In addition, the long chain of islands situated near the center of Chesapeake Bay—Tangier, Smith, South Marsh, and Bloodsworth—is almost entirely made of saltmarshes. Indeed, these island marshes and those along the mainland of the eastern shore account for the most extensive complex of saltmarshes in Chesapeake Bay. In contrast, the land of the western shore is low for only a mile or so, then rises to a series of rolling hills between 20 and 100 feet high. In only a few places along the shore are there saltmarshes between dry land and the Bay's open water.

The floor of Chesapeake Bay is sandy along the shore as are the extensive shallows surrounding the marshy islands located near the Bay's center. Out from shore in deeper waters, the bottom sediments consist of sand mixed with mud, while those in the channels and deep holes are entirely of soft mud. This soft, homogeneous black-and-gray mud accumulates as sediments wash continuously into Chesapeake Bay from the surrounding land.

The main channel, which continues in about the center of the Bay from the previous map section, divides into two branches at about Tangier Island. One branch extends through Tangier Sound into the head of the Nanticoke River, the other extends up the Potomac River. While the deepest section in the Potomac branch is just over 60 feet, that of the Tangier branch is over 100 feet. Up the Bay within the map section on the accompanying pages, the depth in the main channel increases from about 80 feet off Wolf Trap Light, to 110 feet off Great

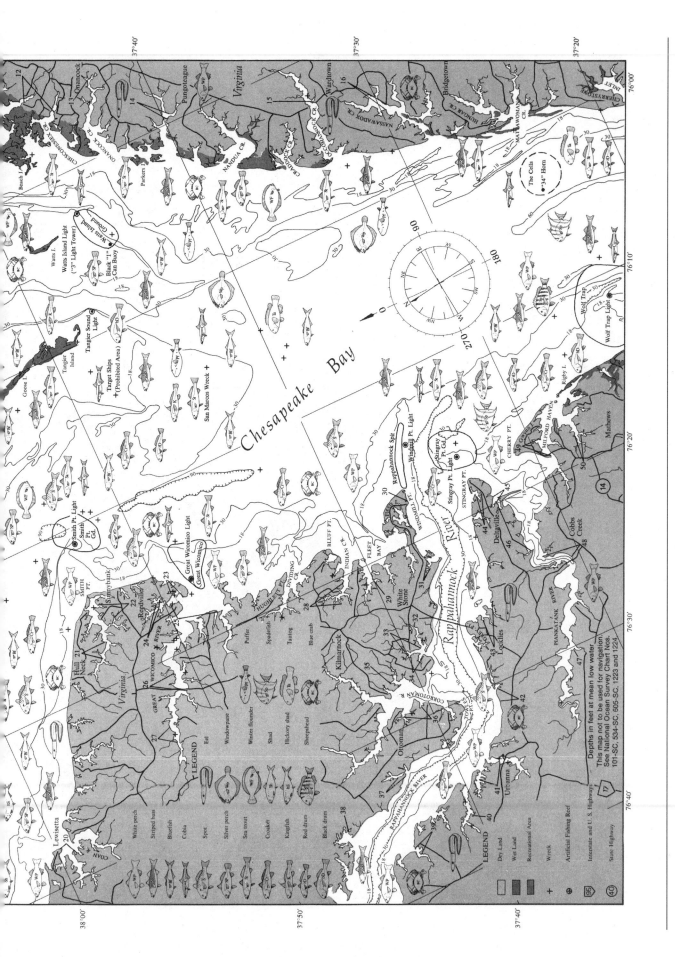

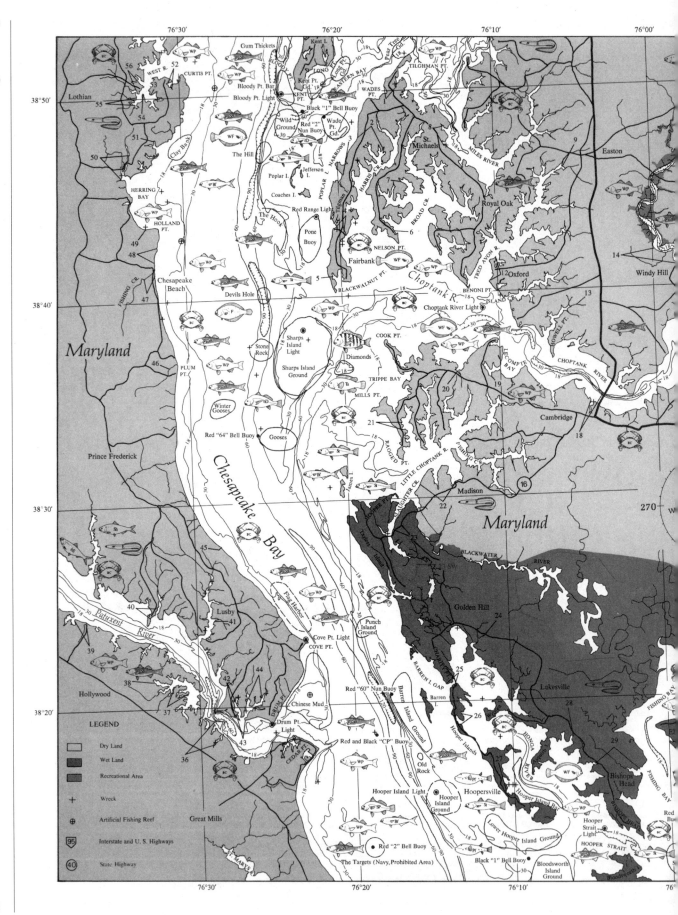

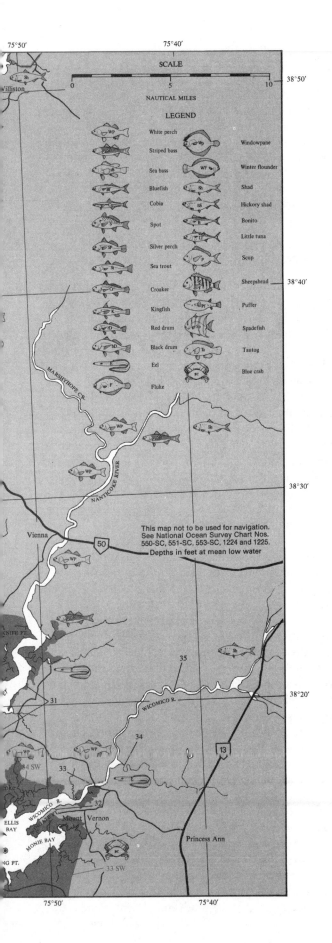

Wicomico Light, to 150 feet off Hooper Island Light.

The salt content of Chesapeake Bay's water increases with depth, and often the deep channels serve as pathways for migrating marine fishes. The salinity of the water also differs from shore to shore, the eastern shore being saltier than the western at any given latitude. Even though there is greater freshwater runoff from the western side, the principal cause of this variation is the earth's rotation. It deflects the water in the Bay to the right, so that salt water moving up the Bay on an incoming tide tends to move along the Eastern Shore, while fresh water draining from the rivers tends to move down along the western shore. The occurrence of clams is an example of how the salinity affects the distribution of aquatic animals. Hard clams or quahogs are found only in water having a salinity greater than about 15 parts per thousand. Since salinities this high persist the year round in Pocomoke and Tangier Sounds, hard clams are found this far up the Bay, even in commercial quantities. Across from Tangier Sound is the Potomac River where soft-shell clams, also called maninose, are abundant. These clams occur in much lower salinities, many in water of only 5 parts per thousand. Since hard clams cannot survive long in such low salinity, they do not occur in the Potomac River.

FISH AND FISHING: WINDMILL POINT TO POINT LOOKOUT

Bottom-fishing and chumming are the most popular methods for catching fish in this portion of the bay. Boats running out of the Rappahannock and Potomac Rivers will head for the shoals and channels, where they anchor up and send out a stream of fresh-ground menhaden. Bluefish and striped bass are attracted to the chum slick, where they find baited hooks waiting. If trout or croaker is the target, the boats will drift over rough bottom using baits such as peeler crab or squid. The Mud Leads are favored for bottom fish while the Middle Grounds attract the chumming fleet.

Charter boats are available out of Deltaville, Reedville, Smith Point and Point Lookout. A few headboats operate from these same points and launch ramps are available. A large fishing pier extends from Point Lookout, and shore fishing is possible along the causeway leading to Point Lookout State Park.

Crisfield is the fishing center along the Eastern Shore, with boats sailing from here into Tangier and Pocomoke Sounds. Weakfish and croaker are available almost everywhere during the summer. The edge of the deep channel through Tangier Sound just west of James Island State Park has been a hot spot for weakfish. Anglers will anchor up right on the drop-off and fish peeler crab baits on the bottom. Late afternoon and evening are best, as the trout seem to move up from the deep water to hunt in the shallows.

171

Pocomoke Sound has numerous areas of rough bottom known as rocks. In days gone by these outcroppings were covered with oysters but now attract other shellfish, which in turn set up a food chain. Weakfish, croaker, spot and striped bass, at the top of this chain, attract the fishermen.

Most of these fish are taken by bottom-fishing with peeler crab but in the fall trollers using wire line and bucktails take rockfish over this structure. Fall is also a good time to cast for striped bass and speckled trout in the shallow areas of the sound.

There are good numbers of charter boats and one or two headboats operating out of Crisfield. Boat ramps are numerous in both Maryland and Virginia, making access quite easy for private boaters.

BLOODSWORTH ISLAND TO KENT ISLAND

LAND CONFIGURATION AND WATER DEPTH

(See chart on pages 170–171)
Within this section both shores of Chesapeake Bay are strikingly different. For the most part, the western shoreline is more even than the eastern and the land rises higher. In the 25 miles between the only large river emptying from the western shore, the Patuxent, and Herring Bay, the shoreline is nearly continuous except where a few small freshwater streams flow into Chesapeake Bay. There, high, sandy hills and rugged cliffs rise abruptly from Chesapeake Bay, some jutting nearly straight up over 125 feet. These cliffs are well known to scientists for their rich deposits of fossilized sharks teeth and other animal remains, perhaps as old as 20 million years. Above Herring Bay the land flattens and is incised by streams and creeks, a form more typical of the rest of Chesapeake Bay's shoreline.

Here the eastern shore of Chesapeake Bay is incised by hundreds of rivers, creeks, coves, and small bays. In the 50 miles, as measured in a straight line from the bottom border of the map on pages 170–171 to its top, the eastern shore has over 1,400 miles of tidal shoreline. The land bordering the shore is nearly flat, rarely rising more than 10 feet or so. Even the series of gently rolling hills that rise in succession for some distance from the shore reach only about 60 feet. Where the land rises gradually from the water, such as from Bloodsworth Island to about Taylors Island, there are extensive saltmarshes. But where it rises abruptly, even though for only a few feet as it does beyond Taylors Island, there are very few saltmarshes. The Choptank is the principal river flowing into this side of the Bay. Smaller rivers, such as the Little Choptank, Tred Avon, Miles, and Wye,

are really arms of the Bay rather than free-flowing streams of fresh water.

As in the previous map section, the floor of Chesapeake Bay is generally sandy along shore, changing to a sand-mud mixture in deeper depths, then to soft mud in the channels and deep holes. The main channel continuing along about the center of the Bay deepens as it approaches Kent Island. There are several places in the channel between Bloodsworth Island and Kent Island with depths of over 100 feet. Off Bloody Point Bar it is 174 feet, the greatest depth in the Bay.

FISH AND FISHING: DRUM POINT TO KENT ISLAND

The mouth of the Patuxent River is one of the better fishing locations in Chesapeake Bay with a great deal of good, fish-holding, structure close to the harbor at Solomons Island. The deep water between the bridge and Drum Point is sheltered on all but the hardest blows. The Chinese Mud just outside the river is a good location for a variety of bottom fish.

On the other side of the bay several shallow rivers empty into the bay through Hooper Strait. The area inside the strait consists of low saltmarsh drained by these rivers, allowing a vast diversity of marine life. Anglers find good action on weakfish, flounder, croaker, spot, speckled trout and blues with most of these fish caught on bottom-fished peeler crab. A few light-tackle experts work bucktails and jigs over grass beds for some fast action on trout, rockfish and blues.

During the spring and fall, trollers pull spoons, plugs and bucktails in the vicinity of Hooper Light for striped bass. During the summer this same area may produce Spanish mackerel and bluefish on small spoons or feathers.

Chesapeake Beach is the next point of entry on the western shore. Most of the boats that sail from here troll the open bay for striped bass, bluefish and Spanish mackerel. The stripers arrive in the early spring and come back in the fall, while the blues and Spanish mackerel are summer visitors. Spoons and bucktails are the lures of choice.

The Choptank River on the Eastern Shore is known far and wide for excellent fishing, with striped bass leading the hit parade. The Stone Rock just offshore from Blackwalnut Point holds weakfish, black drum and blues. Drum like a bucktail tipped with peeler crab, while trolling bucktails is a good method to take both blues and trout.

The entrance to Eastern Bay lies between Tilghman Island and Kent Island. This estuary holds some of the biggest blue crabs in the world but it takes a bit of work using a trot line baited with eel to catch the fattest jimmies.

Bloody Point at the south end of Kent Island is the deepest part of the bay. Some very big bluefish and striped bass have been taken here including the state record rockfish, a 67-pounder, caught on a parachute rig by a 12-year-old boy.

Brick House Bar and Gum Thickets are found along the western shore of Kent Island. Both mark sharp drop-offs—from less than 10 to over 100 feet—where big blues and rockfish cruise the edge looking for food. Trolling with plugs, spoons and bucktails is the most practical method for covering this type of structure.

Over on the western shore, fishermen find shallow water more suitable for bottom-fishing with peeler crab, bloodworms and grass shrimp. Hacketts Bar, Dolly's Lump and Tolly Bar all produce rockfish, white perch, flounder and small blues. The City of Annapolis not only provides all the goods and services required by fishermen but is also a mecca for the sailboat crowd.

On both sides of the bay there are numerous boat ramps as well as marinas, tackle shops, restaurants and motels. Charter boats operate out of Solomons Island, Chesapeake Beach, Annapolis, Kent Narrows, Tilghman Island and Deal. There is a fishing pier on Kent Island and a few rock jetties on the western shore. Otherwise shore fishing is somewhat restricted.

KENT ISLAND TO THE SUSQUEHANNA RIVER

LAND CONFIGURATION AND WATER DEPTH

This section of the Chesapeake Bay is characterized by low, gently rolling country. Save for only a few places where hills rise to over 150 feet, the land is no higher than 60 feet above sea level; and along the shore of the Bay, it is usually less than 20 feet. The shoreline of the Bay appears jagged because of the incisions made by hundreds of rivers, creeks, and small bays. Many of the so-called rivers extending 6 to 8 miles into the interior are actually arms of Chesapeake Bay into which fresh water flows from a few to several dozen small streams. This is especially true along the western shore. At the very upper part of this map section, however, the largest river of all, the Susquehanna, flows into the Chesapeake Bay. Though not as wide as the Potomac or James Rivers farther down Chesapeake Bay, or even half a dozen other lesser rivers, the Susquehanna is by far the most important river in this region. After draining about half of Pennsylvania, a large part of New York, and part of Maryland, and after cutting over 400 miles across the full breadth of the Appalachian Mountains, forming as it flows a series of water gaps in passing through each successive range, it empties an average of 22½ billion gallons of fresh water a day into the Bay. This amounts to over 50% of all the fresh water enter-

ing the Bay. Not only does its discharge determine the salinity of the upper Bay, and thus the distribution of fishes, but also to a great extent it determines the composition and shape of the bottom as well.

FISH AND FISHING: BAY BRIDGES TO THE SUSQUEHANNA RIVER

The northern portion of the Chesapeake Bay can produce everything from smallmouth bass to striped bass, catfish to bluefish, all depending on the season and the salt content of the water.

In the spring, heavy rains lower salinity, and freshwater fish may be taken as far south as the Bay Bridges. During late summer, when rainfall is light, the salinity rises bringing small blues as far north as Turkey Point. These changing conditions can test an angler's skill but will also provide an interesting selection of fish for him to catch.

The recovery of striped bass has put the Bay Bridges back in the spotlight as one of the better places to catch these popular fish. Live eels worked back in the current so they swim around the pilings are very popular and extremely effective. Bucktails and plugs will also work, but nothing outfishes a live eel during the fall run of striped bass.

Rock Hall did not get its name from any geological formation but from the fish that have been landed there for hundreds of years. Drifting eels, peeler crab or bloodworms on Belvidere Shoal or around the mouth of the Chester River will work as well as trolling spoons, plugs or bucktails in the same areas. White perch and catfish may be taken here in the spring.

Moving up the bay, you will find very rough bottom around Pooles Island. An old oyster ground, it is a very good location for rock, white perch, catfish and the occasional bluefish. Jigging with bucktails or bottom-fishing with peeler crab will work, but for larger rockfish try a live eel.

From Pooles Island on up to the head of the bay, largemouth bass and white perch provide most of the action.

The best fishing will be in rivers such as the Gunpowder, Bush, Bohemia, Elk, Northeast and Susquehanna. The Susquehanna Flats between Havre de Grace and Turkey Point were severely damaged by a hurricane in the 1970's but today the grass is coming back and good fishing for striped bass is available in the fall.

Smallmouth bass are taken around the islands upstream from the Route 40 bridge over the Susquehanna River. Largemouth bass stage along piers, pilings and bridges in the towns of Havre de Grace and Perryville. Few fishing locations can offer both species of bass plus an abundance of rockfish all within a few square miles of sheltered waters.

Boat ramps and marinas can be found all along the

bay and in all of the rivers. Charter boats operate out of Rock Hall and a few of the other marinas but not in the numbers of years past. Accommodations vary from luxurious hotels in Baltimore to campgrounds on the Eastern Shore.

FISHING REGULATIONS

As we've noted previously, fishing regulations are relatively perishable. What follow are abstracts of fishing regulations for Maryland and Virginia. This information should be used for general purposes only. Because regulations change frequently, and because the regulations themselves are far more detailed than presented here, all anglers should contact the state agencies listed at the beginning and end of this chapter.

MARYLAND

For Maryland's fishing laws, see page 148.

For Maryland's Tidal-Water Designated Free-Fishing Areas, see page 150.

VIRGINIA

Virginia requires a license to fish the Chesapeake Bay and its tributaries. This does not include the seaside of the eastern shore or Virginia Beach. Any angler between 16 and 65, including anyone fishing on a licensed charter boat, headboat, fishing pier, rental boat, or private boat, must obtain a license. Restrictions are subject to change. For the latest information, call the Virginia Marine Resources Commission in Newport News at 804-247-2247. The VMRC monitors VHF Channel 17. The "hotline" number to report violations is 1-800-541-4646.

Regulations for black drum, cobia, gray trout (weakfish), red drum, summer flounder, and speckled trout have been under review; check for the latest limits and restrictions.

For Virginia's fishing regulations, see page 150.

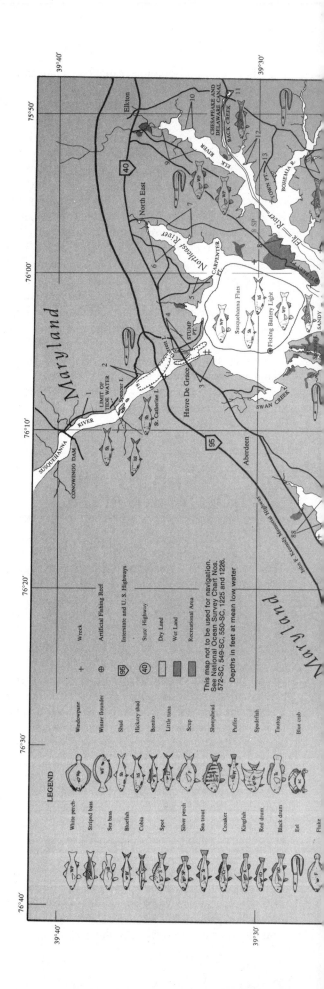

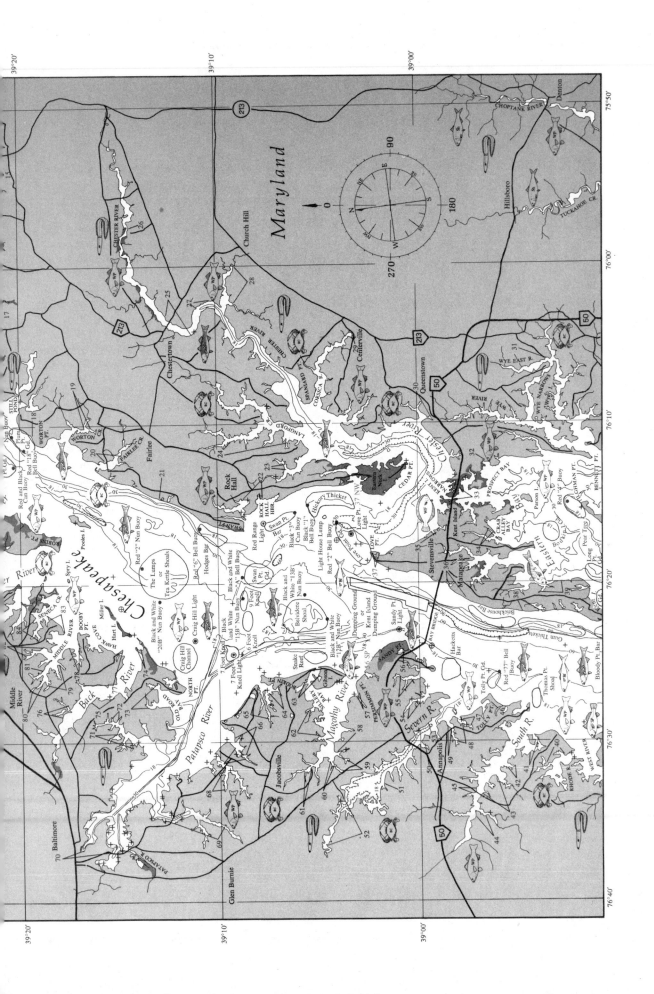

Chesapeake's Fall Flounder Hotspots

by Gary Diamond

Everyone's looking forward to Maryland's upcoming striped bass season, an event that annually attracts more than 60,000 anglers to the fertile waters of Chesapeake Bay. However, with a daily limit of just one rockfish per person, it usually doesn't take long to fill your quota. Ironically, anglers that catch their limit and head back to the launch ramp or dock often pass over large numbers of the best tasting fish inhabiting the area—flounder.

Cool nights and shortened hours of daylight during late September trigger what many fishermen refer to as The Fall Migration, a period when various species of fish gather in large schools and feed heavily just prior to heading south. Flounder are no exception. Although they're not a schooling fish, large numbers of flatties often congregate in relatively shallow water where they'll gorge themselves on bay anchovies, tiny menhaden and baby spot as they slowly migrate toward the Chesapeake's mouth, exiting the bay sometime in mid-December.

By opening day of rockfish season, flounder are constantly foraging in the bay's shallows. They're frequently found at locations easily accessible to small and mid-sized boats, and in some instances, shorebound and wading anglers can also get in on the action.

Additionally, flounder caught this time of year are often among the largest of the entire season. The secret to success is knowing where these hot spots are located and using proven light-tackle fishing techniques, similar to methods effectively utilized by freshwater panfish anglers.

First and foremost, your tackle selection should as light as possible. Light and ultralight spinning or bait-casting outfits are essential for detecting the delicate tap of a hefty flatfish. Their smaller cousins slam a bait like a freight train, while the big guys tend to gently pick up the bait, take a quick taste and at the slightest indication of tension, drop it like a hot potato. This time of

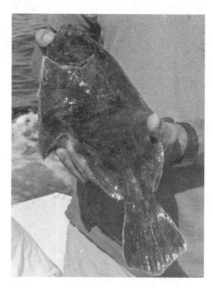

This Chesapeake flounder took a small bucktail tipped with a squid strip. Flounders will bunch up in relatively shallow water and gorge on baitfish while they migrate toward the mouth of Chesapeake Bay. (GARY DIAMOND)

year, flounder are hungry—not stupid.

The reel should be matched to the rod, have a smooth drag system and spooled with nothing heavier than 6- to 8-pound test, premium quality, clear monofilament line. Premium lines have stronger knot strength, finer diameters, less memory and provide increased casting range. The junk lines selling for $2 a pick-up-truck load are just that—junk. Garbage-quality lines have the memory of a Slinky, hook setting characteristics of a size-10 rubber band, diameter of anchor rope, and knot strength of a wet noodle.

When it comes to terminal tackle, most of the more successful anglers feel hardware at the end of your line should consist of nothing more than a sinker and hook. If the sinker's lying on the bottom and the hook is covered with bait, there's nothing to distract or disrupt the flounder's feeding habits. Forget those brass stand-offs, sinker

snaps, big barrel swivels, beads and spinners. No self-respecting flounder will fall for a hook adorned with tacky dime-store jewelry. They're looking for meat—not earring components. In fact, because the water's fairly clear in late September, there's an even chance the added hardware will scare the fish off instead of attracting them to your bait.

Fishing for flounder with light tackle is in many ways similar to fishing for big walleyes in ice-cold water. Essentially, you're fishing over open areas adjacent to abrupt changes in bottom contour. Flats bordering steep channel edges are always good locations to catch foraging flounder. Although these areas might only range in depth from 2 to 12 feet, they often hold flounder of six or more pounds.

If you're fishing with bottom rigs, bait up with a live minnow, squid strip, strip of cut spot or a piece of flounder belly. Position your boat along the shallow edge of the flats, lower your baits to the bottom and drift with the tide or wind, parallel to the edge. At the slightest indication of a strike, set the hook—don't hesitate. Flounder rarely give you a second chance.

Casting small bucktails trimmed with one or more of the above baits can be extremely effective, especially during high and outgoing tides. During an outgoing tide, cast the bucktail to the shallows, retrieving it slowly toward the channel edge. A slight twitch of the rod tip, combined with a slow but erratic retrieve imparts the action of a crippled baitfish, something most flounder find irresistible. Again, if you feel a slight tap or tug, set the hook as if you were trying to break the rod tip. During an incoming tide, cast to the deeper edges, retrieving toward the shallows, mimicking the activities of fleeing baitfish.

Gum Thickets

During the October season the eastern edge of the main shipping channel is always a popular location for trollers seeking striped bass. Just a quarter mile east of the channel you'll find a large, partly submerged stump field in three to six feet of water. The wooded structure attracts hordes of small baitfish which lure lots of flounder during a high tide. Live minnows and squid strips worked close to the stumps and logs often produce a mix of both big stripers and flounder.

Poplar Island Flats

The west side of Poplar Island is littered with hundreds of submerged trees, which form an incredible underwater jungle. Swarms of juvenile spot and croaker inhabit this particular patch of piscatorial real-estate which attracts a variety of gamefish species. Flounder, some weighing more than five pounds, are frequently found lurking among the submerged debris. The flatties are frequently accompanied by big stripers, chopper bluefish and on rare occasions, puppy drum to 18 inches. This is a good area to cast 1/4-ounce bucktails trimmed with live minnows or strips of fresh spot. Caution: This particular area is best fished by small boats on calm days. Large boats with drafts exceeding 18 inches can incur severe hull damage from submerged trees.

Cook Point

The hard bottom flats surrounding Cook Point can be highly productive during low-light conditions. Early morning and late evening fishermen cast small bucktails trimmed with live minnows, squid strips and chunks of peeler crab to lure a mix of big flounder to 22 inches, speckled trout and stripers. The clear waters of the lower Choptank, however, make fishing this area nearly impossible during periods of bright sunlight. During mid-day, head a half mile west to Sharps Island Flats.

Sharps Island Flats

Located at loran-C coordinates 27510.0/42446.0 is what remains of Sharps Island, a sandbar situated in seven feet of water. Although submerged pilings are indicated on NOAA charts, I've never seen them. The bar is surrounded by a series of shallow bottom depressions that resemble spokes of a wagon wheel, radiating outward from the submerged island. Drift-fishing with live minnows or squid strips proves highly effective at this location during both outgoing and incoming tides.

Punch Island Bar (27465.0/42310.0)

Situated along a steep drop-off on the western side of Taylors Island, Punch Island Bar is an isolated location that's a relatively long run from most launch ramps. However, if you have a mid-sized boat, it's a trip that's usually well worthwhile. Large numbers of big flounder often congregate along the edge where the water quickly drops from 17 to 26 feet. It's a great area to drift strips of flounder belly, fresh cut spot and live minnows on bottom rigs.

Hoooper Island Light (27417.0/41192.0)

The relatively shallow channel edge between Hooper Island Light and Richland Point Buoy is always a good bet for lots of big flounder during late September and throughout most of October. It's a great place to drift live minnows and squid strips, which often produce flounder ranging to three pounds, and similar-sized weakfish are often schooled in the vicinity.

Target Ship (27357.5/41041.0)

Chunks of metal litter the bottom adjacent to the U.S. Navy target ship *American Mariner*. The vessel sits on the bottom in 18 feet of water right in the middle of Chesapeake Bay. The partly submerged structure attracts large numbers of flounder, weakfish, snapper bluefish and puppy drum during the fall months. Squid strips and cut spot produce the best action when drift-fished on bottom rigs during outgoing tides.

Point Lookout Pier

A 600-foot-long public fishing pier located at Point Lookout State Park provides shorebound anglers with an excellent opportunity to catch lots of hefty flatfish migrating south. The structure is open year-round and there's no charge for parking or admission. Each fall, a handful of late-season regulars spend their entire weekend fishing for flounder from the pier's far end. It's a great place to take the entire family, explore the park and catch lots of fish.

Blackberry Hang

The shallow flats situated near the mouth of Great Wicomico River are known to local anglers as Blackberry Hang, a location where swarms of baby spot and croaker congregate just prior to migrating south. These juvenile panfish attract lots of big flounder, some of which tip the scales at more than eight pounds.

The Cell (27245.0/41597.0)

Although this is a deep-water area, an artificial reef installed by the State of Virginia has transformed this barren bottom area into one of the most productive fishing locations in the lower Chesapeake. Big flounder, croaker, spot and tautog inhabit this area which is only a short run from nearby Cape Charles Harbor.

Kiptopeke State Park Fishing Pier

Located near the end of the Delmarva Peninsula, this is the largest waterfront state park in Virginia's portion of Chesapeake Bay. A large, modern fishing pier has been constructed adjacent to the old ferry-terminal building, where visiting anglers catch lots of mid-sized flatties, spot, croaker and the occasional tautog.

Currently, both Maryland and Virginia have specific size and creel limits for flounder. Be sure to check your fishing guide book issued with the Chesapeake Bay Sportfishing License for appropriate fisheries laws pertaining to the state in which you're fishing. Then, after catching your legal limit, fillet the fish and savor what some folks refer to as "The best-tasting fish in Chesapeake Bay."

Western Shore Speckled Trout

by Eric B. Burnley

Speckled trout fishing along the western shore of the lower Chesapeake Bay is certainly not a secret but it is not as well known as fishing the creeks and flats on the bayside of Virginia's Eastern Shore. This may change if fishing for specks continues to improve in Mobjack Bay, and the Piankatank and the Rappahannock Rivers, where for the past two seasons trout have been taken in good numbers from spring through the summer and into the fall.

Specks will begin to feed in the spring when the water temperature reaches 55 to 60 degrees and will be even more active once the temperature moves well into the upper 60 degree range. During the early part of the season fresh bait seems to outproduce artificials but during the summer and fall almost everyone will be casting grubs and plugs.

The key to finding trout is locating grass beds and then looking for structure within or adjacent to those beds. The fish will either patrol the edges of the grass or pick a spot inside the beds and wait for their prey to make a fatal error in judgment. The grass beds are normally found relatively close to shore in 2 to 10 feet of water and are making it possible to fish for speckled trout from the beach or while wading. A few anglers will use their boats to reach secluded beds then wade to quickly cover more territory.

The majority of speckled trout fishermen work from shallow-draft boats that are easy to tow and launch and that will quickly cover the open water between fishing holes. Outboards provide the primary power but many of the regulars have installed saltwater-tested electric trolling motors to move over the grass beds in search of specks. I have seen a few hardy souls who still fish from rowboats. This can be very effective, but should the wind switch to the wrong direction it can be a long row back to the dock.

The grass beds are home not only to the speckled trout but also to large numbers of soft crabs recently emerged from their shells. This activity is especially prevalent in May and June as young crabs will shed out more frequently until they reach maturity. At this time of year the most productive method for catching speckled trout is to drift or bottom-fish with soft crab or peeler crab bait.

It may be possible to interest a trout anywhere along a grass bed, but certain structure is more likely to hold fish. When approaching a new area look for the edge of the bed then position the boat uptide or upwind to slowly and quickly drift over the grass. Use your sonar to locate drop-offs or channels and use your eyes to find open bottom inside the grass bed.

The edge of a channel, especially one that runs out from a feeder creek, is a prime location for speckled trout. Anchor your boat so your bait can be worked along the drop-off as the trout will move up from the deeper water looking for food.

Those open areas inside the grass beds are best fished by placing the bait on the open bottom where it can easily be found by patrolling trout. In all cases the boat's motor must be shut off and all hands should rig for silent fishing. Remember you are in very shallow water trying to catch very cautious fish and you do not want to scare them out of the neighborhood.

You prepare your peeler or soft crab by cutting it into segments with a pair of large kitchen shears. Even the sharpest, strongest knife will not handle crab as well as shears. Your bait should not be too large—no more than one or two segments—because the trout feed primarily on young crabs.

If you are fishing over the grass, your crab must be suspended from some sort of float. Adjust the distance from the float to the hook to keep your crab just above the top of the grass. When working in the more open spaces, put the bait on the bottom using a slip-sinker set up similar to a bass fisherman's Car-olina rig. A wide-gap Siwash-style hook, size 5/0 to 7/0 is very effective. Most of the time it will be tied directly to your 12- to 15-pound line, but a few anglers use a 12- to 24-inch leader made of 20- to 30-pound line and secured to the lighter running line with a blood-knot or double uni-knot.

As waters warm during the summer a horde of smaller fish such as spot, croaker and pinfish moves in, making bait-fishing for trout all but impossible. A piece of soft crab or peeler crab will be picked clean off the hook in a matter of seconds by these continuous-eating machines, but their overwhelming presence makes them excellent live baits for trophy-size speckled trout.

Big trout live and feed in the same areas as small trout but prefer larger meals. You need not change your tackle or rigs, simply replace the crab with a live pinfish. You will have to let the trout run with the live bait to give him time to turn it and then swallow it. I always hook my live baits through the eye sockets because this makes a more natural presentation and the hook will be well down in the fishes' gullets as they swallow the bait head first.

Live bait-fishing is a game of waiting. You select a likely looking location, anchor up and wait for a big fish to find your offering. Most anglers demand more action even if the quality of the catch is not as high. For these folks, drifting over the grass beds while casting jigs and plugs provides the action they seek.

In Virginia the MirrOlure is the most popular plug while the Mr. Wiffle rubber tail is the most popular adornment behind a leadhead jig. Plugs that run well suspended just above the grass beds perform better than jigs that sink to the bottom and become fouled with grass. On the other hand nothing is more effective than a leadhead bouncing along the open bottom kicking up little puffs of sand on every hop. Colors seem more important to the angler than to the fish, with red, white, green, smoke and hot pink effective at various times.

Virginia currently has a 14-inch minimum size limit with a ten-fish-per-day bag limit on speckled trout. Most of us seldom catch more than ten specks over 14 inches in a day, but last

year there were reports of anglers catching and releasing 50 or more trout on a tide.

The best action in this shallow water seems to come early and late in the day on a flood tide. If it is overcast and even lightly raining, the fish will remain active all day. The wind is

always a factor, but with the the shape of Mobjack Bay, you can usually find a lee shore to fish.

While less well known than some of the more popular speckled trout locations to our south, Virginia can provide plenty of action along her beautiful western shore. ∎

Lower Bay Sharking

by Gary Diamond

Sharks? In Chesapeake Bay? You're crazy. There's no sharks in Chesapeake Bay," said central Virginia resident Hank Mercer as he impaled a whole, live spot on the point of a heavy, 7/0 hook. The struggling baitfish was slowly lowered into the clear, green water, the rod placed in a vertical holder and everyone sat back and enjoyed the mid-summer sun.

The three anglers patiently awaited for signs of activity at the ends of their lines, but for nearly a half hour, all was quiet. Then it happened. Line began slowly inching from the reel's spool, then stopped as suddenly as it began. "Probably a piece of grass or something on the hook," said Mercer as he leaned back in his seat. Seconds later, the rod bucked, the clicker screamed and line peeled from the spool as if it was hooked to a southbound freight train. Nearly 150 yards had evaporated from the reel before he could grab the rod and set the hook. The ensuing battle lasted only a short time, maybe 20 minutes, but Mercer said it was the longest 20 minutes of his relatively short fishing career. "I thought the shark would rip my arms off. I've never had a fish fight that hard."

A few minutes later, the 75-pound dusky was alongside the boat, exhausted. A tag was carefully inserted just behind the dorsal fin, the leader was cut and this denizen of the deep quickly swam off. "That was incredible," said Mercer. "I wouldn't have believed sharks lived in the lower bay, but I'll be back next year to try this again."

The trio of anglers was fishing within sight of both Cape Charles Har-

bor and the Chesapeake Bay Bridge Tunnel, a place where in years past, anglers by the thousands congregated every spring to fish for black drum. The same location has always held good numbers of big sharks, some to more than 500 pounds, but only a handful of individuals bothered to fish for these tough-fighting gamefish. Even now, when black drum are difficult to find and limits have been placed on most species, only a few visiting anglers bother to fish for the largest species of fish inhabiting Chesapeake Bay.

Several species of shark venture into the confines of the bay every spring and summer. The first to arrive are spawning, spiny dogfish, better known locally as sand sharks or horndogs. This often-maligned fish reaches a maximum weight of approximately 55 pounds and is one of the best-tasting species of shark inhabiting Atlantic coastal waters.

Just prior to spawning, spiny dogfish follow migrating Atlantic mackerel up the coast, feeding on them at their leisure. The spawning urge eventually causes the larger females to enter the mouth of Chesapeake Bay and the back bays behind Virginia's chain of barrier islands. After a few weeks, they give birth to a dozen or more live young, fish that average nearly 12 inches at birth. A few weeks later, the females migrate back to the ocean depths while their offspring will remain inshore to feed on tiny menhaden and other juvenile species.

By early June, large swarms of weakfish inhabit the lower reaches of the Chesapeake. Most will average about 9 to 12 inches with a rare fish

reaching three pounds. They gather in huge schools along the eastern edge of the main shipping channel where they feed on seaworms, mantis shrimp and tiny anchovies throughout most of the summer. It only takes the marauding dusky sharks a few weeks to discover this nearby smorgasbord just inside the mouth of Chesapeake Bay.

The weakfish are eventually joined by swarms of croaker, spot and other panfish species, fish that attract large numbers of predators. One of the largest, the dusky shark, roams the lower bay from the Chesapeake Bay Bridge-Tunnel north to Smith Point. Although this particular species is known to reach lengths exceeding 12 feet, most entering the lower bay rarely exceed 7 feet, weighing less than 250 pounds. However, they can be highly aggressive.

Lower-bay anglers fishing for panfish species often scorn dusky sharks, claiming they're nothing more than a nuisance. Because the sharks are following schools of smaller fish, a spot, croaker or weakfish struggling at the end of someone's line is fair game. The opportunistic shark merely grabs the fish right behind the gills, providing the angler with a very short, exciting battle, leaving them with a fish head for their efforts.

Another species of shark that lurks beneath the fertile waters of Chesapeake Bay is the bull shark. Reaching lengths of 12 or more feet and weighing more than 750 pounds, bull sharks can be found throughout the entire length of the bay. In fact, they're so adaptable that they've been known to travel up to 100 miles into fresh water searching for food. It wasn't too many years ago that an angler fishing for bluefish just above the Chesapeake Bay Bridges at Annapolis spotted what he believed to be a huge shark.

After catching another bluefish, the fisherman quickly impaled the struggling blue on a large hook and lowered it over the side of his 15-foot aluminum boat. It didn't take long for the foraging bull shark to discover the injured blue. Several hours latter, after dragging the lightweight boat the entire length of Kent Island, the massive 10½-foot 550-pound shark was brought alongside. Although no sharks approaching that size have been caught in the upper bay since then, a few in the 250- to 300-pound range have been caught in commercial pound nets situated in Bush River and near Rock Hall. Several years ago, a 750-pounder was found entangled in an illegally set commercial gill net near the Chesapeake Bay Bridges. The net was confiscated, but unfortunately the shark died.

One of the most spectacular species of shark found in the lower bay is the black-tip. Often referred to locally as "spinners," these sharks have the uncanny ability to leap high above the waves when they feel the sting of a hook. The jump is not like that of a tarpon, but rather, it's the twisting, gyrating motion of a fish gone berserk. Nine chances out of 10, it will wrap your line around its sleek body, abrading the mono with its tough hide until the nylon parts with a loud snap.

Most spinners found behind Virginia's barrier islands and near the mouth of Chesapeake Bay rarely exceed 50 pounds. However, on rare occasions, a 150-pounder will be caught near the CBBT or along the oceanside flats of Fisherman's Island National Wildlife Refuge. If you're lucky enough to land one of these majestic fish, place a tag in its back and release it to fight another day. Spinner sharks are lots of fun to catch, but unless blackened, they taste terrible.

Tackle Requirements

Most sharks are caught with heavy tackle, but when you're fishing in relatively shallow water, depths measuring less than 25 feet, heavy gear is unnecessary.

Most heavy-action spinning outfits are more than adequate to land sharks up to 100 pounds, particularly when you're fishing an area where encountering another boat is a rare occurrence. If the shark is exceptionally large, you can attach your anchor line to an anchor-retrieval ball and follow the fish until it's landed. Then you can return, attach the anchor line to a cleat and continue to fish.

Your reel should have a smooth drag system and sufficient line capacity to hold 250 yards of 14- to 20-pound test, premium-grade monofilament. If you're using a spinning outfit, set the drag somewhat loose, allowing the fish to take the bait without encountering much resistance. Once the fish takes off on a run, tighten the drag a little, set the hook and dig in for a long battle.

If you're using a conventional reel, set the drag in the usual manner, freespool line until your bait's properly positioned, leave the gears disengaged and set the clicker. Unless the tide's running extremely strong, the clicker's friction is more than sufficient to hold your bait in position. When the fish hits, engage the gears, set the hook and hang on.

Tag and Release

All species of shark are currently being overfished by commercial fishermen. According to the latest report released by National Marine Fisheries Service, while recreational catches are being severely curtailed, commercial fishing activities for some species are largely ignored. In North Carolina, millions of pounds of spiny dogfish are harvested annually by commercial purse-seine fishermen. Although recreational anglers are limited to one shark daily in Virginia's portion of Chesapeake Bay, the species is being systematically annihilated by commercial netters. There is no catch or minimum size limit on spiny dogfish caught by commercial netters.

In order to help preserve the shark fishery, recreational fishermen and charger captains throughout the nation encourage tag-and-release shark fishing. This means you'll need to purchase a tagging stick at your local tackle shop and procure tags from NMFS.

Tagging kits are available by writing to: Apex Predator Investigation,

National Marine Fisheries Service, South Ferry Road, Narragansett, RI 02882-1199. At this writing, a limited number of the kits were still available, but federal cutbacks have severely curtailed this program.

Tagging a somewhat unhappy shark is not an easy task and if not properly done, can be hazardous to your health. When the fish is alongside the boat, quickly and carefully insert the tag in its back, next to the dorsal fin. Do not tail rope or gaff the fish unless you intend to kill it. Sharks are extremely prone to internal injuries while thrashing around and banging into the side of the boat. Often, they'll swim off, seemingly no worse for wear, but later die from rough handling.

Once the tag is in place, carefully reach down the line with a pair of wire cutters and cut the wire leader a safe distance from the mouth. The shark will usually reject the hook within 24 to 48 hours after being released. DO NOT attempt to revive a lethargic appearing shark by grasping its tail and moving the fish back and forth. Because sharks have no bones, they are the only species of fish that can turn and grab their own tail. They can just as easily grab your arm and inflict a serious or fatal injury.

Next, fill out the tag's card, recording all pertinent information and estimating the shark's length and weight. The cards should be mailed as soon as you return to the dock.

If you have the burning desire to eat shark meat, keep a few smaller fish. Although there is likely little or no difference in taste between a large and small shark, those weighing less than 50 pounds are far safer to gaff and boat.

Large sharks, fish topping 100 pounds, really get upset when you attempt to place a gaff in their jaw. In addition, it's unlikely that you have a cooler large enough to hold a 7-foot shark; consequently, it would probably be lashed to the side of the boat. This means the fish would not be iced down until it dies, thereby making the meat taste somewhat like musty cardboard. Additionally, a shark's highly abrasive skin will virtually destroy a boat's gelcoat in an hour or two of rubbing up and down with the waves.

Small sharks should be buried in ice

immediately upon landing. Once the shark's dead, remove its head and entrails, and rinse the carcass thoroughly in salt water, then ice it down by packing and covering the fish with ice. The fish can then be cut into inch-thick steaks (which taste excellent when charbroiled on a gas grill and seasoned with barbeque sauce, blackening spices, or just salt and pepper). Individually wrapped and frozen steaks retain

a fresh taste, even after two to three months.

Cape Charles, Virginia, is located on the lower end of the Delmarva Peninsula, approximately 12 miles north of the CBBT. Boating anglers will find an excellent launch ramp adjacent to the U.S. Coast Guard Station at Cape Charles and charter fishing boats are available at Kings Creek Marina and in Cape Charles Harbor.

Lower Bay Sharking Locations

The Cell—27245/41595
Old Plantation Light—27220/41470
Cape Charles Reef—27225/41480
Cabbage Patch—27215/41450
Latimer Shoal—27200/41420
Inner Middle Ground—27195/41385
Smith Shoal Inlet Area—27180/41374
Red Can Buoys—27171/41358 ∎

FISHING ACCESS

MARYLAND LAUNCH RAMPS

The following list contains only those launch ramps in counties with access to the Chesapeake Bay and its tributaries. For a listing of state ramps with ocean access, see page 156.

Anne Arundel County
- Truxtun Heights Park (Spa Creek). Off Hilltop Lane at end of Primrose Road.
- Sandy Point State Park (Messick Pond via Chesapeake Bay). U.S. Rte. 50 at Bay Bridge.

Baltimore County
- Cox's Point Park (Back River). Riverside Drive off Eastern Avenue, Rte. 150 in Essex.
- West Inverness Park (Lynch Cove). Inverton Road behind Inverton Elementary School.
- Merritt Park (Patapsco River/Bear Creek). On Dunmanway off Merritt Boulevard.
- Rocky Point Park (Back River/Hawk Cove). End of Back River Neck Road.
- Broening Park (Middle Branch). Rte. 2, Hanover Street near Harbor Hospital.
- Gunpowder State Park-Dundee Creek Marina (Dundee Creek/Gunpowder River). Off Rte. 150 at end of Graces Quarter Road.
- Fort Armistead (Patapsco River). Off Fort Smallwood Road end of Glidden Road.

Calvert County
- Solomons (Patuxent River). South side of Rtes 2 and 4 at Thomas Johnson Bridge.
- Hallowing Point (Patuxent River). At Patuxent River Bridge Rte. 231.

Caroline County
- Choptank Towne Yacht Basin (Choptank River). Rte. 331 east to Maple St. in Preston; end of Choptank Road.
- Daniel Crouse Park (Choptank River). North side Rte. 404 Bridge.
- Federalsburg Marina (Marshyhope Creek). Off Rte. 313 and 318 on Main Street
- Ganey's Wharf (Choptank River). Left on MD Rte. 313 at Greensboro, across bridge turn left into park.
- Hillsboro (Tuckahoe Creek). Rte. 404, in Hillsboro.
- Martinak State Park (Choptank River). Four miles south of Denton off Rte. 404, Deep Shore Road.
- Federalsburg. On River Road at VFW off Rtes. 313 and 318 one mile south of Federalsburg.

Cecil County
- Bohemia River Bridge (Bohemia River). On State Route 213.
- Fredericktown (Sassafras River). Seventeen miles south of Elkton on U.S. Rte. 213.
- Port Deposit (Susquehanna River). Rte. 222 in Port Deposit.
- Elk Neck State Park (Elk River). Ten miles south of North East on Rte. 272.

Charles County
- Friendship Landing (Nanjemoy Creek/Potomac River). End of Friendship Landing Road off Rte. 425 south of Ironside.

- Smallwood State Park-Sweden Point (Potomac River/Mattawoman Creek). One mile south of Marbury on Rte. 224.
- Gilbert Run Park (Wheatley Lake). East of La Plata on Rte. 6 in Dentsville.
- Marshall Hall (Potomac River). Rte. 210 south to Rte. 227 end of Marshall Hall Road.

Dorchester County
- Cambridge (Choptank River). Off Rte. 50 onto Maryland Avenue; Duck Walk-Franklin Street-Trenton Street.
- Taylor's Landing (Slaughter Creek-Little Choptank River). On Rte. 16 at Taylor's Island.
- Crapo (Wingate) (Charles Creek/Honga River). South of Cambridge, Rte. 336 next to Stein's Marina.
- Crocheron (Tedious Creek). Off Rte. 336, Bishop Head and Crocheron Rds.
- Hoopersville-Muddy Hook Cover (Honga River and Chesapeake Bay). Rte. 335 in Hoopersville.
- Shorter's Wharf (Blackwater River). South from Cambridge on Mapledam Road to bridge.
- Toddville Farm Creek (Farm Creek/Fishing Bay). Rte. 336 between Toddville Seafood Company and Meredith & Meredith.
- Vienna (Nanticoke River). End of Race Street.
- Madison Landing (Little Choptank River). On Rte. 16, 12½ miles from intersection Rte. 50 in Cambridge.
- Ragged Point (Chesapeake Bay). Rte. 50 to Rte. 343 to Hills Point left on Ragged Point Road.
- Elliott Island, McCready's Cove (Fishing Bay). End of Wharf Road and McCready's Creek.

- Great Marsh (Choptank River). Cambridge-Somerset Ave.
- Beaver Dam Creek (Chesapeake Bay/Keen Creek). Rte. 16 to Smithville Road.
- Bestpitch (Transquaking River). Off Rte. 50 on Bestpitch Ferry Road.
- New Bridge (Fishing Bay/Chicamacomico River). At Salem left onto Ravenwood Road, left onto New Bridge Road.
- Secretary (Choptank River). End of Temple Street six miles from intersection of Rte. 16 and Rte. 50.
- Wallace Creek (Honga River). Junction Rte. 335 and Rte. 336 next to Gootee's Marina.
- Transquaking River (Transquaking River). On Draw Bridge Road Rte. 397 near Airey.
- Honga River (Tyler's Cove). Chesapeake Bay/Tar Bay/Honga River); 16 miles south of Cambridge on Rte. 335.

Harford County
- Broad Creek Landing (Susquehanna River). Two miles north of Castleton off Rte. 623 on Broad Creek Landing Road.
- Flying Point Park (Bush River). Northeast of Edgewood, Rte. 24 off Willoughby Beach Road on Flying Point Road.
- Glen Cove Marina (Conowingo Lake). Off Rte. 623.
- Havre de Grace; Tydings Park (Susquehanna River). On Commerce Street.
- Otter Point (Bush River). Northeast of Edgewood off Rte. 24 on Otter Park Road.
- Susquehanna State Park; Lapisum Area (Susquehanna River). Off Rte. 155 end of Lapidum Road.
- Mariner Point Park (Foster Branch Creek/Gunpowder River). Rte. 40 to Joppa Farm Road to Kearney Drive.
- Willoughby Beach (Bush River). One mile beyond Flying Point Park at end of Kennard Avenue.
- Jean S. Roberts Memorial Park. Foot of Union Avenue in Havre de Grace.

Kent County
- Betterton (Sassafras River). Public landing at very end of Rte. 292.
- Bogles Wharf (Chester River/Chesapeake Bay). End of Rte. 445 on Eastern Neck Island south of Rock Hall.
- Buckingham Landing (Chester River). 2½ miles north of Chestertown off Rte. 291 end of Buckingham Road.
- Cliff City Wharf (Chester River).

Southwest of Chestertown at end of Rte. 289.
- Fairlee (Fairlee Creek/Chesapeake Bay). From town of Fairlee take Bay Shore Road to Fairlee Public Landing Road.
- Green Lane (Chesapeake Bay). South of Rock Hall off Rte. 445 at end of Green Lane Road.
- Long Cove (Chester River/Langford Creek). In Crosby off Rte. 288.
- Quaker Neck (Chester River). South of Chestertown off Rte. 289 at end of Rte. 661.
- Skinner's Neck (Chester River/Herrington Creek). Rte. 288, off Rte. 20 south of Sharpstown.
- Spring Cove (Swan Creek). North of Rock Hall off Rte. 445 at end of Spring Cove Road.
- Turner Creek (Turner Creek/Sassafras River). Off 213 at Rte. 448 end of Turner Creek Road, North of Chestertown.
- Shipyard Landing (Langford Creek/Chester River). End of Shipyard Lane off Rte. 20 near Edesville.
- Still Pond Creek (Still Pond). Off Rte. 292 to Still Pond Neck Road then to Still Pond Creek Road (permits required).

Montgomery County
- Edward Ferry (Potomac River). Off Rte. 109 south of Poolesville end of Edwards Ferry Road.
- Seneca (Potomac River). Off Rte. 112 and 190 in Seneca on Riley's Lock Road.
- C&O Canal Aqueduct Ramp #2 (Potomac River). Off Rte. 28 on Mouth of Monocacy Road.
- Seneca Creek State Park (Lake Clipper). In Gaithersburg off Clopper Road Rte. 117 (cartop or carryable boats only).

Prince George's County
- Croom Ramp and Pier Patuxent Park (Patuxent River). South of Upper Marlboro off Rte. 382.
- Fort Washington Marina. Washington Beltway I-95 south to Rte. 210 Indian Head Highway to Ft. Washington Road.
- McClure Gun Club Patuxent River Park (Patuxent River). Off Rte. 382 and Mt. Calvert Road on McClure Road.
- Magruder's Ferry Boating Facility Patuxent River Park (Patuxent River).
- Bladensburg (Anacostia River). Rte. 202 next to Port of Bladensburg Marina.

Queen Anne's County
- Deep Landing (Chester River). Off Rte. 544, end of Deep Landing Road three miles west of Rte. 290.
- Southeast Creek (Southeast Creek/Chester River). Near Church Hill off Rte. 213, end of Southeast Creek Road.
- Centreville Landing (Corsica/Chester River). Off 304 in Centreville, on Watson Road.
- Goodhand Creek (Prospect Bay/Kent Narrows). Off Rte. 552 on Goodhand Road.
- Piney Narrows (Chester River/Prospect Bay). Off Rtes. 50 and 301, near Kent Narrows Bridge, next to Piney Narrows Marina.
- Denny's Landing (Cox Creek/Eastern Bay). Off Rtes. 50 and 301, south on Thompson Creek Road.
- Crumpton (Chester River). At end of Market Street.
- Shipping Creek (Shipping Creek/Eastern Bay). South of Stevensville on Rte. 8 end of Shipping Creek Road.
- Matapeake State Park (Chesapeake Bay). On Rte. 8, two miles south of Stevensville off Rtes. 50 and 301.
- Tuckahoe State Park (Tuckahoe Lake). Off Rtes. 480 and 481 on Crouse Mill Road.
- Little Creek (Crab Alley/Eastern Bay). In Dominion, on Kent Island, end of Rte. 552.
- Queenstown (Chester River/Queenstown Creek). Off Rte. 18 to Center Street, at end of 1st Street in Queenstown (permits required).

St. Mary's County
- Bushwood Wharf (Wicomico River). Off Rte. 238 end of Bushwood Road.
- Chaptico Wharf (Wicomico River). Off Rte. 238 south of Chaptico end of Chaptico Wharf Road.
- Clark's Landing (Patuxent River). 2.1 miles south of Hollywood Rte. 235.
- Forest Landing (Patuxent River). Rte. 245, end of Forest Landing Road.
- Leonardtown (Patuxent River). In Leonardtown on Rte. 245, Washington Street.
- Piney Point (St. George Creek/Potomac River). On Rte. 249 near bridge, St. George Landing.
- Point Lookout State Park (Potomac River). End of Rte. 5.
- White Neck Creek (Potomac River). End of Rte. 520 south of Bushwood.
- St. Mary's River State Park. End of Cosoma Road off Rte. 5 south of Leonardtown.

- St, Inigoes (St. Mary's River/Smith Creek). End of Beachville Road off Rte. 5.

Somerset County

- Champ (St. Peters Creek/Manokin River). County Wharf off Rtes. 363 and 627, end of Champ Road.
- Coulbourne Creek (Big Annemessex River). Rte. 357 northwest of Marion end of Coulborne Creek Road.
- Deal Island Chance (Tangier Sound). Deal Island at Upper Thorofare Bridge off Rte. 363.
- Crisfield Ramp (Little Annemessex River). At foot of Brick Kiln Road in Crisfield.
- Rehobeth (Pocomoke River). Off Rtes. 667 and 413 on Rehobeth Road in Crisfield.
- Rumbley (Tangier Sound). Off Rte. 413 end of Rte. 361.
- Shelltown (Pocomoke River). End of Rte. 667 Shelltown Road.
- Smith Island. At Elwell (not accessible by vehicle).
- Mt. Vernon-Webster's Cove (Wicomico River). End of Dorsey Avenue in Mt. Vernon.
- Somers Cove Marina (Little Annemessex River). Crisfield Rte. 413.
- Rumbley Point Boat Ramp (Pocomoke Sound). In Marion off Rte. 357 end of Rumbley Point Road.
- Wenona (Tangier Sound). End of Rte. 363.
- Dames Quarter, Deal Island (Dames Quarter Creek/ Tangier Sound). End of Messick Road, off Rte. 363.
- Jenkin's Creek Wharf (Little Annemessex River). South of Crisfield off Rte. 413 at junction of Calvary and Sackertown Roads.
- Raccoon Point. Off Rte. 13 end of Revells Neck Road.

Talbot County

- Bellevue Boating Ramp (Tred Avon River). End of Rte. 329 next to Bellevue Ferry.
- Neavitt (Broad Creek/Choptank River). End of Rte. 579, southwest of St. Michaels.
- Easton Point Ramp (Tred Avon River). End of Rte. 334 near Easton.
- Wittman-Cummings Creek (Harris Creek/ Choptank River). Rte. 33, through St. Michaels end of Wharf Rd.
- West Harbor Road Boat Ramp (Miles River). Rte. 33 to East Chew Avenue to west Harbor Road in St. Michaels.
- Wye Landing (East Wye River). Off Rte. 662 end of Wye Landing Lane.

- Skipton Landing (East Wye River/Skipton Creek) in Skipton, end of Skipton Landing Road.
- Oak Creek Landing (Miles River). On Rte. 33 in Newcomb, adjacent to the Oak Creek Bridge.
- Claiborne (Chesapeake Bay/Eastern Bay). Four miles northwest of St. Michaels, end of Rte. 451.
- Dogwood Harbor-Tilghman Island (Harris Creek/Choptank River). Off Rte. 33 on Tilghman Island.
- Trappe Landing (La Trappe Creek/Choptank River). End of Trappe Landing Road.
- Windy Hill (Choptank River). End of Windy Hill Road in Bruceville.
- Tuckahoe Creek Bridge (Tuckahoe Creek). Eight miles northeast of Easton on Rte. 328.
- Oxford (Tred Avon Choptank River). End of Tilghman Street in Oxford.

Wicomico County

- Salisbury (Wicomico River). At Shore Stop Market Riverside Drive Ext.
- Cherry Beach (Sharptown). (Nanticoke River). End of Little Water Street in Sharpstown Park off Rte. 313.
- Wetipquin (Nanticoke River). West on Rte. 349 to Wetipquin Creek Bridge.
- Cedar Hill Park-Bivalve Harbor (Nanticoke River). Off Rte. 349 at Bivalve Harbor.
- Leonard Mill Park. Off U.S. Rte. 13, north of Salisbury on Leonard Mill Pond Road.
- Tyaskin (Nanticoke Harbor). Off 349 on Rte. 480 Tyaskin Road.
- Mardela Springs (Barren Creek/Nanticoke River). Off Bridge Street.
- Redden Ferry (Wicomico River). Cooper Road.
- Nanticoke (Nanticoke River). Off Rte. 349 on Harbor Road.

MARYLAND PUBLIC PIERS

Anne Arundel County

- Annapolis City Dock: end of Main Street in Annapolis.
- Galesville Pier and Park: end of Route 255 in Galesville.
- Londontown Public House Pier— Alms House: at historic Alms House at Alms House Creek.
- Deale Pier: on Rockhold Creek off Route 256.

Baltimore County

- Inner Harbor Marina of Baltimore: off Calvert and Light Streets.

- Baltimore Yacht Basin: at Hanover Street Bridge.
- Lancaster Street Boat Hoist and Storage: Baltimore's Inner Harbor on Lancaster Street, foot of Central Avenue.
- Chesterwood Park Pier: on Bullneck Creek in Dundalk.
- Fort Howard Pier: off North Point Road, near Fort Howard Hospital.
- Watersedge Beach Park—Long Point: end of Dundalk Avenue.
- Hull Street: end of Hull Street (South Baltimore).
- Boston Street: east Baltimore end of O'Donell Street.
- Hawthorne Park: end of Midthorne Road.

Calvert County

- Back Creek: at the Calvert Marine Museum.
- Kings Landing: end of Kings Landing Road.

Cecil County

- Perryville Pier: Perryville Community Park.
- North East Community Park: end of Walnut Street.

Charles County

- Southern Park and Pier: off Wilson Road.

Dorchester County

- Municipal Yacht Basin: in Cambridge.
- Long Wharf: end of High Street in Cambridge.
- River Walk: at City Hall in Cambridge.

Harford County

- Congress Avenue: on Congress Avenue in Havre de Grace.
- Lighthouse Pier: end of Lafayette Avenue.
- Lockhouse Pier: on Conesteo Street.

Kent County

- Rock Hall Pier: foot of Sharp Street.
- Wilmer Park: Queen Street in Chestertown.
- Chestertown Boat Landing: foot of High Street.
- Bayside Public Landing: Rock Hall off Bayside Avenue in Rock Hall.

Queen Anne's County

- Romancoke: end of Route 8 off Route 50/301.
- Bennett's Point: off Route 18, end of Bennett's Point Road.

St. Mary's County
- Tonger Basin: on Route 33, just across the Knapps Narrows Bridge.
- Chesapeake Bay Maritime Museum: in St. Michaels.

Wicomico County
- Westside Marina: on Main Street in Salisbury.
- East Prong—Wocomico River: on Carroll Street in Salisbury.
- Riverside Boat Dock: on Carroll Street in Salisbury.

Somerset County
- Pocomoke City Park: off Market Street in Pocomoke City.

VIRGINIA FISHING PIERS

(All telephone area codes are 804.)

Chesapeake Bay Bridge-Tunnel
- Sea Gull Fishing Pier (464-4641)

Norfolk
- Harrison's Boat House & Fishing Pier (587-9630)
- Wolloughby Bay Fishing Pier (588-2663)

Virginia Beach
- Lynnhaven Inlet Fishing Pier (481-7071)
- Virginia Beach Fishing Pier (428-2333)
- Sandbridge Fishing Pier (426-7200)

Lower Peninsula

Hampton
- Buckroe Beach Fishing Pier (851-9146)
- Grandview Fishing Pier (851-2811)

Newport News
- James River Fishing Pier, James River Bridge (247-0364)

VIRGINIA BOAT-LAUNCH RAMPS

The following list contains only those ramps in areas with access to the Chesapeake Bay and its tributaries. For a listing of Atlantic Ocean ramps, see page 156. All area codes 804.

Norfolk/Virginia Beach

Chesapeake Bay Bridge-Tunnel
- Sea Gull Fishing Pier (464-4641)

Norfolk
- Harrison's Boat House & Fishing Pier (587-9630)
- Wolloughby Bay Fishing Pier (588-2663)

Virginia Beach
- Lynnhaven Inlet Fishing Pier (481-7071)
- Virginia Beach Fishing Pier (428-2333)
- Sandbridge Fishing Pier (426-7200)

Lower Peninsula

Hampton
- Buckroe Beach Fishing Pier (851-9146)
- Grandview Fishing Pier (851-2811)

Newport News
- James River Fishing Pier, James River Bridge (247-0364)

Eastern Shore Bayside (Northampton County)

Exmore
- Morley's Wharf Boat Ramp (Occohanocock Creek)
- Nassawadox Creek Ramp (North)

Nassawadox
- Bayford Boat Ramp

Cape Charles
- Cape Charles Municipal Ramp (Cape Charles River)

Tidewater Area

Virginia Beach
- Owl's Creek Ramp (Rudee Inlet)
- Seashore State Park (Broad Bay)

Norfolk
- Willoughby Landing (Ocean View)

Hampton
- Sunset Creek Ramp (Hampton River)
- West Bank Ramp (Hampton River)
- Dandy Point Ramp (Back River)
- Gosnold Hope Park (Back River)

Newport News
- James River Bridge Ramp
- Seafood Industrial Park
- Anderson Park
- Denbigh Park Ramp (Warwick River)
- Deep Creek City Pier (Warwick River)

Poquoson
- Messick Point Landing (Back River)
- Bennett's Creek Landing (Poquoson River)
- Rens Road Ramp (Poquoson River)
- Plum Tree Island NWR

York County
- Back Creek Park
- Back Creek Ramp
- Old Wormley Creek Landing

Gloucester County

Gloucester Point
- Gloucester Point Landing (York River)
- Gaines Point Ramp

Guinea Neck
- Sedges Creek Ramp
- Perrin Creek Ramp
- Monday Creek Ramp
- Jordan Neck Ramp (Monday Creek)
- Brown's Bay Public Ramp
- Severn Holiday Ramp (Severn Creek)

Ordinary
- Timberneck Creek Ramp

Clay Bank
- Clay Bank Ramp
- Aberdeen Creek Ramp

Severn River
- John's Point Ramp
- Bray's Point Ramp

Ware River
- Paynes Wilson Creek Ramp
- Warehouse Landing

Piankatank River
- Deep Point Ramp
- Cypress Shores Ramp

Mathews County

North River
- Auburn Ramp

East River
- Town Point Landing
- Williams Wharf

Horn Harbor
- Horn Harbor Ramp

Winter Harbor
- Winter Harbor Landing
- Old Mill Landing

Milford Haven
- Fitchett's Wharf
- Cedar Lane Ramp
- Queens Creek Ramp

Piankatank River
- Godfrey Bay Public Ramp
- Warehouse Creek Ramp

Middlesex County

Piankatank River
- Jackson Creek Ramp
- Twiggs Ferry Ramp
- Stampers Public Ramp
- Fairfield Public Ramp

Rappahannock River
- Broad Creek Ramp (Deltaville)
- North End Ramp (Deltaville)
- Mill Creek Ramp
- Locklies Ramp
- Whiting Creek Ramp
- Urbanna Creek Ramp
- Mill Stone Ramp (Parrotts Creek)

Lancaster County

Windmill Point
- Windmill Point Landing
- Eastern Branch Ramp (Corrotoman River)

Northumberland County

Glebe Point
- Glebe Point Ramp
- Ball Creek Ramp

Reedville
- Cockrell Creek Landing
- Shell Landing (Cockrell Creek)

Smith Point
- Shipping Point Ramp
- Little Wicomico Ramp (Aphelia)

Coin River
- Rowels Landing
- Forest Landing

Yeocomico
- Lodge Landing
- West Yeocomico Ramp

Westmoreland County

Yeocomico River
- Kinsale Landing Ramp

Bonum Creek
- Bonum's Landing

Lower Machodoc Creek
- Branson Cover

Nomini Bay
- Currioman Dock

Popes Creek
- Popes Creek Ramp
- Westmoreland State Park

Colonial Beach
- Colonial Beach Landing

FISH RECORDS

MARYLAND FISHING RECORDS—CHESAPEAKE BAY DIVISION

Hickory shad: 4 lbs.; Susquehanna River; 1972

White shad: 8 lbs. 2 oz.; Wicomico River

Flounder: 15 lbs.; Buoy #50; 1978

Black drum: 103 lbs. 8 oz.; Buoy #16; 1973

Norfolk spot: 2 lbs.; Tangier Sound; 1978

Channel bass: 74 lbs. 6 oz.; Tangier Sound; 1977

Spotted seatrout: 16 lbs. 8 oz.; Roaring Point; 1977

Weakfish: 16 lbs. 8 oz.; Nanticoke River; 1979

Bluefish (tie): 22 lbs.; off Queen Anne Marina; 1979; Hackett's Point 1986

Striped bass: 55 lbs.; Holland Point Buoy #69; 1978

Yellow perch: 2 lbs. 3 oz.; Marsh Creek; 1979

White perch: 2 lbs. 10 oz.; Dundee Creek; 1979

Chain pickerel: 6 lbs. 8 oz.; Susquehanna River; 1965

Catfish: 19 lbs. 8 oz.; Susquehanna River; 1978

Cobia: 97 lbs. 12 oz.; Middle Grounds; 1969

Carp: 44 lbs. 6 oz.; Morgantown Beach; 1978

Crappie: 3 lbs. 4 oz.; Choptank River-Greensboro; 1981

Croaker: 6 lbs. 3 oz.; Puppy Hole; 1980

For a listing of Virginia gamefish records and tournaments, see page 159.

STATE AGENCIES

MARYLAND

Maryland Office of Tourism and Development
217 East Redwood St.
Baltimore, MD 21202
(410) 336-6611
Maryland Department of Natural Resources
Tidewater Administration
Tawes State Office Building
Annapolis, MD 21401
(410) 974-3765 or (301) 974-3558

VIRGINIA

(Area Code for all phone numbers is 804.)
Virginia Marine Resources Commission Offices
Main Office
2600 Washington Ave.
P.O. Box 756,
Newport News, VA 23607
247-2200
499 Menchville Road,
Newport News, VA 23062
877-1181
30 Jefferson Avenue
Newport News, VA 23707
247-2265
Tidemill Professional Center
Gloucester Point, VA 23063
642-2640
P.O. Box 166, Lancaster
VA 22503 (on Route 3)
462-7200
P.O. Box 117
Heathsville, VA 22473
(on Route 360)
580-2901

6

Commonly
Caught Fish

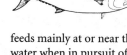

ATLANTIC BONITO, *Sarda sarda*. Bonito, common bonito. Pelagic, schooling and migratory. A rapid swimmer that feeds mainly at or near the surface; often jumping clear of the water when in pursuit of prey. Occur in water warmer than 65°F. Late June or July–mid October; best fishing in August. Both bonito and little tuna, below, move inshore around Montauk, Block Island, Nantucket, and Martha's Vineyard, and an increasing number of fly-fishermen have found these fish both challenging and willing to eat a properly presented streamer. FISHING METHODS: Most are caught at or near the surface by boat anglers 5 to 20 miles from shore while trolling, chumming, jigging, casting, or fly casting; some by anglers casting from shore during late summer. BAITS: Feathers, spoons, plugs, jigs, stripbait, feather stripbait combination and cut fish.

ATLANTIC COD. *Gadus morhua*. Cod. See Atlantic tomcod. Occur near bottom especially over ledges and slopes of shoals. Frequent rock, gravel, shell or sand bottom. During March–April on soft mud-sand. Adult cod generally occur in water colder than 50° to 55°F from near shore to 1,200 feet. Taken all year in depths over 150 feet; November–April in shallower water. Best fishing March–April and November–December in depths of 30 to 210 feet. FISHING METHODS: Bottom-fishing or jigging from boats. A few taken while casting from shore. BAITS: Sand lance, squid, crabs, clams, worms and cut fish; also jigs.

ATLANTIC CROAKER, *Micropogon undulatus*. Croaker, hardhead. Migratory. A few occur in nearly fresh water, but most in salt and brackish water from a few feet below the tide-line to depths of 60 feet. This bottom feeder occurs on mud, sand, gravel or rock bottom and around shellfish beds, rockpiles and wrecks. Mid April or May–late September or October; best fishing June–late August. FISHING METHODS: Bottom-fishing, jigging and chumming from anchored or drifting boats. Some caught by bottom-fishing from shore. Check state regulations on size limit. BAITS: Shrimp, soft or shedder crab, clams and cut fish; also small jigs and weighted bucktails.

ATLANTIC SALMON, *Salmo salar*. Fishable populations of salmon are found in the Machias, Union, St. Croix, East Machias, Dennys, Narraguagus, Sheepscot, Pleasant, and Penobscot Rivers. Most salmon are taken near or above head-of-tide, which requires an inland fishing license and salmon license, but some are taken in the estuaries of these rivers which requires only a salmon license. Salmon fishing is normally restricted to rod and reel and artificial flies. Fishing for "bright" or fresh-run fish extends from May through mid September.

During various growth stages prior to first spawning fish are called smolt, grilse and salmon. After spawning fish are called kelts, slinks or black salmon. Pelagic, schooling, anadromous. Salmon spend most of their lives in the ocean within 300 feet of the surface but migrate to fresh water to spawn. Unlike Pacific salmon, which die after spawning once, Atlantic salmon return to the sea and may spawn as many as 4 times. During the spawning runs they feed very little, if at all, but will strike artificial flies. Runs vary from year to year and from stream to stream. Early runs occur from mid May–late June and late runs from mid July–mid September. Check state regulations on tackle, catch limits and season. FISHING METHODS: Anglers cast from shore or boats for salmon mostly in tidal waters of rivers and river mouths during the spawning migration. BAITS: Dry, wet and streamer flies.

ATLANTIC SPADEFISH, *Chaetodipterus faber.* Bay porgy, porgy, angel-fish. Occur in salt water on sand, shell, gravel or rock bottom and around wrecks, rockpiles, bridges, jetties and breakwaters. May–October. Never abundant, spadefish are caught during the summer only occasionally. FISHING METHODS: Bottom-fishing from boats or shore. BAITS: Clams, worms, mussels, shrimp, crabs and cut fish.

ATLANTIC TOMCOD, *Microgadus tomcod.* Tomcod, frostfish, tommy cod. Distinguished from cod by a rounded tail and the second pelvic ray being about 1½ times the length of the next longest ray. Cod have a slightly concave tail and second pelvic ray is 1¼ times the length of the next longest ray. Usually occur in estuaries, rivers and along the coast in depths less than 36 feet. Frequent sand, mud, gravel, stone or rock bottom. In the fall tomcod move into or toward rivers, where they spawn from November through February. Taken all year; best fishing late October–December. FISHING METHODS: Bottom-fishing or jigging from shore or boats. Also speared during the winter. BAITS: Worms, clams, mussels, cut fish and small jigs.

ATLANTIC WOLFFISH, *Anarhichas lupus.* Catfish, sea catfish, ocean catfish, wolffish. Solitary and sedentary. Occur in water of 31° to 52°F. Wolffish favor a high-relief bottom such as rock outcrops or large stones with intervening mud and sand. Occur from a few feet below the tide-line inshore to over 500 feet offshore. Can be taken throughout the year in depths over 180 feet and during summer in shallower water. FISHING METHODS: Bottom-fishing and jigging from anchored or slow-drifting boats. BAITS: Clams, whelks, crabs, cut fish and diamond jigs.

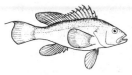

BASS, BLACK SEA, *Centropristis striata.* Sea bass, black bass, blackfish. Migratory and gregarious. Live on or near hard bottom of rocks or shells and around wrecks, pilings and rock jetties. Occur inshore during warm months but during cold months retreat to depths of 400 feet or more to remain in water warmer than 46°F. Scarce north or east of the elbow (Monomoy Point) of Cape Cod.

Season: June–October; best fishing July–September. During the angling season most caught in depths from 10 to 120 feet. FISHING METHODS: Livelining or bottom-fishing from boats. Small fish taken from wharves and jetties. BAITS: Clams, mussels, worms, sand lance, shrimp and pieces of crab, squid or cut fish; also small jigs or weighted bucktails. Large sea bass may strike lures trolled for other fish.

BASS, STRIPED, *Morone saxatilis.* Rock, rockfish, striper. Small fish called school bass; large fish, jumbos. See white perch. Schooling and anadromous. Though many small fish are resident, most large fish are migratory. Occur in rivers, estuaries and the ocean over any type of bottom. In the ocean they usually occur from the tide-line to depths of 45 feet, but during winter some go as deep as 100 feet or more. Striped bass overwinter in rivers, bays or the ocean but are active enough to be taken by anglers only in water warmer than 39°F. Most taken mid March–December, but some all year. Best fishing mid October–December; a smaller run occurs mid March–May. FISHING METHODS: Casting, livelining or chumming from shore; these methods plus trolling and jigging from boats. Check state regulations on size, quantity and season. BAITS: Worms, clams, soft or shedder crab, eels, shrimp, pork rind and live or dead fish; also weighted bucktails, plugs, jigs, spoons, feathers, bucktail flies and imitation eels or worms.

BLUE CRAB, *Callinectes sapidus.* Crab, blue claw crab. Crabs about to shed their shells are called shedders; those immediately after shedding are called soft crabs. Size is usually expressed as the width of the shell across the back measured from spine tip to spine tip. Occur in salt, brackish and a few in fresh water on mud, clay, sand, sand-shell and gravel bottom. Especially abundant in shallow bays and mouths of streams or rivers on muddy sand around eel grass. During warm months crabs frequent shallow water; during cold months they seek deep water and may embed in mud. Active in water warmer than 50°F. Large adult males tend to concentrate in the upper reaches of creeks and rivers, adult females in the bays. Mid May or June–early November; best fishing August–October. Check state laws governing size limits and the taking of egg-bearing females. FISHING METHODS: Hand lines or crab traps from shore or boats. BAITS: Fresh whole and cut fish or scrap meat.

BLUEFISH, *Pomatomus saltatrix.* Blues. Small fish called snappers; large fish called choppers, slammers or jumbos. Pelagic, schooling and migratory. Bluefish occur in water of 50° to 80°F and as deep as 300 feet or more. Fish less than 4 pound are common inshore and offshore of the 90 feet contour; larger fish usually remain offshore of this contour. Late April or May–late November; best fishing June–October or early November. Snapper fishing in estuaries is best August–October. FISHING METHODS: Livelining, chumming and casting from shore; these same methods plus jigging, fly fishing, and trolling from boats. Most caught in water of 64° to 75°F within 90 feet of the surface. BAITS: Spoons, jigs, plugs, feathers, skirts, tube lures and weighted bucktails; also butterfish, silversides, mullet, eels, sand lance and cut menhaden or other fish.

COBIA, *Rachycentron canadum.* Crab-eater, sergeant fish, ling. Sometimes mistakenly called bonito or black bonito. Migratory. Cobia occurring both inshore and offshore are usually solitary or in small aggregations and often found around buoys, wrecks, debris, rockpiles and pilings. Sometimes they are associated with schools of other fish species and sea turtles or large rays. May–mid October; best fishing in July and August. FISHING METHODS: Bottom-fishing, livelining, casting, chumming or trolling from boats. BAITS: Whole spot, eel or shedder crab and cut fish; also spoons, plugs and large weighted bucktails.

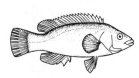

CUNNER, *Tautogolabrus adspersus.* Sea perch, perch, blue perch, choggie. See tautog. Gregarious. Frequent rocky or other hard bottom and shellfish beds; especially plentiful around wharves, pilings, wrecks and headlands. Cunner occur to depths of 250 feet, a few to 400 feet. Abundant south of Casco Bay; become less numerous but of larger size east of Casco Bay. Taken all year but during winter usually in water deeper than 120 feet; during summer most in 30–90 feet. Best fishing May–September. FISHING METHODS: Livelining, bottom-fishing or jigging from shore and boats. BAITS: Worms, clams, mussels, shrimp, snails, and cut fish; also small spoons, spinners and weighted bucktails.

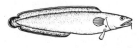

CUSK, *Brosme brosme.* Sedentary and solitary. A bottom dweller that prefers areas with high relief such as rock outcrops. Also occurs on gravel, pebble or mud bottom, but seldom on smooth, clean sand except in the Great South Channel east of Cape Cod. Occurs in water of 33° to 50°F and depths to 700 feet or more. Taken all year. Most are caught from May–October in water of 41° to 46°F and depths of 180 to 300 feet.

The spawning season extends from April through July with a peak in April and May. Cusk eat shrimp and fish and can reach lengths of 32 inches and weights of 20 pounds. Cusk are solitary, deep-water species found on rocky, hard bottom. FISHING METHODS: Bottom-fishing from anchored or slow-drifting boats. BAITS: Clams, whelk, squid, crabs and cut fish. Also taken on weighted bucktails and diamond jigs.

DOGFISH, SMOOTH, *Mustelus canis.* Shark, dogfish, gray dog, smooth dog, miscalled sand shark. Distinguished from other sharks by two spineless triangular dorsal fins of nearly the same size; rounded flat snout; fifth gill opening behind origin of pectoral fin, and small, flat teeth. Migratory. Occur from the tide-line to depths of 600 feet or more in water of 43° to 72°F. Often found on or a few feet above any type of bottom along the open ocean shore or in estuaries; occasionally in fresh water. More active during night than day. Early or mid May–early December. Most abundant during June in depths of less than 60 feet. FISHING METHODS: Bottom-fishing from shore or boats. BAITS: Squid, crabs, worms and cut fish.

DOGFISH, SPINY, *Squalus acanthias.* Dogfish, horndog, dog. Migratory and gregarious. Occur from the surface to depths of 800 feet or more in water of 39° to 62°F. However, usually on or near bottom of any type. Aggregations may be compact or scattered but are usually made up of similar size fish. These sharks are always moving and may erratically appear and disappear from an area. Date of arrival varies from year to year, ranging from April off southern Cape Cod to July at Eastport, Maine, but usually throughout the Gulf of Maine by late June. They depart in September or October. Most are caught by anglers in depths of 10 to 300 feet. FISHING METHODS: Bottom-fishing, livelining, chumming and jigging from shore and boats. BAITS: Any natural bait; some taken on jigs.

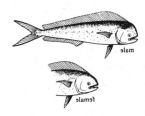

DOLPHIN, *Coryphaena hippurus.* Pelagic, schooling and migratory. A rapid swimmer occurring near the surface in water warmer than 70°F over depths of 60 feet or more. Often found under floating debris and seaweed. Mid June to September or early October; best fishing August–early September. FISHING METHODS: Trolling, casting or chumming from boats. Most are caught 10 miles or more offshore. BAITS: Feathers, spoons, plugs, weighted bucktails, stripbait, feather-stripbait or skirt-stripbait combination, and whole mullet, ballyhoo, squid, eel or cut fish.

DRUM, BLACK, *Pogonias cromis.* Drum; fish less than 8 pounds called puppy drum. The young are characterized by 4 to 6 broad, black bars on their sides. Migratory. In large aggregations during the spring migrations but usually solitary during fall. These bottom feeders occur on any type of bottom but prefer mussel, clam or oyster beds. Often around breakwaters, jetties, pilings, bridge abutments and piers. April–October or mid November; best fishing for large fish in May and June, for small fish in September and October. FISHING METHODS: Bottom-fishing, livelining or chumming from shore or boats. Casting or trolling is also effective for small fish but large fish do not ordinarily take a fast-moving bait. BAITS: Clam, soft or shedder crab, shrimp and cut fish; also spoons, jigs and weighted bucktails.

DRUM, RED, *Sciaenops ocellata*. Channel bass; small ones sometimes called puppy drum. Migratory and schooling. During spring migrations, schools occur in the open bay away from shore; during summer and fall they usually occur close to shore. Late April or May–November; best fishing for large fish mid May–mid June, for small fish August–October. FISHING METHODS: Most are caught by bottom-fishing, casting and trolling from boats; some by bottom-fishing and casting from shore. BAITS: Soft or shedder crab, shrimp, clams, squid and cut mullet, spot or menhaden; also spoons, jigs and weighted bucktails.

EEL, *Anguilla rostrata*. Catadromous. Young (elvers) enter estuaries in the spring. Some remain in the estuaries while others migrate varying distances, sometimes hundreds of miles, up rivers and streams. After living in fresh or brackish water, sometimes for as long as 20 years, they return to the deep ocean to spawn and die. Occur on any type of bottom in ponds, rivers, estuaries and near the ocean shore. Active during warm months and embedded in mud during cold months. FISHING METHODS: By hook and line April—November while bottom-fishing from shore or boats. Speared from boats or through the ice December—March. BAITS: Shrimp, worms, clams, cut fish and whole killifish, silversides or other bait fish. Also taken on small jigs and weighted bucktails.

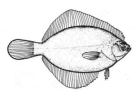

FLOUNDER, SMOOTH, *Liopsetta putnami*. Flounder. Distinguished from winter flounder by a smooth scaleless space between the eyes and 35 to 41 anal fin rays. Winter flounder have scales between the eyes and 44 to 58 anal fin rays. Coastal bottom dweller. Occur chiefly in estuaries and sheltered bays from the tide-line to 90 feet or more in water of 30° to 60°F. Smooth flounder frequent soft mud or clay bottom and muddy sand around eel grass. Most are caught in depths of 10 to 30 feet. FISHING METHODS: Bottom-fishing from shore and from anchored or drifting boats. BAITS: Worms, squid, clams, mussels, shrimp and cut fish.

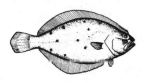

FLUKE, *Paralichthys dentatus*. Fluke, summer flounder; large fish called doormats. See windowpane. Migratory. Live on mud, sand, sand-shell, gravel or rock bottom and around wrecks. During warm months most occur from the tide-line to depths of 100 feet; during cold months they retreat to deeper water, some to 500 feet or more. Small fish occur in brackish water, a few in fresh water; large fish in salt water deeper than 50 feet. Usually feed near bottom but will pursue prey to the surface. May—October or early November; best fishing July—September in water warmer than 61°F. FISHING METHODS: Bottom-fishing and casting from shore; these methods plus chumming, livelining or trolling near bottom from boats. BAITS: Squid, smelt, silversides, clams, worms, cut fish, and live killifish; also spinners, jigs and weighted bucktails.

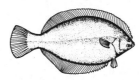

WINTER FLOUNDER, *Pseudopleuronectes americanus*. Flounder, blackback. Often mislabeled halibut or halibut flounder. Many fishermen mistake winter flounder for young summer flounder. A year-round resident. A few occur in fresh water, but most in salt and brackish water from the tide-line to depths of 180 feet in temperatures of 34° to 77°F. Small fish usually live inshore. Large fish live offshore but some enter bays from December through February and leave by April or early May. Occur on mud, sand, shell or gravel bottom; especially mud-sand around eel grass. Most are caught from September—May or early June, but a few all year; best fishing March—May and October—December. FISHING METHODS: Bottom-fishing and chumming from shore and boats. BAITS: Worms, shrimp, clams, mussels, squid, and cut fish.

HADDOCK, *Melanogrammus aeglefinus*. Haddock are normally taken on the offshore banks and ridges and in most of the areas fished by head- and charter boats along the Maine coast. Haddock normally frequent hard bottom but not the areas of ledge and rock. Likewise, haddock do not normally frequent kelp and other areas of heavy marine growth. The haddock is a voracious feeder except at spawning time; the stomachs of haddock have been found to contain most of the known forms of marine life. The same baits used for cod are acceptable to haddock.

In the Gulf of Maine, haddock are known to spawn around the Isles of Shoals, Boon Island, Sheepscot Bay, Wood Island, Cape Elizabeth, Linekin Bay, Mount Desert Island, Cutler, and Petit Manan Island. Peak spawning period along the Maine coast is April, May, and June. Haddock feed on brittle stars, worms, and shrimps. Haddock commonly reach lengths of 30 to 32 inches and weights up to 11 pounds have been reported. Haddock are found at depths of 150 to 450 feet and temperatures of 36°F to 50°F. The Massachusetts record for haddock is 20 pounds, shared by anglers in 1972 and 1974. FISHING METHODS: Bottom-fishing from anchored or slow-drifting boats. BAITS: Sand lance, squid, clams, mussels, worms and cut fish. Occasionally taken on small jigs.

HAKE, SILVER, *Merluccius bilinearis*. Whiting, frostfish. Migratory and schooling. Occur from the surface at the tide-line to depths of 2,400 feet or more in water of 38° to 64°F. Usually remain close to bottom during daylight and move toward the surface or into shallow water at night. Sometimes they drive bait fish ashore and strand themselves in pursuit. Taken in depths over 120 feet all year; in shallower water October March. Best fishing late October—December. FISHING METHODS: Livelining, bottom-fishing or casting from shore; these plus trolling, chumming or jigging from boats. Also speared at night with the aid of a light. BAITS: Clams, worms or cut fish; also jigs, spoons, spinners or plugs.

HAKE, SQUIRREL, *Urophycis chuss*. Ling, frostfish. This bottom fish occurs from the tideline to depths of 1,000 feet on clay, mud or sand bottom; however, during daylight, at least from spring through fall, some congregate on rock or other hard bottom and around wrecks. At night they leave their cover to feed. During warm months small ones are found in all depths, but large ones are usually in 90 feet or more. Taken all year in depths of 120 feet or more. Caught inshore November to June; best fishing April to June and November to December in water of 40° to 50°F. FISHING METHODS: Bottom-fishing and jigging from anchored or drifting boats. BAITS: Sand lance, clams, worms, squid and cut fish; also small jigs.

HAKE, WHITE, *Urophycis tenuis*. Hake, blue hake, sow hake, grey hake, called silver hake in the Cape Cod area. See squirrel hake for distinguishing features. Gregarious and migratory. Fish 8-12 inches are plentiful inshore and offshore in water of 33° to 70°F, but larger fish usually remain in depths over 180 feet in water of 39° to 48°F. Occur to a depth of at least 3,000 feet. Hake frequent soft bottom on the lower slope of banks and ledges as well as the intervening mud floor. Taken all year. Most large fish are caught from mid August—late October or early November. FISHING METHODS: Bottom-fishing and jigging from anchored or slow-drifting boats. BAITS: Clams, mussels, worms, squid, sand lance and cut fish. Large white hake are taken on diamond jigs.

HALIBUT, ATLANTIC, *Hippoglossus hippoglossus*. Fish 50 pounds or less called chicken halibut. Formerly taken only incidentally in the charter and headboat fishery, this species is now being actively sought by some fishing-party skippers. Halibut taken by rod and reel and reaching sizes up to several hundred pounds are capable of providing a good battle and are fine eating. Occur on sand, gravel and clay bottom but prefer sand-gravel or mud-gravel between rock outcrops and ledges. In gullies on gritty clay or clay-sand during March and April. Halibut usually feed near bottom but may pursue prey to the surface. Some are caught attempting to steal a hooked cod, pollock or haddock. Occur in water of 34° to 59°F and depths to 3,000 feet or more. Can be taken in depths over 300 feet all year. Anglers catch most from late March—early November in water of 37° to 48°F and depths of 90 to 270 feet. FISHING METHODS: Bottom- and live-bait fishing or jigging from boats. BAITS: Live or cut fish, clams, crabs, squid, and diamond jigs.

KINGFISH, NORTHERN, *Menticirrhus saxatilis*. Kingfish, roundhead, whiting, king whiting. Mistakenly called mullet or sea mullet. See southern kingfish. An inshore fish occurring from the tide-line to depths of 45 feet in salt and brackish water warmer than 46°–50°F. Congregate on sand, shell or gravel bottom, especially near sand bars or along the edges of channels. Late April or May—

mid November; best fishing August—October. FISHING METHODS: Bottom-fishing from shore; this method plus chumming from anchored or drifting boats. BAITS: Worms, squid, clams, mussels, shrimp, silversides, soft or shedder crab and cut fish.

KINGFISH, SOUTHERN, *Menticirrhus americanus*. Kingfish, roundhead, whiting, king whiting. Mistakenly called mullet or sea mullet. Distinguished from northern kingfish by having 7, rarely 8, soft anal rays; the longest spine of the first dorsal fin in an adult fish extends to just beyond origin of second dorsal fin, and the obscure, oblique bars along the side do not form a V just behind the head. In contrast, northern kingfish usually have 8, sometimes 9, soft anal rays; the longest spine of the first dorsal fin in an adult extends far beyond origin of second dorsal fin, and the dark, oblique bars along the side form a V just behind the head. Northern and southern kingfish are so similar that they are considered the same species by most anglers. Habits, season, fishing methods and baits are the same as for northern kingfish.

MACKEREL, ATLANTIC, *Scomber scombrus*. Mackerel are one of the most sought-after fish in the Maine saltwater sport fishery. Readily available from the shore, bridges, wharves, and boats. When actively feeding, they do so close to the surface where their activities can be observed; also they can easily be caught when feeding, with lures, flies, baits, and jigs. Although it is predominantly a summer fishery in Maine, the mackerel rates very high on the popularity list because of its numbers and ready availability in restricted and protected waters. Mackerel arrive in Maine waters late in May but rod-and-reel fishing seldom gets underway until June. The peak of the season is in July, August, and September.

MACKEREL, CHUB, *Scomber colias*. Mackerel, thimble-eyed mackerel. Distinguished from Atlantic mackerel by having 9–10 dorsal spines, standard body length 3–3½ times head length, and by the silvery sides below mid line mottled with dusky blotches. In contrast the Atlantic mackerel has 11–14, rarely 10, dorsal spines; standard body length 3½–4½ times head length , and the sides below mid line are without dusky blotches. Although smaller and preferring warmer water, chub mackerel are quite similar in most respects to Atlantic mackerel. Most fishermen make no distinction between these two fish. Habits, season, fishing methods and baits are the same as for Atlantic mackerel.

MACKEREL, KING, *Scomberomorus cavalla*. See Spanish mackerel for distinguishing features. Pelagic, schooling and migratory. Occur over any type of bottom in the open ocean; some in inlets and bays when salinities are near that of the open ocean. King mackerel occur throughout the water column in temperatures warmer than 68°F and depths of 50 feet or more, but occasionally venture close enough to shore to be caught from ocean piers. Mid June or July—October; best fishing in August and September. FISHING METHODS: Most are caught by trolling 5 to 15 miles offshore; some while casting or livelining from shore or boats. BAITS: Feathers, stripbait, feather-stripbait or skirt-stripbait combination, spoons, plugs, and whole rigged mullet or ballyhoo.

MACKEREL, SPANISH, *Scomberomorus maculatus*. Distinguished from king mackerel by having scaleless pectoral fins, a lateral line sloping gradually downward under second dorsal fin, and the first dorsal fin having 17 or 18 spines. In contrast, king mackerel have almost completely scaled pectoral fins, a lateral line dipping abruptly downward under the second dorsal fin, and the first dorsal fin has 15 or 16 spines. Pelagic, schooling and migratory. Usually occur near the surface in water warmer than 67°F from the shore to depths of 60 feet. They sometimes pursue bait fish through inlets into estuaries. Mid June or July—October; best fishing in August and early September. FISHING METHODS: Most are caught by trolling or casting from boats within 3 miles of shore, some while casting or livelining from shore. BAITS: Spoons, feathers, stripbait, weighted bucktails, plugs and jigs; also shrimp, squid and whole and cut fish.

MARLIN, WHITE, *Tetrapturus albidus*. Marlin. Pelagic and migratory. Occur in oceanic and continental-shelf water but some come close to shore in water 40 feet deep. Travel in small groups or alone. Mid July—September; best fishing in August. Most marlin are caught near the surface in water warmer than 70°F from 10 to 50 miles offshore. Sight-casting live scup or menhaden on spinning rods is both popular and effective for white marlin. FISHING METHODS: Trolling from boats. Some taken while chumming for other kinds of fish. BAITS: Feathers, stripbait and whole squid, eel, mullet or ballyhoo.

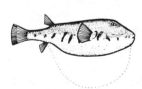

NORTHERN PUFFER, *Sphaeroides maculatus*. Puffer, blowfish or swellfish. An inshore fish found from the tide-line to 30 feet in salt and brackish water. Occur in aggregations on or a few feet above sandy bottom. As the name implies puffers have the ability to inflate themselves with water or air for self-defense. Late May—October; best fishing July—mid September. FISHING METHODS: Bottom-fishing from shore and anchored or drifting boats. BAITS: Worms, clams, mussels, shrimp, squid, cut fish and small crabs.

PERCH, SILVER, *Bairdiella chrysura*. Sand perch, sea perch, perch. Sometimes mistakenly called white perch. See spot. Distinguished from white perch by having 2 anal fin spines and a lateral line extending onto tail. White perch have 3 anal fin

spines and lateral line does not extend to tail. Occur in salt and brackish water on sand, mud or shell bottom; especially sandy mud with eel grass. Adults are migratory; young fish remain inshore the year round. Late May or June—September or early October; best fishing August—September. FISHING METHODS: Bottom-fishing from shore; this method plus livelining and chumming from boats. Usually taken as an incidental fish. BAITS: Worms, shrimp, clams, mussels, soft crab and cut fish; also small weighted bucktails.

PERCH, WHITE, *Morone americanus*. Perch. Distinguished from striped bass by having the spiny and soft dorsal fins connected and the second and third anal fin spines of equal length. In the striped bass the dorsal fins are separated and the second spine of the anal fin is shorter than the third. Schooling and anadromous. Occur in fresh, brackish and salt water from the surface to 35 feet. Most plentiful in estuaries and rivers. During winter found in channels or deep holes. Taken all year; best fishing March—May. FISHING METHODS: Livelining, jigging and casting from shore or boats. BAITS: Worms, clams, shrimp and small silversides or killifish; also small spoons, spinners, jigs and wet or streamer flies.

POLLOCK, *Pollachius virens*. This species ranges the entire coast of Maine; adults are noted for their fighting qualities. Pelagic and schooling. Pollock occur from the surface to 600 feet in water of 31° to 60°F. Juvenile pollock are called "harbor pollock" and are found close inshore, providing a large amount of the wharf, bridge, and float fishery. Adult pollock frequent the deeper offshore waters during winter and summer but in spring and fall are found near the shore in pursuit of bait schools. At this time, they provide outstanding sport and are readily taken on artificial lures as well as fresh baits. Like the adults, the harbor pollock are voracious feeders and are readily taken on flies, lures, and baits.

Pollock feed mainly on krill and small fish, and attain weights of 35 pounds and lengths of 43 inches. The pollock is an active fish which can be found at any level between the surface and the bottom depending upon the season and food supply. The International Game Fish Association record for pollock is 46 pound 10.9 ounces, caught in Maine in 1990. FISHING METHODS: Bottom-fishing and casting from shore or boats; jigging and trolling from boats. BAITS: Sand lance, worms, squid, clams or cut fish and diamond jigs, plastic tubes, spoons, plugs, spinners or flies.

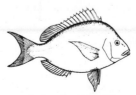

SCUP, *Stenotomus chrysops*. Porgy. Migratory and gregarious. Occur on sand, gravel or rock bottom and near shellfish beds, wrecks or pilings. Scup occur inshore in shallow water during warm months but during cold months retreat to depths of 500 feet or more to remain in water warmer than 45°F. Found near the bottom during daylight but move towards mid depths at night. Late May or June—October; best fishing June—September.

During the angling season most are caught in depths of 10 to 90 feet. FISHING METHODS: Livelining or bottom-fishing from shore and from drifting or anchored boats. BAITS: Clams, mussels, worms, shrimp, squid, cut fish and silversides or killifish; also small spoons, spinners or weighted bucktails. Large scup may strike lures trolled for other fish.

SEA TROUT, SPOTTED, *Cynoscion nebulosus*. Speckled trout, trout, salmon trout. Distinguished from gray sea trout by round dark spots on upper half of body, second dorsal fin and tail. Gray sea trout have dark blotches, often arranged in rows along the back, but without spots on dorsal fin and tail. Schooling and migratory. Occur in salt and brackish water but concentrate along ocean beaches, around inlets, and in shallow estuaries. Favor sandy areas, especially around eelgrass beds, but are found over any type of bottom in water warmer than 50°–54°F. Late May or June—December; best fishing September—early November. FISHING METHODS: Casting, jigging, chumming, and livelining from shore; these methods plus trolling from boats. BAITS: Plugs, weighed bucktails, jigs and spoons; also shrimp, silversides, mullet, live killifish, and soft and shedder crab.

SHAD, AMERICAN, *Alosa sapidissima*. Shad, white shad. Adult females are called roe or roe shad; adult males are called bucks or buck shad. Pelagic, schooling, migratory, anadromous. Although shad spend most of their lives in the ocean, adults ascend to fresh water in the spring to spawn when river temperatures reach 55°F. During the spawning run they take little or no food but will strike some artificial lures. Spawning over, spent fish return to the ocean. March—June or July; best fishing late April—early June. FISHING METHODS: Casting from shore; this method plus trolling and jigging from boats. Angling is usually confined to the freshwater portion of tidal rivers. BAITS: Spoons, spinners, jigs, weighted bucktails and shad darts.

SHAD, HICKORY, *Alosa mediocris*. Shad, hicks. Adult females are called roes; adult males are called bucks. Distinguished from American shad and other herring by the tip of the lower jaw extending noticeably beyond the upper when mouth is closed. Pelagic, schooling, migratory, anadromous. Occur in salt, brackish and fresh water. The spring spawning run of hickory shad into fresh water usually precedes the run of American shad by a few weeks. Late February—November; best fishing late March—early May. A small run usually occurs late August—early October. FISHING METHODS: Casting from shore; this method plus trolling and jigging from boats. Most are caught incidentally with American shad. BAITS: Spoons, spinners, plugs, weighted bucktails and shad darts.

SHARK, BLUE, *Prionace glauca*. Shark. Distinguished from other sharks by the long pointed snout, the long sickle-shaped pectoral fin and the first dorsal fin originating well behind the pectoral fin. To 500 pounds; avg. 125–225 pounds; over 300 pounds unusual. Migratory. A pelagic shark ranging far out at sea, although they occasionally venture close inshore. Frequently seen at the surface swimming lazily or basking in the sun. Early June–mid December; best fishing September–October. Most taken from the upper 60 feet in depths of 120–200 feet. FISHING METHODS: Trolling and chumming from boats. BAITS: Whole or cut fish. Occasionally taken on artificial lures.

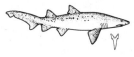

SHARK, SAND, *Carcharias taurus*. Shark, ground shark. Distinguished from other sharks by triangular dorsal fins of equal size, pointed snout, fifth gill opening in front of origin of pectoral fin and sharply pointed teeth. Migratory. A sluggish shark occurring mostly on or a few feet above the bottom; many venture to the tide-line and some enter river mouths. More active during night than day. Late May–November; best fishing late June–early October. Most taken in depths less than 30 feet. FISHING METHODS: Bottom-fishing, livelining and chumming from shore or boats. A few caught while casting from shore at night. BAITS: Squid, crabs, clams, worms and any cut fish.

SHARK, SANDBAR, *Carcharhinus milberti*. Shark, brown shark, ground shark. Distinguished from other sharks by the large first dorsal fin (vertical height exceeds 10% of shark's total length) originating over the middle of equally large pectoral fin, and by a distinct ridge along the back between dorsal fins. Migratory. A bottom dweller common both inshore and offshore. Seen at the surface only when crossing a shoal area or when chummed to the surface. Adult females enter bays in early summer to give birth to their young. Large males remain offshore. A newborn sandbar shark is about 2 feet long and weighs 2½ pounds. June–October; best fishing August–September. FISHING METHODS: Most adult sharks are caught by anglers in depths of 60 to 150 feet by bottom-fishing or chumming; small sharks in bays by bottom-fishing. BAITS: Cut or whole fish, clams, crabs, eels and squid.

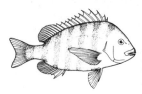

SHEEPSHEAD, *Archosargus probatocephalus*. Sheephead. Aggregate in salt and brackish water on sand, shell, gravel or rock bottom and around jetties, breakwaters, rockpiles and wrecks. Late May–October. Owing to their small numbers and the skill required to hook them, sheepshead are taken only occasionally. FISHING METHODS: Most are caught by bottom-fishing and chumming from boats or shore; some by jigging from boats. BAITS: Crabs, clams, mussels, shrimp and sand bugs; also small jigs and weighted bucktails.

SMELT, AMERICAN, *Osmerus mordax*. Smelt. Pelagic, schooling, anadromous. Feeding ceases during the spawning run in late winter and early spring. Inshore fish that spends nearly all of its life in or near the estuary of its natal stream or river. Spawning occurs in freshwater or slightly brackish streams usually a short distance above tidewater; sometimes in tidewater if obstructions bar upstream movement. Occur from the surface to 30 feet. Taken all year; best fishing March–April and October–December. FISHING METHODS: Taken with hand dip-nets from shore throughout the spawning run; while livelining or jigging from shore or boats the rest of the year. Check state and local laws governing seasons and net-fishing in your area. BAIT: Worms, shrimp, clams, silversides and killifish; also small spoons, spinners and wet or streamer flies.

SMELT, RAINBOW, *Osmerus mordax*. Pelagic, schooling, anadromous. Feeding ceases during the spawning run. Smelt spend nearly all their lives in or near the estuary of their natal stream or river. Occur from the surface to 30 feet. Because of the minimal restrictions of seasons and creel limits on the marine species in Maine, a twelve-month recreational fishery is developing. Smelts, which are resident to most of the major bays and estuaries, are taken in spring by dip net, in summer and fall by rod and hand or handline, and in winter through the ice by hook and line. Major baits are marine worms, small mummichogs, and suckers. A picturesque Maine winter scene is a shanty colony for taking smelts on the ice of a river or bay. Rental "shanties" are equipped with wood heat and electric lights.

SPOT, *Leiostomus xanthurus*. Norfolk spot, Ocean View spot, Cape May goody. Distinguished from silver perch by having a dark shoulder spot and a slightly forked tail. In contrast, silver perch have no such spot and their tails are nearly straight. Most occur in salt and brackish water; a few in fresh water. This bottom feeder usually congregates according to size, and frequents sand or mud bottom and shellfish beds. Adults are migratory; young fish may remain inshore all year, many in deep holes or channels during winter. June–October or mid November; best fishing September–October. Most are caught in bays and inlets; some along the ocean beach. FISHING METHODS: Bottom-fishing from shore; this method plus chumming from boats. BAITS: Worms, shrimp, soft crab, clams and cut fish.

SWORDFISH, *Xiphias gladius*. Broadbill, broadbill swordfish. Pelagic and migratory. Occur in oceanic and continental-shelf water from the surface to depths of 2,100 feet or more. Mid June–September or early October; best fishing late June–late July. Most are caught near the surface in depths of 90 to 250 feet and over offshore canyons when the surface temperature of the water is warmer than 58° to 60°F. The number of swordfish near shore has diminished. FISHING METHODS: Boat anglers usually sight fish at the surface before presenting the bait; some fish caught while blind-trolling or chumming. As many swordfish are caught by angling as are harpooned. BAITS: Whole squid, mackerel, silver hake, eel, butterfish and hake.

TAUTOG. *Tautoga onitis*. Blackfish, tog, slippery bass. See cunner. A gregarious year-round resident living in salt water but occasionally entering brackish water. Occur on rock, gravel or sand bottom and around shellfish beds, wrecks, jetties, breakwaters and pilings. Active during warm months from the tide-line to depths of 250 feet, especially in water of 46° to 65°F; inactive during cold months in depths less than 90 feet and temperatures less than 46°F. All year offshore; late March–mid December inshore. Best fishing April–June and September–November. FISHING METHODS: Bottom-fishing from shore or anchored boats. Most abundant fish in the catch of underwater spear fishermen. BAITS: Clams, worms, mussels, shrimp, crabs and sand bugs.

TUNA, BLUEFIN, *Thunnus thynnus*. Tuna. Fish to 200 pounds called school tuna; those over 200 pounds called tuna or giant tuna. A very highly regulated fishery; a federal permit is required to take bluefin. Pelagic, schooling, migratory. Range from far out at sea to close inshore, but almost always in depths of 100 feet. or more. Large fish occur in water warmer than 54°, most in 55° to 67°F; FISHING METHODS: Trolling from 10 to 60 miles offshore. BAITS: Feathers, spoons and plugs.

TUNA, LITTLE, *Euthynnus alletteratus*. False albacore, mistakenly called albacore. Pelagic, schooling and migratory. A rapid swimmer usually occurring in water warmer than 65°F. Travel in various-sized aggregations from three or four individuals to schools of many thousands. Often found over uneven or broken bottom. July–October; best fishing August–early September. FISHING METHODS: Most taken near the surface from 5 to 30 miles offshore by boat anglers while trolling, chumming or casting. BAITS: Stripbait, feathers, feather-stripbait combination, spoons, fly-casting, jigs and plugs; also squid and whole or cut fish.

TUNA, SKIPJACK, *Katsuwonus pelamis*. Oceanic bonito, arctic bonito, skipjack, striped bonito, watermelon tuna, mush mouth. Pelagic, schooling and migratory. A rapid swimmer usually occurring near the surface in water deeper than 90 feet and warmer than 63°F. Early July–September or early October; best fishing late August–mid September. FISHING METHODS: Most are caught by trolling near the surface over depths of 90 to 600 feet in water of 67° to 78°F. Also taken by casting, jigging or chumming from boats. BAITS: Feathers, spoons, jigs, plugs, stripbait, feather-stripbait or skirt-stripbait combination, and whole or cut fish.

WEAKFISH, *Cynoscion regalis*. Silverhake, Squeteague; small fish called spikes or heads-and-tails, large fish called tide-runners. Pelagic, schooling and migratory. Most abundant in the brackish water of estuaries and in shallow water within three miles of shore, but they occur in the open ocean, some to depths of 300 feet or more during winter. Favor sandy areas, especially around eel grass beds. May to October or early November. Best fishing September to October; a few large fish in June. In the past when this species was abundant, best fishing was in June. Most are caught from the surface to 40 feet. FISHING METHODS: Livelining, casting, chumming and jigging from shore; these methods plus trolling from boats. BAITS: Shrimp, squid, silversides, mullet, soft or shedder crab, worms, clams, mussels, cut fish and live killifish. Also spinners, spoons, plugs, jigs and weighted bucktails.

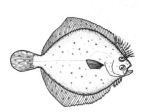

WINDOWPANE, *Scophthalmus aquosus*. Flounder, sand flounder, sand dab, sundial, see-through flounder. Distinguished from the summer flounder by the first 10–12 dorsal fin rays forming a fringed crest. Summer flounder have no fringed crest. A year-round resident in salt or brackish water. Windowpanes frequent sand, sand-mud, sand-shell, gravel and soft mud or clay bottom. Most occur in depths of less than 100 feet but a few are found to 200 feet. Taken all year; best fishing May–November. FISHING METHODS: Bottom-fishing from shore and anchored or drifting boats. BAITS: Shrimp, worms, squid, clams, mussels, silversides and killifish; also weighted bucktails and jigs.

ALL TACKLE WORLD RECORDS

Albacore, 88 lbs. 2 oz., Canary Islands; Spain, Nov. 19, 1977

Amberjack, greater, 155 lbs. 2 oz., Bermuda, June 24, 1981

Barracuda, great, 85 lbs., Christmas Island, April 11, 1992

Bass, black sea, 9 lbs. 8 oz., Virginia, USA, Dec. 22, 1990

Bass, giant sea, 563 lbs. 8 oz., California, USA, Aug. 20, 1968

Bass, striped, 78 lbs. 8 oz., New Jersey, USA, Sept. 21, 1982

Bluefish, 31 lbs. 12 oz., North Carolina, USA, Jan. 30, 1972

Bonefish, 19 lbs., Zululand, South Africa, May 26, 1962

Bonito, Atlantic, 18 lbs. 4 oz., Faial Island, Azores, July 8, 1963

Catfish, gafftopsail, 8 lbs. 12 oz., Florida, USA, March 30, 1991

Cobia, 135 lbs. 9 oz., Shark Bay, Australia, July 9, 1985

Cod, Atlantic, 98 lbs. 12 oz., New Hampshire, USA, June 8, 1969

Croaker, Atlantic, 3 lbs. 12 oz., Florida, USA, Sept. 29, 1992

Cusk, 32 lbs. 13 oz., Sommersel, Norway, July 10, 1988

Cutlassfish, Atlantic, 1 lb. 10 oz., Florida, USA, Aug. 26, 1992

Dogfish, smooth, 17 lbs. 13 oz. New Jersey, USA, July 9, 1988

Drum, black, 113 lbs. 1 oz., Delaware, USA, Sept. 15, 1975

Drum, red, 94 lbs. 2 oz., North Carolina, USA, Nov. 7, 1984

Eel, American, 8 lbs. 8 oz., Massachusetts, USA, May 17, 1992

Flounder, gulf, 4 lbs. 13 oz., Florida, USA, Feb. 4, 1993

Flounder, southern, 20 lbs. 9 oz., Florida, USA, Dec. 23, 1993

Flounder, summer, 22 lbs. 7 oz., New York, USA, Sept. 15, 1975

Flounder, winter, 7 lbs. New York, USA, May 8, 1986

Gar, Florida, 21 lbs. 3 oz., Florida, USA, June 3, 1981

Grouper, black, 113 lbs. 6 oz., Florida, USA, Jan. 27, 1990

Grouper, gag, 71 lbs. 3 oz., Florida, USA, July 12, 1991

Grouper, giant, 263 lbs. 7 oz., Groote Eylandt, Australia, Sept. 9, 1988

Grouper, Nassau, 27 lbs. 8 oz., Bimini, Bahamas, May 30, 1993

Grouper, red, 39 lbs. 8 oz. Florida, USA, June 11, 1991

Grouper, tiger, 14 lbs. 8 oz., Bimini, Bahamas, May 30, 1993

Grouper, warsaw, 436 lbs. 12 oz., Florida, USA, Dec. 22, 1985

Grouper, yellowfin, 34 lbs. 6 oz., Florida, USA, Dec 7, 1988

Grouper, yellowmouth, 8 lbs. 2 oz., Florida, USA, May 4, 1991

Grunt, white, 6 lbs. 8 oz., Georgia, USA, May 6, 1989

Haddock, 11 lbs. 11 oz., Maine. USA, Sept. 12, 1991

Hake, red, 6 lbs. 12 oz., New Jersey, USA, June 5, 1993

Hake, silver, 2 lbs. 4 oz., New York, USA, March 13, 1991

Hake, white, 46 lbs. 4 oz., Maine, USA, Oct. 26, 1986

Halibut, Atlantic, 255 lbs. 4 oz., Massachusetts, USA, July 28, 1989

Hind, red, 6 lbs 1 oz., Florida, USA, Jan. 23, 1993

Hind, speckled, 42 lbs. 6 oz., Florida, USA, Oct. 18, 1987

Hogfish, 19 lbs. 8 oz., Florida, USA, April 28, 1962

Jack, Atlantic, 78 lbs. Argus Bank, Bermuda, July 11, 1990

Jack, crevalle 57 lbs. 5 oz., Barra do Kwanza, Angola, Oct. 10, 1992

Jack, horse-eye, 24 lbs. 8 oz., Florida, USA, Dec. 20, 1982

Jack, yellow, 19 lbs. 7 oz., Florida, USA, Sept. 14, 1985

Jewfish, 680 lbs. Florida, USA, May 20, 1961

Ladyfish, 5 lbs. Florida, USA, Sept. 19, 1993

Mackerel, Atlantic, 2 lbs. 10 oz., Kraakvaag Fjord, Norway, June 29, 1992

Mackerel, Spanish, 13 lbs. North Carolina, USA, Nov. 4, 1987

Mackerel, cero, 17 lbs. 2 oz., Florida, USA, April 5, 1986

Mackerel, king, 90 lbs. Florida, USA, Feb. 16, 1976

Marlin, black, 1,560 lbs. Cabo Blanco, Peru, Aug. 4, 1953

Marlin, blue (Atlantic), 1,402 lbs. 2 oz., Victoria, Brazil, Feb. 29, 1992

Marlin, striped, 494 lbs. Tutukaka, New Zealand, Jan. 16, 1986

Marlin, white, 181 lbs. 14 oz., Victoria, Brazil, Dec. 8, 1979

Mojarra, striped, 2l bs. 4 oz., Florida, USA, Aug. 21,1987

Needlefish, Atlantic, 3 lbs. 4 oz., New Jersey, USA, July 18, 1990

Needlefish, flat, 4 lbs. 4 oz., Florida, USA, July 30, 1986

Permit, 51 lbs. 8 oz., Florida, USA, April 28, 1978

Pollock, 46 lbs. 10 oz., Maine, USA, Oct. 24, 1990

Pompano, 8 lbs. 1 oz., Florida, USA, March 19, 1994

Porgy, black, 7 lbs., Niigata, Japan, March 30, 1992

Porgy, jolthead, 23 lbs. 4 oz., Fla. USA. March 14, 1990

Puffer, oceanic, 7 lbs. New Jersey, USA, Aug. 28, 1991

Runner, blue, 8 lbs. 4 oz., Bimini, Bahamas, Sept. 9, 1990

Sailfish, Atlantic, 135 lbs. 5 oz., Lagos, Nigeria, Nov. 10, 1991

Salmon, Atlantic, 79 lbs. 2 oz., Tana River, Norway, 1928

Salmon, coho, 33 lbs. 4 oz., N.Y. USA, Sept. 27, 1989

Scup, 4 lbs. 9 oz., Massachusetts, USA, June 3, 1992

Seatrout, sand, 1 lb. 1 oz., Florida, USA, Oct. 2, 1993

Seatrout, spotted, 16 lbs. Virginia, USA, May 28, 1977

Shad, American, 11 lbs. 4 oz., Massachusetts, USA, May 19, 1986

Shark, blacknose, 41 lbs. 9 oz., South Carolina, USA, July 30, 1992

Shark, blacktail, 74 lbs. 4 oz., Zululand, South Africa, May 25, 1987

Shark, blacktip, 270 lbs. 9 oz., Malindi Bay, Kenya, Sept. 21, 1984

Shark, blue, 437 lbs., Catherine Bay, Australia, Oct. 2, 1976

Shark, bonnethead, 22 lbs. 13 oz., Texas, USA, July 13, 1991

Shark, bull, 490 lbs., Alabama, USA, Aug. 30, 1986

Shark, dusky, 764 lbs., Florida, USA, May 28, 1982

Shark, great hammerhead, 991 lbs., Florida, USA, May 30, 1982

Shark, lemon, 405 lbs., North Carolina, USA, Nov. 23, 1988

Shark, leopard, 24 lbs. 6 oz., California, USA, Oct. 18, 1991

Shark, porbeagle, 507 lbs., Pentland Firth, Scotland, March 9, 1993

Shark, sand tiger, 350 lbs. 2 oz., South Carolina, USA, April 29, 1993

Shark, sandbar, 260 lbs., Gambia Coast, Gambia, Jan. 2, 1989

Shark, scalloped hammerhead, 234 lbs., North Carolina, USA, March 24, 1990

Shark, shortfin mako, 1,115 lbs., Black River, Mauritius, Nov. 16, 1988

Shark, tiger, 1,780 lbs., South Carolina, USA, June 14, 1964

Shark, white, 2,664 lbs., Ceduna, Australia, April 21, 1959

Sheepshead, 21 lbs. 4 oz., Louisiana, USA, April 16, 1982

Snapper, black, 7 lbs., Little San Salvador, Bahamas, April 24, 1992

Snapper, blackfin, 6 lbs. 4 oz., San Salvador, Bahamas, May 1991

Snapper, dog, (Atlantic), 20 lbs., San Salvador, Bahamas, June 5, 1992

Snapper, gray (mangrove), 17 lbs., Florida, USA, June 14, 1992

Snapper, mutton, 28 lbs. 5 oz., Florida, USA, Sept. 4, 1993

Snapper, red, 46 lbs. 8 oz., Florida, USA, Oct. 1, 1985

Snapper, silk, 18 lbs. 5 oz., Florida, USA, July 12, 1986

Snapper, vermillion, 4 lbs. 8 oz., Florida, USA, March 7, 1993

Snapper, yellowtail, 8 lbs. 8 oz., Florida, USA, July 24, 1992

Snook, common, 53 lbs. 10 oz., Parismina Ranch, Costa Rica, Oct. 18, 1978

Snook, fat, 7 lbs. 4 oz., Florida, USA, Oct. 9, 1992

Spadefish, Atlantic, 14 lbs. Virginia, USA, May 23, 1986

Stargazer, northern, 69 lbs. 12 oz., New Jersey, USA, Aug. 10, 1988

Tarpon, 283 lbs., Lake Maracaibo, Venezuela, March 19, 1956

Tautog, 24 lbs., Virginia, USA, Aug. 25, 1987

Tilefish, blueline, 2 lbs. 6 oz., Florida, USA, May 24, 1992

Tilefish, sand, 2 lbs. 4 oz., Florida, USA, June 23, 1991

Toadfish, oyster, 3 lbs. 10 oz., North Carolina, USA, May 10, 1990

Triggerfish, gray, 13 lbs. 9 oz., South Carolina, USA, Jan. 2, 1992

Triggerfish, ocean, 11 lbs. 11 oz., Harbour Island, Bahamas, Jan. 2, 1992

Triggerfish, queen, 12 lbs., Fla. USA, Aug. 11, 1985

Tripletail, 42 lbs. 5 oz., Zululand, South Africa, June 7, 1989

Trunkfish, 5 lbs. 14 oz., Florida, USA, Nov. 24, 1985

Tuna, bigeye (Atlantic), 375 lbs. 8 oz., Maryland, USA, Aug. 26, 1977

Tuna, blackfin, 42 lbs. Bermuda, June 2, 1978

Tuna, bluefin, 1496 lbs., Nova Scotia, Canada, Oct. 26, 1979

Tuna, skipjack, 41 lbs. 14 oz., Pearl Beach, Mauritius, Nov. 12, 1985

Tuna, yellowfin, 388 lbs. 12 oz., Isla San Benedicto, Mexico, April 1, 1977

Tunny, little, 35 lbs. 2 oz., Cap de Garde, Algeria, Dec. 14, 1988

Wahoo, 155 lbs. 8 oz., San Salvador, Bahamas, April 3, 1990

Weakfish, 19 lbs. 2 oz., New York, USA, Oct. 11,1984

Wolffish, Atlantic, 52 lbs., Massachusetts, USA, June 11, 1986

AN ANGLER'S GUIDE TO SHARKS

After years of being considered something of a second-class gamefish, sharks have attracted the attention of anglers looking for good sport, tough fights, and the thrills that come with gaffing a thrashing catch you've just pulled alongside. Few gamefish can equal the spectacular leaps and swift runs of the mako, and many other shark species are recognized and appreciated for their own special challenges.

Only a few individuals of even the most vicious species of shark ever pursue and attack man, but there is little doubt that all sharks will defend themselves when molested. Not only their teeth, but their rough hides and powerful tails can inflict painful wounds. The fisherman or swimmer who carelessly handles, spears, or otherwise provokes a shark invites injury.

All sharks found off the eastern U.S. are edible. Small sharks and any shark not intended for the dinner table should be tagged and released. According to biologists, makos under 300 pounds are probably immature fish and have not yet spawned.

HOW TO IDENTIFY A SHARK

It is difficult to identify the various species of sharks that inhabit Atlantic coastal waters, and that's where this guide comes in.

The first step is to establish that the fish is in fact a shark. A shark has:

- 5 to 7 paired gill openings located at least partly on the side of the head
- a skeleton composed entirely of cartilage
- jaws, teeth, and paired fins
- a body shape that is typically torpedolike (with the exception of the flattened angel shark)
- a skin, because it's covered with minute toothlike scales similar to the texture of sandpaper.

These features help distinguish sharks

- from lampreys, which lack paired fins and true jaws
- from skates and rays, in which the body is flattened and the gill openings are entirely on the undersurface of the body
- from bony fishes, which have only one pair of gill openings
- from whales and porpoises, which lack gills and scales.

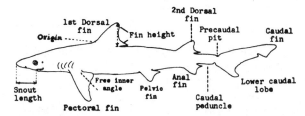

General identifying characteristics of a shark.

Once you're sure that the fish is a shark, the next step is to see how it differs from other sharks. Sharks are distinguished by shape, by size, and often by the presence or absence of the anatomical features shown in the following illustrations. The position and relative size of fins, gill openings, and eyes are important. Each illustration is accompanied by a description that emphasizes these characteristics; an outline drawing of each species is shown on a grid background. It's important to note that the grid divisions show *percentage of total length*, not actual measurements. For example, the drawing of the spiny dogfish shows that its tail is generally about 20 percent of its total length. But a spiny dogfish might be about 4 feet long, while the Greenland shark pictured just above it might be more than 20 feet long.

Species that might cause confusion are shown together to point out differences. To identify your specimen, find an illustration that it resembles, read the distinguishing characteristics, and make your identification. It's important to note that the drawings show only typical examples of each species; an individual shark will not look exactly like the drawing since body proportions vary with size.

A more dependable method is to use the Identification Key that follows on page 206. This key offers a series of alternative descriptions that leads, by successive choices, to the correct identification.

See the following pages for shark descriptions.

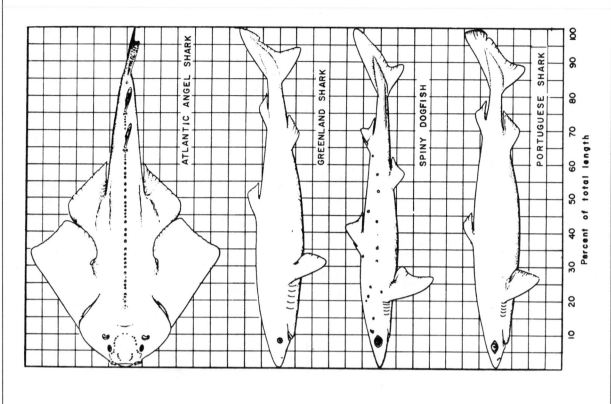

ATLANTIC ANGEL SHARK

GREENLAND SHARK

SPINY DOGFISH

PORTUGUESE SHARK

Percent of total length

Atlantic Angel Shark—*Squatina dumerili*

Distinctive characters: The flattened, skate-like appearance separates this from all other sharks in our area. Distinguished from skates and rays by its sharp teeth and the fact that its gill slits are partly on the side of the body.

Color: Gray above, tinted with red on head and fin margins; white below.

Maximum size: 4 to 5 feet. **Size at birth:** Unknown.

Range: New England to Jamaica.

Remarks: Found in depths of a few feet to several hundred fathoms. Feeds on flatfish, skates, crustaceans, and snails. Most common in summer along middle Atlantic coast (North Carolina to Delaware) but seldom abundant anywhere within its range.

Greenland Shark—*Somniosus microcephalus*

Distinctive characters: Lacks anal fin. The absence of dorsal spines sets this species apart from the next two.

Color: Brown to gray below and above; the back and sides sometimes with indistinct dark bands or whitish spots.

Maximum size: 21 feet. **Size at birth:** Unknown.

Range: Both sides of the Atlantic in arctic and subarctic waters; found south to Cape Cod.

Remarks: A cold-water species abundant along the Greenland and Labrador coasts, occurring in New England waters only as a stray. Seldom taken in waters warmer than 50°F. It feeds on a wide variety of fishes, seals, and carrion.

Spiny Dogfish—*Squalus acanthias*

Distinctive characters: Lacks anal fin. Distinguished from the Greenland shark by the presence of dorsal spines, and from the Portuguese shark by the position of the pelvic fins in relation to the second dorsal.

Color: Slate colored above, pale gray to white below; young specimens with white spots scattered on body.

Maximum size: 4 feet. **Size at birth:** 6½ to 13 inches.

Range: Worldwide in temperate and subarctic latitudes.

Remarks: One of our most common sharks found inshore and to depths up to 100 fathoms. It feeds on smaller fishes, squid, worms, shrimps, and jellyfish. The spines are mildly poisonous.

Portuguese Shark—*Centroscymnus coelolepis*

Distinctive characters: Lacks anal fin. Distinguished from the Greenland shark by the presence of dorsal spines, and from the spiny dogfish by the position of the pelvic fins in relation to the second dorsal.

Colors: Dark brown above and below.

Maximum size: 3 feet 8 inches. **Size at birth:** About 9 inches.

Range: Both sides of the North Atlantic; reported as far north as Grand Banks in the western Atlantic. Southern limit of distribution unknown.

Remarks: Evidently a deep-water species as it has not been reported from waters less than 180 fathoms. Little is known of its habits.

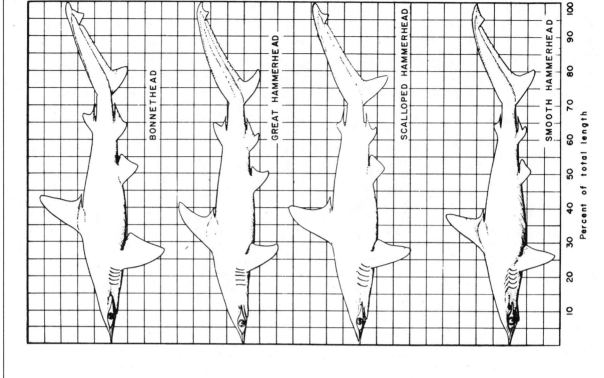

BONNETHEAD

GREAT HAMMERHEAD

SCALLOPED HAMMERHEAD

SMOOTH HAMMERHEAD

Percent of total length

Bonnethead (Shovelhead)—*Sphyrna tiburo*

Distinctive characters: Differs from other hammerheads in having a shovel- (not hammer-) shaped head.

Color: Gray or grayish brown above, paler below; no fin markings.

Maximum size: 6 feet.   **Size at birth:** About 12 inches.

Range: Abundant in tropical and subtropical Atlantic. Found regularly as far north as North Carolina, and as a stray to southern New England.

Remarks: Occurs chiefly in shallow water, often in bays and estuaries. It feeds largely on crabs, shrimps, and small fish.

Great Hammerhead—*Sphyrna mokarran*

Distinctive characters: Head indented at midline as in *Sphyrna lewini* (see below), but the corners of the mouth are about opposite the rear margin of the head; both upper and lower teeth are serrated (saw-edged).

Color: Small specimens brownish gray above and paler below. The dorsals, both caudal lobes, and upper surfaces of the pectorals are dusky toward the tips. Larger specimens are dark olive above and pale olive below.

Maximum size: 15 feet.   **Size at birth:** About 28 inches.

Range: Possibly worldwide in tropical and subtropical seas. Details of distribution in Atlantic unknown; reported as far north as North Carolina.

Remarks: Most specimens recorded offshore. Nothing is known of its diet.

Scalloped Hammerhead—*Sphyrna lewini*

Distinctive characters: Head indented at midline as in the great hammerhead, but the teeth are smooth-edged and the corners of the mouth are behind the rear margin of the head (see above). In the smooth hammerhead (see below) the midline of the head is rounded.

Color: Light gray above shading to white below, the pectorals tipped on their lower surfaces with black.

Maximum size: 13 feet.   **Size at birth:** About 17 inches.

Range: Tropical and warm-temperate Atlantic. Not uncommon in New Jersey waters during the warmer months.

Remarks: This shark is found both inshore and offshore, where it feeds largely on stingrays, skates, and other bottom fishes.

Smooth Hammerhead—*Sphyrna zygaena*

Distinctive characters: Head rounded at midline; teeth of young are smooth-edged, but may become slightly saw-edged in adults. The rear tip of the second dorsal is farther from the base of the tail when compared with the hammerhead (*lewini*) above.

Color: Deep olive or brownish gray above, paler on sides, grayish white below; fins of same color as back with tips dusky.

Maximum size: 14 feet.   **Size at birth:** About 20 inches.

Range: Tropical to warm-temperate belts of Atlantic; north commonly to southern New England and as stray to Massachusetts Bay.

Remarks: Occurs far out at sea as well as close inshore. Its diet consists of stingrays, smaller sharks, shrimp, crabs, and squid.

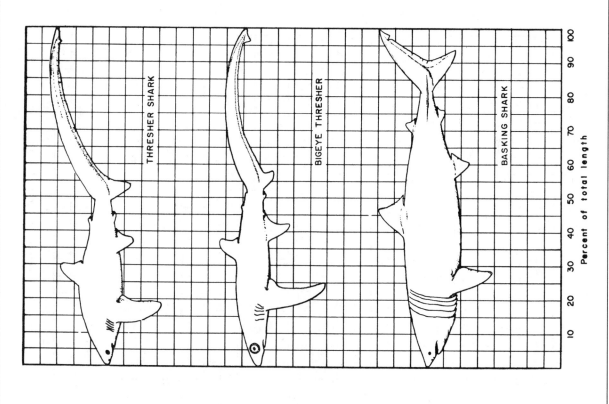

THRESHER SHARK

BIGEYE THRESHER

BASKING SHARK

Percent of total length

Thresher Shark—*Alopias vulpinus*

Distinctive characters: The enormously elongated tail sets the thresher apart from all other Atlantic sharks, except for its close relative, the bigeye thresher (see below).

Color: Back and upper sides vary from brown, through shades of gray to nearly black, becoming white below; lower surface of snout in front of nostrils and the lower surface of pectorals may be of same hue as upper sides.

Maximum size: 20 feet. **Size at birth:** 30 to 49 inches.

Range: In warm temperate and subtropical latitudes. Reported more frequently from southern New England than elsewhere along our east coast.

Remarks: Pelagic species, most often seen at least a few miles offshore. It feeds most commonly on mackerel, bluefish, shad, menhaden, herring, bonito, and squid. Uses tail to group schooling fishes in a tight circle during feeding.

Bigeye Thresher—*Alopias superciliosus*

Distinctive characters: Set apart from *A. vulpinus* (above) by its much larger eyes, longer snout, first dorsal being closer to the base of the tail, and in having only 10 or 11 teeth on a side in each of its jaws (about 20 in *vulpinus*).

Color: Dark gray or brown above, back and upper sides gray or brown; freshly caught specimens may show blue-green iridescence on upper surface of head and body. Rear margin of first dorsal, pectorals, and pelvics dusky.

Maximum size: 18 feet. **Size at birth:** 30 to 43 inches.

Range: Only a few specimens recorded; occurs in both tropical and temperate waters.

Remarks: Extremely large eyes suggest that it is chiefly a deep-water species, but specimens have been seen or caught near the surface. Squid and pelagic fishes are included in its diet. Little is known of the habits of this uncommon shark.

Basking Shark—*Cetorhinus maximus*

Distinctive characters: The combination of a crescent-shaped tail, enormously long gill openings, long gill rakers, and numerous minute teeth sets the basking shark apart from all others.

Color: Grayish brown to slaty gray or nearly black above; underside may be same color or lighter than the back, sometimes with a triangular white patch under the snout and two pale bands on the belly.

Maximum size: 45 feet. **Size at birth:** 5 to 6 feet.

Range: Has been reported in the Gulf of Maine and off northeastern shores. Only one report farther south than North Carolina. In the past, there have been numerous reports of basking sharks off Massachusetts and on occasion off New York and New Jersey.

Remarks: Basking sharks often gather in schools and swim sluggishly near the surface. In the winter it is assumed they retire to deeper water. Their diet consists of plankton which they sift out of the water by means of their gill rakers.

Porbeagle (Mackerel Shark)—*Lamna nasus*

Distinctive characters: Flattened caudal peduncle and crescent-shaped tail. Easily separable from the mako and the white shark by its teeth and by the presence of 2 keels on the caudal fin.

Color: Dark bluish gray above, changing abruptly on the lower sides to white; pectoral fins are dusky on outer half or third, the anal fin white or slightly dusky.

Maximum size: 10 feet. **Size at birth:** About 29 inches.

Range: Northern Atlantic, perhaps as far south as South Carolina.

Remarks: Found inshore as well as offshore, but more abundant in deeper water (40 to 70 fathoms). The porbeagle preys largely on schools of mackerel, herring, and pilchards, following their migrations; also on such groundfish as cod, hake, cusk, flounders, and squid.

Mako—*Isurus oxyrinchus*

Distinctive characters: Flattened caudal peduncle and crescent-shaped tail. The mako is separable from both the porbeagle and the white shark by its teeth and more slender form; also by the relative position of the second dorsal and anal fins.

Color: Deep blue-gray above when fresh caught, but appearing cobalt or ultramarine blue in the water; snow-white below; dirty gray on the lower surface of the pectoral fins.

Maximum size: 12 feet. **Size at birth:** Unknown.

Range: An oceanic species of the tropical and warm-temperate Atlantic; Gulf of Maine to Brazil.

Remarks: Strong-swimming, pelagic shark, known to leap from the water under natural conditions and when hooked. It is a fisheater, preying upon schools of mackerel, herring, and squid. It is considered to be the only natural enemy of the broadbill swordfish.

White Shark—*Carcharodon carcharias*

Distinctive characters: Flattened caudal peduncle and crescent-shaped tail. The large, triangular, saw-edged teeth and more rear-ward position of the anal fin (relative to the second dorsal fin) separate the white shark from the porbeagle and the mako.

Color: Slaty brown, dull slate blue, leaden gray, or even almost black above, shading to dirty white below; may have a black spot in the axil of the pectoral; the dorsals and caudal darker along rear edges.

Maximum size: 36½ feet. **Size at birth:** About 50 inches.

Range: Widespread in tropical, subtropical, and warm-temperate belts of all the oceans.

Remarks: Occurs both inshore and offshore. The white shark feeds often on large prey which it devours practically intact, as illustrated by the presence of other sharks (4 to 7 feet), as well as sea lions, seals, sturgeons, and tuna in the stomachs of some specimens. The white shark is credited with numerous attacks on man in tropical and temperate waters the world over and has thus been given the name "man-eater."

PORBEAGLE

MAKO

WHITE SHARK

Percent of total length

Note: 1st upper and lower tooth of each jaw illustrated above.

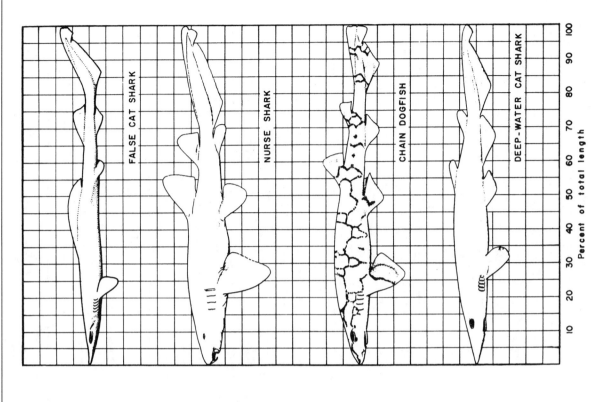

FALSE CAT SHARK

NURSE SHARK

CHAIN DOGFISH

DEEP-WATER CAT SHARK

Percent of total length

False Cat Shark—*Pseudotriakis microdon*

Distinctive characters: Separable from all other Atlantic sharks by the great length of its first dorsal fin.

Color: Uniformly dark brownish gray; darkest on the front margins of fins.

Maximum size: At least 9 feet 8 inches. **Size at birth:** Little known; one female contained embryos 2 feet 9 inches long.

Range: Both sides of the Atlantic, but rarely taken anywhere. Specimens reported from Spain, Portugal, Iceland, New York, and New Jersey.

Remarks: One of the larger deep-water sharks. Most captures have been made in depths of 164 to 807 fathoms, but two specimens (New York and New Jersey) were taken in shallow water. Little is known about its food, size at maturity, or habits.

Nurse Shark—*Ginglymostoma cirratum*

Distinctive characters: Set apart from all other sharks of the western Atlantic by the long barbel on the margin of each nostril and the deep groove connecting the nostril with the mouth.

Color: Yellowish to grayish brown, darker above than below. Small specimens may have dark spots on body or brown crossbars on the fins; adults may or may not retain these markings.

Maximum size: 14 feet. **Size at birth:** About 11 inches.

Range: Common in Caribbean and southern Florida with migrations to North Carolina. Occurs as stray to Rhode Island.

Remarks: Appears chiefly inshore, often in water as shallow as 2 to 10 feet. Sometimes travels in schools and feeds mainly on shrimps, squids, crabs, and small fish.

Chain Dogfish—*Scyliorhinus retifer*

Distinctive characters: Most obviously separated from other sharks by its chainlike color pattern.

Color: Dark reddish brown above, yellowish below, with a very characteristic pattern of sooty black stripes which branch out to form irregularly shaped polygons.

Maximum size: 2½ feet. **Size at birth:** 2 to 3 inches.

Range: Offshore (40 to 125 fathoms) from New York to North Carolina.

Remarks: Lives close to bottom on outer part of the Continental Shelf; seldom if ever strays into shoal water. This is the only common shark on the middle Atlantic Coast which lays eggs; they are described as amber colored, about 2 inches long, ¾ inch wide, with a long tendril at each corner. Little is known of its life history and diet.

Deep-Water Cat Shark—*Apristurus profundorum*

Distinctive characters: Size and position of dorsal fins, large anal fin, and presence of gill rakers protruding from rounded gill openings separate this unusual shark from all other sharks of this region.

Color: Grayish brown above and below.

Maximum size: Unknown; largest specimen measured about 20 inches.

Size at birth: Unknown.

Range: Definitely known only from Continental Shelf off Delaware Bay.

Remarks: Little is known of the habits of this rare species, but the uniform coloration above and below suggest a deep-sea habitat.

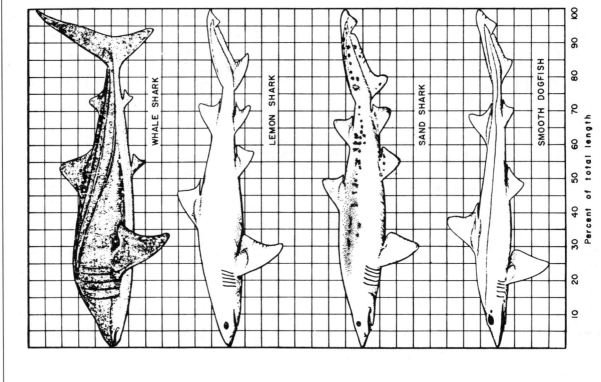

WHALE SHARK

LEMON SHARK

SAND SHARK

SMOOTH DOGFISH

Percent of total length

Whale Shark—*Rhincodon typus*

Distinctive characters: Unique because of its great size and spotted color pattern; its mouth is at tip of snout; prominent ridges on the sides of the body.
Color: Dark gray to reddish or greenish brown and sides; marked with round white or yellow spots and a number of white or yellow transverse bars; white or yellow below.
Maximum size: 45 feet. **Size at birth:** Unknown.
Range: All tropical oceans; reported as far north as Long Island.
Remarks: This offshore species is the largest living fish known to man. It does not bear its young alive, but deposits egg capsules. Its diet is composed mainly of plankton and small fishes.

Lemon Shark—*Negaprion brevirostris*

Distinctive characters: Both dorsal fins triangular and of nearly the same size; distinguished from the sand shark by its blunt snout and by the position and shape of its anal fin, and from the smooth dogfish by its sharp teeth.
Color: Yellowish brown to bluish gray above; white to yellowish below.
Maximum size: About 11 feet. **Size at birth:** About 25 inches.
Range: Occurs regularly from Brazil to North Carolina and as a stray to New Jersey.
Remarks: The diet of this inshore species is not well known; it probably feeds on skates, rays, and a variety of small fishes.

Sand Shark—*Carcharias taurus*

Distinctive characters: Both dorsal fins triangular and of nearly the same size as in the lemon shark (see above) and in the smooth dogfish (see below); easily distinguished from the lemon shark by its more pointed snout, and from the smooth dogfish by its sharp pointed teeth and more rearward position of the first dorsal fin.
Color: Gray-brown above becoming grayish white below; in some specimens darker spots cover the posterior section of the trunk.
Maximum size: 10 feet 5 inches. **Size at birth:** About 36 inches.
Range: Gulf of Maine to Florida.
Remarks: One of our most common large sharks during the summer months. The diet of this inshore species includes black drum, bluefish, butterfish, eels, flatfishes, menhaden, and others; reported to travel in schools and surround other fishes.

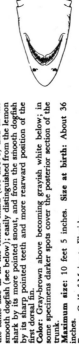

Smooth Dogfish—*Mustelus canis*

Distinctive characters: Both dorsal fins triangular and of nearly the same size. Separated from the lemon and sand sharks (see above) by the position of the first dorsal fin, and from all sharks in this region by its minute, flat, pavementlike teeth. Sometimes confused with the spiny dogfish (see p. 8) from which it is distinguished by the presence of an anal fin and the absence of dorsal spines.
Color: Gray to brown above and grayish white below.
Maximum size: 5 feet. **Size at birth:** About 13 inches.
Range: Cape Cod as far south as Uruguay.
Remarks: One of our most abundant sharks. Preys primarily on crabs, but also on lobsters and small fishes.

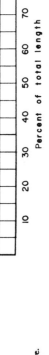

BLUE SHARK

SHARPNOSE SHARK

FINETOOTH SHARK

Percent of total length

Blue Shark—*Prionace glauca*

Distinctive characters: Distinguished from other western Atlantic sharks by the combination of a long pointed snout, a long sickle-shaped pectoral fin, and its blue color.

Color: Blue on upper surface, shading to pure white below.

Maximum size: 12 feet 7 inches. **Size at birth:** About 21 inches.

Range: Worldwide in tropical and temperate seas; common along the northeastern United States during warmer months.

Remarks: Reputedly the most numerous of the large oceanic sharks; it is the one with which sperm whalers were most familiar, and the one around which many superstitions about sharks have developed. Its diet includes herring, mackerel, other small fishes, squid, and garbage.

Atlantic Sharpnose Shark—*Scoliodon terraenovae*

Distinctive characters: Distinguished by its smooth-edged, curved teeth which are similar in both jaws; also by the presence of well-developed labial furrows around corners of the mouth. Differs from the closely related finetooth shark (see below) by its teeth and by the origin of the second dorsal fin which is located over the MIDDLE of the anal fin.

Color: Brownish to olive gray above; white below.

Maximum size: 3 feet. **Size at birth:** 10½ to 16 inches.

Range: Found on both sides of tropical and subtropical Atlantic. Occasionally strays northward to Canada, but it is uncommon north of the Carolinas.

Remarks: This is a shallow-water species that feeds on small fishes, shrimps, and mollusks.

Finetooth Shark—*Aprionodon isodon*

Distinctive characters: Distinguished by its smooth-edged straight teeth which are similar in both jaws; also by the presence of well-developed labial furrows around corners of the mouth. Differs from the sharpnose shark (see above) by the origin of the second dorsal fin which is located over the ORIGIN of the anal fin.

Color: Bluish gray above, shading to gray on sides; white below.

Maximum size: 4 feet or more. **Size at birth:** Unknown.

Range: Tropical species, the majority having been recorded from Florida and the coasts of the Gulf of Mexico. Occasionally strays northward along the east coast of the United States during summer months.

Remarks: Apparently an inshore species which feeds on a variety of small fishes.

Note: Fourth upper and lower tooth of each jaw illustrated above.

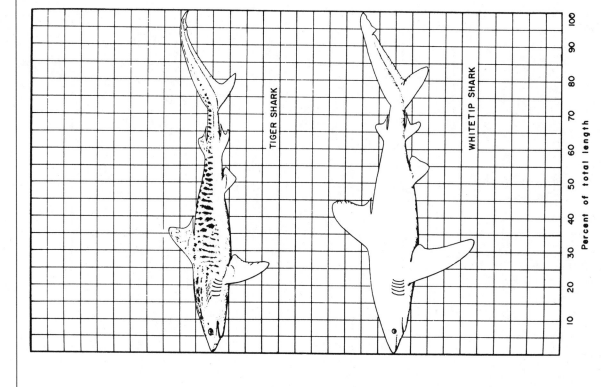

TIGER SHARK

WHITETIP SHARK

Percent of total length

Tiger Shark—*Galeocerdo cuvieri*

Distinctive characters: A low lateral ridge on each side of the caudal peduncle; the short blunt snout and the distinct notch in the rear margin of the teeth distinguish this shark from all others.

Color: Gray or grayish brown, darker above than on sides and belly; small specimens up to about 5 or 6 feet long are marked on back with darker spots, often fusing irregularly into oblique bars on sides and fins. Markings may fade with growth.

Maximum size: 30 feet. **Size at birth:** About 19 inches.

Range: Worldwide in tropical and subtropical seas; not uncommon along New Jersey coasts during warmer months.

Remarks: Occasionally taken far out at sea but more often in coastal waters. Stomach contents of tiger sharks have included squids, horseshoe crabs, stingrays, sharks, and many other fishes, turtles, birds, sea lions, and a remarkable assortment of such garbage as carrion, lumps of coal, tin cans, boards, and empty sacks.

Whitetip Shark—*Pterolamiops longimanus*

Distinctive characters: Set apart from similar species by the broadly rounded first dorsal fin, short snout, white-tipped fins, and rear tip of the anal fin reaching nearly to the lower precaudal pit.

Color: Varying from grayish brown to light gray or pale brown above, and yellowish or dirty white below. In adults the dorsal and pectoral fins are often, but not always, white-tipped. Black-tipped fins are reported on embryos and young specimens.

Maximum size: 12 to 13 feet. **Size at birth:** About 27 inches.

Range: Tropical and subtropical Atlantic, occasionally to Cape Cod.

Remarks: A pelagic species usually found near the surface in offshore waters where the depth exceeds 100 fathoms. Its diet includes squids, dolphin, mackerels, other small schooling fishes, and garbage.

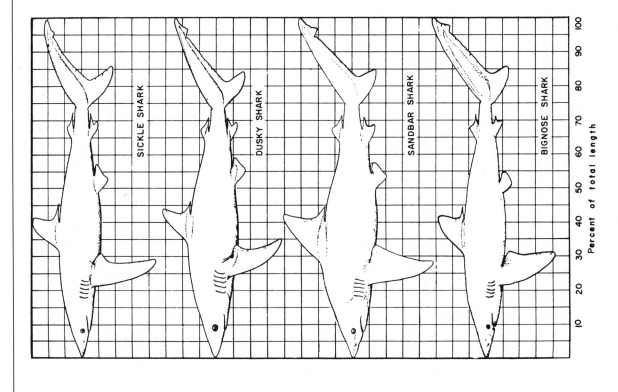

Sickle Shark—*Carcharhinus falciformis*

Distinctive characters: Distinct ridge along back between dorsal fins as in the sharks below, but separable from similar ridged-back species by the longer pelvic fins and the longer free tip of its second dorsal fin. Also, the sickle shark has a smaller eye than the dusky shark, and its first dorsal fin is not as high as in the sandbar shark and is placed farther back.
Color: Black to gray above, grayish white below.
Maximum size: 10 feet. **Size at birth:** Unknown.
Range: Common in the tropical belt of the western North Atlantic; strays northward to Cape Cod in the summer.
Remarks: An offshore species; its diet probably consists of various small fishes and squids.

Dusky Shark—*Carcharhinus obscurus*

Distinctive characters: Distinct ridge along back between dorsal fins. Distinguished from the sickle shark (above) by its shorter pectoral fins, larger eye, and shorter free tip of its second dorsal fin; separable from the sandbar shark (below) by the size and position of its first dorsal fin; and from the bignose shark by its shorter snout.
Color: Lead gray, bluish, or copper above, white below.
Maximum size: 11 feet, 8 inches. **Size at birth:** 38 to 48 inches.
Range: Common in inshore and offshore waters along east coast of United States from Cape Cod to Florida.
Remarks: One of the most common sharks in New Jersey waters. Feeds primarily on bottom fishes including searobins, skates, headfish, and flatfish.

Sandbar Shark (Brown Shark)—*Carcharhinus milberti*

Distinctive characters: Distinct ridge along back between dorsal fins; separated from similar species by its larger first dorsal (vertical height exceeds 10% of shark's total length—less than 10% in sickle, dusky, and bignose sharks), also the first dorsal is further forward in relation to the pectoral fins.
Color: Gray to brown above. Paler below. Fin margins slightly darker.
Maximum size: 7 feet 8 inches. **Size at birth:** About 25 inches.
Range: Common in inshore and offshore waters along east coast of the United States from Cape Cod to Florida.
Remarks: This is the most common large shark reported from New York–New Jersey coastal waters. Adult females enter bays in this area to give birth to their young. Large males are seldom taken and probably remain farther offshore. Its diet is similar to that of the dusky.

Bignose Shark—*Carcharhinus altima*

Distinctive characters: Distinct ridge along back between dorsal fins. This little-known species has a snout length about equal to the width of the mouth (in the sickle, dusky, and sandbar sharks, the length of the snout is less than the width of the mouth).
Color: Grayish brown above, sides a lighter tint; belly dirty white.
Maximum Size: 9 feet. **Size at birth:** About 25 inches.
Range: Reported only from subtropical waters of the western North Atlantic; might occur in local offshore waters as a stray.
Remarks: An offshore species which rarely occurs in depths of less than 50 fathoms. Little is known of its habits.

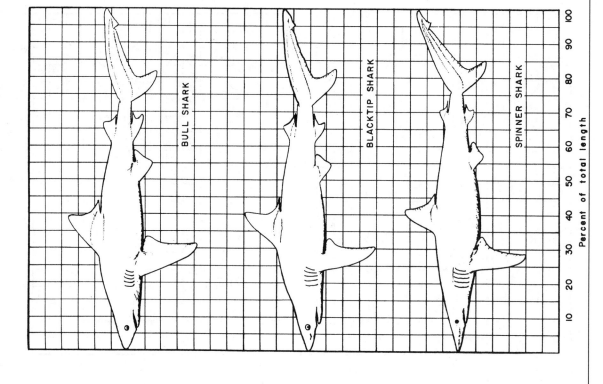

BULL SHARK

BLACKTIP SHARK

SPINNER SHARK

Percent of total length

Bull Shark (Cub Shark)—*Carcharhinus leucas*

Distinctive characters: Lack of ridge along back between dorsal fins separates this from similar species on the preceding page. Absence of black-tipped fins and a snout which is broadly rounded and shorter than the distance between the nostrils separate the bull shark from the blacktip and spinner (see below).

Color: Gray above and white below; lower tips of pectorals sometimes dusky.

Maximum size: 12 feet. **Size at birth:** 28 inches.

Range: Common in tropic waters, strays to Long Island.

Remarks: A sluggish heavy-bodied inshore species, known to enter estuaries and travel up rivers. Feeds on various fishes, other sharks, and garbage.

Blacktip Shark—*Carcharhinus limbatus*

Distinctive characters: Lack of ridge along back between dorsal fins; fins conspicuously tipped with black; differs from the bull shark (above) by its longer snout, and from the spinner (below) by its larger eyes (horizontal diameter ¾ the length of first gill opening) and more forward position of its first dorsal fin.

Color: Gray or ashy blue above, pure white or whitish below; sides with a light wedge-shaped band beginning near the pectoral fins and gradually widening rearward to the pelvic fins where it merges with the white on the belly.

Maximum size: 8 feet. **Size at birth:** 23 to 26 inches.

Range: Southern New England to Brazil, occurring as a stray north of Cape Hatteras, N.C.

Remarks: An active, swift-swimming shark often seen in schools at the surface. It has a habit of leaping from the water and spiraling through the air before falling back into the sea. Feeds on squid, butterfish, menhaden, and other fishes.

Spinner (Large Black-tipped) Shark—*Carcharhinus maculipinnis*

Distinctive characters: Lacks ridge on back between dorsal fins; fins conspicuously tipped with black; differs from the bull shark (above) by its longer snout, and from the blacktip by its smaller eyes (horizontal diameter ¾ the length of first gill opening) and more rearward position of the first dorsal relative to the pectorals.

Color: Similar to that of the blacktip shark.

Maximum size: 8 feet. **Size at birth:** Unknown.

Range: Tropical and subtropical western Atlantic; may stray north of Cape Hatteras.

Remarks: Has the same jumping and spinning habit as the blacktip shark. Little known of its life history and food habits. Probably feeds on squids and small fishes.

IDENTIFICATION KEY

The following key is a series of paired descriptive statements that give contrasting characteristics. Each pair offers two choices; choose the one that best describes the shark you are examining. That selection either names the shark or refers you to another pairing, or couplet. As successive choices are made, the characteristics become more specific. For example, in identifying the smooth hammerhead, your path would be 1B to 2B to 5A to 6B to 7A. Just remember to always begin at the beginning and follow every step until you reach your identification.

Adapted from Anglers' Guide to Sharks of the Northeastern United States *published by the U.S. Department of the Interior.*

1
A. Body flattened; pectoral fins broad and winglike = **Atlantic Angel Shark**
B. Body rounded, torpedo-shaped. *Go to couplet 2.*

2
A. Anal fin absent. *Go to couplet 3.*
B. Anal fin present. *Go to couplet 5.*

3
A. Spine in front of each dorsal fin. *Go to couplet 4.*
B. No spine in front of either dorsal fin = **Greenland Shark**

4
A. Origin of second dorsal fin behind the pelvic fins = **Spiny Dogfish**
B. Origin of second dorsal fin over the pelvic fins = **Portuguese Shark**

5
A. Head expanded sideways like shovel or hammer. *Go to couplet 6.*
B. Head not expanded sideways like shovel or hammer. *Go to couplet 9.*

6
A. Head shovel-shaped = **Bonnethead**
B. Head hammer-shaped. *Go to couplet 7.*

7
A. Front margin of head not notched at midline = **Smooth Hammerhead**
B. Front margin of head notched at midline. *Go to couplet 8.*

8
A. Free rear tip of second dorsal fin shorter than the vertical height of the fin = **Great Hammerhead**
B. Free rear tip of second dorsal fin longer than vertical height of the fin = **Scalloped Hammerhead**

9
A. Tail about as long as entire length of body. *Go to couplet 10.*
B. Tail much less than length of body. *Go to couplet 11.*

10
A. Rear tip of first dorsal fin terminates in front of pelvic fins = **Thresher Shark**
B. Rear tip of first dorsal fin extends at least as far as the pelvic fins = **Bigeye Thresher**

11
A. Keel or ridge on sides of caudal peduncle. *Go to couplet 12.*
B. No keel or ridge on sides of caudal peduncle. *Go to couplet 17.*

12
A. Keel a weakly developed ridge; caudal peduncle nearly round; lower lobe of tail less than half as long as upper lobe. *Go to couplet 13.*
B. Keel strongly developed; caudal peduncle flattened; lower lobe of tail ¾ as long as upper lobe. *Go to couplet 14.*

13
A. Origin of first dorsal fin about opposite rear margin of pectorals; body gray, often with irregular dark bands or spots = **Tiger Shark**
B. Origin of first dorsal fin well behind pectorals; body blue, no dark bands or spots = **Blue Shark**

14
A. Gill slits long—extend almost full height of head and nearly meet on under side of head = **Basking Shark**
B. Gill slits shorter—do not extend full height of head or very far on under side of head. *Go to couplet 15.*

15
A. Second keel below and to rear of main keel; teeth with two small auxiliary points at their base = **Porbeagle**
B. Second keel absent; teeth without auxiliary points at base. *Go to couplet 16.*

16
A. Edges of teeth smooth = **Mako**
B. Edges of teeth serrated (saw toothed) = **White Shark**

17
A. Base of first dorsal fin at least 4 times the height of fin = **False Cat Shark**
B. Base of first dorsal fin much less than 4 times the height of the fin. *Go to couplet 18.*

18
A. Origin of first dorsal fin over or behind origin of pelvic fins. *Go to couplet 19.*
B. Origin of first dorsal fin well in front of origin of pelvic fins. *Go to couplet 21.*

19
A. Origin of first dorsal fin over origin of pelvic fins; a long barbel on each nostril = **Nurse Shark**
B. Origin of first dorsal fin well behind origin of pelvic fins; barbels absent. *Go to couplet 20.*

20
A. Irregular chain-like markings on side of body = **Chain Dogfish**
B. No chain-like markings on sides of body = **Deep-Water Cat Shark**

21
A. Mouth at tip of snout = **Whale Shark**
B. Mouth not at tip of snout. *Go to couplet 22.*

22
A. First and second dorsal fins about equal in size. *Go to couplet 23.*
B. First dorsal fin much larger than second dorsal fin. *Go to couplet 25.*

23
A. All 5 gill openings in front of pectoral fins = **Sand Shark**
B. Last 1 or 2 gill openings over or behind origin of pectoral fins. *Go to couplet 24.*

24
A. Origin of anal fin opposite CENTER of second dorsal fin; teeth flat, blunt (pavement-like) = **Smooth Dogfish**
B. Origin of anal fin opposite ORIGIN of second dorsal fin; teeth pointed and sharp = **Lemon Shark**

25
A. Origin of second dorsal fin about opposite CENTER of anal fin = **Atlantic Sharpnose Shark**
B. Origin of second dorsal fin about opposite the ORIGIN of anal fin. *Go to couplet 26.*

26
A. Maximum length of pectoral fin as great as or greater than distance from tip of snout to last gill opening; fins often white at tips =**Whitetip Shark**
B. Maximum length of pectoral fin less than distance from tip of snout to last gill opening; fins without white tips. *Go to couplet 27.*

27
A. Edges on both upper and lower teeth smooth =**Finetooth Shark**
B. Edges of upper teeth finely to strongly serrated; lower teeth smooth or serrated. *Go to couplet 28.*

28
A. A low but distinct mid-dorsal ridge present in the skin between first and second dorsal fins. *Go to couplet 29.*
B. Mid-dorsal ridge absent. *Go to couplet 32.*

29
A. Length of free rear tip of second dorsal fin more than twice as long as vertical height of the fin =**Sickle Shark**
B. Length of free rear tip of second dorsal fin less than twice as long as vertical height of the fin. *Go to couplet 30.*

30
A. Origin of first dorsal fin behind free inner angle of pectoral fin =**Dusky Shark**
B. Origin of first dorsal fin over or forward of free inner angle of pectoral fin. *Go to couplet 31.*

31
A. Distance from front of mouth to tip of snout less than width of mouth =**Sandbar Shark**
B. Distance from front of mouth to tip of snout about equal to width of mouth =**Bignose Shark**

32
A. Distance between nostrils greater than distance from front of mouth to tip of snout =**Bull Shark**
B. Distance between nostrils less than distance from front of mouth to tip of snout. *Go to couplet 33.*

33
A. Vertical height of first dorsal fin much greater than distance between tip of snout and eye; first gill opening less than 2½ times as long as horizontal diameter of eye; edges of lower teeth finely serrated =**Blacktip Shark**
B. Vertical height of first dorsal fin about equal to distance between tip of snout and eye; first gill opening more than 4 times as long as horizontal diameter of eye; edges of lower teeth smooth =**Spinner Shark**

Part Two

Fishing and Boating Techniques and Gear

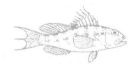

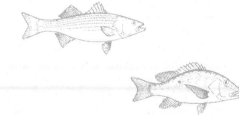

7

Tackle

A host of saltwater gamefish—from half-pound snapper bluefish to 40-pound yellowtails to bluefin tuna weighing nearly half a ton—draw millions of fishermen to the briny each year. They stand in crashing surf and on jetties and piers, and they sail for deeper waters aboard boats of almost every description.

Because of the great differences in weights of saltwater fish, it is important for the fisherman to be armed with balanced tackle that is suited for the particular quarry he is after. Just as the freshwater muskie angler wouldn't use bluegill tackle, the person who's trolling for, say, blue marlin wouldn't use a jetty outfit designed for striped bass.

Balanced tackle—in which rod, reel, line, and other items are all in reasonable proportion to one another—is important for a number of reasons.

For one, a properly balanced outfit—for example, a 9-foot surf rod with a good casting reel and 15- to 25-pound-test line—is a joy to use. Conversely, if you substituted a 5-foot boat rod for the 9-footer in the above outfit and tried to cast, you would soon be turning the air blue. Besides the casting advantage, properly balanced gear makes hooking and playing a fish easier and more effective.

There is still another reason for using balanced tackle. Every fisherman, beginner and expert alike, who tosses or trolls lure or bait in the salt has a chance to sink a hook into a record-size gamefish. The rules of the International Game Fish Association, keeper of the official records of marine gamefish, require that any fish submitted for a record be caught on tackle that is "in reasonable proportion . . . to the line size."

Let's take a detailed look at the various kinds of conventional saltwater gear and how to match up the component parts.

TROLLING REELS

Trolling is the method of fishing in which a lure or bait is pulled along behind a moving boat. It is also a method in which the reel is of paramount importance.

Saltwater trolling reels are sometimes designated by a simple and yet not completely reliable numbering system. This system employs a number followed by a diagonal (/) and then the letter "O" (pronounced "ought"), which merely stands for "ocean." The numbers run from 1 to 16, with each one representing the line capacity of the reel. The higher the number, the larger the reel's line capacity.

It should be noted, however, that these numbers are not standardized—that is, one manufacturer's 4/O trolling reel may have a smaller capacity than another maker's 4/O. A prospective reel buyer would do well to check manufacturers' catalogs to make sure of a reel's line capacity.

Trolling reels are the heavyweights among saltwater reels. Weighing from 18 ounces (for the 1/O size) up to nearly 11 pounds (for the 16/O), they are designed primarily for handling the largest of gamefish (sailfish, marlin, bluefin tuna, swordfish) but are also effective for bluefish, stripers, channel bass, albacore, dolphin, and the like.

These reels have no casting features (such as anti-backlash devices), since their sole function is trolling. Spools are smooth-running, usually operating on ball bearings. The reels are ruggedly built and, of course, corrosion resistant. Unique features include lugs on the upper part of the sideplate for attachment of a big-game fishing harness worn by the fisherman, a U-shaped clamp for more secure union of rod and reel, and, in the largest reels, a lug-and-brace arrangement for extra rigidity.

TROLLING REELS AND LINE CAPACITIES (In Yards)

LINES	REELS									
	1/0	2/0	3/0	4/0	6/0	9/0	10/0	12/0	14/0	16/0
20-lb. mono-filament	350	425								
30-lb. mono-filament	200	275	375							
36-lb. mono-filament				350	600					
45-lb. mono-filament				275	500					
54-lb. mono-filament				200	400					
72-lb. mono-filament					350	500	850			
90-lb. mono-filament						400	600	800	1100	1400
108-lb. mono-filament						300	500	600	1000	1200
20-lb. Dacron	225									
30-lb. Dacron	200	275	350	450						
50-lb. Dacron			200	250	400					
80-lb. Dacron				150	250	400	650	800	1050	1250
130-lb. Dacron						300	450	550	850	1000

The Penn International 80 is typical of a modern trolling reel. Built for 80-pound-test line, the reel has a side lever drag system. A reel of this size is preferred for giant tuna, billfish, sharks, and other big fish. (PENN REEL)

By far the most important feature on a trolling reel is the drag. If a reel is to handle the sizzling runs and line-testing leaps of fish weighing hundreds of pounds, its drag must operate smoothly at all times. And the drag must not overheat or it may bind, causing the line to break.

In most reels the drag is of the star type and consists of a series of alternating metal and composition (or leather) washers. Some quite expensive trolling reels have not one but two drag controls. One is a knob-operated device that lets you preset drag tension to a point below the breaking strength of the line being used. The other is a lever, mounted on the sideplate, that has a number of positions and permits a wide range of drag settings, from very light up to the safe maximum for the line in use. This lever, when backed off all the way, throws the reel into free-spool.

Trolling-reel spools can be graphite composites or made of metal, usually either machined bronze or anodized aluminum, and range in width from $1\frac{5}{8}$ inches (for the 1/O size) to 5 inches (for the 16/O).

Some trolling reels are designed especially for wire and lead-core lines. They have narrow but deep spools and extra-strong gearing.

Other features of trolling reels include a free-spool lever mounted on the sideplate, a single oversize handle grip, and gear ratios ranging from 1.6:1 to as high as 5:1.

TROLLING RODS

Big-game trolling rods have the strength and fittings to withstand the power runs and magnificent leaps of such heavyweights as marlin, sailfish, and giant tuna. The great majority of these rods are of fiberglass and graphite construction.

Almost all blue-water rods have a butt section and a tip section—that is, they seldom have ferrules fitted midway along the "working length" of the rod. In most rods the tip section is about 5 feet long, while butt lengths vary from 14 to 27 inches, depending on the weight of the tip. Standup fighting rods are smaller. Tip sections are usually designated by weight, ranging from about 3 ounces to as heavy as 40 ounces, depending on the line being used and the fish being sought.

Trolling rods are rated according to the line-strength classes of the International Game Fish Association. The eight I.G.F.A. classes are: 6-pound line, 12-pound (line testing, when wet, up to and including 12 pounds), 20-pound (line testing, when wet, more than 12 pounds and up to and including 20 pounds), 30-pound (line testing, when wet, more than 20 pounds and up to and

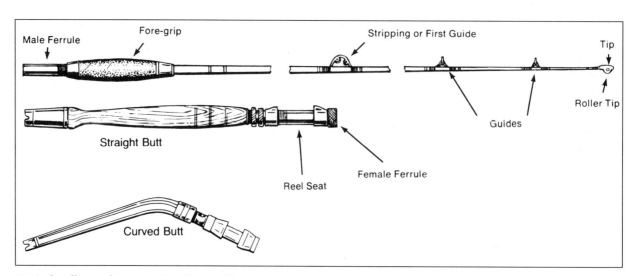

Typical trolling rod construction: designed for strength.

HOW TO MATCH UP OFFSHORE TROLLING TACKLE

This table is meant only as a general guide aimed at helping you put together, in proper balance, the basic elements of a bluewater trolling outfit tailored for fish of a particular weight category. Specific conditions—and your ability and personal preferences—should also be considered.

SPECIES OF FISH	REEL	ROD (Tip-Section Weight, in oz.)	LINE (Lb. Test)
Striped bass, dolphin, wahoo, yellowtail, kingfish, salmon, barracuda, tarpon, school tuna	1/0 to 3/0	3 to 9	12 to 30
Atlantic sailfish, Pacific sailfish, white marlin	3/0 to 6/0	6 to 18	30 to 50
Striped marlin	4/0 to 9/0	6 to 20	30 to 80
Black marlin, blue marlin, swordfish, sharks	6/0 to 14/0	9 to 30	30 to 130
Giant bluefin tuna	9/0 to 16/0	16 to 30	50 to 130

including 30 pounds); 50-pound, 80-pound, 130-pound, and 180-pound.

No rod used in catching a fish submitted for an I.G.F.A. record can have a tip length of less than 5 feet. In the 12-, 20-, and 30-pound classes, a rod's butt length can be no more than 18 inches. In the 50- and 80-pound classes, butt length can be no more than 22 inches. In the 130- and 180-pound classes, butt length can be no more than 27 inches.

The fittings on trolling rods include strong, high-quality guides. The first guide above the reel (called the stripping guide) and the tip guide are of the roller type (either single-roller or double-roller). The middle guides, usually numbering four or five, are of the ring type and are made either of heavily chromed stainless steel or of tungsten carbide (carboloy), which is the most durable material. In some rods all of the guides are rollers. Most roller guides have self-lubricating bearings that can be disassembled for cleaning.

Other features of trolling rods include extra-strong, locking reel seats, and gimbal fittings in the end of the butt that enable the rod to be fitted into a socket on a boat's fighting chair or into a belt harness worn by the fisherman.

CASTING AND BOAT REELS

Conventional (revolving-spool) reels in this category are widely used by saltwater fishermen who cast lures and baits from piers, bridges, jetties, and in the surf, and by sinker-bouncers (bottom fishermen) in boats. Actually an outgrowth and refinement of freshwater baitcasting reels, these reels fill the gap between those freshwater models and big-game trolling reels.

Many surf and jetty casters, especially those who are after big fish, prefer a conventional reel (and rod) over a spinning outfit because the conventional rig is better able to handle heavy lures and sinkers. And a vast majority of bottom fishermen lean toward the revolving-spool reel.

Conventional reels designed for casting have wide, light spools (a heavy spool makes casting difficult) of either metal or a synthetic, and gear ratios ranging from 2:1 to 4½:1. Weights range from about 12 to 22 ounces. In most models the drag is of the star type and there is a free-spool lever mounted on the sideplate. Some of these reels have level-wind mechanisms.

Line capacities range from about 250 yards of 12-pound-test monofilament to 350 yards of 36-pound-test mono. For most surf, jetty, and pier situations, 250 yards of line is sufficient.

A few of these reels have a mechanical brake, magnets, or a thumbing device to help prevent the spool from overrunning during a cast and causing a backlash. In most models, however, as in freshwater baitcasting reels, thumb pressure against the spool is required to control the cast.

Conventional reels designed for deep-sea bottom fishing are quite similar to the casting models but are somewhat heavier and have narrower, deeper spools. They also have larger line capacities and can take heavier lines.

CASTING AND BOAT RODS

In choosing a conventional casting rod, more so than with boat (bottom-fishing) rods, the type of fishing to be done and the fish being sought are critical factors. For casting in the surf, for example, the rod must be long enough so that the fisherman can make lengthy casts and hold the line above the breakers. A rod for jetty use, on the other hand, need not be so long. And if you'll be fishing mainly from piers and bridges, you'll need a rod with enough backbone to lift hefty fish from the water and up over the rail.

However, the beginning fisherman can get a casting rod that will handle most of the situations he'll be facing. A good choice would be one that is 8½ to 9 feet in overall length, of tubular fiberglass (rather than solid fiberglass), and has a rather stiff tip. The stiff tip of a conventional rod lets the angler use a wide range of lure weights and enables him to have more control over big fish.

Conventional casting rods are available in lengths from about 8 to 11½ feet and even longer. A few split-bamboo models are still kicking around the beaches, but most are now made of fiberglass, graphite, Kevlar, or a combination thereof. Recent developments in graphite show that rods of this material can carry an exceptionally wide range of lure weights. In tests, weights of 18 ounces were cast with graphite rods. A majority of these rods are of two-piece construction, breaking either at the upper part of the butt or about midway up the working length of the rod.

These rods are distinguished by the number and arrangement of their guides. In most models, there are only three or four guides, including the tip guide, and all are located in the upper half of the tip section. Why this arrangement? Because these rods are stiffer than most others, fewer guides are required to distribute the strain along the length of the rod. The guides are bunched near the tip because that's where most of the bend occurs when a fish is being played.

Conventional casting rods have sturdy salt-resistant reel seats, usually of anodized aluminum, and butts of hickory, other sturdy woods, cork, or synthetics.

Boat, or bottom-fishing, rods, as their name implies, are designed for noncasting use aboard boats—party boats, charter craft, and private boats. They are also used on piers and bridges, in situations in which lure or bait is simply dropped down to the water.

Boat rods are considerably shorter than casting rods, running from about 4½ to 6½ feet in overall length, with a good length being about 6 feet. Their shortness makes them highly maneuverable, a factor of more than a little importance aboard a crowded party boat, and makes it easier to handle, say, a 30-pound cod while trying to remain upright on a pitching deck.

As with most other modern rods, boat rods are mostly of fiberglass construction, with a growing number of graphite models available. For saltwater angling, most are one-piece. The number of guides on a boat rod depends on length, but there are seldom more than five. Some of these rods, designed for large fish, have a roller tip. Other boat-rod features are similar to those of casting rods.

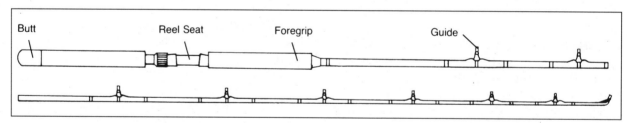

A typical surfcasting rod usually measures from 8 to 14 feet in length and is designed to cast lures and sinkers from 1 to 4 ounces.

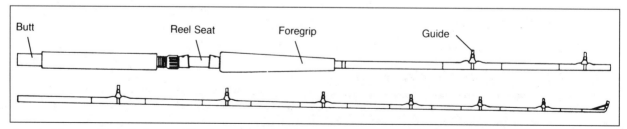

A typical boat rod usually has a stiff action. It measures from 5 to 7 feet and is generally designed for noncasting use, such as on party boats and charter craft.

HOW TO MATCH UP SALTWATER CASTING TACKLE

This table is meant only as a general guide aimed at helping you put together, in proper balance, the basic elements of a saltwater casting outfit tailored for fish of a particular weight category. Specific conditions—and your ability and personal preferences—should also be considered.

SPECIES OF FISH	REEL	ROD TYPE & LENGTH (In Feet)	LINES (Lb. Test)	LURE WEIGHTS (Ounces)
Small stripers, bluefish, weakfish, snook, bonefish, redfish, salmon, pompano, jacks	Light (with star drag)	Popping 6 to 7	8 to 15	½ to 1
Stripers, big bluefish, school tuna, albacore, bonito, salmon, dolphin, wahoo	Medium	Medium-action 6½ to 8	12 to 30	¾ to 3
Channel bass, black drum, tarpon, dolphin, big kingfish, sharks	Heavy	Heavy-action 7 to 8½	18 to 50	1½ to 5
Surf species (bluefish, stripers, drum, channel bass, etc.)	Squidding (Surf-casting)	Surf 8 to 11½	18 to 45	1½ to 6

HOW TO SET DRAG

Drag is what keeps a fish from breaking your line. That sounds simple, but fishermen sometimes lose big fish because they do not know or understand a few basic facts about the drag on their reel.

Many anglers, for example, tighten their drag when a big fish makes a long run and strips off a lot of line. This is wrong. The drag should actually be lightened, because a lot of line in the water as well as a smaller spool diameter will increase the drag. Unfortunately, the reaction of most fishermen is to tighten the drag and stop the fish. Often the result is a lost trophy.

Drag is the resistance of a reel against the fighting pull of a fish, and drag is set at a strain the line can endure without breaking. The drag mechanism usually consists of a series of metal (stainless steel, aluminum, or chromed brass) and composition (leather, cork, plastic, fiber) washers. The washers are stacked, alternating metal and composition, and the friction between the surface areas of the washers creates "drag."

When an angler tightens the drag on his reel, he compresses these washers, creates more friction, and increases drag. Conversely, when he backs off the drag, he lessens friction and lightens drag.

If the size of a fish was the only factor in setting drag, the job would be easy. But there are other consid-erations, such as the friction of the line against the rod guides, resistance of the line being pulled through the water, and the amount of line remaining on the reel spool after a long run.

In addition, not all drags are created equal. They should be smooth, but many are sticky and jerky. In fact, it often takes as much as double the force of the drag setting to get the drag moving. For example, a drag set at 5 pounds may actually take up to 10 pounds of pull before the drag starts moving. It's obvious, therefore, that if you're using 8-pound-test line you should set your drag at about 2 pounds to allow for "starting your drag."

The amount of line on your spool is another factor affecting drag. When the outside diameter of line on your spool is reduced by half, the drag tension is dou-bled. For example, if your drag is set at 2 pounds with a full spool, it will be increased to 4 pounds when a fish makes a long run and strips off half your line.

Long, fast runs will also generate friction and heat between drag washers. This will frequently tighten a drag and add even more tension.

It's also important to remember that a rod held at about 45 degrees will add about 10 percent to the drag you get with the rod pointed directly at the fish. This

You can set the drag on your reel even if you're alone. As Jerry Gibbs demonstrates, fill a bucket with sand, hook a fish scale to the handle and lift with your rod until the scale indicates the correct setting. The accompanying table shows the correct settings for various weight lines.
(VIN T. SPARANO)

increased drag is due to friction between your line and the rod guides. If the rod is held at about 90 degrees, drag will increase about 35 percent of the initial setting.

This is why it is important to lighten the drag and, when possible, point the rod at the fish when it is about to be netted or gaffed. If you hold your rod high and keep a tight drag, a sudden lunge by a fish could break your line. But point the rod tip at the fish and the line will run off the spool more easily, even with the same drag setting.

This technique of lowering the rod is also used when handling thrashing or jumping fish, such as tarpon and marlin. Lowering the rod will lighten drag tension and "cushion" the line from the shock of a jumping fish, a move called "bowing." It's part of the technique that makes it possible to land 100-pound tarpon on 10-pound line.

Taking all the above factors into consideration, how does an angler set his drag so that he can feel reasonably

secure when he hooks a trophy fish? The first step is to determine the minimum and maximum range of drag for the various pound-test lines (see accompanying table). By minimum drag, I mean "starting drag," the amount of pull needed to get the drag moving. If the minimum drag seems light for the pound-test line, remember that there will be other factors increasing your drag beyond this setting, such as rod angle, spool diameter, and amount of line in water. Maximum drag means the heaviest setting you should use while fighting a fish. Never go beyond the maximum for your line class.

Let's take 12-pound-test line and see what factors come into play. Minimum drag is set at 4 pounds, but 8 pounds of pull will likely be required to get that drag started. If the angler holds his rod at 45 degrees or higher, he can add another 10 percent, which brings the drag to 9 pounds. To this figure we also have to add water resistance or line drag, which varies according to amount of line in the water, line diameter, and speed of the fish. With 12-pound line and a fast fish, it can amount to as much as 2 pounds, which brings us up to 11 pounds of drag on our 12-pound line. With only 1 pound of drag to spare, a big fish would likely break the line. It's obvious that you're far better off with a very light drag setting.

Range of Drag

Line	Mininum Draw (lbs.)	Maximum Drag (lbs)
6-lb.-test	1½	4
8-lb.-test	2	5
10-lb.-test	3	6
12-lb.-test	4	8
20-lb.-test	6	12
30-lb.-test	8	15
50-lb.-test	12	25
80-lb.-test	20	40
130-lb.-test	30	50

The first step is to set your drag at the minimum setting. This is easily done at dockside with a reliable fish scale and the help of a friend. Run your line through the guides and tie it to the scale. Ask your friend to hold the scale and back off about 30 feet. Tighten your drag and begin to apply pressure as you would when fighting a fish. Now adjust the drag so that it comes into play when the scale reads the correct minimum drag weight. For example, if you're using 12-pound line, the drag should begin to slip when you apply enough pressure to pull the scale indicator to the 4-pound mark.

Now, with your drag set at 4 pounds, slowly tighten your drag until it comes into play at 8 pounds, which is

Jerry Gibbs, Outdoor Life *fishing editor, puts pressure on a 30-pound-test outfit while Vin Sparano, editor of both the Northeast and Southeast editions of the* Guide to Saltwater Fishing & Boating, *checks the indicator on a fish scale to set drag. Gibbs here is applying 26 pounds of pressure; note the bend in the rod.* (VIN T. SPARANO)

the maximum setting. Note how many turns of the star drag or spool cap are required to bring your drag to maximum setting. Play with the drag, setting it back and forth from 4 to 8 pounds. Do this several times and get the feel of the resistance and pressure you're putting on the line. With enough practice, you'll be able to safely lighten and tighten the drag while fighting a fish.

An easier technique is to leave your drag set at the minimum setting and use your hand or fingers to apply more drag. This is a method many anglers use and it works well. You can practice with your buddy and the scale. With drag at the minimum setting, cup your hand around the spool (assuming you're using an open-face spinning reel), grip it so that the drag does not slip, and apply just enough pressure to pull the scale indicator to the maximum figure. Practice this technique and you'll soon be able to bear down on a fish and gain line without even touching the drag knob.

As mentioned above, you can also cup your hand around the spool of an open-face spinning reel to apply more drag. With conventional reels, use your thumb against the spool and hold the lines against the rod. Make sure you lift your finger when a big fish begins a run, or else you'll get a bad line burn.

Learn to combine this hand technique with "pumping" and you will be able to land big fish on light lines. Pumping a big fish in is not difficult. Let's assume you're using an open-face spinning reel with a light drag. Put your hand around the spool, apply pressure, and ease your rod back into a vertical position. Now drop the rod tip and reel in the slack. Repeat the process and you'll

eventually have your fish at boatside. Always be ready, however, to lower the rod tip and release hand pressure from the spool when you think the fish is about to make a run. When he stops, you begin to pump once again.

One last point: At the end of the day, back off the drag and release all pressure on the washers, or they will lose their physical characteristics and take a set. If this happens, the drag will become jerky and unpredictable. If the washers do take a set, replacing them is then the only solution.

CARE AND REPAIR OF FISHING TACKLE

There's more than a germ of truth in the old saying, "A fisherman is no better than his tackle." Of course, that has also been said of quarterbacks!

Seriously, though, it pays in more ways than one to keep your gear in good working order. For one thing, proper maintenance can add a good many years to the working life of rods, reels, and other tackle on which hard-earned money has been spent. And legions of fishermen have discovered, to their chagrin, that unoiled reels can "freeze up," neglected rods can snap, and rusty lure hooks can give out—just when that lunker comes along.

The following tackle-care tips should help to prevent such problems.

217

KEEP YOUR TACKLE TUNED

I get a pain in the pit of my stomach whenever I look in someone's car trunk and see a couple of fishing rods bouncing around with a tire iron and jumper cables. The same thing happens when I see rods leaning against garage walls and reel drags screwed down tight when not in use. All of these things will wreck tackle. Fishing tackle today is not cheap, and you should learn how to protect your investment.

Today's rods, for example, are designed for long life, but they still require some basic maintenance to keep in good working order. This is especially important for saltwater fishermen. Even the best of tackle can't withstand the corrosive action of salt. Here are the steps that you will need to keep your rod in good shape:

1. Wash the rod, including the guides, thoroughly with soap and fresh water; rinse it with hot water and then let it dry thoroughly. This step should be taken after each use.

2. Clean the guides and ferrules well and give them a very light coating of grease to help prevent oxidation of the metal. I know a charter captain who scrubs all the roller guides with a toothbrush after every trip.

3. New graphite rods usually need nothing more than periodic washing, but I still wax my rods at least once a season with a good car wax.

4. Check the guide wrappings. If they start to look thin or worn, rewrap them. Don't wait until the threads start to unravel. You may not have this problem, however, if you give the wrappings a coat of varnish each season. Two thin coats are better than one. To avoid bubbles in the varnish, apply it with a finger or a pipe cleaner.

5. When you're not using the rod, store it flat or upright without any weight on the tip. If you lean a rod against a wall, it may develop a set or permanent bend. Never store a wet cork-handled rod in a case. Mildew will form on the cork.

Reels are probably the most important piece of fishing gear and probably the most expensive. If you don't want them to fail when you're fighting a big fish, follow this checklist:

1. I rinse off my reels after every trip, and I use lots of soap. Dry your reels thoroughly and oil sparingly.

2. Most important, release drag tension to eliminate fatigue in your drag system.

HOW TO WRAP GUIDES

1. Start by wrapping over the end of the thread toward the guide so thread end is held down by the wrapping. Using the tension from whatever type tension device you are using to hold the wrapping tight, continue to turn the rod so that each thread lies as close as possible to the preceding turn.

2. About 5 to 8 turns from the finish of the wrap, insert the loop of tie-off thread. (This can be 6 inches of heavier thread or a fine piece of nylon leader material.) Finish the wrap over this tie-off loop.

3. Holding wrap tightly, cut the wrapping thread about 4 inches from your rod. Insert this cut end through the tie-off loop. Still holding onto the wrapping thread, pull cut off thread under the wraps with tie-off loop.

4. With a razor blade, trim cut-off end as close as possible to the wrap. With the back of a knife or your fingernail, push wrapping up tight so that it appears solid, and none of the rod or guide shows through.

3. Clean internal gears, but don't attempt to break down the reel completely. More than once, I've had to return a reel to a manufacturer because I couldn't put it back together.

4. If you're not going to use a reel for awhile, give it a light coat of oil and store it in a cloth bag that will allow air to enter and escape. I store reels in Ziploc bags, but I never seal the the bags completely.

ROD-WRAPPING TRICKS OF THE TRADE

Guides and Tension: Guides should be purchased in matched sets to assure uniformity. Feet of guides should be dressed with a file to a fine taper. Next sight your rod; you will note a slight bend, or offset. Apply guides opposite the bend; this will bring it into a straight position. Guides should be affixed with snug wrapping tension, so that you may sight after wrapping and make slight guide adjustments before applying color preserver. Do not wrap guides to the absolute breaking point of the thread. Remember, 10 or 20 wraps of thread exert very heavy pressure on feet of guides. It is possible to damage a blank by wrapping too tight.

Threads: Sizes 2/O to E are most commonly used. Size 2/O or A for fly, casting, or spinning rods. Size E for the heavier freshwater spinning or saltwater rods. Naturally the finer size 2/O thread will make a neater job, but, being lighter, it is not quite as durable.

Trim: You may trim the basic color of your wrap with 5 to 10 turns of another color thread. This is done just as outlined in instructions for basic wrap.

Color Preserver and Rod Varnish: Good color preserver has plastic in it, and should be quite thin in order to penetrate the wrappings. Good-grade varnish is essential to durability of finish. A brush may be used to apply both the color preserver and rod varnish; however, air bubbles are usually present when a brush is used. To maintain a smooth finish, make certain these bubbles are out. A very satisfactory method of minimizing air bubbles is to apply both the color preserver and rod varnish with your index finger. Usually color preserver can be worked in with index finger. This will prevent any shading of the wrapping color.

SELECTING THE TIP TOP AND OTHER GUIDES

In building rods, you get what you pay for; don't skimp on guides, especially for saltwater rods.

Guides are made of various metals, including hardened stainless steel, chrome (or chrome-plated Monel), agate, and tungsten-carbide, with the carbide types being the most durable. Roller guides for heavy saltwater fishing are usually made of stainless steel, Monel, or nickel alloy.

The rod-builder should note that the guides are available in sets tailored to particular rod types and lengths.

SELECTING ROD FERRULES

Ferrules are jointlike devices inserted along the working length of a fishing rod that enable the rod to be dismantled into two or more sections. Ferrules are generally made of metal (nickel, brass, or aluminum), fiberglass, graphite, or a synthetic.

A ferrule set consists of two parts, the male ferrule and the female ferrule. The male section should fit snugly into the female section.

SPACING OF ROD GUIDES

Whether you are building a fishing rod from scratch or refinishing an old favorite, you must pay close attention to the placement of the guides along the working length of the rod.

Putting too many or too few guides on a rod, or placing them improperly, may detract from proper rod action and put undue strain on the line and the rod.

The following chart gives the correct number of guides—and exact spacing measurements—for most spinning, baitcasting, spincasting, and fly rods.

ROD GUIDE DIAMETERS

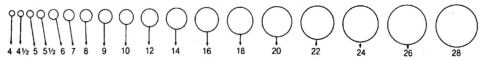

ACTUAL SIZES OF TIP GUIDES IN 1/64"

TYPES OF ROD GUIDES

Snake (Fly Rod)

Ring (Baitcasting/Spincasting)

BRIDGE (Baitcasting Spincasting)

Spinning

Loop or Foulproof (Spinning)

Roller (Big Game)

Fuji (Big Game)

Roller (Big Game)

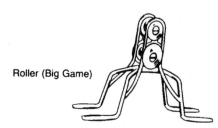

TYPES OF ROD TIPS

Ring with Support
(Spinning, Baitcasting, Spincasting)

Fly Rod

Foulproof (Spinning)

Fuji (Big Game)

Roller (Big Game)

SUGGESTED GUIDE SPACING TABLE

All measurements are from tip of rod down. Figures indicate measurements at the guide ring.

Rod Length & Type	Lure-Weight Range	Fly-Line Weights	1st	2nd	3rd	4th	5th	6th	7th	8th
Spincasting, Baitcasting										
5½-ft.	⅛ to ⅓ oz.		4½"	12"	23"	36"				
6-ft.	⅛ to ⅜ oz.		4	10	18	28	40			
6-ft.	¼ to ¾ oz.		4	8¼	13	18	24½	32⅛	42	
6-ft.	⅜ to 1¼ oz.		3½	7½	12	17⅜	23⅝	31⅞	42½	
6-ft. 4-in.	1/16 to ¼ oz.		4	10	18½	28½	41			
6-ft. 4-in.	⅜ oz.		4	10	18½	28½	41			
6-ft. 4-in.	⅛ to ½ oz.		4	10	18½	28½	41			
6-ft.	⅜ to ⅝ oz.		4	10	18	28	40			
6-ft. 4-in.	¼ to ⅝ oz.		4	10	18½	28½	41			
Fly Rods										
5-ft. 5-in.		5 F, 6 S	5	13	25	40				
6-ft.		5 F, 6 S	3	7½	12	17¾	25	33	42½	
7½-ft.		6 F, 7 S	6	13	21	30	41½	60		
7-ft. 8-in.		6 or 7 F, 7 S	6	13	21	30	43	62		
8-ft.		6 or 7 F, 7 S	6	13	21	30	41	52	66	
8-ft.		7 F, 7 S	6	13	21	30	40	53	66	
8-ft.		7 or 8 F, 7 or 8 S	6	13	21	30	41	53	66	
8½-ft.		7 or 8 F, 7 or 8 S	6	13	21	30	40	56	73	
8½-ft.		7 F, 7 S	6	13	21	30	40	56	73	
8½-ft.		8 or 9 F, 8 or 9 S	6	13	21	30	40	56	73	
9-ft.		7 or 8 F, 7 or 8 S	5	11	18	26	35	45	58½	73
9-ft.		8 or 9 F, 8 or 9 S	5	11	18	26	35	45	58½	73
10-ft.		9 or 10 F, 9 or 10 S	6	13	22	32	43	54½	66½	80½
Spinning Rods										
6-ft.	up to ¼ oz.		5½	15½	27½	40½				
6-ft.	up to ⅜ oz.		3½	10	19	29¼	41½			
6½-ft.	1/16 to ¼ oz.		3½	8½	15	23	33	46		
6½-ft.	⅛ to 1 oz.		5	10⅜	16⅜	23⅜	31⅞	44		
6½-ft.	⅛ to ⅜ oz.		3½	8½	15	23	33	46		
7-ft.*	1/16 to ⅜ oz.	5 or 6 F, 6 S	4	10	18	27½	38½	52½		
7-ft.	1/16 to ⅜ oz.		4	10	18	27½	38½	52½		
6½ ft.	¼ to ⅝ oz.		3½	8½	15	23	33	46		
7-ft.	up to 1½ oz.		4	10	18	27½	38	51		

F = Floating   S = Sinking   * = Combination spin/fly rod

8

Lines, Leaders, and Hooks

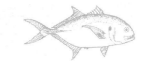

No fisherman is stronger than the line that connects him and his quarry. Fishing lines are made of a wide variety of natural and synthetic materials and as a result differ widely in their characteristics and the uses to which they can be put. No two types of lines, for example, have the same degree of elasticity, abrasion resistance, water absorption, weight, and diameter.

Let's take a look at the physical characteristics of the various lines and the uses for which they are best suited.

MONOFILAMENT (SINGLE-STRAND NYLON)

By far the most widely used fishing line today. It is suitable for everything from blue-water trolling to surf casting to freshwater spinning, and it is the universal material for leaders in both fresh water and salt because of its near-invisibility in water. It is extremely strong and light for its diameter, and it absorbs very little water (3 to 12 percent of its own weight). About the only drawback of monofilament is its relatively high rate of stretch (15 to 30 percent when dry, 20 to 35 percent when wet). For that reason it is not the best choice for such uses as deep-water bottom fishing, in which large fish must be reeled up from considerable depths.

DACRON

A DuPont trademark for a synthetic fiber that is made into a braided line. It is nearly as strong as monofilament but does not stretch as much (about 10 percent). It has virtually the same characteristics whether wet or dry. Its visibility in water is greater than that of monofilament. Dacron's widest uses are as trolling line or for deep jigging.

LINEN

A braided line made from natural fibers and rated according to the number of threads, with each thread having a breaking strength of 3 pounds (6-thread linen has a breaking strength of 18 pounds, 15-thread tests 45 pounds, and so on). This material absorbs considerable water and is stronger when wet. Linen line is subject to deterioration and is heavy and bulky. Very little linen fishing line is made or used today, but because of its negligible stretch and good abrasion resistance it is still preferred by some big-game fishermen.

Braided Fishing Line

by Vin Sparano

The new braided fishing lines sound great the first time we see and hear about them. These lines have small diameter, minimum stretch, and good knot strength. The new braided lines get a high score on two out of three. If you want to use a braided line, you better listen to some sound advice on knots.

There are more than a dozen manufacturers of braided lines, and they all claim their lines are three times as strong as monofilament of the same diameter. This means, of course, that you can get three times as much line on your reel. The smaller diameter also means easier casting with lighter lures. So far, so good.

Braided lines have a stretch factor of less than 5 percent. Monofilament has a stretch factor of about 25 percent, depending on the manufacturer. Minimum stretch is a big deal in fishing. It means sensitivity and fast hook-ups. I've used braided lines on blackfish, a bottom feeder that's tough to hook and keep out of the rocks. The Stren Kevlar braided line worked as predicted. I could feel the hits, and setting the hook was almost instant. The braided line seemed to hold well against the rocks.

So where's the rub with braided lines? It's in the knots! With braided lines, you may only get about 75 percent knot strength, and that's only if you use the right knot. With monofilament, you can get nearly 100 percent with the right knot. Unless you take certain precautions tying knots, the strength-to-diameter ratio of braided lines isn't such a big deal.

Berkley, a line manufacturer that has done a great deal of research on the new braided lines, admits that knots may be the weak link. Good knots are difficult to tie. They are tough to cinch up tight, and they tend to slip.

After considerable research, Berkley recommends the Palomar Knot and the Trilene Knot. The Palomar and Trilene knots are used to tie fishing line to swivels, snaps, hooks, and lures. It's extremely important to wet braided lines before cinching the knot tight. Also, take care to keep the wraps from crossing over one another, and double the length of the tag line.

Stren has another answer to the knot problem in braided lines. This company recommends a glue called Stren Lok-Knot. A drop or two of this adhesive will literally weld a poorly tied knot and eliminate slippage. Stren feels so strongly about the strength of Lok-Knot that it even recommends it for totally knotless connections.

Braided lines have a lot going for them, including small diameter, minimal stretch, and the sensitivity to transmit the slightest nibble. Learning to tie and use the right knots should eliminate any knot problem.

Remember to double the tag end. In fact, it's wise to double braided line before tying any knot. Braided lines are also sharp and hard. Joining braided lines with monofilament may not be suuch a good idea, though further testing may prove otherwise. ■

Palomar Knot

The Palomar Knot is a general-purpose connection used in joining fishing line to swivels, snaps, hooks and artificial lures. The double wrap of line through the eyelet provides a protective cushion for added knot strength.

1. Double the line and form a loop three to four inches long. Pass the end of the loop through hook's eye.

2. Holding standing line between thumb and finger, grasp loop with free hand and form a simple overhand knot.

3. Pass hook through loop and draw line while guiding loop over top of eyelet.

4. Pull tag end of line to tighten knot snugly and trim tag end to about 1/4".

Trilene ® Knot

The Trilene Knot is a strong, reliable connection that resists slippage and premature failures. This knot can be used in joining line to swivels, snaps, hooks and artificial lures. The knots unique double wrap design and ease of tying consistently yields a strong, dependable connection.

1. Run end of line through eye of hook or lure and double back through the eye a second time.

2. Loop around standing part of line 5 or 6 times. Thread tag end back between the eye and the coils as shown.

3. Tighten knot with a steady, even motion without hesitation. Trim tag end leaving about 1/4".

Care of Lines

Check each line for cracking, aging, wear, and rot. If the entire line is no longer serviceable, discard it. If one end has taken all the use, reverse the line. Fly lines tend to crack at the business end after considerable use. If the cracking is confined to the last foot or so, clip off the damaged section or, if the line is a double-taper, reverse it. If the damage is more widespread, replace the line.

Check particularly for nicks and other weak spots in monofilament, and test its breaking strength. If it's weak, replace it.

With braided line, check for dark spots, signifying rot, and test the breaking strength. Replace if weak.

LEAD-CORE

This type of line is made by sheathing a flexible lead core in a tightly braided nylon sleeve. It's suitable for deep trolling in both fresh and salt water, and is especially useful for quickly getting a bait or lure down deep without bulky, heavy sinkers or planers. It's color-coded in 10-yard segments for precise depth control.

WIRE

These lines, too, are designed for deep trolling in both fresh and salt water. They're made of stainless steel, Monel (nickel alloy), bronze, or copper. Wire is popular for downrigger fishing, but because it's heavy enough to sink on its own, it's also used without downriggers and in many cases eliminates the need for a cumbersome drail weight or planer. Since it has no stretch, the angler can jig the rod and give movement to a bait or lure. However, wire is somewhat tricky until a fisherman

FISHING LINE TROUBLESHOOTING CHART

Symptoms	Possible Causes	Recommended Cures
Unexplained line breaks under low stress loads.	a. Nicks or abrasion. If smooth surface and shiny, failure may be line fatigue.	a. Strip off worn line or retie line more frequently.
	b. If surface dull, faded and fuzzy, failure due to sunlight or excessive wear.	b. Replace line.
	c. Wear or stress points on guides and/or reel.	c. Replace worn guides.
Line usually sticky and stretchy.	Line stored in area of high heat. Line damaged by chemicals.	Replace line and change storage areas.
Line has kinks and flat spots.	a. Line spooled under excessive tension.	a. Use lower spooling tension. Make one final cast and rewind under low tension.
	b. Line stored on reel too long without use.	b. Strip out and soak last 50 yards in water.
Excessive curls and backlashes.	Using too heavy mono for reel spool diameter.	Use a more flexible mono or one with a lower pound test or smaller diameter.
Mono stiff and brittle; dry, powdery surface.	Improper storage in either wet or too warm conditions.	Replace line and change storage area.
Line looks good, but losing too many fish.	Faulty or improperly set reel drag. Using too light a break strength for conditions.	Check reel drag. Lubricate or replace washers. Refill with line of higher break strength.
Reel casts poorly.	Not enough line on spool or line is too heavy for reel.	Fill spool with additional line. Use lighter, more limp monofilament.
Line is hard to see.	Line has faded due to excessive exposure to sunlight. Using wrong color line.	Replace line. Switch to high visibility line.

Chart courtesy Berkley, Inc.

This chart was designed to help you quickly find and correct line troubles when you can least afford to have them—on the water. Keep this handy chart in your tackle box.

gets used to it. Kinks can develop, causing weak spots or possibly cutting an unwary angler's hand. Wire line is generally available in a wider range of test weights than lead-core line.

Wire leaders, usually sleeved in plastic, are widely used to prevent line-cutting when fishing for such toothy battlers as pike, muskellunge, and many salt-water species.

LEADERS

There are two basic leader materials, wire and monofilament (single-strand nylon).

Wire leaders—either piano wire (high-carbon or stainless steel) or braided wire—are used generally to protect the line from sharp underwater obstacles and from the teeth, gill plates, and other sharp appendages of both freshwater and saltwater fish.

Some wire leaders, particularly the braided type, are enclosed in a "sleeve" of nylon, which prevents the wire strands from fraying and eliminates kinking.

Some monofilament leaders perform a similar function. Called shock tippets, they are short lengths (6 feet or shorter in most cases) of strong monotesting up to about 100 pounds depending on the size of the fish being sought. Shock tippets protect the line from sharp objects and sharp teeth, but they are also able to withstand the sledgehammer strikes of large fish.

The main purpose of most monofilament leaders, however, is to provide an all-but-invisible link between the end of the line and the lure, bait, or fly. In spinning and spincasting, a leader is seldom necessary, for the line itself is monofilament.

Recommended Leader Strength for Various Species

Mangrove or Gray Snapper	8-pound test
Bonefish	6- or 8-pound test
Tarpon, baby (under 20 pounds)	8-pound test
Tarpon, big (over 20 pounds)	12-pound test
Channel Bass (Redfish)	10-pound test
Striped Bass (to 10 pounds)	8-pound test
Striped Bass (over 10 pounds)	12-pound test
Jack Crevalle	10-pound test
Horse-Eye Jack	10-pound test
Ladyfish	8-pound test
Snook	12-pound test
Spotted Seatrout	10-pound test
Barracuda	12-pound test

Deepwater Fish, by Chumming or Sighting

Dolphin	10-pound test
Mackerel	10-pound test
False Albacore	10-pound test
Bonito	10-pound test
Grouper	10-pound test
Yellowtail	10-pound test
Bermuda chub	10-pound test

Special Leaders For Fish That Might Bite Or Fray Through Leader

Bluefish	10-pound test with 12 inches #4 wire leader added
Sailfish	12-pound test with 12 inches 80-pound-test nylon added
Marlin	12-pound test with 12 inches 100-pound-test nylon added
Tarpon	12-pound test with 12 inches 100-pound-test nylon added
Tuna	12-pound test with 12 inches 100-pound-test nylon added
Barracuda	12-pound test with 12 inches #5 wire leader added
Sharks	12-pound test with 12 inches #5 or #7 heavier wire leader added

HOOKS

Modern hook design and manufacture has come a long way since the first Stone Age bone hooks dating back to 5000 B.C. Today's fishhooks come in hundreds of sizes, shapes, and special designs. They're hardened and tempered, then plated or bronzed to meet special specifications. Some are thin steel wire for use in tying artificial flies; others are thick steel for big-game fish that prowl offshore waters. Avoid stainless steel hooks if you plan to catch and release.

There is no such thing as an all-purpose hook. Fishermen must carry a variety of patterns and sizes to match both tackle and size of fish being hunted. Let's start from the beginning by learning the basic nomenclature of a typical fishhook, illustrated in the accompanying drawing. Even the various parts of a typical fishhook may vary in design to meet certain requirements. There are sliced shanks to better hold bait on the hook, forged shanks for greater strength in marine hooks, tapered eyes to reduce weight of hooks used in tying dry flies, and so on.

225

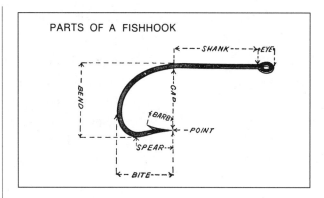

PARTS OF A FISHHOOK

HOOK WIRE SIZE

The letter X and the designations "Fine" or "Stout" are used to indicate the weight or diameter of a hook. For example, a 2X Stout means the hook is made of the standard diameter for a hook two sizes larger, and a 3X Stout is made of the standard diameter for a hook three sizes larger.

When we go to lightweight hooks, the designations are reversed. For example, a 2X Fine means that the hook is made of the standard diameter for a hook two sizes smaller, and so on.

Obviously, the angler seeking the big fish should lean toward the stout hooks, which are not apt to bend or spring when striking the bigger saltwater fish.

SHANK LENGTH

The letter X and the designations "Long" or "Short" are used to specify shank length of a hook. The formula for determining shank length is similar to that used for wire sizes. A 2X Long means the shank of the hook is the standard length for a hook two sizes larger, and a 4X Long for a hook four sizes larger. A 2X Short is a hook that has a shank as short as the standard length of a hook two sizes smaller, and 4X Short for a hook four sizes smaller, and so on.

Picking a hook with the correct shank length depends on the type of fishing you plan to undertake. A short-shank hook is preferred for baitfishing, since it

can be hidden in the bait more easily. The long-shank hook is at its best when used for fish with sharp teeth. A bluefish, for example, would have a tough time getting past the long shank and cutting into the leader. Long-shank hooks are also used in tying streamers and bucktails.

HOOK SIZE

Attempts have been made to standardize hook sizes, but none has been very successful. The problem has been that a hook actually has two measurements—the gap and the length of the shank, both of which vary from pattern to pattern.

Only by studying the various patterns and sizes in the accompanying charts can an angler become sufficiently familiar with hook patterns to pick the right hook for the job.

As a guide, refer to Natural Saltwater Baits on page 240, and note the hook sizes recommended for various species of fish. Match those recommendations with the hook sizes on these pages and compare the differences. With this information, it is not difficult to choose the correct size hook for your type of fishing.

HOOK CHARACTERISTICS

In addition to size and shank length, there are other characteristics of hooks to consider when selecting a hook for a specific purpose. The barb, obviously, is a critical part of the hook. A short barb is quick to set in the mouth of a fish, but it also gives a jumping fish a greater chance of dislodging it. A long barb, on the other hand, is more difficult to set but it also makes it a lot tougher for a fish to shake it loose.

So what guidelines should an angler follow? Let's list some basic recommendations. The all-round saltwater fisherman can't go wrong by using the O'Shaughnessy, Kirby, Sproat, or Siwash patterns. And if you happen to have some Salmon hooks, they're perfectly all right to use with a wire leader for barracuda and other toothy fish.

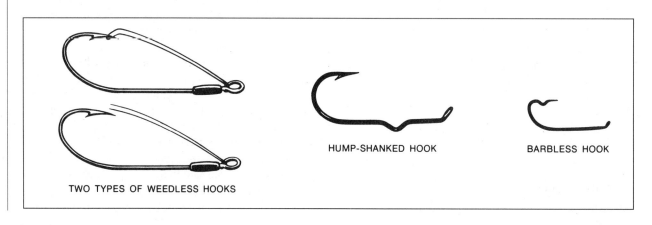

TWO TYPES OF WEEDLESS HOOKS

HUMP-SHANKED HOOK

BARBLESS HOOK

HOOK PART VARIATIONS

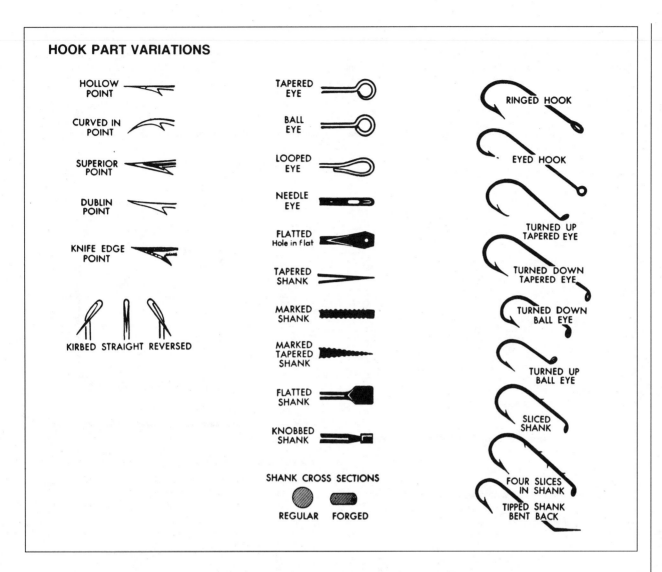

If you're a flounder fisherman, you'll find that the Chestertown and Carlisle patterns are your best bet. The long-shanked Chestertown makes it especially easy to unhook flounders, which may well be a primary reason for using them when fishing for these flatfish.

If you're a baitfisherman, use the sliced shanked Mustad-Beak or Eagle Claw patterns. Those extra barbs on the shanks do a good job keeping natural baits secured to the hook.

Fishermen can also become confused when they see hooks with straight-ringed eyes, turned-up eyes, and turned-down eyes. This should not present a problem. If you're replacing hooks on lures or attaching hooks to spinners use a straight-ringed eye. If you're tying short-shanked artificial flies, pick the turned-up eye, which will provide more space for the hook point to bite into the fish. The turned-down eye is the best bet for standard flies and for baitfishing, since it brings the point of the hook closest to a straight line of penetration when striking a fish.

Curved shanks also lead to some confusion. Without getting into specific details, let's say simply that a curved shank, curved right or left, has its place in baitfishing. The offset point has a better chance of hitting flesh when a strike is made.

When you are casting or trolling with artificial lures or spinners, however, the straight-shanked hook is a better choice, since it does not have a tendency to spin or twist, which is often the case with curved-shanked hooks.

Below and on upcoming pages, you will find various styles of hooks. In most cases, the smallest and largest of hooks in these styles are shown, with intermediate hook sizes indicated by means of horizontal lines and corresponding hook numbers. To match the name and size of an unknown hook, just compare yours to the drawings. (CHART CONCEPT BY JEFF FITSCHEN)

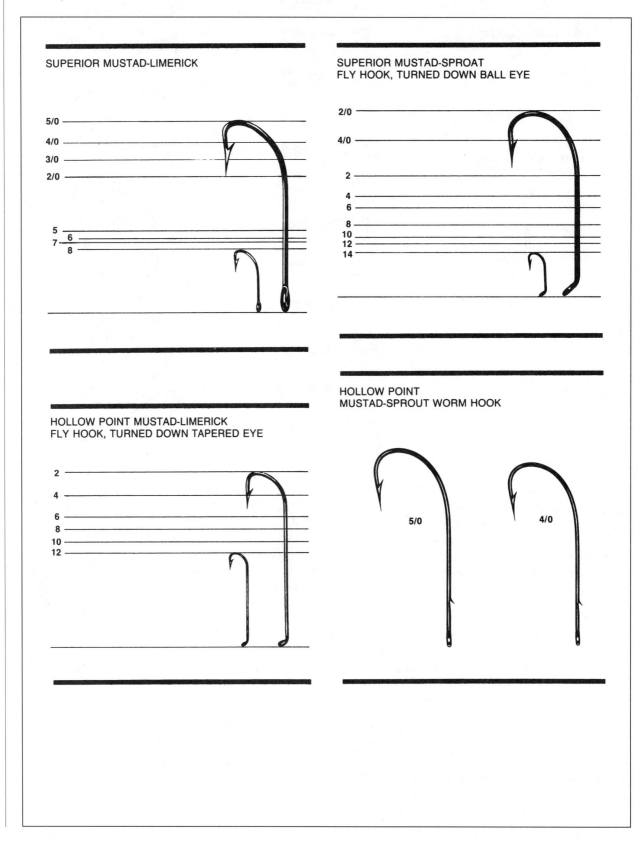

SUPERIOR MUSTAD-LIMERICK

5/0
4/0
3/0
2/0

5
7 — 6
8

SUPERIOR MUSTAD-SPROAT
FLY HOOK, TURNED DOWN BALL EYE

2/0

4/0

2

4
6

8
10
12
14

HOLLOW POINT MUSTAD-LIMERICK
FLY HOOK, TURNED DOWN TAPERED EYE

2

4

6
8
10
12

HOLLOW POINT
MUSTAD-SPROUT WORM HOOK

5/0   4/0

SUPERIOR MUSTAD-CARLISLE

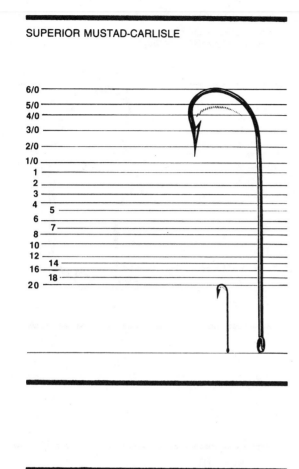

6/0
5/0
4/0
3/0
2/0
1/0
1
2
3
4
5
6
7
8
10
12
14
16
18
20

HOLLOW POINT MUSTAD-WIDE GAP HOOK

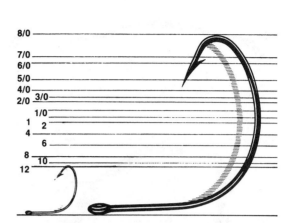

8/0
7/0
6/0
5/0
4/0
2/0   3/0
1/0
1   2
4
6
8
10
12

SUPERIOR MUSTAD-ABERDEEN
CRICKET HOOK

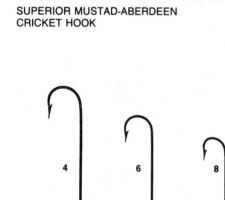

4   6   8

SUPERIOR MUSTAD-O'SHAUGHNESSY

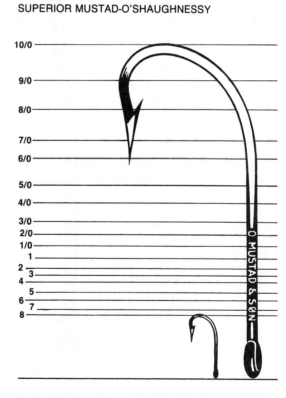

10/0

9/0

8/0

7/0

6/0

5/0
4/0
3/0
2/0
1/0
1
2
3
4
5
6
7
8

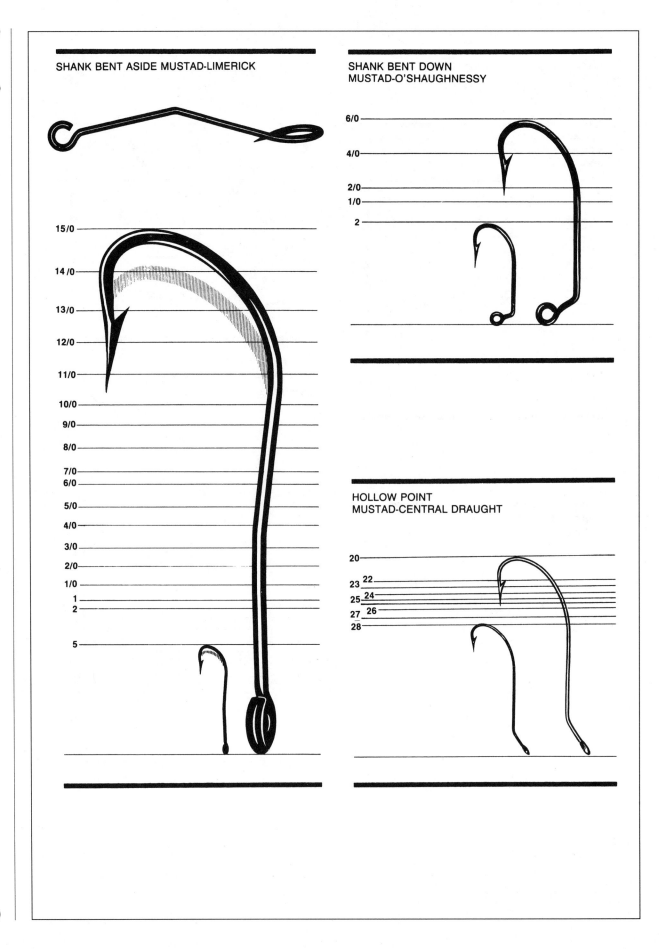

SHANK BENT ASIDE MUSTAD-LIMERICK

**SHANK BENT DOWN
MUSTAD-O'SHAUGHNESSY**

6/0

4/0

2/0
1/0
2

15/0

14 /0

13/0

12/0

11/0

10/0

9/0

8/0

7/0
6/0

5/0

4/0

3/0

2/0

1/0
1
2

5

**HOLLOW POINT
MUSTAD-CENTRAL DRAUGHT**

20
23 22
25 24
27 26
28

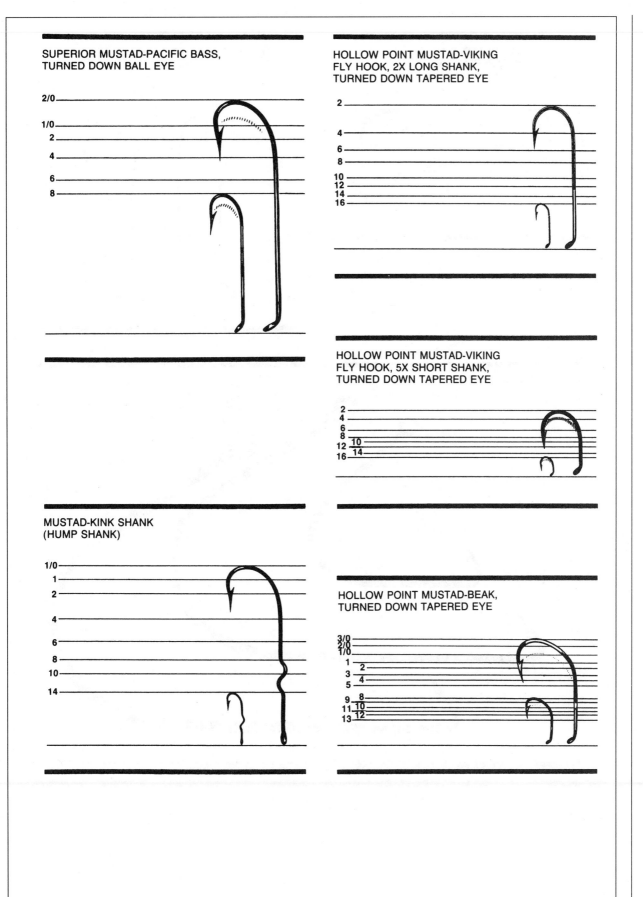

SUPERIOR MUSTAD-PACIFIC BASS,
TURNED DOWN BALL EYE

2/0
1/0
2
4
6
8

HOLLOW POINT MUSTAD-VIKING
FLY HOOK, 2X LONG SHANK,
TURNED DOWN TAPERED EYE

2
4
6
8
10
12
14
16

HOLLOW POINT MUSTAD-VIKING
FLY HOOK, 5X SHORT SHANK,
TURNED DOWN TAPERED EYE

2
4
6
8
12 10
16 14

MUSTAD-KINK SHANK
(HUMP SHANK)

1/0
1
2
4
6
8
10
14

HOLLOW POINT MUSTAD-BEAK,
TURNED DOWN TAPERED EYE

3/0
2/0
1/0
1   2
3   4
5
9   8
11   10
13   12

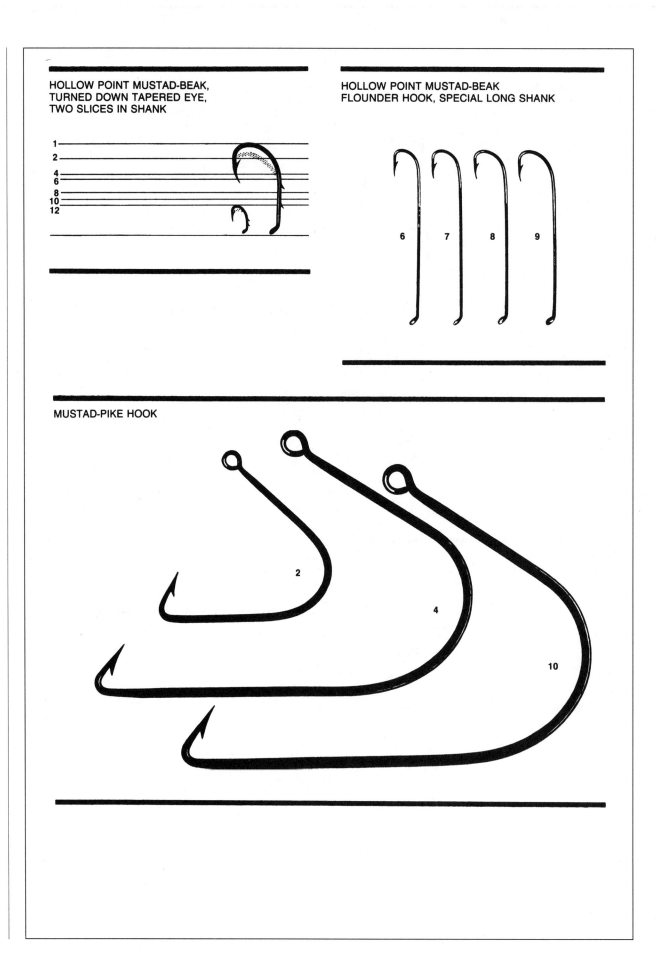

HOLLOW POINT MUSTAD-BEAK,
TURNED DOWN TAPERED EYE,
TWO SLICES IN SHANK

1
2
4
6
8
10
12

HOLLOW POINT MUSTAD-BEAK
FLOUNDER HOOK, SPECIAL LONG SHANK

6   7   8   9

MUSTAD-PIKE HOOK

2

4

10

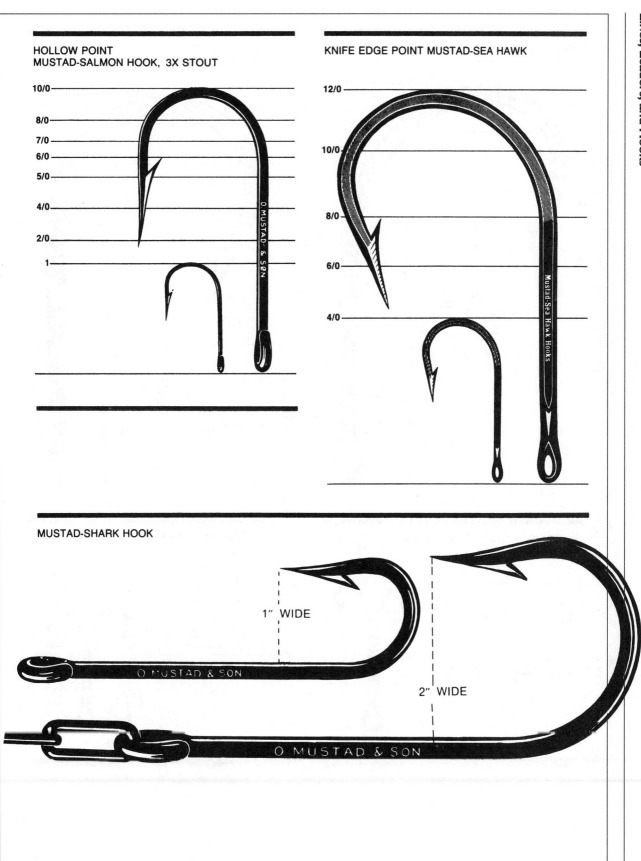

HOLLOW POINT
MUSTAD-SALMON HOOK, 3X STOUT

10/0
8/0
7/0
6/0
5/0
4/0
2/0
1

O MUSTAD & SON

KNIFE EDGE POINT MUSTAD-SEA HAWK

12/0
10/0
8/0
6/0
4/0

Mustad-Sea Hawk Hooks

MUSTAD-SHARK HOOK

1" WIDE

2" WIDE

O MUSTAD & SON

O MUSTAD & SON

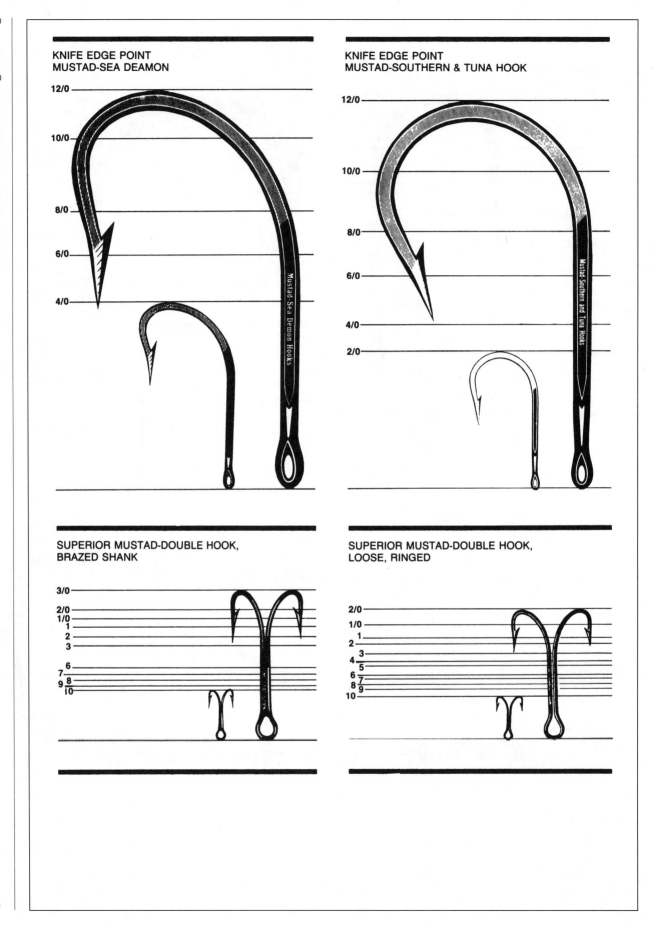

**KNIFE EDGE POINT
MUSTAD-SEA DEAMON**

12/0
10/0
8/0
6/0
4/0

Mustad-Sea Demon Hooks

**KNIFE EDGE POINT
MUSTAD-SOUTHERN & TUNA HOOK**

12/0
10/0
8/0
6/0
4/0
2/0

Mustad Southern and Tuna Hooks

**SUPERIOR MUSTAD-DOUBLE HOOK,
BRAZED SHANK**

3/0
2/0
1/0
1
2
3
6
7
8
9
10

**SUPERIOR MUSTAD-DOUBLE HOOK,
LOOSE, RINGED**

2/0
1/0
1
2
3
4
5
6
7
8
9
10

MUSTAD-TUNA CIRCLE HOOK

6   5   4

**HOLLOW POINT MUSTAD-DOUBLE HOOK,
UNIVERSAL DOUBLE BAIT,
NEEDLE EYE, ROD ATTACHED**

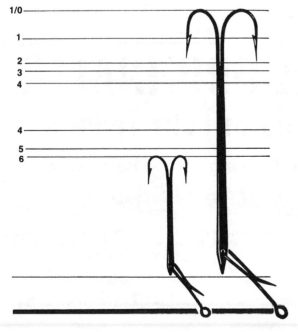

1/0
1
2
3
4

4
5
6

**SUPERIOR MUSTAD-TREBLE
HOOK, SPROAT BEND**

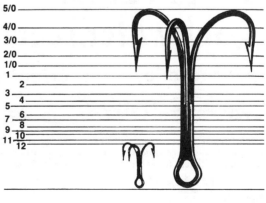

5/0
4/0
3/0
2/0
1/0
1
2
3
4
5
6
7
8
9
10
11
12

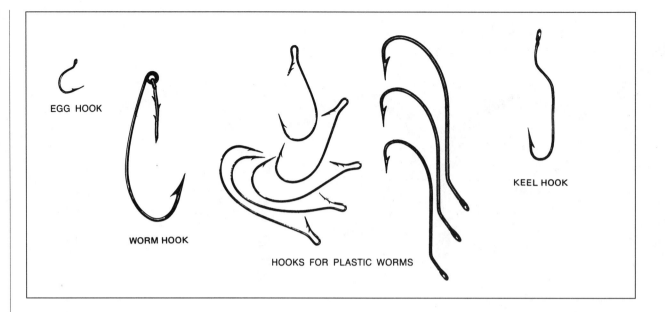

EGG HOOK

WORM HOOK

HOOKS FOR PLASTIC WORMS

KEEL HOOK

FISH WITH THE ORIGINALS!!
Saltwater Legends of Luhr Jensen

Krocodile®

An all-time favorite for casting, trolling or jigging that practically guarantees success. Also available with Tube Tail or Buck Tail.

Crippled Herring®

This versatile lure's natural appearance and action tempts all baitfish-eating species. In sizes up to 20-oz. for the deep, big ones!

Pet® Spoon

A Tony Accetta original whose wounded minnow action has become legend. Available with or without feathered hook.

Hobo®

Another of Tony Accetta's famous salt water lures that features a weedless, feathered hook.

Mr. Champ®

A slab-sided, solid brass lure that casts like a bullet and runs deep. Can be trolled, cast or jigged. Available with Tube Tail or Buck Tail.

Javelin™

A heavy-weight 1 1/4-oz casting minnow specifically designed for surf casting in windy conditions.

Luhr Jensen & Sons
P. O .Box 297
Hood River, OR 97031

Available Now At Your Tackle Counter or Have Your Dealer Write:

LUHR-JENSEN™
"Where Legends Live."

236

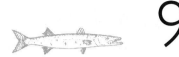

9

Baits and Lures

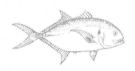

Natural baits are no less important in salt water than they are in fresh water. That fact is well known to anyone who has seen a school of ravenous bluefish slash viciously into a horde of spearing, mossbunkers, or the like.

What natural saltwater baits should you use and when? Those are questions that only time and experience can help you answer accurately. Generally, you will find that it pays to use any bait that is prevalent when and where you are fishing. A few discreet questions at a bait shop in the fishing area will go a long way toward helping you choose a productive bait.

How you rig a saltwater bait can be a vital factor. The primary consideration in rigging most baits is to make them appear as lifelike as possible, whether they are to be trolled, cast out and retrieved, or bounced on the bottom. The upcoming drawings show proven ways to prepare and rig the most popular baits used in salt water.

HOW TO CATCH BAIT AND KEEP IT FRESH

Anglers are often puzzled if they have to catch and keep something other than a dozen worms for a day's fishing. Catching the various baits and keeping them alive and kicking is not difficult.

SEA WORMS

Sea worms, such as blood- and sandworms, are delicate and should be kept in damp seaweed. If they are to be kept for a week or so, spread them out in seaweed and keep them refrigerated. Blood- and sandworms are enemies and should be kept separate. Use a wood partition to divide your bait box into two compartments.

MINNOWS

There are several ways to collect minnows: minnow trap, drop or umbrella net, minnow seine, or the cast net. Remember, saltwater fishing requires saltwater minnows.

Caution: A fishing license is usually required to take bait in fresh water, and many states set limits on the number of baitfish that may be kept. Check the fishing regulations of your state before netting or trapping.

The minnow trap requires the least skill to use. It works on the principle that a small fish will swim into the funnel-like openings after food and be unable to find its way out. For bait, you should wet oatmeal or cornmeal and roll it into balls the size of golfballs.

A minnow seine is fun to use and an effective way to collect bait. A 20-foot net is about right for beginners. Two fishermen wade about 100 feet from the beach and sweep the net along the bottom toward shore. Bait will be trapped and carried up on shore. (VIN T. SPARANO)

The meal will break up gradually in the trap and provide bait for long periods.

The best place to set the trap is in shallow water near a dock or boathouse. On streams, set it near the head or side of a pool where the current is slow.

The drop or umbrella net, which measures 36 by 36 inches, gets more immediate results but may be more difficult to use. Lower it into the water just deep enough so that you can still lift it fast.

A drop or dip net can be used from any dock or bulkhead. Most nets are 36 by 36 inches. Lower it in the water just deep enough so that you can lift it fast. Sprinkle bread crumbs over the net. When minnows gather to fed on the crumbs, lift the net fast and collect your bait.

Sprinkle breadcrumbs over it and let them sink. When minnows begin to feed on the crumbs, lift the net fast. With practice, you'll make good hauls every time.

A minnow seine not only produces a lot of bait, but is fun to use, especially in bays and tidal rivers. A seine is usually 4 feet high and anywhere from 10 to 50 feet long, with lead weights along the bottom and floats on top. A 20-footer is a good size for most purposes. Seining is easy. Two people carry the seine about 100 feet from shore or until depth hits 4 feet or so. Keeping the weighted end of the seine on the bottom, the people sweep toward shore. The seine will belly out, catching everything in its path and carrying bait up on shore, where it can be picked up.

The cast net is one of the most useful tools of both the freshwater and saltwater angler because he can use it to get the bait that he can't buy, and to obtain forage baitfish native to the water that he's fishing—which is the best bait to use under most circumstances.

A few states prohibit the use of cast nets, or restrict sizes or materials. Again, check the fishing regulations of your state before netting.

Monofilament nets, because their nylon strands are stiff, open better than nets made of braided threads. Mono nets also sink faster and are less visible after they're thrown into the water. Generally, they catch more fish, but they're also more expensive.

Cast nets are available in various sizes and types. Experts throw 16-foot and larger nets, but anglers who would only use them occasionally are better off getting one that measures 8 to 10 feet. Bridge nets, popular in the Florida Keys, are short nets with extra lead weights around the bottom. When the net is dropped off a bridge into deep water, its added weight allows it to sink quickly and hold baitfish before they dive.

(continued on page 244)

NATURAL BAITS FOR SALTWATER FISH

SPECIES OF FISH	NATURAL BAITS AND LURES	RECOMMENDED METHODS	HOOKS
Albacore	Feather lures	Trolling	7/0
Amberjack	Strip baits, feathers, spoons, plugs	Trolling, casting	6/0 to 9/0
Barracuda	Bait fish, plugs, feathers, spoons	Trolling, casting	1/0 to 8/0
Bass, California kelp	Sardines, anchovies, clams, mussels, sea worms, shrimp	Trolling, casting, still-fishing	1 to 1/0
Bass, channel	Mullet, mossbunker, crab, clam, spoons, plugs	Casting, still-fishing, trolling	6/0 to 10/0
Bass, giant sea	Cut bait, mullet, mackerel, sardines	Still-fishing, trolling	12/0 to 14/0
Bass, sea	Squid, clam, sea worm, crab, killie	Drifting, still-fishing	1/0 to 5/0
Bass, striped	Sea worm, clam, eel, metal squids, plugs, jigs, live mackerel	Casting, trolling, drifting, still-fishing	2/0 to 8/0
Billfish (sailfish, marlin, swordfish)	Balao, mackerel, squid, bonito, strip baits, feathered jigs	Trolling	4/0 to 12/0
Bluefish	Rigged eel, cut bait, butterfish, plugs, spoons, feathers	Trolling, casting, drifting, still-fishing	3/0 to 8/0
Bonefish	Cut bait (mainly sardine and conch), flies, plugs, spoons	Casting, drifting, still-fishing	1/0 to 4/0
Bonito	Feather lures, spoons	Trolling	4/0 to 6/0
Codfish	Clam, crab, cut bait	Still-fishing, drifting	7/0 to 9/0
Croaker	Sand bugs, mussels, clam, sardine, sea worm	Still-fishing, casting,	1/0 to 6/0
Dolphin	Bait fish, feather lures, spoons, plugs, streamer flies	Trolling, casting	2/0 to 6/0
Eel	Killie, clam, crab, sea worm, spearing	Still-fishing, drifting, casting	6 to 1/0
Flounder, summer	Squid, spearing, sea worm, clam, killie, smelt	Drifting, casting, still-fishing	4/0 to 6/0
Flounder, winter	Sea worm, mussel, clam	Still-fishing	6 to 12 (long-shank)
Grouper	Squid, mullet, sardine, balao, shrimp, crab, plugs	Still-fishing, casting	4/0 to 12/0
Grunt	Shrimp, crab, sea worm	Still-fishing	2 to 1/0
Haddock	Clam, conch, crab, cut bait	Still-fishing	1/0 to 4/0
Hake	Clam, conch, crab, cut bait	Still-fishing	2/0 to 6/0
Halibut	Squid, crab, sea worm, killie, shrimp	Still-fishing	3/0 to 10/0
Jack Crevallé	Bait fish, cut bait, feathers, metal squid, spoons, plugs	Trolling, still-fishing, casting, drifting	1/0 to 5/0
Jewfish	Mullet, other bait fish	Still-fishing	10/0 to 12/0
Ladyfish	Killie, shrimp, flies, spoons, plugs	Trolling, casting, still-fishing, drifting	1/0 to 5/0
Ling	Clam, crab, cut bait	Still-fishing	4 to 2/0
Mackerel	Bait fish, tube lures, jigs, spinners, streamer flies	Trolling, still-fishing, casting drifting	3 to 6
Perch, white	Sea worm, shrimp, spearing, flies, spoons	Still-fishing, casting	2 to 6
Pollack	Squid strip, clam, feather lures	Still-fishing, trolling	6/0 to 9/0
Pompano	Sand bugs, jigs, plugs, flies	Trolling, casting, drifting, still-fishing	1 to 4
Porgy	Clam, squid, sea worm, crab, mussel, shrimp	Still-fishing	4 to 1/0
Rockfish, Pacific	Herring, sardine, mussel, squid, clam, shrimp	Still-fishing, drifting	1/0 to 8/0
Snapper, mangrove	Cut bait, shrimp	Trolling, still-fishing, drifting	1/0 to 6/0
Snapper, red	Shrimp, mullet, crab	Trolling, still-fishing, drifting	6/0 to 10/0
Snapper, yellowtail	Shrimp, mullet, crab	Trolling, still-fishing	4 to 1/0
Snook	Crab, shrimp, bait fish, plugs, spoons, spinners, feathers	Casting, drifting, still-fishing	2/0 to 4/0
Sole	Clam, sea worm	Still-fishing	4 to 6
Spot	Crab, shrimp, bait fish, sea worm	Still-fishing	8 to 10
Tarpon	Cut bait, bait fish, plugs, spoons, feathers	Trolling, casting, drifting, still-fishing	4/0 to 10/0
Tautog (blackfish)	Clam, sea worm, crab, shrimp	Still-fishing	6 to 2/0
Tomcod	Clam, mussel, shrimp	Still-fishing	6 to 1/0
Tuna, bluefin	Mackerel, flying fish, bonito, squid, dolphin, herring, cut bait, feathered jigs	Trolling	6/0 to 14/0
Wahoo	Bait fish, feather jigs, spoons, plugs	Trolling, casting	4/0 to 8/0
Weakfish	Shrimp, squid, sea worm	Still-fishing, casting, drifting, trolling	1 to 4/0
Whiting, northern	Sea worm, clam	Still-fishing, drifting, casting	4 to 1/0
Yellowtail	Herring, sardine, smelt, spoons, metal squids, feather lures	Trolling, casting, still-fishing	4/0 to 6/0

HOW TO RIG SALTWATER BAITS

Two Ways to Hook Live Baitfish

Two-Hook Baitfish Rig for Short-Striking Fish

Hooking Half a Baitfish

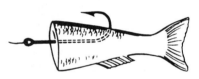

Rigging a Mullet or Grunt for Bottom Fishing

Plug-Cut Baitfish

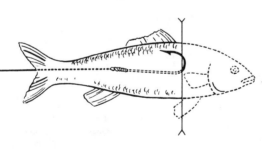

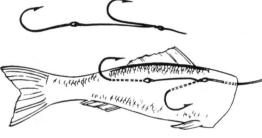

Front part of fish is discarded. Hook with wire leader is threaded through body, and the hook is embedded at the front with its point exposed.

Can be cast out and retrieved like a plug. Especially productive for big snook and tarpon.

Preparing and Using Menhaden as Cut Bait

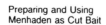

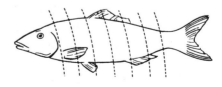

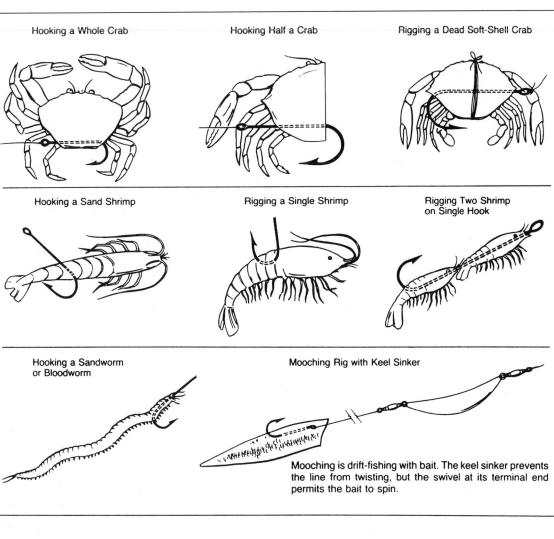

Hooking a Whole Crab

Hooking Half a Crab

Rigging a Dead Soft-Shell Crab

Hooking a Sand Shrimp

Rigging a Single Shrimp

Rigging Two Shrimp on Single Hook

Hooking a Sandworm or Bloodworm

Mooching Rig with Keel Sinker

Mooching is drift-fishing with bait. The keel sinker prevents the line from twisting, but the swivel at its terminal end permits the bait to spin.

SALTWATER BAIT RIGS

Rigging a Whole Unweighted Eel

Hooks are attached to light chain or heavy monofilament, or they can be attached to linen line.

Rigging an Eelskin with Metal Squid

To a Montauk or Belmar-type metal squid, a ring is attached, onto which the eelskin is tied.

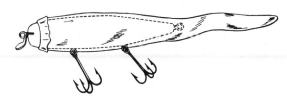

Rigging an Eelskin with Plug

Eelskin is slipped over the plug, whose tail treble hook has been removed. Bottom treble hooks protrude as shown, and skin is tied on at the plug's head.

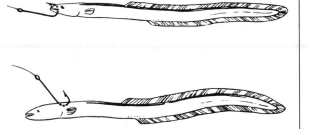

Two Ways to Hook a Live Eel

241

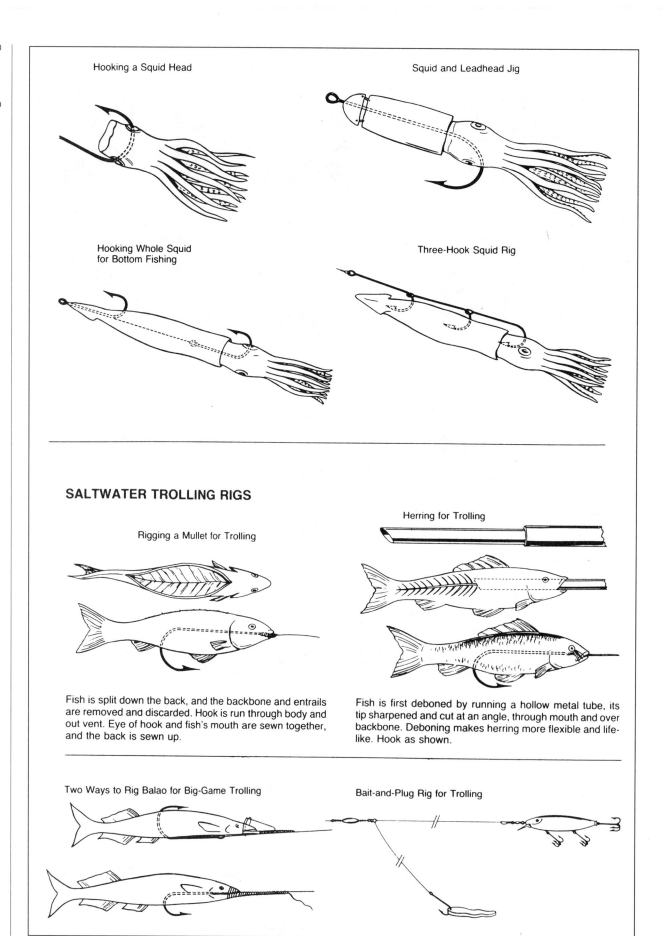

Hooking a Squid Head

Squid and Leadhead Jig

Hooking Whole Squid
for Bottom Fishing

Three-Hook Squid Rig

SALTWATER TROLLING RIGS

Rigging a Mullet for Trolling

Herring for Trolling

Fish is split down the back, and the backbone and entrails are removed and discarded. Hook is run through body and out vent. Eye of hook and fish's mouth are sewn together, and the back is sewn up.

Fish is first deboned by running a hollow metal tube, its tip sharpened and cut at an angle, through mouth and over backbone. Deboning makes herring more flexible and life-like. Hook as shown.

Two Ways to Rig Balao for Big-Game Trolling

Bait-and-Plug Rig for Trolling

Rigging a Whole Eel with Tin Squid for Trolling and Casting

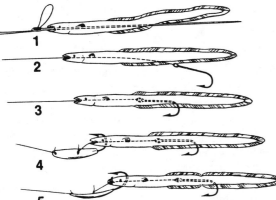

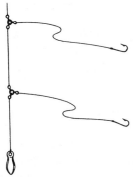

To rig an eel this way, you'll need a long needle with an eye. Form a loop in some relatively heavy line (about 36-pound-test) and run the loop through the needle's eye. Run the needle through the eel from mouth to vent **(Drawing No. 1)**. Pull the loop all the way through the eel, and attach to it a 6/0 to 8/0 hook **(Drawing No. 2)**. Draw protruding line and hook shank into eel **(Drawing No. 3)**. Take a small block-tin squid, and run its hook through the eel's head (or lips) from bottom to top, and tie the line to the eye on the flat surface of the squid **(Drawing No. 4)**. With light line, tie eel's mouth shut, make a tie around the eel's head where the hook protrudes to prevent the hook from ripping out, and make a similar tie around the vent **(Drawing No. 5)**.

MORE SALTWATER BOTTOM RIGS

High-Low
Codfish Rig

Typical
Bottom-Fishing Rig

Spreader Rig
for Bottom Fishing

Fish-Finder Rigs

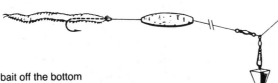

The small piece of cork is used to keep bait off the bottom and away from crabs. Use a wire leader when fishing for sharp-toothed fish, such as bluefish.

Combination Surf Rig

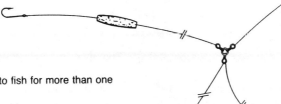

This rig enables the surf angler to fish for more than one species at a time.

243

A plastic bucket is the best storage container for a net. All nets should routinely be rinsed with clean water and cleared of debris.

The proper gripping technique is just as important as the method you use to throw the net. If you're right-handed, you should coil the throwing line and loop it in your right hand. Stretch the net full-length, and grab the net two-thirds of the way down with your left hand. Then bring your right hand (which is still holding the coils) just below your left hand and grasp the net, with your thumb pointing outward. Reach down to the bottom of the net with your left hand, pick up the weighted line at the bottom of the net, and drape the inside of the net over your right shoulder.

Gather about two-thirds of the net in your left hand, and with your feet pointing in the direction in which you'll throw the net, rotate the upper half of your body to the right. You're now ready to cast—just throw the net straight out in front of you.

The next problem is keeping the minnows alive and fresh. The water must be aerated to keep enough oxygen in the bucket for survival, and this can be done in several ways. Water can be aerated by battery-powered devices. You can also aerate the water manually with a tin can. Scoop up a canful of water and pour it back into the bucket from a height of 2 feet. Doing this a dozen times every 15 minutes should provide sufficient oxygen for a couple of dozen minnows.

Bait water must be kept at a constant temperature. In summer, add ice cubes to the water before transporting them. As the ice melts, it will cool the water and add oxygen. Take care, however, not to cool the water too fast.

It is important to avoid abrupt temperature changes, which will kill minnows.

If you plan to troll, keep bait in a bucket designed for trolling. This bucket, built to float on its side, will take water at an angle and aerate it.

If you're stillfishing, use the traditional bucket, which is actually two buckets. The outer bucket is used when transporting minnows. When you start fishing, lift out the insert and lower it into the water. The insert, which floats upright, is vented so that water is constantly changed.

ARTIFICIAL LURES

Fishing with bait is enjoyable, certainly, but there's something about fooling a fish with an artificial that gives most anglers a special charge.

A neophyte fisherman who visits a well-stocked sporting-goods store or tackle shop is confronted with a bewildering array of plugs, spoons, spinners, jigs, flies,

bugs, and others. Some artificials look like nothing that ever swam, crawled, or flew, and yet they catch fish.

Let's look at each type of artificial and see how and why it works and how it should be fished.

PLUGS

Plugs are lures designed to imitate small fish for the most part, though some plugs simulate mice, frogs, eels, and other food on which gamefish feed. Plug action—meaning the way it moves when retrieved by the angler—is important and is something on which manufacturers expend much money and time. Many plugs, particularly the divers, are known as crankbaits because every crank of the reel handle imparts some sort of diving or darting action.

The type, size, and weight of the plug you select is determined by the fish you are after and the kind of fishing outfit you are using. The charts, found elsewhere in this book, on how to match up various kinds of fishing tackle will help the beginner choose the right weight plugs.

There are five basic types of plugs: popping, surface, floating-diving, sinking (deep-running), and deep-diving.

Popping

These plugs float on the surface and have concave, hollowed-out faces. The angler retrieves a popping plug by jerking the rod tip back so that the plug's face digs into the water, making a small splash, bubbles, and a popping sound. Some make a louder sound than others. This sound is especially attractive to some inshore saltwater species, such as striped bass and bluefish. Most popping plugs (and most other plugs) have two sets of treble hooks. Popping plugs are most productive when the water surface is calm or nearly so. They should usually be fished very slowly.

Surface

These plugs float on the surface, but they can be fished with various kinds of retrieves and create a different kind of surface disturbance than poppers do. Designed with an elongated, or bullet-shaped, head, they create surface disturbance by various means, including propellers (at the head or at both head and tail), a wide metal lip at the head, and hinged metal "wings" just behind the head. They can be twitched so that they barely nod, retrieved steadily so that they chug across the water, or skimmed across the top as fast as the angler can turn his reel handle. The proper retrieve depends on the lure's design and, of course, on the mood of the fish. It's best to try different retrieves until you find one that produces. Good saltwater surface plugs include the MirrOlure (float model), which is good for small species, and the Zara Spook.

The Rapala Magnum is typical of deep-running saltwater plugs. It measures 9 inches and weighs 3½ ounces. Plugs of this type are effective on both inshore and offshore fish.

Floating-Diving

These plugs are designed to float when at rest and dive when retrieved. Some float horizontally while others float with the tail hanging down beneath the surface. They are made to dive by an extended lip at the head. The speed of the retrieve determines the depth of the dive. The faster the retrieve, the deeper the dive. Most of these plugs have a side-to-side wobbling action. An erratic retrieve—dive, surface, dive, surface—is often productive, and these plugs are also effective when made to swim just above a submerged weed bed, rock pile, and so on. Good saltwater floater-divers include the Thinfin Silver Shad and larger models of the Rebel Shiner and the Creek Chub Darter.

Sinking (Deep-running)

These plugs sink as soon as they hit the water and are designed for deep work. Some sink slower than others and can be fished at various depths, depending on how long the angler waits before starting his retrieve. Most of these plugs have some sort of wobbling action, and some fairly vibrate when retrieved. Some have propellers fore and aft.

These plugs are excellent fish-finders: the fisherman can start by bouncing them along bottom, and if that doesn't work, he can work them at progressively shallower depths until he finds at what depth the fish are feeding.

The Boone Needlefish has taken its share of striped bass, bluefish, and weakfish in bays, off jetties and from the surf. The Boone T.D. Special is good for salt water at any depth and has proved useful on New Jersey's striped bass. The MirrOlure (sinking model) is a big lure that casts easy and sinks fast. The shiny-sided plug draws strikes from striped bass, bluefish, tarpon, snook, barracuda, and similar inshore species.

Deep-Diving

These plugs may float or sink, but all are designed with long and/or broad lips of metal or plastic that cause the plugs to dive to depths of 30 feet or more as the angler reels in. As with other diving plugs, the faster the retrieve, the deeper the dive. Most of these lures have some sort of wobbling action. They are ideally suited for casting or trolling in deep lakes and at the edges of dropoffs, and they work best in most waters when the fish are holding in deep holes, as fish usually do during the midday in July and August.

Good diving plugs for saltwater include the Atom and the Rebel for casting or trolling, the Creek Chub Surfster for surf casting, and the Stan Gibbs Darter for nearly all inshore species.

SPOONS

Spoons are among the oldest of artificials. If you cut the handle off a teaspoon, you'd have the basic shape of this lure.

Spoons are designed to imitate small baitfish of one kind or another, so flash is an important feature in many of these lures. Most spoons have a wobbling side-to-side action when retrieved.

Many spoons have a silver or gold finish, while others are painted in various colors and combinations of colors. Most have a single free-swinging treble hook at the tail; others have a single fixed hook. Weedless arrangements are becoming more and more popular on both types.

Here are some good saltwater spoons:

Cop-E-Cat: Big mackerel-finish spoon has action similar to the well-known Dardevle, except it is designed for casting and trolling in coastal waters. Trolled deep on wire line it will take bluefish. When it is cast from surf or boat it will take stripers.

Seadevle: Similar to the Cop-E-Cat, except slimmer, this spoon is built for saltwater casting and trolling. Large sizes will get strikes from stripers, bluefish, yellowtails. Small models will catch mackerel, pollack.

Reed R.T. Flash: Well-designed spoon that can be cast, trolled, jigged. Good lure in coastal waters for tinker mackerel, snappers, weakfish, kingfish. Trolled off shore with wire line or trolling lead, it takes bigger inshore species.

Wob-L-Rite: A heavy brass spoon, easy to cast far distances. Wobbles on steady retrieve or can be jigged. Good choice for deep jigging reef species or surf and boat casting.

Tony Accetta Spoon: Available in various sizes, this spoon has proven itself in coastal waters. Usually rigged with pork rind strip, it is an effective trolling and casting lure for nearly all inshore game fish.

SPINNERS

Spinners, like spoons, are designed to imitate baitfish, and they attract gamefish by flash and vibration. A spinner is simply a metal blade mounted on a shaft by means of a revolving arm or ring called a clevis. Unlike a spoon, which has a wobbling action, a spinner blade rotates around the shaft when retrieved.

Good saltwater spinners include the Willow Leaf, particularly effective when trolling blood or sandworms for striped bass, and the Indiana Double-Blade, a multi-purpose spinner rig that can be cast or trolled. The Indiana has been used on party boats drifting cut bait along the bottom for fluke and flounder.

JIGS

Generally speaking, a jig is any lure with a weighted head (usually lead), a fixed hook, and a tail of bucktail (though not always), feathers, nylon, or similar material. Jigs are made in sizes of $1/16$ ounce to 6 ounces and even heavier, and they will take just about any fish that swims in fresh water and salt. Jigs imitate baitfish, crustaceans, and other gamefish forage. In some jigs, the hook rides with the point up, to minimize the chance of snagging.

Jigs, and related lures, take many forms. Here's a look at the most popular types.

Bucktail jigs, such as this Hopkins model, will catch fish at nearly any depth. Cast the jig, let it sink to the bottom, then jig the lure to the surface until you determine the depth at which the fish are feeding. Jigs are sometimes more effective when tipped with cut bait, shrimp, or a plastic worm.

Feathered Jig

Often called Japanese feathers, this jig is commonly used in saltwater trolling and casting. It consists of a heavy metal head with eyes. Through the head runs a wire leader, to the end of which the hook is attached. Running from the head down to the hook is a long tail, usually of feathers. A plastic sleeve covers the feathers for about half their length.

Bonito Jig

Similar to the feathered jig but smaller and having a fixed hook embedded in the metal head. Line is tied to ring on head. Used for saltwater trolling and casting.

Bucktail Jig

Consists of a lead head, embedded hook, and trailing tail of bucktail. Head has ring to which line is attached. Head is painted, with the most popular colors being white, red, yellow, and combinations of those colors. The most popular member of the jig family, bucktail jigs are used on a wide variety of freshwater and saltwater gamefish, especially striped bass, bluefish, and many other bottom-feeders.

Bullet Bucktail Jig

Same as standard bucktail jig except that head is bullet-shaped, coming to a blunt point.

Metal (Block-Tin) Squids

Falling under the general category of jigs are these lures, which are used mostly in salt water for striped bass, bluefish, and the like. Made to resemble baitfish, they have a long, narrow body of block tin, stainless steel, chrome, or nickel-plated lead and either a single fixed hook or a free-swinging treble hook, with or without a tail of bucktail. Most metal squids range in length from 3 to 6 inches. All have bright finishes, usually silvery; in some the finish is smooth, while others have a hammered finish that gives a scalelike appearance. Among the most popular metal squids are types such as the Hopkins (which has a hammered finish; a long, narrow, flat body; and a free-swinging treble hook), the diamond jig (four-sided body, treble hook), and the sand eel (long, rounded, undulating body). A strip of pork rind often adds to the effectiveness of metal squids.

Jig and Eel

Consists of a small metal squid onto which is rigged a common eel, either the real McCoy (usually dead and preserved) or a plastic artificial. These rigged eels range in length from about 6 inches up to a foot or longer. The jig and eel is a deadly combination for striped bass, big snook, redfish, and sea trout. Best retrieve depends on various conditions, but usually a slow, slightly erratic swimming motion is best. Good saltwater jig-and-eel rigs include the Hopkins Swimming Tail, the

Hopkins Shorty ST, the Block Tin Squid, and the Diamond—the mainstay of East Coast deep jiggers.

How do you fish a jig? Most jigs—except the jig-and-eel combination and those designed for trolling—should be retrieved with sharp upward jerks of the rod tip so that they look like fleeing darting bait. Most jigs have little action of their own (though some are designed to wiggle when retrieved), so the angler must impart fish-attracting motion.

Diamond Jig: The mainstay of East Coast deep jiggers. Simple in design, it takes stripers, blues, mackerel, cod, pollock, and similar species. Frequently used in conjunction with one or more surgical tube teasers attached one foot or so above the jig.

Block-Tin Squid: An old favorite, with a pork rind strip, has proven itself a good casting and trolling rig for stripers, bluefish, and other inshore species.

SALTWATER TROLLING LURES

Here are a number of saltwater trolling lures that have proved effective:

Artificial Eel: With lead head and double hooks, weighing six ounces and measuring 18 inches, it's the heaviest artificial eel made. Excellent for big striped bass and other large saltwater gamefish.

Barracuda Jig: A rig more commonly known as Japanese feathers, it is basically a trolling lure for offshore work on billfish, tuna, albacore, and bluefish.

Tony Accetta Pet Spoon: Big with a single fixed hook, this type of lure is more commonly known as a bunker spoon. It can be trolled with large strip of pork rind or an eel. One of the most effective lures for striped bass.

Leisure Lures' Plastic Squid: With long wire leader running through body and attached to single hook, this

---

Care and Repair

Take a close look at your tackle box. It probably represents a bigger investment than your rods and reels. Saltwater lures, for example, cost as much as $30 or so. I fill a bucket to the top with soapy water and drop all the lures I've used in it. Swab them around for a few minutes, then rinse them off with a hose. Let them dry before you put them back in the tackle box or canvas bag.

Examine all hooks on lures and discard rusty hooks and all lures that are beyond repair. A soft-wire soap pad can restore a finsish on plugs, spoons, and spinners. If the hooks are rusty or broken, replace them. It's a good rainy-day project.

Don't leave rusty gear in your tackle box. Rust seems to be contagious. If you see rusty stuff, either clean it or throw it away.

---

rig is designed for offshore trolling for billfish, tuna, albacore, bluefish, and similar species.

Plastic Trolling Lures: A variety of soft and hard-headed ones for canyon and offshore fishing. All are effective for marlin, sailfish, tuna and other bluewater species.

Umbrella Rig: A fishing lure with four wire arms, each supporting two or three surgical-tube lures. A single tube is trailed from the center. Designed to imitate a school of sand eels or baitfish, the umbrella rig is extremely effective on the East Coast for saltwater fish, especially bluefish. The umbrella rig is always trolled.

The Candy Man

by Jerry Gibbs

You ask why a six-foot-three, 260-pound Marine Vietnam vet is frolicking in a rose garden? I'll tell you my theory—but first you should know that this is one extraordinary rose garden, the kind that compels passersby to stop their cars and wander, drawn like hummingbirds to the incredible burst of color vibrating from trellises of climbers and intricate topiaries of

bush plants. Men, it seems, relate to this even more strongly than women. The garden is outside the landmark Shady Rest Restaurant on Route 9 in Bayville, New Jersey, a beautiful rococo device that draws intrigued visitors into the restaurant. It's a tender trap because the food, which centers on sea fare and pasta, is very good.

The garden, I think, reflects its

owner's insatiable infatuation with color, patterns and creative design—abundantly evident inside, as well. Like a bowerbird, Bob Popovics, the ex-Marine turned restaurateur, has created in his Shady Rest a small haven evocative of his passion for fish and the art of angling. Giant aquariums of exotic fish species line the walls. There are handsome fish carvings behind Plexiglas, a gemlike fly-tying display and an exquisite hand-crafted net, the twin of which was presented to former President Bush. Although there's no denying Popovics' passion for angling artifacts that have been elevated to artforms, anglers know his fascination with color, design and fine craftsmanship through the man's own work. It is for his unique, tradition-breaking fly patterns that Bob Popovics has stormed to prominence in the modern angling world. It happened quickly.

In 1970, newly married and back in Seaside Park, New Jersey, after his stint with the First Marine Air Wing Division in Danang, Popovics and his pals Butch Colvin and Jim McGee were into hot bluefish one day, when Bob glanced over his shoulder. "I suddenly saw these bright, thick lines going out like party streamers and realized they were fly lines. I'd never tried it, always wanted to, and told Butch. Within the week he and his dad, Cap, had me in front of Cap Colvin's tackle shop, casting over the street. I got excited right away.

"Soon after, it was my birthday, and Butch came to our house to watch the Ranger-Bruins hockey game. In a cardboard beer flat, he had an old vise, tools, bucktails, feathers. He said 'Happy Birthday!' I told him, 'Ah, Butch, I can't do that; look at these big hands.' He said, 'You're going to learn between periods.' I liked it right away—and then I went crazy over it. Butch made me keep an open mind. There was no tradition in saltwater fly tying. 'We've not been told things we can't do,' he said. 'There's always a way, so do it.'"

Popovics did exactly that, first collaborating with Colvin on a method to produce big extended-body streamers that imitate menhaden (mossbunker), then going on to create an entire family of patterns that hold no traditional allegiance to construction or materials. Go back to the '60s, though, and you'd have no hint that a cult of Popfleye (as he calls his creations), and Popovics enthusiasts were destined to burst onto the fishing scene. Back then there was no

Bob Popovics, creator of the hard-bodied Candy flies, works over a school of breaking stripers in Barnegat Inlet, New Jersey.
(VIN T. SPARANO)

rose garden, and the restaurant was called the Shady Rest Pizza Parlor and Cabins. Although he'd always worked in the family business, young Popovics had just finished schooling as a computer programmer when the invitation from the Marine Corps arrived: "Why don't you join us;" it read, "you don't have to go right away...."

"Fifteen minutes after reading the invite, I went and signed up, and my mother said, 'Oh, God, why the Marines?' Well, it's what I wanted to do."

You have little doubt he has always done just that. Bob is a hands-on, can-do kind of guy with a quixotic artistic flare. A natural leader, he draws a loyal circle of friends now, as he did back in the Corps when stress-reducing R&R took the form of friendly wrestling free-for-alls—the usual drill was several buddies trying to take down big Bob. But there were serious times, too. Popovics' smile vanishes with the memory of pulling a recruit through a personal crisis during an endless night of shelling. "I had to knock him down," he says softly, "then sit on him all night."

As a kid living a block from the Delaware River in Trenton, New Jer-

sey, he'd always fished some. When the family moved to Seaside Park, Bob sometimes joined his surf-fishing father. "I liked it, but I wasn't truly affected by it until I came back from the service," he says. "It wasn't until Alexis and I married that I got wild about it. It was a social thing somehow; all the friends I met—it was all around fishing."

In 1970, there was still much for Bob to learn. Along with fly tying, Butch Colvin began showing Popovics the intricacies of fishing Barnegat Bay. By 1978, computer programming a fast-fading memory, Bob and Alexis became full owners of the Shady Rest and the ceaseless demands of the restaurant business.

Happily, peak restaurant season corresponds with slow fishing periods. "From Memorial Day to Labor Day it's a relentless seven-days-a-week run in the heat at the restaurant," he'll tell you. "After that, we get a migration of mullet that coincides with the migration of people leaving the shore, and that starts the fall fishing season."

Bob fishes locally or up in Martha's Vineyard or maybe a trip out of the country from fall into December, when it's back to the Shady Rest for Christmas season. January through March, he bounces between the restaurant and personal fly-tying appearances. And always, he is plotting new fly patterns based on need, not the orgasmically wild and often purposeless creations of some nonfishing tiers. The simple, durable Candy flies for which he may be best known, are typical.

Tired of losing good flies to the teeth of bluefish, Bob built a creation with a fishform epoxy head that creates a tooth-impervious shield over tying thread and synthetic wing material from shank to hook bend. To prove the pattern's durability, he caught 30 blues on one Candy before retiring it. A chewed epoxy head, he found, can be restored to new with a light coat of Sally Hansen's Hard-As Nails. Eventually, the epoxy head Candies evolved into a family of flies that suggest a variety of forage forms. Many spin fishermen use them as teasers ahead of their plugs.

A shorter version of his big off-shore fly came after a frustrating late-season day in the surf with bass feeding on rainfish (bay anchovies). "There were bass that looked 40 pounds, but we couldn't get them to eat. That night, I realized I'd thrown everything at them but something big. I came up with a slightly downsized version of my offshore Big Boy. At first light the next morning, with a raw north wind going, I took a 12-pound fish on the new pattern. My hands were so cold I couldn't take out the hook. The next fish just annihilated the fly. My hands were so cold I couldn't control the reel. I think it was the biggest bass I've ever had on, and I blew it. But the Cotton Candy fly was born!"

The stuff that seals your bathtub figured in another of Bob's break-through patterns. It is silicone that coats a fleece head, soft and squishy-feeling.

"I loved soft-plastic baits for fresh-water bass," Bob tells me. "These are like that. After it cured I threw the first one in the water. It floated. What a great mullet imitation waking on the surface, I thought. Squeeze the trapped air from the head and the fly sinks. So many ways to fish it. Rub on a little fresh silicone to fix the tears from fish teeth. I call them Siliclones."

The new flies have obvious fresh-water application for pike, muskies, bass, but more was yet coming. Exhausted from his creative high with the Siliclones, Popovics felt he'd hit the wall with new patterns, but friend Ed Jaworowski wouldn't let him rest. "What we need is a real swimming fly," Jaworowski insisted.

"Well, my friend Sal Ribarro had been fooling around with hard lips to make flies swim—even tried women's artificial fingernails. I'd messed with other kinds of hard lips before, but they're tough to pull from the water. But now I had silicone, and the next day I had the fly."

I want to know about the lip and Bob says, "Oh, yeah, the Poplips. It's really a Siliclone with one extra step—a fleece beard covered with silicone to make a lip that bends back a little on the pick-up. That makes it easier casting than a hard lip. But they swim . . . man, the first time I saw one go, I just started chuckling.

At a table in the Shady Rest, we're joined by Sal Ribarro and Bob's police officer pal Lance Erwin, who relates how the Poplips fly is supreme during conditions that would also favor swimming plugs—easy swells, gentle currents. Because the lip digs in, swells or wind don't ruin the retrieve, as can happen with normal streamers.

There are so many more patterns. What's his favorite? "I like the Surf Candy a lot, and the Siliclones," Bob thinks aloud. "But maybe the Banger. It is the Banger. I've never had to create another popper after that!"

Bob leaps from the table for the kitchen and returns with a pizza, which he has made himself. He places it on the table, watching, pleased.

"He won't let anybody else make the pizza when he's got friends," Sal says. It turns out to be wonderful pizza.

When the Salt Water Fly Rodders of America disbanded about 1978, local flyfishers had no real home. Popovics' reputation was growing, and by 1987 he was regularly receiving calls from strangers with technical questions, and local anglers began visiting his home on Tuesday nights for informal tying sessions.

"From a handful of guys, we were getting more than 50 people in the house. There'd be people tying, standing in the hallway, crowded in the bathroom, waiting on the steps for a chance at the vises. I said, 'Ah well, we've got a problem. We've got to start a club.'"

The Atlantic Salt Water Fly Rodders was born in April 1992. At a recent count, there were 177 members. An average of 100 members attend summer meetings centered on tying and casting clinics.

The Shady Rest is festive and busy at this evening hour. Non-angling din-ers gaze happily at the saltwater exotics staring back at them behind aquarium glass. Others admire the bonito and sailfish carvings, the tarpon and snook dioramas. At the bar, big screen images come from the TV via projector. Not just ball games: At Christmas, there's a sing-along tape and jigs and reels on St. Patrick's Day.

In this bright place, everyone seems to be having a good time. It's the Popovics rich talent for attraction, just as the man's fascinating fly creations continue drawing enthusiasts from across the United States—including, not insignificantly, the fish.

Many of Popovics' flies—including the Siliclones, Candies, Cotton Candy and Ultra Shrimp, plus a kit to produce the Bangers—are available through Umpqua Feather Merchant dealers. For those nearest you, contact the company at Box 700, Glide, OR 97443 (503-496-3512).

Popovics fly patterns are included in the following books: *Salt Water Fly Tying* by Frank Wentink; *Flies for Bass & Panfish* by Dick Stewart and Farrow Allen; *Flies for Saltwater* by Dick Stewart and Farrow Allen; *Saltwater Fly Patterns* by Lefty Kreh; *A Fly-Fisher's Guide to Saltwater Naturals and Their Imitation* by George V. Roberts Jr. ∎

10

Rigs

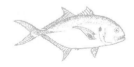

SWIVELS, SINKERS, FLOATS

The items of fishing gear covered here are various components of the rigs shown previously. These accessories are as important as links in a chain, so buy the best you can afford. A well-constructed snap swivel of the correct size, for example, won't literally come apart at the seams under the surge of a good strike.

Swivels come in many forms and sizes, but basically a swivel consists of two or three round metal eyes connected in such a way that each eye can rotate freely and independently of the others. Swivels perform such functions as preventing or reducing line twist, enabling the angler to attach much more than one component (sinker and bait, for example) to his line, and facilitating lure changes.

Sinkers, like swivels, come in many shapes and weights. Usually made of lead, they are used to get a bait (or lure) down to the desired depth.

Floats are lighter-than-water devices that are attached to the line. They keep a bait at a predetermined distance above the bottom and signal the strike of a fish. Floats are usually made of cork or plastic and come in many forms.

SWIVEL DESIGNS

Barrel Swivel

The basic **barrel swivel** is used to join line and leader.

Big-Game Swivel

The **big-game swivel** is for heavy fish. It also comes with locking snap.

Snap Swivel

The **snap swivel** is used to join line and lure.

Coastlock Snap Swivel   Interlock Snap Swivel   Ball-Bearing Swivel

Coastlock snap swivel's end of wire snap hooks around itself, and spring tension keeps the snap locked. This is preferred over the standard snap swivel for sizable fish. The **interlock snap swivel** is stronger than the standard swivel. A **ball-bearing swivel** is less apt to bind than a standard swivel.

Connecting Link   Three-Way Swivel   Cross-Line Swivel

The **connecting link** is used to attach a sinker to a terminal rig and can also be used as a component in a fishfinder rig.

McMahon Snap Swivel   Corkscrew Snap Swivel   Duolock Snap Swivel   Cross-Lok Snap Swivel

SINKER DESIGNS

Split-Shot Sinker   Egg Sinker   Clincher Sinker

With the **split-shot sinker,** line is inserted in slot, and split is pinched on. Split-shot sizes range from BB to OO. Split shot finds widest use in freshwater. With the **egg sinker,** line goes through a hole drilled through the core; can be used as basis of a fish-finder rig since line slides freely through the hole. With the **clincher sinker,** line is inserted in the slot, and the "wing" on each end is pressed over the line.

Pyramid Sinker   Bank Sinker   Dipsey Sinker   Diamond Trolling Sinker

Sharp edges on a **pyramid sinker** dig into sand and mud, resisting pressures of tidal currents and wave action and helping the angler "hold bottom." A **bank sinker** is preferred for fishing when and where tide and waves are no problem; also good for fishing from rocks and jetties, for its rounded edges are apt to slide over rock crevices rather than hang up.

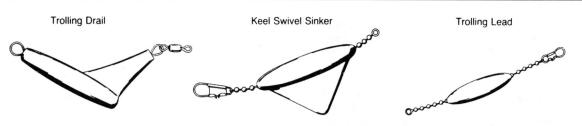

Trolling Drail   Keel Swivel Sinker   Trolling Lead

Trolling drail eliminates line twist, gets bait down deep. **Keel swivel sinker,** used for trolling, eliminates line twist.

TROLLING DEVICES

The trolling planer is a heavily weighted device with metal or plastic "wings" that permit trolling at considerable depths. The bait-walker sinker keeps the bait moving near the bottom but not dragging on the bottom. The downrigger assembly shown has a terminal rig with cable, cannon ball, and multi-bead release.

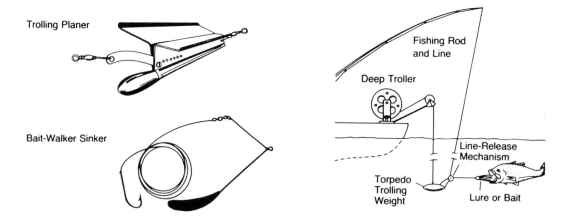

Trolling Planer

Bait-Walker Sinker

Fishing Rod and Line

Deep Troller

Line-Release Mechanism

Torpedo Trolling Weight

Lure or Bait

FLOAT DESIGNS

Plastic Ball Float   Cork Ball Float   Caro-Line Float

In the **plastic ball float,** a spring-loaded top section, when depressed, exposes a small U-shaped "hook" at the bottom into which line is placed. Releasing the top section reseats the "hook" holding the line fast. The **Caro-line cork float** has a doubled length of line running through it lengthwise. The fishing line is run through the loop, and then the loop is pulled through the cork body, seating the line. The Caro-line float is generally used in surf fishing to keep a bait off the bottom and away from crabs.

KNOTS

Anyone who aspires to competence as a fisherman must have at least a basic knowledge of knots. Most anglers know and use no more than half a dozen knots. However, if you fish a lot, you are sure to run into a situation that cannot be solved efficiently with the basic ties. The aim of what follows is to acquaint you with knots that will help you handle nearly all line-tying situations.

All knots reduce—to a greater or lesser degree, depending upon the particular knot—the breaking strength of the line. Loose or poorly tied knots reduce line strength even more. For that reason, and to avoid wasting valuable fishing time, it is best to practice tying the knots at home. In most cases, it's better to practice with cord or rope; the heavier material makes it easier to follow the tying procedures.

It is important to form and tighten knots correctly. They should be tightened slowly and steadily for best results. In most knots requiring the tyer to make turns around the standing part of the line, at least five such turns should be made.

Now let's take a look at the range of fishing knots. Included are tying instructions, the uses for which each knot is suited, and other information.

BLOOD KNOT

Used to connect two lines of relatively similar diameter. Especially popular for joining sections of monofilament in making tapered fly leaders.

1. Wrap one strand around the other at least four times, and run the end into the fork thus formed.

2. Make the same number of turns, in the opposite direction, with the second strand, and run its end through the opening in the middle of the knot, in the direction opposite that of the first strand.

3. Hold the two ends so they do not slip (some anglers use their teeth). Pull the standing part of both strands in opposite directions, tightening the knot.

4. Tighten securely, clip off the ends, and the knot is complete. If you want to tie on a dropper fly, leave one of these ends about 6 to 8 inches long.

STU APTE IMPROVED BLOOD KNOT

Excellent for joining two lines of greatly different diameter, such as a heavy monofilament shock leader and a light leader tippet.

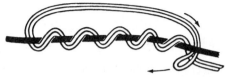

1. Double a sufficient length of the lighter line, wrap it around the standing part of the heavier line at least five times, and run the end of the doubled line into the "fork" thus formed.

2. Wrap the heavier line around the standing part of the doubled lighter line three times, in the opposite direction, and run the end of the heavier line into the opening, in the direction opposite that of the end of the doubled line.

3. Holding the two ends to keep them from slipping, pull the standing parts of the two lines in opposite directions. Tighten the knot completely, using your fingernails to push the loops together if necessary, and clip off the ends.

DOUBLE SURGEON'S KNOT

Used to join two strands of greatly unequal diameter.

1. Place the two lines parallel, with ends pointing in opposite directions. Using the two lines as a single strand, make simple overhand knot, pulling the two strands all the way through loop, and then make another overhand knot.

2. Holding both strands at each end, pull the knot tight and clip off the ends.

IMPROVED CLINCH KNOT

Used to tie flies, bass bugs, lures, and bait hooks to line or leader. This knot reduces line strength only slightly.

1. Run the end of the line through the eye of the lure, fly, or hook, and then make at least five turns around the standing part of the line. Run the end through the opening between the eye and the beginning of the twists, and then run it through the large loop formed by the previous step.

2. Pull slowly on the standing part of the line, being careful that the end doesn't slip back through the large loop and that the knot snugs up against the eye. Clip off end.

DOUBLE-LOOP CLINCH KNOT

Same as Improved Clinch Knot except that line is run through eye twice at the beginning of the tie.

TRILENE® KNOT

Used in joining line to swivels, snaps, hooks and artificial lures, the Trilene Knot is a strong, all-purpose knot that resists slippage and premature failures. It is easy to tie and retains 85–90 percent of the original line strength. The double wrap of monofilament line through the eyelet provides a protective cushion for added safety.

1. Run the end of the line through the eye of the hook or lure and double back through the eye a second time.

2. Loop around the standing part of the line five or six times.

3. Thread the tag end back between the eye and the coils as shown.

4. Pull up tight and trim the tag end.

SHOCKER KNOT

Used to join two lines of unequal diameters.

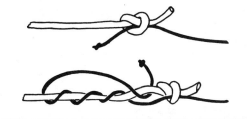

JANSIK SPECIAL KNOT

This is a terminal-tackle connecting knot that is popular with muskie anglers.

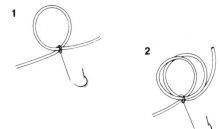

1. Run about 5 inches of line through eye of hook on lure; bring it around in a circle and and run it through again. **2.** Make a second circle, parallel with the first, and pass end of line through eye a third time.

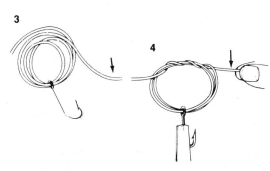

3. Bend standing part of line (identified by arrows) around the two circles. Bring tag end around in a third circle and wrap it three times around the three parallel lines. **4.** Hold hook, swivel, or lure with pliers. Hold standing line with other hand and tag end in teeth. Pull all three to tighten.

ARBOR KNOT

The Arbor Knot provides the angler with a quick, easy connection for attaching line to the reel spool.

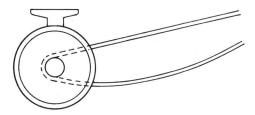

1. Pass line around reel arbor.

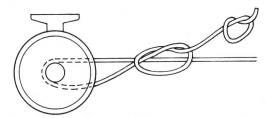

2. Tie an overhand knot around the standing line. **3.** Tie a second overhand knot in the tag end.

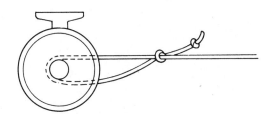

4. Pull tight and snip off excess. Snug down first overhand knot on the reel arbor.

MULTIPLE CLINCH KNOT

Used to join line and leader, especially in baitcasting. This knot slides through rod guides with a minimum of friction.

A loop is tied in the end of the line. Then leader is run into the loops, around the entire loop four times, and then back through the middle of the four wraps.

DOUBLE IMPROVED CLINCH KNOT

Same as Improved Clinch Knot except that line is used doubled throughout entire tie.

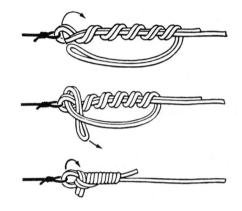

PALOMAR KNOT

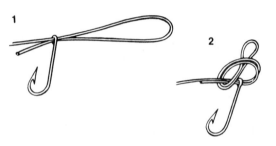

1. Pass line or leader through the eye of the hook and back again to form 3- to 5-inch loop. 2. Hold the line and hook at the eye. With the other hand, bring the loop up and under the double line and tie an overhand knot, but do not tighten.

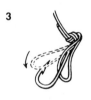

3. Hold the overhand knot. With the other hand, bring the loop over the hook. 4. Pull the line to draw the knot to the top of the eye. Pull both tag end and running line to tighten. Clip tag end off about ⅛ inch from knot.

KING SLING KNOT

This offers the angler an easy-to-tie end loop knot that is used primarily as a connection for crank baits. This knot allows the lure to work freely, making it more lifelike, and resulting in more strikes.

1. Insert tag end of line through artificial bait so that it extends 8 to 10 inches.

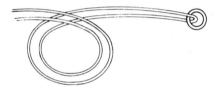

2. Hold the tag end and the standing line in your left hand, and form a loop.

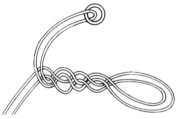

3. With the bait in your right hand make four turns around the tag end and the standing line above the loop.

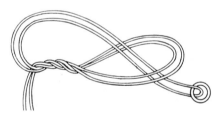

4. Bring the bait down and through the loop.

5. To tighten, hold line above the bait at desired loop length and pull the tag end and the standing line at the same time. 6. Trim the tag end.

DOUBLE SURGEON'S LOOP

This is a quick, easy way to tie a loop in the end of a leader. It is often used as part of a leader system because it is relatively strong.

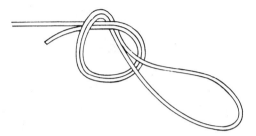

1. Double the tag end of the line. Make a single overhand knot in the double line.

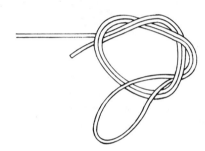

2. Hold the tag end and standing part of the line in your left hand and bring the loop around and insert through the overhand knot again.

3. Hold the loop in your right hand. Hold the tag end and standing line in your left hand. Moisten the knot (don't use saliva) and pull to tighten.

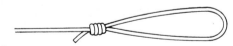

4. Trim off the tag end.

WORLD'S FAIR KNOT

An easy-to-tie terminal tackle knot for connecting line to swivel or lure.

1. Double a 6-inch length of line and pass the loop through the eye.

2. Bring the loop back next to the doubled line and grasp the doubled line through the loop.

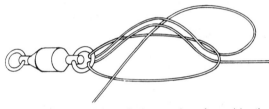

3. Put the tag end through the new loop formed by the double line.

4. Bring the tag end back through the new loop created by Step 3.

5. Pull the tag end snug, and slide the knot up tight. Clip the tag end.

257

PERFECTION LOOP KNOT

Used to make a loop in the end of line or leader. Make one turn around the line and hold the crossing point with thumb and forefinger **(Drawing 1)**. Make a second turn around the crossing point, and bring the end around and between loops *A* and *B* **(Drawing 2)**. Run loop *B* through loop *A* **(Drawing 3)**. Pull upward on loop *B* **(Drawing 4)**, tightening the knot **(Drawing 5)**.

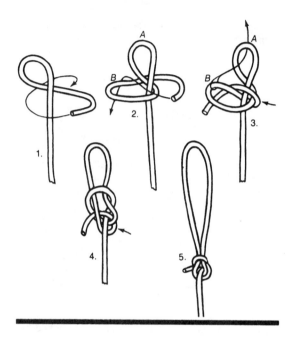

TUCKED SHEET BEND

Joins fly line and leader when leader has an end loop.

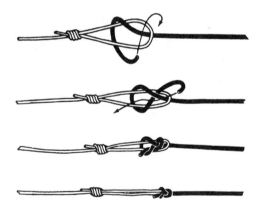

TURLE KNOT

Used to tie a dry or wet fly to a leader tippet. Not as strong as the Improved Clinch Knot, but it allows a dry fly's hackle points to sit high and jauntily on the surface of the water.

1. Run end of leader through eye of hook toward the bend, and tie a simple overhand knot around the standing part of the line, forming a loop.

2. Open the loop enough to allow it to pass around the fly, and place the loop around the neck of the fly, just forward of the eye.

3. Pull on the end of the leader, drawing the loop up tight around the neck of the fly.

4. Tighten the knot completely by pulling on the main part of the leader.

DROPPER LOOP KNOT

This knot is frequently used to put a loop in the middle of a strand of monofilament.

1. Make a loop in the line and wrap one end overhand several times around the other part of the line. Pinch a small loop at point marked X and thrust it between the turns as shown by the simulated, imaginary needle.

2. Place your finger through the loop to keep it from pulling out again, and pull on both ends of the line.

3. The knot will draw up like this.

4. Finished loop knot.

OFFSHORE SWIVEL KNOT

1. Slip loop of double-line leader through the eye of the swivel. Rotate loop ½ turn to put a single twist between loop and swivel eye.

2. Pass the loop with the twist over the swivel. Hold the loop end, together with both strands of double-line leader, with one hand. Let the swivel slide to the other end of the double loops now formed.

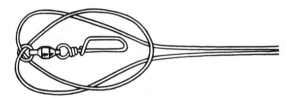

3. Still holding loop/lines, use other hand to rotate swivel through center of both loops. Repeat at least five times.

4. Continue holding strands of double-line leader tightly, but release the end of the loop. As you pull on swivel, loops of line will begin to gather.

5. To draw knot tight, grip the swivel with pliers and push the loops toward eye with fingers, still keeping strands of leader pulled tight.

THE UNI-KNOT SYSTEM

The Uni-Knot System consists of variations on one basic knot that can be used for most needs in freshwater and saltwater. The system was developed by Vic Dunaway, editor of *Florida Sportsman* magazine and author of numerous books. Here's how each variation is tied, step by step.

A. TYING TO TERMINAL TACKLE

1. Run line through eye of hook, swivel, or lure at least 6 inches and fold it back to form two parallel lines. Bring the end of the line back in a circle toward the eye.

2. Turn the tag end six times around the double line and through circle. Hold double line at eye and pull tag end to snug up turns.

3. Pull running line to slide the knot up against the eye.

4. Continue pulling until knot is tight. Trim tag end flush with last coil of the knot. This basic Uni-Knot will not slip.

B. LOOP CONNECTION

Tie the same basic Uni-Knot as shown above—up to the point where coils are snugged up against the running line. Then slide knot toward eye only until the desired loop size is reached. Pull tag end with pliers to tighten. This gives a lure or fly free, natural movement in the water. When fish is hooked, knot slides tight against eye.

C. JOINING LINES

1. With two lines of about the same diameter, overlap ends for about 6 inches. With one end, form Uni-Knot circle and cross the two lines at about the middle of the overlap.

2. Tie basic Uni-Knot, making six turns around the lines.

3. Pull tag end to snug the knot.

4. Use loose end of the overlapped line to tie second Uni-Knot and snug it up in the same manner.

5. Pull the two lines in opposite directions to slide the two knots together. Pull tight and snip tag ends close to outermost coils.

D. JOINING LEADER TO LINE

1. Using leader no more than four times the pound-test of the line, double the end of line and overlap with leader for about 6 inches. Make Uni-Knot circle with the doubled line.

2. Tie a Uni-Knot around leader with the doubled line, but use only three turns. Snug up.

3. Now tie a Uni-Knot with the leader around doubled line, again using only three turns.

4. Pull knots together tightly. Trim tag ends and loop.

E. JOINING SHOCK LEADER TO LINE

1. Using leader of more than four times the pound-test of the line, double the ends of both leader and line back about 6 inches. Slip line loop through leader loop far enough to permit tying Uni-Knot around both strands of leader.

2. With doubled line, tie a Uni-Knot around doubled leader, using only four turns.

3. Put finger through loop of line and grasp both tag end and running line to pull knot snug around leader loop.

4. With one hand, pull long end of leader (not both strands). With the other hand, pull both strands of line (as arrows indicate). Pull slowly until knot slides to end of leader loop and slippage is stopped.

F. DOUBLE-LINE SHOCK LEADER

1. As a replacement for Bimini Twist or Spider Hitch, first clip off amount of line needed for desired length of loop. Tie the two ends together with an overhand knot.

2. Double the end of the running line and overlap it 6 inches with knotted end of the loop piece. Tie a Uni-Knot with the tied loop around the double running line, using four turns.

3. Now tie a Uni-Knot with the doubled running line around the loop piece, again using four turns.

4. Hold both strands of double line in one hand, both strands of loop in the other. Pull to bring knots together until they barely touch.

5. Tighten by pulling both strands of loop piece (as two arrows indicate) but only main strand of running line (as single arrow indicates). Trim off both loop tag ends, eliminating overhand knot.

G. SNELLING A HOOK

1. Thread line through the hook eye for about 6 inches. Hold line against hook shank and form Uni-Knot circle. Make as many turns as desired through loop and around line and shank. Close knot by pulling on tag end.

2. Tighten by pulling running line in one direction and hook in the other. Trim off tag end.

LOOP KNOT

Tie overhand knot in line, leaving loop loose and sufficient length of line below loop to tie rest of knot. Run end through hook eye and back through loop in line, and then tie another overhand knot around standing part. Pull tight.

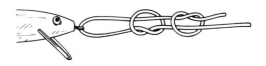

DAVE HAWK'S DROP LOOP KNOT

Used to attach lure to line or leader via a nonslip loop that will permit freer lure action than would a knot snugged right up to the eye of the lure.

1. Tie overhand knot about 5 inches from end of line, pull tight, and run end through the lure eye.

2. Bring end back parallel with standing part of line, bend end back toward lure, and then make two turns around the parallel strands.

3. Slowly draw the knot tight, and then pull on the lure so that the jam knot slides down to the overhand knot.

END LOOP

Used to form a loop in the end of a line.

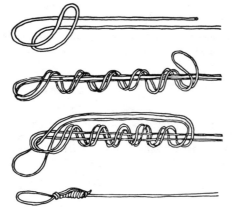

BUFFER LOOP

Used to attach lure to line or leader via a nonslip loop.

1. Tie simple overhand knot in line, leaving loop loose and leaving end long enough to complete the knot, and then run end through eye of lure.

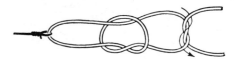

2. Run end back through loose loop, and make another overhand knot, using end and standing part of line.

3. Tighten overhand knot nearest to lure eye, and then tighten second overhand knot, which, in effect, forms a half hitch against first knot.

4. Finished knot.

BIMINI TWIST

Used to create a loop or double line without appreciably weakening the breaking strength of the line. Especially popular in bluewater fishing for large saltwater fish. Learning this knot requires practice.

1. Double the end of the line to form a loop, leaving yourself plenty of line to work with. Run the loop around a fixed object such as a cleat or the butt end of a rod, or have a partner hold the loop and keep it open. Make 20 twists in the line, keeping the turns tight and the line taut.

2. Keeping the twists tight, wrap the end of the line back over the twists until you reach the V of the loop, making the wraps tight and snug up against one another.

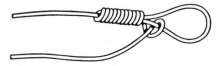

3. Make half hitch around one side of loop and pull tight.

4. Then make a half hitch around the other side of the loop, and pull this one tight.

5. Now make a half hitch around the base of the loop, tighten it, clip off excess line at the end, and the Bimini Twist is complete.

HAYWIRE TWIST

Used to tie wire to hook, lure, or swivel, or make loop in end of wire.

Run about 4 inches of the end of the leader wire through the eye of the hook, lure, or swivel, and then bend end across standing part of wire as in **Drawing 1**. Holding the two parts of the wire at their crossing point, bend the wire around itself, using hard, even, twisting motions. Both wire parts should be twisted equally **(Drawing 2)**. Then, using the end of the wire, make about 10 tight wraps around the standing part of the wire **(Drawing 3)**. Break off or clip end of wire close to the last wrap so that there is no sharp end, and job is complete **(Drawing 4)**.

SPIDER HITCH

Serves same function as the Bimini Twist. But many anglers prefer the Spider Hitch because it's easier and faster to tie—especially with cold hands—and requires no partner to help, nor any fixed object to keep the loop open. And it's equally strong.

1. Make a long loop in the line. Hold the ends between thumb and forefinger, with first joint of thumb extending beyond your finger. Then use other hand to twist a smaller reverse loop in the doubled line.

2. Slide your fingers up line to grasp small reverse loop, together with long loop. Most of small loop should extend beyond your thumb tip.

3. Wind the doubled line from right to left around both thumb and small loop, taking five turns. Then pass remainder of doubled line (large loop) through the small loop.

4. Pull the large loop to make the five turns unwind off thumb, using a fast, steady pull—not a quick jerk.

5. Pull the turns around the base of the loop tight and then trim off the tag end.

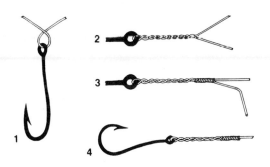

Saltwater Fishing Techniques

WATER TEMPERATURE AND FISH

There is no doubt left in anglers' minds of the importance of water temperature and its direct bearing on the activities of fish. Water temperature will tell you where the fish gather and where they feed at various times of the year.

It is a scientifically proven fact that every species of fish has a preferred temperature zone or range and it will stay and generally feed in this zone.

Taking temperature readings of water is not difficult, whether you use a sophisticated electronic thermometer or an inexpensive water thermometer lowered into the water on a fishing line. One electronic thermometer has a probe attached to a cable that is marked at regular intervals, so depth and temperature can be read simultaneously.

The inexpensive water thermometers can also do the job, and many also indicate depth by inserting a water pressure gauge in the thermometer tube. With these thermometers, allow at least 30 seconds to 1 minute for a reading. Also, the fishing line attached to it should be marked off in regular intervals, say 5 feet, so you can determine just how deep you are lowering the thermometer in the water.

The accompanying Preferred Temperature Table shows popular saltwater gamefish and baitfish and their preferred temperature zones. Look up the fish you are seeking and the water temperature it prefers. Then begin taking temperature readings from the surface on down, at 5-foot intervals, until you locate the correct zone and depth. Concentrate your efforts at that depth and you'll soon come to discover how important this water temperature business is.

SALTWATER GAMEFISH

Species	Lower Avoidance	Optimum	Upper Avoidance
Albacore (Thunnus alalunga)	59°	64° (17.8 C)	66°
Amberjack (Seriola dumerili)	60°	65° (18.3 C)	72°
Atlantic bonito (Sarda sarda)	60°	64° (17.8 C)	80°
Atlantic cod (Gadus morhua)	31°	44°–49° (6–8 C)	59°
Atlantic croaker (Micropogon undulatus)			100°
Atlantic mackerel (Scomber scombrus)	45°	63° (17 C)	70°
Barracuda (Sphyraena barracuda)	55°	75°–79° (24–26 C)	82°
Big-eye tuna (Thunnus obesus)	52°	58° (14.4 C)	66°
Blackfin tuna (Thunnus atlanticus)	70°	74° (23.3 C)	82°
Black marlin (Makaira indica)	68°	75°–79° (24–26 C)	87°
Bluefin tuna (Thunnus thynnus)	50°	68° (20 C)	78°
Bluefish (Pomatomus saltatrix)	50°	66°–72° (19–22 C)	84°
Blue marlin (Makaira nigricans)	70°	78° (26 C)	88°
Bonefish (Albula vulpes)	64°	75° (23.9 C)	88°
Dolphinfish (Coryphaena hippurus)	70°	75° (23.9 C)	82°
Fluke or summer flounder (Paralichthys dentatus)	56°	66° (18.9 C)	72°
Haddock (Melanogrammus aeglefinus)	36°	47° (8 C)	52°
Horn shark (Heterodontus francisci)		75° (24 C)	
Kelp bass (Paralabrax clathratus)	62°	65° (18.3 C)	72°
King mackerel (Scomberomorus cavalla)	70°		88°
Opaleye (Girella nigricans)		79° (26.1 C)	86°
Permit (Trachinotus falcatus)	65°	72° (22.2 C)	92°
Pollock (Pollachius virens)	33°	45° (8.3 C)	60°
Red drum (Sciaenops ocellata)	52°	71° (22 C)	90°
Red snapper (Lutjanus blackfordi)	50°	57° (13.8 C)	62°
Sailfish (Istiophorus platypterus)	68°	79° (26 C)	88°
Sand seatrout (Cynoscion arenarius)	90°	95° (35.0 C)	104°
Sea catfish (Arius felis)			99°
Skipjack tuna (Euthynnus pelamis)	50°	62° (16.7 C)	70°
Snook (Centropomus undecimalis)	60°	70°–75° (21–24 C)	90°
Spotted seatrout (Cynoscion nebulosus)	48°	72° (22 C)	81°
Striped bass (Morone saxatilis)	61°	68°	77°
Striped marlin (Tetrapturus audax)	61°	70° (21 C)	80°
Swordfish (Xiphias gladius)	50°	66° (19 C)	78°
Tarpon (Megalops atlantica)	74°	76° (24.4 C)	90°
Tautog (Tautoga onitis)	60°	70° (21 C)	76°
Weakfish (Cynoscion regalis)		55°–65°	78°
White marlin (Tetrapturus albidus)	65°	70° (21.1 C)	80°
White sea bass (Cynoscion nobilis)	58°	68° (20.0 C)	74°
Winter flounder (Pseudopleuronectes americanus)	35°	48°–52° (9–11 C)	64°
Yellowfin tuna (Thunnus albacares)	64°	72° (22.2 C)	80°
Yellowtail (Seriola dorsalis)	60°	65° (18.3 C)	70°

SALTWATER BAITFISH

Species	Lower Avoidance	Optimum	Upper Avoidance
Atlantic silverside (Menidia menidia)			90°
Atlantic threadfin (Polydactylus octonemus)			92°
Bay anchovy (Anchoa mitchilli)		82° (27.8 C)	92°
California grunion (Leuresthes tenuis)	68°	77° (25.0 C)	93°
Gulf grunion (Leuresthes sardina)	68°	89° (32 C)	98°
Gulf menhaden (Brevoortia patronus)			86°
Pacific silversides such as jacksmelt and topsmelt (Atherinopsis sp)	72°	77° (25 C)	82°
Rough silverside (Membras martinica)			91°
Skipjack herring (Alosa chrysochloris)	72°		84°
Spot (Leiostomus xanthurus)			99°
Tidewater silverside (Menidia beryllina)			93°

Mark Sosin's Top Tips for Chumming Reefs and Wrecks

Chumming is becoming more popular every year as the tactic to attract—and catch—game fish that lurk around bottom structure.

Chumming ranks as one of the most effective ways to locate and attract fish that live around reefs and wrecks. Almost every species, from billfish to bottom dwellers, responds enthusiastically to a free dole of tasty tidbits.

But successful chumming is more than merely hanging a frozen block of ground-up fish over the side or simply tossing a handful of chunks behind the boat. Those skippers who chum on a daily basis have honed this technique into an art form. Here are some of their key tactics.

Choosing the Spot

Position is everything, whether you are anchoring near underwater structure or drifting a reef line. To be effective, the chum must reach the fish. A near miss doesn't count. You'll often see top captains such as Bouncer Smith of Pembroke Pines, Florida, and Ken Harris of Key West move their anchor four or five times before they begin to chum.

The trick is to calculate the lie of the boat in relation to the target and the force of the current. There must be a flow of water, and you have to be on the upcurrent side of the structure. How far upcurrent is the primary question. Picture an inclined plane from the stern of the boat to the submerged structure. Chum will follow this route as it sinks. A strong current reduces the angle of the plane, carrying the chum much farther before it reaches the bottom. The opposite is true as the water slows. Your job is to anchor over a spot that assures the chum will reach bottom right at the structure. If it doesn't, the results may be frustrating.

Drifting involves more than a random approach. Learn to position the boat so that wind and current will take it over the structure you want to fish. You may find fish at a certain depth along the reef, and should therefore concentrate on that zone. One approach is to work from shallow to deep; another is to drift parallel to the edge of the reef, where predators prowl.

If the boat is being pushed too fast, fish may find the chum long after you are out of range, particularly if you are using live chum. Capt. David Doll of Fort Lauderdale remedies this by using sea anchors and even his engines to help control the drift rate.

Types of Chum

Personal preference, availability, and even the species you target determine the type of chum you should use. Options range from frozen blocks of ground-up fish to chunks to shrimp-boat bycatch to live bait, and, in some cases, even ground-up lobster heads.

No matter what type of chum they use, most reef and wreck anglers will also hang a mesh bag of block chum over the side. Ken Harris is an exception. He pursues large individual fish, and relies on shrimp-boat bycatch or live bait to attract them. The ground chum attracts swarms of smaller fish that he would rather not have in his slick.

Researchers report that the sound of smaller fish feeding frequently attracts larger predators. That's why block chum can be effective in many situations. Capt. Tom Greene of Lighthouse Point, Florida, insists on sweetening any slick with small goodies, such as glass minnows. Capt. Neil Grant of Sunshine Key, Florida, feels that live glass minnows flashing in the water creates an important visual attraction.

Over a reef, ground chum often tempts ballyhoo and speedos (frigate bonito). On the back side of the reef, you'll usually find mackerel and little tunny in the chum slick. If you do raise these species, it pays to net or catch some and then put them out as bait.

Work the Water Column

When trying to pull fish out of deeper water or when working the entire water column, David Doll has a neat trick. He puts a heavy weight on the end of some stout line and ties several mesh bags of chum to the line, staggered at various depths.

When targeting some bottom species, Tom Greene attaches a 10-pound sash weight to the end of a garden hose, lowers it to the bottom, and then pumps water through the hose with an extra bilge pump or salt water washdown. The water stirs up the bottom, much as a ray would, which attracts species that feed on bottom-dwelling critters.

Some veterans make chum containers that hold a handful of small baitfish. The device has a sinker and a trip mechanism. The first load of baitfish is released near the bottom. Subsequent drops are let go at higher and higher levels. This helps to bring game fish to the surface.

Commercial yellowtail fishermen mix their chum with sand so it will sink quickly. They then make chum balls with the sand, put the hooked bait in the middle, and wrap the fishing line around the outside. The ball is placed in the water carefully and dropped a measured distance. By lifting on the rod, you unwind the line and break the ball at the depth you want. This puts out a small cloud of chum with your bait in the middle. It's a deadly technique, but your boat won't be a pretty sight at the end of the day.

Chumming Rhythm

"I develop a rhythm when I chum," says Ken Harris, "and the fish quickly adjust to it. You must be consistent with that rhythm and keep the slick going at the same pace, no matter how busy you are aboard the boat."

The majority of skippers caution against over-chumming. Bouncer tosses in a fresh chunk or two at about the time the last pieces drift out of sight.

Harris talks about being stingy. He puts out far fewer pieces of chum than the number of big fish might be able to see. This stimulates competition.

A steady stream of chum keeps the fish well back in the slick. When you follow a slower rhythm, the fish tend to swim closer to the source, hoping to find the next piece before a competitor does.

The same theory holds when chumming with live bait, such as pilchards. Fish are extremely sensitive to feeding activity, even if they don't find something every time. The sound of a few predators crashing live bait causes the others to hang around for the next handout.

Mesh Size

Professional skippers who use frozen blocks of chum pay attention to the mesh size of their chum bags. This determines how fast the chum will be dispersed. As an example, a bag with ½" mesh should release a seven-pound block of chum in 30 to 40 minutes. Smaller mesh will lengthen the process.

Those who target yellowtail want to create a cloud of chum, and therefore opt for much larger mesh sizes. Some anglers buy landing-net replacement bags with one-inch or two-inch mesh, string a line around the top, and make their own chum bags.

Coastal tackle shops sell blocks of frozen chum. You certainly have the option of grinding your own and freezing it in various size containers. Understand from the beginning that it's a messy job. That's why most captains buy their chum already frozen. Besides, many spouses don't appreciate chum in their food freezers.

David Doll does suggest, however, that you freeze any small baitfish you don't use on a trip. These make wonderful chunks for a future adventure. That includes offshore baits, such as ballyhoo, which can also be cut into chunks.

People Food and Pet Food

When fishing for bottom species over reefs, some anglers use both people food and pet food as chum. Capt. Penny Banks has his own recipe. He cooks five-gallon buckets of macaroni, which he then ladles into the water for yellowtail and snappers. Corn has become a staple in some areas, either used alone or mixed with natural chum for yellowtails. Raw oats and cooked oatmeal find favor with some, while others beef up their chum with bread.

Aboard some boats, bulk bags of dog food are laced with menhaden oil and then used in place of other types of chum. Dog food does not have to be refrigerated. Cans of cat food contain acceptable chum for some species. A number of different scents (in addition to bunker oil) and fish attractants can be used to enhance artificial chum or natural chum.

How to Hook a Bait

Chumming and fishing the slick should be tailored to specific species. If you are using chunk baits, make sure each piece is trimmed neatly, and insert the hook in one corner. When that doesn't work, try burying the hook, so most of it is hidden in the bait. My own preference is to use relatively small hooks. I don't want the weight of the hook to make the bait sink more quickly than the natural chum, and therefore miss

the concentration of fish. The same theory applies when using whole, small, dead fish as bait. Place the hook carefully and strategically.

With live bait, Bouncer Smith has a system that makes sense. His first choice is to place the hook low in the body near the head. With a pilchard, for example, the hook is inserted right under the pectoral fins. When you pull on the line, it forces the bait to dive deeper, which should put it right in the strike zone.

When the current slows, Bouncer hooks the bait low and near the tail so that it will swim away from him when he tightens the line. In a strong current, the bait is hooked near the dorsal fin. The secret, according to Bouncer, is to place the hook in an off-center position so the fish has trouble swimming. This causes it to send out more distress vibrations, which attracts predators.

How to Fish a Chum Slick

Fishing a chum slick seems simple enough, but it takes a bit of practice to do it right. All you're trying to do is put the bait where the fish are and make it appear the same as the free-drifting chum. If your boat is anchored, the current is carrying the chum away at a given rate and it is sinking at the same time. The bait must follow this same path, because the fish are going to be somewhere along the chum trail.

The technique involves pulling slack line off the reel before you put the bait in the water. As the current starts to carry the bait away from the boat, watch the line. Just before it becomes taut, strip some more slack line into the water. If you allow the line to tighten, the bait will stop drifting and rise in the water column, away from the chum line. Fish become suspicious of any morsel that rises or stops in the current.

When you first start chumming, fish tend to appear well back in the slick. Therefore it makes sense to drift your bait a long distance before reeling in and starting again. Sometimes it takes a while to attract anything, so be patient.

If the fish get finicky and stop feeding, Ken Harris recommends you stop fishing for a while and just chum.

By watching the line, you can also detect a strike before you feel it. As soon as the line moves faster than the current, you'll know a fish has picked up the bait. In some instances, you may want to lower the rod tip and wait for the line to come tight before setting the hook. Other times, it makes sense to reel rapidly until you feel the fish on the other end.

With live bait, the tactics change. You can hold a live bait stationary in the slick, because it continues to swim around. Unless the fish are chasing everything to the surface, you may want to put a small sinker ahead of the live bait to force it deeper.

If you are chumming and drifting, David Doll recommends that you cover the water column. He likes to fish baits at various depths and distances from the boat. Some of his rigs will have sinkers, while others won't. It's a matter of experimenting until he finds the setup that works.

Light Lines

Fish can suddenly become fussy feeders. Leader diameter, hook size, bait type, or any number of other factors may convince them to ignore the standard rigs. We once ran some crude experiments on a school of yellowtail that were visible behind the boat.

Unless we offered them a bait on six-pound line with no leader, they refused to bite. You could put two identical tidbits side by side and they would always turn down the one fished on heavier line.

When the fish get selective, skippers like Bouncer Smith and Tom Greene switch to very light lines and smaller baits and eliminate leaders. For toothy critters, such as king mackerel, they use long-shanked hooks, which help somewhat in preventing bite-offs. A few fish may be lost in the process, but it beats getting skunked. Tom may even use a fresh water bass hook designed for plastic worms, since it has a long shank and bait-holder barbs.

Fishing Artificials

Chumming provides the perfect setting for fishing artificial lures. You have the option of standing ready until some oversized predator suddenly appears in the slick, or you can simply work a lure blindly. You can allow some soft plastic baits that resemble the chum to drift back without imparting any motion. Most artificials, however, work best when cast and retrieved through the chum. To be effective, you have to get the lure down to the fish or pick a time when your quarry is aggressive enough to hit something on the surface.

Leadheads let you work different depths. If you choose a swimming plug, make sure it will dive down to the same level as the chum. On active fish, try a topwater chugger. It represents a smaller baitfish feeding on surface chum. In a slick, the big guys often ignore the chum and feed on the smaller species that are feasting on the handouts. Keep in mind, however, that even sailfish and marlin will ingest chunks of dead fish from time to time.

Retrieves should be somewhat erratic with lures, and the speed should match the preferences of the targeted species. If you're after king mackerel, try a fast retrieve. Cobia, on the other hand, might prefer a slower presentation.

Most fly fishermen now prefer to dead-drift their flies back in the chum slick, unless they spot a specific fish to cast to. It's a technique that's proven extremely successful. Prior to 1966, I had never heard of this method. Fishing over a reef in Bermuda for yellowfin tuna back then, I watched the fish refuse a moving fly over and over. Finally, it occurred to me to let it drift naturally with the chum. The closest tuna to the fly picked it up instantly.

Chumming combines the very basic approach of establishing a food source for fish with more sophisticated subtleties. The difference in results can usually be traced to small details rather than major mistakes. Professional captains who chum successfully on a daily basis stick with a game plan and refuse to cut corners. Follow their suggestions and you'll also enjoy some exciting days over the wrecks and reefs. ∎

Reading the Ocean

by Ed Jaworowski

Locating fish in the ocean constitutes the angler's first order of business, surpassing tackle choice, fly selection or technique in importance. Fly anglers in particular, because of the limited effective range of their tackle, need all the help they can get to improve their odds in a seemingly endless sea; shore-based anglers even more so.

Several facts compound an already difficult chore. First, most ocean gamefish don't have homes. Their movements are largely determined by the movement of the food supply and tides. Second, their habits are greatly affected by the physical makeup of the areas in which they feed. This primer will remove some of the mysteries of tides and structure. Reading the ocean, like reading a trout stream, is an indispensable skill for the salt water angler and the first requirement for salt water anglers.

Tides represent the single biggest difference between freshwater and saltwater fishing. Though gamefish may temporarily take up residence around structure—inlets, seawalls, rock jetties, sand bars and the like—they will invariably move on with the next tide, following migrating food forms that also obey tidal influences. Any angler who hopes to score with any consistency in the salt must have at least a rudimentary knowledge of the way tides work. However subtle, tidal movements establish what amount to the equivalent of freshwater rivers. Here are some of the basics and suggestions on how to fit it all into your fishing.

The gravitational pulls of the moon and, to a lesser degree, the sun, cause ocean waters to move, building higher in some areas while getting lower in others. As a rule, a section of coast will experience two high tides and two low tides in each 24- to 25-hour period. A low will follow a high every six to six and one-half hours. Each day the highs and lows will therefore occur about an hour later than the previous day. This also means that at a given time and day each week, the tide will be nearly the exact opposite from what it was the previous week. If you had good fishing on the incoming tide on Saturday morning at daybreak, remember that you will have the opposite tide the following Saturday at the same time.

During different times of the month tides also vary. When the new moon (the darkest time of the month) and the full moon occur, expect the highest highs and lowest lows. Such tides are called "spring tides." It means during the six hours of tidal flow between the highs and lows you will note faster flows and stronger pulls. During the first and last quarters of the moon the tides are weaker, current flows slower and differences less great—lower highs and higher lows. Such tides are called "neap (or nip) tides."

Here's a typical scenario. If the new

Striped bass fishing at dusk along a rocky Martha's Vineyard beach.
(ED JAWOROWSKI)

moon occurs on the 1st of the month and the full moon about two weeks later, on the 15th, you will experience the highest and lowest tides and strongest pulls at those times of the month (stronger over the full moon). During the week preceding each of those phenomena tides wax stronger, waning each successive day following. During the weeks of the first and last quarters (approximately the 8th and 22nd) the tides will be gentler. Also, on any given day, if a high tide occurs at 6:00 A.M. expect the next low around noon and the next high 6 to 7:00 P.M.

The change of water level from high to low will also vary with geographic locale. Consider the Atlantic coast. On Florida flats, only a few inches may separate low tide from high tide, particularly during the neap tide periods. On the Bay of Fundy, Nova Scotia, on the other hand, there may be more than a 25-foot difference; the flooding tide comes in so quickly that a man walking rapidly can't outpace it. Mid-Atlantic coastal states commonly show four- to six-foot tidal variations. As a rule, tide variations diminish closer to the equator.

Tide tables are approximations based upon a couple of dozen factors, in addition to time of month, time of day and moon phase, and changes in some of these may alter the predicted times. Other contributing factors affecting fish behavior are wind, weather,

light intensity, bait availability, barometric pressure, currents. The wind is one of the strongest. A strong and persistent wind following the waves can make a high tide occur much earlier than predicted and reach much higher onto the shore. Obviously, when blowing against the tide, it can have the opposite results, actually holding the ocean back. I've seen 150 yards of a New Jersey beach exposed when it should have been under a few feet of water, totally because of a strong northwest wind.

Changes in atmospheric pressure will affect the water. Low barometric pressure will allow the surf to rise higher and develop more violent wave action. We've all seen what happens to the ocean during a hurricane, a period of very low barometric pressure.

All this data may seem confusing to the newcomer to saltwater fishing but it's really no more so than learning about freshwater insect hatches or differences in fly dressings. On the other hand, knowledge of tides can be more important than either of those concerns; if you fish where there is no water or can't get to the feeding grounds, you're not apt to catch many fish.

Here is a random list of additional ideas for the angler to consider.

- When you plan to fish an area, consider how the tide will affect the water there. During times of strong tidal flow, bait will be caught and forced to collect in rips around jetties and inlets; the bait can't swim against the flow.

- During spring tides, high waters will flood grass beds in the bays and tear loose a lot of eel grass and other vegetation. The effect is less during neap tide periods. Grass buildup is generally also greater the closer you fish to an inlet.

- One change of tide can dirty the water or can clear a surf, by bringing or removing grass or cloudy water.

- Usually, more whitewater tends to develop when the tide is dropping. It tends to disappear on a rising tide.

- My experience has been that tides are less a factor when fishing farther from shore. Inshore, moving water, whether incoming or outgoing, is nearly always superior to the static water you get at flood or ebb tide. A moving tide tends to concentrate bait; static water allows it to disperse.

- Great changes in water temperature can affect fishing. If deeper offshore water is cooler, a strong tide may move it inshore, displacing the shallower warmer water and turn fish off.

- Know the contour of the beach you fish. When the tide drops, gamefish will make every effort to get out to deeper water rather than risk being cut off by a sand bar. If the bar is a hundred yards from shore, the fish will be out of range at low tide. If you can't wade to the bar, plan on fishing the area closer to shore at higher tide, when the fish can get over the bar.

- Note that the times of the highs and lows along the coast will be approximately the same along the beach for many miles.

Back on the bays, estuaries and creeks, however, tides may be two, three or four hours different. Tide tables will tell you how to make the necessary adjustments. Get a tide table for the area you are considering fishing. Bait and tackle shops will carry them. You can also consult local newspapers. Learn how to read the tables and consider them a basic part of your equipment.

As with tides, learning to read structure will increase your odds dramatically. Even when the arrival of bait and favorable tides indicate the likelihood of gamefish in the area, narrowing the possible spots demands some skill in recognizing structure and understanding why some spots are more likely to be productive than others.

Like freshwater bass, stripers gravitate to rocks, weeds, and bars. Bluefish often feed close to underwater lumps, ridges or wrecks. Snook hide among mangroves, weakfish seek out bottom depressions or jetties and false albacore like rips and strong flows. All these gamefish regularly position themselves where structure will concentrate food, making it easy to locate, ambush or trap. Just what constitutes structure?

Basically any bottom formation or contour (like a sand bar or drop-off), rocks, wrecks, bridge and pier pilings, weeds, even waves. Structure may be natural or artificial, temporary or permanent. One of the most obvious forms of structure is the jetty or groin, usually a man-made, rocky finger jutting out from the beach. Jetties cause waves to break, loosening shellfish and organisms on which the fish feed. They also provide places for forage fish to hide as well as causing and directing currents. The biggest mistake you can make when fishing from jetties is to cast out and away. Nearly all feeding takes place close to and among the rocks. Cast parallel to the rocks and smack your offerings down right in the foaming water. Rubber-headed Siliclone flies are especially deadly in this situation.

All kinds of pilings also give shelter to bait. Some are best fished from a boat and most produce best at night, so scout out your spots at day. It's amazing how bold fish become in the dark, swimming around boat docks and harbors they would never approach in daylight. Look for older pilings, as new piers and docks haven't yet developed encrustations that provide food for the chain. White perch, weakfish and stripers particularly like docks, piers and bridges. At night, they lie on the edge of the shadows and assault bait attracted to lights shining on the water. You are very apt to see and hear surface activity then. I've taken scores of small stripers all around the piers and terminals in New York Harbor, the East River and the Brooklyn waterfront!

Many back bays are marked by sod banks, grass covered islands and cutouts of land laced by narrow streams. Fish take up position any place a smaller flow dumps water into a larger area. If you can walk the sod banks (some are mucky and nearly impossible to walk), stay back from the edge. Not only might it give way, you could spook the fish, which like to hang under the overhang and rush out to snatch bait. A small boat, even a cartopper with a small outboard is adequate to fish among the sod banks in many areas. Nautical charts of the areas you plan to fish provide invaluable assistance in locating channels, holes and dropoffs and bars.

Some oceanfront structure is obvious. Reading other forms requires more experience. Look first at the contour of the beach. Is it pretty straight, north-south, or scalloped out with indentations and cuts? Straighter beaches generally don't attract bait so well. They have fewer points to obstruct wave flow and form holes and pockets, thus fewer ambush points. Storms and heavy wave action may create new holes and sand bars—or destroy them. Routinely check out and explore the beaches you want to fish. They can change in short order. Also take note of the slope of the beach. Flatter beaches have less bottom structure, hence less cover for fish. Steeper beaches allow bait to move closer to the shore.

Bars running parallel to the beach

commonly draw fish, yet some provide great fishing on the inshore side, while others are fishless. The difference usually depends on breaks in the bar. If you see white water breaking over a bar within 100 or 200 yards of the shore, forming a deep trough close to the beach, check to see if there are any cuts (marked by darker colored water) through which fish can get back to the safety of deeper water. Without such cuts, fish have little opportunity to get over the bar, usually only for the brief periods of high water and then generally only at night.

On the other hand, fish will stay and feed in deep troughs close to the beach right through low water, so long as they have the opportunity to get back beyond the bar through a cut or channel. Thick weed masses also serve as structure. They form slack pockets in the current where bait can hide and fish can feed, just like weed beds in a smallmouth stream. A drift over a bay

or ocean bottom with an electronic depth finder/fish locator is a real eye opener. Fish will register in the tiniest of pockets or holes, more so if they can hide behind vegetation anchored to the bottom. However, even clear bottoms can hide fish in depressions; waves and currents flow over them.

Finally, waves themselves sometimes represent a form of structure. Surf turbulence can conceal gamefish stalking forage. An understanding of how wave action works shows how this can be so. As a wave moves toward the shore, the water particles swirl down and back up in a circular path, equal in diameter to the height of the wave. For example, as a three-foot wave moves toward the shore, the water particles near the surface go down and around in a three-foot clockwise pattern, nearly returning to their starting position as the wave itself rolls along. Sand particles, grass and other suspended matter are also

moved around by this turbulence. A striped bass can readily move into striking range concealed by this mass of confusion and visual disturbance.

Incidentally, you can estimate the depth of water on a bar over which a wave breaks. Normally a wave breaks when it reaches a depth equal to its own height up to one and a half times its height. Thus, a four-foot wave will break when it runs into bottom interference four to six feet down. The most effective way to fish a turbulent surf is to let your fly wash around on a semi-slack line, simulating the naturals which lose much their ability to swim in the strong currents.

Reading an ocean is fascinating and challenging. As with all fishing, the more you understand the environment in which the fish feed, in the long run, the more fun you will have and the more successful you will be. ■

Salt Water Sportsman's Guide to Releasing Fish

by Tom Richardson

Gather round, you skeptics, we've got news for you. Released fish *do* survive. Problem is, many anglers simply don't know how to release a fish properly. There's a lot of confusion, not to mention controversy, about what to do. Today we're going to set the record straight.

Before we get into the best ways to release specific species, there's a few general rules that apply across the board. Much of the following was gleaned from a fact sheet entitled "Guidelines To Increase Survival of Released Sport Fish," written by Cornell University researchers Mark Malchoff, Michael Voiland, and David

MacNeill. It's is an excellent source of information for anyone interested in proper catch-and-release procedure, and can be obtained by sending $1 (ppd.) to the Media Services Resource Center—Fish, Cornell University, 7 Business and Technology Park, Ithaca, NY 14850.

Stress and wounding, say the authors, are the two major causes of angling mortality in fish. Stress is most often caused by "vigorous physical exertion (which) causes lactic acid to accumulate in the fish's muscles as a result of fighting the rod and reel. If the animal is able to restore its blood acid (pH) level to pre-stress or normal lev-

els, normal physiological processes return and the fish may live to fight another day. In some cases, blood chemistry balance is not restored and the fish may die—perhaps as long as 72 hours after the catch.

"Since the amount of lactic acid generated is directly proportional to the duration and intensity of muscular activity, a quick retrieve and capture of the fish would thus tend to lessen muscular exertion and metabolistic stress." In other words, the quicker you can get the fish to the boat and release it, the better its chances of survival. This would certainly seem to refute the idea that light tackle is more "sporting."

Hook wounds were listed as the second major cause of fishing mortality. The researchers found that wounds to the gill and stomach areas were the most deadly. Intermediate mortalities were caused by injury to the lower jaw, isthmus (the triangular "throat" section connecting the head and body), and eye regions. Finally, hooks imbedded in the snout, the upper jaw, the corner of the mouth, and the cheek caused the lowest level of mortality. The pamphlet also states that baited hooks were more likely to cause serious injuries than lures, and that the use of barbless hooks and single hooks, being easier to remove, cause less out-of-water stress (oxygen deprivation, excess handling) than barbed hooks or treble hooks. Also important is the type of metal the hook is made of. For instance, some hooks erode faster than others, and there is some evidence that tin/cadmium hooks may poison the fish if left embedded in the tissue.

Other causes of physical stress include the removal of protective slime, low salinity, high and low water temperature, depressurization, and internal injury caused by rough handling. These factors, alone and in combination with physical exertion, can increase mortality.

General recommendations are also given in the Cornell pamphlet concerning the best way to release fish. For example, the authors say not to remove the fish from the water if at all possible, and recommend the use of hook-removal devices, such as needle-nose pliers and J-shaped dehookers. Also important is minimizing the time a fish spends out of the water: if a hook is difficult to remove, it's better to cut the line or leader as close to the mouth as possible rather than struggle with the fish. Do not touch the gills or soft underbelly, and if you must handle the fish, always do so with wet hands or wet gloves to keep the protective mucous coating intact.

Additional tips include covering a fish's eyes with a wet cloth or towel to calm it down, placing the fish on a soft, wet surface (i.e., foam or carpeting) if it

A quick fight and a quick release, with a minimal amount of handling, is the best way to ensure a fish's survival.

has to be brought aboard, and releasing the fish with a headfirst plunge from several feet above the water if it appears healthy after capture.

I found that almost all of the above recommendations were shared by the fishermen and biologists I interviewed for this article. Let's take a look now at how these experts practice release on some specific species.

Releasing Striped Bass

If there's anyone qualified to answer questions on how to release striped bass, it's Captain Al Anderson of Point Judith, Rhode Island. During his 27 years as a charter captain, Anderson has released a total of 3,102 fish. A few days before I spoke with him, Anderson had tagged and released his 1,700th bass for the American Littoral Society and had recently learned of the 70th recapture of stripers he's tagged.

Anderson, who began tagging striped bass in 1967, has a finely honed method of tag and release. "First, we recognize very quickly if the fish is a keeper or not," he says. "If it looks undersized, or just barely legal, we land the fish with a (soft cotton) net. Then we lift it out of the water and place it on the wet, carpeted deck where a

saltwater hose is kept running. This helps keep the fish's protective slime from being rubbed off. Then we quickly place a wet towel over the fish's head to calm it down."

Anderson makes sure he has his yardstick and tagging equipment ready to go, so he won't waste valuable time. If the angler wants a picture taken, he'd better be ready to shoot. "If the cameraman isn't ready, too bad," says Anderson. "That fish goes right back in the water."

After the fish has been measured and tagged, Anderson releases it by dropping it headfirst, "like a torpedo," from three or four feet above the water. This is to give the fish a head start and get water flowing through its gills. The entire process, from the time the fish is brought aboard to the time it's released, takes roughly 15 to 20 seconds—quick and efficient with a minimal amount of handling.

Remember that Anderson only removes the fish from the water to tag it or to remove a hard-to-reach hook. If you aren't going to tag your fish, try to keep it in the water to give it oxygen and reduce the risk of slime removal caused by handling. Bringing the fish onboard can also result in internal injury if it's allowed to flop around violently. (How many times have you fumbled a slippery fish and sent it skittering across the deck?)

Schoolie stripers that have been hooked in the lip can be safely released by lifting them out of the water by the leader and using a J-shaped dehooker to extract the hook. With this device, you never have to touch the fish, and it only spends a few seconds out of the water. Large fish should not be lifted out of the water by the leader.

Incidentally, the J dehooker is also the preferred method among many charter captains for releasing bluefish. It's convenient, not only because you avoid handling the fish, but also to avoid the sharp teeth. After you get the hang of using the J dehooker, it's unbelievable how fast you can release a fish and get back in the action.

Striped bass that have been fought to exhaustion, as often happens in surf fishing or when using light tackle, have to be treated more carefully. If possible, do not take an exhausted fish out of the water to remove the hooks. For instance, it's poor practice, in Anderson's opinion, to drag a surf-caught fish onto the beach, where a lot of slime can be rubbed off and where sand can irritate the gills. If the hooks are difficult to remove on a severely exhausted fish, cut the line or clip the hook from the lure rather than wrenching it out and handling the fish excessively.

It's also important to revive an exhausted fish before letting it go, even if it takes quite a while. Holding the fish's lower jaw with your thumb and supporting its body with your other hand, revive the fish by gently "swimming" it back and forth in the water so that oxygen can wash over the gills. "You know the fish is reviving when it bites down on your thumb and shakes its head," says Anderson. Anderson recalls catching bass from the rocks along Narragansett Bay and letting the fish recover in a small tidal pool before sending it back out into the surf. It would be interesting to see if letting an exhausted bass recover in a large livewell might not also be beneficial.

As previously mentioned, water temperature and salinity can affect fishing mortality. This was proved with striped bass in experiments conducted by Keith Lockwood at the University of Maryland. Using hook-caught bass, Lockwood and his associates discovered that the higher the water temperature and the lower the salinity, the lower the survival rate. Therefore, stripers that are caught during periods of hot weather, such as in summer, or in rivers and estuaries where salinity is lower, should be handled with much greater care.

King Mackerel

Randy Gregory, a technician with the North Carolina Department of Marine Fisheries (NC-DMF), uses many of the same release techniques as Anderson, except that his specialty is king mackerel. Gregory, who says the NC-DMF tagged and released roughly 1,500 kings last year, agrees that when it comes to a successful release, time is of the essence. "If you keep a king mackerel out of the water for more than a minute," he says, "you would probably cut its chances of survival by 50 percent. If it takes more than 30 seconds to remove the hook, cut the line."

Like Anderson, Gregory says it's best not to remove the fish from the water if you know you're going to release it. Try to remove the hooks over the side of the boat or clip the line close to the hook if it can't be reached. "Handle them as little as possible," he says. "King mackerel have really soft skin and a lot of slime, which serves as protection against bacteria and parasites. When you break the integrity of that coating, it allows bacteria to grow and the fish has to work harder to replace the slime."

As for removing the hook, Gregory warns not to rip it out of the fish, even if this seems like the quickest and easiest way to get it out. If the hook, or hooks, are lodged very deep, tearing them out could cause severe internal injury, especially to the delicate gill area. Since so much blood courses through the gills, tearing them could cause the fish to bleed to death, or the blood could attract predators.

When Gregory has to bring a fish onboard to tag it, he likes to place it on a wet surface, such as in his specially designed king mackerel trough that's filled with wet foam. Like Anderson, he folds a wet towel over the fish's head and body to calm it down and to keep the skin moist. Holding the fish upside down by its tail also has a calming effect, he says. Any time Gregory has to handle a fish, he makes sure that his hands or gloves are wet to protect the slime. After the tagging has been completed, Gregory releases the fish using the head-first-plunge method—"almost like you're chucking a spear," he says.

According to Gregory, one of the best methods for bringing a king aboard is with a tail rope, since it doesn't harm any organs or remove a lot of slime; however, he admits it may take some practice to master the device. Because king mackerel are so fast, you have to place the rope loop around the head of the fish first. That means the loop has to be passed around the rod and reel and down the line. When the loop is parallel with the eyes, quickly cinch it shut and it should end up around the tail after the fish shoots forward. If you decide against using a tail rope, then netting the fish is preferable to lifting it by the leader, especially if it's a "smoker."

Gregory and the North Carolina DMF are working to get more North Carolina anglers involved in the tagging program. The DMF actively recruits the help of sport fishermen through tournaments and lectures, and last year the number of kings released by anglers rose to around 300. For more information, call Gregory at the NC-DMF, (919) 726-7021.

Billfish

But what about releasing bigger game, such as billfish? To find out, I spoke with John Jolley, former head of the State of Florida's East Coast Marine Lab. From 1970 to 1980, one of the lab's primary missions was assessing the stocks of Atlantic sailfish in the western North Atlantic, and Jolley and his team collected and tagged hundreds of specimens. Although Jolley's current job involves the assessment of a different stock, the Wall Street kind, he still tags and releases sailfish whenever he has the time to go fishing.

Jolley says that a quick fight and a quick release, with a minimal amount of handling, is the best way to ensure survival. The longer a fish is fought, the more exhausted it will be and the longer it will take to recover, thus making it susceptible to predation. Using 20-pound-test tackle, Jolley says he's usually able to bring a fish to the boat within 20 minutes, without backing down. If the fight reaches the 30-minute mark, he advises putting on some extra pressure and/or backing down to get the fish in.

Jolley tries to avoid touching the fish at all during the release. In fact, he never even bills the fish, because he says this can cause injury when the fish slams against the side of the boat. He also says not to cram the stomach back inside the mouth if the sailfish has everted it during the fight; the fish will swallow it later. With the boat moving slowly forward, he grabs the leader, wraps the fish in, and clips the leader next to the mouth, leaving the hook in the fish. By doing this, the fish maintains its forward momentum and usually swims off with plenty of vigor. Only if the fish appears to be completely exhausted and begins to float belly up does Jolley advise grabbing its bill and swimming it along beside the moving boat.

While Jolley takes exceptional care to release his sailfish, he realizes that all of them may not make it, particularly those that have sustained injury to the eye. But at the same time he points out how tough these fish really are. "Survival is actually higher than we once thought," he says, and offers the example of a badly injured sailfish he had once tagged and released. The fish had suffered severe eye damage and was bleeding from the gills. Even worse, it was brought aboard so it could be fitted with a sonic tag. Jolley was sure the fish would sink to the bottom and die; however, he and his crew tracked the sail for six hours before it was finally eaten by a shark.

To Bill or Not to Bill

Salt Water Sportsman's, George Poveromo has also released his share of sailfish, a lifetime total estimated at 300. However, Poveromo differs from Jolley in that he prefers to bill the fish, primarily for safety reasons. He argues that a billfish, especially if it's brought in quickly and is still green, can pose a real threat to the person handling the

leader if it decides to greyhound or jump next to the boat.

When Poveromo leaders a billfish to the boat, he does so very gently to avoid causing any internal injuries if the hook has been swallowed. "The worst thing you can do is manhandle a fish to the boat or try to snap-jerk the leader to break it," which he says is practiced by some tournament anglers who want to get back in the action quickly. While Poveromo is leadering the fish, he's always prepared to drop the leader if it makes a last-ditch run. After getting the fish next to the boat, he grabs the thick base of the bill, keeping his thumbs opposed, so the fish can't snap the bill by thrashing. This positioning also gives him more leverage to control the fish. When he's got control, he looks to see where the hook is located and then removes it with his pliers. If the hook is lodged too deeply to reach, he clips the leader next to the mouth.

Throughout the process, the boat is kept slowly moving forward to maintain the flow of water through the mouth and over the gills. After he removes the hook, Poveromo holds the fish in the water until he feels it swimming under its own power, then gives it a little shove forward to get it going. A little trick he uses is to reach back and give the fish a quick squeeze on the base of its tail, which causes the sailfish to shoot ahead quickly. This reaction may be a flight instinct used to escape an attacking predator, and seems to be enough to get a sluggish fish moving under its own power.

Poveromo releases white marlin the same way as sails, but he says that blue marlin have to be handled with a little more caution due to their size and the type of rigs used. If double-hook rigs are used, he always checks to see where the hooks are embedded *before* he grabs the bill. The last thing you want is a 12/0 hook through your hand and a green marlin threatening to take off at boatside. Poveromo also says he makes every attempt to remove a double-hook rig, since the loose hook could actually wire the fish's mouth

shut by later swinging around, causing it to drown.

Like many other big-game fishermen, Poveromo believes that trolling lures are better suited for catch and release than natural bait, since they're less likely to be swallowed and lodge in a critical area. Trolling lures rigged with single hooks, which are becoming increasingly popular, are even better for release.

Both Poveromo and Jolley agree that a billfish should never be lifted up by the gill plate or bent over the gunwale to remove a hook or have a picture taken. More importantly, the fish should never be brought onboard, which could result in internal injuries, allow lots of slime to be removed, and cause severe trauma. Keep in mind that a billfish's (or any fish, for that matter) body is designed to be supported by water, and that removing it from that medium can compress and damage the organs.

Sharks

The same holds true for sharks, especially big sharks, according to Jack Casey, a biologist with the National Oceanographic and Atmospheric Administration in Narragansett, Rhode Island. Casey says that large sharks may actually be more susceptible to injury than small ones if removed from the water or retrained with a tail rope or gaff. (Aquarium cases, in which large sharks were injured while being transported from one tank to another, support this.) Allowing a shark to bang against the side of the boat or roll itself tightly in a leader can also cause internal damage.

Still, Casey is quick to dispel the myth that released sharks don't survive. "That notion," he says, "is a bunch of bull." For evidence he points to NOAA's extensive shark-tagging program, which began in 1962. To date, over 100,000 sharks have been tagged and released in the NOAA program, most of them by sport fishermen. So far, Casey's department has recorded a four-percent (over 4,500) return rate on the tagged fish.

Over the years, Casey has seen many healthy sharks with four or five old hooks in their jaws. He's also recorded plenty of recaptures of sharks released from commercial long-lines, and told me that several sharks in the program had been recaptured over three times!

When it comes to gut-hooked fish, Casey admits that the returns have been fewer, although he's seen recaptured sharks that have survived with hooks lodged in their gullets. The problem is that many times a swallowed hook increases the risk of infection. Because of this, he believes the use of stainless steel hooks may be more harmful than other hook types, since they are extremely slow to erode. To avoid gut-hooking, Casey advocates setting up on the fish quickly after it has taken the bait, so it doesn't have time to swallow the hook.

Finally, Casey recommends leaving the hook in the fish by cutting the leader close to the mouth. Again, the main objective is to get the fish in quickly and release it. Unless you've had some practice at it, trying to wrench the hook out of a shark's mouth can only cause more trauma. And considering the value of sharks as a game fish, hooks are cheap.

Shallow-Water Game Fish

Fly fishermen and light-tackle inshore enthusiasts pay attention: Paul Tejera has some advice to offer. During his nine years as a light-tackle guide in South Florida and the Keys, Tejera has gained a lot of experience in releasing shallow-water game fish. In fact, he estimates that 90 percent of the fish his clients catch are released.

To give a fish its best chance of survival, Tejera tries to keep it in the water at all times. He says using a net can rub off lots of slime and bringing the fish in the boat can only cause further injury through oxygen deprivation and by allowing the fish to flop around.

"With bonefish, I try not to bring them in the boat at all," says Tejera. With permit, he says you can lift the fish briefly out of the water by its caudal peduncle to remove the hook. This reduces slime removal.

Since most of Tejera's clients use light tackle, the fish are usually exhausted by the time they are brought to the boat. Therefore, he doesn't advocate the method of dropping the fish headfirst to release them. "You really have to spend a lot of time with them and make sure they've recovered," he says. Tejera's method is to hold the fish by the tail and swim it gently back and forth. In some cases he'll let the fish swim off a little ways and then grab it by the tail again and continue to revive it. He'll do this several times until he feels confident that the fish will be able to make it on its own.

Tejera stresses the importance of making sure a flats fish is completely recovered before its allowed to swim off on its own, otherwise it's a prime target for sharks. A released fish will instinctively head for the deeper water beyond the flat to seek safety; ironically, that's where sharks usually wait to pick off weak and injured fish.

Reds Are Tough, Snook Aren't

"Redfish," Tejera says, "are tough. I don't worry as much about them as the other species. In fact a lot of times the redfish will stay alive in your livewell all day long. They're one of the easiest species to release safely."

Tough they may be, but they're not immune to sharks. In fact, Tejera warns *anglers* to be careful of barracuda and sharks while reviving a fish. He points to the unfortunate case of a fisherman who spent several weeks in the hospital after a large barracuda sliced his arm while attacking a red he was releasing.

In regards to survival rates following release, A.G. Woodward, a fisheries biologist with the Georgia Department of Natural Resources, offers this encouraging data. Between 1988 and 1989, 513 sub-legal, hook-caught redfish were

placed in tanks and observed for a minimum of two weeks. Of the 394 mouth-hooked reds, 92 percent survived. Fish that had been hooked in the gill and throat exhibited a 68 percent survival rate and the 52 gut-hooked fish had a survival rate of 47 percent.

With only five months of open snook season and strict size limits, anglers in southern Florida should certainly be aware of how to release these valuable game fish successfully. Particularly important is water temperature—not so much high temperature (as with striped bass), but low. Tejera says that snook caught during periods of cold weather have to be handled very carefully. Usually these fish are heavily stressed by the low water temperatures to begin with and may not be able to recover from a lengthy battle on light tackle. Handle these fish as little as possible, always keep them in the water, and make sure they're able to swim off vigorously, otherwise they could end up as shark bait, too.

As for the practice of lipping a healthy snook caught in optimum water temperatures, Tejera says that he doesn't have any evidence that it's harmful to the fish. "At least you're not touching the gills or rubbing off any slime when you do that," he says. "What usually happens, though, is that the person will lift the snook up to remove the hook or take a photo and the fish will shake. Then, of course, the person immediately drops the fish. That's worse than if you used a net and didn't drop the fish."

Releasing Tarpon

When it comes to tarpon, Tejera speaks out strongly against the common practice of lip-gaffing. "My latest project," he says, "is getting people not to lip-gaff. Usually, you will rip six to eight inches of jaw membrane before the hook catches around the hard lip cartilage." And for what? To get back the fly or lure? Consider yourself lucky enough to get the fish to the boat in the first place, and cut the line.

Another practice Tejera believes should be stopped, even though he used to do it himself, is the ceremonial removal of a trophy scale from the tarpon's back. Tejera says that he's seen some tarpon with big clumps of growth where a scale has been removed.

To revive a tarpon, Tejera grasps it firmly by the lower lip and swims it back in forth, keeping the fish facing into the current. He'll also raise the tarpon's head to give it a gulp of air once and a while, "since that's what they do naturally." Again, Tejera stresses the importance of making sure a tarpon that's exhausted after being fought on light tackle has completely recovered before it's allowed to swim off. "The fish that are hurt the least are the ones caught near the bridges on heavy tackle: there the fight may last five minutes. It's the fly-rodders that really exhaust them the most."

And an exhausted tarpon, Tejera says, is a prime target for hammerhead sharks. "Where you find tarpon," he warns, "There's always a hammerhead lurking nearby. And a tired tarpon is a hammerhead's favorite meal. If a fish is bleeding, it's automatically dead." To make sure a tarpon is able to make it on its own, Tejera has spent up to 20 minutes reviving it. "I've even gone into the water to revive a fish that's really exhausted," he says. Uh, what about those hammerheads, Paul?

Pacific Salmon

Although Tony Floor, spokesman for the Washington State Department of Fisheries, admits that the Northwest hasn't been very forward-thinking when it comes to catch and release, he says that anglers—particularly salmon anglers—had better start getting used to it. "Due to a recent downward spiral in native coho salmon stocks," he says, "anglers are going to be required, like it or not, to release the native fish."

Floor admits that it's going to cause a lot of controversy. However, he was quite confident that it's the only answer. "The next step down from

here is putting native cohos on the Endangered Species List, and we want to avoid that at all costs." Anglers will likely be required to release all native cohos, but may keep hatchery fish, which can be identified by the one missing ventral fin that was removed prior to release from the hatchery.

For those who want to get used to releasing fish, there's no need to wait. Jump right in and get some practice! Floor recommends obtaining some sort of dehooking tool, such as a pair of needlenose pliers or a J-shaped dehooker. Try to keep the fish in the water while you remove the hook and handle the fish as little as possible. If you have to handle the fish, only do so with wet hands, and be particularly careful not to touch the gills. The proper way to hold a salmon is by grasping the caudal peduncle (base of the tail) with one hand and gently cupping the other hand under the belly, just behind the gills. If the hook is deeply embedded and you can't get to it, cut the line near to the mouth. Another quick way to release a jaw-hooked salmon without touching it is to grab the hook with a dehooking tool, lift the fish out of the water, and twist the hook so the salmon simply falls into the water. If the hook has been removed quickly, and the salmon is not exhausted from the fight, it will usually zip right off.

If you're not confident with your dehooking abilities and need to bring the fish aboard, Floor recommends using a cotton-mesh net rather than one made of nylon, since cotton removes less slime and scales. In fact, anglers may be *required* to have a cotton-mesh net and some sort of dehooking tool on board their vessel in the future.

Sport fishermen in Washington have been required to use barbless hooks now for ten years. In fact, many expert salmon anglers now *prefer* them to barbed hooks, since they penetrate easier. As far as Floor knows there haven't been any studies on treble hooks versus single hooks. However,

he says that trebles are "hellish on the head and mouth areas," and feels that barbless singles give the fish the best chances of survival.

Deep-Water Bottom Fish

Finally, we come to the most controversial issue of them all: how to release deep-dwelling reef and bottom fish. Although the jury's not out yet on this one, initial studies offer some encouraging data. For instance, several studies involving red snapper caught off the Gulf Coast oil rigs in water approximately 100 feet deep showed a very high rate of survival if the fish had no hook injuries and weren't eaten on the way back to the bottom. In fact, most of the snappers had no problem returning to the bottom on their own. Some of the snappers were kept in cages on the bottom and observed for several days after release with no ill effects observed.

The bad news is that fish caught in depths over 100 feet showed a rapid increase in mortality after being observed in cages, and many of the "free-released" fish weren't able to return to the bottom because of the buoyancy caused by expanded stomach gas. It appears that the deeper the water, the higher the mortality due to injuries caused by decompression.

What about the practice of deflating the fish's abdomen so it can return to the bottom? According to Ron Schmied, special assistant for NMFS's Southeast Regional Office, and who also put together a video on how to release fish called *Pass it On* with *Salt Water Sportsman's* Senior Editor Mark Sosin, deflating a fish is better than leaving it floating on the surface, where it's susceptible to predation and exposure to the sun. It's the same principle as leaving the hook in a gut-hooked fish: sure, it isn't the ideal situation, but at least the fish has a chance.

Another biologist who advocates abdomen deflation is Dr. Ray Wilson of the University of South Florida. Wilson is currently studying hook-caught groupers (red, gag, and scamp) taken from South Florida's offshore reefs, and has found that release survival is relatively high if the fish are taken in less than 200 feet of water. Here the process of decompression and recompression doesn't seem to affect survival. Any deeper than 200 feet, however, and decompression injury becomes a factor and survival rate rapidly decreases.

"Don't have the attitude that you're throwing away a good fish," Wilson says, regarding a common misconception shared by many bottom fishermen. If you can get the fish in quickly so it's not completely exhausted, and deflate (aspirate) the abdomen (not the swim bladder, which is destroyed when the fish is brought to the surface), the fish has a good chance of surviving. Wilson recommends using a clean hypodermic needle (around 14 gauge) to deflate the abdomen, because it has a hole in the center that allows the gas to bleed off. Naturally, you need to remove the back of the syringe for it to work. If you can't obtain a needle, a *clean* ice pick, bait-stitching needle, or a debarbed hook will work in a pinch. Later, the puncture hole will heal.

"Remember," says Wilson, "that the only thing you're doing by deflating the abdomen is assisting the descent— so the fish is no longer buoyant. Some fish do have the energy to overcome that buoyancy." If a fish is still fighting hard when you get it to the boat, first see if it's able to descend on it's own. If not, then you should aspirate the abdomen.

The best way to deflate, or aspirate, a grouper is to turn the fish over on its back and insert the needle (or other device) on either side of the centerline just forward of the anus. (Many people confuse the large bulbous sac protruding from the mouth of a grouper or snapper as the swim bladder. This is actually the stomach of the fish that has been everted by the expanding gas and should not be punctured.) Then gently massage the gas out of the abdomen

General Rules for Safe Release

- Bring the fish to the boat quickly.
- Keep the fish in the water if possible. Always keep large fish, such as billfish and sharks, in the water.
- Small fish can be lifted from the water briefly and the hook removed with a dehooking tool.
- Cut the line or leader as close to the mouth as possible if the hook is difficult to remove.
- Use single, barbless hooks. Change trebles to singles on plugs or clip off two of the barbs on a treble to maintain balance.
- If you have to handle the fish, only do so with wet hands to keep the protective mucous coating intact.
- Don't touch the gills.
- Minimize time kept out of water.
- Lay the fish on a wet surface if it has to be brought onboard.
- Cover the fish's head with a wet towel to calm it.
- Take time to revive an exhausted fish.
- Deflate (aspirate) bottom fish only if they are unable to descend on their own.

and return the fish to the water. If the fish appears to be too exhausted to swim, Wilson says you can keep it in a live well just long enough for its breathing to return to normal. Groupers are surprisingly hardy, I was interested to learn, and have a fairly good chance of surviving if returned to the water in under three minutes. Some red grouper have been kept out of the water for up to five minutes and survived release.

Pacific Rockfish

West Coast rockfish are another deep-water species that present a similar release problem. I spoke with Farron Wallace, a fisheries biologist with the Washington Department of Marine Fisheries, who expressed surprise that I would even choose to cover the release of rockfish, since apparently very few sport fishermen in the Northwest practice it. Wallace told me that any rockfish taken from below 60 feet generally don't seem to be able to overcome the buoyancy of expanded gas. "Above that depth," he said,

"they're usually pretty lively and don't seem to have a problem getting back down."

When asked about the practice of gas deflation, Wallace said he wasn't aware of any studies being done, but directed me to the Seattle Aquarium and its Senior Biologist Pat McMahon. McMahon told me that his staff has experimented with deflation techniques using hypodermic needles (14 gauge) and says it does work with rockfish. He says that rockfish caught below 100 feet are unable to make it back down on their own, but seem to have no problem after deflation. (Unfortunately, I was unable to uncover any data concerning survival after release.) McMahon says that with rockfish, the needle should be inserted about two scales below the fish's lateral line behind the pectoral fin. The needle should also be angled toward the head as it's inserted into the musculature. Again, as with grouper and snapper, deflation should only be practiced if the fish is unable to descend on its own.

Some West Coast bottom fishermen have expressed concern over releasing lingcod. Fortunately, ling have no swim bladder and do not have a problem returning to any depth.

So there you have it, our rather exhaustive treatise on how to release

fish. Unfortunately, space did not allow us to cover every game fish, but the general principles of safe release can be applied to most every species. We hope the article has been instructive, that it has convinced you that released

fish survive, and that it will get you to release more of your fish. Of course, not every released fish will survive, but you can increase the number that do.

■

Saltwater Fly Fishing With Lefty Kreh

by Gary Diamond

When anglers talk of fly fishing experts, especially in saltwater, they usually refer to Lefty Kreh, a man who for more than four decades, has been considered the world's leading authority. Lefty has fished in all 50 states, throughout Central America, South America, Europe, Iceland, Australia, New Guinea, New Zealand and a number of small islands in both the South Pacific and Caribbean. He's the author of more than a dozen fly fishing books, several videos, holds a staff position on six major outdoor magazines and served on the boards of national fly fishing organizations, where he received numerous awards.

Kreh can do things with a fly rod that most folks only dream about. His fly casting techniques have been taught to avid fly fishermen throughout the world and his fishing success is unmatched. At one time, Kreh held nearly a dozen saltwater fly fishing records, many of which were on species found right in our own back yard. Lefty is one of the few fishermen fortunate enough to land a white marlin, blue marlin, sailfish, bluefin tuna, yellowfin tuna and a host of other big game species on a fly rod.

Before racing to the nearest tackle shop and purchasing a fly rod, Kreh said, "It's important to know that for most saltwater fly fishing, especially in the mid-Atlantic and New England states, you only need two fly rods. First, a size #8 for smaller species such as weakfish, white perch, yellow perch,

Fly fishing expert Lefty Kreh with an albacore. Lefty can do things with a fly rod that most folks only dream about. (GARY DIAMOND)

flounder and false albacore. When the wind is high, or you want to chase larger fish, you'll need a size #10. Modern 10 weight rods made by top manufacturers, such as Sage, Loomis, Orvis and others, can usually handle 10 or 11 weight lines equally as well and they'll whip any striped bass you'll ever catch."

Heavier Rods

Kreh added "There's a tendency for striped bass fishermen, especially those in the Northeast, to use heavier fly tackle than necessary. Some fishermen use size 12 or 13 weight rods, but the problem is, most people can't cast a

heavy rod for long periods of time." Because striped bass fishing usually requires casting large, wind-resistant flies, often for extended periods of time, lighter weight rods are preferred. However, when the winds are howling from an easterly direction, heavier rods and lines are often a necessary evil.

Two-Handed Rods

Kreh said this problem was recently solved when a lightweight, graphite version of a 200-year-old salmon fishing rod was introduced by a few manufacturers. "You can now buy a 14-foot, two-handed fly rod that only weighs 9 ounces." said Kreh. "There are a number of advantages to using a two-handed fly rod but until recently, very few people in the Northeast knew they existed. They're really great for striper fishing in the surf."

"When you're fishing from the beach, there are a number of advantages to fishing with a two handed rod. First, a person can cast 25 to 30 feet farther with a 12 to 14 foot rod than they can with a 9 footer. The reason is quite simple. The increased length of the rod makes the tip move a greater distance at a higher velocity, thereby increasing your casting range. This is really helpful when you're trying to catch big blues or stripers in the surf. If you make longer casts, you'll cover more water, which means you'll usually catch more fish."

Kreh says another distinct advantage of using the long, two-handed fly rod is it's ability to keep the line above the waves, preventing the surf from dragging and curling your line. Additionally, Kreh added, "The longer rod makes it easier to pick your line up and make a back-cast. If you're near the end of your retrieve and you're fighting the wave action, it's difficult to lift your line from the water, get it airborne and make a cast. With the longer 12 or 14 foot rod, this problem is minimized."

Kreh says a lot of fly fishermen have a false impression of the casting techniques used with a two-handed rod. In reality, the basic casting procedure is nearly identical to double hauling. Merely hold the rod's foregrip with your casting hand, grasping the line between your index finger and thumb. Grip the rod butt with your other hand and with a short, quick motion, shove it forward as you pick the line from the water for your back-cast. When the line's straight behind you, pull the butt toward your elbow to initiate your power cast. It's that easy.

Kreh says the average person can easily pick 60 feet of line off the water using this technique. The ensuing forward or power cast often travels well over 100 feet. Kreh says special fly lines designed for two-handed rods are now available from Scientific Anglers and Courtland. These lines have designations such as Extra-Long Belly Taper and Special Rocket Taper for two handed rods.

Tippet

"Most fishermen don't really understand the function of a leader, especially when it comes to saltwater fly fishing." said Lefty. "A leader plays several roles, the most important, an invisible connection between the line and fly. However, there are additional, but very important considerations. First, the tippet, which is the smallest part of the leader, has to match the fly. If you were to use a heavy length of monofilament for a tippet and a relatively small fly, it would kill the fly's action, which reduces the number of fish you'll catch. Therefore, tippet is not only an integral part of this invisible connection, but it's weight determines the fly's action."

Leader Length

"If you're fishing for striped bass in a clear New England river or a coastal Long Island back cove that's flat calm, you'll need a longer leader than if you were fishing offshore or in the surf," said Kreh. "The reason behind the extended length is to place the fly line's impact on the water well away from the fly. In calm, clear water, a leader measuring 10 to 12 feet works well."

"Unfortunately, God never lets us fly fish in salt water without first making the weather windy. When the winds are high, the water will be rough and under these conditions substantially shorter leaders are equally as effective," Kreh said. "If you're fishing the surf and conditions are relatively calm, a 9-foot leader is acceptable. When the water's surface is dead calm, you'll do best with a 12- to 13-foot leader. If the surface is choppy, 7 to 8 feet is fine, especially when you're using sinking line."

Kreh added, "If you're using sinking lines, leaders should never be longer than seven to eight feet. The problem is the fly line sinks, but the monofilament leader tends to float. If I want my fly deep, I prefer a maximum leader length of just three to four feet with most types of sinking fly line."

Topwater Versus Sinking Flies

"When you're fishing in water less than 15 feet deep, most of the food consumed by predator fish is consumed on or near the bottom," said Kreh. "Obviously, if you're fishing on the open ocean, pelagic species will feed up and down the water column, but most of the time, they'll feed 10 to 20 feet beneath the surface."

"The major problem you'll encounter when saltwater fly fishing is casting a sufficient distance to get the fly deep, where the fish are feeding." Kreh says most of the time, sinking and fast sinking lines produce far more strikes than floating lines. Because of this, Kreh prefers shooting heads, specially constructed lines that frequently outperform standard weight forward designs because of their decreased wind resistance and improved casting ability.

Kreh says if you encounter situations where floating lines and popping bugs can be productive, such as a school of breaking bluefish or stripers actively feeding on the surface, be sure to attach the popper with a loop knot. This allows the bug to splash erratically as it's being retrieved, giving it the appearance of an injured baitfish. Kreh says the loop knot also aids in lifting the fly from the water's surface before casting.

Line Backing

"I use 30 pound Dacron line for backing. The reason is, 30-pound Dacron resists abrasion much better than 20-pound. Although some anglers use 20-pound Dacron backing because they can put more line on their spool, in most instances, the added length isn't necessary. I've been fishing hard with a fly rod since 1949 and with the exception of some ocean species such as sailfish, tuna and huge tarpon, I have never had a fish run off 200 yards of backing. In fact, any fish that lives within two or three miles of the coast, with the exception of tarpon, will never take 200 yards of backing, plus an additional 30 yards of fly line from your reel. The only advantage to having a lot of backing is it increases the spool's diameter which allows you to recover line at a greater rate. With 200 yards of 30-pound Dacron backing, you can land just about any fish that swims within two miles of shore."

Kreh says never, under any circumstances, use monofilament backing. When under stress, monofilament line stretches, decreases it's diameter and buries itself into the bed of line remaining on the spool. The compressed line eventually becomes weakened and catches within the line's folds, causing it to break when a big fish makes a hard run. Not only do you lose the fish, but in addition, you could lose your $35 fly line.

Kreh says the most important aspect of backing is making sure it's installed properly on the spool. "Most people put backing on a reel by allowing the line to run between their thumb and forefinger while winding it on. Ironically, a lot of novice saltwater fly anglers lose big fish because of this. If the backing isn't extremely tight, it packs down in the folds of the line and snags when the fish takes off on a long run. You should use cotton or leather work gloves, hold the line as tight as possible and make sure it's put on evenly."

Night Fishing

"Some of the most productive fly fishing in the Northeast, especially for big stripers, takes place at night, a time when fish often migrate into the surf to feed. The problem with night fishing is there's no way of telling how much line you have retrieved. If too much line is retrieved, it's impossible to make another cast until you've worked sufficient line out with several false casts. Wouldn't it be nice if you knew exactly how much line was out, then make a single false cast and place the fly right where you want it? It's easy to do during the day when you can see the line, but at night, it's nearly impossible."

Kreh, known by his peers as a creative genius, developed a Braille-type method of marking his fly line so he knows exactly how much line is out while fishing in total darkness. "All you have to do make a few casts during the day and at the point where you normally pick up the line to make another cast, mark it with a pen. Then, using a short length of 10-pound test monofilament line, tie a tight nail knot over the mark. The monofilament will compress the fly line enough so you won't

have to coat the area with Goop or Rubber Cement and to make it pass through the rod guides. At night, when you're striping line in, you'll feel that tiny nail knot as it touches your fingers and know it's time to make another cast." Kreh says the same technique is great for anglers casting Slime Line, a clear fly line that's nearly invisible.

Stripping Baskets

"Most saltwater fly fishermen quickly discover the value of a stripping basket when they're fishing the surf. Good baskets are commercially available, but for $5 you can make one from a plastic dishpan or Tupperware container. All you do is cut a couple of slots in one side and pass a belt through the slots so the pan can be attached to your waist. Then turn the pan over and with a small diameter, heated nail, punch a couple dozen holes through the bottom. Then cut some 2-inch strands of 100 pound monofilament leader, heat one end with a match until a ball is formed and place a piece of mono in each hole. Then, using epoxy or hot melt glue, put a dab at the base of each strand of mono to hold it in place. Now the inside of the striping basket has a bunch of tiny monofilament fingers projecting upward and preventing your line from tangling as you walk. Without a stripping basket, you'll spend a lot of time untangling line from your feet."

Casting Accuracy
Makes a Difference

"More often than not, casting accuracy determines your saltwater fly fishing success," Kreh said. "In many instances, especially when you're fishing offshore, you're casting a swirl or trying to place your fly as close as possible to a weed-line. If you can't see the line, how can you determine where it's going to hit?" This is one of the reasons Kreh prefers using fluorescent colored fly lines, colors that sharply contrast with both the sky and water.

"If you're fishing properly, you're not throwing fly line directly over the fish. In most instances, you're casting to a spot some distance away from them, to a point where the fly will be intercepted as it's being retrieved. Another big advantage of fluorescent line is after you've hooked a big fish, if the captain has to chase it with the boat, he's not as likely to run over a bright line he can readily see." Kreh added.

Fly Selection

When it comes to which flies to use for a specific species of fish, it's tough to beat the Lefty's Deceiver, a large streamer made from a combination of bucktail hair and long, slender hackle feathers. Although several variations of Lefty's famous fly have been adapted to various fishing situations, the basic pattern he created nearly three decades ago is still effective on a variety of big game, saltwater species.

"One of the advantages of fishing with a deceiver, a fly I designed for catching stripers, is you can make it very large but still maintain a good profile that's easy to cast. Lets face it, big fish tend to take big flies. The Deceiver's a good fly, but more recently, the Clouser Deep Minnow has become one of the best flies you can use in the Northeast. In fact, during the past three years, I've caught 63 different species of fish in fresh and salt water with this particular pattern. It's the single best underwater fly that has been developed in the past 25 years."

"If you're fishing for striped bass, one of the best flies you can use is a chartreuse and white Clouser Deep Minnow measuring about five inches long. During the past two years, especially in the Northeast, this has been a red-hot striped bass fly. That's because sand eels are one of the favorite foods of striped bass and a sparsely dressed Clouser minnow, tied in the same colors as the eel, is one of the best imitations I've ever seen. It's a good idea to tie a bunch of them with different sized lead eyes so you can cover a variety of depths," Kreh added.

"When you're fishing for false albacore and bonito, a very small Clouser minnow, one measuring about two inches long with fairly small lead eyes, has been responsible for some of the best albacore action from North Carolina to New England. During the fall, both species travel close to shore and if you have a good selection of deceivers, Clouser minnows and a few big popping bugs, that's all the flies you'll need to catch all the fish you can handle. Sure, there are lots of other flies that work in saltwater, but if you have these three, you probably won't need the others.

Lefty's Tips for Catching Big Fish

Cobia: "There's a couple secrets to catching big cobia with a fly rod. First of all, cobia will hit a large popping bug faster than any other fly. A 3/0 popper with a face the size of a quarter is just about right for cobia—they rarely take a small fly.

"Teasing cobia is probably the best way to catch them. You can do this by catching a small baitfish, hook it to a heavy boat rod and drag it around near a buoy. Cobia are like sharks in that they're readily attracted to sounds made by a struggling baitfish. If there's a cobia in the area, it won't be long until it appears right under the baitfish. Lift the baitfish from the water and cast your popping bug in the same spot. Unless the fish is spooked by the boat, it will hit the popper like a freight train."

Striped Bass: "Most fly fishing for striped bass in Maryland and Virginia is done in the shallows from a small boat. The fishing usually takes place in Chesapeake Bay tributaries such as the Choptank and Potomac, where big schools are often found during late summer and fall. The best action is usually during the late afternoon and early evening when baitfish frequently congregate on the surface," he said.

"If you see stripers actively feeding—birds diving, fish breaking—toss a big deceiver or popping bug in their general direction and you're going to catch lots of fish. This is fast fishing and the fish don't always cooperate by staying on top for long periods of time. It's a good idea to have a fly rod rigged and ready to cast at all times.

"A trick I use is to take a five-gallon plastic bucket, put it near the transom and then make the longest cast you possibly can, strip the line into the bucket and hook the fly on the rod handle. When you find a school of fish, unhook the fly, make a false cast and the line will shoot out of the five gallon bucket without getting tangled. If it's windy or you're chasing moving schools of fish at high speeds, put a little water in the bucket. It will keep both your fly line and the bucket from blowing out of the boat.

"From New Jersey north to New England, several striped bass fishing options are available to fly rod fishermen. One of the most exciting is catching them from the surf, which is better in the fall than any other time of year. When you hook a big striper in just three or four feet of water, it goes completely berserk.

"There are lots of small boat fishing opportunities for big stripers also, especially in places like Barnegat Bay where big fish can be found in grass beds and near rock piles. These are great places that are often only accessible to 14- to 16-foot aluminum skiffs powered with small outboards.

"One of the best things about fishing from a small boat is you can go way up into a river system or work the edge of a flats or fish drop-offs of small coves. Striped bass love to lay on a drop-off, whether it's in Chesapeake Bay, Barnegat Bay or Penobscot River, if you can locate a drop-off, you can catch stripers close to the bottom. In New England, there are lots of quiet bays formed where river mouths drop back off the coast. It's in these little sloughs, creeks and coves where big stripers feed on baitfish and crabs all

summer long. On calm, overcast days, striper fishing in these locations can be fantastic."

Kreh added: "Jetties are always a good place to fish for striped bass and most of the time, you don't need a boat in order to catch fish. Stripers school near jetties in spring, summer and fall, but here's a trick that will make fly fishing from a jetty easier. Buy an eight foot by eight foot piece of half inch mesh netting, tie a six- to eight-ounce sinker to each corner and lay it over the rocks. Now you can drop your fly line on the netting and it won't get snagged in the boulders. Some people use tarps, but when the wind get under a tarp, it's gone—wind doesn't effect the netting."

Lefty says it's extremely important to read the water by looking for structure that impedes tidal flow and forms turbulent, backwater eddies. "It's the tide that carries the baitfish and they'll congregate on the downtide side of jetties, rock piles, sand bars and other forms of shallow structure, places where they don't have to expend lots of energy to survive. That's why big stripers are usually found in the same locations."

Bluefish: "Bluefish are tough to catch, mainly because they're constantly on the move, trying to find something to eat. Bluefish are essentially eating machines, but unless you're lucky enough to stumble across a migrating school of blues hitting everything that moves, they're difficult to catch. The best way I know to catch bluefish, especially on a fly rod is in a chum slick. It's a lot easier to attract fish to you, than it is for you to find them in the open ocean."

Kreh's technique for catching big blues is unique. His secret to success is to use sinking line, a relatively short leader and a short length of coffee-colored, stainless tippet. "Sometimes I'll tie on a fly that imitates the baitfish attracted to the chum, but my most effective fly looks like a fresh chunk of ground menhaden. The fly is just a 1/0 hook wrapped with enough lead wire

281

to make it sink with the chum. The hook is then wrapped with dark brown and red maribou to make it look like a large piece of chum drifting in the slick. Let the fly drift freely for 30 to 40 feet, flowing with the chum line. If you don't get a strike, retrieve the line and drop the fly at the beginning of the slick. It's just like nymph fishing for freshwater trout. The fish hit on a slack line and it takes fast reflexes to set the hook before it discovers something's wrong with the bait."

Billfish: Lefty is among a handful of individuals who can brag of catching both blue and white marlin on a fly rod. "The hardest billfish to catch is a white marlin. They're a fast-swimming fish that feeds while it's moving extremely fast. The only time it hits a slow bait is after it has been stunned or injured during the chase. That's why they're impossible to catch from a drifting boat."

Kreh says most marlin, blue and white are taken by first luring the fish with a large teaser trolled at high speeds. When a marlin attacks the teaser, the mate drags lure within fly casting range while the boat's still in motion. A large streamer, often measuring 10 to 12 inches, is then dropped behind the teaser. "If your equipment is perfectly matched, your drag's smooth as silk and the hook is razor sharp, you might get lucky enough to sink the

hook beyond the barb. The fish will jump and you'll likely spend the next several hours chasing a marlin all over the ocean," added Kreh.

Tuna: "The easiest tuna to catch on a fly rod is yellowfin and bonito. The bonito are often found close to shore and accessible to small boat anglers. At certain times, especially during late summer and early fall, you'll find them breaking a few miles offshore. Toss a big streamer several feet in front of the fish, strip your line as fast as possible and when they hit, hang on. Bonito are a lot of fun on any kind of light tackle, but they're fantastic on a fly rod," he said.

"The few yellowfin tuna I've taken on a fly were mid-sized, 25 to 50 pounders. Like most saltwater fish with deeply forked tails, they're extremely powerful, but because they don't jump, tuna also have lots of stamina, making them tougher to land than a similar sized marlin." Kreh says when yellowfins are feeding on the surface, they'll slam a big streamer, but after fighting and landing that first fish, few anglers are willing to battle another.

Dolphin: "Dolphin are easy to find and one of the most exciting species you'll encounter while fly fishing in salt water. The secret to success is finding the right kind of bluewater structure. If you're lucky enough to locate an offshore weed line, there's an even chance you'll find lots of dolphin hiding

in it's shadow. You'll also find them lurking in the shade of lobster pots, fish pots, under offshore buoys and beneath floating debris. If you can't locate floating structure, you can make your own by merely placing sheets of newspaper on the water at intervals of 50 to 100 feet. Two or three sheets sandwiched together will float for six or seven hours, but they'll eventually disintegrate, therefore they're not causing pollution. Mark the coordinates on your loran and return to the site within an hour or two. When conditions are right, you'll find a hefty dolphin under every other sheet.

"The easiest way to catch dolphin with a fly rod is to cast from a drifting boat. Simply toss a big streamer close to the weed line or newspaper sheets, let it sink a few feet and retrieve it at a rapid rate. If there's a dolphin under the structure, your fly doesn't have a prayer of making it back to the boat. Most of these fish are only 12- to 20-pounders, but once in a while, a 40- to 50-pounder shows up. If it hits your fly, dig your heels in for a long and exciting battle."

Lefty says fly fishing is an exciting and often new way for many anglers to catch many species of fish that were once reserved only to those fishing with heavy tackle. "It's the ultimate challenge for all saltwater fishermen." ∎

Bottom Bouncing

by Mark Sosin and George Poveromo

Searching for fish along the floors of oceans, bays and sounds ranks as the most popular form of saltwater fishing, and for good reason. Bottom fishing usually offers plenty of action, which can range from rigging gear and baiting hooks to judging when to set up on a pernicious fish that's been

nibbling away at an offering. In contrast to trolling or other specialized forms of fishing, there's always something to keep an angler's mind occupied, and the odds are greater for finding more consistent fishing. Furthermore, most benthic fish provide good to excellent tablefare.

Locating Structure

The concept behind successful bottom fishing is based on an angler's ability to uncover structure that is likely to hold fish. Structure can be defined as wrecks, reefs, rockpiles, depressions in the bottom's contour, weed growth, bridges and assorted rubble, pilings and even channel edges. Anything that offers sanctuary is likely to be an ecosystem that harbors both bait and gamefish. As algae and micro organisms begin to flourish on or near such points, smaller fish move in to feed and seek shelter and, in turn, attract larger fish. Depending on the size and location of the structure, a complete community is often maintained, with the larger benthic fish establishing their own niches within the boundaries. If such territorial fish are removed from the system, there will be others that'll quickly replace them.

Expert anglers realize how critical structure is to success. It's not unusual for them to run long and hard before settling down to fish, with the excessive travel time often rewarded with quality catches. Probably the most valuable aid when it comes to bottom fishing is a dependable chart recorder. Used by all professional captains and an ever-increasing number of recreational anglers, a recorder offers the advantages of illustrating an entire water column. It shows whether a bottom's composition is hard (rocky) or soft (muddy), the exact zone in which the fish are holding and, to some degree, it differentiates between bait and gamefish.

When ferreting out productive structures in an unfamiliar region, anglers should first study a navigational chart. By doing this homework, which includes chatting with local baitshop personnel, one can pencil in, and then locate, several proven areas. The chart recorder helps to pinpoint the exact spot by monitoring the bottom's contour. Furthermore, anglers often run to such spots with their recorders on. They may burn excessive amounts of paper in the process but there's always the possibility of uncovering fish and new structures along the way.

Loran has greatly simplified the ability to find and return to a hot area. In addition, the coordinates of the more popular points are often public knowledge, reducing the amount of effort and headaches associated with

Joey, left, and Nick Andelora with four keeper fluke (summer flounder) caught by bottom bouncing squid and spearing bait in the channels of New Jersey's Barnegat Bay. Fluking is an ideal way to introduce any youngster to fishing. (VIN T. SPARANO)

trying to locate them by other means. A professional captain will always study a chart recorder for structure, placing the loran coordinates of promising areas into the unit's memory. Over the years, these captains have logged hundreds of spots in the pages of their loran books. By taking the time to record their findings, they have literally created a fishing circuit. A captain now has the option of lining up several prominent spots within striking distance of each other. If one point fails to produce fish, he'll simply plug in another set of coordinates and continue on his way. It may take a few years to master, but recreational anglers can build their own collection of numbers, as well as determine what spots are best during the course of the year.

Different Strokes for Different Folks

By developing a basic understanding of the most popular fish frequenting a region, you should have an advantage that will reflect in your catch. Focus on the seasons, the types of structure that appeal to them, the best baits, and

coordinating your terminal gear with the size and species of the fish.

For example, blackfish is a very popular Northeastern groundfish that takes up residence around scattered rocks in sounds and shallow offshore waters, becoming more abundant between spring and fall. These scrappy warriors, often less than four pounds, lurk around structure for protection and to feed on various types of mussels and clams. Anglers fishing Long Island Sound off Rowayton, Connecticut, particularly around Green's Ledge, Budd Reef and The Cows off Shippan Point (just north of the Stamford breakwater), benefit from abundant rockpiles that maintain healthy populations of these tasty fish.

Black seabass are similar to blackfish except that they prefer slightly greater depths and are more prominent offshore of the Carolina and Virginia coastlines. From the Carolinas southward through the Gulf of Mexico, groupers and snappers take over as the most valuable bottom fish.

Wreck Dwellers

Artificial reefs and shipwrecks have improved local fisheries by replacing portions of the bottom that have been damaged, and by adding structure to otherwise barren areas. Most wrecks and artificial reefs are situated offshore, although an increasing amount of attention is being given to developing inshore programs. Species visiting or taking up residence around these points run the gamut from amberjack, barracuda, cobia (ling), snapper, and grouper from the Gulf of Mexico to the Carolinas. Cod, pollack and hake take over in the cooler waters off the New England coast.

Seasons will determine the arrival of migratory species. Peaks can range from the winter in the extreme southern portion of Florida to the spring and early summer off the Southeast and Gulf of Mexico states to mid-summer and early fall off the Northeast. Because of the vast ecosystems supported by these wrecks, pelagic species sometimes linger around the ones situated near deep water. Dolphin, kingfish and mackerel may visit sights in the Gulf of Mexico and Southeastern states, and every now and again there might be a smattering of sailfish and tarpon off some of the South Florida wrecks.

Deep Dwellers

The ultra deep species that reside on the bottom near and beyond the Continental Shelf make up a small recreational fishery due to the vast depths and currents that must be encountered to get a bait down to them. Tilefish are probably the most popular and abundant species, followed by hake and cusk in the Northeast. Since it's sometimes necessary to make a set depth nearing 2,000 feet, especially for the latter two species, electric reels are used to lower and haul up the heavily weighted rigs. You will occasionally find recreational anglers fishing for tilefish in waters around 400 feet deep with electric reels or downriggers that have enough cable to reach them.

Inshore Fish

Inshore species are located in a manner similar to their offshore counterparts, but their structure will consist of scattered debris, channel edges, depressions, oyster bars, etc. The prestigious striped bass is a prime example of an inshore species that frequents shelves and rocky points. It is especially fond of structure at the mounts of rivers or canals that dump fresh and brackish waters into bays and sounds. Compared to blackfish, which can sometimes be found around offshore rocks, striped bass rarely travel seaward.

Gulf coast and southeastern bay anglers know that the popular sheepshead can be found around hard bottom. Alabama's Mobile Bay is just one productive system that yields great numbers of these fish. The remains of the old Dauphin Island bridge and the surrounding oyster beds attract some

real heavyweights that may break five or six pounds. The tasty fish feed mainly on crustaceans that abound around such structure.

Species such as flounder or fluke (summer founder) are fond of structure, too. However, in comparison to hard bottom, these fish enjoy muddy bottoms that are adjacent to shallow flats, as well as various holes, depressions or channels. Their flat configuration and coloration permit them to blend into the ocean floor. This camouflage offers both protection and the ability to attack unsuspecting baitfish such as blood and sand worms, mussels, killifish and sand eels. The fluke grows considerably larger than the winter flounder, with doormats weighing more than ten pounds. It'll frequent sections of inlets and shoals where moderate to swift currents abound.

The Fun Fish Species

If the most sought-after species take a breather, there are always the "fun fish" that will do their best to turn an otherwise unproductive day into a memorable outing. Some of these lesser-known fish aren't recommended for quality tablefare, but practically all of them will put up a determined scrap with anglers who are willing to scale their tackle accordingly. Day savers can include pinfish, which are caught over grassy flats, white perch, grunts, sea robins, and blowfish. All species are prominent inshore and over some offshore structures and are usually under two pounds. Their willingness to consume a variety of small cut baits make them the perfect challenge for youngsters who are just beginning to experience the thrill of salt water angling.

Getting to the Fish

Although some inshore fish, such as flounder, striped bass, porgies and blackfish, can be taken by anglers from bridges, piers or in the surf, increased fishing pressure has limited the better catches to boatowners. After locating

a potential area, an angler must select the baits and use them in conjunction with the proper rigs to get them down to the fish. Always obtain the freshest bait possible. Bottom fish, particularly grouper and snapper, rely heavily on their sense of smell and it often takes the scent of a fresh bait to convince a finicky member to eat. While you may take your fair share of fish on frozen bait, there's no denying that a fresh bait will be the decisive factor in producing fish on slow days.

An experienced bait fisherman always takes into consideration what's happening around him. That is, he's monitoring the water conditions to find out what the fish are feeding on and using the bait that's the most abundant within an area. By "matching the hatch," an angler can increase his chances of catching fish. There are many species that go on a selective feeding pattern, consuming those baits that they have rounded up or which thrive in a system. Striped bass is just one species that tends to specialize at times. Veteran anglers know they'll score more consistently using the predominant bait.

Understand that fish frequenting grass flats or soft bottoms are often pursuing shrimp, crabs or bloodworms and those over rockpiles are ferreting out crabs, mussels and a variety of baitfish. Try tempting the fish with their natural food first, switching strategies only after there's a lull in the activity. Furthermore, it often requires alternating baits when fish become wise to a certain offering. For example, grouper fished over the rockpiles in the Gulf of Mexico are noted for turning off to a specific type of bait that's repeatedly lowered into their domain. That's why successful anglers begin by using only one type of offering, such as Spanish sardines, and switching to another, usually squid, mullet or live pinfish, when the fish cease feeding. By doing so, they can effectively take advantage of a concentration of fish.

Neatness counts in trimming baits. There's more to presenting natural

Saltwater Fishing Techniques

baits than cutting a chunk from a fish and lowering it to the bottom. Consider the current and how much more enticing a strip of squid or mullet will be as it flutters in front of a fish's lair. Baits can be trimmed to create a swimming action, and even to conceal a hook, such as a ballyhoo plug. A streamlined bait will cut accurately through a swift tide, appealing more to fish than a bulky one that resists the flow. Above all, pack several different types of baits on each outing. You'll not only have a greater chance of supplying the fish with what they want, but have an adequate back-up supply that can even be used for chum.

Terminal Gear

Successful bottom fishing requires a precise balance of terminal gear tailored to the desired species. Many fishermen make the mistake of employing gear that is too heavy for their quarry. Such overkill results in fewer strikes, affects a bait or lure's action, and reduces the sensitivity to feel a fish pick up an offering. Whenever applicable, use the lightest monofilament leaders that can handle a species and the least amount of lead that will hold an offering at the bottom. Depending upon the structure and the size of the fish, you may even consider scaling down to light tackle, such as 10- or 12-pound test line. The smaller diameter of a light line allows it to sink quicker than a heavier one and increases its sensitivity. Also, the lighter the monofilament leader, the less hardware a fish is likely to notice.

There will be certain situations that will prohibit the use of light gear. When fishing near wrecks or abrupt structures for large fish such as grouper or snapper, it's often necessary to employ heavy gear to horse the fish away from a potential cutoff. However, by utilizing a monofilament leader that tests slightly above the actual fishing line, you can still benefit by keeping visibility minimal. If an angler is fishing a wreck for grouper averaging 15 or 20

pounds and uses 30-pound test line, his leader's breaking strength should be 40 or 50 pounds. If he uses a 20-pound test outfit, he should reduce his leaders to around 30- or 40-pound test. Grouper don't possess dentures that are detrimental to fishing lines and it's often beneficial to use light to moderate strength leaders for them. Even with toothy fish such as mackerel or kingfish, you'll draw more strikes by using predominantly monofilament leaders. To reduce the risk of a cut-off and still maintain low visibility, tie a three or four inch wire trace leader to the monofilament with an Albright Special knot.

Sinkers come in a variety of sizes and shapes to cover most bottom applications. Among the standard selections that attach directly to the fishing line are the split shots (a small lead that is crimped on a fishing line) and the rubbercore sinker (which is attached by running the fishing line through its groove with a rubber cap or stop at each end to hold it in place). The egg sinker is the common choice of bottom fishermen. If the lead is small enough, it can ride just above the eye of a hook. Otherwise, most applications will find it resting on a swivel or the knot joining the fishing line and leader.

The pyramid sinker is often used in swift currents. In contrast to the weight styles mentioned above, the pyramid actually anchors itself in the bottom, leaving the bait to ride freely just above it. Like the egg sinker, the pyramid can be rigged as slider by running the fishing line through its eye. It also can be used as a base for specialty rigs where two or more hooks are featured.

The type of terminal arrangement an angler chooses will depend on the species and his sporting virtues. For example a rig for striped bass can consist of an egg sinker just above a three or four foot stretch of 60-pound test monofilament leader and a 6/0 or 7/0 live bait hook. The bait can be a live menhaden, or the head section of one. Rigs for blackfish, grouper and seabass

can be as simple as a 2/0 hook, a foot or so of 30- or 40-pound-test monofilament leader, and an adequate amount of lead to maintain a proper depth. A more complex dropper rig would incorporate a pyramid sinker at its base and about three or four feet of 60-pound-test monofilament leader equally divided by a pair of three-way swivels, each featuring about a two foot dropper line with a hook.

There are anglers who are fond of a spreader rig, particularly with flounder. Such an instrument is constructed with a three way swivel dividing 20 to 24 inches of stiff wire. The fishing line is tied to the swivel's top eye with a few inches of monofilament and a bank or pyramid sinker attached to the bottom. A dropper hook is then secured to each end of the wire bar.

Regardless of the rigs, hook sizes should be geared to the species of fish. A large hook shows more hardware and requires a serious effort to drive it home, especially with species blessed with bony jaws. Take the time to hone each hook before placing it into action, inspecting it for sharpness throughout the day.

Deep Jigging

Deep jigging involves the art of coaxing a fish to strike an artificial. It's a popular form of fishing that is often associated with light tackle. The advantage of deep jigging is that you work not only the ocean bottom, but the entire water column. Grouper anglers in South Florida, the Bahamas, and the Keys continually see action from pelagic species such as kingfish, mackerel, barracuda and even a sailfish over the deep, offshore reefs. In addition, the boat usually drifts along a reef, allowing an angler to cover more ground and increase his chances of finding fish.

Deep jigs come in a variety of sizes and shapes. The two most prominent designs include the lima bean and arrow heads. The lima bean style features compressed sides that give it a fluttering action when worked through

285

the water. The arrow tends to track straight and accurately. The latter design also penetrates a water column quicker because it exposes less surface area. Jigging spoons are more prominent in northern waters. Like the lead heads, they, too, come in various weights and two main designs that give them an inherent action. The diamond jig slices through the water quickly, while those featuring flat sides maintain a swimming like motion.

To maximize a jig's action and potential, use the lightest weight possible to reach bottom. Depending upon the species, opt for the lightest monofilament leader that can accomplish the job. If you have to use wire to prevent a cut-off, try a trace of about for or five inches. Pay particular attention to the knot, making sure there's an adequate loop for the jig to swing on. Ditto with wire. Never snug a knot against a lead's eye ring, for it will only hinder its performance.

A productive drift pattern is one that covers the shallow and deep sections of a reef. Depending upon the wind and tide, begin your drift at one extreme, repositioning yourself only after you clear the opposite end. By covering various depths and working closely with a chart recorder, you'll be able to discover the most productive zones to concentrate on. For benthic species, a jig should be allowed to reach bottom before being retrieved back to the surface with a hopping motion. It often pays to let the jig sink back to the bottom a second time after initially retrieving it about 20 feet. A solid strike will get an angler's attention in a hurry. Fish often strike a jig on its descent, reducing an angler's ability to "feel" the fish. It there's the slightest interference with a jig destined for the bottom, engage the reel's drag, take up the slack line, and strike if there's any resistance.

Often frowned upon by purists, sweetening a jig with a natural bait is almost a surefire way of luring bottom dwellers into feeding. Sweeteners can include strips of cut bait trimmed so

that they flutter attractively with the jig's motion, or whole baits that are impaled on a hook. Tipped jigs can be retrieved in a fashion listed above or left on the bottom until a fish consumes it. A second hook can even be added to guard against short strikes. Trailing hooks feature open eyes that can be closed with pliers after they've been attached to the lead hook. The lead hook is inserted under the bait's lower jaw and out the upper membrane with the barb of the second hook positioned inside the mid section.

Party Boats

Party or drift boats provide access to bottom fish and are an inexpensive alternative to chartering a private craft. They offer a great day on the water with friends when you don't feel like going through the motions of preparing your own craft. Prices on these boats vary, but you can expect to pay an average of $12 to $25 dollars per person for a half- or full-day ticket respectively. The fishing strategies will also vary with what's running at the time. If migratory species are in, expect the drift and tackle to be geared towards to them. Although you can still drop a bait to the bottom, the odds are that the boat won't be positioned over prime ground fish spots.

Check with a party boat captain in advance to learn what's running, his strategy for the week, prices, and the type of gear he has available. Chances are reservations aren't required and, unless you prefer your own gear, tackle is usually available at a nominal rental fee. Ditto terminal gear. Also, find out what baits he'll have on board, packing your own if you believe a different offering may stack the deck in your favor. Party boats make their money on the number of fishermen they host. Therefore, heavy tackle (30- and 40-pound-test conventional gear), is the norm. If you plan on bringing light tackle, it may be best to consult the captain in advance. If the "rail" is lean, he may let you follow through with your quest.

Otherwise, a disaster is almost sure to occur if a fish hooked on light tackle skirts its way across and tangles the lines of about 40 other paying customers.

Productive positions or hot seats aboard a party boat are those that happen to be near the fish when they're passing through, or right above an edge, shelf, wreck or structure. Many anglers swear by the stern, although their preference may be based on the fact that they're not sandwiched between other anglers, and that their baits can be drifted or worked in the relatively uncrowded waters off that section. If you desire a stern slot, make certain you arrive at the dock well ahead of time to secure it. And by all means, make sure you board the craft at least 15 minutes before departure. Party boat captains adhere precisely to their designated schedule to maximize actual fishing time.

The backbone of any drift boat is the mate. This hard-working lad must cater to the needs of the ship's party. He's in charge of rigging tackle, baiting hooks, untangling lines, keeping anglers happy, cleaning fish for anglers, and keeping the boat and its gear in ship shape and Bristol fashion. He's only too happy to explain the most productive techniques for the designated species, simply looking for a little consideration in the form of a tip back at the dock.

Party boat techniques are as simple as using a strip of bait or a whole fish on a hook and sending it down with the aid of a weight. The idea is to keep the bait just above the bottom which is usually accomplished by taking a few turns on a reel after it reaches its destination. Periodically, drop the bait back down to the bottom to compensate for any line planing due to current. After several minutes, it becomes necessary to reel up, check the bait, and re-drop it to keep an advantageous angle with the bottom. Deep jigging techniques also will produce, although it can become very difficult to entice a fish to strike an artificial when there's plenty of natural bait to be had. Some drift boat captains will go so far as to deploy a live bait or two in hopes of capturing a shark, billfish or other trophy fish for mounting purposes. If you desire to fish a live bait, make arrangements with the captain at least a day or so in advance.

Some drift boats even offer weekend bottom fishing expeditions to remote regions at very attractive rates, especially those sailing from South Florida and the Keys. Drift boats operate half- and full-day trips, as well as some night outings.

Fighting Strategies

Bottom fish can be pursued with almost any type of gear. The smaller members frequenting grass beds, oyster bars, bridges, etc., are enjoyable to wrestle on lines less than 10-pound test. The bigger gladiators are a different story. Depending on an angler's skill, he may attempt to challenge some of these critters on bait-casting gear spooled with lines testing between 12- and 15 pounds. However, when large fish abound over potentially dangerous structures, it often requires stiff rods and a minimum of 20 pound test line to have a chance at them.

The strategy with bottom fish, even with the smaller species on ultra light gear, is to go toe-to-toe with them immediately after setting the hook. By placing as much strain on your tackle as you can and still keeping within the line's breaking strength, you'll have a better chance of disorienting the fish enough o move it away from any structure. Any delays will give the fish a fighting chance, and usually enough time to react and charge into its lair. If a fish holes up, try throwing slack in the line for a few minutes, then engaging the reel's drag and "horsing" the fish after the line becomes taut. There are no guarantees, but sometimes this trick is worthy of a try. The most critical stage of the battle usually ends about ten or 15 feet above the bottom. It's a game of reflexes and judgment that becomes mastered after a few seasons in the field. ∎

Fishing by the Birds

by Al Ristori

The modern angler has a multitude of fishing aids arrayed before him when he goes to sea, and they can greatly increase his chances of making a good catch. Yet, all too often, these same fishermen fail to use the powers of observation that were the only stock in trade of their predecessors. Though few fishermen are also birders, they're well-advised to become more acquainted with our feathered friends as they'll often lead us to fish which we'd otherwise be unaware of.

The most important aspect of successful saltwater fishing is being at the right place at the right time. The water volume we cover is huge, and every clue must be considered in order to narrow down the search. No matter how high the tower of the boat, your visibility is of little consequence when compared with that of any bird—and you can bet that their sight is a lot better besides. Best of all, their services in leading us to fish are completely free.

Whether you're fishing for stripers and blues, or marlin and tuna, the assistance provided by seabirds can make or break your effort on many occasions. The trick is to learn what birds will prove helpful for various species in your area and how to interpret their behavior.

Among the most reliable fish indicators in tropical and semi-tropical seas is the frigate, also known as man-o-war. This bird, which can have a wing spread of up to eight feet, is unable to dive for fish. However, there is no

Frigates take advantage of a shrimp trawler's riggers as they wait for trash to fall into the Gulf of Mexico off Key West. (AL RISTORI)

better fish spotter in the world. The frigate hovers far up in the sky and will track a single billfish until it pushes a bait fish to the surface, where it can be plucked off by the swooping bird. If there are no other signs to work with, I'll always steer toward any frigate spotted.

Frigates put me into some of the most exciting striped marlin fishing I've seen off Salinas, Ecuador, years ago as the birds targeted marlin balling bait fish. More recently, those birds led to action with marlin off the coast of La Guaira, Venezuela, as they dove on schools of bait driven so far up on the surface that the frigates could fly in one after another and easily pick off a fish on each pass. On another day off La Guaira, large dolphin were scattered over a wide area offshore of the bank, but our skipper was able to race to each pair as they chased bait to the surface by watching the actions of the frigates. That timing was critical, as the balao were blasted immediately and after the fish were boated it was time to race to another swooping frigate for a sure hook-up.

Feeding isn't usually easy for frigates, and they are notorious pirates—stealing fish from lesser birds. That propensity has to be accounted for as the birds may end up well away from the predator fish you're seeking in the course of a fight for an already captured bait.

Frigates aren't usually much of a problem for fishermen, but that's not the case at Christmas Island. That mid-Pacific bonefishing hot spot has its own species of frigate (*Fregata andrewsi*), which is extremely aggressive. They would dive on plugs trolled along the surface of the lagoon, and while casting plugs I'd have to watch out on my back-cast as frigates would swoop down to grab the plug from the tip of the rod. After the cast was made, it became a question of whether a giant trevally would hit before a frigate nabbed the popper.

Frigates aren't the only birds that can be a hindrance to anglers at times. Boobies can be a real pain when

trolling bait in the tropics, as they don't give up easily. There were many occasions in the Galapagos Islands when we had to stop trolling balao because blue-footed boobies wouldn't stay off them. After first picking up a balao and having it pulled away, they'd typically fly off far ahead of the boat as if they were leaving—but would then make a big circle and sneak back in for the same bait. However, boobies don't seem to be as aggressive on plugs as the frigates which often feed with them in the same areas. Boobies are found in most tropical seas and are related to the gannets. They also can plunge below the surface to pick off fish, but make shallower, more angled dives than gannets.

The most fascinating and wide-spread sea bird is the tiny storm petrel. Actually there are 22 species of this smallest web-footed sea bird that is better known to sailors as Mother Carey's chickens. According to David Saunders in his *Sea Birds* (Grosset & Dunlap, N.Y., 1973), petrels were probably named after St. Peter, because they seem to walk on the surface while feeding. Saunders suspects that the popular name may have evolved from the words *Mater Cara*, which is an appellation of the Blessed Virgin Mary.

Wilson's petrel is the most common species of storm petrel, and may well be the most numerous bird in the world. Shark fishermen of the northeast see these constantly flying birds picking at the tiniest scraps in their shark chum slicks, but few realize that the 6-inch petrels migrate north all the way from the Antarctic. Though they have no meaning while in chum slicks, petrels have earned their nickname of "tuna birds" by leading fishermen to everything from schools of smaller tunas up to a single feeding giant. Never overlook a concentration of petrels while trolling!

Sharkers have no problem with storm petrels, but they're occasionally plagued with shearwaters. Those long-winged, slender sea birds are great

divers and can pick off baits at considerable depths. Most of the time you'll just see one or two fly by and check out any chunks which may be in the slick. However, there are times when flocks will sit around the boat and defy you to get a bait in the water. Unlike gannets and pelicans, shearwaters have no need to dive out of the air in order to get below the surface. They can sit on the water and spot a bait well below before swimming down to it like a winged fish.

Shearwaters are excellent tuna indicators when diving on actively-feeding fish, and even when sitting in the water in flocks. It's been my experience that shearwaters rarely rest for long, and a flock on the water indicates very recent action in the area.

Pelicans were once considered threatened, but it would be hard to prove that point in Florida where those big-billed birds hang around boats to grab baits and try to push fishermen aside at cleaning tables in order to swallow anything not protected. I've seen them in the summer as far north as Sandy Hook, N.J., and they've become a permanent winter resident at Hatteras, N.C., even when water temperatures drop into the forties.

Pelicans aren't a very reliable guide to predators in shallow waters because they have the ability to dive on bait fish, sticking their heads underwater in order to scoop up the prey without the aid of predator fish chasing them to the surface. In both the Atlantic and Pacific I've often spotted masses of diving pelicans near shore only to find they were happily feeding in skinny water. Under such circumstances, it's likely the crashing of those awkward-looking birds as they hit the water would probably scare off predators in any case.

On the other hand, pelicans diving in deeper waters are always worth a look for a variety of coastal and oceanic game fish. Off Cabo San Lucas, at the tip of Mexico's Baja California, pelicans dive on baits chased up by striped marlin and the entire fleet will start a high speed chase toward even a single diving pelican.

Sea gulls are the sea bird most familiar to shorebound fishermen, and they can be very effective fish spotters. Like the frigate, gulls can't dive and must look for easy pickings. In the case of the gull, those pickings can be literally anything and they've earned the nickname "flying rats." Yet, gulls are pretty reliable indicators of feeding fish, since they have to wait for dead and dying bait fish pushed up by predators.

Sea gulls are particularly important to striped bass and bluefish anglers in the Northeast. Even a novice fisherman would realize that gulls are probably over feeding fish, but those sitting on the water also may provide a valuable clue that something has recently gone on or is about to happen.

A valuable example of that occurred during a November striper run in Raritan Bay. As the birds got active after sun-up, they clued us into the portion of the open bay where bass would briefly chase bunkers. However, after the action was over, Tony Arcabascio of Staten Island noted that the sitting birds were also a good indication—and almost every time we dropped a live bunker near even a few sitting gulls we raised at least one bass from seemingly dead water.

On the negative side, gulls can be a big problem for anglers attempting to cast lures at breaking fish. Not only do they often try to grab surface plugs, but the cast line may get tangled in their wings. As with all sea birds which get tangled in lines or hooked, it's important to avoid being bitten by sharp beaks. The trick is to drop a cloth over the bird's eyes. Without sight, they usually remain quite calm and you'll be able to get everything cleared so the bird can fly away unharmed.

It was on Cape Cod that I learned how sea gulls can help in navigation. At the time I was running a Mako 19 and fishing for stripers in the fall off Monomoy Island at Chatham. Rather than running the dangerous inlet, I would return on the calm back side of Monomoy. However, fog was a regular problem, and combined with darkness it was difficult to follow the winding channel through the flats. Yet, I found it was possible to do so in practically zero visibility by stopping to listen for and smell the sea gulls standing on the exposed flats I had to avoid.

Terns are close relatives of the gulls, but these slender birds with long wings and forked tails are much more active. They are very good fish indicators, but can fool you when bait is close to the surface since they're agile enough to plunge partly beneath the surface in order to nab sand eels, rainfish, etc. without any help from predators. Though terns have webbed feet, they prefer to stand on shore or floating objects rather than resting on the water. When terns are in the area, they'll find bluefish long before the gulls arrive, so keep an eye on them.

Since terns can feed on tiny objects, they're often attracted to weed lines. Anything different in the ocean is always worth checking out, as weed lines often indicate contrasting currents and temperature variations. However, terns may be actively picking away in weed lines when there are no predators about. By observing them closely, you'll soon be able to tell at a glance when terns are picking on undisturbed bait fish or working over baits being pushed to the surface—at which time they fly and dip much more erratically.

An illustration of that occurred after the perfect combination of a northeaster followed by a cool, clearing northwester during a recent October when I joined Capt. Frank Rose on his *Miss Diane* from Point Pleasant as Stu Wilk and other marine biologists from the Sandy Hook Marine Lab sought out specimens of fall bluefish for analysis of possible contaminants. There was plenty of bait being marked on Rose's fishfinder in the Shrewsbury Rocks area, but we were surprised to find no bluefish where they should have been thick—a preview of what turned out to be the first fall without a real bluefish migration in decades.

By noon there was considerable tern action on that bait, but it didn't look frantic enough. Purple clouds of bait could be spotted just under the surface and the terns would dive on them every time the school moved just a bit higher and within reach. Sea gulls were sitting on the water, which normally wouldn't be the case if bluefish were feeding.

Though sea birds know enough to stay clear of the sharp-toothed, ravenous blues, which may hit anything in the course of wild feeding, they're probably unaware of their real enemies. Goosefish (angler, monkfish) gained their name by making meals of sitting birds, and tiger sharks seem to be fond of sea gulls. In the course of releasing a 600-pounder from my boat off Montauk I watched it spit up hundreds of gull feathers while I was holding it on the leader for photos—and Captain Bob Rocchetta saw a tiger eat a sea gull off the surface the next day.

Gannets are the cold water, high-diving relatives of the tropical boobies. Measuring up to three feet in length, the North Atlantic gannet circles 100 feet above the water before diving headlong with folded wings to nail the prey well below the surface. Those spectacular dives are punctuated with three-foot splashes that look like bombs being dropped into the water from a distance. Gannets can handle large prey, and should prosper now that the herring population is rebuilding after being decimated by foreign trawlers in the 1960s and 1970s. These birds become abundant in the fall, and can clue anglers into migrating schools of striped bass from great distances.

During the late 1960s, I used to run across to Nantucket with the late Captain Bud Henderson, and we'd spot gannets from a mile or more away. Gulls and gannets made it look like a garbage dump at sea as they fed on herring and squid driven to the surface by acres of stripers. There are no longer such vast schools of bass, and these days there's usually a lot more bait than predators, but gannets will still find those sub-surface bait concentrations that may well have bass below them.

Off the New Jersey coast, we usually start seeing gannets in November. There's no greater assurance that bait is available, though most of the time they're feeding without help from the striped bass we seek. As with the terns, there's a more erratic pattern to the gannet's movements when they're actually on feeding fish—and sea gulls tend to join them quickly when easy pickings are available.

The height of the dive is another indication with gannets as well as with many other birds as to how high the bait and predators are. When birds are flying high they're broadening their range of vision as well as the depth they can see below the surface—a good indication that bait fish are deep. On the other hand, birds fly lower and dives are shallower when bait is close to the surface and, hopefully, being pushed to the surface by the fish we seek.

Though I have a reputation to protect and even in my most desperate hours of fishlessness have never slipped

Bird	Fish Indicated	Behavior
Frigate	Oceanic predators	Check out area they circle over
Pelican	Oceanic predators	Race to diving birds
Gannet	Striped bass	Diving from great heights
Shearwater	Tuna	Troll by even sitting flocks
Petrel	Tuna	Flock to tuna on surface
Sea Gull	All predators	Raucous and erratic

NOTE: Sea birds may react differently in various areas, depending on the bait and predators involved. This table only reflects personal observations of bird behavior in many areas around the world where I've fished. In every case, the angler must decipher the behavior of sea birds in his area—which could be quite different.

to such depths, I must note that the unwary can also be fooled by birds with just a bit of help from certain fishermen who carry bread, oatmeal, or a few dead baits that can be spread upon the waters to create a feeding flurry—drawing boats to an otherwise dead area while they slip off to the real hot spot.

The foregoing only briefly touches

on the many sea birds that are far better fishermen than any human being, and whose skills can be utilized by anglers to make themselves look a lot smarter. Keep your eyes peeled whenever you're at sea or on the beach, and there'll be many occasions when you'll be thanking sea birds for saving the day.

■

A Guide to Offshore Fish-Fighting Teamwork

by George Poveromo

The fight exceeded the three-hour mark before the swordfish began to tire. The weary angler, strapped in the fighting chair with an 80-pound-class outfit, kept at it throughout that still, starlit June evening. He was sure this fish was going to be his. It was 2:30 A.M., but reports of the exciting battle kept the anglers in the 17-boat fleet glued to their radios. As the fish neared the radio went silent.

Then it happened. Instead of a joyous victory shout over the VHF, a depressed voice declared that the fish was gone. I later learned the story. According to the angler's father, when

the swordfish surfaced behind the boat, the captain left the helm to help wire and gaff the fish. But the fish wasn't entirely beaten. With the boat stationary, it was able to swim underneath the transom and cut the line on the lower unit. Had someone remained at the wheel, things might have turned out differently.

Big sportfishing boats, especially those on the tournament circuit, generally have experienced crews who know their roles intimately. But what about the guys in the midsized boats? Do they stand a chance of landing a big fish with a small crew?

Absolutely! All you need is a game plan.

Beating a trophy fish requires quality tackle, an experienced angler, and a sharp boat handler. I've seen and heard of many big fish that were successfully played to the boat, only to have a miscue end the fight on the prop, lower unit, or hull. In fact, it's all too common an occurrence, primarily because the crew isn't aware of the importance of keeping a skilled helmsman at the wheel.

Helmsman is Team Captain

The helmsman's responsibility is to lead the fish to the wireman, giving him a

Fighting a big fish takes teamwork between the anglers and captain, a fact especially true on small boats. (GEORGE POVEROMO)

good, clean angle to work with, while being ready to counter any last-second surges by speeding up, backing down, or spinning around.

Several factors determine when and how the helmsman should assist his crew. Aboard my boat, for instance, I generally have friends who have fished with me for many years. We all know the drill, and any one of us could take over the wheel if necessary.

When trolling, I won't alter the boat's speed and direction on a hook-up. In my opinion, this helps set the hook by getting the stretch out of the monofilament, while leaving the remaining baits working for a possible second hook-up.

Once He's Hooked

Once the hook is firmly set, I shift to neutral. If it's a small to medium fish hooked on heavy tackle (30- or 50-pound test), we'll immediately remove only the lines that might interfere with the fight. For example, if the fish eats the port outrigger bait and swims away from the bait spread, the long center rigger and the port flat line are quickly removed from the water. I like to keep

at least one bait out throughout the fight, which might pick up another fish. In the above case, this would be the starboard outrigger bait and/or the starboard flat line.

If the fish charges the boat, throwing slack in the line, I'll throttle forward, steering the boat to keep the fish off the port stern quarter. Should the fish take off in the opposite direction, I'll remain in neutral and let the angler play the fish, unless he's losing too much line. Once the fish settles down, I'll either stay in neutral, except to adjust the boat to keep the fight off the port stern quarter, or slowly back down a few feet at a time to help the angler regain line (at this point the extra line is reeled in so it won't be run over). I never back down faster than the angler can reel to keep a tight line.

Big-Fish Tactics

If a big fish is hooked, such as a marlin, a big wahoo, or a big tuna, the helmsman's ability becomes critical. He must react immediately—not after most of the spool has been emptied. Our plan, since we're fishing out of an outboard-

powered center console, requires the helmsman to shift into neutral once the hook has been firmly set, then pivot the boat around to chase the fish. While the angler moves to the bow, all remaining lines are quickly reeled in and the outfits stored away. An uncluttered cockpit and gunwales are a must!

If fighting the fish from the bow is a problem, the angler can remain in the cockpit and quarter the fish off the bow during the chase. This is a more practical approach in rough seas or aboard an outboard-powered cuddy or cabin boat. Or, if you have an inboard-powered boat that has the speed and agility, you can simply back down quickly.

One important note: Once the fish is under control and settles into the depths, the angler can move back to the cockpit for the remainder of the fight. By keeping the fish off the stern, the helmsman can lead it to the wire-man more effectively, and can quickly counter any last-second runs (a helmsman trying to lead in a fish from the bow always runs the risk of losing control at boatside).

Communicate!

Communication between the helmsman and the angler is crucial throughout the battle. During the chase, the helmsman must gauge his speed: He mustn't charge ahead too quickly, so that the angler can't keep pressure on the fish, or pursue too slowly, so that line can't be gained efficiently. It's a fine balance, and the angler has to let the helmsman know how he's doing. Also, if the fish stops or abruptly alters course, the angler must alert the helmsman immediately.

I become concerned when the spool is nearly half empty, and prefer to start chasing the fish before it gets that far. Some people wait until a reel is at least half spooled before giving pursuit, but I believe this subjects the line to a substantially greater drag pressure, and increases the chance of its getting nicked or cut by a piece of flotsam. I also feel that you begin to lose control of the fish.

When the Fish Goes Deep

When a big fish sounds, such as a tuna, a marlin, or a big dolphin, it can drive even an experienced crew nuts. Once again, the helmsman becomes invaluable. It's up to him to talk with the angler and be aware of what the fish is doing. To keep the line away from the engines on an outboard-powered boat, he must keep the fish off to the side of the stern. On an inboard boat, he must keep the fish either off to the side or well off the transom, where the angler can pump and wind without the line rubbing against the gunwale. The helmsman must also know when to throttle away, establish a more vertical angle, or hold above a stubborn fish, should the angler decide to pivot pump from the chair.

Equally important is knowing how to compensate for a fish that has sounded and managed to cross underneath the boat. In this case, the boat should be spun forward and around the line's entry into the water (if the angler is in the stern), or backed down so the bow spins away from the line's entry into the water. If a fish crosses underneath the boat and begins jumping or running at the surface (where the prop might cut the line on such a maneuver), the angler should dip his rod tip in the water and move to the bow while the helmsman backs down and away from the line's entry into the water.

Planing Him Up

Sometimes the battle becomes deadlocked. It happens with marlin and tuna, and especially big dolphin on light tackle. Here, the helmsman can help by "planing" the fish towards the surface. This is done by slowly throttling forward as the angler backs off the drag a little. After about 100 feet, shift back into neutral. Slowly back down half the distance, letting the angler re-adjust the drag and

gain line. Then motor forward another 100 feet and repeat the process. You'll soon know if the fish has been planed up towards the surface or if its rhythm has been broken. If not, continue the planing process.

One trick that helps the helmsman determine how much line is being gained is to lay a half-inch-long strip of colored string or mono onto the spool as the angler attempts to pump up the fish. As the fishing line is reeled onto the spool, it buries the marker. As long as the marker isn't fully exposed, you're making headway. Add a second marker if another stand-off is reached. Aside from letting the helmsman know the effectiveness of his moves, the marker is a great psychological boost for a tired angler.

Boatside Manners

Arguably, fish are more likely to be lost on the strike and next to the boat than at any other time during the fight. The latter situation is more critical because of the boat (which can become an obstacle) and the person(s) who must handle the fish. There's not much a helmsman can do about a bad gaff shot or a poor wiring job, but he can help the crew by leading the fish directly to them. During the final stages of battle, the helmsman should put the boat in gear and lead the fish in off a stern quarter. Keep the fish coming at a steady angle and swimming forward by inching ahead, occasionally shifting into neutral and letting the angler take up line.

When the leader comes up, shift into neutral and let a crew member take control and lead the fish alongside the boat. Don't relax yet; he may have to turn the leader loose, forcing you to react to the fish's actions. Once the fish is completely under control, that's the time to leave the helm and do the gaffing or releasing honors—if you're short-handed.

Throughout all this, the angler should back off the drag slightly, so the tension won't hinder the crew's efforts,

and be ready in case the fish makes a sudden surge. He should *never* put down the rod or get out of the chair.

The above describes the handling techniques we use on my boat, and they can be applied to most forms of offshore fishing, from trolling to live-baiting. As mentioned, my friends all know what to do when a fish strikes, and that's a big advantage. If you haven't formulated a similar game plan on your boat, do so.

When a big fish decides to eat, there's no time for assigning duties on the spot. If you're at the helm, the ball's in your court, and your performance might be the deciding factor in whether or not your angler comes home a winner. ∎

Boaters don't have a clean record when it comes to accidents afloat. Do you know why? It has little to do with the prerequisites of fishing and hunting, but much to do with neglecting to control the boat and guard personal safety aboard. A sportsman who has not schooled himself in basic boating safety and safe habits will forget about it when the action gets lively. Here's your chance to start right.

IMPORTANT EQUIPMENT

BASIC TOOL KIT

Every boat must be equipped to get home on its own. The exact selection of tools, spare parts, and supplies necessary must be suited to your boat and motor and to problems you are most likely to encounter.

Ordinary pliers

Diagonal-cutting pliers

Screwdrivers

Combination open-end
 and box wrenches in
 sizes ⅜ to ¾ inch

Vise-grip pliers

Long-nose electrician's
 pliers

Spark-plug wrench to fit

Sharp knife

SPARE PARTS

Spark plugs of correct specifications

Distributor cap, rotor, condenser, point set

Fuel pump and filter

Oil filter

Water-pump impeller

V-belts to match each size used

Spare fuel lines, cocks, and fittings

Gaskets and hoses

Bailing-pump diaphragm

Fuses and bulbs to double for each used

ALL-PURPOSE KIT

50-ft. chalk line

Molly screws and pot
 menders for small
 cracks and holes

Nails, screws, bolts
 and nuts, washers

Hose clamps

Electrical tape

Insulated wire

Cotter pins

Packing

Elastic plastic bandage
 material

Small blocks of wood
 that can be carved

Machine oil

12

Safe Boating

OUTBOARD MOTOR TROUBLESHOOTING CHECKLIST

Check gas supply and tank pressure; squeeze bulb several times.

Check to be sure propeller is not wrapped in weeds, line, or net. If line is wrapped around prop, try slow reverse to loosen it; then cut off pieces until you can pull the rest free.

Look for loose ignition wire at battery terminals.

Remove ignition wire from any spark plug; crank the motor; spark should jump from wire end to engine head; if no spark, check back to ignition switch.

If you have a hot spark, look into fuel feed; pull gas feed line off from side of outboard; blow through line until you hear bubbles in tank.

Clean the carburetor bowl and fuel filter.

Did you remember to add oil to gas tank in right proportion?

SAFE BOATING PROCEDURES

First, it is important to know your boat. Get familiar with its equipment and discover its limitations. If it's a livery rental, check it over completely before you push off.

Make a habit of checking off safety equipment aboard. First, locate the safety items required by law. Then compare your optional equipment with the Coast Guard's list of recommended equipment in the same section.

Count the life preservers, and make sure that each passenger has one that will keep him afloat in the water.

Check the fuel supply, the condition of the tank and feed line. Make sure the spark is strong and regular. Take along at least 1½ times as much fuel as you estimate you will need. If you run into heavy waves, your boat will take more fuel to go the same distance.

Carry a map you can read—a proper chart if the water is a large one—and a compass that is reliable near machinery.

Put tackle, guns, decoys, nets and other gear where they are secure and won't clutter walkways and footing. There is a bonus for the sportsman who keeps everything in place on board: He always knows where to find it when the action gets hot.

Do not overload your boat. Make sure you have safely adequate freeboard before casting off. Look ahead

to water conditions and weather changes you might encounter.

Keep an alert lookout. If you have a boat over 20 feet, name your mate and agree he'll keep lookout any time you can't. You have more to watch for than other boats and shallow water. Watch for obstructions such as big rocks and floating logs.

Swimmers are hard to see in the water. Running through swimmers or a swimming area is the most sensitive violation a boat can make. If in doubt, give beaches and rafts a wide swing.

Your wake is potent. You can swamp small craft such as a canoe or rowboat, damage shorelines and shore property, disturb sleepers, and ruin fish and wildlife sport for hours by running fast through small passages and shallows.

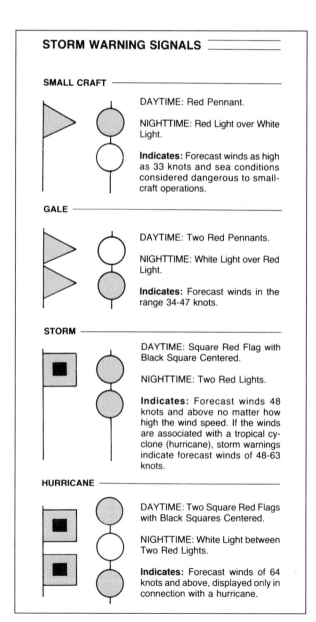

STORM WARNING SIGNALS

SMALL CRAFT

DAYTIME: Red Pennant.

NIGHTTIME: Red Light over White Light.

Indicates: Forecast winds as high as 33 knots and sea conditions considered dangerous to small-craft operations.

GALE

DAYTIME: Two Red Pennants.

NIGHTTIME: White Light over Red Light.

Indicates: Forecast winds in the range 34-47 knots.

STORM

DAYTIME: Square Red Flag with Black Square Centered.

NIGHTTIME: Two Red Lights.

Indicates: Forecast winds 48 knots and above no matter how high the wind speed. If the winds are associated with a tropical cyclone (hurricane), storm warnings indicate forecast winds of 48-63 knots.

HURRICANE

DAYTIME: Two Square Red Flags with Black Squares Centered.

NIGHTTIME: White Light between Two Red Lights.

Indicates: Forecast winds of 64 knots and above, displayed only in connection with a hurricane.

Storm warning signals.

Learn the Rules of the Road and obey them at all times. Copies are available free from the Coast Guard. Most collisions are caused by those "onetime" violations.

Make sure at least one other person aboard knows how to operate the boat and motor in case you are disabled or fall overboard.

Know a plan of action you will take in emergencies—man overboard, a bad leak, motor won't run, collision, bad storm, or troublesome passenger.

Storm signals and danger signs are often informal. Learn to read the weather, and keep alert to what passing boats are trying to tell you.

Wear your life preserver—or at least make sure children and nonswimmers wear theirs. In any case, don't sit on life preservers.

In a capsizing, remember that you are safer if you stay with the boat, where you can be seen. It will help you stay afloat until help arrives.

Under U.S. Coast Guard legislation, it is illegal for anyone to build, sell, or use a craft that does not conform to safety regulations. Check with your dealer, and check with yourself to make sure your boat measures up.

LOADING YOUR BOAT

There are several things to remember when loading a boat: distribute the load evenly; keep the load low; don't overload; don't stand up in a small boat; and consult the "U.S. Coast Guard Maximum Capacities" label. On boats with no capacity label, use the following formula to determine the maximum number of persons your boat can safely carry in calm weather:

The length of your vessel is measured in a straight line from the foremost part of the vessel to the aftermost part of the vessel, parallel to the centerline, exclusive of sheer. Bowsprits, bumpkins, rudders, outboard motors, brackets and similar fittings are not included in the measurement.

Wind Speed/ Sea Height Relationships

Winds	Sea Conditions
0–3 knots	Sea like a mirror
4–6 knots	Ripples, less than 1 foot
7–10 knots	Smooth wavelets, 1–2 feet
11–16 knots	Small waves, 2–4 feet
17–21 knots	Moderate waves, many whitecaps, 4–8 feet
22–27 knots	Large waves, spray, 8–13 feet
28–33 knots	Heaped seas, foam from breaking waves, 13–20 feet
34–40 knots	High waves, foam blown in well-marked streaks, 13–20 feet
41–47 knots	Seas rolls, spray may reduce visibility, 13–20 feet
48–55 knots	Very high waves, white seas, overhanging crests, 20–30 feet
56–63 knots	Exceptionally high waves, 30–45 feet
Over 63 knots	Air filled with foam, sea completely white, over 45 feet

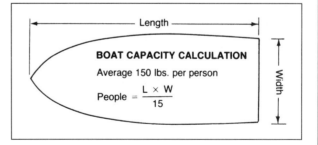

FLOAT PLAN

File a float plan. Tell someone where you are going and when you plan to return. Tell them what your boat looks like and other information that will make identifying it easier should the need arise. Make copies of the following Float Plan and leave it with a reliable person who can be depended upon to notify the Coast Guard, or other rescue organization, should you not return as scheduled. Do not, however, file float plans with the Coast Guard.

1. NAME OF PERSON REPORTING AND TELEPHONE NUMBER.

2. DESCRIPTION OF BOAT. TYPE _____ COLOR _____
   TRIM _____ REGISTRATION NO. _____
   LENGTH _____ NAME _____ MAKE _____
   OTHER INFO. _____

3. PERSONS ABOARD _____

   NAME   AGE   ADDRESS & TELE. NO.

4. ENGINE TYPE _____ H.P. _____
   NO. OF ENGINES _____ FUEL CAPACITY _____

5. SURVIVAL EQUIPMENT: (CHECK AS APPROPRIATE)
   PFDs _____ FLARES _____ MIRROR _____
   SMOKE SIGNALS _____ FLASHLIGHT _____ FOOD _____
   PADDLES _____ WATER _____ OTHERS _____
   ANCHOR _____ RAFT OR DINGHY _____ EPIRB _____

6. RADIO YES/NO TYPE _____ FREQS. _____

7. TRIP EXPECTATIONS: LEAVE AT _____ (TIME)
   FROM _____ GOING TO _____
   EXPECT TO RETURN BY _____ (TIME) AND IN
   NO EVENT LATER THAN _____

8. ANY OTHER PERTINENT INFO. _____

9. AUTOMOBILE LICENSE _____ TYPE _____
   TRAILER LICENSE _____ _____ COLOR AND MAKE OF
   AUTO _____
   WHERE PARKED _____

10. IF NOT RETURNED BY _____ (TIME) CALL THE
    COAST GUARD, OR _____ (LOCAL AUTHORITY)
    TELEPHONE NUMBERS _____

Taking Your Small Boat Offshore

by Capt. John N. Raguso

Like the Siren's call to the ancient Greek mariners, the lure of the sea is strong. But the sea is also a fickle mistress who is unforgiving to those foolish anglers who would take her "sometimes" benign nature for granted, ignoring the fury that she can often vent without warning to the unsuspecting. With the single-minded specter of crossing paths with a large billfish, high-flying mako, or schools of powerful tuna, many anglers often go further than either their skills or boat's capabilities should take them in pursuit of their sport, which creates a potentially perilous situation.

I've been driving small 19- to 24-foot outboard-powered fishing boats offshore in search of big game sportfishing opportunities since the mid-70s. While I may not take as many calculated risks in downsized craft as some, I have been known to "press the envelope" of sanity on more than one occasion. As recently as this past season, my 24-foot Grady-White Explorer has been as distant as 84.99 nautical miles from the closest Long Island inlet, working the mouth of the fabled Hudson Canyon for tuna and billfish.

And why would anyone in their right mind want to do this in a relatively tiny, peanut-sized craft? Well, for starters, not everyone can afford those 40- and 50-foot gold-plated, super sportfishing platforms that ply the exotic waters of this planet. Plus, some of the smaller boats, with their deep-vee hulls, beefy laminate schedules, foam flotation and outboard power, are actually safer in some respects than their bigger sisters, who if given the right set of circumstances, will sink unceremoniously like the proverbial rock.

Small 22- to 25-foot outboard boats have the advantage over many of their larger, more cumbersome sister craft in numerous ways. They require less horsepower to achieve cruising speeds, typically use less fuel per mile traveled and are a lot easier on the pocketbook. But when you're 50 miles from the nearest inlet when a hostile squall line comes your way, being on that efficient, affordable and economical little fishing boat might be the last place you'd ever want to be! Well, no one ever said that going offshore in a small boat was going to be easy, but it can be eminently do-able. Let's take a closer look on how to improve your odds out there in the big blue.

A Deep-Vee with Twin Power and Plenty of Fuel

Venturing 40 to 50 miles and more offshore demands that your boat can handle the constant stress and pounding of the often-merciless sea conditions that prevail this far off the beach. Modified vee hulls just won't cut it out here, as a tight 3- to 5-foot sea will certainly loosen a few fillings and desensitize numerous brain cells in the process. And a stiff 20-knot crosswind on your beam will make a walkaround or cuddy cabin boat seem like an open center console with no canvas, unless your mini-hull can knock the wind and spray back down and away from the cockpit.

Some of the older classics, like the 23-foot SeaCraft, 24-North Coast and 25-foot Blackfin hulls are still found where big fish roam, but a new generation of bluewater chariots like the new Grady-White SeaV2 hulls, and the latest 1995 vintage running bottoms from Pursuit, Boston Whaler, Regulator, Wahoo, Contender, Ocean Master and Fountain all have what it takes to get you out there and back. A deep-vee design, with 50-degrees or more of entry angle, a raised forward "Carolina" sheer with plenty of flare, offering wide, reversed chines and tapering back to at least 20-degrees of aft deadrise is the minimum hull you should consider for this specialized duty. An 8.5 to 9.5-foot beam is nice, since it usually offers a bit more stability and cockpit space to fight the catch-of-the-day.

Anyone who ventures offshore with only one engine is either truly mad or is just waiting to become a statistic. Even though small boats should always take long distance trips in pairs or threes, don't always count on your friends being there to help you when tragedy strikes. You must always be able to control your own destiny, and this starts by going with twin outboard power on the transom. The optimum bluewater set-up is either twin V-4s or V-6s, depending on your hull's horsepower requirements and efficiency. Remember, the concept of twin outboards is truly maximized when you set up your rig to plane home on one powerplant, with the other tilted up and out of the way.

If your platform cannot perform this simple but essential task, your initial capital investment, and subsequent higher fuel and maintenance bills, will be a continuation of this less-than-desirable situation. Work closely with both the manufacturer of your hull, as well as your local dealer, to set your boat up with the appropriate combination of engines and props that will achieve this critical objective. Laboring home at 8 mph at displacement speeds, while gulping gas at your most inefficient consumption rate, might put you too close to the bottom end of your precious fuel supply.

A viable alternative to the downside of this first scenario is to rig your offshore sportfishing vessel with a single

V-6, ensuring a "get-home" strategy with a 20- to 30-h.p. outboard kicker. These larger mid-sized outboards typically have the push necessary to move your hull along at the typical 6.5- to 8-mph displacement speeds you're likely to experience in average offshore sea conditions.

Just remember to install the largest blade diameter, lowest-pitch prop you can find for this auxiliary outboard, which will enable your mill to operate in its designed rpm range and provide maximum performance. If you go this route, be sure to get a heavy duty bracket (like the 40-h.p. version offered by the Garelick Co.) and run the engine at the marina every few weeks to ensure that the little kicker will start right up when you really need it the most. I've run seven different offshore rigs set up this way (versus a trio of twin-outboard platforms), and the lower investment cost, fuel economy over the life of the vessel, and lower overall maintenance costs were right for my situation. I had to come back on auxiliary power from 53 miles offshore once, but I made it back in slightly under 8.5 hours, powered along by a Mercury 25 kicker.

One of the most important considerations for your offshore chariot, the one factor that will truly enable you to roam far and wide in search of your dream catch, is your fuel capacity. Based on my experience rigging 11 offshore fishing machines in the 21- to 24-foot class, if you run a single primary V-6 outboard, you should have at least a 150- to 160-gallon fuel capacity onboard. This will allow you roughly 9 hours of cruising at a consumption rate of roughly 12 gallons-per-hour (108 gallons), plus a generous 6 hours of trolling time at 5 gph (30 gallons), for a total of 138 gallons of fuel used. With about 140 gallons of usable fuel on the 150 gallon fuel cell, you're pushing the envelope a bit too much, and will probably have to sacrifice a little fishing range or trolling time to leave a safety margin, just in case you hit rough weather.

Looking at a typical twin V-6 rig,

assuming 150s or 175s as your power choice, you should opt for an onboard fuel capacity of somewhere between 180 to 200 gallons. At 16 gph for the twin V-6s, figure you'll require the same 9 hours of cruising range (144 gallons). Add 6 hours of trolling time at approximately 7 gph (42 gallons), and you can see that the 186-gallon total would once again necessitate either shortening your trip or your trolling time, or maybe a little of both, especially when you factor-in usable fuel and a 10% buffer for inclement weather.

Safety Gear and Electronics

An "EPIRB" emergency radio beacon can also be a big lifesaver when the going gets rough. There are two types of these Emergency Position Indicating Radio Beacons on the market. Most bluewater anglers are probably familiar with the Class B EPIRBs, which simultaneously transmit emergency signals on two distress frequencies, 121.5 and 243.0 mHz, for recognition by other vessels, aircraft and satellites.

The cost for these Class B units will typically be in the $200 to $300 range, and they are an excellent investment for those who frequent the bluewater.

Looking at the next step up in capability, many offshore aficionados have been opting for the more costly, but more effective, combination 406.0 and 121.5 mHz EPIRBs. These more advanced units comply fully with all USCG requirements, with the major difference in capability being the addition of the 406.0 mHz frequency, which transmits both a positive ID of your vessel and your location to within a fairly narrow-focused 3-mile radius. If you do experience some trouble, the likelihood of the rescue team knowing you're out there and then finding you right away is greatly enhanced. Once help has entered the 3-mile zone of your original 406.0 mHz signal, the 121.5 mHz beam allows rescuers to easily home in on your pulsing distress frequency, if a visual recognition hasn't already been established.

As far as other electronics are concerned, I share the same philosophy as one of the most ancient mariners, Noah, when he was outfitting his fabled ark for the original 40 days and nights journey—take two of everything! I still prefer the accuracy of loran-C over GPS for my primary navigation functions, especially when wreck fishing 40 or 50 miles offshore. The theoretical 10- to 15-meter repeatable accuracy of GPS is neat, but with the Department of Defense playing with the "selective availability" switch with increasing regularity, the signal from the orbiting navigation satellites is scrambled to provide a usable accuracy of ± 100 meters. Compare this figure to loran's ± 50- to 75-foot repeatability, and the old reliable loran-C workhorse navigation system gets my vote, especially when trying to find a 15-foot patch of rocky bottom in 200 feet of water. Since I've been taking more and more charters to the edge of the continental shelf, I typically employ a handheld GPS unit as a backup, just in case my primary Loran-C takes an unannounced vacation. For depth sounders, I usually run two units, one a LCD graph and the other a small 6" color CRT, with each sounder offering both narrow and wide-beam transducers, and operating on different frequencies to prevent "cross-talk." Looking at my VHFs, my primary radio is hooked-up to the best cell-wave antenna I can afford, plus I carry a spare handheld VHF, with a BNC-to-PL259 antenna adapter, so the smaller VHF can use its big brother's main antenna for increased range. I also pack a portable emergency replacement antenna that can be hoisted up on the center rigger, just in case the 8-foot cell wave runs into harm's way.

Yet another invaluable tool for the offshore angler is a FloScan fuel flow gauge. I make excellent use of mine, and it is one of the main reason's I can confidently venture 85 miles offshore (in favorable weather conditions) and know to within a few gallons, how much fuel I have consumed from my Grady 24's 150-gallon onboard fuel cell.

Type I life jackets are an absolute

must, as they will most likely keep the wearer in a face-up position when floating in the open ocean waters, even if unconscious. For cold-water fishing in the early spring and late fall, I've even gone to the extent of purchasing thermal float coats and bib trousers, which will keep you alive for a few hours when swimming in 50-degree waters. According to research conducted by the Mustang Manufacturing Company, one of the leading makers of offshore survival gear, the projected survival time of the average person swimming in 45- to 50-degree water is less than an hour. There are two basic survival problems that result from cold-water immersion, even when you are wearing a lifejacket or other PFD. The first is the initial shock of cold water on your skin, which can cause you to gasp or take sharp and rapid breaths. If your head is under water when this occurs, you may drown. The second problem, hypothermia, is more subtle, but equally as terminal in its effect. Most people can safely lose 5.5 degrees Fahrenheit of body temperature, but as your body cools to below 93 degrees Fahrenheit, you start to lose your mental and physical functions.

Unconsciousness will likely occur when your body temperature drops below 86 degrees Fahrenheit. Wearing flotation clothing that provides insulation from cold-water immersion can greatly enhance your odds for survival.

I've also installed a portable strobe light to each of my five Type I PFDs that I keep aboard my *MarCeeJay*. These strobes feature a super bright 80-pulse-per-minute flash that will last up to 24 hours of continuous use from a standard 9-volt alkaline battery, with a visibility of over 3 miles. Hey, for roughly $28 bucks each, you can't go wrong, especially on a dark, moonless night!

Rough Weather Ahead

After entertaining my charters with the thrill of five canyon adventures without incident this past season, the last excursion turned out to be a real "adventure." NOAA was calling for 20- to 25-knot offshore winds for the afternoon of our last trip and the accompanying 6-foot seas. However, the weather pattern prior to this dire forecast had seen light and variable winds with a 1-foot sea. Against the advice of some fellow charter skippers, as dawn broke the eastern horizon, we headed southeast for the 70-mile trek to the edge. The ride out was absolutely glorious—we averaged 25.5 knots and made the run in less than 3 hours. And the fish didn't disappoint us either. We tomahawked over two dozen 5- to 10-pound dolphin casting live killies under a few productive lobster pots and trolled-up a pair of cooperative 40-pound yellowfins, losing a few others to fight for another day. Come 2:30 P.M., the seas were still only 2 to 3 feet, but the wind was starting to "freshen" just a bit. My sixth sense said it was time to leave, while we still had the chance to make a good run of speed, but then we came upon the opportunity of a lifetime.

We had heard numerous Jersey and Long Island boats talking on the VHF about their experiences with large blue marlin, spooling 50-pound outfits and rasping through 300-pound leaders, and three of our dolphin had fresh slash marks on their sides from aggressive billfish. Suddenly, thirty yards to starboard, the caudal fin of the largest billfish I had ever seen anywhere broke the surface, looking like the periscope of a German U-Boat that used to prowl these same waters 50 years ago. As we approached, we could clearly see the unmistakable shape and colors of a huge blue marlin, as it gently surfed down the building southwest swells. As we brought the boat alongside to within spitting distance of the billfish, it appeared that this 13-footer was in a trance, probably up on the surface to get some sun while it digested a big meal, and didn't even recognize our presence. At that point, my young son Marc decided to take some action and made a sharp starboard turn, dragging the tuna clones and psychobeads directly over the big blue's head.

Well, that sure woke it up! It lit up like a neon sign, dove down into the deep and resurfaced some 50 yards away. We played a game of leapfrog with this fish for over 20 minutes without any luck before I decided to pull the plug. It would have spooled my 30- and 50-pound outfits anyway. Only 15 miles into our return trip, all hell broke loose, and NOAA's weather predictions came through in spades. We slugged it out for the better part of 55 miles in hissing, breaking 6-foot seas, but they were fortunately at my stern quarter, providing some added push back to port. Although we took a few waves over the hardtop when we reached shallower water, we made it back without incident and were lucky to do so!

My best advice when venturing offshore in small boats is to be cautious. Remember, no fish is worth your life—and be sure to know the capabilities of your boat in case rough weather hits. Carry the best PFDs you can afford—as a charter skipper, I'm required to carry Type I vests aboard for every passenger—and be sure to put them on *before* you're stuck in a compromising position, not after it's too late! If the seas are too big to handle running a straight course home, employ a modified zig-zag route, like the way a sailboat might tack down a course, and take the waves on a 30- to 45-degree angle on your bow. To save the wear and tear on vessel and crew, you might also consider slowing down your speed to bare planing attitude, which might be somewhere between 12 and 15 knots, depending on your hull and power configuration.

If the seas are too rough for a return trip back to port, bring your bow into the waves at roughly a 15- to 25-degree angle and use only enough throttle to keep bare steerage while you ride out the worst of the storm—old salts call this "heaving to." Never turn your engine off, if you can help it, as you'll turn sideways to the surfing seas and increase your chances of "broaching." A sea anchor run off the bow can provide a big assist in helping to keep your nose into the slop, especially if you lose power. If given the option, head to deeper water during a storm, where the waves will have a tendency to be a bit less steep and farther apart. Make sure your vessel has a reliable high-capacity bilge pump of at least 1500 gph or more. My 24-footer has two of these aboard, and I check their operation at least once every few weeks. If you have to make a turn in rough seas, try to count the rhythm and duration of the waves and look for a flat spot, particularly after a big sea has passed, to make your move and do it quickly.

In Conclusion

Heading offshore in a 22- to 25-foot outboard boat and enjoying our coastal fishery on a budget is something that just about anyone can do, if done within reasonable parameters. You need a good hull, with a proven rough-water running bottom, super solid construction and a long range fuel capacity. Carrying extra fuel in portable containers is just asking for trouble. You also need the right electronics and safety equipment, plus the knowledge and ability to bring vessel and crew back safely to port, even when the weather turns against you. Hey, it's a real "rush" to catch the big ones 60 miles off the beach from a miniature platform, but no fish that's ever swam the oceans is worth the lives of you and your crew. Enjoy your sport, but be safe out there!

∎

Why Boats Sink

by Vin Sparano

The mere thought of a boat sinking out from under its skipper and his passengers will send chills down the back of the toughest boater. Will he calmly handle the situation or will he go to pieces and panic? Why did it happen? What did he do wrong?

According to Boat/U.S., boaters should worry more about sinking at the dock than out on the water. Statistics show that three out of four recreational boat sinkings happen right at the dock. I thought that was a surprising statistic until a few weeks ago when I climbed into a 14-foot aluminum boat to bail out a foot or so of rain water. It simply did not occur to me that my weight, plus the weight of the water concentrated in the stern, plus the weight of the Yamaha outboard motor, would push the transom below the surface and water would gush into the boat. It took only a second to realize my mistake and I quickly shifted my weight to bring the transom out of the water. It would have been embarassing to sink my boat right there at the dock, but it can and does happen to a lot of boaters every year. Fortunately, most dockside sinkings can be prevented.

First, never depend completely on an automatic float switch to turn on your bilge pump when water gets into your hull. Bilge pumps and switches, because of their location, get dirty and will sometimes jam in the off position and not turn on your pump at all or get stuck in the on positon and kill your battery. Both cases are bad news and could sink an unattended boat.

Check your bilge pump and switches before every trip. In fact, I replace my automatic float switch every other year. These switches are inexpensive and easy to wire to a bilge pump.

Learn how to tie your boat correctly at the dock, especially in tidal water. If your boat swings or drifts too freely at the dock, it could get stuck under the dock and get pushed under the water when the tide rises.

Make it a point of learning every through-hull underwater fitting on your boat. Draw the locations of the fittings on a piece of paper and check them every time the boat is out of the water. Look inside the hull. Do all the fitting have seacocks? Do they all work? Do you close them when you leave the boat unattended? Do you keep them well-lubricated? It's this kind of maintenance and attention that will keep your boat afloat.

Remember that your boat can take on water from above the waterline as well as from below. Check all deck fittings, fastenings and hatches. Not all boat manufacturers use a good sealant on fastenings and some of them leak. Hose down your cabin and decks, then look for leaks inside and in the hull. If you see a leak, fix it. You can sink from rain water just as easily as from a leak below the surface.

I have found that water from washings at the dock can sometimes get trapped in the hull. To get this water out, try this trick: When your bow lifts up, just before you get on plane, manually switch on your bilge. If you have to, keep the bow high until all the bilge water rushes to the pump and gets pumped out.

Continually check all hoses and clamps. Clamps are cheap. If they look rusty, replace them. In fact, you should keep an assortment of different size clamps in your tool box. Pay special attention to hoses that have sharp bends. If any look stressed or kinked, replace them. Replacing a hose when your boat in on a trailer is easy. It's a panic problem, however, if it happens five miles from shore. It's also a good idea to double clamp all hoses.

If you're shopping for a boat, look for designs with self-bailing cockpits. This means the deck is above the waterline. Any water coming into the boat will drain out the transom and not stay in the boat or hull. This is a comforting thought in a heavy sea. Most of the tough breed of small fishing boats built for offshore fishing have this feature. Many small, less-expensive ski boats, however, do not have self-bailing cockpits.

Make sure your transom drains, transom wells and scuppers are clean and not clogged with dirt. Water must be allowed to drain out. The best time to check these drains and flush them out is when you're washing your boat with a hose and good water pressure.

Maintenance of through-hull fittings, seacocks, hoses, bilge pumps and switches is easy. Make a checklist and do it often. This is especially important if you leave your boat unattended for long periods of time.

If you leave your boat in the water, you should also get a mooring cover that protects your boat from bow to stern. This kind of full cover will give you peace of mind the next time it storms and your boat is 50 miles away at a marina where your boat may not get any attention. ∎

Why Boats Blow Up

by Vin Sparano

A day on the water can be an exhilarating experience. But, when things go wrong with your boat, it can also be a frightening experience. The thought of a fire or explosion on a boat is even more terrifying. If you're far from land, there is no safe place to run.

Fires and explosions can only come from faulty fuel systems or human error. Fortunately, both are avoidable if you take certain precautions.

First, let's start with the deck. Is your gas cap clearly labeled GASOLINE? As farfetched as it sounds, there are cases on record where a clueless gas attendant has pumped gasoline into a rod holder or into a water tank.

All boats must have an overside drain or tank vent for your fuel tank. Make sure that excess fuel or fumes at the gas dock will not find their way into your boat or bilge. Make sure your vent has a mesh screen in place, which could keep fumes from igniting in the fuel line.

If your fill hose is worn or frayed, replace it. But make certain you buy the right hose. It should be stamped "USCG TYPE A2," which is fire resistant. Your filler cap should also be grounded with an electrical wire from the fill opening to the tank, so that any static electricity from the dock hose will flow to the ground without causing a spark.

It's critical that you run your blower to clear your bilge of gas fumes before starting your engine. Check the blower hose and make sure it's not crushed or broken or twisted. After you've run your blower, sniff the bilge with your nose, which is probably the best fuel detector of them all. If you have any doubts, don't start your engine. This is especially true at the fuel dock, where most explosions and fires occur.

If you're buying a new or used boat, check the fuel tanks. Any tank over seven gallons should have a label with the manufacturer's name, date of manufacture, capacity, and material. It should also state: THIS TANK HAS BEEN TESTED UNDER 33 CFR 183.580. If you can't find this label, avoid the boat or have the tank replaced.

Even if you have all the right fittings and parts, you can still get into trouble if you are careless. According to BOAT/U.S., explosions are most likely to occur at the fuel dock, when a leak in the fill or vent system may not be discovered until the tank is topped off.

When you refuel, take certain precautions. First, close all hatches and turn off the battery switch and stove. Fill the tank yourself, if you can, and never fill it to the very top. If you do, and the gas expands, you could get spillage in your boat and bilge. After refueling, run the blower for a full five minutes or longer, then sniff the bilge with your nose before starting the engine.

If you use outboard-motor tanks, take them out of the boat and do your refueling on the dock. This is the safest procedure. Unfortunately, most inboard and stern-drive boats don't have this option.

Let's suppose, for example, that you don't notice a fuel leak until it is too late and you're out on the water with a bilge full of gas. Do you know what to do?

Here's the best and only procedure. Do not start the engine or use any electrical equipment other than your VHF radio and this should be only after you turn off all other electrical circuits. Next, turn off your battery switch

301

and have all your passengers put on lifejackets and stay on deck. Finally, call the Coast Guard and describe your problem and situation. They will instruct you on the next step.

If you find gas has leaked into your boat at the dock, order all guests off the boat. Turn off the battery switch and shore power. Notify the marina manager and call the fire department.

Don't wreck your day or endanger your guests because you don't know how to handle a gas emergency. Most of these precautions are simple common sense. ■

Man Overboard!

by Vin Sparano

Most fishermen will have their boats in the water before warm summer temperatures arrive. They will push the season and launch for trout, flounder and other species that will start biting in early spring. One truth that is hard to accept is the fact that most fishermen are not dedicated boatmen. Fishermen are usually interested more in fishing than boating... and this means a potential danger to themselves and their passengers.

One distinct danger is falling overboard into cold water. Even if you are a good swimmer, the effects of cold water may be more than your body can handle. Cold water, according to BOAT/U.S., can rob your body of heat very quickly. When your body temperature drops, hypothermia becomes a very real threat to life.

Don't be misled into believing that water has to be 35 degrees to be dangerous to someone falling overboard. Cold water is anything under 70 degrees. When water temperature drops to as low as 35, survival is usually based on the physical condition of the victim.

Panic and shock are the first and most dangerous hazards to a fisherman falling overboard. Cold water can shock the body and sometimes induce cardiac arrest. Remember how your breath was taken away when you dived into the pool? The same reaction happens when you fall head first into cold water. Your first gasp for air will fill your lungs with water. You may also

become disoriented for a minute or two before you realize what is happening to you.

If at all possible, get back into your boat as quickly as possible. Your life may depend on it. Unless you have a big boat, this may not be as difficult as it sounds. The majority of fatal boating accidents involve small boats with outboard motors. Most small boats, even if capsized, can be righted and re-entered.

Small boats are legally bound to have enough flotation to support all occupants. If you can, right the boat, climb back into it and bail out the water. If you can't right the boat, climb onto the hull and hang on. It's critical that you get out of the cold water.

If the boat slips away and you can't reach it, there are certain precautions to take in the water until help arrives. Unless there is no chance for a rescue, do not try swimming. It will drain body heat and, if you're like most people, you will not be able to swim very far in cold water.

Your best bet is to remain still and get into a protective position to conserve heat and wait for a rescue. This means protecting your body's major heat loss areas, such as your head, neck, armpits, chest and groin. If there is more than one person in the water, huddle together to preserve body heat.

Treatment of cold-water victims varies. First signs of hypothermia are intense shivering, loss of coordination, mental confusion, blue skin, weak

pulse, irregular heart beat and enlarged pupils. If the victim is cold and only shivering, dry clothes and blankets may be all that is necessary.

If the victim is semi-conscious, move him to a warm place and into dry clothes. Make him lie flat with his head slightly lower than the rest of his body, which will make more blood flow to the brain. You can also warm the victim with warm towels to the head, neck, chest and groin.

Of course, it's always easier to avoid problems by taking a few simple precautions. First, wear a lifejacket at all times when out on the water during cool weather. Whenever possible wear several layers of wool for insulation. Wool, even when wet, will retain body heat.

If you suddenly find yourself in the water, make sure your lifejacket is snug. Keep clothing buttoned up. The water trapped in your clothes will be warmed by your body heat and keep you warm. ■

Stormy Weather for Captains

by Vin Sparano

I've just read about a terrible boating tragedy that could have been avoided. Eight men in a 28-foot pleasure craft got caught in 20-foot seas and 70-m.p.h. winds 30 miles off the New Jersey coast. In a miraculous Coast Guard rescue, seven men were saved, but one man was never found.

The wife of a survivor told reporters, "I don't understand why the captain took the boat out. The captain didn't want to go. He said it was too windy."

I'll venture a guess why the captain took the boat out. It was probably a long-planned fishing trip, no one wanted to be disappointed and the weather didn't look bad at the dock.

I live and fish in New Jersey. I remember that day and I also remember a weather forecast that would have kept me at the dock. I don't care how many friends showed up to go fishing. I would have treated them to breakfast at a local diner and sent them home. They would be disappointed, but alive. The open water is no place to prove that you have more guts than brains.

Never forget that if you own and run a boat, you are also the captain, and totally responsible for the safety of your passengers. If someone gets hurt on your boat, you have to take the blame.

I get scared when I see a boat pass me with young children sitting on the bow with their feet hanging over the side. One bumpy wake and a child could be easily killed by the prop. I get angry when I see a boater pulling a water skier in a channel with heavy boat traffic.

I also wonder what is going through the minds of small-boat operators who disappear in ground swells as they head offshore when a small-craft advisory flag is flying in plain view. I also say a prayer when I see a family overload a rental boat and head for a day of fishing with two inches of freeboard.

High winds and rough water can turn a pleasant day into a life-threatening nightmare. The best way to stay out of trouble is to learn how to read the warnings, wind and water. And it's equally important to know when to cancel a trip and stay home. This advice is even more important to hunters and fishermen who tend to use smaller boats and go out in marginal weather.

Rule No. 1: Check the weather. The National Weather Service issues marine forecasts every six hours with details of winds, seas, weather and visibility. If you have a VHF radio, check the weather frequently on Channels WX-1, WX-2 or WX-3. Marine forecasts on these channels are broadcast continuously. Heavy static on your AM radio may also indicate nearby storms.

The National Weather Service also posts visible warnings at prominent locations along shore, including Coast Guard stations, lighthouses, yacht clubs and marinas. Although the Weather Service has, unfortunately, discontinued the official system of displaying these warnings, you can still find them at some shore installations. Learn where these warnings are displayed in your area and check them before leaving the dock. Here are the warnings and what they mean:

SMALL CRAFT ADVISORY—Daytime warning signal is a single red pennant. Nighttime signal is a red light over a white light. A Small Craft Advisory means winds as high as 33 knots and sea conditions dangerous to small craft. Small craft generally means boats under 25-feet, but I have seen winds that would keep a 40-footer at the dock. You must use your judgment.

GALE—Daytime signal is two red pennants. Nighttime display is a white light over a red light. Gale means winds in the 34 to 47-knot range.

STORM—Daytime signal is a single square red flag with a black square in its center. Nighttime signal is two red lights, displayed vertically. Storm means winds 48 to 63 knots

HURRICANE—Daytime signal is two red flags with black centered squares. Nighttime warning is a white light displayed vertically between two red lights. Hurricane winds are 64 knots and higher.

One of the problems with weather forecasts is that they are not always right. Sometimes you may have to make judgment calls on your own. Learn to read simple weather signs. Watch for dark threatening clouds which nearly always indicate a thunderstorm or squall. Any steady increase in wind or sea is another sign of bad weather.

If you're on the water, don't wait too long to make a decision. Calm winds and water can turn into a gusty electrical storm in as little as 30 minutes.

You can determine the distance of an approaching thunderstorm, in miles, by counting the seconds between the lightning flash and the thunder and dividing by five. For example, if it takes 10 seconds to hear the thunder, the storm is about two miles away.

If you've taken all precautions and you still get caught in a storm, pinpoint your location or write down your loran numbers on a chart before heavy rain reduces your visibility. Watch for other boats, secure hatches, lower antennas and outriggers, stow all loose gear and, most important, make sure everyone is wearing a lifejacket.

Once the storm hits, try to take the first and heaviest gusts of wind on the bow of the boat. Approach waves at a 45-degree angle to keep the propeller underwater and reduce pounding. If there is lightning, unplug the radio and electrical equipment. Stay away from metal objects and order your passengers to stay low. If you don't lose power, you should be able to ride out almost any storm. ■

How Not to Get Seasick

by Vin Sparano

I haven't been seasick in the last 15 years or so. The night before a trip, I stay away from alcohol and get a good night's sleep. The following morning, I sip a cup of black coffee before I get on the boat. If I still feel good by 10 A.M., I'll start to eat . . . but never before. Will this simple formula work for you? To be quite honest, I don't know.

Finding a cure for seasickness is often a matter of trial and error. Everyone has a different approach. Some fishermen are convinced that a full stomach before a fishing trip is the best way to avoid seasickness and that may work for some people. It doesn't work for me. I can, however, tell you what doesn't work for everyone. Stay out late, overindulge, get on a boat tired and hung over and I can guarantee that you will get sick in even a small chop.

In simplest terms, seasickness is the inability of your body to adjust to motion. Your body has a built-in gyroscope to keep you on even keel, much the way a gyroscope keeps a rocket upright as it travels in space. This system works on solid ground, but on a rocking boat or a bumpy airplane, the mechanism sometimes fails and you get seasick.

This means, of course, that when you start feeling seasick, you should try to reduce movement as soon as possible. If you are on a boat, sit in the center and at the stern, where movement will be minimized. It also helps to keep your eye on a stationary object, such as a bridge or tower on the shoreline. You are trying to send a message to your brain that you are not really rocking and have no reason to be seasick. It sometimes works.

Fight the urge to go into a cabin. There is nothing stationary in a cabin, you have no fixed object and you will likely get sicker. In fact, if you get seasick and head for the cabin, you will probably be there for the rest of the day.

Over the years I've heard of dozens of concoctions to cure seasickness. Some may be effective for some people, but most wacky formulas don't work. A doctor once suggested cold stewed tomatoes and saltines, a formula that originated aboard an oil tanker. I suggested it to a friend and he still got sick. It could, however, work for you.

Fortunately, modern medicine has made great strides in helping people cope with an illness that will make you feel like dying. These seasick drugs fall into two categories: antihistamines and scopolamine. These drugs are designed to inhibit the flow of nerve impulses from the vestibular system to the brain. Which drug will work for you? You may have to try them all until you find the one that works best for you.

Antivert and Bonine are non-prescription antihistamines that you take every 24 hours. They will make you drowsy. Marezine is another antihistamine, but it is taken every four to six hours.

Dramamine is the old standby. If the weather forecast calls for rough seas, I will take a Dramamine tablet with my cup of black coffee one hour before I get on a boat. It works for me. A antihistamine that is taken every four hours, Dramamine is a non-prescription drug and it will make you drowsy. On my last trip to a pharmacy, however, I did see a Dramamine formula that the company claims will not make you drowsy.

Phenergan and Mepergan are prescription antihistamines that will effectively prevent and treat seasickness, but ask your doctor about side effects. In some people, they can cause considerable drowsiness.

Transderm Scop is a comparatively new and perhaps the most effective drug in fighting and preventing seasickness. It's an patch on the skin behind the ear that slowly releases scopolamine into your system for days. The side effects can sometimes be severe, however, and should be discussed with your doctor.

There's a lot you can do to protect yourself from getting seasick. First, accept the fact that everyone will eventually get seasick. When someone brags that he never gets seasick, don't believe him. His time at the rail has not yet arrived! There is also no reason to be apologetic or embarrassed about getting seasick.

Finally, never poke fun at someone who is seasick, especially a youngster. You may get paid back on your next trip! ■

Get Ready for Hurricanes

by Vin Sparano

Don't wait for a 12-hour warning to start preparing your boat for a hurricane. Do it now! You may need more time than you think to work out a plan of action that will secure and protect your boat in a storm. Now is the time to think about extra lines and special storm gear.

Even the best plan of action, however, cannot guarantee that your boat will survive a hurricane. In 1992 Hurricane Andrew, for example, proved so violent that boats and people were helpless in its path. Fortunately, not all hurricanes are killers and there are some precautions you can take to keep storm damage to a minimum.

Most boaters believe their real threat of damage comes from wind and waves. This isn't so. Most boat damage comes from storm surge, which means high water. In fact, storm surge accounts for nine out of 10 hurricane-related deaths.

The safest place for your boat is out of the water. If you have a trailer, load your boat on it and take it home. If the boat and trailer fit in your garage, park it there and leave your car outside. Your boat is lighter than your car and can get blown off your trailer in hurricane winds. If you must leave your boat and trailer outside, put it where it will get the best protection from the wind, trees and electrical lines. Let some air out of the trailer tires, block the wheels and make sure the boat is strapped securely to the trailer.

You have two options when you leave your boat on a trailer. First, if it's a heavy boat, take out the drain plug to allow rain water to drain quickly out of the hull. If your boat is light, however, and you are concerned that it may blow off the trailer, leave the drain plug in and fill the hull with water from a garden hose to add more weight. Don't put in too much water or you will damage the hull. Remember that rain will add more water and weight.

Don't trust storage racks, even if your marina says it's a safe place. There may be other lighter boats that could be blown off their cradle and into your boat. Tell your marina to take your boat out of the rack and block it securely in a safe area. Your marina may balk at this, but be insistent.

If you are forced to leave your boat in the water, make sure it is tied securely, which means double lines. Most boats require five lines: two bow lines, two stern lines and one spring line. If a hurricane is approaching, you will need 10 lines. It's also wise to go up one size larger than your normal dock lines. Line your boat with as many rubber fenders as you can find to protect the craft boat from the dock. Always give your lines chafe protection where they will come in contact with the boat or cleats. Neoprene hose is best, but canvas wrapped in place with duct tape will do in a pinch.

If your slip is a small one, look around for a bigger one that's empty and ask your marina if you can use it. The more distance you put between your boat and the pilings and bulkhead, the safer it will be.

Mooring or anchoring in a protected harbor that is not crowded is a safe way to ride out a hurricane, but only if the mooring is a permanent installation and you back it up with two additional storm anchors.

When you leave your boat, take all loose gear and electronics with you and use duct tape to seal all hatches, windows, vents and doors. When you feel your boat is ready for a hurricane, the next step is an important one: Go Home! When hurricane-force winds hit your boat at 100 miles per hour, there will be nothing you can do.

You can now track a hurricane by phone, which may give you enough warning to secure your boat. When a hurricane is headed your way, you can get official hurricane advisories issued by the National Oceanic and Atmospheric Administration (NOAA). A phone call to Boat/U.S. Weather Watch will connect you to the NOAA Hurricane Center in Miami, Florida. Just dial 1-900-933-BOAT. The cost is 98 cents per minute, a small price for a hurricane warning. ■

GET... SCHRADE TOUGH

... AND GET A GRIP ON A FILLET KNIFE THAT'S A KEEPER !

Built Schrade Tough, this Old Timer® Safe-T-Grip™ was designed by fishermen for fishermen. The 147OT Pro Fisherman sports a super-sharp 7 1/2" Schrade+ stainless steel blade. The Sure grip handle is ergonomically designed for easy, safe, and comfortable use. Comes with a weather-resistant ballistic cloth sheath. Get your hand around the Pro Fisherman from Schrade... It's a Keeper!

SCHRADE CUTLERY®
Est. 1904
Built To Last A Lifetime.

Made in U.S.A. © 1995 Imperial Schrade Corp., 7 Schrade Court, Ellenville, N.Y. 12428

SIGNALING THE FUTURE

While there's a great deal going on in the world of marine electronics, it's nothing compared to what's about to happen in the near future. To determine the direction of technology, we interviewed numerous manufacturers and put together a summary—their "sense-of-the-industry."

As late as 1995, industry surveys showed there was still consumer hesitancy to switch over from loran to GPS. But GPS and loran manufacturers agree that the market for the satellite-based system is still just barely tapped. Only 10 percent of all boatowners currently own a GPS unit.

Look for better interfacing abilities from "multi-talkers." That's where your instruments can talk in both directions rather than information traveling in one direction only. You'll find this makes your navigation display far easier to use. Also expect to see displays themselves getting larger, night lighting improving, and more disparate instruments hooked together.

GPS

Trimble NT 200

Trimble has introduced its NT family of navigation instruments—the NT 100 GPS, the NT 200 Chart Plotter and the NT 200D, a chart plotter with a built-in differential receiver. The Trimble plotters are Navionics-based cartography units with an interesting twist. They have bi-directional NMEA ports, meaning they can talk to and receive input from other electronics. A small "Smart Card" is used to store data. You can store, LAT/LON, Course over ground, Speed, Time, Position, heading, and cross-track error updates every five seconds and not run out of memory for two days. **Trimble Navigation, 645 North Mary Ave., Sunnyvale, CA 94086, (408) 481-8000.**

Northstar 941X GPS

The 941X is completely waterproof, with a built-in, dual-channel differential beacon receiver, descriptive waypoint names (Nantucket Harbor), heat-resistant LCD display that will never turn black, 24-hour graphic tide display for over 3,000 locations, graphic steering director with waypoint markers, and a feature called Nav Log that is an interactive database telling you how you are progressing on your trip. Northstar provides many useful functions that no one else has. **Northstar, 30 Sudbury Rd., Acton, MA 01720, (508) 897-6600.**

Electronics

by Dean Travis Clarke

Micrologic Mariner Plus GPS

This is an LCD GPS unit that you can virtually use without reading the manual. There are loads of prompt messages. You can save 500 waypoints by number or name, automatically record your position, speed, day, date, and time periodically in your data log, and read your position in converted TDs. There's even a readout of how accurate your position fix is in meters or feet. The Mariner Plus can be connected to the Micrologic ML-9100 Differential receiver for DGPS accuracy. **Micrologic, 9174 Deering Ave., Chatsworth, CA 91311, (818) 998-1216.**

Magellan Meridan XL

Nervous about changing over from loran to GPS? Magellan's Meridian XL will help you over the hurdle. This tiny handheld GPS will automatically readout your position in converted TDs. In addition, this tiny handheld provides a track plotter, five different navigation screens, 200-waypoint memory, detachable antenna, and differential GPS capability. Magellan is also introducing a very small fixed-mount GPS, the Nav 1200, and a new C-Map-based electronic chart plotter, The Chartmate. **Magellan, 960 Overland Ct., San Dimas, CA 91773, (909) 394-5000.**

Magellan's Meridian XL has a wide-screen and features easy-to-read displays, large keys and user-friendly operation, making it ideal for the boater looking for a handheld GPS receiver.

VHF

We've all heard about Digital Selective Calling and agree it will be an excellent technology. The problem at the moment is there are only two Coast Guard DSC stations operating and there's no timeline for total system function. Budget constraints are hurting the program. But the turn-of-the-century should see a final mandate in effect.

Long-term, the most significant change in marine radio communications is going to be the low-earth orbit cellular telephone system: when the whole earth is connected via cellular phone with no "out-of-coverage area" even in the middle of the ocean; when instead of using just an EPIRB and hoping someone is listening, you'll suddenly have two-way communications. It probably won't affect VHF substantially since VHF is free and cellular has no provision for vessel-to-vessel traffic. But you can bet it will hammer the Single Sideband business. And it isn't that far off, either. A company called OrbComm already has the earth stations, the assigned frequency space, the satellites ready to launch, the launch dates—it's just around the corner.

ICOM IC-M10 Handheld VHF

How annoying is it to have a supposedly fully charged handheld VHF whose NiCad batteries die when you use it for a half-hour or so? Battery memory is the real stumbling block with handhelds. ICOM now has an innovative unit, the IC-M10, that has all the features of most fixed-mount VHFs. But this handy unit uses alkaline batteries. Never worry about charging again. Also new this year are ICOM's M-15 waterproof handheld—a truly waterproof radio, and the IC-M58 DSC VHF, with emergency calling. Simply press a single button and a continuous, pre-programmed distress call goes out containing your boat's identification, the time, and your vessel's position. And if you want total privacy in your radio transmissions, you can get the optional voice scrambler. **ICOM America, 2380-116th Ave., Bellevue, WA 98004, (206) 454-8155.**

Shakespeare NAV-COM 6000 VHF RADIO

Shakespeare's SE-6000 integrates a Digital Selective Calling VHF radio, with GPS, loran, and electronic compass sensors, displays all the information on a large, highly-visible screen, and can even direct your autopilot. The microphone has buttons to change display readouts. When another radio calls you, the 6000 will act as a receptionist, storing the call information until you are ready to call them back. **Shakespeare, PO Box 733, Newberry, SC 29108, (800) 800-9008.**

Standard Horizon Eclipse VHF

No company has a richer history making radios than Standard. Their new Horizon Eclipse is the smallest fixed-mount VHF in the world! And the Eclipse is loaded with useful features like mike-mounted channel switching, automatic weather alert interruption, instant access to both channel 9 and channel 16, several scanning modes, and an LCD display that comprises almost 25 percent of the face so those of us with eyesight that isn't what it once was can see the channel with ease. Also, unlike other companies' warranty promises, Standard will cover water damage. Chances are good that you won't have any. **Standard Communications, PO Box 92151, Los Angeles, CA 90009-2151, (310) 532-5300.**

LORAN

There's still question about what will ultimately happen to loran. Many European and third-world nationals are distrustful of the U.S. Deptartment of Defense having total control of all GPS satellites. Foreign government representatives question what would happen if we suddenly decided to shut the system down for any reason. Their shipping, aircraft and land-based users would all be stuck.

Throughout the rest of the world, loran is still on the upswing. There are new chains developing and it appears the system is here to stay for the foreseeable future outside the U.S.

However, the U.S. government has no budget to operate two navigation systems. What may happen is some agency other than the Coast Guard, or perhaps even a private enterprise may take over loran's operation. But according to Magellan's Vern Bennet, a former loran station operating chief in southeast Asia, "The Coast Guard will never, ever, turn over control of loran to *anyone!*"

Some people feel loran just isn't taken as seriously as it once was. The association of government officials, academicians, engineers, and international users that promotes loran, called the Wild Goose Association, has changed its name. It is now the International Loran Association.

Si-Tex XJ-9 Loran

This new loran has the *real* answer for those making a switch from loran to GPS. It can interface with the Si-Tex GPS-10 and you can then scroll between real loran and GPS—no conversion algorithms from Lat/Lon to TDs. However, as a straight loran receiver, the XJ-9 has a four-line display, all the normal navigation information, memory for 20 "instant positions" for your daily fishing hotspots as well as 89 waypoints 10 reversible routes and single-button Man Overboard calculations

and readout. Si-Tex, PO Box 6700, Clearwater, FL 34618, (813) 576-5734.

ELECTRONIC CHART SYSTEMS

As Navionics' Dr. Guiseppe Carnevali said, and to a fault, everyone agreed: "The dramatic evolution that we will witness in the next several years can be summarized in one word: 'Awareness.'"

You simply can't imagine how much simpler, safer, and more comfortable using an electronic chart plotter is compared to a straight alpha-numeric readout as in GPS or loran. The human mind likes processing graphic images better than digital data. The world is becoming increasingly aware of electronic charting—not just in boats—but in automobiles, hiking, surveying, interstate commerce, aviation, agriculture and other uses you couldn't even imagine. And every new system introduced has more features and handles information better than the last. Look for "vending machines" that will sell updated charts you can download to your cartridge. Also, every chart you need can be had on one or two CD-ROM disks.

What does ECS really do for you? It relaxes you. It is so easy you can let your mind dwell on fishing rather than navigating. Just a glance at the ECS display will tell you everything you could ever want to know about your location and where you're going.

MarineTek SeaMax Chart GPS/Dual-Frequency Sounder

Heading in the right direction of all your onboard electronics information available from one display, Marinetek's SeaMax Chart System combines a color fish finder, a Navionics-based chart plotter, and a Trimble-engineered GPS engine. Colors are very bright, the resolution is excellent, and SeaMax has an automatic transducer that constantly tunes both transducer frequencies at the same time for optimum signal. Another great feature is the ability to recall a particular track and re-sail that track with cross-track error display. You'll be absolutely certain you're hitting the exact spot where you hooked that last fish. **Marinetek, 2300E Zanker Rd., San Jose, Ca 95131, (408) 526-9288.**

Maptech Pilot

Resolution Mapping introduces their newest electronic charting systems, the Maptech Pilot and Professional. Both display full-color versions of the real charts you're used to. However, the Pilot has half the features of the Professional. But don't scoff. The Pilot has everything the average navigator will ever use and costs less. The Maptech difference is you can use this system on any personal computer with a CD-ROM drive, rather than needing a special expensive instrument dedicated only to navigation. Otherwise, this system does virtually everything the other electronic chart plotters do. The flexibility you have in planning trips at home is amazing. **Maptech, 35 Hartwell Ave., Lexington, MA 02173, (617) 860-0430.**

Cetrek ChartPilot 775

The new Cetrek ChartPilot 775 is a combination autopilot and chart plotter, and is one of the easiest systems to use. It contains the best "onscreen" instructions, a display that covers most of the front of the case for super visibility, and interface ability second to none. Use the trackball to lay out your course line, press the button and the autopilot steers you there. **Cetrek, 640 North Lewis Rd., Limerick, PA 19468, (610) 495-7011.**

KVH Quadro Chart Plotter

KVH, maker of some of the world's best electronic compasses, has broadened its navigation product line with the Quadro LCD GPS Chart Plotter. This compact, splashproof display uses Navionics' seamless cartography, has an automatic zoom, loads of memory and built-in world chart. But the most innovative part is the Quadro's ability to connect with KVH's instrument system. With this feature, your chart plotter can also figure in depth, boat and wind speed, and will even drive your autopilot. KVH has come one step closer to a total navigation suite in one instrument. **KVH Industries, 110 Enterprise Center, Middletown, RI 02842, (401) 847-3327.**

Datamarine Chartlink LCD & CRT

Datamarine's new electronic chart systems are available with a VGA display in either a LCD or CRT forms. Datamarine can interface with most other manufac-

turer's equipment, not just Datamarine's. However, it does offer interface ability with all their performance instruments including depth, water temperature, and speed through the water as well as over ground—a good way to determine drift speeds. Waypoint and route storage is substantial internally—but infinite on storage cartridges. Both units offer the option of a built-in GPS or the ability to plug into your existing GPS engine. **Datamarine International, 53 Portside Dr., Pocasset, MA 02559-1900, (508) 563-7151.**

Raytheon Chart Plotters

These C-Map-based chart plotters are available in numerous configurations. The 600XX and RT units can be interfaced with radar for a "real world" electronic view. The 610EST interfaces with a color fish finder and the 610T boasts a huge 14-inch color monitor. Additionally, all can be hooked up to SeaTalk instruments, allowing them to provide depth, speed, wind direction and speed, velocity made good, course made good, speed over ground, distance log, and true wind direction. They also come with a Man Overboard feature that, at the touch of a button, locks the position into memory, sounds an alarm, and gives constant readout of distance and bearing to the position. **Raytheon, 676 Island Pond Rd., Manchester, NH 03109-5420, (603) 647-7530.**

VIDEO DEPTH SOUNDERS

One of the greatest demands from the users of fish finders is visibility—they're just too danged hard to read—from a distance, from any angle other than straight on, in sunlight, or at night.

Other things you can look forward to that will improve sounders is new software and interfacing with GPS and other navigation instruments. For example, have you ever gotten frustrated because your sounder scrolls at pretty much the same speed no matter how fast you're going? Why can't it stop when I stop? Expect to see real time scrolling that will show the bottom passing under your boat at the same speed at which you are traveling. Also, there will be a better perspective. Where is the boat? Which way are the fish traveling? How far back are those marks? All common questions. New software will address these difficulties, offering information so excellent, you'll wonder how you ever managed before.

Furuno FCV-667 Color Video Sounder

Furuno has several new products: Chart Plotters, LCD sounders, combination chart plotters/sounders/GPS units, and autopilots, to name but a few. But one very interesting product for offshore fishermen is the FCV-667 color sounder. It's very compact, having only a six-inch screen. But while the display is small, the capabilities

The Furuno GP-1800 is a combination LCD and GPS Plotter. It will track up to eight satellites and uses Furuno chart cards. The GP-1800 will also select and display the most appropriate chart.

are large. Dual-frequency operation (50/200 kHz) from a single transducer, A-scope, eight color levels, auto-mode, and numerous zoom adjustments. An ideal unit for anglers with little instrument space. Also new from Furuno are their GP-1800, a full-featured chart plotter, and their FAP-300 autopilot. **Furuno, PO Box 2343, South San Francisco, CA 94083, (415) 873-9393.**

Apelco Fishfinder

Apelco's new 460 pumps out 800 watts of power for bottom readings at 600 feet while the 530 puts out an impressive 2,400 watts for reaching the bottom through 900 feet of saltwater. Both units offer Bottom Lock for reading the bottom and a selected distance above. The White Line feature distinguishes bottom fish from the actual bottom, and Bottom Coverage allows the anglerto see where the fish actually are relative to the boat and just how much of the bottom is represented on the screen. **Apelco, 676 Island Pond Rd., Manchester, NH 03109-5420, (603) 647-7530.**

Interphase Probe, Sea Scout, and Echoscan

These new depth sounders from Interphase are specialists indeed. The Probe scans from just below the water's surface ahead to directly below to show you what you are approaching. It also shows you exactly how far ahead the structure is. The Sea Scout tracks the bottom directly below the boat and scans a 90-degree arc from one side of your bow to the other like a searchlight, to detect bait and schools of fish. The EchoScan 8 scans from side-to-side beneath the boat to see structure and fish on either side you might otherwise miss. **Interphase Technologies, 1201 Shaffer Rd., Santa Cruz, CA 95060, (408) 427-4444.**

Humminbird Wide Vision

Wide Vision solves the problems offshore fishermen have with most depth sounders. It reaches bottom at 1,000 feet. It has exceptionally clear display resolution, it allows a very quick glance to determine the exact depth a fish is marked at. It has a screen you can actually see while wearing polarized sunglasses. It gives a constant water temperature and speed readout and is waterproof. In fact, the unit is so good, it took Humminbird a half year to catch up with the demand. Also available this year is Humminbird's new DC5-S handheld VHF. It's not just waterproof. It's submersible. With a full 25-watt output and exceptional saltwater corrosion resistance, this radio is the ideal radio for small boats and an indispensable backup on larger offshore vessels. **Humminbird, 3 Humminbird Lane, Eufala, AL 36027, (205) 687-6613.**

Lowrance X-70A 3D

This 3,000-watt unit has the potential to reach 1,000 feet down to show you fish, bottom composition, and structure. Lowrance has incorporated all the performance

The Humminbird Wide 3D Vision is a three-dimensional sonar that also offers a two-dimensional mode that can be viewed simultaneously. This unit will read bottoms down to 1,000 feet.

and versatility of their 2D picture in their 3D display. The 3D signal will lock onto the bottom rather than being fooled by baitfish or thermoclines. In fact, the X-70A 3D has 2D-mode with all its benefits, allowing the 3D to provide greater information about contour and perspective—the best of both worlds. And no one has better visibility in direct sunlight than Lowrance with their super-twist display. **Lowrance, 12000 E. Skelly Dr., Tulsa, OK 74128-2486, (918) 437-6881.**

MISCELLANEOUS

Simrad Robertson AP3000 Autopilot

This is a Robertson autopilot specially designed for boats less than 40 feet long. Robertson's proprietary "Autotune" feature monitors rudder movement and vessel response for instant and accurate course adjustment. Good for mechanical or hydraulic systems, the AP3000 also offers selectable night vision backlighting in red, green or white. If you want the real story on Simrad Robertson autopilots, ask almost any professional charter boat captain. He probably has one. **Simrad, 19210 33rd Ave. West, Lynnwood, WA 98036, (206) 778-8821.**

Roffer's Ocean Fishing Forecasts Go Online

Roffers, one of the top satellite image-based fishing spot forecasters has gone on-line with an electronic bulletin board. Those of you who modem your way through on-line services and the Internet will appreciate a peek at the numerous menu items such as fishing articles, offshore analyses, expert's forums, satellite imagery, shareware and free filesource, an electronic mailbox and frequent weather update announcements. **Roffers, 2871 SW 69th Ct., Miami, FL 33155-2829, (800) 677-7633.**

Alden Satfind 406 Survival EPIRB

Small, rugged and ideal for smaller offshore fishing boats. Controls are easy to use even in stressful situations. It can be mounted in any position, is water-activated as well as manually. Each unit is coded to broadcast information identifying you, your boat, its size, emergency contacts, and now, with a built-in GPS receiver, constant position readouts. It also broadcasts on 121.5 MHz so aircraft and shipping can home in on your beacon. **Alden Electronics, 40 Washington St., Westborough, MA 01581-0500, (508) 366-8851.**

FloScan 9000 Fuel Computer

Some of the most crucial information to have when you're running offshore is how much fuel you have and how fast are you using it. FloScan's new fuel-management system provides real-time information on miles per gallon, gallons per hour, and total gallons used. Combined with integral RPM input, you can easily build your own performance curves—or simply set your throttles for the most efficient fuel consumption. And unlike the performance charts you see in magazines, these figures are on your boat with all your gear, tackle, ice and anglers aboard. **FloScan, 3016 NE Blakely St., Seattle, WA 98105, (800) 522-3610.**

ACR Mini-B2 EPIRB

Touted as the smallest floating Class B EPIRB, ACR's Mini-B2 broadcasts simultaneously on 121.5 MHz (civilian) and 243.0 MHz (military) Search and Rescue homing frequencies. Operating battery life is 48 hours and the long-life lithium batteries have a replacement life of six years. The Mini-B2 measures an incredible 6″ × 2.6″ × 1.6″ so will fit on even the smallest offshore center console — the type of boat that should really have an EPIRB aboard. **ACR Electronics, 5757 Ravenswood Rd., Ft. Lauderdale, FL 33312, (305) 981-3333.**

Shakespear Art-1 Antenna Tester

Shakespeare has an invaluable antenna tester for a price everyone can afford and simple enough for a child to use. Simply plug this meter between your radio and antenna. It will give you a constant readout of output, the antenna's efficiency (Standing Wave Ratio-SWR) and whether your radio's signal will be transmitted properly. A switch lets you pick between forward or reflective power and a calibrator knob allows you to adjust your SWR for the optimum signal. This should be standard equipment with every radio. **Shakespeare, PO Box 733, Newberry, SC 29108, (800) 800-9008**

Autohelm LCD Radar

Autohelm presents its new ST50, a waterproof, liquid crystal display radar with 16-mile range. In addition to the normal information a radar provides, the ST-50 offers navigation data on waypoints, tide and wind, Electronic Bearing Line (EBL) and Variable Range Marker (VRM), both "big ship" anti-collision features that are extremely helpful. The ST-50 also interfaces with Raytheon's 600XX system, making it a C-Map-based chart plotter. **Autohelm, 676 Island Pond Rd., Manchester, NH 03109-5420, (603) 647-7530.**

ITT Night Mariner Monocular

Night Vision just became affordable. ITT Night Vision has a monocular that sells for about half what the large binocular unit does. And though it's certainly personal preference (meaning loads of people disagree with me), I find it easier to run a boat while looking through the monocular than the binocular. For those who want magnification in addition to their night sight, ITT introduces their 150 DX kit; a 3-way lens offering 3X, 2X and .42 wide angle magnification. Also available now are other lenses to further boost magnification. **ITT Night Vision, 7635 Plantation Rd., Roanoke, VA 24019, (800) 448-8678.**

FIELD CARE AND DRESSING OF FISH

If you sit down at the dinner table and bite into a poor-tasting fillet from a fish you caught, there's a good chance that the second-rate taste is your own fault. In all probability, the fish was not handled properly from the moment it came out of the water. Fish spoil rapidly unless they are kept alive or quickly killed and put on ice.

Here are the necessary steps involved in getting a fresh-caught fish from the water to the table, so that it will retain its original flavor.

First, the decision to keep a fish dead or alive depends on conditions. For example, if you have no ice in your boat, you'll want to keep all fish alive until it's time to head home. Under no circumstances should you toss fish into the bottom of the boat, let them lie there in the sun, then gather them up at the end of the day. If you try that stunt, the fillets will reach your table with the consistency of mush and a flavor to match. Instead, put your fish on a stringer as quickly as possible and put them back into the water, where they can begin to recover from the shock of being caught. (This is something you will want to avoid in shark-filled waters; in that case, make sure you bring a large cooler and lots of ice.)

Use the safety-pin type stringer and run the wire up through the thin almost-transparent membrane just behind the fish's lower lip. This will enable the fish to swim freely, and the fish will recover from this minor injury should you decide to release it at the end of the day.

Do not shove the stringer under the gill cover and out of the mouth. This damages gills and kills fish fast. Also avoid cord stringers, where all fish are bunched in a clump at the end of the cord. Use the safety-pin stringer. It does its job well.

If you're rowing or trolling slowly, you can probably keep the stringer in the water. If you have a big boat and motor, however, it's a good idea to take the stringer into the boat for those fast runs to other hotspots. If the run is fairly long, wet down the fish occasionally. But don't tow a fish in the water at high speed—you'll drown it.

If a fish has been deeply hooked and appears to be dying slowly, however, it's best to kill the fish immediately, gut it, and keep it on ice.

Killing a fish quickly is simple. Holding the fish upright, impale it between the eyes with the point of your knife or rap it on the head with a heavy stick. The important factor is killing it quickly, since the more slowly it dies the more rapidly the flesh will deteriorate.

 14

From Hook to Table: Field Care and Nutrition

If you're surf fishing, bury your catch in the damp sand to keep it cool and out of the sun. Just remember to mark the spot. (VIN T. SPARANO)

If you're a surf fisherman, you can bury your catch in the damp sand. Just remember to mark the spot. A burlap sack occasionally doused in the surf also makes a practical fish bag. The important factor is to keep the fish cool and out of the sun.

Regardless of the various ways to keep fish cool, they should first be cleaned properly. With a bit of practice and a sharp knife, the job can be done in less than a minute.

Take a sharp knife, and insert it in the anal opening on the underside of the fish. Slit the skin forward from there to the point of the V-shaped area where the forward part of the belly is attached to the gills. Put your finger into the gills and around that V-shaped area, and pull sharply to the rear. You will thus remove the gills and all or most of the entrails. Then, with the fish upside down, put your thumb into the body cavity at the anal opening, and press the thumbnail up against the backbone. Keeping the nail tight against the bone, run your thumb forward to the head, thereby removing the dark blood from the sac along the backbone.

That completes the cleaning process—unless you want to remove the fins. This is easily done with a knife but is even easier with a small pair of wire clippers or scissors.

One more tip. More good fish meat is probably ruined during the drive home than during any other point in the trip from the water to the plate. Take the time to ice the fish properly for the drive home. Here's how:

Don't pack the fish in direct contact with the ice. The ice is sure to melt, and the fish, lying in the water, might well deteriorate, becoming soft and mushy. It's far better to put the fish in plastic bags, seal the bags so that they are watertight, and then pack the bags in the ice. The fish will stay cool—and dry—until you get home.

When you get the fish home, scale or skin them. For saltwater fish, prepare a heavy brine solution, and brush them thoroughly (a pastry-type brush works well) with the brine until they are clean.

Separate the fish into lots, each of which will make a meal for yourself or your family, and wrap each lot in good freezer paper, sealing tightly to prevent freezer burn. Freeze the fish as quickly as possible.

Some fishermen prefer not to field-dress their fish, but to fillet and skin them. This method, which appears difficult but is actually quite simple, has a number of advantages. First, gutting the fish is not necessary since entrails are left intact and never touched with a knife. Second, messy scaling is also an eliminated step because the fillet is skinned and the skin discarded, scales and all. Finally, and perhaps most important, the fillets are bone free.

Filleting is also a good idea for fishermen on extended trips. Head, entrails, fins, and skin are left behind and only clean and meaty fillets are brought home.

FISH COOKING TIPS

How Much To Cook
The following is an estimate of how much to cook per person, depending on appetite and course of meal served:

Whole or round fish—¾ pound
Dressed or cleaned fish—½ pound
Fillets or steaks—4 to 6 ounces
Crab meat, scallops and peeled shrimp—¼ pound
Unpeeled shrimp or whole squid—½ pound
Crab or lobster, live—1 to 2 pounds
Oysters or clams, shucked—¼ pint
Oysters or clams, in the shell—6 pieces

How Long to Cook?
The 10-Minute Rule: The main point to remember when cooking any seafood is not to cook it too long. Overcooked fish and shellfish becomes tough and dry, and much of the delicate flavor is lost.

FISH: "The 10-Minute Rule" is a good rule of thumb for timing all types of fish cookery, except deep drying and microwaving. Measure the fish at its thickest point. For every inch of thickness, allow 10 minutes cooking time. Double the cooking time for frozen fish that has not been thawed. Observe the changes in the fish as it cooks. Fish is done when it has just turned opaque and it starts to flake when prodded with a fork. Properly cooked fish will be firm yet moist.

Five Basic Cooking Methods
Sautéing: One of the easiest and quickest ways to cook fish, sautéing is ideal for thin fillets, fish steaks, and small whole fish as well as shrimp, scallops, and oysters. Heat a small amount of vegetable oil, butter, or mar-

garine in a heavy skillet. Dip seafood in seasoned flour and shake off excess. Sauté over medium-high heat until browned; turn and brown the second side. Serve immediately.

Baking: Baking requires little attention and works well for almost any fish. Melt a small amount of butter or margarine in a shallow baking pan. Season fish with herbs, salt, and pepper and turn in pan to coat with butter. Bake at 450°F, allowing 10 minutes per inch of thickness.

Broiling/Grilling: Steaks and fillets of firm fish or whole fish may be placed directly on an oiled broiler pan or on the well-oiled grill of an outdoor barbecue. A hinged fish basket is recommended for fragile fish. Cook 4 to 6 inches from the source of heat, turning once and basting frequently to prevent drying. Allow 10 minutes cooking time per inch of thickness.

Poaching: Fish simmered gently in a flavorful poaching liquid can be served either hot or chilled.

Place a whole fish, steaks, or fillets in a boiling liquid to cover. Reduce heat, cover and simmer gently, allowing about 10 minutes per inch of thickness. Remove skin from whole fish while it is warm.

Microwaving: An excellent and quick method for a variety of seafood.

Cut fish into equal portions to facilitate even cooking. Place in shallow microwave-proof dish with thinner parts overlapping in the center to make an even layer. Cover with heavy-duty waxed paper. Allow approximately 3 minutes per pound cooking time at highest setting for boneless fish and 2 to 3 minutes per pound for shellfish. Rotate dish halfway through cooking time. Allow 3 to 5 minutes covered "standing time" to finish cooking.

A Guide to Cooking Fish

Species	Fat or Lean	Broil	Bake	Boil Steam Poach	Fry/ Sauté
Alewife	Fat	.....	Best	Good	
Barracuda	Fat	Good	Best	.....	Fair
Bluefish	Fat	Good	Best	.....	Fair
Bonito	Fat	Good	Best	.....	Fair
Buffalo Fish	Lean	Good	Best	.....	Fair
Bullheads	Lean	.....	Fair	Good	Best
Cod	Lean	Best	Good	Fair	.....
Croaker (Hardhead)	Lean	Good	Fair	.....	Best
Drum (Redfish)	Lean	.....	Best	Good	.....
Eels	Fat	.....	Good	Fair	Best
Flounder	Lean	Good	Fair	.....	Best
Fluke	Lean	Good	Fair	.....	Best
Grouper	Lean	.....	Best	.....	.....
Haddock	Lean	Best	Good	Fair	.....
Hake	Lean	Fair	Best	Good	.....
Halibut	Fat	Best	Good	Fair	.....
Herring, Lake	Lean	Good	Fair	.....	Best
Herring, Sea	Fat	Best	Fair	.....	Good
Hog Snapper (Grunt)	Lean	Good	.....	.....	Best
Jewfish	Lean	.....	Best	.....	.....
Kingfish	Lean	Best	Good	Fair	.....
King Mackerel	Fat	Best	Good	.....	.....
Ling Cod	Lean	Best	Good	Fair	.....

(continued on page 316)

A Guide to Cooking Fish

Species	Fat or Lean	Broil	Bake	Boil Steam Poach	Fry/ Sauté
Mackerel	Fat	Best	Good	Fair	.....
Mango Snapper	Lean	Good	.....	.....	Best
Mullet	Fat	Best	Good	.....	Fair
Pollock	Lean	Fair	Good	Best	.....
Pompano	Fat	Best	Good	.....	Fair
Porgies (Scup)	Fat	Good	Fair	.....	Best
Redfish(ChannelBass)	Lean	Good	Best	.....	.....
Red Snapper	Lean	Good	Best	Good	.....
Rockfish	Lean	.....	Good	Best	.....
Rosefish	Lean	.....	Good	.....	Best
Salmon	Fat	Good	Best	Fair	.....
Sablefish(Black Cod)	Fat	.....	......	Good	.....
Sardines	Fat	.....	Best	.....	.....
Sea Bass	Fat	Best	Fair	.....	Good
Sea Trout	Fat	Best	Good	.....	Fair
Shad	Fat	Good	Best	.....	Fair
Shark (Grayfish)	Fat	.....	Best	Good	.....
Sheepshead					
(Freshwater)	Lean	.....	Good	Best	.....
(Saltwater)	Lean	Best	Good	.....	Fair
Smelts	Lean	Good	Fair	.....	Best
Snapper	Lean	Good	Best	Fair	.....
Snook	Lean	Good	Best	.....	.....
Sole	Lean	Good	Fair	.....	Best
Spanish Mackerel	Fat	Best	Good	.....	Fair
Spot	Lean	.....	.....	.....	.....
Striped Bass	Fat	.....	Good	Best	.....
Sturgeon	Fat	Good	Best	Fair	.....
Swordfish	Fat	Best	Good	Fair	.....
Tautog (Blackfish)	Lean	Best	Good	.....	Fair
Tuna	Fat	Fair	Best	Good	.....
Weakfish (Sea Trout)	Lean	Best	Good	.....	Fair
Whiting(Silver Hake)	Lean	.....	.....	Best	.....
Whitefish	Fat	Good	Best	.....	Fair
Yellowtail	Fat	Good	Good	Best	.....

Note: All Shellfish are Lean

Index

317